International Fisheries Law

Offering a practical exploration of persistent and new challenges relating to contemporary international fisheries law, this book examines emerging and unresolved issues in international fisheries law.

Covering a wide range of international legal aspects related to fisheries governance, it offers practical perspectives that go beyond the existing debates in this field. An expert team of contributors offers a comprehensive study of current challenges in fisheries governance, institutional law frameworks, procedural aspects and trade and enforcement issues. The book enriches fisheries law scholarship, outlining the capacity of international law to address challenges in international fisheries law and policy, highlighting the critical importance of fisheries to many states, coastal communities and economies globally.

The book's chapters have been meticulously selected, focusing on policy and practical considerations. The result is a comprehensive edited collection covering the main persistent challenges in international fisheries law, making it an essential reading for all those interested in the conservation, integrated management and sustainable use of living resources globally.

Bjørn Kunoy is Professor of International Law at the University of the Faroe Islands. He is also Special Legal Adviser, Ministry of Foreign Affairs & Trade, Faroe Islands.

Tomas Heidar is President of the International Tribunal for the Law of the Sea and Director of the Law of the Sea Institute of Iceland.

Constantinos Yiallourides is Associate Professor (Senior Lecturer) in International Law at Macquarie University, Sydney. He is also Research Leader in Law of the Sea at the British Institute of International & Comparative Law (BIICL), London.

International Fisheries Law

Persistent and Emerging Challenges

Edited by Bjørn Kunoy, Tomas Heidar and Constantinos Yiallourides

Routledge
Taylor & Francis Group
LONDON AND NEW YORK

First published 2025
by Routledge
4 Park Square, Milton Park, Abingdon, Oxon OX14 4RN

and by Routledge
605 Third Avenue, New York, NY 10158

Routledge is an imprint of the Taylor & Francis Group, an informa business

British Library Cataloguing-in-Publication Data
A catalogue record for this book is available from the British Library

ISBN: 978-1-032-79445-7 (hbk)
ISBN: 978-1-032-79446-4 (pbk)
ISBN: 978-1-003-49203-0 (ebk)

DOI: 10.4324/9781003492030

Typeset in Times New Roman
by Apex CoVantage, LLC

Contents

Contributors

Ethan Beringen Postgraduate Researcher at Macquarie Law School, Macquarie University, Sydney

Kathleen Claussen Professor, Georgetown University Law Center

Daniela Diz Associate Professor, International Ocean Governance, The Lyell Centre, Heriot-Watt University

Meggan Engelke-Ros Senior Attorney, National Oceanic and Atmospheric Administration

Adriana Fabra Senior Advisor, The Pew Charitable Trusts

James Harrison Professor of Environmental Law, University of Edinburgh

Tomas Heidar President of the International Tribunal for the Law of the Sea. Director of the Law of the Sea Institute of Iceland

Valerie Hughes International Trade Law Consultant and Arbitrator

Ben Juratowitch KC Barrister, Essex Court Chambers

Bjørn Kunoy Professor of International Law, University of the Faroe Islands. Special Legal Adviser, Ministry of Foreign Affairs & Trade, Faroe Islands

Dita Liliansa Research Fellow, Ocean Law and Policy Programme at the Centre for International Law (CIL), National University of Singapore (NUS)

Alina Miron Professor, University of Angers

Erik J. Molenaar Deputy Director, Netherlands Institute for the Law of the Sea (NILOS) and Associate, Utrecht Centre for Water, Oceans and Sustainability Law (UCWOSL), Utrecht University

Clarisse Morgan Director, Rules Division, World Trade Organization (WTO)

Sean D. Murphy Manatt/Ahn Professor of International Law; George Washington University; Former Member, United Nations International Law Commission

Kentaro Nishimoto Professor of International Law at the School of Law, Tohoku University, Japan

Mercedes Rosello Senior Lecturer, University of Lincoln

Iain Sandford Partner, Sidley Austin LLP, Geneva

Valentin J. Schatz Junior Professor of Public Law and European Law, Faculty of Sustainability, Leuphana University of Lüneburg

Andrew Serdy Professor of the Public International Law of the Sea, University of Southampton, United Kingdom

Yoshifumi Tanaka Professor of International Law, Faculty of Law, University of Copenhagen, Denmark

Osvaldo Urrutia Senior Lecturer of International Law at the Faculty of Law, P. Universidad Católica de Valparaíso (PUCV, Chile) and former Chairperson of the SPRFMO Commission (2017–2021)

Eva R. van der Marel Associate Professor, UiT the Arctic University of Norway

Ariane Vincent Managing Associate, Sidley Austin LLP, Geneva

Constantinos Yiallourides Associate Professor, Macquarie University, Sydney; British Institute of International & Comparative Law, London

Samuel Wordsworth KC Barrister, Essex Court Chambers

Foreword

It is both an honour and a pleasure to provide a foreword to this important new book on persistent and emerging challenges in contemporary international fisheries law. The editors are to be congratulated on having assembled such a distinguished group of contributors to this book. They include many of the leading experts in the field, both academics and practitioners. They share their knowledge, experience and insights in discussing and analysing a wide range of topics: regional fisheries management organisations; dispute settlement, particularly with reference to such organisations; IUU fishing; shared, straddling and highly migratory fish stocks; trade issues; climate change; and the implications of the recently concluded BBNJ Agreement for fisheries management. The various chapters assess the adequacy of the present law, review issues with its practical implementation, and, where appropriate, make proposals for its reform and future development.

Effective fisheries management faces more challenges today than ever. This book offers many suggestions as to how those challenges may be met. It will therefore be essential reading for all those with an interest in international fisheries law, especially for those tasked with managing fish stocks sustainably and equitably.

Robin Churchill

Editors' Preface

In the aftermath of the adoption of the United Nations Convention on the Law of the Sea in 1982, international fisheries law has considerably developed. The most significant development was the adoption in 1995 of the UN Fish Stocks Agreement, an implementing agreement under the Convention relating to the conservation and management of straddling and highly migratory fish stocks. From what was initially a quasi-vacuum, firm regulations are now established which operate on generally accepted principles of the modern law of the sea. A number of multilateral and regional treaties have been adopted, consecrating rules and principles on which the conservation and management in regard to high seas fisheries and also, as appropriate, EEZ fisheries rely. The instrumentalisation of a rules-based system is also apparent in the creation of a high number of regional fisheries management organisations that play an important role in ensuring autonomous regional developments of international fisheries law. This development does not only arise from the implementation of multilateral treaties such as the Port State Measures Agreement but extends also to the adoption and subsequent implementation of a broad range of non-binding instruments, such as voluntary guidelines that are adopted at the FAO and the United Nations General Assembly sustainable fisheries resolutions. Yet, while international fisheries law is constantly in progress, several challenges persist notwithstanding international efforts that have been invested to take the necessary and appropriate measures to overcome such challenges, one of which relates to IUU fishing. Further, due to climate change-related reasons, new challenges arise, which, together with other problems, call for further attention in order to ensure a widespread ecosystem-based conservation and management regime applicable to international fisheries.

In the autumn of 2019, the idea arose to convene a conference on international fisheries law to discuss persistent and emerging challenges in this field to be organised by the University of the Faroe Islands together with the Law of the Sea Institute of Iceland. The objective was to gather leading and recognised experts in their respective fields but also promising young talents. The speakers represented different regions of the world with an equal gender-based representation. The conference was initially scheduled to be held in Tórshavn, Faroe Islands, in the late summer of 2020 but the COVID-19 pandemic forced the organisers to postpone the conference to the spring of 2021, and again to the summer of 2022.

The conference was finally held from 23–25 June 2022. While initially unfortunate, this delay, in retrospect, proved to be fortunate. With the easing of pandemic restrictions, speakers and a large number of attendees were able to participate in the conference. But also, on matters of substance, the postponement proved beneficial. First, only four days prior to the launch of the conference in 2022, the WTO Members had adopted a multilateral agreement prohibiting harmful fisheries subsidies, considered decisive in the widespread depletion of the world's fish stocks. Second, only two weeks prior to the launch of the conference, the FAO adopted the Voluntary Guidelines for Transshipment. Third, the BBNJ Agreement, although not yet finalised at the time, was in an advanced stage of negotiation. These developments allowed for their timely discussion, which would not have been possible had the conference occurred as originally scheduled.

Following the highly successful conference, it was decided to invite speakers from the conference and a few additional experts to contribute papers for the production of this book, which includes 23 chapters, organised into eight thematic sections. The general aim of the book is to make a contribution to international fisheries law. On the one hand, collecting in a single book different thematic questions of acute relevance for international fisheries which previously have not been dealt with jointly. On the other hand, to enrich the literature within this field with a view to contribute to the further development of international fisheries law. In cooperation with the authors, the topics were carefully and narrowly defined in order to address well-identifiable legal questions that relate to persistent and emerging challenges in international fisheries law. The editors are very grateful to all the authors for accepting to contribute to this book and for providing solid, research-based and thought-provoking chapters, all of which were finalized and submitted in a timely manner.

Finally, the editors wish to thank the publisher Taylor & Francis for accepting the book proposal they submitted in early 2023 and are grateful for the excellent and professional commitment throughout the work.

Bjørn Kunoy, Tórshavn, 29 February 2024
Tomas Heidar, Hamburg, 29 February 2024
Constantinos Yiallourides, Sydney, 29 February 2024

Abbreviations

ABMT	Area-Based Management Tool
ABNJ	Areas Beyond National Jurisdiction
BBNJ Agreement	Agreement Under the United Nations Convention on the Law of the Sea on the Conservation and Sustainable Use of Marine Biological Diversity of Areas beyond National Jurisdiction
CAOFA	Agreement to Prevent Unregulated High Seas Fisheries in the Central Arctic Ocean
CBD	Convention on Biological Diversity
CBS Convention	Convention on the Conservation and Management of Pollock Resources in the Central Bering Sea
CCAMLR	Commission for the Conservation of Antarctic Marine Living Resources
CCSBT	Commission for the Conservation of Southern Bluefin Tuna
CMM	Conservation and Management Measure
CNCP	Cooperating Non-Contracting Party
COFI	Food and Agriculture Organization Committee on Fisheries
COP	Conference of the Parties
DSB	Dispute Settlement Body
DSU	Dispute Settlement Understanding
EBSA	Ecologically or Biologically Significant Marine Area
EEZ	Exclusive Economic Zone
EIA	Environmental Impact Assessment
EU	European Union
FAO	Food and Agriculture Organization of the United Nations
FAO Code of Conduct	Food and Agriculture Organization Code of Conduct for Responsible Fisheries

FAO Compliance Agreement	Food and Agriculture Organization Agreement to Promote Compliance with International Conservation and Management Measures by Fishing Vessels on the High Seas
Fish Stocks Agreement	Agreement for the Implementation of the Provisions of the United Nations Convention on the Law of the Sea of 10 December 1982 relating to the Conservation and Management of Straddling Fish Stocks and Highly Migratory Fish Stocks
FPZ	Fisheries Protection Zone
GATT	General Agreement on Tariffs and Trade
GFCM	General Fisheries Commission for the Mediterranean
IATTC	Inter-American Tropical Tuna Commission
ICCAT	International Commission on the Conservation of Atlantic Tunas
ICES	International Council for the Exploration of the Sea
ICJ	International Court of Justice
IFBs	Instruments, Frameworks, and Bodies
IGC	Intergovernmental Conference
ILC	International Law Commission
IOs	International Organisations
IOTC	Indian Ocean Tuna Commission
IPHC	International Pacific Halibut Commission
IPOA-IUU	Food and Agriculture International Plan of Action to Prevent, Deter and Eliminate Illegal Unreported and Unregulated Fishing
ITLOS	International Tribunal for the Law of the Sea
IUU	Illegal, unreported, and unregulated fishing
JNRFC	Joint Norwegian Russian Fisheries Commission
MCS	Monitoring, Control, and Surveillance
MMPA	United States' Marine Mammal Protection Act
MOU	Memorandum of Understanding
MPA	Marine Protected Area
MSY	Maximum Sustainable Yield
NAFO	Northwest Atlantic Fisheries Organization
NASCO	North Atlantic Salmon Conservation Organization

NEAFC	North-East Atlantic Fisheries Commission
NOAA	United States' National Oceanic and Atmospheric Administration
NPAFC	North Pacific Anadromous Fish Commission
NPFC	North Pacific Fisheries Commission
OECMs	Other Effective Area-Based Conservation Measures
Port States Measures Agreement	Food and Agriculture Organization Agreement on Port State Measures to Prevent, Deter and Eliminate Illegal, Unreported and Unregulated Fishing
PrepCom	Preparatory Committee
PSC	Pacific Salmon Commission
REIO	Regional Economic Integration Organisation
RFMA	Regional Fisheries Management Arrangement
RFMO	Regional Fisheries Management Organisation or Arrangement
SEAFO	South East Atlantic Fisheries Organisation
SIOFA	Southern Indian Ocean Fisheries Agreement
SPRFMO	South Pacific Regional Fisheries Management Organisation
SPS Agreement	WTO Agreement on the Application of Sanitary and Phytosanitary Measures
SPS	Sanitary and phytosanitary
STB	Scientific and Technical Body
TAC	Total allowable catch
TBT Agreement	Agreement on Technical Barriers to Trade
UNCLOS	United Nations Convention on the Law of the Sea
UNGA	United Nations General Assembly
VME	Vulnerable marine ecosystem
VMS	Vessel monitoring systems
Voluntary Guidelines for Flag State Performance	Food and Agriculture Organization Voluntary Guidelines for Flag State Performance 2015
WCPFC	Western and Central Pacific Fisheries Commission
WTO Agreement	Marrakesh Agreement establishing the World Trade Organization
WTO	World Trade Organization

Cases

List of International Cases

Aegean Sea Continental Shelf (Greece v. Turkey), Judgment of 19 December 1978 [1978] ICJ Rep 3.

Allegations of Genocide under the Convention on the Prevention and Punishment of the Crime of Genocide (Ukraine v. Russian Federation), Provisional Measures, Order of 16 March 2022 [2022] ICJ Rep 211.

Applicability of the Obligation to Arbitrate under Section 21 of the United Nations Headquarters Agreement of 26 June 1947, Advisory Opinion [1988] ICJ Rep 12.

Application for Review of Judgement No. 158 of the United Nations Administrative Tribunal, Advisory Opinion, [1973] ICJ Rep 166.

Application for Review of Judgment No. 333 of the United Nations Administrative Tribunal, Advisory Opinion [1987] ICJ Rep 18.

Application of the Convention on the Prevention and Punishment of the Crime of Genocide (The Gambia v. Myanmar), Preliminary Objections, Judgment [2022] ICJ Rep 477.

Application of the International Convention on the Elimination of All Forms of Racial Discrimination (Georgia v. Russian Federation), Preliminary Objections [2011] ICJ Rep 70.

Case concerning Land Reclamation by Singapore in and around the Straits of Johor (Malaysia v. Singapore) Case No. 12, Provisional Measures, Order of 8 October 2003, ITLOS.

Case concerning the Barcelona Traction, Light and Power Company, Limited (Belgium v. Spain), Second Phase (Judgment) [1970] ICJ Rep. 3.

Certain Activities Carried Out by Nicaragua in the Border Area (Costa Rica v. Nicaragua) and Construction of a Road in Costa Rica along the San Juan River (Nicaragua v. Costa Rica), Judgment [2015] ICJ Rep 665.

Certain Activities Carried Out by Nicaragua in the Border Area (Costa Rica v. Nicaragua), Compensation, Judgment [2018] ICJ Rep 15.

Certain Questions of Mutual Assistance in Criminal Matters (Djibouti v. France) [2008] ICJ Rep. 177.

Chagos Marine Protected Area Arbitration (Mauritius v United Kingdom), Award of 18 March 2015, XXXI RIAA 359–606.

Dispute Concerning Coastal State Rights in the Black Sea, Sea of Azov, and Kerch Strait (Ukraine v. Russian Federation), PCA 2017–06, 21 February 2020.

Dispute concerning delimitation of the maritime boundary between Mauritius and Maldives in the Indian Ocean, Case No. 28, Preliminary Objections, Judgment of 28 January 2021, ITLOS.

Dispute concerning the Detention of Ukrainian Naval Vessels and Servicemen (Ukraine v. the Russian Federation), Award on Preliminary Objections, PCA Case 2019–28, 27 June 2022.

Dispute regarding Navigational and Related Rights (Costa Rica v. Nicaragua), Judgment [2009] ICJ Rep 213.

Fisheries Jurisdiction (United Kingdom v. New Zealand), Merits, Judgment [1974] ICJ Rep 3.

Fisheries Jurisdiction Case (Federal Republic of Germany v. Iceland), Merits, Judgment [1974] ICJ Rep 1.

Fisheries Jurisdiction Case (Spain v. Canada), Jurisdiction of the Court, Judgment [1998] ICJ Rep 432.

Fisheries Jurisdiction Case (United Kingdom v. Iceland), Merits, Judgment [1974] ICJ Rep 3.

Fisheries Jurisdiction Case (United Kingdom v. Iceland), Jurisdiction of Court, Judgment, [1973] ICJ Rep 3.

Gabcikovo-Nagymaros Project (Hungary/Slovakia), Judgment [1997] ICJ Rep 7.

Legal Consequences of the Separation of the Chagos Archipelago from Mauritius in 1965 Advisory Opinion [2019] ICJ Rep 95.

Methanex Corp. v. United States of America, UNCITRAL, Partial Award on Jurisdiction, 7 August 2002.

Military and Paramilitary Activities in and against Nicaragua (Nicaragua v. United States of America), Jurisdiction and Admissibility, Judgment [1984] ICJ Rep 392.

MOX Plant Arbitration (Ireland v United Kingdom), Procedural Order No 4, 14 November 2003, PCA.

North Sea Continental Shelf cases (Federal Republic of Germany v. Denmark and Netherlands), Judgment [1969] ICJ Rep 3.

Nuclear Tests Case (Australia v. France) Judgment of 20 December 1974 [1974] ICJ Rep 253.

Pulp Mills on the River Uruguay (Argentina v. Uruguay), (Judgment) [2010] ICJ Re 14.

Request for an Advisory Opinion Submitted by the Sub-regional Fisheries Commission (SRFC), Case No. 21, Advisory Opinion, ITLOS.

Review Panel established under the Convention on the Conservation and Management of High Seas Fishery Resources in the South Pacific Ocean), Findings and Recommendations, 5 July 2013, PCA Case 2013–14.

Review Panel established under the Convention on the Conservation and Management of High Seas Fishery Resources in the South Pacific Ocean, Findings and Recommendations, 1 July 2023, PCA Case 2023–33.

South China Sea Arbitration (Philippines v. China), Award on Jurisdiction and Admissibility, 29 October 2015, PCA Case 2013–19.

South West Africa Cases (Liberia v. South Africa), Second Phase, Judgment [1966] ICJ Rep 6.

Southern Bluefin Tuna (New Zealand v. Japan; Australia v. Japan), Cases Nos. 3 and 4, Provisional Measures, Order of 27 August 1999, [1999] ITLOS.

The Atlanto-Scandian Herring Arbitration (The Kingdom of Denmark in respect of the Faroe Islands v. The European Union), PCA Case 2013–30.

The Bay of Bengal Maritime Boundary Arbitration between the People's Republic of Bangladesh and the Republic of India, Award of 7 July 2014, PCA Case 2010–16, XXXII RIAA 1.

The MOX Plant Case (Ireland v. United Kingdom), Case No. 10, Provisional Measures, Order of 3 December 2001, ITLOS.

Whaling in the Antarctic (Australia v. Japan), Declaration of Intervention of New Zealand, Order of 6 February 2013 [2013] ICJ Rep 3.

WTO Case Law

European Communities – Trade Description of Scallops (DS14), WTO Case No. DS14–1996.

United States – Import Prohibition of Certain Shrimp and Shrimp Products (DS58), WTO Case No. DS58–1996.

Australia – Measures Affecting Importation of Salmon (DS18), WTO Case No. DS18–1997.

United States – Countervailing Duty Investigation of Imports of Salmon from Chile (DS97), WTO Case No. DS97–1997.

Chile – Measures Affecting the Transit and Importation of Swordfish (DS193), WTO Case No. DS193–2000.

European Communities – Trade Description of Sardines (DS231), WTO Case No. DS231–2002.

United States – Customs Bond Directive for Merchandise Subject to Anti-Dumping/Countervailing Duties (DS345), WTO Case No. DS345–2004.

European Communities – Anti-Dumping Measures on Farmed Salmon from Norway (DS337), WTO Case No. DS337–2005.

United States – Anti-Dumping Measures on Certain Shrimp from Ecuador (DS335), WTO Case No. DS335–2005.

Japan – Measures on the Importation of Dried Laver and Seasoned Laver (DS323), WTO Case No. DS323–2006.

United States – Provisional Anti-Dumping Measures on Shrimp from Thailand (DS324), WTO Case No. DS324–2006.

European Communities – Definitive Safeguard Measure on Salmon (DS328), WTO Case No. DS328–2006.

United States – Measures Concerning the Importation, Marketing and Sale of Tuna and Tuna Products (DS381), WTO Case No. DS381–2008.

European Communities – Measures Prohibiting the Importation and Marketing of Seal Products (DS400/DS401), WTO Case No. DS400 and DS401–2009.

United States – Measures Affecting the Importation of Shrimp and Shrimp Products from Viet Nam (US – Shrimp (Viet Nam)), WTO Case No. DS404–2010.

United States – Anti-Dumping Measures on Certain Shrimp from Viet Nam (DS429), WTO Case No. DS429–2011.

European Union – Measures on Atlanto-Scandian Herring (EU – Herring), WTO Case No. DS469–2013.

Korea – Import Bans, and Testing and Certification Requirements for Radionuclides (DS495), WTO Case No. DS495–2016.

United States – Anti-Dumping Measures on Fish Fillets from Viet Nam (DS536), WTO Case No. DS536–2018.

International Legal Instruments

1920 – Treaty concerning the Archipelago of Spitsbergen, 9 February 1920.

1945 – Constitution of the Food and Agriculture Organization of the United Nations (FAO) (16 October 1945) 145 BSP 910.

1945 – Charter of the United Nations, 24 October 1945, 1 UNTS XVI.

1949 – Agreement for the Establishment of the General Fisheries Commission for the Mediterranean, 6 December 1949, 126 UNTS 237.

1959 – North-East Atlantic Fisheries Convention, 24 January 1959.

1960 – United Nations General Assembly, 'Declaration on the Granting of Independence to Colonial Countries and Peoples' (14 December 1960) A/RES/1514(XV).

1966 – International Convention on the Elimination of All Forms of Racial Discrimination, 7 March 1966, Treaty Series, 660 UNTS 195, entered into force 4 January 1969.

1966 – International Convention for the Conservation of Atlantic Tunas, 14 May 1966.

1969 – Vienna Convention on the Law of Treaties, 23 April 1969, 1155 UNTS 331 (VCLT).

1974 – United Nations General Assembly, 'Charter of Economic Rights and Duties of States', 12 December 1974, Resolution 3281 (XXIX).

1975 – Agreement between the Government of the Kingdom of Norway and the Government of the Union of Soviet Socialist Republics on Co-operation in the Fishing Industry (JNRFC Agreement), 11 April 1975.

1978 – Convention on Cooperation in the Northwest Atlantic Fisheries (NAFO Convention), 24 October 1978, 1135 UNTS 369.

1978 – Convention on Future Multilateral Co-Operation in the North-East Atlantic Fisheries (NEAFC Convention), 24 October 1978, 17799 UNTS.

1979 – Convention on Long-Range Transboundary Air Pollution, 13 November 1979, 1302 UNTS 217.

1980 – Convention for the Conservation of Antarctic Marine Living Resources, 20 May 1980, 1329 UNTS 47.

1982 – Convention for the Conservation of Salmon in the North Atlantic Ocean (NASCO Convention), 2 March 1982.

1982 – United Nations Convention on the Law of the Sea (UNCLOS), 10 December 1982, 1833 UNTS 3, entered into force 16 November 1994.

1985 – Treaty between the Government of the United States of America and the Government of Canada Concerning Pacific Salmon (1985) – 1469 UNTS 357.

1992 – Convention on Biological Diversity, 5 June 1992, 1760 UNTS 79, entered into force 29 December 1993.

1993 – Agreement for the establishment of an Indian Ocean Tuna Commission, 15 November 1993, 1927 UNTS 329.

1993 – Agreement to Promote Compliance with International Conservation and Management Measures by Fishing Vessels on the High Seas, 24 November 1993, UNTS 2221, entered into force 24 April 2003.

1994 – Marrakesh Agreement Establishing the World Trade Organization, 15 April 1994, 1867 UNTS 154, entered into force 1 January 1995.

1995 – Agreement for the Implementation of the Provisions of the United Nations Convention on the Law of the Sea of 10 December 1982 relating to the Conservation and Management of Straddling Fish Stocks and Highly Migratory Fish Stocks (1995) – 2167 UNTS 3.

1997 – Convention on the Law of the Non-Navigational Uses of International Watercourses, 21 May 1997, 2999 UNTS 77.

1999 – Agreement between the Government of Iceland, the Government of Norway, and the Government of the Russian Federation Concerning Certain Aspects of Co-operation in the Area of Fisheries, 15 May 1999.

2000 – Convention on the Conservation and Management of Highly Migratory Fish Stocks in the Western and Central Pacific Ocean (WCPFC Convention), 5 September 2000, 2275 UNTS 43.

2001 – Convention on the Conservation and Management of Fishery Resources in the South East Atlantic Ocean, 10 April 2001, 2221 UNTS 189, entered into force 13 April 2003.

2001 – International Law Commission, 'Draft Articles on Responsibility of States for Internationally Wrongful Acts, with commentaries', 2001, II Yearbook of the International Law Commission.

2006 – Southern Indian Ocean Fisheries Agreement, 7 July 2006, 2835 UNTS 409.

2009 – Convention on the Conservation and Management of High Seas Fishery Resources in the South Pacific Ocean, 14 November 2009, 2899 UNTS 211.

2010 – Arrangement between the Government of Republic of Indonesia and the Government of Australia on Consular Notification and Assistance, 10 March 2010.

2010 – Treaty between the Kingdom of Norway and the Russian Federation concerning Maritime Delimitation and Cooperation in the Barents Sea and the Arctic Ocean, Murmansk, 15 September 2010.

2012 – Convention on the Conservation and Management of High Seas Fisheries Resources in the North Pacific Ocean (NPFC Convention), 24 February 2012.

2012 – Convention on the Determination of the Minimal Conditions for Access and Exploitation of Marine Resources within the Maritime Areas under Jurisdiction of the Member States of the Sub-Regional Fisheries Commission, 1 June 2012, entered into force 16 September 2012.

2015 – Paris Agreement, 12 December 2015, 3156 UNTS 79, entered into force 4 November 2016.

2017 – United Nations General Assembly Resolution on the 'International Legally Binding Instrument under the United Nations Convention on the Law of the Sea on the Conservation and Sustainable Use of Marine Biological Diversity of Areas Beyond National Jurisdiction' 24 December 2017 (A/RES/72/249).

2018 – Agreement to Prevent Unregulated High Seas Fisheries in the Central Arctic Ocean (CAOFA Agreement), 3 October 2018.

2019 – Food and Agriculture Organization of the United Nations Agreement on Port State Measures to Prevent, Deter and Eliminate Illegal, Unreported and Unregulated Fishing, 22 November 2019, entered into force 5 June 2016.

2020 – Trade and Cooperation Agreement between the European Union and the United Kingdom, 30 December 2020, entered into force 1 May 2021.

2021 – United Nations General Assembly Resolution on Sustainable Fisheries: A/RES/76/71 (9 December 2021).

2022 – Protocol Amending the Marrakesh Agreement establishing the WTO, Agreement on Fisheries Subsidies, 17 June 2022, not yet in force.

2023 – Agreement under the United Nations Convention on the Law of the Sea on the Conservation and Sustainable Use of Marine Biological Diversity of Areas Beyond National Jurisdiction (BBNJ Agreement), 19 June 2023, A/CONF.232/2023/4, opened for signature on 20 September 2023, not yet in force.

FAO Reports & Guidelines

1995 – FAO, 'Code of Conduct for Responsible Fisheries' (1995) C 95/20/Rev 1.

2001 – FAO, 'International Plan of Action to Prevent, Deter and Eliminate Illegal, Unreported and Unregulated Fishing' (2001).

2001 – FAO, 'The Reykjavik Declaration on Responsible Fisheries in the Marine Ecosystem' (October 2001).

2002 – FAO, 'Report of the Norway-FAO Expert Consultation on the Management of Shared Fish Stocks' (Bergen, Norway, 7–10 October 2002).

2016 – FAO, Fisheries and Aquaculture, 'Report of the 32nd Session of the Committee on Fisheries' (Rome, 11–15 July 2016), report no 1167.

2014 – FAO, 'Voluntary Guidelines for Flag State Performance' (June 2014).

2017 – FAO, 'Voluntary Guidelines for Catch Documentation Schemes' (July 2017).

2018 – FAO, Fisheries and Aquaculture Report, 'Report of the 33rd Session of the Committee on Fisheries' (Rome, 9–13 July 2018), FIAP/R1249.

2018 – FAO, 'Global Study on Transshipment: Regulations, Practices, Monitoring and Control' (Rome, June 2018).

2021 – FAO, Fisheries and Aquaculture, 'Report of the 34th Session of the Committee on Fisheries' (Rome, 1–5 February 2021), report no 1336.

2021 – FAO, Fisheries and Aquaculture, 'Report of the Expert Consultation on Voluntary Guidelines for Transshipment' (Virtual meeting, 11–15 October 2021), Report no 1363.

2022 – FAO, Fisheries and Aquaculture, 'Report of the Technical Consultation on Voluntary Guidelines for Transshipment' (Rome, 30 May–3 June and 7 July 2022), report no 1385, Appendix E.

2022 – FAO, 'Voluntary Guidelines for Transshipment' (2022).

Part I

Introduction

1 International Fisheries Law

Persistent and Emerging Challenges

Bjørn Kunoy, Tomas Heidar and Constantinos Yiallourides

1. Introduction: International Fisheries Law in the Face of Evolving Issues

In 1954, the world's population stood at 2.8 billion, increasing to 4.1 billion by 1974 and to 8.2 billion by 2024.[1] Over the past seven decades, the population has tripled, and projections suggest a sustained upward trajectory, with an anticipated 10 billion people by the year 2050.[2] The expansion of the world's population means that food production must steadily increase to avoid widespread hunger and malnutrition. Yet, the challenges are numerous, most notably, climate change, overexploitation of living marine resources and diminishing arable land. Living marine resources play a key role in human food supply. This is illustrated by the fact that fish represents approximately 20% of the animal protein consumed worldwide.[3] While aquaculture has developed significantly during the last 30 years, reaching an annual worldwide production of approximately 90 million tonnes, in comparison to 20 million tonnes in 1995, capture fisheries production remains important, levelling approximately an annual 90 million tonnes production.[4] Capture fisheries production amounts to around 25% of the annual meat production levelling about 370 million tonnes.[5] The importance of seafood in the general human food chain exemplifies the necessity to ensure a comprehensive international legal framework, providing for sustainable conservation and management of all living marine resources.

1 United Nations Population Fund, *World Population Dashboard*. www.unfpa.org/data/world-population-dashboard.

2 ibid; Infographic, 'World Population Day: What will the world look like in 2050?', *Aljazeera* (11 Jul 2023) <www.aljazeera.com/news/2023/7/11/world-population-day-what-will-the-world-look-like-in-2050>.

3 FAO, *The State of World Fisheries and Aquaculture 2022. Towards Blue Transformation* (2022). https://doi.org/10.4060/cc0461en.

4 ibid.

5 ibid; see also Hannah Ritchie and Max Roser, 'Fish and Overfishing: How are Fish Stocks Changing Across the World? How Much is Overfished?' (first published October 2021). https://ourworldindata.org/fish-and-overfishing.

DOI: 10.4324/9781003492030-2

Many changes have taken place in the international legal fisheries regime since the 200-nautical mile fisheries jurisdiction zones were established in the 1970s, more than 50 years ago. Among the achievements are first and foremost the adoption in 1982, and subsequent entry into force in 1994, of the United Nations Convention on the Law of the Sea ('UNCLOS')[6] and the UN Fish Stocks Agreement ('UNFSA'), adopted in 1995 and entered into force in 2001.[7] Other achievements account the Code of Conduct for Responsible Fisheries adopted in 1995 by the Food and Agriculture Organization of the United Nations ('FAO')[8], the FAO Technical Guidelines for Responsible Fisheries, adopted in 2006[9], the FAO International Guidelines for the Management of Deep-Sea Fisheries in the High Seas, adopted in 2008,[10] the conclusion of the Agreement to Promote Compliance with International Conservation and Management Measures by Fishing Vessels on the High Seas, adopted in 1993 and entered into force in 2003,[11] the conclusion of the Agreement on Port State Measures to Prevent, Deter and Eliminate Illegal, Unreported and Unregulated Fishing ('Port State Measures Agreement'), adopted in 2009 and entered into force in 2016,[12] the adoption in 2014 of the FAO Voluntary Guidelines for Flag State Performance,[13] and, more recently, the adoption in 2022 of the FAO Voluntary Guidelines for Transshipment.[14] Further, in June 2023, the United Nations adopted a new treaty under UNCLOS, the Agreement on the Conservation and Sustainable Use of Marine Biological Diversity of Areas beyond National Jurisdiction ('BBNJ Agreement').[15] The BBNJ Agreement may play a role in the

6 United Nations Convention on the Law of the Sea (UNCLOS) adopted 10 December 1982, 1833 UNTS 3, entered into force on 16 November 1994.

7 Agreement for the Implementation of the Provisions of the United Nations Convention on the Law of the Sea of 10 December 1982 relating to the Conservation and Management of Straddling Fish Stocks and Highly Migratory Fish Stocks ('UNFSA') (1995), 4 August 1995–2167 UNTS 3, entered into force 11 December 2001.

8 FAO, 'Code of Conduct for Responsible Fisheries' (1995). www.wto.org/english/tratop_e/rulesneg_e/fish_e/1995_fao_ccrf.pdf.

9 FAO, 'Technical Guidelines for Responsible Fisheries: Food and Agriculture Organization' (2006). www.fao.org/documents/card/en?details=6a4a1130-e111-5abf-99dd-c4226eef5ea2/.

10 FAO, 'International Guidelines for the Management of Deep-Sea Fisheries in the High Seas: Food and Agriculture Organization' (2008). www.sprfmo.int/assets/Meetings/Meetings-before-2013/Scientific-Working-Group/SWG-06-2008/7e88751513/SPRFMO6-SWG-INF01-FAO-Deepwater-Guidelines-Final-Sep20.pdf.

11 'Agreement to Promote Compliance with International Conservation and Management Measures by Fishing Vessels on the High Seas: Food and Agriculture Organization' (1993). www.fao.org/iuu-fishing/international-framework/fao-compliance-agreement/en/.

12 'Agreement on Port State Measures to Prevent, Deter and Eliminate Illegal, Unreported and Unregulated Fishing ('PSMA')' (22 November 2009, entered into force 5 June 2016). www.fao.org/port-state-measures/en/.

13 FAO, 'Voluntary Guidelines for Flag State Performance ('VGFSP')'. www.fao.org/iuu-fishing/international-framework/voluntary-guidelines-for-flag-state-performance/en/.

14 FAO, 'Voluntary Guidelines for Transshipment: Food and Agriculture Organization' (2022). www.fao.org/3/cc6029en/cc6029en.pdf.

15 United Nations, 'Demonstrating the "Power of Multilateralism", Intergovernmental Conference Adopts Historic New Maritime Biodiversity Treaty', *United Nations* (19 June 2023). https://press.un.org/en/2023/sea2181.doc.htm.

international regime applicable to high-seas fisheries. Finally, to combat unsustainable fisheries, the World Trade Organization ('WTO') has, in 2022, adopted a new binding multilateral Agreement on Fisheries Subsidies, which marks a significant step as it sets a prohibition on harmful fisheries subsidies which are a key factor in the widespread depletion of the world's fish stocks.[16]

The UN General Assembly has also been paying an ever-closer attention to sustainable fisheries. Since 2003, the General Assembly has adopted an annual resolution consecrating principles relevant to ensuring sustainable fisheries governance. Its actions have also generated an impetus among relevant States to establish regional fisheries management organisations ('RFMOs') where these did not yet exist. Two such RFMOs were created, in 2012[17] and 2015,[18] in regard to high seas areas of the South and North Pacific Oceans, respectively, establishing conservation and management mandates that extend up to almost 80 million square kilometres. The actions undertaken by the General Assembly have also resulted in performance review mechanisms, which the RFMOs in general terms can be seen to follow. Yet, despite the establishment of over twenty RFMOs worldwide and the success of some RFMOs in improving the status of certain fish stocks, the percentage of stocks fished at biologically unsustainable levels has been increasing.

In some cases, the overexploitation occurring within the spatial mandate of relevant RFMOs results from poor compliance with obligations that have been undertaken therein. Elsewhere, this arises from structural problems applicable to the relevant RFMO, disallowing effective RFMO management. One such characteristic is the lack of general dispute settlement provisions within several RFMOs allowing States with quasi-full discretion to lodge objections to management measures that are adopted by the RFMO. Most often, this results in the adoption of unilateral quotas, the implication of which is that the cumulative catches by far exceed the scientifically advised total catch. One such RFMO is the North-East Atlantic Fisheries Commission ('NEAFC') in which Member States may unilaterally and almost in full discretion lodge objections to any management measure, and by so doing making that management measure inapplicable to the objecting Member State.[19] Accordingly, while there are RFMOs in which the precautionary approach is an overarching principle, difficult to get around, where objections may be lodged according to the discretion of a relevant Member State, the precautionary approach, or for that matter any sound conservation approach to fisheries, loses its practical value. Yet, most RMFOs that are recently established have incorporated

16 World Trade Organization (WTO), 'Plurilateral Agreement on Fisheries Subsidies: World Trade Organization' (2022). www.wto.org/english/tratop_e/rulesneg_e/fish_e/fish_factsheet_e.pdf.

17 'Convention on the Conservation and Management of High Seas Fishery Resources in the South Pacific Ocean ('SPRFMO')' (adopted 2009, entered into force 2012). https://treaties.un.org/pages/showDetails.aspx?objid=0800000280363a44.

18 North Pacific Fisheries Commission ('NPFC'). www.npfc.int.

19 'Convention on Future Multilateral Cooperation in North-East Atlantic Fisheries' (adopted 1980, entered into force 1982). www.neafc.org/system/files/Text-of-NEAFC-Convention-04.pdf.

compulsory dispute settlement provisions. Accordingly, Member States of these RFMOs may not at their discretion lodge objections and establish opposable unilateral quotas that may otherwise risk rendering nugatory the conservation and management measures adopted by such RFMOs. The South Pacific Regional Fisheries Management Organisation ('SPRFMO') and the North Pacific Fisheries Commission ('NPFC') are two such illustrations. Further, some older RFMOs, such as the North Atlantic Fisheries Organization ('NAFO'), have amended their constitutive treaties in order to incorporate quasi-compulsory dispute settlement provisions, significantly diminishing the discretion of Member States of the RFMOs to lodge an objection to a conservation and management measure. These are important tools in order to avoid overexploitation of fish stocks, and to further bolster cooperation among all Member States of the relevant RFMOs.

The role that RFMOs play in preventing, deterring and eliminating illegal, unreported and unregulated fishing ('IUU fishing') cannot be overestimated. They have taken a leading role in implementing the Port State Measures Agreement, preventing not only vessels that are sighted in their convention areas from accessing any ports of the Member States but also entering into memorandums of understanding with other RFMOs providing that vessels listed by an RFMO are to be promptly placed on the IUU list of the cooperating RFMO. Yet, the operation of many of the RFMOs is by no means to be seen as an easy ride. The challenges are numerous, including, but not limited to, fundamental public international law questions relating to the exercise of self-determination, and jurisdictional spatial overlaps with other RFMOs, all of which are dependent on close cooperation among the relevant RFMOs. The role that RFMOs have been given to ensure effective tools to combat IUU fishing is likely in the aftermath of the FAO Voluntary Guidelines for Transshipment to be reproduced in the elaboration of rules on transshipment within the operation of the relevant RFMOs.

Accordingly, RFMOs cannot but be seen as pillars in the establishment of a modern law applicable to high-seas fisheries. Yet, while the success is obvious, there are also emerging challenges arising as a result of climate change and ocean acidification, the effects of which are not limited to high-seas fisheries. The advent of climate change and its observable impacts on the world's oceans challenges the narrative that there is a measurable point at which target fish species can be maximally and sustainably caught allowing, in principle, exploitation to be continued indefinitely. This is the thinking behind maximum sustainable yield. This arises as ocean warming and acidification are expected to alter species distributions, abundance, and ecosystem structures, resulting in greater uncertainty in ocean ecosystems, which are already difficult for scientists to monitor. This poses difficult challenges in determining and setting a total allowable catch based on attaining a maximum sustainable yield. These changes are also susceptible to result in changes to migratory patterns of fish stocks, not only rendering further complex the delicate undertaking to agree on compatible measures in regard to straddling fish stocks, in other words, stocks that straddle areas under national jurisdiction and the high seas, but further burdens the process to agree on the allocation of a shared resource. The emerging challenges appearing from climate change become accordingly linked to persistent challenges that have existed for a number of years and addressed with a variable degree of success. These are the jurisdictional limitations within UNCLOS and the UN Fish Stocks Agreement to address the conduct of coastal States in regard to fisheries management, so far that the conduct in question relates to their sovereign rights to manage and exploit those parts of the stocks that are (also) within their maritime areas under national jurisdiction. This difficulty prompts the question of whether a request for an advisory opinion from the International Tribunal for the Law of the Sea (ITLOS) can plausibly be seen as a remedy for the challenges that follow the application of the compatibility requirement, as further exacerbated by climate change, or, alternatively, relying on compulsory conciliation proceedings, are to be considered as a way forward.

2. Aim of the Book

The previously cited broad considerations demonstrate that the evolution of the international legal regime governing fisheries over the past half-century reflects a dynamic and complex response to the escalating challenges of conserving and managing living marine resources. Advancements in the international law of the sea, including through the adoption of various new agreements and soft law instruments, signify a collective effort to respond to these challenges. Yet, significant challenges remain.

RFMOs have played, and continue to play, a crucial role in combating overfishing and illegal fishing activities. However, the rapid growth of the world population, coupled with the pressing need for sustainable food sources, the emerging and ever-intensifying threats of climate change and ocean acidification and their various impacts on marine biodiversity and fish migration patterns, present new and multifaceted challenges. These developments underscore that the management of our oceans need continuous adaptation and innovation, as well as stronger cooperation among nations to ensure the long-term sustainability of marine fishery resources.

This book seeks to present and explore both theoretical and applied perspectives on persistent and emerging challenges in contemporary international fisheries law. It brings together a highly knowledgeable group of contributors, including established authorities in international law and the law of the sea, as well as emerging talents representing diverse legal traditions and various regions across the world. While some of the topics have received little or no previous attention, other topics have been addressed elsewhere but remain relevant due to their persisting and unresolved character in international fisheries law.

This book is not intended to replace existing materials but to complement them, and hopefully, it will bring the issues to the attention of a broader audience. Nor is it designed to provide an exhaustive exposition of all the challenges in international fisheries law. Many topics covered in this book could benefit from further exploration, and numerous others could have been included if not for the limitations of time and space.[20]

20 Climate change, for instance, is dealt with at several points but considerations on the intersection of climate change and fisheries law could easily form a voluminous book of their own.

Contributors were invited to analyse the various factors contributing to international fisheries governance challenges, institutional law frameworks, as well as substantive and procedural aspects for addressing them. In addition to highlighting important developments in the field, contributors were invited to systematically evaluate diverse areas of international fisheries law that may require further modification or advancement to address persistent and emerging pressures on oceans. Accordingly, various chapters assess the adequacy of existing legal frameworks in light of advanced scientific knowledge, scrutinising whether they effectively tackle new challenges. They also examine the presence of governance and compliance mechanisms necessary for the effective implementation of the law in its current state and foreseeable evolving dimensions. Finally, various chapters have proposed future-oriented perspectives and solutions to rectify identified regulatory weaknesses, gaps or barriers hindering cooperation for sustainable fisheries management. In some instances, existing legal instruments may need refinement, adaptation or improvement, while in other areas entirely new perspectives are required.

As such, this book aims to enrich international fisheries law scholarship and to form a valuable documentary source for all readers interested in understanding these persistent and emerging challenges in international fisheries law and where future solutions might lie.

3. Structure of the Book

The book is composed of 23 chapters, organised into eight thematic sections. Section I introduces the overall scope, aim and structural organisation of the book, drawing insights from the discussions throughout the book. Section II focuses on governance and institutional challenges in RFMOs. Section III explores dispute settlement mechanisms in RFMOs. Section IV addresses issues pertaining to combating IUU Fishing. Section V covers a range of substantive and procedural aspects in fisheries disputes, followed by trade-related measures and fisheries in Section VI. Section VII examines the BBNJ process and its implications for international fisheries management. Finally, Section VIII presents selected perspectives on the intersection of climate change and international fisheries law.

3.1. Section II: Governance and Institutional Challenges in Regional Fisheries Management Organisations

Section II of the book addresses selected challenges in RFMOs, including issues of decolonisation, overlapping geographical mandates and non-compliance. *Valentin J. Schatz* provides an analysis of the United Kingdom's involvement in the Indian Ocean Tuna Commission ('IOTC') in the Chagos Archipelago, a territory claimed by Mauritius. The analysis serves as a case study to investigate the participation of former colonial powers in RFMOs on behalf of overseas territories subject to decolonisation claims by other RFMO members. The chapter provides an overview of the international legal framework for RFMO participation and examines the legal status and incomplete decolonisation of the Chagos Archipelago. It also provides a useful legal analysis of Mauritius' challenge to the UK's IOTC membership within the IOTC's legal and institutional framework. *Erik J. Molenaar* addresses the issue of overlapping geographical mandates of RFMOs in the context of the gradual evolution of international law. Overlapping mandates can lead to conflicts, especially in areas with shared target species or differing fishing techniques impacting non-target species or habitats. The analysis explores the reasons for such overlaps, the potential conflicts, and the arrangements developed to avoid conflicts and ensure complementarity. Special attention is given to the evolving geographical and species overlap between NEAFC and the Joint Norwegian-Russian Fisheries Commission. Finally, *Adriana Fabra* focuses on the primary objective of RFMOs to promote cooperation among States for effective fisheries conservation and management and explains the challenges faced by RFMOs in ensuring member compliance. As Fabra observes, despite the establishment of over twenty RFMOs, there has been an increase in the percentage of stocks fished at unsustainable levels since 1974. The analysis investigates the reasons for non-compliance, explores the inadequacies in identifying and addressing non-compliance, and seeks to provide solutions based on outcomes from expert workshops and subsequent recommendations by specialists in RFMO compliance.

3.2. Section III: Dispute Settlement Mechanisms in Regional Fisheries Management Organisations

Section III of the book examines various dispute settlement perspectives in RFMOs. *Samuel Wordsworth KC* emphasises the relationship between dispute settlement mechanisms under UNCLOS and those embedded in existing RFMOs. The chapter underscores the necessity of determining which RFMOs can offer a pathway to compulsory jurisdiction through Part XV of UNCLOS. Additionally, it explores the consideration of UNCLOS provisions as part of the applicable law in disputes arising within RFMOs. *James Harrison* provides a detailed analysis of emerging dispute settlement principles and practices within RFMOs. The analysis encompasses diplomatic and legal mechanisms, as well as innovative procedures found in RFMO treaties. These include dispute prevention tools and ad hoc technical panels designed to address disputes related to high-seas fish stocks. The chapter also highlights persistent challenges arising from the multilateral and technical nature of high-seas fisheries disputes. Finally, *Osvaldo Urrutia* explores the objection procedure within SPRFMO. Over SPRFMO's ten-year existence, the objection mechanism has been triggered three times concerning allocation decisions in regard to the jack mackerel fishery. The cases involve objections raised by Russia in 2013, Ecuador in 2018, and Russia again in 2023. The chapter contextualises the objection mechanism structure, summarises the three cases, and evaluates the Review Panel's recommendations, assessing their effectiveness in resolving short- and long-term allocation conflicts among SPRFMO members.

3.3. Section IV: Combating Illegal, Unreported and Unregulated (IUU) Fishing

Section IV of the book comprises three chapters offering critical insights into persistent and emerging challenges in combating IUU Fishing. *Eva R. van der Marel and Mercedes Rosello* explore the important role of RFMOs in combating IUU fishing, focusing in particular on IUU fishing vessel listing cooperation, exchange of information and current RFMO practices. Their chapter further analyses these practices against the duty to cooperate as a fundamental aspect of international environmental law. They analyse the international legal personality of RFMOs and the corresponding obligations they may have in addressing IUU fishing. Importantly, the analysis in this chapter explores whether the practice of cross-listing should be part of RFMOs' duty to cooperate, concluding that this may be undesirable without additional safeguards. *Dita Liliansa* provides an insightful overview of Indonesia's enforcement measures against IUU fishing vessels. She explains that despite its substantial control over living marine resources, Indonesia faces both persistent and emerging challenges in combating IUU fishing within its EEZ. The chapter further examines Indonesia's efforts in enforcing national laws and regulations over living resources in its EEZ and addresses law enforcement practices in undelimited areas. *Meggan Engelke-Ros* focuses on transshipment as part of an integrated scheme of monitoring measures. She explains that transshipment, in other words, the direct transfer of fish from one vessel to another at sea or in port, is crucial for fishing operations but also poses increasing challenges related to IUU fishing. The chapter discusses measures developed by States and RFMOs to monitor and control transshipment, emphasising its impact on IUU fishing. Engelke-Ros expertly highlights the integration of these measures into broader monitoring schemes and reviews recent voluntary guidelines adopted by the FAO for the control of transshipment.

3.4. Section V: Substantive and Procedural Aspects in Fisheries Disputes

Section V of the book addresses selected substantive and procedural challenges in international fisheries disputes as well as gaps in existing compulsory dispute settlement mechanisms. *Ben Juratowitch KC* focuses on the limitations concerning the compulsory settlement of fisheries disputes in the EEZ under Article 297(3)(a) of UNCLOS. The chapter carefully examines the scope of this limitation, considering relevant treaty terms and case law pertinent to Article 297(3)(a). It concludes by raising interpretative questions as an 'emerging' challenge in international fisheries law. *Alina Miron* explores compulsory conciliation proceedings concerning disputes over the conservation and management of fish stocks. She investigates the operation and potential application of compulsory conciliation procedures under UNCLOS. A conclusion is drawn that despite its inclusion in UNCLOS, conciliation has only played a marginal role in the dispute settlement system under UNCLOS. Conciliation has never been resorted to in fisheries-related disputes. This is because States have increased access to judicial means and specialised bodies, established under sectorial or regional conventions. Such means seem to be preferred to a method of dispute settlement which remains, in the end, amicable. *Yoshifumi Tanaka* examines the uncertainty surrounding the applicability of compulsory procedures to international disputes over fish stocks straddling the EEZ and high seas. The chapter analyses the intractability of disputes concerning straddling fish stocks before examining the jurisdiction of adjudicative bodies acting under Part XV of UNCLOS from three viewpoints: the consent of States, the effective settlement of international disputes and safeguarding common interests of the international community or community interests. *Constantinos Yiallourides* discusses the scope of obligations in Article 63(1) of UNCLOS on the management of shared fish stocks. He outlines the substantive and procedural aspects of Article 63(1) and explores persistent and emerging challenges to its implementation. The chapter emphasises the due diligence obligations incumbent on States to seek to exchange information, consult with other affected EEZ States, and negotiate meaningfully and in good faith with a view to arriving at a cooperative agreement. *Sean D. Murphy* concludes this section with a chapter on straddling and highly migratory fish stocks. The chapter explores the legal framework surrounding the 'compatibility requirement' for conservation and management measures and identifies ambiguities impeding international cooperation. It suggests considering whether an RFMO should seek an advisory opinion from ITLOS to clarify the nature and scope of the compatibility requirement. While doubts have been raised about addressing abstract legal questions through advisory proceedings, Murphy argues that an advisory opinion could allow for a more granular legal understanding as to how States should be cooperating in the conservation and management of straddling fish stocks and highly migratory species.

3.5. Section VI: Trade-Related Measures and Fisheries

Section VI of the book explores the intersection between international trade regulations and fisheries management. *Valerie Hughes* probes the role of public international law in shaping decisions made by the WTO, particularly focusing on cases involving living marine resources. She examines instances where public international law was deemed inappropriate for resolving WTO disputes and explores ways to better enhance fisheries conservation and management through trade-related dispute resolution. *Clarisse Morgan* discusses the WTO Agreement on Fisheries Subsidies, a significant development adopted at the 12th Ministerial Conference in 2022. The Agreement aims to promote ocean sustainability by prohibiting harmful fisheries subsidies and addresses the issue of IUU fishing. She explains how the provisions of the Agreement obligate WTO members to cease subsidising vessels or operators found engaged in IUU fishing, fostering transparency in IUU findings and subsidy-related measures. *Iain Sandford and Ariane Vincent* provide a focused analysis of international trade rules, particularly those of the WTO, and how these seek to achieve a balance between disciplining measures affecting trade for economic goals while allowing regulatory space for other policy objectives. Using trade in marine resource products as a case study, they analyse how adjudicators and negotiators have applied rules strictly to economic objectives while allowing flexibility for health protection, environmental and 'moral' considerations. The chapter concludes by discussing the implications of this varying application on security, and predictability, and outlines choices available to policy makers and litigants in structuring, defending, or challenging trade measures. Finally, *Kathleen Claussen* examines how the United States (U.S.) implements the import provisions of the Marine Mammal Protection Act (MMPA). The U.S. Government is restructuring obligations for fisheries exporting to the U.S., requiring them to meet a specified level of marine mammal protection. This approach aims to balance environmental and animal advocacy concerns with business and foreign trade considerations. The chapter uses the MMPA's Import Rule as an example to highlight the persistent challenges faced by governments in reconciling conflicting public policy aims and international commitments in the realm of trade and environmental protection.

3.6. Section VII: The Biodiversity Beyond National Jurisdiction Process (BBNJ Process) and Implications for Fisheries Management

In **Section VII** of the book, two chapters provide insights into the negotiations leading up to the conclusion of the BBNJ Agreement and the broader implications on international fisheries management. *Daniela Diz* explores diverse perspectives on the relationship between the BBNJ Agreement and RFMOs operating under their respective conventions. She specifically addresses the non-undermining concept in relation to the BBNJ Agreement and RFMOs' mandates related to area-based management tools ('ABMTs'), with a focus on marine protected areas ('MPAs') and other effective area-based conservation measures ('OECMs'). OECMs, a concept emerging under the Convention on Biological Diversity ('CBD'), are increasingly gaining attention from RFMOs. Accordingly, Diz further explores the potential role of the BBNJ Agreement in facilitating cross-sectoral cooperation to ensure that OECMs identified by RFMOs can deliver biodiversity conservation outcomes. *Kentaro Nishimoto* concentrates on the changes that may occur in the functioning of RFMOs upon the entry into force of the BBNJ Agreement. He reviews the relevant provisions of the Agreement and their relationship with instruments, frameworks and bodies ('IFBs'), including RFMOs. The chapter identifies and discusses mechanisms through which the BBNJ Agreement aims to establish a more coherent governance system for areas beyond national jurisdiction ('ABNJ'), including creating a platform for interaction among IFBs, issuing non-binding recommendations, and influencing Parties' behaviour within IFBs. In conclusion, Nishimoto observes that while RFMOs will continue to play their roles in managing high-seas fisheries resources, they will be invited and expected to interact within the new legal framework under the BBNJ Agreement. Thus, their performance could come under increased scrutiny regarding possible recommendations regarding ABMTs/MPAs or guidelines and/or standards on environmental impact assessments ('EIAs') adopted under the BBNJ framework.

3.7. Section VIII: Climate Change and Fisheries

Finally, **Section VIII** focuses on selected challenges for international fisheries law arising as a result of anthropogenic climate change. The first of two chapters on this topic, by *Ethan Beringen*, explores the foundational principles of current international fisheries law, and how the Anthropocene concept challenges the continued relevance of these principles. He explains that human activities are the primary driver of planetary change, particularly in climate, which in turn makes oceans susceptible to various persisting stressors. These include ocean warming, acidification and sea-level rise, as well as other threats to marine biodiversity, such as overfishing, shipping and pollution. The chapter concludes that foundational narratives underpinning international fisheries law will need to be rethought in the context of the emerging conditions of the Anthropocene Ocean. The book concludes with a chapter by *Andrew Serdy*, focusing specifically on the implications of climate change on the management of straddling and shared fish stocks. He argues against the necessity for a radical transformation of international fisheries law to address the consequences of fish stocks redistributing across international boundaries due to climatic cycles. Instead, he underscores the need for States and RFMOs to enhance the responsiveness of allocative regimes through pre-agreed mechanisms. The chapter questions the assumption that fish stocks will not move or will move in one direction only and rather emphasises the importance of avoiding the reopening of settled EEZ boundaries. Serdy suggests that the transferability of quotas may be a solution, contingent on a more robust foundation for rights claimed from participation in high seas fisheries.

Part II

Governance and Institutional Challenges in Regional Fisheries Management Organisations

2 Decolonizing RFMOs

The Case of The United Kingdom's IOTC Membership on Behalf of the Chagos Archipelago

Valentin J. Schatz

1. Introduction

States participate in regional fisheries management organisations or arrangements (RFMOs)[1] because of economic interests in exploiting fish stocks falling within the scope of the relevant RFMO's competence or other interests, such as conservation, social, or political aims.[2] Legal and institutional analysis of RFMOs usually focuses on their primary mandate to adopt conservation and management measures (CMMs),[3] together with related measures on issues such as monitoring, control and surveillance, compliance and enforcement, governance, and science.[4] One issue which has – to this author's knowledge – attracted limited scholarly commentary so far is the role – if any – of RFMOs in relation to the decolonisation of, and sovereignty disputes related to, overseas territories of former colonial powers.[5]

1 For an explanation of the institutional differences between regional fisheries management organisations and regional fisheries management arrangements, see James Harrison, 'Key Challenges Relating to the Governance of Regional Fisheries' in Richard Caddell and Erik Molenaar (eds), *Strengthening International Fisheries Law in an Era of Changing Oceans* (Hart 2019) 83–6. This chapter refers to RFMOs as including regional fisheries management organisations or arrangements unless indicated otherwise.

2 On RFMOs generally, see Rosemary Rayfuse, 'Regional Fisheries Management Organizations' in Donald Rothwell et al. (eds), *The Oxford Handbook of the Law of the Sea* (OUP 2015).

3 See Agreement for the Implementation of the Provisions of the United Nations Convention on the Law of the Sea of 10 December 1982 relating to the Conservation and Management of Straddling Fish Stocks and Highly Migratory Fish Stocks, 4 August 1995, 2167 UNTS 3, entered into force 11 December 2001 (Fish Stocks Agreement), art 10(a). Art 1(1)(b) of the Fish Stocks Agreement defines 'conservation and management measures' as 'measures to conserve and manage one or more species of living marine resources that are adopted and applied consistent with the relevant rules of international law as reflected in [UNCLOS] and [the Fish Stocks Agreement]'.

4 Fish Stocks Agreement, art 10(b) to 10(m); Erik Molenaar, 'Regional Fisheries Management Organizations' in Marta Ribeiro, Fernando Bastos and Tore Henriksen (eds), *Global Challenges and the Law of the Sea* (Springer 2020) 89.

5 There are limited exceptions, see Gabriela Oanta, 'European Union – Falkland Islands Fisheries Relations Post Brexit' (2022) 52 *Ocean Development & International Law* 325; Bruno Arpi and Jeffrey McGee, 'Fishing Around the South Georgia Islands and the "Question of the Falklands/Malvinas": Unprecedented Challenges for the Antarctic Treaty System' (2022) 143 *Marine Policy* 1. For a dispute settlement perspective, see Marco Benatar, 'Not Like the Others? The Position of

DOI: 10.4324/9781003492030-4

Most remaining overseas territories of former colonial powers are coastal or even island territories.[6] Most are located in Africa.[7] In the absence of a universally accepted definition of the expression 'overseas territories', this chapter uses a broad understanding which includes 'all territories that in some way are politically dependent on a relatively distant metropolitan State and were or are significant, as such, from the perspective of international law'.[8] Former colonial powers, most prominently the United Kingdom (UK) and France, enjoy RFMO membership as 'coastal States' on behalf of some overseas territories. These former colonial powers thereby influence the fisheries policy of not only these overseas territories themselves, but also of the region falling within the spatial mandate of the relevant RFMO. If another RFMO member claims sovereignty over the overseas territory, particularly as a territory pending decolonisation, the ensuing dispute can affect the RFMO's ability to exercise its fisheries conservation and management mandate.[9] Moreover, such disputes can politicise the functioning of the RFMO on issues which do not fall within the RFMO's competence, meaning that the RFMO may not be able to address adequately these issues.

This chapter uses the UK's participation in the Indian Ocean Tuna Commission (IOTC) on behalf of the Chagos Archipelago, which is contested by Mauritius, as a case-study to examine the issue of RFMO participation by former colonial powers on behalf of overseas territories subject to decolonisation claims by other RFMO members. The IOTC is an RFMO mandated to conserve and manage highly migratory fish stocks – particularly tuna – in most of the Indian Ocean.[10] For reasons of space, this chapter will not discuss the law of decolonisation, a concept described as 'a process that signifies the attainment of independence of colonial territories, mandates, trusteeship territories, non-self-governing territories, and the remnants in these categories'.[11] Rather, this chapter, first, provides an overview of

Associated States and Dependent Territories in Fishing Disputes' (2020) 22 *International Community Law Review* 471.

6 See generally Gregor Novak, 'Overseas Territories, Australia, France, Netherlands, New Zealand, United Kingdom, United States of America' (last updated July 2017), in Anne Peters (ed), *Max Planck Encyclopedia of Public International Law* (OUP online 2024).

7 See generally Malcolm Shaw, *Title to Territory in Africa: International Legal Issues* (OUP 1986).

8 ibid, para 1.

9 See, for example, Bruno Arpi and Jeffrey McGee, 'Fishing Around the South Georgia Islands and the "Question of the Falklands/Malvinas": Unprecedented Challenges for the Antarctic Treaty System' (2022) 143 *Marine Policy* 4–9.

10 IOTC, 'Competence: Area and Species' (2022). https://iotc.org/about-iotc/competence accessed 1 October 2023.

11 Rahmatullah Khan, 'Decolonisation' (last updated May 2011) in Anne Peters (ed), *Max Planck Encyclopedia of Public International Law* (OUP online 2024), para 1. See also UNGA, 'Declaration on the Granting of Independence to Colonial Countries and Peoples' (14 December 1960) A/RES/1514(XV). For detailed analysis of the concept of self-determination, see, for example, Rosalyn Higgins, *Problems and Process: International Law and How We Use It* (Clarendon 1995) 111–28; Antonio Cassese, *Self-determination of Peoples: A Legal Reappraisal* (CUP 1996); Christian Walter, Antje von Ungern-Sternberg and Kavus Abushov (eds), *Self-Determination and Secession in International Law* (OUP 2014); Miriam Bak Mckenna, *Reckoning with Empire: Self-Determination*

the international legal framework on participation in RFMOs. Next, it examines the legal status and pending decolonisation of the Chagos Archipelago. The remainder of this chapter analyses Mauritius' challenge to the UK's IOTC membership on behalf of the Chagos Archipelago within the IOTC's legal and institutional framework.

2. Rules of Participation in RFMOs: An Overview

Generally speaking, two sets of rules of international law governing participation in RFMOs must be distinguished. First, a global legal framework for participation is laid down in the 1982 United Nations Convention on the Law of the Sea (UNCLOS),[12] and, more specifically, the Agreement for the Implementation of the Provisions of the United Nations Convention on the Law of the Sea of 10 December 1982 relating to the Conservation and Management of Straddling Fish Stocks and Highly Migratory Fish Stocks (Fish Stocks Agreement)[13] – although with 93 States Parties, the Fish Stocks Agreement remains far from UNCLOS' near-universal participation status.[14] Second, the constitutive instruments of RFMOs often contain more specific rules on participation in the relevant RFMO, which implement and complement the global legal framework.[15]

Whenever an RFMO within the meaning of the Fish Stocks Agreement has the competence to establish CMMs for particular straddling fish stocks or highly migratory fish stocks, both 'relevant' coastal States and States fishing for the relevant fish stocks in the high seas must either a) become members of the RFMO or b) agree to apply the CMMs established by the RFMO. In the latter case, they obtain so-called cooperating non-contracting party (CNCP) status.[16] If a State fails to opt for either avenue of cooperation with respect to an existing competent RFMO,[17] the

---

in International Law (Brill 2022); Tom Sparks, *Self-Determination in the International Legal System: Whose Claim, to What Right?* (Bloomsbury 2023).

12 United Nations Convention on the Law of the Sea (UNCLOS), 10 December 1982, 1833 UNTS 3, entered into force 16 November 1994. See Stefán Ásmundsson, 'Freedom of Fishing on the High Seas, and the Relevance of Regional Fisheries Management Organisations (RFMOs)' in Myron H. Nordquist, John N. Moore and Ronán Long (eds), *Challenges of the Changing Arctic: Continental Shelf, Navigation, and Fisheries* (Brill 2016) 509.

13 'Consolidated Table Recapitulating the Status of the Convention and of Its Implementing Agreements'. www.un.org/depts/los/reference_files/StatusTablesEnglish.pdf accessed on 08 January 2024.

14 See further Erik Molenaar, 'Non-Participation in the Fish Stocks Agreement: Status and Reasons' (2011) 26 *International Journal of Marine and Coastal Law* 195.

15 It is beyond the scope of this chapter to provide an in-depth analysis of the relevant provisions of the Fish Stocks Agreement and the constitutive instruments of RFMOs and their implementation in practice. For an in-depth discussion, see Erik Molenaar, 'Participation in Regional Fisheries Management Organizations' in Richard Caddell and Erik Molenaar (eds), *Strengthening International Fisheries Law in an Era of Changing Oceans* (Hart 2019) 103.

16 Fish Stocks Agreement, art 8(3).

17 An RFMO does not have competence have all parts of the sea and species of fish, see, for example, Katherine Seto et al., 'Fishing Through the Cracks: The Unregulated Nature of Global Squid Fisheries' (2023) 9 *Science Advances* 1.

State will be prohibited from fishing in the high seas for the stocks covered by the RFMO's CMMs.[18] As a corollary of the obligation to become an RFMO's member or CNCP to fish lawfully for a stock, States with a 'real interest in the fisheries concerned' have a qualified right to participate in the relevant RFMO.[19]

The Fish Stocks Agreement does not define the expression 'real interest in the fisheries concerned'. Therefore, considerable ambiguity remains as to the requirements that a State must fulfil to enjoy a qualified right of participation in an RFMO.[20] Here, it suffices to state that, based on the first sentence of Article 8(3) of the Fish Stocks Agreement, 'relevant coastal States' have a 'real interest'.[21] A teleological and systematic interpretation of this undefined expression shows that it covers all coastal States with EEZs adjacent to high seas areas within the RFMO's area of competence, in which the straddling stock (Article 63(2) of UNCLOS) or highly migratory stock (Article 64 of UNCLOS) under the RFMO's substantive mandate is permanently or temporarily present.[22]

To safeguard this qualified right of participation, the design and application of an RFMO's 'terms of participation' in practice must conform with the legal framework for participation laid down in the Fish Stocks Agreement – at least as far as States Parties to the Fish Stocks Agreement are concerned. Specifically, the RFMO's terms of participation must not preclude from membership or participation States which have a 'real interest' and the terms must not 'be applied in a manner which discriminates against' States or groups of States with a 'real interest'.[23] If an RFMO's legal framework contains exclusionary rules of participation which violate these rules, or if the RFMO's applicable rules are applied in an exclusionary fashion *in practice*, affected States with a 'real interest' may arguably ignore (parts of) the CMMs adopted by the relevant RFMO and adopt alternative effective CMMs which comply with their international obligations instead.[24]

18 Fish Stocks Agreement, art 8(4).

19 Fish Stocks Agreement, art 8(3).

20 Erik Molenaar, 'The Concept of "Real Interest" and Other Aspects of Co-operation Through Regional Fisheries Management Mechanisms' (2000) 15 *International Journal of Marine and Coastal Law* 475, 493–501.

21 ibid, 495; Erik Molenaar, 'Participation in Regional Fisheries Management Organizations' in Richard Caddell and Erik Molenaar (eds), *Strengthening International Fisheries Law in an Era of Changing Oceans* (Hart 2019) 103, 114.

22 Erik Molenaar, 'The Concept of "Real Interest" and Other Aspects of Co-operation through Regional Fisheries Management Mechanisms' (2000) 15 *International Journal of Marine and Coastal Law* 475, 495; Valentin J. Schatz, Alexander Proelss and Nengye Liu, 'The 2018 Agreement to Prevent Unregulated High Seas Fisheries in the Central Arctic Ocean: A Critical Analysis' (2019) 34 *International Journal of Marine and Coastal Law* 195, 240.

23 Fish Stocks Agreement, art 8(3).

24 Erik Molenaar, 'The Concept of "Real Interest" and Other Aspects of Co-Operation Through Regional Fisheries Management Mechanisms' (2000) 15 *International Journal of Marine and Coastal Law* 475, 493; Andrew Serdy, *The New Entrants Problem in International Fisheries Law* (CUP 2016) 62.

3. Legal Status and Pending Decolonisation of the Chagos Archipelago

The Chagos Archipelago is an outstanding step in the completion of the decolonisation of former British colonies.[25] The UK administers the archipelago as the so-called British Indian Ocean Territory (BIOT) and has leased one of its atolls, Diego Garcia, to the United States for use as a military base.[26] Mauritius has pursued a campaign to decolonise the Chagos Archipelago in multiple international forums. This campaign is briefly summarised here for context.[27]

In 1965, in the wake of Mauritius' demand for independence (ultimately achieved in 1968), the UK detached the Chagos Archipelago from Mauritius and assured that the archipelago would be returned to Mauritius once it no longer served a military purpose.[28] The United Nations General Assembly (UNGA), inter alia, condemned this move. The UNGA reaffirmed 'the inalienable right of the people of the Territory of Mauritius to freedom and independence in accordance with UNGA Res 1514 (XV)'.[29] It invited the UK 'to take no action which would dismember the Territory of Mauritius and violate its territorial integrity'.[30] Thereafter, UK sovereignty over the Chagos Archipelago remained contested. In the past decade, Mauritius increasingly raised this issue in international organisations and before international courts and tribunals. In 2015, Mauritius instituted proceedings against the UK on the establishment of a marine protected area in the Chagos Archipelago. An arbitral tribunal established under Annex VII of UNCLOS found that it lacked jurisdiction to make determinations concerning sovereignty over the Chagos Archipelago, but it confirmed the binding nature of the UK's undertaking to return the archipelago to Mauritius 'when no longer needed for defence purposes'.[31]

25 See generally Pietro Sullo, 'Decolonisation: British Territories' (last updated February 2013) in Anne Peters (ed), *Max Planck Encyclopedia of Public International Law* (OUP online 2024).

26 Ebrahim Afsah, 'Diego Garcia (British Indian Ocean Territory)' (last updated March 2009) in Anne Peters (ed), *Max Planck Encyclopedia of Public International Law* (OUP online 2024), paras 1–10.

27 For more detailed analysis, see Stephen Allen (ed), *The Chagos Islanders and International Law* (Hart 2014); Thomas Burri and Jamie Trinidad (eds), *The International Court of Justice and Decolonisation: New Directions from the Chagos Advisory Opinion* (CUP 2021); Philippe Sands, *The Last Colony: A Tale of Race, Exile and Justice from Chagos to the Hague* (Weidenfeld and Nicolson 2022).

28 Niko Pavlopoulos, 'Chagos (Advisory Opinion)' (last updated March 2021) in Anne Peters (ed), *Max Planck Encyclopedia of Public International Law* (OUP online 2024), paras 5–12.

29 UN General Assembly, *Question of Mauritius*, A/RES/2066, UN General Assembly, 16 December 1965, para 2 https://treaties.un.org/doc/source/docs/A_RES_2065-Eng.pdf

30 ibid, para 4.

31 *Chagos Marine Protected Area Arbitration (Mauritius v. United Kingdom)*, Award, PCA Case No 2011–03, 18 March 2015, paras 445–8, but see the Dissenting and Concurring Opinion of Judges Kateka and Wolfrum, paras 68–80. For a discussion, see, for example, Mario Gervasi, 'The Interpretation of the United Nations Convention on the Law of the Sea in the *Chagos Marine Protected Area Arbitration*: The Influence of the Land Sovereignty Dispute' in Angela del Vecchio and Roberto Virzo (eds), *Interpretations of the United Nations Convention on the Law of the Sea by International Courts and Tribunals* (Springer 2019) 191.

In 2019, following a request by the UNGA,[32] the International Court of Justice (ICJ) rendered an advisory opinion, in which the Court held, inter alia, that the UK

> is under an obligation to bring an end to its administration of the Chagos Archipelago as rapidly as possible, thereby enabling Mauritius to complete the decolonization of its territory in a manner consistent with the right of peoples to self-determination.[33]

Shortly thereafter, the UNGA in Resolution 73/295 welcomed the ICJ's advisory opinion and demanded the UK to 'withdraw its colonial administration from the Chagos Archipelago unconditionally within a period of no more than six months from the adoption of the present resolution, thereby enabling Mauritius to complete the decolonisation of its territory as rapidly as possible'.[34] Of particular importance here, the UNGA called upon the United Nations and all its specialised agencies, as well as all other international, regional and intergovernmental organisations,

> to recognize that the Chagos Archipelago forms an integral part of the territory of Mauritius, to support the decolonization of Mauritius as rapidly as possible, and to refrain from impeding that process by recognizing, or giving effect to any measure taken by or on behalf of, the 'British Indian Ocean Territory'.[35]

In 2021, a Special Chamber of the International Tribunal for the Law of the Sea (ITLOS) relied on the ICJ's advisory opinion and the UNGA resolution in a case brought by Mauritius against the Maldives (ostensibly concerning the delimitation of the maritime boundary between the Chagos Archipelago and the Maldives). The Special Chamber stated, inter alia, the following:

> While the process of decolonization has yet to be completed, Mauritius' sovereignty over the Chagos Archipelago can be inferred from the ICJ's determinations [and that] it is inconceivable that the United Kingdom, whose administration over the Chagos Archipelago constitutes a wrongful act of a continuing character and thus must be brought to an end as rapidly as

32 UN General Assembly, 'Request for an advisory opinion of the International Court of Justice on the legal consequences of the separation of the Chagos Archipelago from Mauritius in 1965', Resolution 71/292 adopted by the General Assembly on 22 June 2017 https://digitallibrary.un.org/record/1290265?ln=en&v=pdf.

33 *Legal Consequences of the Separation of the Chagos Archipelago from Mauritius in 1965*, Advisory Opinion, ICJ Rep 2019, para 178. For a discussion, see, for example, Niko Pavlopoulos, 'Chagos (Advisory Opinion)' (last updated March 2021) in Anne Peters (ed), *Max Planck Encyclopedia of Public International Law* (OUP online 2024); Victor Kattan, 'The Chagos Advisory Opinion and the Law of Self-Determination' (2020) 10 *Asian Journal of International Law* 12; Thomas Burri and Jamie Trinidad (eds), *The International Court of Justice and Decolonisation: New Directions from the Chagos Advisory Opinion* (CUP 2021).

34 UN General Assembly, 'Advisory opinion of the International Court of Justice on the legal consequences of the separation of the Chagos Archipelago from Mauritius in 1965' Resolution 73/295 adopted by the General Assembly on 22 May 2019 https://digitallibrary.un.org/record/3806313?ln=es&v=pdf.

35 ibid, paras 6–7.

> possible, and yet who has failed to do so, can have any legal interests in permanently disposing of maritime zones around the Chagos Archipelago by delimitation.[36]

By doing so, the Special Chamber was the first UNCLOS tribunal to proceed to the merits of a claim implicating a territorial sovereignty dispute.[37] This suggests that the UK's claim to sovereignty was a 'mere assertion' in light of the 'authoritative determination' in the ICJ's advisory opinion, which had 'legal effect'.[38] Regardless of whether one considers the Special Chamber's judgment persuasive,[39] the judgment did not *decide* the sovereignty dispute. Instead, it merely stated that no such dispute existed for the purpose of determining its jurisdiction. Further, the judgment has *no* binding legal effect vis-à-vis the UK as a non-party to the proceedings.[40]

Overall, one may conclude – in line with the ICJ's advisory opinion – that the UK is obliged to bring to an end its illegal administration of the Chagos Archipelago and to return it to Mauritius. Once the decolonisation process is completed, Mauritius will have full sovereignty over the Chagos Archipelago. In a change of foreign policy, the UK agreed in November 2022 to begin negotiations with Mauritius 'on the exercise of sovereignty over the British Indian Ocean Territory (BIOT)/ Chagos Archipelago'.[41] However, in December 2023, it was reported that the UK planned to discontinue these negotiations.[42]

36 *Dispute concerning Delimitation of the Maritime Boundary between Mauritius and Maldives in the Indian Ocean (Mauritius/Maldives),* Preliminary Objections, Judgment of 28 January 2021, ITLOS Case No 28, paras 246–7.

37 *Dispute concerning Delimitation of the Maritime Boundary between Mauritius and Maldives in the Indian Ocean (Mauritius/Maldives),* Preliminary Objections, Judgment of 28 January 2021, ITLOS Case No 28, Separate and Dissenting Opinion of Judge ad hoc Oxman, paras 25–33. See also Valentin J. Schatz, 'The Status of Crimea and the Sea of Azov as a Jurisdictional Hurdle in *Ukraine v. Russia*: A Comment on the UNCLOS Annex VII Arbitral Tribunal's Award concerning Preliminary Objections' (2021) 46 *Review of Central and East European Law* 400, 413–4.

38 *Dispute concerning Delimitation of the Maritime Boundary between Mauritius and Maldives in the Indian Ocean (Mauritius/Maldives)*, Preliminary Objections, Judgment of 28 January 2021, ITLOS Case No 28, paras 243–6.

39 The judgment has been criticised given that, first, the ICJ's advisory opinion did not in fact determine that Mauritius had sovereignty over Chagos and, second, the ICJ's advisory opinion and the subsequent UNGA's resolution are not legally binding. See, for example, Fabian Eichberger, 'The Legal Effect of ICJ Advisory Opinions Redefined?: The Mauritius/Maldives Delimitation Case – Judgment on Preliminary Objections' (2021) 22 *Melbourne Journal of International Law* 383, 394–400.

40 See UNCLOS, arts 296(2) and art 33(2) of Annex VI.

41 UK Parliament, '"British Indian Ocean Territory/Chagos Archipelago", Statement Made by James Cleverly, Secretary of State for Foreign, Commonwealth and Development Affairs' (3 November 2022). https://questions-statements.parliament.uk/written-statements/detail/2022-11-03/hcws354 accessed 1 October 2023.

42 Driver, 'UK Drops Plans to Hand Chagos Islands Back to Mauritius', *The Telegraph* (1 December 2023). www.telegraph.co.uk/world-news/2023/12/01/uk-drop-plan-to-hand-chagos-islands-back-mauritius/; Lewis and Brunnstrom, 'Cameron, Blinken Say They Discussed 'vital' US Air Base at Diego Garcia', *Reuters* (8 December 2023). www.reuters.com/world/cameron-blinken-say-they-discussed-vital-us-air-base-diego-garcia-2023–12–07/.

4. The UK's IOTC Membership on Behalf of the Chagos Archipelago

Prior to the UK's withdrawal from the European Union (EU), that is, between 1973 and 2020, the UK's interests as an Indian Ocean *fishing* State were represented through the EU because of the EU's exclusive competence over the Common Fisheries Policy (CFP).[43] Conversely, the UK acted itself on behalf of the BIOT as an Indian Ocean *coastal* State because the BIOT was excluded from the scope of the CFP and, thus, was not subject to the EU's exclusive competence.[44] This also applied to the IOTC. The UK became a member of IOTC 'in respect of the British Indian Ocean Territory only' on 31 March 1995.[45] After Brexit, the UK sought independent membership of the IOTC as a *flag* State, in addition to its previous *coastal* State status. However, its membership on behalf of the Chagos Archipelago was challenged by Mauritius and cast in doubt.[46]

4.1. Requirements of IOTC Membership

The IOTC Agreement's membership criteria must be understood in the context of the IOTC's establishment and operation within the FAO's institutional framework. The IOTC was established under Article XIV of the FAO Constitution.[47] This special institutional arrangement is explicitly acknowledged by Article I of the IOTC Agreement and has important ramifications for various aspects of the IOTC Agreement, including its provisions on membership. There are two different paths to IOTC membership. The first is for members and associate members of FAO.[48] The second is for States that are not members of FAO but are members of the UN, any of the UN's specialised agencies, or the International Atomic Energy Agency.[49] Besides the path for associate members of FAO, both sets of eligibility requirements concern *States*. States must either be Indian Ocean *coastal* States ('coastal States . . . situated wholly or partly within the [IOTC Area of Competence]'[50])

43 Consolidated Version of the Treaty on the Functioning of the European Union [2012] OJ C326/47, art 3(1)(d).

44 At the time, this was stated in ibid, art 355(2) in conjunction with Annex II.

45 FAO, 'Note from the Legal Office of FAO' (2019) IOTC-2019-S23–14[E], 1.

46 Gabriela Oanta, 'Resolving the United Kingdom and European Union Membership of Regional Fisheries Management Organisations Post Brexit' (2021) 36 *International Journal of Marine and Coastal Law* 355, 363–4.

47 See Constitution of the Food and Agriculture Organization of the United Nations (FAO) (16 October 1945) 145 BSP 910, art XIV <www.fao.org/3/k8024e/k8024e.pdf>; FAO, 'Regional Fishery Bodies (RFB): Indian Ocean Tuna Commission (IOTC)' (2022). www.fao.org/fishery/en/organization/rfb/iotc accessed 8 January 2024. See also, with respect to attempts to 'emancipate' the IOTC from the FAO, William Edeson, 'An International Legal Extravaganza in the Indian Ocean: Placing the Indian Ocean Tuna Commission outside the Framework of FAO' (2007) 22 *International Journal of Marine and Coastal Law* 485.

48 Agreement for the Establishment of the Indian Ocean Tuna Commission (25 November 1993) 1927 UNTS 329 (IOTC Agreement), art IV(1).

49 ibid, art IV(1)–(2).

50 ibid, art IV(1)(a)(i) and (2)(a)(i).

or *fishing* States (States 'whose vessels engage in fishing in the [IOTC Area of Competence] for stocks covered by [the IOTC Agreement]'[51]). Regional economic integration organisations (REIOs) may also become members of the IOTC if they are members of FAO and an Indian Ocean coastal or fishing State 'has transferred competence over matters within the purview of [the IOTC Agreement]' to the REIO in question.[52] Currently, the EU is the only REIO member of FAO[53] and IOTC.[54]

Based on the aforementioned, a *coastal* State's IOTC membership has both geographical and legal elements. Geographically, at least part of the relevant State (which would include parts of any maritime zone of exclusive fisheries rights and jurisdiction) must be situated in the IOTC Area of Competence. Legally, the State must have sovereignty over the territory in question (and, by extension, the relevant maritime zones generated by this territory).[55] Moreover, the relevant State's maritime zones must have been established in conformity with the law of the sea (and thus be opposable to the other IOTC members).[56]

4.2. Positions of Mauritius and the UK

There is no doubt that the Chagos Archipelago is within the IOTC Area of Competence. However, Mauritius has challenged for many years the UK's sovereignty over the Chagos Archipelago and, thus, the UK's right to membership as an IOTC *coastal* State.[57] These challenges intensified following the adoption of UNGA Resolution 73/295 in 2019.[58] From an institutional perspective, it is notable that the UK considers the subject to be a 'bilateral issue' and that the IOTC 'is not an appropriate forum for Mauritius to raise this'.[59] The UK has expressed regret over 'the continued use of this important multilateral forum by the Republic of Mauritius to address a bilateral matter', which it says 'only serves to distract from the important

51 ibid, art IV(1)(b)(ii) and (2)(b)(ii).

52 ibid, art IV(1)(c).

53 FAO, 'The Development Law Service: Membership of FAO' www.fao.org/legal-services/membership-of-fao/en/ accessed 8 January 2024.

54 IOTC, 'Structure of the Commission: Commission Contracting Parties (Members)' www.iotc.org/about-iotc/structure-commission accessed 8 January 2024.

55 See, for example, Irini Papanicolopulu, 'The Land Dominates the Sea (Dominates the Land Dominates the Sea)' (2018) 47 *Questions of International Law Zoom-In* 39.

56 See, for example, *Fisheries Jurisdiction (United Kingdom of Great Britain and Northern Ireland v. Iceland)*, Judgment, ICJ Rep 1974, para 54.

57 See, for example, IOTC, 'Report of the Eighteenth Session' (Colombo, 1–5 June 2014) IOTC–2014–S18–R[E]. https://iotc.org/sites/default/files/documents/2014/06/IOTC-2014-S18-RE.pdf accessed 8 January 2024, 59; IOTC, 'Report of the 22nd Session' (Bangkok, 21–25 May 2018) IOTC–2018–S22–R[E], 28–31. https://iotc.org/sites/default/files/documents/2018/06/IOTC-2018-S22-RE.pdf accessed 8 January 2024.

58 See, for example, UNGA, 'Advisory Opinion of the International Court of Justice on the Legal Consequences of the Separation of the Chagos Archipelago from Mauritius in 1965: Report of the Secretary-General' (18 May 2020) A/74/834, 18–20.

59 IOTC, 'Report of the 22nd Session' (Bangkok, 21–25 May 2018) IOTC–2018–S22–R[E], 30–1. https://iotc.org/sites/default/files/documents/2018/06/IOTC-2018-S22-RE.pdf accessed 8 January 2024.

work of IOTC members'.[60] On the other hand, Mauritius is of the view that the status of the Chagos Archipelago has an impact on the fisheries-related work of the IOTC and is 'not academic'.[61] Mauritius cites the potential impact of a coastal State status on allocation of fishing opportunities based on proposals for an allocation mechanism currently under consideration.[62]

At the IOTC Commission's annual session in 2022, Mauritius reiterated

> that the United Kingdom cannot claim membership of the IOTC as a coastal State since the Chagos Archipelago forms an integral part of the territory of Mauritius as authoritatively determined by the [ICJ], the [UNGA], the [ITLOS], and the legal advisor of the FAO.[63]

Conversely, the UK reiterated 'its position that it remained a coastal State given its sovereignty over "BIOT"'.[64]

4.3. *Instruments of Acceptance: Role of the Depositary*

To become a contracting party to the IOTC Agreement, an instrument of acceptance must be deposited with the FAO Director-General,[65] who serves as the depositary of the IOTC Agreement.[66] For coastal or fishing FAO members, FAO associate members, and REIOs falling under Article IV(1)(a)(iii) of the IOTC Agreement, no further decision by the IOTC Commission is required for the acceptance to be effective.[67] By contrast, acceptance by other coastal or fishing States only becomes effective once the IOTC Commission has approved the membership application by a two-thirds majority of its members.[68]

As a result, for FAO members and associate members and for REIOs which qualify for membership under Article IV(1)(a)(iii) of the IOTC Agreement, it is the task of the FAO Director-General as depositary to ensure that the instrument of acceptance fulfils the eligibility criteria of the IOTC Agreement.[69] However, the

60 ibid, 31.
61 ibid, 30.
62 ibid.
63 IOTC, 'Report of the 26th Session' (Seychelles, 16–20 May 2022) IOTC–2022–S26–R[E]. https://iotc.org/sites/default/files/documents/2022/11/IOTC-2022-S26-RE_-_Final.pdf accessed 8 January 2024, para 8.
64 ibid, para 7.
65 IOTC Agreement, art XVII (1) and (2).
66 IOTC Agreement, art XXIV. On the role of the FAO Director General specifically as the IOTC Agreement's depositary, see William Edeson, 'An International Legal Extravaganza in the Indian Ocean: Placing the Indian Ocean Tuna Commission outside the Framework of FAO' (2007) 22 *International Journal of Marine and Coastal Law* 485, 492–500.
67 IOTC Agreement, art XVII (1).
68 IOTC Agreement, arts XVII (2) and IV(2).
69 Vienna Convention on the Law of Treaties, 23 April 1969, 1155 UNTS 331, entered into force 27 January 1980 (VCLT), art 77(1)(d). See Fatsah Ouguergouz, Santiago Villalpando and Jason

scope of the depositary's powers to interpret the relevant treaty and make determinations on statehood or sovereignty is unclear and contested.[70] Importantly, the depositary is obliged to act 'impartially' in performing its functions.[71] The depositary's non-acceptance of an instrument establishing consent to be bound by a treaty is not usually final and binding, but merely temporary.[72] Rather, where the depositary and the State seeking membership disagree, the depositary must bring the question to the attention of the organisation and/or its members, which may take a decision on the matter (provided that the rules of the organisation allow for such a decision).[73]

After Brexit, the UK submitted a new instrument of acceptance to the depositary on 22 December 2020 per Article IV(1)(a) of the IOTC Agreement (i.e., based on FAO member status). The depositary accepted this instrument and the IOTC Agreement entered into force for the UK as a fishing State on 22 December 2020.[74] However, the FAO Legal Counsel subsequently made clear that the FAO and the FAO Director-General (as depositary of the IOTC Agreement) were implementing UNGA Resolution 73/295 and, therefore, recognised that 'the Chagos Archipelago forms an integral part of the territory of Mauritius'.[75] On this basis, the FAO Legal Counsel concluded that '[i]f an instrument was deposited at this time by the United Kingdom purporting to extend the application of the IOTC Agreement to the 'BIOT', such an instrument would not be accepted by the Depositary'.[76]

Morgan-Foster, 'Article 77' in Olivier Corten and Pierre Klein (eds), *The Vienna Conventions on the Law of Treaties: A Commentary* (OUP 2011), para 46; Helmut Tichy and Philip Bittner, 'Article 77: Functions of Depositaries' in Oliver Dörr and Kirsten Schmalenbach (eds), *Vienna Convention on the Law of Treaties: A Commentary* (Springer 2018), paras 15 and 19.

70 ibid, para 37; Fatsah Ouguergouz, Santiago Villalpando and Jason Morgan-Foster, 'Article 77' in Olivier Corten and Pierre Klein (eds), *The Vienna Conventions on the Law of Treaties: A Commentary* (OUP 2011), paras 47–8.

71 VCLT, art 76(2); Richard Caddell, 'Depositary' (last updated June 2006) in Anne Peters (ed), *Max Planck Encyclopedia of Public International Law* (OUP online 2024), para 8.

72 Fatsah Ouguergouz, Santiago Villalpando and Jason Morgan-Foster, 'Article 77' in Olivier Corten and Pierre Klein (eds), *The Vienna Conventions on the Law of Treaties: A Commentary* (OUP 2011), para 53.

73 See VCLT, art 77(2); Helmut Tichy and Philip Bittner, 'Article 77: Functions of Depositaries' in Oliver Dörr and Kirsten Schmalenbach (eds), *Vienna Convention on the Law of Treaties: A Commentary* (Springer 2018), para 39; Fatsah Ouguergouz, Santiago Villalpando and Jason Morgan-Foster, 'Article 77' in Olivier Corten and Pierre Klein (eds), *The Vienna Conventions on the Law of Treaties: A Commentary* (OUP 2011), paras 53, 67–73. An important example of restraint by depositaries is that of UN Secretaries-General, who 'have consistently refused to take any decision on accepting instruments of ratification or accession from entities whose statehood is in question', see Peter Tzeng, 'Incidental Jurisdiction in International Adjudication and Incidental Determinations by International Organizations' (2022) 116 *AJIL Unbound* 186, 187, with further references.

74 FAO, 'Note from the Legal Counsel of the Food and Agriculture Organization of the United Nations ("FAO") in Relation to Agenda Item 4 of the Agenda for the 26th Session of the Indian Ocean Tuna Commission ("IOTC"), Proposed by Mauritius: "Clarification of the Status of the United Kingdom's Membership in the IOTC"' (2022) IOTC-2022-S26-REF01, 1.

75 ibid.

76 ibid, 2.

Indeed, the wording of the UK's new instrument of acceptance was ambiguous and did not contain 'further specification as to whether the instrument was deposited [with respect to coastal and/or flag State status]'.[77] In other words, it did not make clear whether the UK intended to a) *extend* its IOTC membership as a coastal State (on behalf of the BIOT) to *additional* membership as a fishing State (on behalf of the UK as such) or b) *replace* its original instrument with an instrument seeking fishing State status only. This raised the question of whether the original instrument could still be regarded as valid. In this respect, the FAO Legal Counsel stated:

> From a legal perspective, it would be anomalous to consider the 1995 instrument as remaining valid simply on the basis that it was valid at the time of deposit, bearing in mind that it is inconsistent with the position that 'the Chagos Archipelago forms an integral part of the territory of Mauritius'.[78]

These statements show a remarkable lack of restraint by the depositary. This can be explained by the specific political and legal context described previously – bearing in mind, however, that, as noted previously, neither the existing juridical pronouncements nor the UNGA resolution are legally binding. That said, during the 26th IOTC Session in 2022, the FAO Legal Counsel reiterated her previously stated view that 'the continued membership of a Member of the Commission appears to be a matter for the Commission'.[79] In other words, it is for the IOTC Commission – as the principal IOTC decision-making body – to take a decision on the UK's membership. This view is in line with the function of the depositary described previously.

4.4. Determination of Withdrawal by the IOTC Commission

The position of the FAO Legal Counsel finds additional support in the IOTC Agreement. The IOTC Agreement specifies that existing membership is not immune from review through the RFMO. If a member ceases to meet the IOTC Agreement's eligibility criteria, the IOTC Commission is empowered to 'determine that the Member is deemed to have withdrawn from this Agreement effective as from the date of that determination'.[80] This power granted to the IOTC Commission does not have an (explicit) equivalent in the constitutive instruments of other RFMOs. The legal effect of a withdrawal determination terminates the relevant member's status as a contracting party to the IOTC Agreement and as a member of the IOTC, with an accompanying loss of rights and obligations under the IOTC Agreement.[81]

77 ibid, 1.

78 ibid, 2.

79 FAO, 'Note from the Legal Office of FAO' (2019) IOTC-2019-S23–14[E], 2.

80 IOTC Agreement, art IV(4). See also FAO, 'Note from the Legal Office of FAO' (2019) IOTC-2019-S23–14[E], 2.

81 See VCLT, arts 5 and 70(1) and (2).

4.4.1. *Substantive Requirements*

Article IV(4) of the IOTC Agreement comes into play if a member ceases to meet the IOTC Agreement's eligibility criteria 'for two consecutive calendar years'. With respect to the eligibility criteria described in Section 4.1, this provision was likely originally intended to cover determinations that a member's vessels no longer engage in fishing in the IOTC Area of Competence.[82] This would align with the Fish Stocks Agreement's 'real interest' requirement.[83] However, interpreting the wording of Article IV(4) of the IOTC Agreement in line with the customary international rules of treaty interpretation reflected in Article 31(1) of the Vienna Convention on the Law of Treaties suggests that the IOTC Commission can also determine a loss of 'coastal State' status, whether because of a change in the scope of the IOTC Area of Competence or a loss of territory through cession or decolonisation. There is also no reason to suggest that the IOTC Commission cannot determine a *partial* withdrawal of membership where membership was based both on fishing and coastal State status. A partial determination would not be merely symbolic as 'coastal State' status has legal consequences, including for allocating fishing opportunities. Of course, it is true that RFMOs' subject-matter mandate typically does not include decisions on statehood or territorial sovereignty. That said, a determination of withdrawal could be based on the explicit competence under Article IV(4) of the IOTC Agreement and, thus, would not be *ultra vires*.

The UK's continued sovereignty over the Chagos Archipelago until the completion of the decolonisation process could pose an obstacle as the UK retains control over the territory and maritime zones of the Chagos Archipelago during this period. Therefore, the UK, arguably, has not yet lost its 'coastal State' status in the strict sense. UNGA Resolution 73/295, but not the ICJ's advisory opinion, contradicts this legal situation to some extent. However, the predominant view in the literature and in the jurisprudence of international courts and tribunals remains that UNGA resolutions, such as Resolution 73/295, are not legally binding *per se*, but can, for example, 'be relevant for ascertaining the existence and contents of a rule of customary international law'.[84] For this reason, it is doubtful whether the IOTC, as suggested by its chairperson at the annual session in 2019, 'as a specialised institution of the UN would need to abide by the Resolution of the [UNGA]'.[85]

82 IOTC Agreement, art IV(1)(b)(ii) and (2)(b)(ii).

83 Fish Stocks Agreement, art 8(3).

84 *Dispute Concerning Coastal State Rights in the Black Sea, Sea of Azov, and Kerch Strait (Ukraine v. Russian Federation)*, Award on Preliminary Objections, PCA Case 2017–06, 21 February 2020, paras 172–7. See also *South West Africa Cases*, Second Phase, Judgment, ICJ Rep 1966, para 98; *Legality of the Threat or Use of Nuclear Weapons*, Advisory Opinion, ICJ Rep 1996, para 70; Christian Tomuschat, 'United Nations, General Assembly' (last updated April 2019) in Anne Peters (ed), *Max Planck Encyclopedia of Public International Law* (OUP online 2024), para 22; Marko Divac Öberg, 'The Legal Effects of Resolutions of the UN Security Council and General Assembly in the Jurisprudence of the ICJ' (2005) 16 *European Journal of International Law* 879.

85 IOTC, 'Report of the 23rd Session' (Hyderabad, 17–21 June 2019), IOTC–2019–S23–R_rev1[E]. https://iotc.org/sites/default/files/documents/2019/10/IOTC-2019-S23-RE_Rev1_FINAL.pdf accessed 8 January 2024, para 9.

To circumvent this problem, the IOTC Commission could determine that the UK is no longer an IOTC 'coastal State' on behalf of the Chagos Archipelago, for the purposes of the IOTC Agreement, because the UK is obliged to complete the decolonisation process by returning the Chagos Archipelago to Mauritius. Even if such a withdrawal determination would constitute a violation of the IOTC Agreement and/or the Fish Stocks Agreement, the UK would be in a difficult legal and political position if it sought to challenge such a decision.[86]

4.4.2. Consultations

The IOTC Commission may determine withdrawal only 'after consultation with the Member concerned'.[87] The IOTC Agreement does not specify the substantive or procedural requirements of such 'consultation'. The wording of the provision suggests that the IOTC Commission *itself* must consult with the relevant member. However, a more reasonable interpretation would be to expect consultations between members *in the framework of* the IOTC Commission (e.g., at an annual or special session). While Mauritius had raised the issue on various occasions, the IOTC Commission only formally agreed at its annual session in 2022 'that its consultation with the United Kingdom has started and the final determination in accordance with Article IV(4)of the IOTC Agreement will be made at S27'.[88] However, nothing in the wording of Article IV(4) of the IOTC Agreement suggests that the IOTC Commission must take such a decision for the consultations to start or the consultation requirement to be fulfilled. Nonetheless, the chairperson was hesitant to determine that consultations had taken place in accordance with this provision. To avoid such confusion in the future, it would be advisable for the IOTC to incorporate more detailed directions into its procedural rules.[89]

At the IOTC Commission's annual session in 2023 in Mauritius, the UK claimed that 'there has not been adequate consultation between the United Kingdom and the IOTC' and expressed its willingness 'to engage fully in these consultations and commits to clarify the status of its membership before the end of the year'.[90] In response, Mauritius did not object to the proposed arrangement 'in a spirit of

86 For reasons of space, this chapter cannot explore the possibility that the UK might be estopped from challenging the decision in light of its obligation to return the Chagos Archipelago. See, for example, Thomas Cottier and Jörg Müller, 'Estoppel' (last updated September 2021) in Anne Peters (ed), *Max Planck Encyclopedia of Public International Law* (OUP online 2024).

87 IOTC Agreement, art IV(4).

88 IOTC, 'Report of the 26th Session' (Seychelles, 16–20 May 2022) IOTC–2022–S26–R[E]. https://iotc.org/sites/default/files/documents/2022/11/IOTC-2022-S26-RE_-_Final.pdf accessed 8 January 2024, para 11.

89 IOTC, 'Rules of Procedure' (2022). https://iotc.org/sites/default/files/documents/2022/06/IOTC_Rules_of_Procedure_2022.pdf accessed 8 January 2024.

90 IOTC, 'Report of the 27th Session of the Indian Ocean Tuna Commission' (Mauritius, 8–12 May 2023), IOTC-2023-S27-R. https://iotc.org/sites/default/files/documents/2023/07/IOTC-2023-S27-RE.pdf accessed 8 January 2024, para 11.

flexibility'.[91] Accordingly, the IOTC Commission formally noted the UK's 'commitment to clarify the status of its IOTC Membership before the end of the year' and requested the IOTC Secretariat 'to notify [contracting parties and CNCPs] as soon as a communication on this matter is received'.[92]

4.4.3. Decision-making

A final point of interest is the question of decision-making for determinations of withdrawal. The IOTC Commission takes its 'decisions and recommendations' by a 'majority of the votes cast', unless another provision of the IOTC Agreement states otherwise.[93] Article IV(4) of the IOTC Agreement does *not* state otherwise. Therefore, the threshold for a determination of withdrawal is (only) a simple majority or, per the normal approach at the IOTC, consensus. However, given the UK's objection during the IOTC Commission's annual session in 2022, there was no consensus on Mauritius' proposal to determine the UK's withdrawal from IOTC as a 'coastal State' on behalf of the Chagos Archipelago. Mauritius argued that the UK, as the member whose membership was at issue, should not be allowed to object (and, thus, prevent consensus) or vote. However, in the absence of guidance in IOTC's rules of procedure, the chairperson was not prepared to entertain Mauritius' argument. No procedural mechanism existed to clarify this point quickly.

Interestingly, although a vote can be requested by a single member, Mauritius did not request a vote. The discussions at the annual sessions in 2022 and 2023, as well as intimations by various delegates, suggest that Mauritius lacked sufficient support for a vote. Mauritius may also have lacked support from most developing coastal States in the Indian Ocean – even though these States are otherwise sympathetic to Mauritius' decolonisation cause and voted in support of Mauritius at the UNGA. The reason for this restraint appears to be that RFMO delegations frequently lack a mandate to vote or to make statements on matters of territorial sovereignty, which require specific instructions at the ministerial level – usually from the Ministry of Foreign Affairs. Where such instructions have not been received, RFMO delegations are likely to abstain from voting. The chairperson of the IOTC also hinted at this problem at the IOTC Commission's annual session in 2019 by stating that 'the delegates present may not have had proper guidance from their capitals'.[94]

5. Conclusion

This chapter has used Mauritius' challenge to the UK's membership in the IOTC on behalf of the Chagos Archipelago as a case study to examine the problem of former

91 ibid, para 12.
92 ibid, para 13.
93 IOTC Agreement, art VI(2).
94 IOTC, 'Report of the 23rd Session' (Hyderabad, 17–21 June 2019), IOTC–2019–S23–R_rev1[E] https://iotc.org/sites/default/files/documents/2019/10/IOTC-2019-S23-RE_Rev1_FINAL.pdf accessed 8 January 2024, para 9.

colonial powers' participation in RFMOs on behalf of overseas territories subject to decolonisation claims by other RFMO members. It has shown that such disputes can pose considerable obstacles to RFMOs' ability to exercise their fisheries conservation and management mandate. At the same time, questions of decolonisation and/or sovereignty are not entirely detached from the functioning and mandate of RFMOs. Examples include the issue of allocation of fishing opportunities based on coastal and flag State status and, more generally, the obligations of coastal States under Articles 63(2) and 64 of UNCLOS and Articles 7 and 8 of the Fish Stocks Agreement.

From this perspective, RFMO membership on behalf of an overseas territory pending decolonisation necessarily involves decisions which have – often lasting – impacts on the marine living resources and the marine environment within the maritime zones of the overseas territory and the adjacent high seas. This challenges the legitimacy, although not necessarily the legality, of former colonial powers' RFMO membership. RFMOs do not exist in a distinct and confined legal framework. Therefore, RFMOs are arguably suitable cooperative fora for aspects of decolonisation disputes, at least insofar as decolonisation disputes – which are arguably by nature non-bilateral – implicate issues falling within the ambit of the RFMO. However, RFMOs generally face difficulties in addressing such disputes. These difficulties are partly due to RFMOs' limited subject-matter mandate and to legal and institutional frameworks that do not adequately allow for reconsidering the membership status of existing members.

In this respect, Mauritius' challenge to the UK's membership in the IOTC on behalf of the Chagos Archipelago is unique in several ways. The illegality of the UK's detachment of the Chagos Archipelago from Mauritius is relatively straightforward – when compared to, for instance, some of the French overseas territories in the Indian Ocean.[95] This illegality formed the basis of Mauritius' subsequent political and legal victories in various international fora, including before UNGA and the ICJ. UNGA Resolution 73/295, which addressed all international organisations, including the FAO (as a specialised agency of the UN) and the IOTC (as an RFMO established in the framework of FAO), created a growing impetus within IOTC. Most importantly, the FAO – as depositary of the IOTC Agreement – cited UNGA Resolution 73/295 as the main reason to consider that the UK could no longer claim 'coastal State' status on behalf of the Chagos Archipelago.

This, in turn, bolstered Mauritius' position at the IOTC because the IOTC Agreement, exceptionally for a RFMO, contains a procedure to determine the withdrawal of a member. There is inherent legal tension between, on the one hand, the IOTC's fulfilment of the UNGA's call to support the lawful decolonisation process by determining the UK's partial withdrawal and, on the other hand, the UK's (temporary) sovereignty over the Chagos Archipelago – and associated eligibility as an IOTC 'coastal State' member – pending completion of the decolonisation process.

95 See generally Makane Mbengue, 'Decolonisation: French Territories' (last updated May 2011) in Anne Peters (ed), *Max Planck Encyclopedia of Public International Law* (OUP online 2024).

Ultimately, no decision on the matter was taken at the annual sessions in 2022 and 2023. Given the most recent political developments, it is unclear whether Mauritius will call for a vote on the UK's membership as a coastal State or whether the UK will voluntarily renounce to the coastal State element of its membership as part of or in preparation for an agreement between the UK and Mauritius on the return of the Chagos Archipelago. One way to accommodate the legally intricate transitional period of decolonisation would be for the UK, as the former colonial power, to seek temporary CNCP status rather than member status on behalf of the overseas territory.

6. Acknowledgements

Parts of this chapter are based on legal opinions commissioned by Sustainable Fisheries and Communities Trust (SFACT) in 2021 and 2022, which have been expanded and revised for publication. The views expressed in the chapter are those of the author and are not necessarily shared by SFACT.

3 Overlapping Geographical Mandates of RFMOs

*Erik J. Molenaar**

1. Introduction

Regional fisheries management organizations (RFMOs)[1] are regional intergovernmental mechanisms for the conservation and management of fisheries resources. The origins of RFMOs can be traced back to the early 20th century. In recent decades, they have, arguably, become the preeminent institutions of international fisheries law.[2] The issue of overlapping geographical mandates of RFMOs must be viewed in light of the evolution of international law, which has proceeded in a gradual manner with little attention to hierarchy. This evolution and the phenomena to which it led – such as the 'fragmentation of international law', 'regime complexes', and 'polycentricity'[3] – also apply to international fisheries law and RFMOs.

Almost all RFMOs are entirely separate, autonomous, or 'stand-alone' bodies which have been negotiated and established outside the scope of an overarching intergovernmental body.[4] The global component of international fisheries law consists of key

* The author is very grateful to Darius Campbell, Robin Churchill, Alf Håkon Hoel and various other persons for providing information or comments on drafts.

1 Unless specified otherwise, the acronym RFMO comprises a regional fisheries management arrangement (RFMA). Together they are denoted as RFMO/As. See also the text accompanying footnote 18.

2 See Erik Molenaar, 'Regional Fisheries Management Organizations' in Marta Chantal Ribiero, Fernando Loureiro Bastos and Tore Henriksen (eds) *Global Challenges and the Law of the Sea* (Springer 2020) 81.

3 See the Report of the Study Group of the International Law Commission, 'Fragmentation of International Law: Difficulties Arising from the Diversification and Expansion of International Law' (18 July 2006) A/CN.4/L.702; Tomasz Widłak 'Polycentric vs. Fragmented: A Neo-Kelsenian Order of Global Law' (2019) 10 *Transnational Legal Theory* 229.

4 The only exceptions are the Commission for the Conservation of Antarctic Marine Living Resources (CCAMLR) – which is part of the Antarctic Treaty System – and the Indian Ocean Tuna Commission (IOTC) and the General Fisheries Commission for the Mediterranean (GFCM) – which have been established under the Food and Agriculture Organization of the United Nations (FAO). Table 1 in the main text contains the acronyms and full names of all the RFMOs mentioned in this chapter. On the question as to whether CCAMLR qualifies as an RFMO, see footnote 20 and accompanying text below

DOI: 10.4324/9781003492030-5

instruments like the United Nations Convention on the Law of the Sea (UNCLOS),[5] the Agreement for the Implementation of the Provisions of United Nations Convention on the Law of the Sea of 10 December 1982 relating to the Conservation and Management of Straddling Fish Stocks and Highly Migratory Fish Stocks (the Fish Stocks Agreement),[6] and bodies such as the United Nations General Assembly and the Committee on Fisheries of the Food and Agriculture Organization of the United Nations (FAO). Even though this global component establishes the framework and minimum requirements for RFMOs, they retain broad autonomy at the operational level.

Overlapping geographical mandates of RFMOs can lead to working at cross-purposes and even conflicts. This could, for instance, arise in relation to fishing in the geographical area of overlap (hereafter, 'overlap area') for the same target species, or for different target species but using fishing techniques or gears which have impacts on non-target species or benthic habitats for which at least one of the RFMOs involved has adopted conservation and management measures (CMMs). In this scenario, differences in the composition of the membership of the RFMOs and their CMMs could easily lead to problems. One example here is the fishing for Southern bluefin tuna (*Thunnus maccoyii*) pursuant to the CMMs of the Commission for the Conservation of Southern Bluefin Tuna (CCSBT), which occasionally takes place in the regulatory area of the Commission for the Conservation of Antarctic Marine Living Resources (CCAMLR) (see Table 3.1 for a list of RFMOs). Among other things, CCAMLR's conservation measures to avoid seabird bycatch used to be (or still are) more stringent than the CMMs of CCSBT. Fishing in CCAMLR's regulatory area, pursuant to CCSBT's CMMs, could then be regarded as undermining the effectiveness of CCAMLR.[7]

As explained in Part 2 of this chapter, geographical overlaps between regional fisheries management organisations and arrangements RFMO/As[8] are quite common due to their species-based and area-based specialisations. One would assume that this is different for RFMO/As with the same species mandate. When a new RFMO/A is negotiated, it would in principle be logical to choose geographical boundaries which coincide with the geographical boundaries of already existing 'adjacent' RFMO/As with the same species mandate. An example is the South Pacific Regional Fisheries Management Organisation (SPRFMO). During the negotiations to establish SPRFMO, between 2006 and 2009, the northern boundary of the regulatory area

5 United Nations Convention on the Law of the Sea (UNCLOS), 10 December 1982, 1833 UNTS 3, entered into force 16 November 1994.

6 Agreement for the Implementation of the Provisions of the United Nations Convention on the Law of the Sea of 10 December 1982 relating to the Conservation and Management of Straddling Fish Stocks and Highly Migratory Fish Stocks (Fish Stocks Agreement), 4 August 1995, 2167 UNTS 3, entered into force 11 December 2001.

7 See Alan Hemmings, 'Regime Overlap in the Southern Ocean: The Case of Southern Blue Fin Tuna and CCSBT in the CCAMLR Area' (2006) 3 *New Zealand Yearbook of International Law* 207; 'Arrangement between the CCAMLR and Commission for the Conservation of Southern Bluefin Tuna (CCSBT)' (30 October 2015) www.ccsbt.org/system/files/EC25_16_ActivitiesWithOtherOrganisations_0.pdf accessed 11 December 2023.

8 See footnote 18 and accompanying text.

of CCAMLR – which had already become effective in 1982 – was chosen as the southern boundary of SPRFMO's regulatory area. Such adjacency between RFMO/As can also give rise to the need to cooperate on the management of transboundary fish stocks. An example is the cooperation between the North-East Atlantic Fisheries Commission (NEAFC) and the Northwest Atlantic Fisheries Organization (NAFO) on the stock of redfish (*Sebastes mentella)* in the Irminger Sea.[9]

Whereas negotiations to establish new RFMO/As commonly result in adjacency to existing RFMO/As with the same species mandate, and occasionally result in overlaps, they can also lead to gaps in high seas coverage. Examples are the high seas gaps in the Pacific Ocean between the regulatory areas of SPRFMO and the North Pacific Fisheries Commission (NPFC) which remained at the end of the NPFC's negotiations, and the high seas gaps in the Indian Ocean which remained after the conclusion of the negotiations on the Southern Indian Ocean Fisheries Agreement (SIOFA).[10] These gaps could explained by the lack of interest of coastal States to participate in the negotiations and the future RFMO,[11] or the lack of support among the delegations involved in negotiations to extend the geographical scope of the RFMO as that would require inviting more coastal States.

The objective of this chapter is to examine the present occurrence of overlapping geographical mandates of RFMOs and arrangements which have been developed to avoid working at cross-purposes and conflicts and ensure complementarity. These arrangements can be regarded as regime interactions aimed at addressing problems caused by the fragmentation of international (fisheries) law and polycentricity. As will become clear, arrangements can be treaty-based or not, and be focused on determining primacy or rather on cooperation and coordination. In view of space constraints, it is not possible to discuss arrangements on primacy or on cooperation and coordination between RFMOs with overlapping geographical mandates in a manner that is both comprehensive and in-depth. This chapter, therefore, focuses on one case study of RFMOs with overlapping geographical and species mandates, in which treaty-based primacy arrangements are absent. The selected case study is on NEAFC and the Joint Norwegian Russian Fisheries Commission (JNRFC). The chapter first provides an overview of RFMOs and treaty-based primary arrangements. It then discusses RFMOs with overlapping geographical and species mandates. Finally, the chapter focuses on the case study of NEAFC and JNRFC before drawing some conclusions.

9 See Performance Review Panel, 'Report of the North East Atlantic Fisheries Commission, NEAFC' (2006) 13. https://nammco.no/wp-content/uploads/2018/01/neafc_pr-2006.pdf.

10 Southern Indian Ocean Fisheries Agreement, 7 July 2006, entered into force 21 June 2012; https://www.fao.org/treaties/results/details/en/c/TRE-000038/.

11 For instance, Mexico in relation to the North Pacific Fisheries Commission (NPFC), 'Record of the 7th Multilateral Meeting on Management of High Seas Fisheries in the North Pacific Ocean' (Bellevue, Washington, USA, 5–7 August 2009) 4. www.npfc.int/sites/default/files/2017-02/7th%20Meeting%20Report.pdf.

Table 3.1 Acronyms and full names of all RFMO/As mentioned in this chapter

Tuna RFMOs	
CCSBT	Commission for the Conservation of Southern Bluefin Tuna
IATTC	Inter-American Tropical Tuna Commission
ICCAT	International Commission on the Conservation of Atlantic Tunas
IOTC	Indian Ocean Tuna Commission
WCPFC	Western and Central Pacific Fisheries Commission
Other Particular Species RFMO/As	
CBS Convention	Convention on the Conservation and Management of Pollock Resources in the Central Bering Sea[12] (Conference of the Parties)
IPHC	International Pacific Halibut Commission
NASCO	North Atlantic Salmon Conservation Organization
NPAFC	North Pacific Anadromous Fish Commission
PSC	Pacific Salmon Commission
All or Other/Residual Species RFMO/As	
CAOFA	Agreement to Prevent Unregulated High Seas Fisheries in the Central Arctic Ocean[13] (Conference of the Parties)
CCAMLR	Commission for the Conservation of Antarctic Marine Living Resources
GFCM	General Fisheries Commission for the Mediterranean
JNRFC	Joint Norwegian Russian Fisheries Commission
NAFO	Northwest Atlantic Fisheries Organization
NEAFC	North-East Atlantic Fisheries Commission
NPFC	North Pacific Fisheries Commission
SEAFO	South East Atlantic Fisheries Organisation
SIOFA	Southern Indian Ocean Fisheries Agreement[14] (Meeting of the Parties)
SPRFMO	South Pacific Regional Fisheries Management Organisation

2. RFMOs and Treaty-Based Primacy Arrangements

Article 1(i) of the Agreement on Port State Measures to Prevent, Deter and Eliminate Illegal, Unreported and Unregulated Fishing defines an RFMO as ‘an intergovernmental fisheries organization or arrangement, as appropriate, that has the competence to establish conservation and management measures’.[15] An RFMO can be distinguished from the broad concept of a regional fishery body used by FAO.[16] This is because RFMOs (1) relate to marine fisheries rather than inland fisheries

12 Convention on the Conservation and Management of Pollock Resources in the Central Bering Sea (16 June 1994, entered into force 8 December 1995) 34 *International Legal Materials* 67.

13 Agreement to Prevent Unregulated High Seas Fisheries in the Central Arctic Ocean (CAOFA), 3 October 2018, *OJ* 2019, L 73/3, entered into force 25 June 2021.

14 See footnote 10.

15 Agreement on Port State Measures to Prevent, Deter and Eliminate Illegal, Unreported and Unregulated Fishing, (22 November 2019, entered into force 5 June 2016). www.fao.org/treaties/results/details/en/c/TRE-000003/.

16 See, FAO, ‘What are Regional Fishery Bodies (RFBs)?’ www.fao.org/fishery/en/topic/16800/en accessed 11 December 2023.

and (2) have a mandate to impose legally binding CMMs on their members or participants, rather than merely exercising an 'advisory' mandate – whether primarily science-oriented (e.g., the International Council for the Exploration of the Sea (ICES)) or management-oriented (e.g., the Western Central Atlantic Fishery Commission).[17]

There are different types of RFMO/As and key distinctions between them, for instance between an RFMO and a regional fisheries management arrangement (RFMA).[18] Whereas the former establish an intergovernmental organisation, the latter commonly establish a Conference of the Parties or a Meeting of the Parties as their principal decision-making body. At the time of writing, there were, arguably, four RFMAs: the CAOFA, the CBS Convention, JNRFC, and the SIOFA. The view that the CBS Convention and the SIOFA are RFMAs is widely held. However, the same is not necessarily true for the CAOFA and JNRFC, even though it is submitted that strong arguments exist in support of this view.[19] Finally, reference should be made to the well-known debate on the qualification of CCAMLR. Arguably, the prevailing view is that CCAMLR is 'more than an RFMO', in particular due to its integration in the Antarctic Treaty System.[20] This view is also followed here.

For this chapter, the principal distinction among RFMOs is between, first, those with a mandate limited to particular (groups of) species throughout their range(s) of distribution, and second, those with a mandate for all or other (or: residual) species in a particular geographical area. The first group has a species-based specialisation and the second group can be regarded as primarily having an area-based specialisation (see Table 3.1). The first group includes the five tuna RFMOs (CCSBT, IATTC, ICCAT, IOTC, and WCPFC); three RFMOs with a mandate limited to one or more salmon species (NASCO, NPAFC, and PSC); one single-species RFMO (IPHC); and one single-species RFMA (the CBS Convention). The second group – RFMOs with a primarily area-based specialisation – are referred to in this chapter as the 'All or Other/ Residual Species' RFMOs. Of this group, ten have a geographical mandate which includes high seas areas or consists exclusively of high seas: the CAOFA, CCAMLR, GFCM, JNRFC, NAFO, NEAFC, NPFC, SEAFO, the SIOFA, and SPRFMO.

Geographical overlaps between RFMOs are common due to their species-based and area-based specialisations, and many high seas areas in the world have a double or even triple layer of RFMOs. The Northwest Pacific, for example, is covered by three RFMOs: NPAFC, NPFC, and WCPFPC. As geographical overlaps may lead to working at cross-purposes and conflicts, the constitutive instruments of some RFMOs recognise the primacy of other RFMOs. These treaty-based primacy

17 Erik Molenaar, 'Regional Fisheries Management Organizations' in Marta Chantal Ribiero, Fernando Loureiro Bastos and Tore Henriksen (eds), *Global Challenges and the Law of the Sea* (Springer 2020) 81, 85–6.

18 See footnote 1.

19 Erik Molenaar, 'Regional Fisheries Management Organizations' in Marta Chantal Ribiero, Fernando Loureiro Bastos and Tore Henriksen (eds) *Global Challenges and the Law of the Sea* (Springer 2020) 81, 90–2.

20 ibid, 92–6.

arrangements are only found in the constitutive instruments of 'All or Other/Residual Species' RFMOs.

Of the group of ten 'All or Other/Residual Species' RFMOs mentioned previously, the following six have treaty-based primacy arrangements: NAFO, NEAFC, NPFC, SEAFO, the SIOFA and SPRFMO. All primacy arrangements are included in the constitutive instruments' definitions of target species, for which the term 'fishery resources' is used. All definitions include fish, molluscs, crustaceans and (other) sedentary species.[21] They exclude other species. As regards NPFC and SPRFMO – which are the newest RFMOs – the definitions also include the residual categories of 'other marine species caught by fishing vessels within the Convention Area' and 'other living marine resources as may be decided by the Commission', respectively.[22] All six arrangements exclude sedentary species within the meaning of Article 77(4) of UNCLOS.[23] However, this cannot be regarded as a primacy arrangement vis-à-vis RFMOs.

In the case of SEAFO and the SIOFA, the primacy arrangements relate only to 'highly migratory species listed in Annex I' of UNCLOS, which are excluded from the scope of the term 'fishery resources'.[24] This exclusion, therefore, covers not only tuna and tuna-like species but also oceanic sharks and cetaceans.

Additional exclusions – whether explicit or implicit – are contained in the primacy arrangements of the four other 'All or Other/Residual Species' RFMOs. As regards NEAFC, which is discussed in more detail below, the exclusion concerns 'anadromous stocks', which implicitly recognises the primacy of NASCO. The phrase, 'in so far as they are dealt with by other international agreements' reflects NEAFC's residual mandate.[25] NAFO has a similar arrangement, which also excludes 'anadromous and catadromous stocks' and contains the phrase 'in so far as they are managed under other international treaties'.[26] SPRFMO's primacy arrangement also

21 Except for NAFO.

22 Convention on the Conservation and Management of High Seas Fisheries Resources in the North Pacific Ocean (NPFC Convention), 24 February 2012, entered into force 19 July 2015, www.npfc.int; art 1(h); Convention on the Conservation and Management of High Seas Fishery Resources in the South Pacific Ocean (SPRFMO Convention), 14 November 2009, entered into force 24 August 2012, www.sprfmo.int; art 1(1)(f).

23 As regards NEAFC, this is a consequence of the phrases 'area(s) under the jurisdiction of a Contracting Party' in arts 5 and 6 of the NEAFC Convention, which also cover outer continental shelves (Convention on Future Multilateral Cooperation in the North-East Atlantic Fisheries (NEAFC Convention), London, 18 November 1980, 1285 UNTS 129, entered into force 17 March 1982; as amended. Consolidated version available at www.neafc.org). As regards NPFC, this is complemented by the exclusion of 'indicator species of vulnerable marine ecosystems as listed in, or adopted pursuant to, Article 13, paragraph 5 of this Convention', NPFC Convention, art 1(h)(i).

24 Convention on the Conservation and Management of the Fishery Resources in the South East Atlantic Ocean (SEOFA Convention), 20 April 2001, 2221 UNTS 189, entered into force 13 April 2003, art 1(1) and the SIOFA, art 1(f).

25 NEAFC Convention, art 1(b).

26 Convention on Cooperation in the Northwest Atlantic Fisheries – originally named 'Convention on Cooperation in the Northwest Atlantic Fisheries' – (NAFO Convention), 24 October 1978, 1135 UNTS 369, entered into force 1 January 1979; as amended; consolidated version available at www.nafo.int, art I(f).

excludes 'anadromous and catadromous species' and 'marine mammals, marine reptiles and sea birds'.[27] The primacy arrangement of NPFC is a bit different, as it excludes 'catadromous species', 'marine mammals, marine reptiles and seabirds' and 'other marine species already covered by pre-existing international fisheries management instruments within the area of competence of such instruments'.[28] The last phrase implicitly recognises the primacy of the two Pacific tuna RFMOs (IATTC and WCPFC) as well as the anadromous species covered by NPAFC.

The following four RFMO/As do not have fully-fledged treaty-based primacy arrangements: the CAOFA, CCAMLR, GFCM, and JNRFC. Of these four, the constitutive instruments of GFCM and JNRFC do not define their species mandate in any way. The case of JNRFC is discussed in more detail in Part 4 of this Chapter.

3. RFMOs with Overlapping Geographical and Species Mandates

Among the five tuna RFMOs, there are overlaps between geographical and species mandates between the following:

- CCSBT and ICCAT, which has led to an informal understanding by which ICCAT de facto recognises the primacy of CCSBT over the southern bluefin tuna;[29]
- CCSBT and IOTC, which has led the IOTC to recognise the primacy of CCSBT over Southern bluefin tuna;[30]
- CCSBT and WCPFC, which has led WCPFC to recognise the primacy of CCSBT over Southern bluefin tuna through, inter alia, a Memorandum of Understanding (MOU) between CCSBT and WCPFC;[31]
- IATTC and WCPFC with respect to the south-west part of the IATTC's regulatory area, and the south-east part of the WCPFC's regulatory area, in which

27 SPRFMO Convention, art 1(1)(f).

28 NPFC Convention, art 1(h).

29 See 'Report of the Independent Performance Review of ICCAT' (2016). www.iccat.int/documents/other/0-2nd_performance_review_tri.pdf accessed 11 December 2023, 70.

30 Report of the 'First Special Session of the Indian Ocean Tuna Commission Rome, Italy, 21–24 March 1997', *FAO Fisheries Report No 554* (1997). www.fao.org/fishery/docs/CDrom/IOTC_Proceedings(1999-2002)/files/proceedings/miscellaneous/ComReportsTexts/IOTC%20First%20Special%20Session.pdf, para 31. See also IOTC Resolution 98/03 'on southern bluefin tuna' which was revoked by IOTC Resolution 14/01 but whose essence is still in effect (as confirmed by the purpose of the IOTC Working Party on Temperate Tunas described here: www.iotc.org/science/wp/working-party-temperate-tunas-wptmt).

31 See, Western and Central Pacific Fisheries Commission, 'Relations with Other Organisations'. www.wcpfc.int/relations-other-organisations accessed 11 December 2023. See Convention on the Conservation and Management of Highly Migratory Fish Stocks in the Western and Central Pacific Ocean (WCPFC Convention), 5 September 2000, 2275 UNTS 43, entered in force 19 June 2004, art 22 (2)–(3).

most of the maritime zones of French Polynesia are located.[32] This has, inter alia, led to an MOU between IATTC and WCPFC;[33] and

- IOTC and WCPFC with respect to an area around and south of the Australian island of Tasmania.[34] This has, inter alia, led to an MOU between the IOTC and WCPFC.[35]

In addition, there are overlaps between geographical and species mandates between 'All or Other/Residual Species' RFMOs as well as between tuna RFMOs and 'All or Other/Residual Species' RFMOs. These include the following:

- CCAMLR and CCSBT, which has led to an arrangement between them, which focuses on cooperation and consultation without recognising the primacy of either;[36]
- GFCM and ICCAT;[37]
- NASCO and the CAOFA;[38]

32 See Convention for the Strengthening of the Inter-American Tropical Tuna Commission Established by the 1949 Convention Between the United States of America and the Republic of Costa Rica, 14 November 2003, entered in force 27 August 2010, https://www.iattc.org/; art III. See also WCPFC Convention, art 3(1).

33 Western and Central Pacific Fisheries Commission, 'Relations with Other Organisations'. www.wcpfc.int/relations-other-organisations accessed 11 December 2023. See WCPFC Convention, art 22 (2)–(3).

34 See Agreement for the Establishment of the Indian Ocean Tuna Commission, 25 November 1993, entered into force 27 March 1996, https://www.fao.org/treaties/results/details/en/c/TRE-000022/; art II; WCPFC Convention, art 3(1).

35 Western & Central Pacific Fisheries Commission, 'Relations with Other Organisations'. www.wcpfc.int/relations-other-organisations accessed 11 December 2023. See WCPFC Convention, art 22 (2)–(3). See also WCFPC, '18th Regular Session of the Commission Summary Report' (29 November–7 December 2021). https://meetings.wcpfc.int/node/15036 accessed 11 December 2023, paras 46–8.

36 'Arrangement between the CCAMLR and Commission for the Conservation of Southern Bluefin Tuna (CCSBT)' (30 October 2015). www.ccsbt.org/system/files/EC25_16_ActivitiesWithOtherOrganisations_0.pdf accessed 11 December 2023.

37 Some years ago – as least as early as 2018 –GFCM discontinued the earlier practice of endorsing ICCAT Recommendations relevant to the Mediterranean, see, e.g. GFCM Compendium of Decisions for 2014 (on file with author), section 1.4. The Memorandum of Understanding between GFCM and ICCAT that was under consideration at the time of writing does not contain a recognition of primacy and also no other arrangements to avoid overlap and ensure complementarity, see 'Draft Memorandum of Understanding between the ICCAT and FAO on Behalf of the GFCM' (8 November 2019). www.iccat.int/com2019/ENG/PLE_109_APP1_ENG.pdf accessed 11 December 2023.

38 See Convention for the Conservation of Salmon in the North Atlantic Ocean (NASCO Convention), 2 March 1982, 1338 UNTS 33, entered in force 1 October 1983, art 1(1); and CAOFA, art 1(b). See also, Jean-Jacques Maguire, Philip McGinnity and Erik Molenaar, 'Report of the Third NASCO Performance Review' (14 March 2023) 7 and 9. https://nasco.int/wp-content/uploads/2023/03/CNL2317_Report-of-the-Third-NASCO-Performance-Review.pdf accessed 11 December 2023.

- NEAFC and ICCAT in relation to sharks, which has led to some cooperation and coordination between them;[39]
- NEAFC and JNRFC, as discussed in Part 4 of this Chapter; and
- NEAFC, JNRFC, and the CAOFA.[40]

4. NEAFC and JNRFC

4.1 The 1959 NEAFC Convention

NEAFC was originally established by the 1959 NEAFC Convention, which entered into force in 1963.[41] Its Convention Area was identical to that of the current (1980) NEAFC Convention,[42] and was also subdivided into three regions governed by a separate Regional Committee.[43] NEAFC's species mandate covered 'all species of sea fish and shellfish, but not . . . sea mammals'.[44] This, therefore, included not only tuna and tuna-like species but also Atlantic salmon (*Salmo salar*). Whereas NEAFC was actively engaged in the regulation of Atlantic salmon, this appears not

39 See NEAFC Convention, art 1(b). See also the various NEAFC Recommendations relating to sharks, in particular, 'Recommendation on Conservation and Management Measures for Spurdog (Squalus acanthias) in ICES Subareas 1, 10, 12 and 14 for 2023 and 2024 (Rec. 05:2023)' (1 January 2023). https://leap.unep.org/en/countries/national-legislation/recommendation-conservation-and-management-measures-spurdog-0 accessed 11 December 2023. See also the provisions relating to elasmobranchs included in the Protocol of 18 November 2019 (not in force, www.fao.org/treaties/results/details/en/c/TRE-000262/ accessed 11 December 2023) to amend the International Convention for the Conservation of Atlantic Tunas, 14 May 1966, 673 UNTS 63, entered into force 21 March 1969, as amended by Protocols adopted in 1984 and 1992, which both entered into force; ICCAT Recommendation 19–01, 'On Fishes Considered to be Tuna or Tuna-Like Species or Oceanic, Pelagic and Highly Migratory Elasmobranchs'. www.iccat.int/Documents/Recs/compendiopdf-e/2019-01-e.pdf accessed 11 December 2023; and various other various ICCAT Recommendations relating to sharks. See also NEAFC, 'Report of the Working Group on the Future of NEAFC' (25–27 February 2020). www.neafc.org/system/files/WGFN%20Report%20final.pdf accessed 11 December 2023, para 10.9; NEAFC, 'Report of the Working Group on the Future of NEAFC' (15–16 June 2021). www.neafc.org/system/files/WGFN-2021-01_Report%28Final%29.pdf accessed 11 December 2023, paras 4.10–4.12; NEAFC, 'Report of the 41st Annual Meeting of the NEAFC' (15–18 November 2022). www.neafc.org/system/files/Report%20AM_2022%20final_0.pdf accessed 11 December 2023, paras 9.55–9.56.

40 See the second sentence of art 14(4) of the CAOFA and its preambular paragraph starting with 'UNDERLINING'. See also the discussion in Erik Molenaar, 'The CAOF Agreement. Key Issues of International Fisheries Law' in Thomas Heidar (ed), *New Knowledge and Changing Circumstances in the Law of the Sea* (Brill/Nijhoff 2020) 446, 455–60. Note also that the Norway-United Kingdom Arrangement and the Norway-EU Arrangement discussed further down also apply to the 'Atlantic segment' of the high seas portion of the central Arctic Ocean, and thereby also negatively impact on the future operation of the CAOFA (see also the text accompanying footnote 94).

41 North East Atlantic Fisheries Convention, 24 January 1959, 486 UNTS 157, entered into force 27 June 1963 (1959 NEAFC Convention).

42 See art 1 of the 1959 NEAFC Convention and the 1980 NEAFC Convention.

43 1959 NEAFC Convention, arts 1(2) and 5, and the Annex.

44 1959 NEAFC Convention, art 7(3).

to have been the case for tuna and tuna-like species. ICCAT was formally established in 1969, but its constitutive instrument had already been adopted in 1966 and the negotiations must have started several years before.

NEAFC's performance left much to be desired, among other things due to the frequent use of the objection procedure, weak arrangements on enforcement and compliance, and a lack of political will to follow scientific advice provided by ICES as well as to take the necessary difficult decisions on total allowable catches (TACs).[45] During the mid-1970s, NEAFC's performance was eroded further by the phenomenon of 'creeping coastal state jurisdiction', which led to increasingly wider claims to exclusive fishery zones and eventually culminated in the general acceptance of 200 nautical miles (nm) maritime zones by the mid-1970s. This enormous expansion of coastal State maritime zones – which, inter alia, deprived the North Sea of any areas of high seas – meant that the focus of attention shifted to cooperation between adjacent and opposite coastal States.

4.2 The JNRFC Agreement

In the context described previously, Norway and Russia established the bilateral JNRFC in April 1975 through the JNRFC Agreement[46] and established 200 nm maritime zones in December 1976[47]. The bilateral cooperation through JNRFC was also of critical importance in light of the absence of an agreed maritime boundary between Norway and Russia in the Barents Sea. This maritime delimitation issue was only resolved in 2010.[48]

Nothing in the title, preamble, or body of the JNRFC Agreement is explicitly devoted to its geographical scope. This instrument – and thereby the mandate of JNRFC – is therefore not exclusively confined to the maritime zones of Norway and Russia, the adjacent high seas areas, or the Barents Sea. Fisheries for species whose distributional ranges extend into the high seas pocket of the Barents Sea (the so-called 'Loophole') or beyond the Barents Sea into the Norwegian Sea, the Greenland Sea, or the central Arctic Ocean – including the high seas portion of the

45 Sevaly Sen, 'The Evolution of High-Seas Fisheries Management in the North-East Atlantic' (1997) 35 *Ocean & Coastal Management* 85, 88–91.

46 Agreement between the Government of the Kingdom of Norway and the Government of the Union of Soviet Socialist Republics on Co-Operation in the Fishing Industry (JNRFC Agreement), 11 April 1975, 983 UNTS 7, entered into force 11 April 1975. See art III(1).

47 Royal Decree of 17 December 1976 relating to the establishment of the Economic Zone of Norway; and Decree dated 10 December 1976 of the Presidium of the Supreme Soviet of the USSR 'On Provisional Measures to Conserve Living Resources and Regulate Fishing in the Sea Areas Adjacent to the Coast of the USSR', *Gazette of the Supreme Soviet of the USSR*, 1976, No 50, 728.

48 Treaty between the Kingdom of Norway and the Russian Federation concerning Maritime Delimitation and Cooperation in the Barents Sea and the Arctic Ocean, Murmansk, 15 September 2010, UNTS Reg 49095, entered into force 7 July 2011.

Norwegian Sea (the so-called 'Banana Hole') and the high seas portion of the central Arctic Ocean – therefore fall in principle within JNRFC's mandate.[49]

The JNRFC Agreement does not define the species mandate of JNRFC. It merely contains a reference to 'the living resources of the sea' in its preamble. Its constitutive instrument therefore provides JNRFC with an essentially unlimited species mandate. The practice of JNRFC has confirmed this, for instance by regulating the harvesting of harp and hooded seals.[50] The absence of a treaty-based primacy arrangement meant that the establishment of JNRFC created geographical and species overlaps with NEAFC and ICCAT. The preamble to the JNRFC Agreement nevertheless reaffirms the two parties' support for cooperation with the parties to the 1959 NEAFC Convention. The absence of a reference to ICCAT could be due to the non-occurrence of ICCAT species in proximity to the areas on which JNRFC focused when it was established, or to the fact that neither States were then members of ICCAT. The JNRFC Agreement implies that each contracting party is a member of the JNRFC,[51] but contains no provisions on accession to the Agreement or membership of JNRFC by other parties.

4.3 The 1980 NEAFC Convention

In November 1976 the members of the then-European Economic Community (EEC) agreed to combine their concerted establishment of 200 nm maritime zones with further developing the EEC's Common Fisheries Policy.[52] Among other things, the European Commission was given a mandate to represent the EEC at the international level and negotiate agreements with third States on behalf of the EEC. This meant that the EEC would have to replace its Member States in RFMOs and that arrangements would have to be made to enable the EEC to obtain membership of such RFMOs. This development, and the establishment of 200 nm maritime zones in the North-East Atlantic, led to a decision to commence negotiations to replace the 1959 NEAFC Convention with an entirely new convention, which

49 See also Agreement between the Government of the Union of Soviet Socialist Republics and the Government of the Kingdom of Norway Concerning Mutual Relations in the Field of Fisheries, 15 October 1976, 1157 UNTS 146, entered into force 21 April 1977, art 7 which reads:

> In accordance with the Agreement of 11 April 1975 between the Government of the USSR and the Government of Norway on co-operation in the fishing industry, the Contracting Parties undertake to co-operate directly and through appropriate international organizations to ensure responsible management and conservation of the living resources of the sea, particularly in respect of: (a) Stocks of fish and other living resources occurring within the areas specified in article 1 of this Agreement, (b) Such stocks as occur in areas of the high seas situated beyond the limits of the areas specified in article 1 of this Agreement and adjacent to them, and (c) Other such stocks having a relation of mutual dependence with the stocks referred to in subparagraphs (a) and (b).

50 As reflected in the 'Protocols of the Annual JNRFC Meetings'. www.jointfish.com/OM-FISKERI KOMMISJONEN/PROTOKOLLER.html accessed 11 December 2023.

51 JNRFC Agreement, art III(1).

52 Council Resolution of 3 November 1976 on certain external aspects of the creation of a 200-mile fishing zone in the Community with effect from 1 January 1977, OJ C 105, 7 May 198181, 1.

was eventually opened for signature in 1980 and entered into force in 1982. The negotiations on the NASCO Convention also concluded in 1982, and NASCO was eventually established in 1983.

As noted already, the Convention Area of the 1980 NEAFC Convention was identical to that of the 1959 NEAFC Convention. Due to the expansion of coastal State fisheries jurisdiction, however, the size of the high seas component of the 1980 NEAFC Convention had shrunk significantly and now consisted of only four high seas areas: a large (unnamed) area in the south-west; the Banana Hole; the Loophole; and the 'Atlantic segment' of the high seas portion of the central Arctic Ocean. Together, these four high seas areas form the NEAFC's Regulatory Area.[53]

NEAFC membership had decreased markedly under the new convention as the EEC had replaced EEC Member States and decreased further due to subsequent accessions to the EEC and its successors. By 2007, NEAFC had only five members: Denmark (in respect of the Faroe Islands and Greenland), the European Union (EU), Iceland, Norway, and Russia. The most recent change in membership occurred on 7 October 2020, when the United Kingdom obtained membership following its withdrawal from the EU.[54]

Despite the overlapping geographical and species mandates of the NEAFC and JNRFC, their members have largely managed to avoid conflicts and working at cross-purposes and, rather, act complementarily. As regards their species overlap, NEAFC has been focusing in practice mostly on pelagic species (e.g. Norwegian spring-spawning (Atlanto-Scandian) herring, North-East Atlantic mackerel, blue whiting), redfish, deep-sea species such as orange roughy (*Hoplostethus atlanticus Collett*) and various shark species (for which directed fishing is largely prohibited).[55] Conversely, JNRFC's management measures relate mostly to demersal fish species (e.g. cod (Norwegian Arctic cod and coastal cod), (North-East Arctic) haddock and Greenland (North-East Arctic) halibut), but also cover (Barents Sea) capelin, northern shrimp (*Pandalus borealis*), redfish, harp and hooded seals, as well as red king crab (*Paralithodes camtschaticus*) and snow crab.[56]

These species specialisations of NEAFC and JNRFC are directly related to the range of distribution of these species. This meant that, in practice, JNRFC focused primarily on the Loophole and NEAFC primarily on the Banana Hole and the high seas area in the southwest of the NEAFC Regulatory Area.

Reference should also be made to the so-called 'Coastal State Agreements' on North East Atlantic mackerel, Atlanto-Scandian herring, and blue whiting, which

53 NEAFC, 'NEAFC Scheme of Control and Enforcement' (11 February 2021). https://faolex.fao.org/docs/pdf/mul190964.pdf accessed 11 December 2023, art 1(b).

54 NEAFC, 'Report of the 39th Annual Meeting of the NEAFC' (10–13 November 2020). www.neafc.org/system/files/AM_2020_Final-REPORT.pdf accessed 11 December 2023, para 4.2. See also NEAFC, 'AM 2020–23 Instrument of Accession Letter by FCO'. www.neafc.org/system/files/AM_2020-23_Instrument-of-Accession_NEAFC%28sm%29.pdf.

55 See the NEAFC Recommendations currently in force, in particular Recommendation 5:2023 on Spurdog (*Squalus acanthias*).

56 See note 50.

were previously in effect.[57] These agreements were negotiated by different groupings of NEAFC members outside of the framework of NEAFC, even though they related to NEAFC's most commercially important fish stocks. The agreements aimed to establish the component of the overall TAC earmarked for coastal State maritime zones as well as their allocation between the participants. They, thereby, effectively determined the high seas component of the overall TAC as well, which is subsequently endorsed by NEAFC and complemented by a determination of its allocation among NEAFC members. At the time of writing, coastal State negotiations had not been able to secure many successful outcomes for a considerable number of years.

A unique feature of the practice of JNRFC is its encouragement of non-members to discontinue, or not to commence, fishing for particular species in the Loophole, and thereby not to exercise their entitlements under international law to fish in the high seas and to be involved in high seas fisheries management.[58] In return, Norway and Russia – individually and collectively through JNRFC – have provided allocations (of fishing opportunities) to be fished in their maritime zones and have discontinued withholding privileges, such as access to their ports. This practice notably culminated in the trilateral Loophole Agreement between Iceland, Norway and Russia.[59] It is aimed at avoiding unregulated high-seas fishing and thereby undesirable effects on the two coastal States' rights and interests over straddling fish stocks. At the same time, however, this practice can also be seen as creeping coastal State jurisdiction.

4.4 Recent Developments

When the United Kingdom obtained NEAFC membership in October 2020, the number of members went from five to six. This also had important consequences

57 See 'Multilateral Agreement – Coastal States'. https//oceans-and-fisheries.ec.europa.eu/fisheries/international-agreements/northern-agreements_en#multilateral-agreement-coastal-states accessed 11 December 2023.

58 These entitlements are, inter alia, laid down in UNCLOS, art 116, and Fish Stocks Agreement, art 8(3).

59 'Agreement Between the Government of Iceland, the Government of Norway and the Government of the Russian Federation Concerning Certain Aspects of Co-operation in the Area of Fisheries' (15 May 1999, entered into force 15 July 1999) 41 *Law of the Sea Bulletin* (1999), 5; 'Protocol between the Government of Iceland and the Government of the Russian Federation Under the Agreement between the Government of Iceland, the Government of Norway and the Government of the Russian Federation Concerning Certain Aspects of Co-Operation in the Area of Fisheries' (15 May 1999, entered into force 15 July 1999) 14 *International Journal of Marine and Coastal Law* 488–490; Convention on the Conservation and Management of Pollock Resources in the Central Bering Sea (16 June 1994, entered into force 8 December 1995) 34 *International Legal Materials* (1995), 67 and 'Protocol between the Government of Norway and the Government of Iceland Under the Agreement between the Government of Iceland, the Government of Norway and the Government of the Russian Federation Concerning Certain Aspects of Co-operation in the Area of Fisheries' (15 May 1999, entered into force 15 July 1999) 41 *Law of the Sea Bulletin* 56. See in this context Robin Churchill, 'The Barents Sea Loophole Agreement: A 'Coastal State' Solution to a Straddling Stock Problem' (1999) 14 *International Journal of Marine and Coastal Law* 467. Interestingly, Churchill notes at 471 that Iceland rejected an earlier proposal by Norway and Russia for a dedicated regime for the Loophole.

for decision-making on NEAFC Recommendations, which requires a two-thirds majority.[60] With five NEAFC members, proposals could be blocked by just two members; now this requires three members. Moreover, at the time of writing, it has already become clear that Brexit, the United Kingdom's revival as an independent North East Atlantic coastal State, and the consequential diminished significance of the EU as a North East Atlantic coastal State was having extensive repercussions on the intergovernmental relationships and balance of power in North East Atlantic fisheries.

By the end of 2020, the long-standing complementarity between NEAFC and JNRFC had already come under pressure because of actions from within both bodies to assert greater authority over fishing in the Loophole and the Banana Hole. One of these actions relates to fishing for northern shrimp by using a so-called 'collecting bag' in which other demersal species, such as Arctic cod and Greenland halibut, are separated from the target species and led to a separate cod-end.[61] As regards Arctic cod caught by EU fishing vessels, these are deducted from the quota allocated by JNRFC to the EU.[62] As regards Greenland halibut, however, EU fishing vessels do not have a (by-catch) quota allocated by JNRFC and Norway and Russia view these by-catches as undermining JNRFC.[63] The EU nevertheless sets its own by-catch quota for the high seas,[64] but would presumably be open to discuss the possibility of a mutually agreeable (by-catch) quota for high seas areas. In 2019, 2020, and 2021, Norway and Russia tabled proposals within NEAFC to ban

60 Cf, NEAFC Convention, arts 3(9), 5(1) and 8(1).

61 See ICES, 'NEAFC Request to ICES to Define the Fisheries that Use Collection Bags in the NEAFC Regulatory Area (ICES Subareas 1 and 2) and to Assess Their Impact on Species Caught and Bycaught', *ICES Special Request Advice* (7 January 2022). https://ices-library.figshare.com/articles/report/NEAFC_request_to_ICES_to_define_the_fisheries_that_use_collection_bags_in_the_NEAFC_Regulatory_Area_ICES_subareas_1_and_2_and_to_assess_their_impact_on_species_caught_and_bycaught/18640088 accessed 11 December 2023.

62 Council Regulation (EU) 2022/109 of 27 January 2022 fixing for 2022 the fishing opportunities for certain fish stocks and groups of fish stocks applicable in Union waters and for Union fishing vessels in certain non-Union waters, OJ L 21, 31.1.2022, 104 (ICES Area 1 and 2b includes the waters around Svalbard). See similarly Council Regulation (EU) 2023/194 of 30 January 2023 fixing for 2023 the fishing opportunities for certain fish stocks, applicable in Union waters and, for Union fishing vessels, in certain non-Union waters, as well as fixing for 2023 and 2024 such fishing opportunities for certain deep-sea fish stocks, *OJ L* 28, 31 January 023, 127.

63 See the 'Agreed Record of Fisheries Consultations between the European Union and Norway for 2022' (9 December 2022). https://assets.publishing.service.gov.uk/media/63935cce8fa8f546da1bf3e8/Agreed_record_of_fisheries_consultations_between_the_European_Union__Norway_and_the_United_Kingdom_for_2023.pdf, section 5.1.4.

64 See Council Regulation (EU) 2022/109 of 27 January 2022 fixing for 2022 the fishing opportunities for certain fish stocks and groups of fish stocks applicable in Union waters and for Union fishing vessels in certain non-Union waters, *OJ L* 21, 31.1.2022, 108 (1766 tonnes); Council Regulation (EU) 2023/194 of 30 January 2023 fixing for 2023 the fishing opportunities for certain fish stocks, applicable in Union waters and, for Union fishing vessels, in certain non-Union waters, as well as fixing for 2023 and 2024 such fishing opportunities for certain deep-sea fish stocks, *OJ L* 28, 31 January 023, 132.

the use of collecting bags in shrimp fisheries in the NEAFC Regulatory Area,[65] but none of these were adopted.

Another relevant action relates to fishing for redfish in the Banana Hole. For 2022, JNRFC set a TAC of 67,210 tonnes for this species, of which 10% was set aside for non-members. Of this 10%, 4,1% was earmarked for the Fisheries Protection Zone (FPZ) around Svalbard and 5,9% for the Banana Hole.[66] Whereas Norway and Russia made a corresponding proposal within the NEAFC in 2021, the EU proposed that 25% of the TAC agreed by JNRFC would be made available for the NEAFC's Regulatory Area.[67] None of these proposals within NEAFC were adopted.

The next major development was the adoption of two bilateral non-legally binding arrangements: the Norway – United Kingdom Arrangement on Fisheries Cooperation in December 2021,[68] and the Norway – EU Ad-hoc exploratory consultations in relation to the fisheries in ICES areas 1 and 2 in April 2022 (hereafter Norway-United Kingdom Arrangement and Norway-EU Arrangement).[69]

Even though the arrangements do not explicitly define their geographical scope, it is clear from both texts as well as the title of the Norway-EU Arrangement that they are limited to ICES areas 1 and 2. Within these areas, the arrangements apply to all areas within and beyond national jurisdiction, including therefore the FPZ, all other coastal State maritime zones – in particular exclusive economic zones, other 200 nm zones derived therefrom, and continental shelves – as well as high seas areas. The latter comprise the Banana Hole, the Loophole, and the Atlantic segment of the high seas portion of the central Arctic Ocean.

65 See, for example, NEAFC, 'Report of the 38th Annual Meeting of the NEAFC' (12–14 November 2019). www.neafc.org/system/files/Report_AM-2019_FINAL_plus_List-of-Annexes_0.pdf accessed 11 December 2023, para 12.40; NEAFC, 'Report of the 39th Annual Meeting of the NEAFC' (10–13 November 2020). www.neafc.org/system/files/AM_2020_Final-REPORT.pdf accessed 11 December 2023, paras 8.49–8.52; NEAFC, 'Report of the 40th Annual Meeting of the NEAFC' (9–12 November 2021). www.neafc.org/system/files/Report%20AM_2021%20Final.pdf accessed 11 December 2023, paras 9.46–9.49.

66 See JNRFC, 'Protocol of the 51st Annual Session' (2021). www.jointfish.com/content/download/512/6950/file/51-norsk.pdf accessed 11 December 2023, 5–6; NEAFC, 'Report of the 40th Annual Meeting of the NEAFC'(9–12 November 2021). www.neafc.org/system/files/Report%20AM_2021%20Final.pdf accessed 11 December 2023, paras 9.15–9.19; and 'Agreed Record of Fisheries Consultations between the European Union and Norway for 2022' (9 December 2022). assets.publishing.service.gov.uk/media/63935cce8fa8f546da1bf3e8/Agreed_record_of_fisheries_consultations_between_the_European_Union__Norway_and_the_United_Kingdom_for_2023.pdf section 5.1.3.

67 NEAFC, 'Report of the 40th Annual Meeting of the NEAFC' (9–12 November 2021). www.neafc.org/system/files/Report%20AM_2021%20Final.pdf accessed 11 December 2023, para 9.16.

68 'Arrangement between the United Kingdom and Norway on fisheries cooperation (Norway – United Kingdom Arrangement)' (20 December 2021). www.regjeringen.no/contentassets/8e674a19756e44518c4641287b28e4db/uk-norway-arrangement-20.12.2021-fpz.pdf accessed 11 December 2023.

69 'Ad-hoc exploratory consultations in relation to the fisheries in ICES areas 1 and 2 (Norway – EU Arrangement)' (28 April 2022). www.regjeringen.no/contentassets/70a18c8e8d7542558dbffdc76e95ca55/ad-hoc-exploratory-consultations-in-relation-to-the-fisheries-in-ices-areas-1-and-2.pdf accessed 11 December 2023.

The arrangements were intended to resolve disputes between Norway, on the one hand, and the United Kingdom and the EU on the other hand, regarding fishing for Arctic cod in the FPZ around Svalbard. These disputes arose in December 2020 when Norway reduced the combined allocations of the EU and the United Kingdom by about 30% in comparison to the allocation which the EU and its predecessors had received for a period of 35 years (1986–2020).[70] The EU allocation consisted of a fixed percentage of 3.77% – based on historic catches during the reference periods 1967–76 and 1968–77 – of the TAC set by JNRFC. This long-standing practice had been very successful in setting aside the dispute on the geographical scope of the Spitsbergen Treaty,[71] which continues to exist between Norway and various other parties to this treaty.[72]

Norway argued that the 30% reduction it effectuated in December 2020 was merely a direct consequence of Brexit, as the United Kingdom had become an independent actor within the domain of international fisheries law on 1 January 2021.[73] The main difficulty with this argument, however, is that it is unable to explain the rationale for subsequently making the 30% reduction available to Norwegian and Russian vessels, to be split on a 50–50% basis.[74] While bilateral negotiations to resolve the dispute continued between Norway and the United Kingdom, and between Norway and the EU, the fishing companies which held these cod quotas under the laws and regulations of the United Kingdom, the EU, and EU Member States challenged the actions of the Norwegian government before the Oslo City Court in August 2021.[75] Around the same time, the EU submitted a proposal within NEAFC to add Arctic cod in ICES areas one and two to the list of regulated species by NEAFC.[76] Norway and Russia took the view that this was a political issue and that the proposal was not acceptable.[77] Eventually, the negotiations between Norway and the United Kingdom, and between Norway and the EU successfully

70 Legal Notice J-219–2020, 'Forskrift om regulering av fisket etter torsk i fiskevernsonen ved Svalbard i 2021' (1 January 2021). www.fiskeridir.no/Yrkesfiske/Regelverk-og-reguleringer/J-meldinger/Utgaatte-J-meldinger/j-219-2020 accessed 11 December 2023. Note the difference between these numbers and the 34 864 tonnes agreed by JNRFC in October 2020, JNRFC, 'Protocol of the 50th Annual Session' (2020). www.jointfish.com/content/download/512/6950/file/50-norsk.pdf accessed 11 December 2023, Appendix 4.

71 Treaty concerning the Archipelago of Spitsbergen, 9 February 1920, 2 League of Nations Treaty Series 7 (1920), entered into force 14 August 1925.

72 See, inter alia, Robin Churchill and Geir Ulfstein, 'The Disputed Maritime Zones Around Svalbard' in Myron Nordquist, John Norton Moore and Thomas Heidar (eds), *Changes in the Arctic Environment and the Law of the Sea* (Martinus Nijhoff 2010) 551; Erik Molenaar, 'Fisheries Regulation in the Maritime Zones of Svalbard' (2012) 27 *International Journal of Marine and Coastal Law* 3.

73 Norwegian Note Verbale dated 4 May 2021, on file with author.

74 Letter from Synnøve Liabø of the Norwegian Directorate of Fisheries, dated 8 February 2021, on file with author.

75 Case No 21–117819TVI-TOSL/05.

76 NEAFC, Doc. PE 2021–02–33, on file with author.

77 NEACF, 'Report of the Permanent Committee on Monitoring and Compliance' (14–16 September 2021). www.neafc.org/system/files/Report%20PECMAC-02%202021_final.pdf accessed 11 December 2023, para 4.43.

concluded in December 2021 and April 2022, respectively, through the adoption of the two aforementioned bilateral arrangements. The case before the Oslo City Court was therefore withdrawn.

The two arrangements are short, one-page documents containing four to six paragraphs which lay down various commitments. Some commitments relate more generally to fisheries management and the rights and responsibilities of coastal States in their maritime zones.[78] The recognition or acknowledgement by the United Kingdom and the EU of the sovereign rights and jurisdiction of Norway in the FPZ around Svalbard is balanced by noting the long-term interests of the United Kingdom and the EU in the Arctic region.[79] These long-term interests must be understood as references to the historic catches of vessels from the United Kingdom and the EU in what is now the FPZ.

More directly relevant to this chapter, the arrangements include the following acknowledgement:

> the established fisheries management regime in the ICES areas 1 and 2 in waters north of the 62°N line has over decades secured the sustainable management of marine living resources and been beneficial for the coastal States and vessels from other States through different arrangements.[80]

It is submitted that, in conjunction with the references to 'other international instruments relating to management of fisheries',[81] this must be understood as an acknowledgment of the success of Norway's fisheries management in the FPZ around Svalbard and of JNRFC more broadly. This can to some extent also be regarded as comprising implicit acknowledgements of the legitimacy and legality of the role of JNRFC in the established regime as such – including in the three high seas pockets in ICES areas 1 and 2 – as well as of the practices by Norway and Russia which amount to creeping coastal State jurisdiction in the context of fisheries.

These explicit and implicit acknowledgements relating to JNRFC are complemented by commitments by the United Kingdom and the EU to fish only for certain (amounts of) species as directed by Norway and Russia individually or collectively through JNRFC (see the following). These commitments are balanced by a commitment by Norway to restore the long-standing allocation of Arctic cod that was interrupted in December 2020.[82] The corresponding commitment of the United Kingdom is not to:

> authorise vessels flying the flag of the United Kingdom in ICES areas 1 and 2 to fish for species and quotas, other than those allocated to the United

78 Norway-United Kingdom Arrangement, paras 1–2; Norway-EU Arrangement, para 1.

79 Norway-United Kingdom Arrangement, paras 3 and 5; Norway-EU Arrangement, paras 1 and 3.

80 Norway-EU Arrangement, para 2. Similar wording is included in the Norway-United Kingdom Arrangement, para 4.

81 Norway-United Kingdom Arrangement, para 2; Norway-EU Arrangement, para 1.

82 Norway-United Kingdom Arrangement, para 5; Norway-EU Arrangement, para 3(a).

> Kingdom by the coastal States in the area, without cooperating and consulting with those coastal States. This commitment does not apply to fishing in ICES area 2 on stocks to which the United Kingdom is a coastal State.[83]

It is submitted that the words 'coastal State(s)' must be understood as references to Norway and Russia, even though they are not mentioned. Other coastal States relating to ICES areas one and two – besides Norway, Russia and the United Kingdom – are Denmark/Faroe Islands, Denmark/Greenland, and Iceland. As the Norway-United Kingdom Arrangement is a bilateral instrument and is not legally binding, it obviously cannot bind – legally or politically – the United Kingdom vis-à-vis non-parties, consistent with the *pacta tertiis* principle. In case of species managed jointly by Norway and Russia through JNRFC, however, the United Kingdom will in reality not only be cooperating and consulting directly with Norway, but indirectly also with Russia.

The corresponding commitment of the EU is laid down in paragraph 3(c) of the Norway-EU Arrangement which stipulates that:

> With the same objective of ensuring sustainable fishing, following consultations, Norway will set limitations in ICES areas 1 and 2 for redfish, cod, haddock, and Greenland halibut, for both directed fisheries and as by-catch. On this basis, in a coordinated manner, the Union will fix quotas and adopt necessary technical regulations for the same areas and species.[84]

A notable difference between the wording used here and that in the corresponding commitment of the United Kingdom is that Norway is explicitly mentioned, rather than being implicitly covered through references to 'coastal State(s)'. This difference can be explained not so much by the principle of *pacta tertiis* as discussed previously, but by the fact that the final stages of the negotiations between Norway and the EU took place when Russia was in the midst of waging its full-scale war against Ukraine, which had started on 24 February 2022. Any commitment by the EU vis-à-vis Russia, even remotely implicit, would clearly have been hugely undesirable. As already noted, however, the regulation of the four designated species is not done by Norway alone, but together with Russia through JNRFC. When Norway sets limitations on the catches of these four species – whether through directed fishing or by-catch – by EU fishing vessels, it does in fact no more than implement regulation of JNRFC. In a sense, Norway performs the function of an 'executive' arm of JNRFC.

Both arrangements contain a provision that makes the continuation of Arctic cod allocations by Norway to the United Kingdom and the EU conditional on the latter two carrying out the provisions of the arrangements.[85] This clearly serves to

83 Norway-United Kingdom Arrangement, para 6.

84 Norway-EU Arrangement, para 3(c).

85 Norway-United Kingdom Arrangement, para 5; Norway – EU Arrangement, para 3(d).

give Norway a 'stick' in case it takes the view that the United Kingdom and/or the EU have not complied with Norway's directions. But, if Norway were to actually use that stick in practice, it would obviously create a dispute with the United Kingdom and/or the EU.

The global geopolitical order which existed when the Norway-United Kingdom Arrangement was adopted in December 2021 had fundamentally changed by the time the Norway-EU Arrangement was adopted in April 2022. The successful conclusion of the latter negotiations, despite the EU's apparent initial resistance to agree to concessions similar to those made by the United Kingdom in December 2021, can be interpreted in different ways. On the one hand, it may have been significantly driven by the exposure of the EU's energy vulnerability and acute dependence on energy imports from allies with abundant energy resources, such as Norway. On the other hand, it may also have been driven by the EU's confidence – based on repeated Norwegian assurances – that the Norway-EU Arrangement would establish a new process where outstanding fisheries issues could be resolved by serious and good faith negotiations by both sides. Such an interpretation attributes significant weight to the words 'following consultations' and 'in a coordinated manner' in paragraph 3(c) of the Norway-EU Arrangement.

The EU's hopes and expectations for better cooperation with Norway, unfortunately, did not materialise during the period between the adoption of the Norway-EU Arrangement in April 2022 and the time of writing in October 2023. Whereas the 52nd Annual JNRFC Meeting in October 2022 did not produce unexpected outcomes on the issues at hand,[86] the EU and Norway clashed repeatedly during the 41st Annual NEAFC Meeting in November 2022. Regarding redfish in the Banana Hole, the EU tabled a machine translation of the official Norwegian text of the Protocol of the 52nd Annual JNRFC Meeting in 2022.[87] This triggered strong criticism by Norway, to which the EU responded by criticising Norway's continued close cooperation with Russia despite Russia's war against Ukraine.[88] The EU and Norway both tabled proposals on redfish in the Banana Hole. Neither attracted the necessary majority, but the United Kingdom (together with Norway and Russia) voted in favour of Norway's proposal, and no other NEAFC member supported the EU's proposal.[89] A proposal by the EU on Greenland halibut – presumably the first ever tabled at NEAFC – did not attract support from any other NEAFC member

86 See JNRFC, 'Protocol of the 52nd Annual Session' (2022). www.jointfish.com/content/download/512/6950/file/52-norsk.pdf accessed 11 December 2023, Annex 3 and 4.

87 NEACF, 'Protocol for the 52nd Session in the Mixed Norwegian-Russian Fisheries Commission' (17–24 October 2022). www.neafc.org/system/files/AM_2022-82_EU-protokoll-52-Mixed-Norwegian-Russian-Fisheries-Commission.pdf accessed 11 December 2023; NEAFC, 'Protocol of the 52nd Session of the Joint Norwegian-Russian Fisheries Commission: Key Sections' (2022). www.neafc.org/system/files/AM_2022-83_EU-summary-of-doc-AM_2022-82_0.pdf.

88 NEAFC, 'Report of the 41st Annual Meeting of the NEAFC' (15–18 November 2022). www.neafc.org/system/files/Report%20AM_2022%20final_0.pdf accessed 11 December 2023, paras 9.12–9.15.

89 ibid, paras 9.17–9.20.

either.[90] Finally, both the EU and Norway tabled proposals on the use of collecting bags. To the dismay of the EU, the Norwegian proposal to prohibit the use of collecting bags was adopted (with the EU and Iceland voting against); leading the EU to use its right to opt-out from the Recommendation.[91]

These events at the Annual NEAFC Meeting in November 2022 also underlined the failure of various bilateral meetings between the EU and Norway convened earlier. Following the Annual NEAFC Meeting, Norway decided to provide the EU a lower Arctic cod quota than the EU would have otherwise received based on the long-standing practice mentioned previously, as reflected in paragraph 3(a) of the Norway-EU Arrangement.[92] Presumably, Norway justified its decision by invoking the 'stick' in paragraph 3(d) of the Norway-EU Arrangement in response to the EU's decision to set its own TACs for Greenland halibut and redfish[93] and to continue to allow the use of collecting bags.

The aforementioned account suggests that, at the time of writing, the Norway-United Kingdom Arrangement had performed satisfactorily for both Parties, but the Norway-EU Arrangement did not. It therefore seems that only the Norway-United Kingdom Arrangement has strengthened the role of JNRFC and the authority of Norway and Russia through creeping coastal State jurisdiction – in the three high seas areas covered by the arrangements. At the same time, the Norway-United Kingdom Arrangement has weakened NEAFC – and the CAOFA[94] – and the authority of high-seas fishing States there. By maintaining its position on Greenland halibut, redfish and collecting bags, the EU avoided a similar impact for

90 ibid, paras 9.43–9.46.

91 ibid, paras 9.62–9.69. As confirmed by the NEAFC Secretary to the author in an email dated 29 September 2023. Iceland also opted out.

92 Legal Notice, 'Forskrift om regulering av fissket etter torsk i fiskevernsonen ved Svalbard i 2023' https://lovdata.no/dokument/LTI/forskrift/2023-03-31-463 accessed 11 December 2023, para 3. The amount is 3907 tonnes, and only for the period 1 January – 31 March 2023. The EU's quota should have been 15629 tonnes; almost exactly three times the quota of the United Kingdom, Council Regulation (EU) 2023/194 of 30 January 2023 fixing for 2023 the fishing opportunities for certain fish stocks, applicable in Union waters and, for Union fishing vessels, in certain non-Union waters, as well as fixing for 2023 and 2024 such fishing opportunities for certain deep-sea fish stocks, *OJ L* 28, 31 January 2023, 10 and 127. See also the amendment included in Council Regulation (EU) 2023/1062 of 1 June 2023 amending Regulation (EU) 2023/194 fixing for 2023 the fishing opportunities for certain fish stocks, applicable in Union waters and, for Union fishing vessels, in certain non-Union waters, as well as fixing for 2023 and 2024 such fishing opportunities for certain deep-sea fish stocks, *OJ L* 143, 2 June 2023, 1 and 3. Subsequently, Norway issued a new notice allocating 12,415 tonnes to the EU, Legal Notice J-71–2023, 'Forskirft Forskrift om regulering av fisket etter torsk i fiskevernsonen ved Svalbard i 2023' (28 January 2023). www.fiskeridir.no/Yrkesfiske/Regelverk-og-reguleringer/J-meldinger/Gjeldende-J-meldinger/j-71-2023 accessed 11 December 2023.

93 See Council Regulation (EU) 2023/1062 of 1 June 2023 amending Regulation (EU) 2023/194 fixing for 2023 the fishing opportunities for certain fish stocks, applicable in Union waters and, for Union fishing vessels, in certain non-Union waters, as well as fixing for 2023 and 2024 such fishing opportunities for certain deep-sea fish stocks, *OJ L* 143, 2 June 2023.

94 See footnote 40. It should be noted that the United Kingdom was not a party to the CAOFA at the time of writing.

the Norway-EU Arrangement; albeit at the cost of its Arctic cod quota. The difference between the positions of the EU and the United Kingdom in this regard is at least partially linked to the fact that the United Kingdom is a coastal State to the Banana Hole, and the EU is not. Quite remarkably, Russia's war in Ukraine does not seem to have had a significant effect on the positions of either the United Kingdom or Norway on these fisheries issues.

Other considerations for the EU may have included the need to safeguard the broader positions and interests of the EU and its Member States vis-à-vis the Spitsbergen Treaty. A new development in this regard is Norway's plan to commence deep seabed mining on its (outer) continental shelf in the North-East Atlantic, including on the continental shelf around Svalbard.[95]

5. Conclusions

The phenomenon of overlapping geographical mandates of RFMOs must be viewed in light of the evolution of international law, which has proceeded in a gradual manner with little attention to hierarchy. This evolution and the phenomena to which it has led – such as the 'fragmentation of international law', 'regime complexes' and 'polycentricity' – also apply to RFMOs, as almost all of them are entirely separate, autonomous or 'stand-alone' bodies.

Overlaps in the geographical mandates of RFMOs can lead to working at cross-purposes and even conflicts. As this chapter has shown, geographical overlaps between RFMOs are quite common due to their species-based and area-based specializations. To avoid working at cross-purposes and conflicts, and to ensure complementarity, the constitutive instruments of six of the ten so-called 'All or Other/Residual Species' RFMOs (with a geographical mandate which includes high seas areas or consists exclusively of high seas) recognise the primacy of species-based RFMOs. The CAOFA, CCAMLR, GFCM and JNRFC do not have treaty-based primacy arrangements.

One would assume that there are no, or at least very few, geographical overlaps between RFMOs with the same species mandate. In reality, however, a considerable number of geographical overlaps exist between tuna RFMOs as well as between 'All or Other/Residual Species' RFMOs. Many, but not all, of these overlaps are addressed through formal recognitions or informal understandings of the primacy of one of the RFMOs or instruments (such as MOUs) between them on cooperation and coordination.

The geographical and species overlap between NEAFC and JNRFC is neither addressed by primacy arrangements – whether treaty-based or otherwise – nor by formal or informal arrangements on cooperation and coordination. For a

95 See info at 'Åpning av områder for mineralvirksomhet på deler av norsk kontinentalsokkel' (20 June 2023). www.regjeringen.no/no/tema/energi/olje-og-gass/kunnskapsinnhenting-og-konsekvensutredning/apning-av-omrader-for-mineralvirksomhet-pa-deler-av-norsk-kontinentalsokkel/id2871504/ accessed 11 December 2023.

considerable period of time since the establishment of JNRFC in 1975 and the continuation of NEAFC under a new constitutive instrument in 1982, the members of the two RFMO/As managed to avoid conflicts and work at cross-purposes, and to act complementarily. This was achieved by focusing on different species and geographical areas. In recent years, however, this long-standing complementarity has come under pressure by actions from within both bodies to assert more authority over fishing in the Loophole and the Banana Hole. One example is the dispute which arose in December 2020 between Norway, on the one hand, and the United Kingdom and the EU, on the other hand, on fishing for Arctic cod in the FPZ around Svalbard. The dispute was intended to be resolved by the adoption of two non-legally binding arrangements: the December 2021 Norway-United Kingdom Arrangement and the April 2022 Norway-EU Arrangement. The future impact, if any, of these arrangements on the roles of JNRFC, NEAFC, and the CAOFA in the Loophole, the Banana Hole, and the Atlantic segment of the high seas portion of the central Arctic Ocean depends above all on how they will be implemented.

4 Challenges in RFMO Compliance Review Mechanisms

*Adriana Fabra**

1. Introduction

The principal objective of regional fisheries management organisations or arrangements (RFMOs) is to promote cooperation among States to ensure effective conservation and management of fisheries resources.[1] Over 20 RFMOs have been established to manage some of the world's fisheries and some RFMOs have succeeded in improving the status of certain fish stocks.[2] However, according to data from the Food and Agriculture Organization of the United Nations (FAO), the percentage of stocks fished at biologically unsustainable levels increased from 10% in 1974 to 35.4% in 2019.[3] Effective RFMO management of internationally shared fisheries resources is particularly important in this context.

* This chapter is directly based on the reports of three Virtual Expert Workshops on Best Practices in Compliance in RFMO held in 2020 and 2021 and on the 2022 report titled 'Approaches to Evaluate and Strengthen RFMO Compliance Processes and Performance: A Toolkit and Recommendations' developed by an Expert Review Group. These initiatives were convened by the Pew Charitable Trusts, in collaboration with the International Seafood Sustainability Foundation (ISSF), under the guidance of a Steering Committee comprised of Holly Koehler (Vice President for Policy and Outreach, ISSF); Gerald Leape (Principal Officer, The Pew Charitable Trusts); Lara Manarangi-Trott (Compliance Manager, Western and Central Pacific Fisheries Commission); Osvaldo Urrutia (Senior Lecturer, Universidad Católica de Valparaíso); Mark Young (Executive Director, International MCS Network); and this author. The author is co-writer of materials for the Expert Workshops, including report of the Expert Workshops. The author is thankful to Holly Koehler, Robin Davies, Laura Eeles, and Gerald Leape for their valuable comments to this chapter. All opinions in this chapter are attributable solely to the author.

1 See in particular, Agreement for the Implementation of the Provisions of the United Nations Convention on the Law of the Sea of 10 December 1982 relating to the Conservation and Management of Straddling Fish Stocks and Highly Migratory Fish Stocks, 4 August 1995, 2167 UNTS 3, entered into force 11 December 2001 (Fish Stocks Agrement), art 8. The constitutive agreements of most RFMOs are in line with these objectives.

2 Terje Løbach et al (eds), 'Regional Fisheries Management Organisations and Advisory Bodies: Activities and Developments, 2000–2017', *Food and Agriculture Organization of the United Nations (FAO) Fisheries and Aquaculture Technical Paper 561* (Rome 2020).

3 FAO, 'The State of World Fisheries and Aquaculture: Towards Blue Transformation' (Rome 2022) 46–47, 52 and Figure 23 https://openknowledge.fao.org/handle/20.500.14283/cc0461en.

DOI: 10.4324/9781003492030-6

Different reasons explain the failure of some RFMOs to achieve their objectives. One reason is poor compliance by RFMO members of their obligations.[4] For example, members can repeatedly fail to submit required data and information; implement agreed measures; and effectively follow up on and remedy their own identified instances of non-compliance. Non-compliance shows poor accountability and responsibility by individual RFMO members. When not effectively addressed, non-compliance is also a manifestation of poor performance by the RFMO as a whole.

Independent performance reviews of several RFMOs have noted the need to improve the frameworks and actions to ensure compliance. Such actions could include following up on infringements or infractions and improving the functioning of RFMO compliance committees and assessment processes.[5] Resolutions by the United Nations General Assembly have requested international support for increased enforcement and compliance capabilities for RFMOs and members.[6] They have also highlighted specific areas where RFMOs need to improve their members' compliance.

RFMOs have progressively strengthened their mechanisms to monitor, assess, and support members' compliance. In recent years, new tools and processes have been reviewed, developed, tested, or implemented. While some compliance review frameworks are common to most RFMOs, the specific tools and processes RFMOs choose to implement vary widely.[7] In particular, there are important differences in their levels of transparency, in the tools and processes adopted to support compliance

4 The term 'member' applies to both RFMO members and cooperating non-members. The latter are subject to the same obligations as members.

5 See Holly Koehler, 'Tuna RFMO Compliance Assessment Processes: A Comparative Analysis to Identify Best Practices', *ISSF Technical Report 2023–05* (June 2023) 5. On the issue of performance reviews, see also 'Fourteenth Round of Informal Consultations of States Parties to the Agreement for the Implementation of the Provisions of the United Nations Convention on the Law of the Sea of 10 December 1982 Relating to the Conservation and Management of Straddling Fish Stocks and Highly Migratory Fish Stocks' (15 August 2019) ICSP14/UNFSA/INF.3.

6 United Nations General Assembly (UNGA), 'Sustainable Fisheries, Including Through the 1995 Agreement for the Implementation of the Provisions of the United Nations Convention on the Law of the Sea of 10 December 1982 Relating to the Conservation and Management of Straddling Fish Stocks and Highly Migratory Fish Stocks, and Related Instruments' (9 December 2021) A/RES/76/71, para 244 and paras 24, 25, 87, 108, 168, 170, 175, 176, 179, among others; UNGA, 'Sustainable Fisheries, Including Through the 1995 Agreement for the Implementation of the Provisions of the United Nations Convention on the Law of the Sea of 10 December 1982 Relating to the Conservation and Management of Straddling Fish Stocks and Highly Migratory Fish Stocks, and Related Instruments' (8 December 2020) A/RES/75/89, para 244 and others; UNGA, 'Sustainable Fisheries, Including Through the 1995 Agreement for the Implementation of the Provisions of the United Nations Convention on the Law of the Sea of 10 December 1982 Relating to the Conservation and Management of Straddling Fish Stocks and Highly Migratory Fish Stocks, and Related Instruments' (10 December 2019) A/RES/74/18, para 244 and others.

7 Holly Koehler, 'Tuna RFMO Compliance Assessment Processes: A Comparative Analysis to Identify Best Practices', *ISSF Technical Report 2023–05* (June 2023) 4–5.

review, and in the types of responses enacted in instances of non-compliance. Considering that RFMOs have implemented or are developing a range of tools and systems, examining and comparing these different approaches can provide useful feedback on the tools and practices which contribute to better compliance in RFMOs.

1.1. Expert Workshops

In this context, The Pew Charitable Trusts, in collaboration with the International Seafood Sustainability Foundation, convened three virtual Expert Workshops in 2020 and 2021 on RFMO compliance processes and performance (Expert Workshops). These workshops aimed at identifying challenges in current RFMO compliance review mechanisms and potential solutions to strengthen these processes and improve member compliance. The first workshop identified the principal drivers of compliance and non-compliance. The second and third workshops focused on two areas identified by workshop participants as key for compliance: 1) transparency in the compliance review mechanisms and 2) the effectiveness of responses, including sanctions, to instances of non-compliance. These workshops were attended by highly qualified specialists in the field, including chairs of RFMO compliance committees and RFMO compliance officers, coming from ten different RFMOs,[8] and experts from international organisations, academia, and civil society.[9]

Three publicly available reports present key takeaways from these three workshops and two high-level panels convened in conjunction with the workshops.[10] These workshop reports provide information which facilitates comparison among different RFMOs, points to potential useful practices, and assists in systematising the elements of any compliance review mechanism. These reports have been

8 Participants attended in their individual capacity and under the Chatham House Rule. Participants included compliance officers, chairs of compliance committees or executive directors of the following RFMOs: Commission for the Conservation of Antarctic Marine Living Resources, Commission for the Conservation of Southern Bluefin Tuna, Inter-American Tropical Tuna Commission, International Commission for the Conservation of Atlantic Tunas, Indian Ocean Tuna Commission, North East Atlantic Fisheries Commission, North Pacific Fisheries Commission, South East Atlantic Fisheries Organisation, South Pacific Regional Fisheries Management Organisation, and Western and Central Pacific Fisheries Commission.

9 The list of participants at the Expert Workshops and at expert panels organised jointly with the Workshops are provided in the Expert Workshop's reports.

10 'Virtual Expert Workshop on Best Practices in Compliance in RFMOs: 2020 Report' (September 2020). www.pewtrusts.org/-/media/assets/2021/04/virtual-expert-workshop-on-best-practices-in-compliance-in-rfmos.pdf accessed 23 September 2023 (First Expert Workshop); 'Second Virtual Expert Workshop on Best Practices in Compliance in RFMOs: The Role of Transparency in Improving RFMO Compliance' (March 2021). www.pewtrusts.org/-/media/assets/2021/07/pew_issf_secondcomplianceworkshopreport_july2021.pdf accessed 23 September 2023 (Second Expert Workshop); 'Third Virtual Expert Workshop on Best Practices in Compliance in RFMOs' (November 2021). www.pewtrusts.org/-/media/assets/2022/05/2021-third-workshop-report.pdf accessed 23 September 2023 (Third Expert Workshop).

circulated as information papers at some RFMO meetings, and their content discussed in RFMO plenary sessions and workshops.[11]

1.2. Toolkit and Recommendations to Evaluate and Strengthen RFMO Compliance Processes and Performance

The outcomes of the Expert Workshops provided the basis for a toolkit and recommendations for improving RFMO compliance, issued by an independent Expert Review Group.[12] The Group's recommendations are reflected in a 2022 report titled 'Approaches to Evaluate and Strengthen RFMO Compliance Processes and Performance: A Toolkit and Recommendations'.[13] This report was presented during compliance committee meetings of some RFMOs, including the Inter-American Tropical Tuna Commission, the Western and Central Pacific Fisheries Commission, and the International Commission for the Conservation of Atlantic Tunas. This toolkit provides principles to guide compliance review processes, recommendations to evaluate and strengthen these mechanisms, and a methodology to assist RFMOs in assessing the effectiveness of their compliance processes.

Some of these principles and recommendations are already being implemented or developed by RFMOs. Other principles and recommendations could be relevant in the framework of new reforms. The Expert Review Group's toolkit is considered later in this chapter.

1.3. What are Compliance Review Mechanisms?

Most RFMOs have a compliance review mechanism in place, through an RFMO compliance committee or a similarly named body. This mechanism may include

11 See workshop reports and presentations submitted to the Technical and Compliance Committee of the Western and Central Pacific Fisheries Commission, '17th Regular Session of the Technical and Compliance Committee' (September 2021). meetings.wcpfc.int/meetings/tcc17 accessed 23 September 2023; International Commission for the Conservation of Atlantic Tunas, 'Message from the Chair of ICCAT's Compliance Committee' (November 2021). www.iccat.int/com2021/ENG/COC_325_ENG.pdf accessed 23 September 2023; International Commission for the Conservation of Atlantic Tunas, 'Expert Workshops on Best Practices in Compliance in RFMOs' (1–2 June 2022). www.iattc.org/GetAttachment/5d23d4f0-6804-4796-91f3-9f0457844e02/OTM-37-PRES_Expert-workshop-on-best-practice-in-compliance-in-RFMOS.pdf accessed 23 September 2023.

12 The Expert Review Group under the coordination of Gerald Leape (Principal Officer, The Pew Charitable Trusts) included Duncan Currie (Director, Globelaw); Robert Day (International Fisheries Advisor and Consultant); Jung-re Riley Kim (Policy Officer/Negotiator, Ministry of Oceans and Fisheries, Korea); Holly Koehler (Vice President for Policy and Outreach, ISSF); Sarah Lenel (Fisheries Advisor and Consultant); Masa Miyahara (Advisor to the Ministry of Agriculture, Forestry and Fisheries, Japan); and Penelope Ridings (Legal Advisor, Western and Central Pacific Fisheries Commission).

13 See 'Approaches to Evaluate and Strengthen RFMO Compliance Processes and Performance: A Toolkit and Recommendations' (July 2022). www.pewtrusts.org/-/media/assets/2023/07/approaches-to-evaluate-and-strengthen-rfmo-compliance-processes-and-performance-a-toolkit-and-recomm.pdf accessed 23 September 2023 (A Toolkit and Recommendations).

subsidiary bodies or small working groups tasked with further assisting the process. Some of these mechanisms were established decades ago, such as the compliance committee of the International Commission for the Conservation of Atlantic Tunas set up in 1995. Other compliance committees have been created more recently, such as the North Pacific Fisheries Commission which became operative in 2016. Compliance review bodies can be established in an RFMO's constitutive agreement or through subsequent RFMO measures. Currently, most RFMO compliance committees meet once a year for approximately two or three days.

Compliance committees review all aspects related to the implementation of the RFMO's conservation and management measures (CMMs) and particularly compliance with these measures by RFMO members. RFMOs recognise different functions or objectives for their compliance committees, but these typically include monitoring and reviewing compliance; identifying problem areas related to the implementation of CMMs; and making recommendations to solve these problems, including through adopting new CMMs. On the compliance review process, most RFMOs follow three main steps: 1) collecting information relevant to compliance; 2) reviewing and assessing compliance; and 3) stipulating some consequences in instances of non-compliance.[14]

Participants at the Expert Workshops valued positively the contribution of compliance review mechanisms for strengthening an RFMO's overall performance. However, the majority of participants considered that these mechanisms had room for improvement.[15]

This chapter addresses three main questions. First, what are the problems hindering the effectiveness of compliance review mechanisms? Second, what solutions could help address these problems? Third, are there challenges in implementing these solutions and, if so, how could these be overcome? To answer these questions, this chapter considers the reports of the Expert Workshops and the toolkit and recommendations of the Expert Review Group.

2. Problems in Compliance Review Mechanisms

Participants at the Expert Workshops identified challenges in all three key stages of compliance review mechanisms: information management, compliance assessment, and determination of consequences for non-compliance. They also identified structural or cross-cutting difficulties related to RFMO governance structures, the clarity and consistency of CMMs, transparency, and resources to support improved compliance, notably capacity-building and using technological solutions.

14 Holly Koehler, 'Tuna RFMO Compliance Assessment Processes: A Comparative Analysis to Identify Best Practices', *ISSF Technical Report 2023–05* (June 2023) 10.

15 Pre-workshop survey to the First Virtual Expert Workshop on Best Practices in Compliance in RFMOs, on file with the author. In the survey, 30% of respondents considered that compliance review mechanisms conduct their activities 'poorly'.

This section provides a short summary of the principal challenges in compliance review mechanisms identified at the Expert Workshops. It first describes challenges in cross-cutting areas and then, discusses challenges related to the compliance review mechanisms themselves.

2.1. *Cross-Cutting Issues*

2.1.1. *RFMO Governance*

An effective compliance review mechanism requires up-to-date and efficient RFMO institutional arrangements. The basic architecture of most RFMOs has not evolved over time. Certain institutional aspects if not addressed, can hinder efforts to improve compliance review mechanisms.

Participants at the Expert Workshops identified the following main challenges in governance structures:

- Lack of adequate regulation in constitutive treaties, conservation measures, rules of procedure, and other instruments to support new approaches to compliance review;
- Lack of adequate mandate by key bodies involved in compliance review mechanisms to contribute more effectively to compliance reviews, such as RFMO Secretariats, by providing preliminary assessments of compliance;
- Lack of effective cooperation between RFMOs and with other multilateral organisations, which prevents RFMOs from benefiting from data-sharing agreements and hinders technical cooperation between RFMO Secretariats or the harmonisation of regulations; and
- Lack of adequate rules on data access and confidentiality, which could for instance facilitate the use of third-party data to assess compliance.

2.1.2. *Clarity and Consistency of CMMs*

The lack of clarity in CMMs is at the root of many compliance problems. CMMs are often unclear or ambiguous because of rushed negotiations or the need to reach political compromises. At times, measures can overlap with, duplicate, or contradict other CMMs. Occasionally, they are translated inaccurately, unnecessarily complex, and devoid of concrete guidance to facilitate their practical implementation. These shortcomings create difficulties for members to implement the measures and report on them correctly and efficiently. These shortcomings also make assessments more uncertain and less objective and complicate setting clear consequences for non-compliance. In addition, the number of CMMs can be daunting, particularly for members with less capacity to monitor their implementation.

2.1.3. *Transparency*

Participants at the Expert Workshops identified transparency as a cornerstone of an effective compliance mechanism and noted that most RFMOs are not sufficiently transparent in sharing information and giving access to compliance review processes.[16] Transparency is tied to the notion of accountability and should lead to better compliance as public scrutiny breeds self-correcting behaviour. However, there is a flip side to high levels of transparency: the fear of having information used against RFMO members, or outside the RFMO, can disincentive information-sharing and the opening-up of decision-making processes. Political dynamics, particularly mistrust, compromise transparency.

In practice, in the context of compliance review mechanisms, RFMOs do not facilitate access to all information and to all stakeholders. Information which goes in and out of the RFMO is often restricted, particularly information on compliance assessment outcomes and on follow-up action by members. In some RFMOs, some information is not available to all RFMO members. RFMOs may provide access to large amounts of not particularly useful information, but greater transparency would be achieved if information-sharing was more accurate, complete, and timely. On assessment and decision-making processes, significant progress has been made in many RFMOs to facilitate participation by non-members (so-called 'observers'). However, in certain RFMOs, observers are not given access to compliance review bodies and decision-making processes remain opaque. Procedural rules do not always give clarity on whether contributions from observers are considered in compliance reviews.

2.1.4. Capacity-Building

Some RFMO members lack the legal framework, infrastructure, and human and material resources to implement fully the measures to which they are bound. Limited capacity also impacts the quality of the compliance review process itself, as compliance meetings can represent a significant burden on some members and impact their staff capacities, for example, to fulfil their reporting obligations. Capacity building is relevant not only to prevent situations of non-compliance but also to help members resolve situations of non-compliance constructively.

Despite ongoing efforts in RFMOs to develop the capacity of their members, overall, there are not enough resources earmarked for capacity-building. In addition, some of the existing programmes are not sufficiently effective because they are not adequately targeted or lack active engagement by the recipient State. RFMO Secretariats, which are responsible for supporting members in compliance review mechanisms, notably in fulfilling their reporting obligations, are generally understaffed and short of technological and other material resources.

16 Pre-workshop questionnaire on transparency, Second Virtual Expert Workshop 3 March 2021. On file with the author. Seventy-nine per cent of respondents considered that RFMOs are not sufficiently transparent and noted that levels of transparency significantly vary between RFMOs.

2.2. *Challenges in the Compliance Review Processes*

2.2.1. Data Collection, Information Management, and Reporting

2.2.1.1. DATA COLLECTION

Information forms the basis of any compliance review mechanism. Information must reach the RFMO Secretariats so it can be used to assess compliance; be managed efficiently and effectively to ensure meaningful assessments; and be made available to members and other stakeholders in a useful manner.

In practice, information is often lacking or of poor quality. If data is poor, the basis upon which compliance decisions can be made will also be poor. Some members frequently provide incomplete information or fail to submit their required reports altogether. At the same time, reporting requirements in many RFMOs have gradually increased over the years and the amount of information required at times from members can be overwhelming. Information provided to the RFMO can also be imprecise and unverifiable. Most compliance reviews are based on information which is self-reported by members. RFMO Secretariats have limited access to independent sources to verify that information, for instance through civil society, scientific institutions, or other RFMOs.

2.2.1.2. INFORMATION MANAGEMENT AND REPORTING

Some RFMOs are starting to incorporate technological solutions into their information management and reporting processes. Examples include enabling members to make online submissions of information and automatically generating some reports by the RFMO Secretariats. However, most of the information processing continues to be done manually by RFMO staff. The data used for assessments comes from different sources and in different formats. This often makes the data difficult to filter, compare, or corroborate, particularly when there is a lack of data processing resources.

RFMO Secretariats dedicate most resources to processing large amounts of information. As a result, Secretariats have limited capacity to provide other forms of support to RFMO members or to develop a more active role in analysing the compliance information. Some RFMOs are developing more systematic forms of analysis. However, overall, RFMOs pay insufficient attention to identifying trends in compliance or assessing risks which could support the organisation's compliance reviews.

Some compliance reports are extremely comprehensive, comprising hundreds of pages to be reviewed for each annual compliance meeting. They often provide administrative or superfluous information and do not focus on compliance priorities. As noted during the Expert Workshops, information could be presented in formats that are easier to manage and understand.

2.2.2. Compliance Assessment Processes

There are some developments in RFMOs to establish criteria to assist with compliance assessments. In this regard, there are initiatives to develop 'audit' or assessment points in CMMs, which could make the assessment process more objective, and to set hierarchies of obligations and infractions, which may help prioritise review processes. However, most compliance review processes tend to conduct exhaustive reviews of all CMMs in force, year after year. This inevitably leads to more simplified assessments, which may suffice to tackle the most serious cases of non-compliance.

Criteria to assess compliance tend to focus on members meeting their individual obligations. Such criteria, typically, do not consider broader implications, such as the impact of those failures on the overall performance of the RFMO and its ability to achieve its objectives. In addition, given the ambiguity of some CMMs, certain assessments may be prolonged and fail to reach any concrete outcome.

2.2.3. Outcomes of Compliance Assessment Processes

Participants at the third Expert Workshop noted that existing outcomes in situations of non-compliance are not satisfactory and do not provide sufficient incentives for better compliance. The problem can be partly explained by some of the weaknesses described previously, such as the poor quality of information used for compliance review and the lack of clarity and specificity of CMMs. Additionally, most of these processes generally take place at the annual meeting of the RFMO. There is little room for prior consultations with members on potential situations of non-compliance. This leads to higher levels of politicisation in the deliberations and less suitable responses to instances of non-compliance. Overall, current compliance review mechanisms lack adequate 'carrots' and 'sticks', particularly in cases of serious and pervasive non-compliance. Furthermore, these processes lack sufficient transparency, particularly around the criteria that are followed to determine the consequences of non-compliance.

3. Potential Solutions to Improve Compliance Review Mechanisms

Participants at the Expert Workshops identified a range of initiatives which could improve the effectiveness of compliance review mechanisms. The Expert Review Group developed these recommendations, extracting seven guiding principles and a set of recommendations structured around ten core elements of compliance review processes. These ten core elements cover all problem areas identified in the previous section. This section provides a summary of these principles and recommendations.[17] It, then, discusses how such solutions could be implemented.

17 More solutions can be found in A Toolkit and Recommendations; First Expert Workshop; Second Expert Workshop; and Third Expert Workshop.

3.1. Principles

Participants of the Expert Workshops and the Expert Review Group identified seven underlying principles which should be applied across all elements of any compliance review process.[18] To ensure their long-term success, these compliance review mechanisms should be:

1. *Fair and impartial*: they should be undertaken consistently, based on clear rules, and afford an equal opportunity to participate to all members, recognising their differences in capacity;
2. *Legitimate*: they should aim at supporting the RFMO in achieving its objectives, through adequate consultation and good understanding among members, and not focus on individual penalties;
3. *Transparent*: transparency at all levels of an RFMO and between all actors involved can increase fairness and impartiality and make processes more legitimate and, eventually, more effective;
4. *Targeted*: considering the high volume of activity and information, they should prioritise certain obligations for assessments and any compliance responses should reflect the severity of the instance of non-compliance;
5. *Effective*: they should result in improved compliance by enacting rigorous follow-up mechanisms in situations of non-compliance and by monitoring compliance and implementation trends over time;
6. *Efficient*: they should minimise unnecessary administrative burden and costs to all involved and, as a result, promote fairness among RFMO members, including by relying on electronic platforms; and
7. *Cooperative*: they should support and promote cooperation within the RFMO, among RFMOs, and with other organisations to increase information-sharing and work towards harmonisation of certain criteria and processes.

3.2. Recommendations

The Expert Review Group identified ten core elements of compliance review processes and structured its recommendations around those ten elements.[19] The following is a description of the main recommendations which can support an effective implementation of the compliance review processes and ensure they achieve their purpose and operate along agreed principles.

A block of recommendations is directed at strengthening the governance structures of RFMOs by:

1. *Establishing the necessary institutional framework and governance rules in the RFMO*, to ensure that these processes are set by clear and stand-alone

18 A Toolkit and Recommendations, section 2.3.
19 A Toolkit and Recommendations, sections 2.5 and 3.

instruments, supported by the RFMO's overarching governance structure, with guarantees, among others, that RFMO Secretariats have adequate mandates to assist effectively RFMO members in compliance review processes;
2. *Improving the quality and applicability of CMMs*, by, notably, preventing duplications and inconsistencies between measures, improving their applicability by making them clearer, incorporating audit points and implementation guidance, and automating simple compliance assessment processes; and
3. *Ensuring that decision-making rules do not prevent inaction or deadlocks*, as decision-making is currently predominantly based on consensus, by, for example, enabling RFMO members to take decisions binding onto a non-compliant member.

Other important recommendations concern the use of information necessary to assess compliance. In particular, the Expert Review Group recommended mechanisms to

1. *Ensure that information used for compliance review is of the right quality and quantity*, including that it is timely, accurate, and verifiable with third-party data; and
2. *Improve the collation, analysis, and presentation of data*, by reviewing and adapting RFMO rules to facilitate the work of RFMO Secretariats and incorporate technological solutions to strengthen database management and the presentation of information.

Another pillar of any effective compliance review mechanism is to *establish effective consequences for non-compliance and follow-up actions*. This can ensure that first, adequate and proportionate consequences for non-compliance are pre-established according to different types of infringements and, second, robust and transparent follow-up mechanisms to report on action taken by members and the RFMO are implemented when a situation of non-compliance is identified.

To improve processes, the Expert Review Group recommended that RFMOs:

1. *Incorporate tools to make the compliance review process more effective, efficient, and clearer*, by setting hierarchies in obligations and infractions, focusing on priority areas through risk assessment, adopting a compliance monitoring schedule, and incorporating monitoring and assessment of less complex matters between annual sessions; and
2. *Establish effective monitoring, evaluation, and review mechanisms*, so that, in a context of openness and transparency, the RFMO can track trends on the implementation of CMMs and monitor follow-up actions to assess the effectiveness of compliance review processes. This information can be used to carry out a 'health check' of the RFMO, review measures, procedures, and priorities and strategically improve the performance of the RFMO, also in the context of a performance review.

Finally, two recommendations relate to actions to improve the performance of RFMOs and their members in all phases of the compliance review process:

1. *Develop capacity-building* by ensuring that capacity-building initiatives, which are one of the possible responses in situations of non-compliance, are targeted, engage recipient countries, are monitored, and their effectiveness assessed; and
2. *Improve cooperation among RFMOs*, through memoranda of understanding and through informal collaboration among RFMOs' staff, to share data to cross-verify information, centralise some data collection and publication systems, and harmonise reporting requirements and assessment criteria among RFMOs as much as possible.

3.3. How to Implement These Solutions?

Introducing changes to compliance review mechanisms, such as those mentioned previously, is possible. Indeed, several RFMOs are already implementing some of these tools and are developing new mechanisms. However, strengthening these systems requires time and the ability to overcome challenges, which could pull the RFMO in the opposite direction. While many external and internal factors can drive or block progress in an international organisation, participants at the Expert Workshops identified two important obstacles: mistrust among members and the perception that compliance review mechanisms are tools for punishment.

3.3.1. Overcoming Perceptions of Unfairness and Mistrust

Perceptions of political imbalance, unfairness, and mistrust can prevent meaningful development in compliance review mechanisms, particularly on issues related to transparency and the adoption of consequences in cases of non-compliance. Like other international organisations, particularly those concerned with the management of natural resources, RFMOs are complex entities. RFMO members must reconcile competing interests over resources (particularly between coastal States and distant water fishing nations) and diffuse tensions between the need to follow scientific advice and respond to economic interests – in a continuously changing environment. There is often an underlying perception of unfairness in the management and allocation of resources and in the way negotiations are done, where some members may have a disproportionate influence and some deals are concluded behind closed doors.

How then could trust be built in the context of RFMO compliance review mechanisms? While complex political dynamics are inevitable in any international organisation, participants at the Expert Workshops identified concrete steps which could improve confidence in the system and amongst members:

1. *Support reforms through collective and cooperative mechanisms*, including among RFMOs, while ensuring that all members participate in these processes

and are provided with necessary assistance, and take advantage of opportunities for virtual meetings;

2. *Begin reforms for persistent and most serious types of non-compliance*, which damage the integrity of the RFMO and undermine the conservation of resources, as addressing these types of non-compliance first could harness support for other reforms; and
3. *Engage global multilateral bodies in developing international standards or guidelines for compliance review mechanisms*, including the FAO, as these international standards could provide a common framework in which to establish specific RFMO reforms.

3.3.2. Overcoming Perceptions that Compliance Review Mechanisms are 'Courts'

Participants at the Expert Workshops noted that there is a general perception among RFMO members that compliance review bodies are disciplinary in nature and focused on finger-pointing. Some emphasised that 'RFMOs are not courts'. This notion, combined with the mistrust noted previously, undermines transparency, as there is the perception that information can be used against a member, including outside the RFMO. Discussing compliance matters once a year in a multilateral context can place members on the defensive. In addition, these concerns can make some members reluctant to adopt 'audit points' and to support pre-establishing consequences for non-compliance with CMMs.

Participants in all Expert Workshops acknowledged that penalties are necessary to respond to certain infringements. However, they noted that these measures should be applied as part of a collective effort to improve the performance of the RFMO and not to weaken individual members. As a way forward, the following actions could be considered:

1. *Change the narrative on compliance review mechanisms*, by emphasising their benefits for the overall performance of the RFMO. This can be achieved by introducing some RFMO 'health checks' providing indicators of progress in the performance of the RFMO related to members' compliance. Some participants suggested changing the names of some of these processes to remove their focus on 'compliance'.
2. *Provide more opportunities for members to resolve some of the compliance problems between annual sessions*, as members should be able to address these situations intersessionally in collaboration with the RFMO Secretariat.
3. *Address uneven playing fields and challenges in implementation of CMMs* by strengthening the capacity of Secretariats to assist the membership and by increasing targeted capacity-building assistance to members.

3.3.3. Taking it in Steps

Participants at the Expert Workshops acknowledged that changes in compliance review mechanisms cannot happen overnight for political, economic, and technical reasons. To foster a sense of trust and of constructive review, experts noted that these changes could be taken incrementally by:

1. *Adopting reforms in a stepwise approach*, for example by firstly addressing less controversial issues and issues on which members share common concerns;
2. *Taking reforms that suit the specific RFMO*, as while some degree of harmonisation among RFMOs is desirable, there can be no 'one-size-fits-all' approach; and
3. *Developing case studies on compliance*, which can demonstrate how compliance regimes can be strengthened.

4. Conclusions

While there are challenges, RFMOs are taking important steps to strengthen compliance review mechanisms. Different RFMOs are implementing or developing different instruments. Taken together, these instruments offer a good catalogue of initiatives that all RFMOs can monitor and learn from. The new set of 'Approaches to Evaluate and Strengthen RFMO Compliance Processes and Performance' developed following the Expert Workshops may point to initiatives which have not yet been considered by RFMOs.

However, progress to implement these reforms should be made rapidly. All too often RFMOs fail to take the necessary science-based measures to achieve their fisheries conservation and management objectives. Low levels of compliance exacerbate this problem. To achieve their objectives, RFMOs require a system based on reliable and accurate information, where every member is doing its part. Otherwise, failures in compliance can become a failure of the RFMO itself.

As pointed out in the Expert Workshops, 'RFMOs don't exist in a vacuum'.[20] They are an integral part of the framework established for the conservation and management of living resources by the United Nations Convention on the Law of the Sea, and further developed by the Fish Stocks Agreement.[21] RFMOs are also an important piece of the recent legally binding instrument on the conservation and sustainable use of marine biological diversity in areas beyond national jurisdiction.[22]

Scrutiny of RFMO performance should be intensified, not only within each RFMO, through its performance reviews, but also at the global level, for example within the frameworks of the UN Fish Stocks Agreement Review Conference and the FAO. International courts and tribunals are also relevant fora which could consider the failure by RFMOs and/or their members to comply with their international obligations.

20 Third Expert Workshop, 8.

21 United Nations Convention on the Law of the Sea (UNCLOS), 10 December 1982, 1833 UNTS 3, entered into force 16 November 1994, arts 63, 64, 118, 119; Fish Stocks Agreement.

22 UNGA, 'International Legally Binding Instrument under the United Nations Convention on the Law of the Sea on the Conservation and Sustainable Use of Marine Biological Diversity of Areas Beyond National Jurisdiction' (24 December 2017) A/RES/72/249.

Part III

Dispute Settlement Mechanisms in Regional Fisheries Management Organisations

5 Dispute Settlement Mechanisms in RFMOs and Under UNCLOS

Samuel Wordsworth KC

1. Introduction

Dispute settlement mechanisms in regional fisheries management organisations or arrangements (RFMOs) can engage – or impede[1] – jurisdiction under Part XV of the United Nations Convention on the Law of the Sea (UNCLOS). As a separate matter, UNCLOS may be agreed to play a role as part of the applicable law in a dispute under a given RFMO. On jurisdiction under Part XV of UNCLOS, which is the principal focus of this chapter, Article 288(2) of UNCLOS provides that:

> A court or tribunal referred to in Article 287 shall also have jurisdiction over any dispute concerning the interpretation or application of an international agreement related to the purposes of this Convention, which is submitted to it in accordance with the agreement.

Two obvious points should be made. First, the 'related to the purposes' criterion is a low bar, and RFMOs will qualify, not least because the purposes of UNCLOS include equitable and efficient utilisation of living resources as well as their conservation.[2] Second, jurisdiction turns on the terms of the given international agreement. Article 288(2) opens a door, but States may or may not choose to enter.

Thus far, there has been no headlong rush for this particular door, no doubt, as concerns fisheries disputes. This is largely for the reasons listed by Churchill some 15 years ago in his 2007 paper on the jurisprudence of the International Tribunal for the Law of the Sea (ITLOS) on fisheries disputes.[3] In brief, these are the fact that fisheries disputes may derive more from policy choices than departure from legal rules; issues of locus standi and the jurisdictional impact of Article 297(3) of UNCLOS with respect to the exclusive economic zone; and a

1 See the controversial decision of the majority in Southern Bluefin Tuna, Award on Jurisdiction and Admissibility, 4 August 2000, XXIII RIAA 1.

2 United Nations Convention on the Law of the Sea (UNCLOS), 10 December 1982, 1833 UNTS 3, entered into force 16 November 1994, Preamble, fourth para.

3 Robin Churchill, 'The Jurisprudence of the International Tribunal for the Law of the Sea Relating to Fisheries: Is There Much in the Net' (2007) 22 *International Journal of Marine and Coastal Law* 383.

DOI: 10.4324/9781003492030-8

lack of resources necessary to bring or substantiate a claim. The latter may be of particular significance. All the more so where the potential respondent State has greater economic power, such that a power imbalance means that little if any political scope for bringing a claim.[4] States are also traditionally unwilling to subject themselves to compulsory dispute settlement save where they have no choice, for example as a respondent in a claim brought pursuant to some form of investment treaty. It is notable that many States now seek to restrict or withdraw altogether from compulsory arbitration in this area of treaty law.

The chapter examines the extent to which jurisdiction under Article 288(2) of UNCLOS may be open with respect to RFMOs where the parties to those agreements are also parties to the 1995 Fish Stocks Agreement.[5]

2. Article 30(2) of the Fish Stocks Agreement: Initial Points

Article 30(2) of the Fish Stocks Agreement provides that

> The provisions relating to the settlement of disputes set out in Part XV of the Convention apply *mutatis mutandis* to any dispute between States Parties to this Agreement concerning the interpretation or application of a subregional, regional or global fisheries agreement relating to straddling fish stocks or highly migratory fish stocks to which they are parties, including any dispute concerning the conservation and management of such stocks, whether or not they are also Parties to the Convention.[6]

There are two useful points to emphasise before considering how this provision impacts on existing RFMO.

First, the application of Part XV of UNCLOS is to be *mutatis mutandis*. It may allow a court or tribunal considering its jurisdiction a certain leeway when

4 Cf., *The Atlanto-Scandian Herring Arbitration (The Kingdom of Denmark in Respect of the Faroe Islands v. The European Union)*, PCA Case 2013–30, although this was a dispute precipitated by the European Union imposing trade sanctions against the Faroe Islands.

5 The website of the International Tribunal for the Law of the Sea (ITLOS) lists the Fish Stocks Agreement and the agreements of eleven RFMOs as treaties which may confer jurisdiction on ITLOS, 'International Agreements Conferring Jurisdiction on the Tribunal'. www.itlos.org/en/main/jurisdiction/international-agreements-conferring-jurisdiction-on-the-tribunal/ accessed 18 December 2023. See further Nigel Bankes, 'The Jurisdiction of the Dispute Settlement Bodies of the Law of the Sea Convention With Respect to Other Treaties' (2021) 52 *Ocean Development and International Law* 346, including on whether a further consent is needed to establish compulsory jurisdiction. Note also that the list on ITLOS' website does not give a complete picture given the potential jurisdictional impact of Article 30(2) of the Fish Stocks Agreement. It could be of use to State officials and practitioners not well-versed in this area of law for the list on ITLOS' website to identify that potential impact.

6 Agreement for the Implementation of the Provisions of the United Nations Convention on the Law of the Sea of 10 December 1982 relating to the Conservation and Management of Straddling Fish Stocks and Highly Migratory Fish Stocks (Fish Stocks Agreement), 4 August 1995, 2167 UNTS 3, entered into force 11 December 2001, art 30(2).

considering the interplay between Article 30(2) and the given fisheries agreement. This may be particularly important when addressing perceived conflicts between the obligation accepted by States under Article 30(2) and obligations with respect to dispute settlement under a fisheries agreement. One should also bear in mind that Part XV contains its own carefully drafted jurisdictional allocation provisions at Articles 281 and 282.

Second, the relevant fisheries agreement must be one 'relating to straddling fish stocks or highly migratory fish stocks'. This begs the question of how close this relation must be. As a matter of ordinary meaning, the formula 'relating to' appears broad. It does not suggest that the principal subject matter of the given fisheries agreement must be straddling or highly migratory fish stocks. In the separate opinion of Judge Shahabuddeen in the *Headquarters Agreement* case before the International Court of Justice (ICJ),[7] which refers to the dissenting opinion of Judge Schwebel in the *Yakimetz* case, the term 'relating to' is interpreted as meaning 'has reference to' or 'is connected with'.[8] In the *Methanex* case, which concerned another jurisdictional gateway, the tribunal held that 'relating to' required some form of legally significant connection.[9] On this basis, it would appear enough that the relevant agreement regulated straddling or highly migratory stocks in some way.

ITLOS has interpreted the word 'concerning', which is arguably narrower than 'relating to', as meaning 'having a bearing on', which is again very broad.[10] However, in interpreting the military activities exception in Article 298 of UNCLOS, the Annex VII tribunal in *Coastal State Rights* contrasted 'concerning' with the use of 'arising out of' or 'arising from' in other provisions of UNCLOS.[11] It stated that 'the term "concerning" circumscribes the military activities exception by limiting it to those disputes whose subject matter is military activities'.[12] A reluctant respondent State would certainly say that this is analogous and that Article 30(2) of the Fish Stocks Agreement is intended to cover only agreements which have as their subject matter straddling or highly migratory stocks. The position of the Annex VII

7 *Applicability of the Obligation to Arbitrate under Section 21 of the United Nations Headquarters Agreement of 26 June 1947*, Advisory Opinion, ICJ Rep 1988, Separate Opinion of Judge Shahabuddeen, para 63.

8 *Application for Review of Judgment No 333 of the United Nations Administrative Tribunal*, Advisory Opinion, ICJ Rep 1987, Dissenting Opinion of Judge Schwebel, para 113–4. See also *Aegean Sea Continental Shelf (Greece v. Turkey)*, Judgment, ICJ Rep 1978, para 76, where 'relating to the territorial status of Greece' is 'to be understood as a generic term denoting any matters properly to be considered as comprised within the concept of territorial status under general international law'.

9 *Methanex v. United States of America*, Partial Award of August 2002, paras 137–9, on the gateway to protection under Chapter 11 of the North American Free Trade Agreement, 17 December 1992, entered into force 1 January 1994.

10 *M/V Louisa (Saint Vincent and the Grenadines v. Kingdom of Spain)*, Judgment, ITLOS Rep 2013, para 83.

11 *Dispute Concerning Coastal State Rights in the Black Sea, Sea of Azov, and Kerch Strait (Ukraine v. the Russian Federation)*, Award on Preliminary Objections, PCA Case 2017–06, 21 February 2020, paras 330–1.

12 ibid, para 330.

tribunal in the recent *Detention of Ukrainian Naval Vessels and Servicemen* award appears to have been a little more nuanced: it analysed the prior cases as evidencing that 'there must be a close connection or relationship between the subject of the dispute and the military activities referred to'.[13]

3. Article 30(2) of the Fish Stocks Agreement: The Rules Governing the Interplay with Dispute Settlement Provisions in Other Treaties

In his 2007 paper, Robin Churchill looked at the then-concluded fisheries agreements.[14] He noted that the application of Article 30(2) of the Fish Stocks Agreement to such treaties may depend on the principles of *lex posterior* and *lex specialis*.[15] In applying the *lex posterior* rule, reference may be had to Article 30 of the Vienna Convention on the Law of Treaties (VCLT).[16] Article 30 reflects the default principle that a later treaty can be taken to express the most recent and most accurate reflection of the parties' intentions.[17] The principle of *lex specialis* has now been applied with some regularity by the ICJ and other international tribunals, for example when applying competing human rights and rules of international humanitarian law in the context of an armed conflict.[18]

However, there may be a question as to the usefulness of these two principles in the specific context of Article 30(2) of the Fish Stocks Agreement. The concept of *lex posterior* is predicated on there being some incompatibility between provisions in the earlier and the later treaty. This is reflected in the express wording of Article 30(3) of the VCLT, which provides for application of the earlier treaty 'only to the extent that its provisions are compatible with those of' the later treaty. Courts and tribunals may, in general, be hesitant to make a finding of incompatibility, because treaty parties may be presumed not to have intended to act incompatibly with their pre-existing obligations.[19] Additionally, the principles of *lex posterior* and *lex specialis* are default rules in the sense that either rule could readily fall away depending on express treaty wording. Article 30(2) of the VCLT expressly provides for

13 *Dispute Concerning the Detention of Ukrainian Naval Vessels and Servicemen (Ukraine v. the Russian Federation)*, Award on Preliminary Objections, PCA Case 2019–28, 27 June 2022, para 107.

14 Robin Churchill, 'The Jurisprudence of the International Tribunal for the Law of the Sea Relating to Fisheries: Is There Much in the Net' (2007) 22 *International Journal of Marine and Coastal Law* 383.

15 ibid, 394–8.

16 Vienna Convention on the Law of Treaties (VCLT), 23 April 1969, 1155 UNTS 331, entered into force 27 January 1980.

17 Article 30 of the VCLT applies with respect to successive treaties relating to the same subject matter. There might be an argument as to whether a constitutive treaty establishing a RFMO would meet that criterion insofar as concerns the Fish Stocks Agreement or UNCLOS.

18 See, for example, *Legality of the Threat or Use of Nuclear Weapons*, Advisory Opinion, ICJ Rep 1996, para 25; *Legal Consequences of the Construction of a Wall in the Occupied Palestinian Territory*, Advisory Opinion, ICJ Rep 2004, para 106.

19 Sir Robert Jennings KC and Arthur Watts KCMG KC (eds), *Oppenheim's International Law: Volume 1 Peace* (OUP 2008) 1275.

this in the context of *lex posterior*. Alexander Orakhelashvili, in the *Commentary* on the VCLT edited by Olivier Corten and Pierre Klein, describes Article 30(2) as a form of conflicts rule and notes that:

> In order to avoid normative controversies, states often insert in treaties priority clauses to determine which treaty applies in which circumstances, and how far one treaty is supposed to prejudice the applicability of another, or defer to it. If such clauses are not inserted, then the later treaty is supposed to prevail over the earlier one.[20]

In the context of Article 30(2) of the Fish Stocks Agreement, both of these points lead to Articles 281 and 282 of UNCLOS, which are conflicts rules with respect specifically to competing jurisdictional provisions. Their application follows directly from the express wording of Article 30(2) of the Fish Stocks Agreement, which refers without distinction to 'provisions relating to the settlement of disputes set out in Part XV'. As a result, the issues of how any jurisdiction conferred by Article 30(2) of the Fish Stocks Agreement will interact with the dispute settlement provisions in 'subregional, regional or global fisheries agreement relating to straddling fish stocks or highly migratory fish stocks' could be decided in most cases by the *mutatis mutandis* application of Articles 281 and 282 of UNCLOS. Thus, there would be little need to refer to the more general principles of *lex posterior* and *lex specialis*.[21]

4. The *mutatis mutandis* application of Articles 281 and 282 of UNCLOS

Article 281(1) of UNCLOS provides that:

> If the States Parties which are parties to a dispute concerning the interpretation or application of this Convention have agreed to seek settlement of the dispute by a peaceful means of their own choice, the procedures provided for in this Part apply only where no settlement has been reached by recourse to such means and the agreement between the parties does not exclude any further procedure.

This breaks down into four elements: (i) identification of a dispute; (ii) whether there has been an agreement to seek settlement by other means; (iii) whether a

20 Alexander Orakhelashvili, 'Article 30 1969 Vienna Convention' in Olivier Corten and Pierre Klein (eds), *The Vienna Conventions on the Law of Treaties: A Commentary* (OUP 2011) 786.

21 For a discussion of conflicts clauses and *lex posterior* in the context of the Convention on international trade in endangered species of wild fauna and flora (CITES), 3 March 1973, 993 UNTS 243, entered into force 1 July 1975, see Erik Franckx, 'The Protection of Biodiversity and Fisheries Management: Issues Raised by the Relationship between CITES and LOSC' in David Freestone, Richard Barnes and David Ong (eds), *The Law of the Sea: Progress and Prospects* (OUP 2006) 210; see Margaret Young, *Trading Fish, Saving Fish* (CUP 2011) 151–4.

settlement has been reached; and (iv) whether the agreement excludes any further procedure.

As to (i), where, in the context of a given fisheries agreement and Article 30(2) of the Fish Stocks Agreement, Article 281 is being applied *mutatis mutandis*, the 'dispute' it refers to would presumably be taken as the 'dispute concerning the interpretation or application of' that fisheries agreement.

As to (ii), the Commission in the *Conciliation between Timor-Leste and Australia* persuasively reasoned that the agreement to which Article 281(1) refers must be a legally binding agreement. As the Commission explained, this is consistent with the wording of Article 282.[22] Thus, the Commission could not accept

> that a reading of Article 281 that would permit a non-binding agreement to preclude the application of the compulsory dispute settlement provisions of Part XV would be consistent with the fact that Part XV of the Convention is itself a binding agreement.[23]

As to (iii), whether a settlement has been reached by recourse to the agreed means is just a yes/no question of fact. According to the Annex VII tribunal in the *South China Sea*, 'Article 281 does not require parties to pursue any agreed means of settlement indefinitely. It only requires parties to abide by any time limit set out in their agreement'.[24] Absent any agreed time limit (to which Article 281(2) would apply), Article 281 appears to envisage no more than a good faith and unsuccessful attempt at settlement through the agreed means. There is no requirement for persistent attempts at settlement. However, the references to 'recourse to such means' and 'further procedure' support that there should be some attempt to seek settlement through the agreed means.[25]

As to (iv), the question of whether the given agreement excludes any further procedure; this was determinative in the decision of the Annex VII tribunal to reject jurisdiction in the *Southern Bluefin Tuna* case, as will be discussed further below.

22 *Timor Sea Conciliation (Timor-Leste v. Australia)*, Report and Recommendations of the Compulsory Conciliation Commission between Timor-Leste and Australia on the Timor Sea, PCA Case 2016–10, 9 May 2018. In *Maritime Delimitation in the Indian Ocean (Somalia v. Kenya)*, Judgment, ICJ Rep 2017, paras 126–8, the ICJ focused on the formulation 'or otherwise' in Article 282 of UNCLOS, concluding that Article 282 thus encompasses agreement to the jurisdiction of the Court through an optional clause declaration. This does not detract from the Commission's reasoning.

23 *Timor Sea Conciliation (Timor-Leste v. Australia)*, Decision on Australia's Objections to Competence, PCA Case 2016–10, 19 September 2016, paras 56–7. See also *South China Sea Arbitration (Philippines v. China)*, Award on Jurisdiction and Admissibility, PCA Case 2013–19, 29 October 2015, paras 212–9.

24 *South China Sea Arbitration (Philippines v. China)*, Award on Jurisdiction and Admissibility, PCA Case 2013–19, 29 October 2015, para 220.

25 See also, for example, *Southern Bluefin Tuna (New Zealand v. Japan; Australia v. Japan)*, Provisional Measures, Order of 27 August 1999, ITLOS Rep 1999, para 59–60.

The chapter looks at three examples from the pool of current fisheries agreements, both to identify the problems with a *lex posterior* or *lex specialis* approach and to identify how the application of Articles 281 and 282 of UNCLOS appears sufficient to regulate apparent incompatibilities.

4.1. Example 1: The IOTC Agreement

As the first example, Article XXIII of the 1993 Agreement for the Establishment of the Indian Ocean Tuna Commission (IOTC Agreement) provides that:

> Any dispute regarding the interpretation or application of this Agreement, if not settled by the Commission, shall be referred for settlement to a conciliation procedure to be adopted by the Commission. The results of such conciliation procedure, while not binding in character, shall become the basis for renewed consideration by the parties concerned of the matter out of which the disagreement arose. If as the result of this procedure the dispute is not settled, it may be referred to the International Court of Justice in accordance with the Statute of the International Court of Justice, unless the parties to the dispute agree to another method of settlement.[26]

According to a *lex posterior* approach, the first step would be to identify which treaty came second in time. If the date of adoption is taken as the appropriate date for identifying what is *lex posterior*, as is consistent with the negotiating history of the VCLT and the views of many commentators,[27] the Fish Stocks Agreement, adopted in 1995, is the later treaty in time. However, if it is the date of entry into force which is relevant, as asserted by Orakhelashvili,[28] the IOTC Agreement is the *lex posterior*. The existence of these conflicting approaches – both of which have a plausible basis – may itself suggest that *lex posterior* can be an unsatisfactory tool for identifying the intention of treaty parties, in particular, if its application can readily be avoided through bespoke jurisdiction allocation provisions.

Article XXIII of the IOTC Agreement could also be seen as a form of *lex specialis*, particularly given the compulsory reference to conciliation. However, it does not establish consent to the jurisdiction of any court or tribunal. As a *lex specialis*, it could not therefore guarantee the resolution of a dispute. Further, Kenya's arguments on *lex specialis* and *lex posterior* in *Maritime Delimitation in the Indian Ocean (Somalia v. Kenya)* got no traction before the ICJ. From a reading of the judgment, the ICJ appeared interested only in the wording of the optional clause declarations before it and Article 282 of UNCLOS.

26 Agreement for the Establishment of the Indian Ocean Tuna Commission, 25 November 1999, 1927 UNTS, entered into force 27 March 1996, art XXIII.

27 See, for example, Ian Sinclair, *The Vienna Convention on the Law of Treaties* (Manchester University Press 1984) 98; Anthony Aust, *Modern Treaty Law and Practice* (CUP 2013) 204.

28 Alexander Orakhelashvili, 'Article 30 1969 Vienna Convention' in Olivier Corten and Pierre Klein (eds), *The Vienna Conventions on the Law of Treaties: A Commentary* (OUP 2011) 786.

By contrast, for the (many) States which are parties to the IOTC Agreement and the Fish Stocks Agreement, the treaty obligation under Article 30(2) of the Fish Stocks Agreement appears available to secure compulsory jurisdiction. There is no material obstacle to applying the provisions relating to the settlement of disputes in Part XV of UNCLOS *mutatis mutandis* to disputes concerning the interpretation or application of the IOTC Agreement. The key conflicts provision could then be Article 281. Applying Article 281 in this context would give full effect to the IOTC parties' agreement to conciliation, which is formulated in compulsory terms, unlike the reference to the ICJ. It would only be where such conciliation fails to result in a settlement that the Part XV procedures could apply. Article 282 would not have any impact as Article XXIII of the IOTC Agreement does not constitute an agreement that a 'dispute, shall, at the request of any party to the dispute, be submitted to a procedure that entails a binding decision'.[29]

A further – if more difficult – argument would be that applying Article 287 of UNCLOS *mutatis mutandis*, the parties expressed a choice through Article XXIII in favour of the ICJ as the relevant court or tribunal under Part XV. However, if the disputing parties both considered that there was some form of compulsory jurisdiction under Part XV, the parties could agree on the specific forum (although the jurisdictional objection in *Somalia v. Kenya* shows that States may litigate over the specific forum). In practice, it may be that whichever forum had to consider an objection, in other words, whichever forum was first seised by the claimant State – whether the ICJ or an Annex VII tribunal as the default tribunal in the absence of the requisite Article 287 declarations – would find that it had jurisdiction.[30]

Article 30 of the Fish Stocks Agreement on the applicable law is also of importance. Where, pursuant to Article 30(2) of the Fish Stocks Agreement or a fisheries agreement, the provisions on the settlement of disputes in Part XV of UNCLOS apply *mutatis mutandis*, this must also engage Article 293(1) of UNCLOS. According to Article 293(1), '[a] court or tribunal under this section shall apply this Convention and other rules of international law not incompatible with this Convention'. Applying it *mutatis mutandis* would likely mean taking the reference to 'the Convention' as referring to the given fisheries agreement which is the subject matter of the dispute. On that basis, the substantive provisions of UNCLOS would

29 As indeed confirmed in the IOTC's Second Performance Review, see IOTC, 'Minutes of the 2nd Session of the 2nd IOTC Performance Review Panel' (Mahé, 14–8 December 2015). www.fao.org/3/bf694e/bf694e.pdf accessed 18 December 2023, para 177.

30 Note the trenchant criticisms of the Court's reasoning in *Maritime Delimitation in the Indian Ocean (Somalia v. Kenya)*, Dissenting Opinion of Judge Robinson, ICJ Rep 2017, para 35. Judge Robinson rejects the argument that the ICJ should accept jurisdiction as such might be refused by an Annex VII tribunal:

> In any event, the Court should not indulge in speculation. The Court's function is to determine whether on the basis of the law and facts the Annex VII Tribunal or the Court itself has jurisdiction. Speculation that the Tribunal will not accept jurisdiction is not a sufficient reason for the Court to conclude that it has jurisdiction; neither is it a sufficient reason for the Court to determine that the Annex VII Tribunal does not have jurisdiction. It is simply not a proper consideration.

only be applicable as the second category, in other words, as 'other rules of international law not incompatible'.[31] However, Article 30(5) of the Fish Stocks Agreement would also come into play with possibly far-reaching effects on applicable law. Article 30(5) provides that:

> Any court or tribunal to which a dispute has been submitted under this Part shall apply the relevant provisions of the Convention, of this Agreement and of any relevant subregional, regional or global fisheries agreement, as well as generally accepted standards for the conservation and management of living marine resources and other rules of international law not incompatible with the Convention, with a view to ensuring the conservation of the straddling fish stocks and highly migratory fish stocks concerned.

This establishes no less than five potential sources of substantive law or standards. Although there must be a question on whether provisions of UNCLOS can be considered as 'relevant', if both parties to the dispute are not also parties to UNCLOS (cf. Articles 30(1) and 30(2) of the Fish Stocks Agreement). Further, the jurisdiction of a tribunal constituted pursuant to Article 30(2) of the Fish Stocks Agreement would be to decide 'any dispute between States Parties to this Agreement concerning the interpretation or application of' a qualifying subregional, regional, or global fisheries agreement. As noted by the tribunal in *Mox Plant*, there is a cardinal distinction between the scope of jurisdiction and the law a court or tribunal can apply on the merits.[32] It is questionable whether Article 30(5) could expand the scope of the dispute to cover a new allegation of breach of UNCLOS or the Fish Stocks Agreement.

4.2. Example 2: The Antigua Convention and Related Examples

To move to a second example, Article XXV of the 2003 Convention for the Strengthening of the Inter-American Tropical Tuna Commission (the Antigua Convention) provides that

1. The members of the Commission shall cooperate in order to prevent disputes. Any member may consult with one or more members about any dispute related to the interpretation or application of the provisions of this Convention to reach a solution satisfactory to all as quickly as possible.
2. If a dispute is not settled through such consultation within a reasonable period, the members in question shall consult among themselves as soon as possible in

31 There is a debate as to whether this second category is intended to capture anything more than *renvois* and secondary rules such as those concerned with State responsibility.

32 The cardinal distinction between the scope of jurisdiction and the law that a court or tribunal is to apply on the merits was emphasised by the Annex VII tribunal in the *Mox Plant case* (*Ireland v. United Kingdom*), Order No 3, PCA Case 2002–01, 24 June 2003.

> order to settle the dispute through any peaceful means they may agree upon in accordance with international law.[33]

This provision includes mandatory elements, but only on cooperation to prevent disputes and consultation.

On a *lex posterior* analysis, it would be critical that this provision is a later treaty compared to the Fish Stocks Agreement. Yet when identifying the intent of the parties to this provision and to the Fish Stocks Agreement, the wording of Article 30(2) of the Fish Stocks Agreement does not suggest that it applies only to prior agreements. Likewise, there is nothing in Article XXV of the Antigua Convention suggesting any attempt to exclude the impact of Article 30(2) of the Fish Stocks Agreement. It has been suggested that Article 30(2) operates to amend other dispute settlement provisions,[34] but this is questionable. The provision in the fisheries agreement is left unaffected, while Article 30(2) merely appears to provide an alternative and mandatory form of dispute settlement for parties to the Fish Stocks Agreement who are also parties to the given fisheries agreement. This alternative mandatory form of dispute settlement would aim at establishing the painstakingly negotiated provisions of Part XV of UNCLOS as a form of overarching set of provisions, which include Articles 281 and 282.

This is not to suggest that Article 30(2) of the Fish Stocks Agreement is itself a conflict of laws rule which would fall within Article 30(2) of the VCLT and displace the default rule of *lex posterior*. Article 30(2) of the VCLT provides that '[w]hen a treaty specifies that it is subject to, or that it is not to be considered as incompatible with, an earlier or later treaty, the provisions of that other treaty prevail.' Yet, Article 30(2) of the Fish Stocks Agreement operates to incorporate Articles 281 and 282 of Part XV of UNCLOS, which do fit within Article 30(2) of the VCLT.

Applying Article 281 to Article XXV of the Antigua Convention, there is no agreement to settle the dispute by other means, save through consultation. Further, the obligation of consultation is arguably no more than a provision to exchange views on the means of settlement. Hence, the gateway appears open to Part XV dispute settlement.

Various other treaties pre-date or post-date the Fish Stocks Agreement which appear to fall into the same category (and which could be usefully signposted in some way on the ITLOS website), namely:

1. The Convention on the Conservation and Management of Pollock Resources in the Central Bering Sea, Article XIII of which contains the same basic terms as Article XXV of the Antigua Convention.[35]

33 Convention for the strengthening of the Inter-American Tropical Tuna Commission established by the 1949 Antigua Convention between the United States of America and the Republic of Costa Rica, June 2003, entered into force 27 August 2010.

34 See, for example, Nigel Bankes, 'The Jurisdiction of the Dispute Settlement Bodies of the Law of the Sea Convention With Respect to Other Treaties' (2021) 52 *Ocean Development and International Law* 346, 359.

35 Convention on the Conservation and Management of Pollock in the Central Bering Sea, 16 June 1994, entered into force 8 December 1995.

2. The Barents Sea Loophole Agreement.[36]
3. The Federated States of Micronesia Arrangement for Regional Fisheries Access, Article 19 of which reflects the language of Article 283 of UNCLOS.[37]
4. The Arrangement for the Conservation and Management of the Western Pacific Purse Seine Fishery, Article 10(2) of which provides for settlement through peaceful negotiations.[38]
5. The Convention on Fisheries Co-operation among African States Bordering the Atlantic Ocean, Article 21 of which provides for settlement by peaceful means in accordance with the United Nations Charter.[39]
6. The Convention for the Conservation of Southern Bluefin Tuna and, subject to a question of whether its parties would accept that it could fall within Article 30(2) of the Fish Stocks Agreement, the Convention on the Conservation of Antarctic Marine Living Resources.[40] Both Conventions provide for consultation; give scope for mutual consent to refer the dispute to the ICJ or to arbitration; and include wording, which was carefully analysed in *Southern Bluefin Tuna*, that 'failure to reach agreement on reference to the International Court or to arbitration shall not absolve Parties to the dispute from the responsibility of continuing to seek to resolve it by any of the various peaceful means'.[41]

The decision of the Annex VII tribunal in *Southern Bluefin Tuna* is not inconsistent with this conclusion. Even if one did not find the separate opinion of Judge Keith and the reasoning in the *South China Sea* award more convincing,[42] the tribunal stated its view that had the Fish Stocks Agreement been in force, it would have gone far towards resolving the procedural as well as the substantive issues in the case. The tribunal appears to have envisaged that the considerations of *lex posterior* and *lex specialis* underlying its reasoning would have limited or no application

36 Barents Sea Loophole Agreement, 15 May 1999.

37 Federated States of Micronesia Arrangement for Regional Fisheries Access, 14 November 1994, entered into force September 1995.

38 Palau Arrangement for the Management of the Western Pacific Purse Seine Fishery, 2 October 1992, entered into force 1 November 1995.

39 Convention on fisheries cooperation among African States bordering the Atlantic Ocean, 5 July 1991, entered into force 1995.

40 Convention on the Conservation of Antarctic Marine Living Resources, 20 May 1980, 1329 UNTS, entered into force 7 April 1982, which is often seen not as a RFMO but rather a *sui generis* organisation that is part of the Antarctic Treaty System. It is questionable whether any State party to this Convention would ever wish to invoke Article 30(2) of the Fish Stocks Agreement for this reason. Otherwise, Article 30(2) could offer an avenue for disputes, such as that arising out of the 2021 failure of the Commission to agree a catch for Patagonian toothfish, with the consensus being blocked by Russia despite the fact that a catch limit had been recommended by the Scientific Committee based on the best scientific information available. Both Russia's actions and the United Kingdom's subsequent licensing of vessels have been the subject of criticism.

41 Southern Bluefin Tuna, Award on Jurisdiction and Admissibility, 4 August 2000, XXIII RIAA 1, para 23.

42 *South China Sea Arbitration (Philippines v. China)*, Award on Jurisdiction and Admissibility, PCA Case 2013–19, 29 October 2015, paras 219–25.

where Article 30(2) of the Fish Stocks Agreement applied.[43] Here, reference to Article 281 of UNCLOS would still be required but applied *mutatis mutandis*. Further, the fact that the parties to the Convention for the Conservation of Southern Bluefin Tuna had not provided for compulsory dispute settlement would not carry the same great weight that the tribunal accorded to it.[44]

4.3. Example 3: The South Pacific Tuna Treaty and Related Examples

As a third example, one can consider one of the fisheries agreements which may engage Article 282 of UNCLOS where the Fish Stocks Agreement applies between disputing parties because the provision is, at least arguably, made for binding dispute settlement.

Pursuant to Article 6.2 of the 1987 Treaty on Fisheries between Certain Pacific Island States and the United States (the South Pacific Tuna Treaty),

> Any dispute between the Government of the United States and the Government of one or more Pacific Island parties in relation to or arising out of this Treaty may be submitted by any such party to an arbitral tribunal for settlement by arbitration no earlier than one hundred and twenty (120) days following a request for consultations under Article 6.1. Unless the parties to the dispute agree otherwise, the Arbitration Rules of the United Nations Commission on International Trade Law as at present in force, shall be used.[45]

Between parties to both the South Pacific Tuna Treaty and the Fish Stocks Agreement, Article 30(2) of the Fish Stocks Agreement provides for the application of Part XV of UNCLOS. In turn, Part XV, pursuant to Article 282, applied *mutatis mutandis*, prioritises the agreement to submit to an arbitral tribunal as this is 'a procedure that entails a binding decision'. The same would apply for Article 18 of the Western Indian Ocean Tuna Organization Convention, which also provides for mandatory arbitration, pursuant to the rules of the place of arbitration. A default power is allocated to the Board to 'appoint an independent person to establish the tribunal'.[46] However, Article 14(3) of the Framework Agreement for the Conservation of the Living Marine Resources of the High Seas of the South Pacific may lead

43 Southern Bluefin Tuna, Award on Jurisdiction and Admissibility, 4 August 2000, XXIII RIAA 1, para 71.

44 See, for example, ibid, paras 57–8.

45 Treaty on Fisheries between the Governments of Certain Pacific Island States and the Government of the United States of America, 2 April 1987, entered into force 15 June 1988.

46 Pursuant to the Agreement for the Establishment of the Indian Ocean Tuna Commission, 25 November 1993, 1927 UNTS, entered into force 27 March 1996, art 18(1): 'Any dispute regarding the interpretation or application of this convention, if not settled by the parties or the Board shall be referred to an arbitration tribunal.' The default power of the Board is located in Article 18(3).

to a different result.[47] Although this allows either party to 'solicit a binding arbitration procedure', and provides for arbitration as a form of default, Articles 14(1) and 14(2) allow for or apply in default of other procedures agreed by the parties.[48] This procedure could be taken as agreement to Part XV, which would apply as the choice made before getting to the stage of a default to arbitration.

Eight agreements are more straightforward in providing directly for the settlement of disputes as provided for in Part XV of UNCLOS and/or the Fish Stocks Agreement: the Convention on the Conservation and Management of Highly Migratory Fish Stocks in the Western and Central Pacific Ocean;[49] the Convention on the Conservation and Management of Fishery Resources in the South East Atlantic Ocean;[50] the Southern Indian Ocean Fisheries Agreement;[51] the Convention on Future Multilateral Co-Operation in the North East Atlantic Fisheries;[52] the Agreement to Prevent Unregulated High Seas Fisheries in the Central Arctic Ocean;[53] the Convention on the Conservation and Management of High Seas Fishery Resources in the South Pacific Ocean;[54] the Convention on Future Multilateral Co-Operation in the North West Atlantic Fisheries;[55] and the Convention on Conservation and Management of High Seas Fisheries Resources in North Pacific Ocean.[56]

47 Framework Agreement for the Conservation of the Living Marine Resources of the High Seas of the South Pacific, 14 August 2000.

48 See ibid, arts 14(1) and (2),

> 1. Disagreements among the States Parties as to the interpretation or application of the provisions established in this Agreement, or in its complementary instruments, shall be resolved in the first instance through the dispute-settlement procedures set forth in Article 33 of the Charter of the United Nations, *or in other international instruments in force for the States Parties*. 2. If an agreement cannot be reached, disputes must be submitted either to a conciliation commission or to a technical arbitration body, *unless both parties have agreed upon a different procedure* (emphasis added).

49 Convention on the Conservation and Management of Highly Migratory Fish Stocks in the Western and Central Pacific Ocean, 5 September 2000, 2275 UNTS, entered into force 5 September 2000, art 31.

50 Convention on the Conservation and Management of Fishery Resources in the South East Atlantic Ocean, 20 April 2001, 2221 UNTS, entered into force 20 April 2001, art 24.

51 Southern Indian Ocean Fisheries Agreement, 7 July 2006, 2835 UNTS, entered into force 21 June 2012, art 20.

52 Convention on Future Multilateral Co-Operation in the North East Atlantic Fisheries, 18 November 1980, 1285 UNTS, entered into force 17 March 1982, in accordance with the new art 18 bis.

53 Agreement to Prevent Unregulated High Seas Fisheries in the Central Arctic Ocean, 3 October 2018, entered into force 25 June 2021, art 7.

54 Convention on the Conservation and Management of High Seas Fishery Resources in the South Pacific Ocean, 14 November 2009, 2899 UNTS, entered into force 24 August 2012, art 34.

55 Convention on Future Multilateral Co-Operation in the North West Atlantic Fisheries, 24 October 1978, 17799 UNTS, entered into force 1 January 1979, in accordance with the amended art XV.

56 Convention on Conservation and Management of High Seas Fisheries Resources in North Pacific Ocean, 24 February 2012, entered into force 19 July 2015, art 19.

One final agreement to consider with respect to the potential application of Article 282 *mutatis mutandis* is the Agreement for the establishment of the General Fisheries Commission for the Mediterranean, which provides at Article XVII:

> Any dispute regarding the interpretation or application of this Agreement, if not settled by the Commission, shall be referred to a committee composed of one member appointed by each of the parties to the dispute, and in addition an independent chairman chosen by the members of the committee. The recommendations of such a committee, while not binding in character, shall become the basis for renewed consideration by the parties concerned of the matter out of which the disagreement arose. If as the result of this procedure the dispute is not settled, it shall be referred to the International Court of Justice in accordance with the Statute of the Court or, in the case of a Regional Economic Integration Organization that is a Member of the Commission, it shall be submitted to arbitration unless the parties to the dispute agree to another method of settlement.[57]

This appears to provide for compulsory dispute settlement – although it does not expressly provide for unilateral submission. A respondent State might take the view that it had an obligation to refer the dispute, but that such referral should not be understood as consent to a unilateral submission, such that it could elect to be in breach and block compulsory dispute settlement. Where the language of a treaty requires, expressly or implicitly, that the State take an additional step before consent or referral is completed (and there is no default mechanism), one can argue that the consent to adjudication or arbitration is not complete. In these circumstances, Article 30(2) of the Fish Stocks Agreement could, however, act as a form of insurance policy. If a recalcitrant State took this position, it would be exposed to the argument that Part XV was engaged, and Article 282 would not act as a bar as it only applies where there is a unilateral right to submit a dispute. In practice, the existence of Article 30(2) may stop a State from adopting this position in the first place.

5. Conclusion

Article 30(2) of the Fish Stocks Agreement further opens the gateway established by Article 288(2) of UNCLOS. Its potential impact is significant, including with

57 Agreement for the establishment of the General Fisheries Commission for the Mediterranean As amended by the General Fisheries Council for the Mediterranean at its First Special Session (May 1963), at its Thirteenth Session (July 1976), at its Twenty-second Session (October 1997) and by the General Fisheries Commission for the Mediterranean at its Thirty-eighth Session (May 2014) and approved by the FAO Conference at its Twelfth Session (December 1963) and by the FAO Council at its Seventieth Session (December 1976), at its Hundred and Thirteenth Session (November 1997) and at its One Hundred and Fiftieth Session (December 2014), entered into force on 20 May 2014.

respect to the considerable number of regional fisheries agreements where it appears that compulsory jurisdiction may now be established through the application of Article 30(2). However, the reluctance to compulsory jurisdiction, identified and explained by Churchill long ago, endures. It remains to be seen when – or whether – the impact of Article 30(2) of the Fish Stocks Agreement as a source of jurisdiction will be analysed in future cases.

6 Emerging Dispute Settlement Principles and Practices in RFMOs

James Harrison

1. Introduction

Today, regional fisheries management organisations or arrangements (RFMO) are accepted as the main forum for States to cooperate to conserve and manage shared fish stocks, particularly straddling stocks and highly migratory stocks,[1] and discrete high seas stocks. The main functions of RFMOs are to obtain scientific advice on relevant fish stocks and to agree on appropriate conservation and management measures to ensure these stocks' long-term sustainability.[2] Their decisions are often technical in character but involve striking a difficult balance between the interests of the various States and actors concerned. Inevitably, disagreements and disputes will arise over the exercise of these functions. This chapter considers how such disputes should be addressed.

The answer to this question will, of course, depend on the nature of the dispute. Not all fisheries disputes are exclusively legal in character. First, disputes may arise over the interpretation of the scientific evidence available for a stock or the broader marine environment. Resolving such differences often requires specific expertise. Second, disputes may also arise over the types of measures which should be adopted to promote the conservation and management of the relevant fish stock. Such disputes can relate to differences on the technical conservation measures to be adopted and differences on allocation. Disputes over-allocation have been described as 'the most difficult issue that every fishery has to face.'[3] Disputes over allocation often

1 Agreement for the Implementation of the Provisions of the United Nations Convention on the Law of the Sea of 10 December 1982 relating to the Conservation and Management of Straddling Fish Stocks and Highly Migratory Fish Stocks (Fish Stocks Agreement), 4 August 1995, 2167 UNTS 3, entered into force 11 December 2001, art 8. See also Rosemary Rayfuse, 'Regional Fisheries Management Organisations' in Donald Rothwell et al. (eds), *The Oxford Handbook on the Law of the Sea* (OUP 2015) 442; Michael Lodge and Satya Nandan, 'Some Suggestions Towards Better Implementation of the United Nations Agreement on Straddling Fish Stocks and Highly Migratory Fish Stocks of 1995' (2005) 20 *International Journal of Marine and Coastal Law* 345, 355.

2 Fish Stocks Agreement, art 10.

3 Michael Lodge and Satya Nandan, 'Some Suggestions Towards Better Implementation of the United Nations Agreement on Straddling Fish Stocks and Highly Migratory Fish Stocks of 1995' (2005) 20 *International Journal of Marine and Coastal Law* 345, 373.

DOI: 10.4324/9781003492030-9

turn on different perceptions of equity. This means that 'failure to achieve an agreement cannot readily be rectified by reference to a legal tribunal'[4] and recourse to other diplomatic dispute settlement mechanisms may be more appropriate. Yet, associated legal questions may still arise about whether the measures to be adopted are, for example, discriminatory or within the powers of an organisation. Finally, some disputes primarily raise questions of law. Thus, disputes may arise over whether a particular State or fishing entity has complied with the conservation and management measures or other applicable rules of international law, such as the duty to cooperate. These disputes may be more appropriate for submission to traditional means of legal dispute settlement. The key point is that States must choose a dispute settlement option which suits the nature of the dispute they face.

High seas fisheries disputes may arise under multiple legal instruments.[5] Yet, this chapter focuses on the mechanisms available under RFMO agreements to settle disputes arising under those instruments. The Fish Stocks Agreement explicitly provides that one of the functions of RFMOs is to 'promote the peaceful settlement of disputes.'[6] This chapter addresses two key issues arising in the context of RFMO dispute settlement. First, it considers the multitude of procedures available and their interrelationship. Second, it considers how various actors can participate in dispute settlement procedures, given that many fish stocks are common resources shared by multiple States and other fishing entities.

2. Diversity of Dispute Settlement Procedures

Since the conclusion of the Fish Stocks Agreement in 1995, there has been a clear trend towards strengthening dispute settlement procedures within RFMOs to provide for compulsory binding settlement. Most of the treaties negotiated after the Fish Stocks Agreement include compulsory dispute settlement clauses. Many of these treaties simply make reference to Part VIII of the Fish Stocks Agreement or Part XV of the United Nations Convention on the Law of the Sea (UNCLOS).[7] Amendments to

4 Thomas Clingan, 'Compulsory Settlement of Fisheries Disputes' in Giulio Pontecorvo (ed), *Fisheries Conflicts in the North Atlantic* (Ballinger 1974) 194.

5 See, for example, Southern Bluefin Tuna Arbitration, Award on Jurisdiction and Admissibility, 4 August 2000, XXIII RIAA 1, para 52: 'it is a commonplace of international law and State practice for more than one treaty to bear upon a particular dispute [and] there is frequently a parallelism of treaties.' See further the chapter by Sam Wordsworth in this collection.

6 Fish Stocks Agreement, art 10(k).

7 United Nations Convention on the Law of the Sea (UNCLOS), 10 December 1982, 1833 UNTS 3, entered into force 16 November 1994. See, Convention on the Conservation and Management of Highly Migratory Fish Stocks in the Western and Central Pacific Ocean, 5 September 2000, 2275 UNTS 43, entered into force 19 June 2004, art 31; Convention on the Conservation and Management of Fishery Resources in the South East Atlantic Ocean 10 April 2001, 2221 UNTS 189, entered into force 13 April 2003, art 24; Convention on the Conservation and Management of High Seas Fishery Resources in the South Pacific Ocean, 14 November 2009, 2899 UNTS 211, entered into force 24 August 2012, art 34; Convention on the Conservation and Management of High Seas Fisheries Resources in the North Pacific Ocean, 24 February 2012, entered into force 19 July 2015, art 19;

this end have also been adopted for some existing RFMOs, including the North East Atlantic Fisheries Commission in 2004,[8] the North West Atlantic Fisheries Organisation in 2007,[9] and the International Commission for the Conservation of Atlantic Tunas in 2019.[10] The cross-reference to UNCLOS and the Fish Stocks Agreement means that no single dispute settlement forum is prescribed. Rather, States have the option to make a declaration choosing one or more of the following fora: the International Court of Justice (ICJ), the International Tribunal for the Law of the Sea (ITLOS), Annex VII arbitration, or Annex VIII special arbitration.[11] Annex VIII special arbitration includes recourse to a panel of fisheries experts. In the absence of matching declarations and unless otherwise agreed, disputes may be submitted to Annex VII arbitration.[12] It is significant that Annex VII arbitration remains the default under most RFMO treaties, particularly in given certain procedural issues connected with fisheries disputes, as discussed in the following section.

There are some exceptions to this trend of compulsory dispute settlement. These include the General Fisheries Commission for the Mediterranean (GFCM), the Inter-American Tropical Tuna Commission, the Commission on the Conservation of Antarctic Marine Living Resources, the Indian Ocean Tuna Commission, and the Commission for the Conservation of Southern Bluefin Tuna. Some of these RFMO treaties do provide for recourse to courts and tribunals, but only with the express consent of all parties to a dispute.[13] In other cases, the treaty provides for disputes to be submitted to alternative non-binding mechanisms, such as conciliation.[14]

Where an RFMO does provide for compulsory adjudication, it does not follow that compulsory adjudication should always be the primary means of dispute settlement. Article 280 of UNCLOS enshrines the principle of freedom of choice

Southern Indian Ocean Fisheries Agreement, 7 July 2006, 2835 UNTS 409, entered into force 21 June 2012, art 20.

8 See '2004 Proposal to amend the Convention on Future Multilateral Cooperation in North East Atlantic Fisheries, Not Yet in Force' (24 July 2003). www.neafc.org/system/files/EU-proposal-to-amend-the-Convention-2004.pdf accessed 5 September 2022.

9 See 'Amendment to the Convention on Future Multilateral Cooperation in the Northwest Atlantic Fisheries' (28 September 2007, entered into force on 18 May 2017). https://archive.nafo.int/open/gc/2007/gcdoc07-04.pdf accessed 5 September 2022.

10 See 'Protocol to amend the International Convention for the Conservation of Atlantic Tunas, Not Yet in Force' (4 December 2019). https://eur-lex.europa.eu/legal-content/EN/TXT/PDF/?uri=CELEX:22019A1204(01)&rid=7 accessed 5 September 2022.

11 UNCLOS, art 287(1).

12 UNCLOS, art 287(3)-(4)

13 Convention for the Conservation of Antarctic Marine Living Resources, 20 May 1980, 1329 UNTS 47, entered into force 7 April 1982, art XXV; Convention for the Conservation of Southern Bluefin Tuna, 10 May 1993, 1819 UNTS 359, entered into force 20 May 1994, art 16(2); Agreement for the Establishment of the General Fisheries Commission for the Mediterranean, 6 December 1949, 126 UNTS 237, entered into force 20 February 1952, art 19(3); Agreement for the establishment of an Indian Ocean Tuna Commission, 15 November 1993, 1927 UNTS 329, entered into force 27 March 1996, art XIII.

14 Agreement for the establishment of an Indian Ocean Tuna Commission, 15 November 1993, 1927 UNTS 329, entered into force 27 March 1996, art XXIII.

over dispute settlement methods. This principle is also reflected in most RFMO treaties, either by incorporating Article 280 or other language.[15] The requirement that States consult on other possible dispute settlement mechanisms prior to commencing litigation further encourages States to exercise this freedom of choice.[16] The obligation to consult has not been interpreted too strictly.[17] Yet, its effect is to incentivise States to consider the type of dispute settlement process most appropriate to resolve the dispute at hand at an early stage.

A further principle introduced by the Fish Stocks Agreement, and incorporated into many RFMO treaties, seeks to prevent a dispute escalating to the stage where formal dispute settlement procedures are required. Thus, according to Article 28 of the Fish Stocks Agreement:

> States shall cooperate in order to prevent disputes. To this end, States shall agree on efficient and expeditious decision-making procedures within subregional and regional fisheries management organizations and arrangements and shall strengthen existing decision-making procedures as necessary.

Article 28 makes a clear link between dispute prevention and decision-making procedures. It follows that dispute prevention methods will depend in part on the nature of the decision-making procedures employed by RFMOs. Some RFMO treaties simply encourage consultations to avoid disputes.[18] Other RFMO treaties implicitly encourage dispute prevention by promoting consensus decision-making, either as a requirement to adopt measures[19] or as an objective to pursue before resorting to majority voting.[20] By its nature, consensus implicitly pushes the parties to employ informal dispute prevention methods to overcome differences of opinion.[21]

Other treaties provide more elaborate dispute prevention mechanisms. The clearest example is the Convention of the Western and Central Pacific Fisheries Commission (WCPFC). For decisions which must be adopted by consensus, the

15 E.g., Convention for the Strengthening of the Inter-American Tropical Tuna Commission, 14 November 2003, entered into force 27 August 2010, art XXV(2).

16 UNCLOS, art 283.

17 See, for example, Chagos Marine Protected Area Arbitration, Award, XXXI RIAA 359, 18 March 2015, para 385: 'It is not necessary for the Parties to comprehensively canvas the means for the peaceful settlement of disputes set out in either the UN Charter or the Convention.' Neither does it require parties to 'continue with an exchange of views when it concludes that the possibilities of reaching agreement have been exhausted'; *Land Reclamation in and around the Straits of Johor (Malaysia v. Singapore)*, Provisional Measures, Order of 8 October 2003, ITLOS Rep 2003, para 47.

18 Convention for the Strengthening of the Inter-American Tropical Tuna Commission, 14 November 2003, entered into force 27 August 2010, art XXV(1).

19 For example, Convention for the Conservation of Antarctic Marine Living Resources, 20 May 1980, 1329 UNTS 47, entered into force 7 April 1982, art XII(1).

20 For example, Convention on Future Multilateral Cooperation in the Northwest Atlantic Fisheries, 24 October 1978, 1135 UNTS 369, entered into force 1 January 1979, art XIII.

21 Barry Buzan, 'Negotiating by Consensus: Developments in Technique at the United Nations Conference on the Law of the Sea' (1981) 75 *American Journal of International Law* 324.

WCPFC Convention provides that where 'the Chairman determines that there would be an objection to [a] proposal, the Commission may appoint a conciliator for the purpose of reconciling the differences in order to achieve consensus on the matter.'[22] Thus, conciliation takes place before the decision is adopted in order to promote consensus and avoid deadlock. In practice, the procedure does not appear to be used. Instead, the Chair of the Commission often plays a conciliation role.[23] For decisions which can be adopted by a majority vote, the WCPFC Convention provides that 'if it appears to the Chairman that all efforts to reach a decision by consensus have been exhausted, the Chairman shall fix a time during that session of the Commission for taking the decision by a vote.'[24] This provision resembles the 'cooling-off' period which was integrated into the decision-making procedures at the Third United Nations Conference on the Law of the Sea and which allowed the bureau of the Conference to engage in active diplomacy to address outstanding issues, pending a final vote.[25] It, thus, seeks to maximise the opportunities to avoid serious disagreement on measures.

Another example of a dispute prevention mechanism built into an RFMO treaty is Article 19(2) of the Statute of the GFCM:

> If the parties concerned cannot reach agreement in accordance with paragraph 19.1, they may jointly refer the matter to a committee composed of one representative appointed by each of the party of the dispute, and in addition the Chairperson of the Commission. The findings by such committee, while not binding in character, shall constitute the basis for renewed consideration by the Contracting Parties concerned of the matter out of which disagreement arose.

The precise procedures to follow can be adapted to the individual dispute as 'the committee may adopt such rules of procedures as it deems necessary for effective and expeditious proceedings, including decisions on the methods of work it will follow.'[26] However, consensus is promoted and the procedure is limited to 90 days unless the parties mutually agree to extend it.[27] However, the rules of procedure

22 Convention on the Conservation and Management of Highly Migratory Fish Stocks in the Western and Central Pacific Ocean, 5 September 2000, 2275 UNTS 43, entered into force 19 June 2004, art 20(4).

23 At the twelfth meeting of the Western and Central Pacific Fisheries Commission, the Chair indicated that they were 'investigating the possibility of a conciliation process to work through [the] issues', but the discussions were instead escalated to a Head of Delegation meeting. The session ended without any agreement. See, WCPRC12 Summary Report (2016), paras 306–307, 315.

24 Convention on the Conservation and Management of Highly Migratory Fish Stocks in the Western and Central Pacific Ocean, 5 September 2000, 2275 UNTS 43, entered into force 19 June 2004, art 20(3).

25 See, for example, Satya Nandan, *Reflections on the Making of the Modern Law of the Sea* (NUS Press 2021) 146.

26 Agreement for the Establishment of the General Fisheries Commission for the Mediterranean, 6 December 1949, 126 UNTS 237, entered into force 20 February 1952, Rules of Procedure, Rule XVIII(8).

27 ibid, Rule XVIII(9).

explicitly provide that a decision shall be adopted at the end of the process and prohibit committee members from abstaining. This raises interesting questions about the role of the Chair of the GCFM. On the one hand, the Chair may be considered an impartial member whose function is to facilitate a compromise between the disputing parties.[28] On the other hand, the Chair must take a position at the end of the process if consensus is not forthcoming. Ultimately, the findings of the committee are not binding, and the matter will be remitted to the GFCM. Therefore, this mechanism does not guarantee a successful settlement of disagreements. Moreover, the voluntary nature of this mechanism is also highlighted by the rules of procedure which allow a party to refuse to submit a disagreement to the committee.[29]

Dispute prevention procedures may also apply after a decision has been adopted. This is particularly the case where a party objects to a decision, thus indicating that a disagreement persists. Extensive use of objection procedures has led sometimes to fully-fledged legal proceedings between RFMO members.[30] This inspired some procedural reforms to deescalate such disputes. In many cases, raising an objection will trigger a procedure whereby the RFMO's central decision-making body is invited to reconsider the measure. Thus, the Convention of the South East Atlantic Fisheries Organisation provides that 'in the event that any Contracting Party [makes an objection to a measure], the Commission shall meet at the request of any other Contracting Party to review the measure.'[31] The same situation prevails in the Convention of the North Pacific Fisheries Commission (NPFC). However, to try to break the deadlock, the NPFC Convention provides that

> the Commission shall, at its expense, invite to that meeting two or more experts who are nationals of non-members of the Commission and who have sufficient knowledge of international law related to fisheries and of the operation of [RFMOs] to provide advice to the Commission on the matter in question.[32]

Involving technical experts may 'establish common parameters and promote confidence-building'[33] which could facilitate a compromise between the NPFC's various members. However, the experts' intervention is limited to presenting their

28 They have been described as 'an independent chairperson'; First General Fisheries Commission for the Mediterranean Performance Review (2011), para 4.4.2.

29 Agreement for the Establishment of the General Fisheries Commission for the Mediterranean, 6 December 1949, 126 UNTS 237, entered into force 20 February 1952, Rules of Procedure, Rule XVIII(2).

30 See, for example, the Estai Incident and related litigation, *Fisheries Jurisdiction Case (Spain v. Canada),* Judgment, ICJ Rep 1998.

31 Convention on the Conservation and Management of Fishery Resources in the South East Atlantic Ocean 10 April 2001, 2221 UNTS 189, entered into force 13 April 2003, art 23(1)(f).

32 Convention on the Conservation and Management of High Seas Fisheries Resources in the North Pacific Ocean, 24 February 2012, entered into force 19 July 2015, art 9(g).

33 Rolf Einar Fife, 'Contributions of LOSC Jurisprudence to Reaching and Justifying a Negotiated Outcome – and Contributions of Negotiated Settlements to the Law of the Sea' (2023) 38 *International Journal of Marine and Coastal Law* 363, 369.

opinion. The experts do not play a formal conciliatory role or formally propose a settlement. This function is left to the members of the NPFC and, particularly, the Chair. Ultimately, these procedures simply prolong discussions in the RFMO. The procedures do not trigger any external mechanism to assist in the settlement of the dispute.

As well as promoting dispute prevention, an increasing number of RFMO treaties encourage alternative dispute settlement procedures falling short of formal litigation. So-called ad hoc technical panels are a common example.[34] This process takes the dispute outside of the formal framework of the RFMO's governing body to an impartial forum involving experts. The dispute can be submitted to an ad hoc panel either at the request of one party,[35] or all parties to the dispute.[36] These procedures, where experts are directed to settle the dispute, are designed to be quicker and cheaper than litigation. Timeframes are often short to 'ensure expeditious resolution of the dispute and to avoid undue interference with the work of RFMOs.'[37] Such expert panels differ from courts and tribunals in that they cannot formally settle the dispute. However, the nature of a panel recommendation will depend upon the relevant treaty. In many cases, the panel report is not binding and, where there is no resolution, the dispute can be submitted to further compulsory procedures. In the WCPRFC Convention, the Commission must 'modify or amend its decision in order to conform with the findings and recommendations of the review panel or it may decide to revoke the decision.'[38] Thus, recommendations have some force, whilst leaving it to the Commission to come up with a new measure. In the Convention on the Conservation and Management of High Seas Fishery Resources in the South Pacific Ocean, a Member must either accept the results of the panel process or institute formal dispute settlement proceedings.[39] Ad hoc technical panels were primarily envisaged to resolve disagreements on objections to conservation

34 See generally Valentin J. Schatz, 'Ad Hoc Technical Panels: Regional Fisheries Management Organisations (RFMOs)' in Hélène Ruiz Fabri (ed), *Max Planck Encyclopedia of International Procedural Law* (OUP 2022).

35 Convention on the Conservation and Management of Highly Migratory Fish Stocks in the Western and Central Pacific Ocean, 5 September 2000, 2275 UNTS 43, entered into force 19 June 2004, art 20(6) referring to 'A member which has voted against a decision or which was absent during the meeting at which the decision was made'; Convention on the Conservation and Management of Fishery Resources in the South East Atlantic Ocean 10 April 2001, 2221 UNTS 189, entered into force 13 April 2003, art 23(2)(f): 'any contracting party.'

36 Convention on the Conservation and Management of Fishery Resources in the South East Atlantic Ocean 10 April 2001, 2221 UNTS 189, entered into force 13 April 2003, art XV(3).

37 Rosemary Rayfuse, 'Settling Disputes in Regional Fisheries Management Organisations: Dealing with Objections' in Hèlène Ruiz Fabri et al. (eds), *A Bridge over Troubled Waters: Dispute Resolution in the Law of International Watercourses and the Law of the Sea* (Brill 2020) 260.

38 Convention on the Conservation and Management of Highly Migratory Fish Stocks in the Western and Central Pacific Ocean, 5 September 2000, 2275 UNTS 43, entered into force 19 June 2004, art 20(9).

39 Convention on the Conservation and Management of High Seas Fishery Resources in the South Pacific Ocean, 14 November 2009, 2899 UNTS 211, entered into force 24 August 2012, Annex II, para 10.

and management measures[40], and they have only been used in this context to date[41], the Fish Stocks Agreement suggests that any technical dispute may be submitted to ad hoc expert panels.[42] Some treaties provide for a broader range of disputes to be submitted to a panel.[43]

Multiple options are available to resolve fisheries disputes. This raises the question of how these different procedures could interact. There is no formal hierarchy between different dispute settlement mechanisms. Yet, questions may arise in practice about the interrelationship between diplomatic methods of dispute settlement and litigation. This may be particularly true when a treaty allows a party to trigger unilaterally compulsory and binding dispute settlement procedures.

As a general principle, that a matter is subject to ongoing diplomatic negotiations does not impede the start of dispute settlement proceedings.[44] Therefore, the fact that the political organs of an RFMO are continuing to discuss a matter should not prevent recourse to litigation. However, the situation may differ where parties to a dispute have agreed to submit a dispute to another form of settlement, albeit non-binding. This issue is addressed by Article 281 of UNCLOS.[45] Article 281 is incorporated by reference into different RFMO treaties.[46] According to this provision, a court or tribunal will not have jurisdiction where parties agreed to submit the dispute to another non-binding dispute resolution mechanism, unless and until no settlement has been reached, and provided that the parties have not

40 For example, Convention on the Conservation and Management of Highly Migratory Fish Stocks in the Western and Central Pacific Ocean, 5 September 2000, 2275 UNTS 43, entered into force 19 June 2004, art 20(6).

41 See the chapter by Osvaldo Urrita Silva in this collection.

42 Fish Stocks Agreement, art 29.

43 For example, Convention on Future Multilateral Cooperation in the Northwest Atlantic Fisheries, 24 October 1978, 1135 UNTS 369, entered into force 1 January 1979, art 15(3) referring to 'a dispute [concerning] the interpretation or application of a measure adopted by the Commission.' However, Article 15(2) on disputes relating to the interpretation or application of the Convention also notes the possibility of submitting such disputes to ad hoc panel proceedings. See also Convention for the Strengthening of the Inter-American Tropical Tuna Commission, 14 November 2003, entered into force 27 August 2010, Convention, art XXV(3) which generally provides for referral of 'disputes of a technical nature' to an ad hoc panel by mutual consent.

44 See, for example, *Military and Paramilitary Activities in and against Nicaragua (Nicaragua v. United States of America)*, Jurisdiction and Admissibility, Judgment, ICJ Rep 1984, para 106: 'even the existence of active negotiations in which both parties might be involved should not prevent . . . the Court from exercising [its] functions under the . . . Statute of the Court'.

45 UNCLOS art 281(1) provides

> if the States Parties which are parties to a dispute concerning the interpretation or application of this Convention have agreed to seek settlement of the dispute by a peaceful means of their own choice, the procedures provided for in this Part apply only where no settlement has been reached by recourse to such means and the agreement between the parties does not exclude any further procedure.

In practice, a question has arisen as to whether further procedures can be implicitly excluded. See Natalie Klein and Kate Parlett, *Judging the Law of the Sea* (OUP 2022) 48–58; see also the chapter by Sam Wordsworth in this collection.

46 See footnote 7.

agreed to exclude any further procedure. For example, if parties submit a dispute to mediation, a court or tribunal will not have jurisdiction under Article 281 until the mediation process is complete and does not bring a successful outcome.[47] Similarly, reference to an ad hoc technical panel will arguably fall within the scope of Article 281. This means that States cannot commence litigation until panel proceedings have been completed and the RFMO has met to consider the recommendations.[48] This is consistent with the text of some RFMO treaties which explicitly allows parties to pursue dispute settlement if they do not agree with the panel's recommendations.[49]

3. Multi-Party Litigation and Relevant Principles of Dispute Settlement

RFMO treaties tend to prioritise dispute prevention and alternative forms of dispute resolution. However, litigation will remain a dispute settlement option in many cases. In many respects, disputes concerning international fisheries law resemble other international legal disputes. However, certain features of fisheries disputes may pose challenges for resolution through adjudication or arbitration. In particular, the shared nature of high seas fish stocks means that multiple actors may be involved in a dispute, contrary to the 'basic assumption' underlying most international judicial procedures that disputes are bilateral in nature.[50] The multiplicity of potential parties explicitly recognised in many RFMO treaties, which refer to 'disputes between two or more contracting parties.'[51] This raises questions over which contracting parties will have standing to bring a claim and the different ways in which parties may become involved in dispute settlement proceedings.

In some situations, contracting parties may bring a claim to protect their own individual interests affected by the alleged unlawful conduct and there is no doubt that an injured state may bring such a claim. It is more controversial whether a party that has not suffered any direct injury from an action has standing to bring a claim.

On the one hand, many of the obligations in RFMO treaties are now widely recognised as *erga omnes (partes)*, which all parties to a treaty have an interest in their performance.[52] This is not explicit in the treaties themselves but can be deduced

47 UNCLOS, art 284(4) further provides that 'unless the parties otherwise agree, when a dispute has been submitted to conciliation, the proceedings may be terminated only in accordance with the agreed conciliation procedure.'

48 See Tullio Treves, 'A System for Law of the Sea Dispute Settlement' in Richard Barnes, David Freestone and David M Ong (eds), *The Law of the Sea: Progress and Prospects* (OUP 2006) 423.

49 Convention on the Conservation and Management of High Seas Fishery Resources in the South Pacific Ocean, 14 November 2009, 2899 UNTS 211, entered into force 24 August 2012, Annex II, para 10.

50 Penelope Ridings, 'The Intervention Procedure in Whaling in the Antarctic: A Threat to Bilateralism?' (2014) 32 *Australian Yearbook of International Law* 97, 97.

51 For example, Convention on Future Multilateral Cooperation in the Northwest Atlantic Fisheries, 24 October 1978, 1135 UNTS 369, entered into force 1 January 1979, art XV(2).

52 See, for example, Yoshifuma Tanaka, 'The Legal Consequences of Obligations Erga Omnes in International Law' (2021) 68 *Netherlands International Law Review* 1, 6. Indeed, obligations

from the content and character of the relevant obligations.[53] In this respect, many obligations relating to high-seas fish stocks are integral in nature. This means that all parties must perform this obligation to meet the objectives of the treaties. The International Law Commission suggested that 'when an obligation can be defined as an "integral" obligation, the breach by a State necessarily affects all the other parties to the treaty.'[54] It would follow that a strong connection exists between the integral nature of obligations and their character as *erga omnes* obligations.

On the other hand, even if one accepts that RFMO treaties establish *erga omnes* obligations, the question of standing in relation to this category of obligation is controversial. The ICJ cast serious doubts on the subject in *South West Africa Cases*, where it rejected the standing of Liberia and Ethiopia to bring claims to uphold the Mandate for South West Africa.[55] In doing so, the ICJ roundly rejected 'the equivalent of an "actio popularis", or right resident in any member of a community to take legal action in vindication of a public interest,' which in its view 'is not known to international law as it stands at present.[56] Yet, the ICJ's finding must be understood against the specific background of the case. Neither Liberia nor Ethiopia was a party to the agreement establishing the Mandate. Therefore, they sought to invoke rights conferred by that instrument on non-parties. Thus, the ICJ found that 'not being parties to the instruments of the mandate, [the Applicants] could draw from them only such rights as these unequivocally conferred, directly or by a clearly necessary implication.'[57] At the same time, the ICJ appeared to accept that a party to a treaty with a relevant jurisdictional clause was in principle 'entitled to enjoy rights under all the provisions of the instrument concerned.'[58]

---

relating to the protection of the environment of the high seas, of which fish stocks form part, have been explicitly recognised as having an *erga omnes* character, see *Responsibilities and Obligations of States Sponsoring Persons and Entities With Respect to Activities in the Area*, Advisory Opinion, 1 February 2011, ITLOS Rep 2011, para 180.

53 Article 33 of the International Law Commission, Draft Articles on Responsibility of States for Internationally Wrongful Acts, November 2001 states that:

> The obligations of the responsible State . . . may be owed to another State, to several States, or to the international community as a whole, depending on the particular character and content of the international obligation and on the circumstances of the breach.

Any analysis must be conducted at the level of the obligation, rather than the instrument; see, for example, *Nuclear Tests (Australia v. France)*, Judgment ICJ Rep 1974, Joint Dissenting Opinion of Judges Onyeama, Dillard, Jiménez de Aréchage and Sir Humphrey Waldock, para 117; *Questions relating to the Obligation to Prosecute or Extradite (Belgium v. Senegal)*, Judgment, ICJ Rep 2012, Declaration of Judge Donoghue, para 12.

54 Commentary to Article 33 in James Crawford, *The International Law Commission's Articles on State Responsibility: Introduction, Text and Commentaries* (CUP 2002) 209.

55 *South West Africa Cases (Liberia v. South Africa)*, Second Phase, Judgment, ICJ Rep 1966.

56 ibid, para 88.

57 ibid, para 32.

58 ibid, para 66. Even this distinction was controversial and has been criticised by numerous commentators, see, for example, Rosalyn Higgins, 'The International Court and South West Africa' (1966) 42 *International Affairs* 573, 583, describing the distinction between particular provisions and conduct provisions as 'hitherto unpropounded in international law.'

In later case law, the ICJ adopted a more lenient position on standing for parties to a relevant treaty to bring claims in the protection of a common interest. Thus, in *Questions relating to the Obligation to Prosecute or Extradite*, the ICJ accepted that any party to the treaty could bring a claim based upon a provision establishing an *erga omnes* obligation.[59] It struck a similar result in *Application of the Convention on the Prevention and Punishment of the Crime of Genocide*.[60] There, the Court expressly rejected drawing a distinction between the right to invoke the responsibility of a State and standing to bring a claim before a court or tribunal, finding that this distinction had 'no basis in law.'[61] In the marine environmental context, the Australian claims in the *Whaling* case illustrate a sort of public interest claim successfully brought forward without any objection to the State's standing to do so.[62]

Given this contemporary case law, standing to bring a claim to uphold *erga omnes* obligations under RFMO treaties should be recognised by a court or tribunal. Failure to do so would significantly undermine the objectives of international fisheries law. The recognition of such common interests could, however, complicate dispute settlement as more than one State will have an interest.[63] This presents the challenge of how to manage multi-party litigation in an international context.

Multi-party litigation is not unknown at the international level. The very first case to come before the Permanent Court of International Justice resulted from a single joint application filed by the United Kingdom, France, Italy and Japan.[64] Multi-party proceedings can also be initiated through individual applications which are later joined. In this respect, the rules of procedure of the ICJ and ITLOS provide that those judicial bodies may 'at any time direct that the proceedings in two or more cases be joined.'[65] One example is the *Southern Bluefin Tuna Cases*, which allowed ITLOS to grant a single order in the provisional measures proceedings.[66] In the arbitral proceedings, the proceedings seemingly began with separate

59 *Questions relating to the Obligation to Prosecute or Extradite (Belgium v. Senegal)*, Judgment, ICJ Rep 2012, para 69. See however, the Separate Opinion of Judge Skotnikov, para 19 and Dissenting Opinion of Judge Xue, para 17.

60 *Application of the Convention on the Prevention and Punishment of the Crime of Genocide (The Gambia v. Myanmar)*, Preliminary Objections, Judgment, ICJ Rep 2022, para 112.

61 ibid, para 108.

62 See, for example, Cymie Payne, 'Responsibility to the international community for marine biodiversity beyond national jurisdiction' (2022) 11 *Cambridge Journal of International Law* 24, 43. See also James Harrison, *Saving the Oceans Through Law* (OUP 2017) 24–25.

63 Eirini-Erasmia Fasia, 'No Provision Left Behind – Law of the Sea Convention's Dispute Settlement System and Obligations Erga Omnes' (2021) 20 *The Law and Practice of International Courts and Tribunals* 519, 534. See also Yoshifuma Tanaka, 'The Legal Consequences of Obligations Erga Omnes in International Law' (2021) 68 *Netherlands International Law Review* 1, 26.

64 *SS Wimbledon Case* (1923) PCIJ Rep, Series A, 20.

65 ICJ Rules of Procedure, art 47; ITLOS Rules of Procedure, art 47.

66 *Southern Bluefin Tuna (New Zealand v. Japan; Australia v. Japan)*, Order of 16 August 1999, ITLOS Rep 1999. For a similar situation in another earlier law of the sea case, see *North Sea Continental Shelf (Federal Republic of Germany/Denmark; Federal Republic of Germany/Netherlands)*, Order of 26 April 1968, ICJ Rep 1969.

notifications for each party but the claims were joined by mutual agreement of all parties, including Japan as the respondent.[67]

Different issues could arise from joining separate claims by parties in the same interest. In particular, it may impact the composition of the forum hearing the dispute. For proceedings before a permanent judicial forum, parties in the same interest may jointly choose an ad hoc judge, provided that there is not already a judge of the nationality of any of these parties.[68] In the context of arbitration, two States bringing a claim in the same interest must select their arbitrator by agreement.[69] Joining separate claims by parties will also impact the organisation of proceedings. Thus, in the *Southern Bluefin Tuna* Arbitration, Australia and New Zealand were both represented by their own agent and counsel. However, they coordinated their pleadings by presenting a single set of submissions to the tribunal and providing joint answers to the tribunal's questions. As noted by one of the participants, there are advantages and disadvantages to running such a joint litigation strategy:

> having additional parties . . . can add momentum to that position – but there is a balance to be had. It can be easier to run a case [as a single party] because there is no additional layer of consultation.[70]

Of course, this assumes that participants in joined proceedings are acting in the same interest, but this cannot be taken for granted. The rules of procedure of the ICJ and ITLOS make clear that whether parties are in the same interest is decided by the judges.[71] This implies that parties could be found to have separate interests, in which case each could presumably appoint an ad hoc judge if a judge of their nationality is not already on the bench. This outcome is more explicit in the case of arbitration. The Annex VII arbitral rules provide that 'where there are several parties having separate interests or where there is disagreement as to whether they are of the same interest, each of them shall appoint one member of the tribunal'.[72] This is on the proviso that 'the number of members of the tribunal appointed separately by the parties shall always be smaller by one than the number of members of the tribunal to be appointed jointly by the parties.' This language implies that there may be more than one applicant with distinct interests in a single proceeding. Of course, this approach could be cumbersome where numerous parties with separate interests are involved in a single proceeding. It would also most certainly increase the cost of the proceedings. As a result, parties would be best advised to agree on

67 See, for example, Southern Bluefin Tuna Arbitration, Award on Jurisdiction and Admissibility, 4 August 2000, XXIII RIAA 1, para 1.

68 ICJ Rules of Procedure, art 36(1); ITLOS Rules of Procedure, art 20(1).

69 See UNCLOS, Annex VII, art 3(g).

70 Bill Campbell QC, 'International Dispute Resolution: Australian Perspectives and Approaches' (2017) 35 *Australian Yearbook of International Law* 1, 14.

71 ITLOS Rules of Procedure, art 20(2).

72 UNCLOS, Annex VII, art 3(g).

suitable arrangements to ensure that all interests are represented without excessively increasing the size of the tribunal.

Indeed, where separate interests are involved, joinder may not be appropriate, even if similar claims are made against a single respondent. In *Icelandic Fisheries*, the ICJ treated the United Kingdom and Germany as separate parties. In reaching this decision,

> the Court took into account the fact that while the basic legal issues in each case appeared to be identical, there were differences between the positions of the two Applicants, and between their respective submissions, and that joinder would be contrary to the wishes of the two Applicants.[73]

Unusually, Germany was refused an ad hoc judge because its interests were sufficiently close to those of the United Kingdom.[74] This refusal underlines that the question of joinder goes beyond merely analysing whether the parties are in the same interest.

Where a formal joinder is not prescribed, courts and tribunals have flexible powers to manage separate proceedings in related cases. Thus, the rules of procedure of the ICJ and ITLOS provide, in identical terms, that they may 'direct common action' in relation to the written or oral proceedings, including the calling of witnesses.[75] Falling short of directing common action, the ICJ decided in *Icelandic Fisheries* to hold the public hearings in the two cases immediately following each other.[76] Such steps allow a court or tribunal to ensure that decisions made in individual cases are reached in a consistent manner.

Coordination is more complex if proceedings are initiated before different courts or tribunals, which is a possibility given the diversity of available procedures discussed previously. Even then, courts and tribunals can use their procedural powers to manage possible tensions. One example is the *MOX Plant Arbitration*, which was suspended pending the outcome of parallel litigation proceedings before the Court of Justice of the European Union.[77]

More States may also become involved in litigation where a State joins a case as an intervenor. Before the ICJ and ITLOS, a party to a treaty may intervene as of right where the subject matter of the dispute is the treaty's interpretation.[78] RFMO parties are likely to have a right to intervene on this basis.

73 *Icelandic Fisheries (Federal Republic of Germany v. Iceland)*, Merits, Judgment, ICJ Rep 1974, para 8.

74 *Icelandic Fisheries (Federal Republic of Germany v. Iceland)*, Jurisdiction, Judgment, ICJ Rep 1973, para 7.

75 ICJ Rules of Procedure, art 47; ITLOS Rules of Procedure, art 47.

76 *Icelandic Fisheries (Federal Republic of Germany v. Iceland)*, Merits, Judgment, ICJ Rep 1974, para 8.

77 MOX Plant Arbitration, Procedural Order No 4, 14 November 2003. See generally Yuval Shany, *The Competing Jurisdictions of International Courts and Tribunals* (OUP 2003).

78 ITLOS Statute, arts 31–32; ICJ Statute, arts 62–63.

Intervenors do not formally become a party to the proceedings, and they do not have a right to appoint an ad hoc judge.[79] However, they will be bound by the interpretation adopted in the case. Intervention is also arguably possible where claims are brought to arbitration. The relevant rules do not explicitly foresee a right of intervention for Annex VII arbitration, but it has been persuasively argued that a tribunal could allow such intervention based on its discretion to 'determine its own procedure' under Article 5.[80] In contrast, the RFMO treaties which provide for arbitration by consent tend to foresee explicitly the possibility of intervention.[81] This language acknowledges that fisheries disputes may impinge the interests of multiple actors. The advantage of intervention is that it does not require all parties to agree in advance on a single forum. Instead, it allows other parties to contribute to proceedings once these have commenced. However, intervention depends on a single party being willing to bring the claim in the first place. Moreover, the right of the intervenor is limited to commenting on the legal issues surrounding the interpretation of the treaty.[82] Intervenors cannot comment on the facts or other related matters.

In principle, any contracting party may intervene in a case involving the interpretation of the relevant treaty. The ICJ held that a court or tribunal 'cannot limit the number of intervening States . . . since this would encroach on the rights of States to intervene.'[83] However, challenges may arise if many contracting parties

79 Nor is the participation of an intervenor in support of a party likely to affect this party's ability to appoint an ad hoc judge if they do not have a judge of their nationality on the court or tribunal, see *Whaling in the Antarctic (Australia v. Japan: New Zealand Intervening)*, Order of 6 February 2013, ICJ Rep 2013, paras 18 and 21.

80 See, for example, Judith Levine and Garth Schofield, 'Navigating Uncharted Procedural Waters in a Rising Sea of Cases at the Permanent Court of Arbitration' in Stephen Minas and H Jordan Diamond (eds), *Stress Testing the Law of the Sea* (Brill 2018) 114–115; Sir Michael Wood and Eran Sthoeger, 'Third Party Intervention and Involvement in Inter-State Arbitration' in Hélène Ruiz Fabri et al. (eds), *A Bridge Over Troubled Waters: Dispute Resolution in the Law of International Water Courses and the Law of the Sea* (Brill 2020) 61–82.

81 See Convention for the Conservation of Antarctic Marine Living Resources, 20 May 1980, 1329 UNTS 47, entered into force 7 April 1982, Annex, para 4, stating, 'Any Contracting Party which is not a Party to the dispute may intervene in the proceedings with the consent of the arbitral tribunal.' See also Convention for the Conservation of Southern Bluefin Tuna, 10 May 1993, 1819 UNTS 359, entered into force 20 May 1994, Annex, para 4; Agreement for the Establishment of the General Fisheries Commission for the Mediterranean, 6 December 1949, 126 UNTS 237, entered into force 20 February 1952, Annex, para 5.

82 In practice, the ICJ has been willing to limit interventions going beyond these matters; see *Allegations of Genocide under the Convention on the Prevention and Punishment of the Crime of Genocide (Ukraine v. Russian Federation)*, Order of 5 June 2023, para 84: 'intervention under Article 63 of the Statute is limited to the construction of the provisions in question at the relevant stage of the proceedings' and

> to the extent that . . . declarations also address other matters, such as the existence of a dispute between the Parties, the evidence, the facts or the application of the Convention in the present case, the Court will not consider them.

For a more hesitant approach, see Dissenting Opinion of Judge Xue, para 23.

83 *Allegations of Genocide under the Convention on the Prevention and Punishment of the Crime of Genocide (Ukraine v. Russian Federation)*, Order of 5 June 2023, para 50.

seek to intervene. In such cases, a court or tribunal may need to take steps to manage the process,[84] so as to 'organise the proceedings in a manner which ensures the equality of the parties and the good administration of justice.'[85]

An alternative mechanism to facilitate multi-party proceedings in the context of fisheries disputes is to request an advisory opinion from ITLOS.[86] Advisory proceedings are particularly flexible when it comes to participation. There is no formal distinction between applicant and respondent. A wide variety of actors, including inter-governmental organisations, can also potentially take part in the proceedings. For example, in the advisory opinion request submitted to ITLOS by the Sub-Regional Fisheries Commission, 22 States, the European Union and seven inter-governmental organisations made written submissions during the first round and many of them also participated in the oral proceedings.[87]

To date, no RFMO responsible for managing high-seas fish stocks on the high seas has been granted a power to request an advisory opinion from ITLOS. However, such a power could easily be conferred on such a RFMO. The relevant rules of procedure provide that 'the Tribunal may give an advisory opinion on a legal question if an international agreement related to the purposes of the Convention specifically provides for the submission to the Tribunal of a request for such an opinion.'[88] There is little doubt that an agreement concerning fisheries conservation and management is 'related to the purposes of the Convention'.[89] Further, there is considerable flexibility as to the manner in which a power to request an advisory opinion could be conferred on RFMO. It is unlikely to require a formal amendment to the RFMO's constituent instrument, as the term 'agreement' in Article 138 of the ITLOS rules of procedure implies flexibility in terms of the required degree of formality.[90] Thus, RFMO members could conclude a separate agreement specifically

84 Such as setting deadlines and determining applications as far as possible by written procedure, see ibid, paras 20 and 22.

85 ibid, para 52. In particular, the parties to the dispute must be given a fair opportunity to respond to interventions.

86 See ITLOS Rules of Procedure, art 133, which applies mutatis mutandis to advisory proceedings conducted under Article 138. See generally on the suitability of advisory opinions for dealing with common interest claims, Eirini-Erasmia Fasia, 'No Provision Left Behind – Law of the Sea Convention's Dispute Settlement System and Obligations Erga Omnes' (2021) 20 *The Law and Practice of International Courts and Tribunals* 519, 544.

87 See ITLOS, 'Request for an Advisory Opinion Submitted by the Sub-Regional Fisheries Commission (SRFC) (Request for Advisory Opinion Submitted to the Tribunal)'. https://www.itlos.org/en/main/cases/list-of-cases/case-no-21/> accessed 26 August 2022.

88 ITLOS Rules of Procedure, art 138.

89 See, for example, Doo-Young Kim, 'Advisory Proceedings Before the International Tribunal for the Law of the Sea as an Alternative Procedure to Supplement the Dispute-Settlement Mechanism Under Part XV of the United Nations Convention on the Law of the Sea' (2010) 7 *Issues in Legal Scholarship*, 6.

90 See, for example, discussion in the commentary to Conclusion 4 of the Draft Conclusions on Subsequent Agreements and Subsequent Practice in Relation to the Interpretation of Treaties with commentaries, Yearbook of the International Law Commission (2018), vol II, part Two. Cf Maria Garcia

authorising the RFMO to request an advisory opinion from ITLOS to meet the requirements of Article 138.[91]

Advisory opinions are not formally binding, but their legal authority should not be underestimated. ITLOS itself has said of ICJ's advisory opinions that 'judicial determinations in advisory opinions carry no less weight and authority than those in judgments.'[92] Moreover, States and organisations can also 'commit themselves in advance to act upon and give effect to advisory opinions.'[93] In this way, in concluding an agreement to confer the power to request an advisory opinion on a RFMO, States could agree to treat the opinion as legally binding. This would be a helpful solution to address any disputes concerning the legality of a RFMO's actions, where multiple parties are likely to have an interest in the proceedings. Yet, advisory jurisdiction should not be used to circumvent contentious procedures.[94] Therefore, an advisory opinion would be less appropriate to deal with differences on the compliance of particular members with their obligations under an RFMO treaty.

Adjudication and arbitration are not the only procedures permitting participation by multiple actors. The ad hoc panel process discussed in the previous section also has flexible rules on participation. In the North West Atlantic Fisheries Organisation's panel process, the process identifies particular disputing parties involved in establishing the panel. However, it makes clear that 'where another Contracting Party wishes to become Party to a dispute, it may join the process of constituting an ad hoc panel, unless the original Parties to the dispute disagree'.[95] Further, even if a member does not wish to become a party to the dispute, it 'may attend all hearings of the ad hoc panel, make written and oral submissions to the ad hoc panel and receive the submissions of each Party to the dispute.'[96] The Organisation may also participate directly in the process, in particular by providing information to the

García-Revillo, *The Contentious and Advisory Jurisdiction of the International Tribunal for the Law of the Sea* (Brill 2015) 312.

91 See, for example, Philippe Gautier, 'Urgent Proceedings before the International Tribunal for the Law of the Sea' (2009) 7 *Issues in Legal Scholarship*, 19, going as far as saying that 'such an agreement could, for example, be recorded in the decision taken by the competent body.'

92 *Dispute concerning delimitation of the maritime boundary between Mauritius and Maldives in the Indian Ocean (Preliminary Objections)*, Judgment, ITLOS Rep 2021, para 203.

93 See, for example, Convention on Privileges and Immunities of the United Nations, 13 February 1946, 90 UNTS 327, entered into force 17 September 1946, art 8, stating, 'The opinion given by the Court shall be accepted as decisive by the parties.' See Manley Hudson, 'The Effect of Advisory Opinions of the World Court' (1948) 42 *American Journal of International Law* 630, 631; Louis B Sohn, 'A Tribunal for the Sea-Bed or the Oceans' (1972) *Heidelberg Journal of International Law* 253, 259.

94 Nevertheless, advisory opinions have sometimes tackled the question of individual state responsibility, for example, *Legal Consequences of the Separation of the Chagos Archipelago from Mauritius in 1965*, Judgment, ICJ Rep 2019, para 177. For discussion of the appropriateness of such proceedings, see the Dissenting Opinion of Judge Donohue and the Declaration of Judge Gevorgian.

95 Convention on Future Multilateral Cooperation in the Northwest Atlantic Fisheries, 24 October 1978, 1135 UNTS 369, entered into force 1 January 1979, Annex II, para 3.

96 ibid, Annex II, para 5.

panel.[97] Similar rules apply to the dispute prevention mechanisms under the GFCM discussed previously.[98] Therefore multi-actor participation is facilitated across the spectrum of dispute settlement mechanisms available under RFMO treaties, which emphasises this key characteristic of high seas fisheries disputes.

4. Conclusion

Dispute prevention and dispute settlement have come to play a prominent role in the institutional design of RFMOs. This has been particularly true since the conclusion of the Fish Stocks Agreement, which has inspired much of the practice discussed in this chapter. Yet, the discussion has highlighted that there is no single forum for the settlement of disputes under RFMO treaties. Rather, there has been a proliferation of options, including conciliation or similar procedures, ad hoc panels for technical disputes, and increased availability of traditional forms of adjudication and arbitration. Disputing parties must choose carefully depending on the nature of the dispute, the types of issues it raises, and the options for participation by relevant actors. Given this variability, one author has concluded that 'one should probably not expect much consistency or predictability in the practice of the various bodies and organisations and their members.'[99] At the same time, there are commonalities, particularly on participation, where procedural questions can be addressed through common principles on fairness and judicial propriety applicable across various forums.

Despite the widespread availability of dispute settlement procedures under the treaties surveyed in this chapter, there is very little practice associated with them. The exceptions are review panels automatically triggered if an objection is made.[100] It appears that States prefer to deal with their disputes through diplomatic means. Such diplomacy may take place bilaterally or through the RFMO itself.[101] This observation underlines the essential point that, just because dispute settlement

97 See, for example, Review Panel established under the Convention on the Conservation and Management of High Seas Fishery Resources in the South Pacific Ocean, Findings and Recommendations, CMM 01–2023, 1 July 2023, paras 24, 30, 32, 25.

98 Agreement for the Establishment of the General Fisheries Commission for the Mediterranean, 6 December 1949, 126 UNTS 237, entered into force 20 February 1952, Rules of Procedure, Rule XVIII.

99 Jean-François Pulvenis de Séligny-Maurel, 'Regional Fisheries Bodies and Regional Fisheries Management Organisations and the Settlement of Disputes concerning Marine Living Resources' in Lilian del Castillo (ed), *From Grotius to the International Tribunal for the Law of the Sea* (Brill 2015) 712.

100 For example, Convention on the Conservation and Management of High Seas Fishery Resources in the South Pacific Ocean, 14 November 2009, 2899 UNTS 211, entered into force 24 August 2012, art 17(5)(a).

101 See, for example, the example provided in Jean-François Pulvenis de Séligny-Maurel, 'Regional Fisheries Bodies and Regional Fisheries Management Organisations and the Settlement of Disputes concerning Marine Living Resources' in Lilian del Castillo (ed), *From Grotius to the International Tribunal for the Law of the Sea* (Brill 2015) footnote 47.

options exist, it does not mean that these options will be used. Recourse to dispute settlement involves strategic choices on the part of States and other actors, who may, for a variety of reasons, prefer keeping their disagreements within diplomatic forums.[102] It is therefore difficult to evaluate fully the effectiveness of these procedures in the absence of concrete cases.

However, dispute settlement mechanisms should not be discounted as irrelevant. The very possibility of submitting a dispute to an international court or tribunal could have a subtle effect on the negotiating positions of relevant actors. As observed by Örebech, Sigurjonsson and McDorman, 'the binding nature of the dispute settlement regime may be employed to hasten a negotiated solution or to alter the negotiating dynamic of states in dispute.'[103] From this perspective, the evolution of dispute settlement within RFMOs, including the increased availability of compulsory binding procedures, is an important development in international fisheries law.

At the same time, dispute settlement cannot solve all differences arising in fisheries management. Dispute resolution procedures typically focus on a relatively narrow set of short-term issues. Therefore, the emphasis on dispute prevention in the Fish Stocks Agreement and RFMO treaties deserves significant emphasis. As noted by the recent decision of a Review Panel established under the Convention on the Conservation and Management of High Seas Fishery Resources in the South Pacific Ocean, 'the further strengthening of the deliberative and negotiating processes would contribute to the effectiveness of [conservation and management measures].'[104] In other words, dispute settlement procedures are not a substitute for effective decision-making processes.

102 See generally, Shirley Scott, 'Litigation Versus Dispute Resolution Through Political Processes' in Natalie Klein (ed), *Litigating International Law Disputes* (OUP 2014) at 24–41; Robin Churchill, 'The General Dispute Settlement System of the UN Convention on the Law of the Sea: Overview, Context and Use' (2017) 48 *Ocean Development and International Law* 216, 225–226. For a more general study, see Sara McLaughlin Mitchell and Andrew Owsiak, 'Judicialization of the Sea: Bargaining in the Shadow of UNCLOS' (2021) 115 *American Journal of International Law* 579.

103 Peter Örebech, Ketill Sigurjonsson and Ted L. McDorman, 'The 1995 United Nations Straddling and Highly Migratory Fish Stocks Agreement: Management, Enforcement and Dispute Settlement' (1998) *Internal Journal of Marine and Coastal Law* 119, 133. See also Robin Churchill, 'Trends in Dispute Settlement in the Law of the Sea: Towards the Increasing Availability of Compulsory Means' in Duncan French et al. (eds), *International Law and Dispute Settlement* (Bloomsbury 2012) 149.

104 Review Panel established under the Convention on the Conservation and Management of High Seas Fishery Resources in the South Pacific Ocean, Findings and Recommendations, CMM 01–2023, 1 July 2023, para 144.

7 The Objection Procedure in the South Pacific Regional Fisheries Management Organisation

*Osvaldo Urrutia**

1. Introduction

The use of adversarial inter-State dispute settlement mechanisms is infrequent when it comes to international fisheries management. The United Nations Convention on the Law of the Sea (UNCLOS)[1] and the Agreement for the Implementation of the Provisions of the United Nations Convention on the Law of the Sea of 10 December 1982 relating to the Conservation and Management of Straddling Fish Stocks and Highly Migratory Fish Stocks (Fish Stocks Agreement) provide detailed provisions.[2] However, recourse to permanent courts and arbitral tribunals to solve conflicts related to transboundary fisheries seems to be the exception rather than the rule. This context contrasts with the contentious dynamics of regional fisheries management organisations or arrangements (RFMOs), where multidimensional and often structural disagreements are pervasive amongst Member States.

Decision-making rules lie at the chore of managing conflict in international organisations. RFMOs have traditionally adopted two approaches: consensus or voting with the possibility of objecting and preventing the adopted decision from applying to a dissatisfied State.[3] RFMOs in the first group have dealt with internal

* The content of this chapter incorporates SPRFMO updates up to 28 September 2023.The author wishes to thank the book's editors for their constructive comments on an earlier version of this chapter. All errors remain the author's responsibility.

1 United Nations Convention on the Law of the Sea (UNCLOS), 10 December 1982, 1833 UNTS 3, entered into force 16 November 1994.

2 Agreement for the Implementation of the Provisions of the United Nations Convention on the Law of the Sea of 10 December 1982 relating to the Conservation and Management of Straddling Fish Stocks and Highly Migratory Fish Stocks (Fish Stocks Agreement), 4 August 1995, 2167 UNTS 3, entered into force 11 December 2001.

3 Examples of organisations whose decisions are adopted by consensus only include the Commission for the Conservation of Antarctic Marine Living Resources and the Inter-American Tropical Tuna Commission. Convention on the Conservation of Antarctic Marine Living Resources, 20 May 1980, 1329 UNTS 47, entered into force 7 April 1982, art XII. Convention for the Strengthening of the Inter-American Tropical Tuna Commission established by the 1949 Convention between the United States of America and the Republic of Costa Rica, 14 November 2003, entered into force 27 August 2010, art IX(1). An organisation that allows its members to object without the need to justify its decisions is the North East Atlantic Fisheries Commission, Convention on Future Multilateral

DOI: 10.4324/9781003492030-10

differences by accepting that consensus inevitably means the common lowest denominator. In the second group, RFMOs have allowed members to free ride from a joint decision by simply objecting, which can bring frustrating challenges. Neither approach alone is satisfactory. As a result, tensions and arguments can linger for years, affecting inter-State dynamics and undermining sustainability goals.

Against this background, treaties establishing modern RFMOs have designed novel decision-making rules and additional mechanisms to deal with disputes among their members. They have allowed decisions by qualified majorities and created objection procedures for dissatisfied members to challenge these decisions under specific and limited grounds. The objection procedure in the South Pacific Regional Fisheries Management Organisation (SPRFMO) is a highlight in the landscape of RFMOs.[4] Article 17 and Annex II of the SPRFMO Convention set up a system whereby any member can object to a decision of the SPRFMO Commission subject to specific requirements and conditions. These objections are heard by a Review Panel following a detailed and structured process. In the SPRFMO's first decade, this mechanism has been triggered three times to contest allocation decisions, the most controversial topic in RFMOs' practice: in 2013 by Russia, in 2018 by Ecuador, and then again in 2023 by Russia. Three other RFMO Conventions have objection procedures: the Western and Central Pacific Fisheries Commission (WCPFC), the Northwest Atlantic Fisheries Organization (NAFO), and the North Pacific Fisheries Commission (NPFC).[5] However, only the SPRFMO's objection mechanism has been set in motion.

The paper assesses the objections raised before the three Review Panel procedures of the SPRFMO before the Permanent Court of Arbitration. It first summarises the primary outcomes and assesses the broader impacts of the SPRFMO objection procedure to solve effectively conflicts among its members. It then evaluates lessons learned and challenges arising from the SPRFMOs objection procedure by examining whether the Review Panel's recommendations solved short-term and long-term issues associated with the SPRFMO's allocation conflicts that triggered these cases in the first place. Overall, this chapter suggests that the SPRFMO experience offers positive takeaways for other RFMOs.

Cooperation in the Northeast Atlantic Fisheries, 18 November 1980, 1285 UNTS 129, entered into force 17 March 1982, art 12.

4 Convention on the Conservation and Management of High Seas Fishery Resources in the South Pacific Ocean (SPRFMO Convention), 1 February 2010, 2899 UNTS 211, entered into force 24 August 2012.

5 Convention on the Conservation of Highly Migratory Fish Stocks in the Western and Cen-tral Pacific Ocean, 5 September 2000, 2275 UNTS 40532, entered into force 19 June 2004, art 20(6)–(9) and Annex II. Convention on Cooperation in the Northwest Atlantic Fisheries, 24 October 1978, 1135 UNTS 369, entered into force 1 January 1979, including amendments adopted in 2007, entered into force in 2017, art XIV. Convention on the Conservation and Management of the High Seas Fisheries Resources in the North Pacific Ocean, 24 February 2012, entered into force 19 July 2015, art 9(1).

2. The SPRFMO Objection Procedure: A Quick Overview

The SPRFMO Convention was adopted in 2009 and entered into force in 2012.[6] It is a modern and forward-looking text with several innovative and progressive provisions. A critical feature concerns decision-making: it is based on consensus with the possibility of voting on questions of substance and adopting decisions by a three-fourths majority.[7] A member dissatisfied with the majority vote can object to a SPRFMO Commission's decision. Once objected, the decision does not become binding on that member as the objection process proceeds before a Review Panel.

Several features make the SPRFMO's procedure sophisticated. For example, unlike in the WCPFC and partially the NPFC, the SPRFMO's Review Panel can deal with complaints about allocation schemes because participatory fishing rights decisions can be adopted by majority voting. Also, unlike in the NAFO and NPFC Conventions, establishing a panel is not optional: the panel must be appointed once an objection has been submitted. Other features also deserve to be highlighted, including procedural and substantive.

2.1. Procedural and Substantive Rules

A central feature which makes the SPRFMO's objection procedure efficient is its short timeframe to deliver results. The Review Panel is established 30 days after the end of the 60-day objection period, which starts when the Secretariat notifies the annual decisions to Commission members.[8] Once established, the Review Panel must carry out its work and deliver its findings and recommendations within 45 days. As a former Chairperson of the SPRFMO Commission observed, this framework 'ensures that the issue is resolved promptly or is formally submitted to binding dispute settlement in accordance with Part VIII of the UN Fish Stocks Agreement'.[9]

Another positive element – shared by the WCPFC, the NAFO, and the NPFC – relates to the grounds for objection. Only two grounds are allowed: the decision must unjustifiably discriminate against the Commission member or be inconsistent

6 The SPRFMO Convention has 17 members: *Australia, Belize, Chile, China, Cook Islands, Cuba, Ecuador, the European Union, the Kingdom of Denmark in respect of the Faroe Islands, the Republic of Korea, New Zealand, Panama, Peru, the Russian Federation, Chinese Taipei, the United States of America, and Vanuatu.* The primary competence of this organisation is over straddling stocks: jack mackerel, squid, and bottom fisheries such as orange roughy.

7 SPRFMO Convention, art 16(2)(b).

8 The Review Panel will consist of three members appointed from the list of fishery experts drawn up and maintained by the Food and Agriculture Organization of the United Nations under Annex VIII UNCLOS or a similar list maintained by the SPRFMO Secretary. The Chairperson and the Commission member which presented an objection shall each appoint one member. The objecting member and the Chairperson of the Commission agree on the third member.

9 Bill Mansfield, 'Consensus: A Good Goal but a Bad Rule? Decision Making in Regional Fisheries Management Organisations and the Implementation of the UN Fish Stocks Agreement' *ANZSIL Perspective No 5* (May 2016) 2. www.anzsil.org.au/resources/Perspective/ANZSIL%20Perspective%20No%205.pdf accessed 4 December 2023.

with the provisions of the SPRFMO Convention or other relevant international law as reflected in UNCLOS or the Fish Stocks Agreement.[10] In the NAFO or WCPFC, the distinction between the grounds has no bearing on the role of the Review Panel. However, this distinction is significant in the SPRFMO because the Review Panel acts differently depending on each objection's category. The objecting member must also and simultaneously adopt alternative measures equivalent to the decision it objected to, and the Review Panel must respond to them.[11]

2.2. *The Role of the Review Panel*

The SPRFMO Convention regulates the Review Panel's role for each objection ground in detail.

2.2.1. *Findings of Discrimination*

If the Review Panel finds that the decision is discriminatory, it will decide on the alternative measures presented by the objecting member. If these proposed measures have an equivalent effect *vis-a-vis* the objected decision, these alternative measures shall bind the objecting member instead of the SPRFMO decision.[12]

However, if the objecting State's proposed alternative measures do not have an equivalent effect, the Review Panel will recommend new measures.[13] The objecting member may then accept them or request an extraordinary meeting of the Commission, where members may confirm or modify the Review Panel's recommendations. Depending on the outcome of the meeting, the objecting member may again implement the amended findings or institute binding dispute settlement procedures under Article 34 of the SPRFMO Convention.[14]

A critical element in the SPRFMO Convention to balance the organisation's multilateral interest and the objecting State's rights is the 'equivalent effect' of the proposed alternative measures.[15] The dissatisfied member should be careful in this move: if the measures are equivalent, the dispute will end in its favour, but if not, the Review Panel will need to recommend new measures. In the latter case, the

10 SPRFMO Convention, art 17(2)(c).
11 SPRFMO Convention, art 17(2)(b)(ii).
12 SPRFMO Convention, Annex II, para 10(a).
13 SPRFMO Convention, Annex II, para 10(c).
14 SPRFMO Convention, art 34(2): where a dispute is not resolved through amicable means, 'the provisions relating to the settlement of disputes set out in Part VIII of the 1995 Agreement shall apply, mutatis mutandis, to any dispute between the Contracting Parties.'
15 SPRFMO Convention, art 17(2)(b):

> A member of the Commission that presents an objection shall at the same time: (i) specify in detail the grounds for its objection; (ii) adopt alternative measures that are equivalent in effect to the decision to which it has objected and have the same date of application; and (iii) advise the Executive Secretary of the terms of such alternative measures.

objecting State would have little option but to accept them as taking the matter to the Commission is unlikely to be in the State's interest.

Another conspicuous element is the Commission's lack of any significant role when there is a finding of discrimination. Members which did not challenge the decision have no explicit role. The Review Panel can indirectly impose a new measure on the Commission members who did not object to the initial decision by adopting alternative measures which are accepted by the objecting member – as happened, for example, after Russia objected in 2013. Only the objecting member, if still dissatisfied, can request an extraordinary meeting of the Commission. This framework offers a reasonable chance to correct a majority management decision and make it acceptable to the rest of the Commission.

2.2.2. *Findings of Inconsistency with the SPRFMO Convention, UNCLOS, or the Fish Stocks Agreement*

Given the seriousness of a finding of inconsistency, an extraordinary Commission meeting must occur to reconsider the original decision.[16] The new or modified decision will then become binding on the members under the general rules of the Convention.[17] If the Commission maintains the original decision, the objecting member may implement this decision or institute dispute settlement proceedings under Article 34 of the SPRFMO Convention.[18]

Two aspects of these rules deserve attention. The first one concerns the alternative measures presented by the objecting State. The SPRFMO provisions ask that the dissatisfied member propose alternative measures, but these proposals do not play any role when the Review Panel concludes there is inconsistency with the relevant treaty law. The second one is that the Review Panel's conclusions are still framed as recommendations, notwithstanding that a finding of inconsistency is tantamount to saying that the original Commission's decision was contrary to international law. The recommendations do not impose an obligation to amend the original decision. Instead, the SPRFMO Commission must meet and decide 'in the light of those findings and recommendations.'[19] This approach may be a questionable aspect of the SPRFMO objection procedure, which favours the collective decision over its consistency with international law.

2.2.3. *Rejecting the Objection*

If the Review Panel rejects the grounds for objection, the objecting member can either implement the decision or institute dispute settlement proceedings under Article 34 of the SPRFMO Convention.[20] Yet, the panel can still find that the

16 SPRFMO Convention, Annex II, para 10(f).
17 SPRFMO Convention, Annex II, para 10(g).
18 SPRFMO Convention, Annex II, para 10(h).
19 SPRFMO Convention, Annex II, para 10(f).
20 SPRFMO Convention, Annex II, para 10(i).

alternative measures the objecting State offered have an equivalent effect to the objected decision. The Review Panel may then recommend that such measures be binding on the objecting member instead of the original Commission's decision.[21] However, the SPRFMO Convention still weighs the rights of the Commission, the objecting State, and the Review Panel's role by requiring that the Commission accept such recommendations at the Commission's next meeting.[22]

In short, objection procedures are distinct from traditional dispute settlement mechanisms. They represent an attempt to balance the RFMO's collective goals and the sovereign rights of its members. The SPRFMO mechanism offers comparative advantages when it comes to its scope, procedural aspects, detailed substantive rules, and the Review Panel's role. As one scholar put it, '[w]hen compared with other RFMO conventions, the SPRMFO Convention establishes by far the most comprehensive formal procedure for resolving disputes over objections.'[23]

3. The Objection Procedure Cases in Practice: Summary and Assessment

This part briefly reviews the practice of the SPRFMO objection procedure to assess its role in solving disagreements between a member and the majority. The three objection procedures triggered under the SPRFMO to date took place under the auspices of the Permanent Court of Arbitration. In all three cases, Russia and Ecuador objected to SPRFMO decisions invoking the grounds of discrimination and inconsistency and proposed alternative measures.

3.1. Russia (2013)

Managing and allocating fishing rights in the jack mackerel fishery have been among the primary concerns of SPRFMO since the first negotiations to adopt the 2009 Convention started in the mid-2000s. At the SPRFMO meeting held in January 2013, the Commission established a total catch limit of 360,000 tonnes, relying only on the catches in 2010 as a benchmark.[24]

The origin of Russia's objection was around choosing 2010 as the reference year for granting fishing rights for the 2013 season.[25] In 2010, Russia reported

21 SPRFMO Convention, Annex II, para 10(j).

22 ibid.

23 Rosemary Rayfuse, 'Settling Disputes in Regional Fisheries Management Organisations: Dealing with Objections' in Helene Ruiz Fabri et al. (eds), *A Bridge over Troubled Waters: Dispute Resolution in the Law of International Watercourses and the Law of the Sea* (Brill Nijhoff 2020) 264.

24 SPRFMO, CMM 1.01, 'Conservation and Management Measure for *Trachurus murphyi*' (2013). www.sprfmo.int/assets/Meetings/Archived-Meetings/Meetings-2013-plus/Commission-Meetings/1st-Commission-Meeting-2013-Auckland-New-Zealand/Annex-G-CMM-1-v2.01-Conservation-and-management-measures-for-Trachurus-murphyi.pdf accessed 4 December 2023, para 6.

25 Whether it was an allocation exercise under SPRFMO Convention, art 21 was debated. See Andrew Serdy, 'Implementing Article 28 of the UN Fish Stocks Agreement: The First Review of a

catches from one vessel only: 41,315 tonnes of jack mackerel caught from a vessel then-called Lafayette.[26] Subsequent inspections discovered the Lafayette could not catch fish and was only suitable for transshipments. As a result, the 2013 decision, by voting, assigned Russia no individual quota.[27] Russia objected to this exclusion from the shares in the catch limit of jack mackerel. Russia invoked the two grounds for objection: discrimination and inconsistency with relevant treaty law.

Russia developed two arguments. First, it questioned the Commission's powers to review the data presented by other parties.[28] Russia accepted that catches were transferred to the Lafayette, but argued that these should be 'counted' as its own.[29] Second, and more significantly, Russia claimed that the Commission 'wrongfully only took into account 2010 data' and failed to consider 'Russia's historical catch and significant contribution to scientific research' as mandated by Article 21(1) of the SPRFMO.[30] Russia criticised the Commission's decision to choose only one year to grant fishing rights.[31]

Russia proposed alternative measures. It first suggested that its fishing rights for 2013 should be 19,944 tonnes, based on the proportional reduction that all members undertook, taking 2010 catches as the baseline. At the hearings, Russia rephrased and complemented this proposed measure. Irrespective of the actual catch of jack mackerel by the Russian fishing vessels in 2013, Russia argued that if the SPRFMO limit of 360,000 tonnes were reached, Russia would 'cease fishing' for this resource in the Convention area.[32]

The Review Panel found a way forward that would prove acceptable for everyone, even if this meant not fully addressing the contentious issue of the Russian catches' provenance. First, the Review Panel concluded that it had no 'sufficient basis to determine the source of the portion' of the Lafayette's catches.[33] It could not discuss the extent to which other vessels transhipped them to the Russian-flagged ship. Second, on the substantive issue, the panel concluded that 'no convincing argument' had been to justify not allocating any catch to Russia, which resulted in

Conservation Measure in the South Pacific Regional Fisheries Management Organisation' (2016) 47 *Ocean Development and International Law* 1, 17–8.

26 Later known as the *Damanzaihao* and currently as *Vladivostok 2000*.

27 SPRFMO, CMM 1.01, 'Conservation and Management Measure for *Trachurus murphyi*' (2013). www.sprfmo.int/assets/Meetings/Archived-Meetings/Meetings-2013-plus/Commission-Meetings/1st-Commission-Meeting-2013-Auckland-New-Zealand/Annex-G-CMM-1-v2.01-Conservation-and-management-measures-for-Trachurus-murphyi.pdf accessed 4 December 2023, Tables 2 and 3; Review Panel established under the Convention on the Conservation and Management of High Seas Fishery Resources in the South Pacific Ocean (Objection by the Russian Federation), Findings and Recommendations, PCA Case 2013–14, 5 July 2013, paras 25–47.

28 Review Panel established under the Convention on the Conservation and Management of High Seas Fishery Resources in the South Pacific Ocean (Objection by the Russian Federation), Findings and Recommendations, PCA Case 2013–14, 5 July 2013, para 53.

29 ibid, paras 47 and 63.

30 ibid, para 62.

31 ibid, para 62.

32 ibid, paras 85–6.

33 ibid, para 91.

'unjustifiable discrimination'.[34] Third, it decided that the SPRFMO decision was 'not inconsistent' with 'the provisions of the Convention or other relevant international law as reflected in the 1982 Convention or the 1995 Agreement.'[35]

Finally, the Review Panel recommended a slightly different alternative measure. First, Russia should be allowed to authorise vessels to catch jack mackerel in the Convention Area in 2013. Second, such vessels should only catch jack mackerel if and when Russia had concluded, from data reported by the SPRFMO, that it was 'likely' that the 2013 catches had not reached the total allowable of 360,000 tonnes, and only until the SPRFMO informed members that this total allowable catch had been reached.[36]

The Review Panel thus recommended an alternative measure of equivalent effect to the objected decision while respecting the allocations granted to other members. At the same time, it critically recognised Russia's right to participate in the fishery and indirectly questioned the SPRFMO's wisdom in setting 2010 as the only year to determine fishing rights.

3.2. Ecuador (2018)

Ecuador acceded to the SPRFMO Convention on 11 May 2015. Before that date, Ecuador did not operate – or only sporadically and incidentally operated – in the jack mackerel fishery.

The objection presented by Ecuador represented a typical example of the new entrant problem.[37] The SPRFMO had agreed on a five-year allocation decision in 2017 after complex, protracted negotiations, and Ecuador did not obtain its desired allocation. Ecuador requested in January 2017, during the annual SPRFMO meeting, 4,590 tonnes in addition to the 1,100 tonnes the Commission had initially allocated in 2015 (a total of 5,690 tonnes).[38]

The SPRFMO's 2017 allocation decision, adopted for five years, gave Ecuador a low allocation of 0.2% of the total allowable catch (1,179 tonnes at the time).[39] Ecuador did not object back then but requested an increase in 2018, like the one it had made in 2017. At that meeting, several SPRFMO members regarded this move as a means of reopening the 2017 agreement. The Commission rejected Ecuador's proposal and maintained the allocation percentages agreed in 2017.[40]

When raising its objection, Ecuador's arguments relied on the criteria Article 21 of the SPRFMO Convention set for allocating fishing rights. Ecuador complained

34 ibid, para 92.

35 ibid, paras 93 and 100.

36 ibid, para 100(c).

37 See Andrew Serdy, *The New Entrants Problem in International Fisheries Law* (CUP 2016).

38 Review Panel established under the Convention on the Conservation and Management of High Seas Fishery Resources in the South Pacific Ocean (Objection by the Republic of Ecuador), Findings and Recommendations, PCA Case 2018–13, 5 June 2018, para 30.

39 ibid, para 32.

40 SPRFMO, CMM 01–2018, 'Conservation and Management Measure for *Trachurus murphyi*' (2018). https://pcacases.com/web/sendAttach/2373 accessed 4 December 2023, Table 2.

that the Commission based its allocation decisions entirely on historical catches. Criticising this approach, Ecuador underlined its geographical position as a coastal and developing nation.[41] It sought a bigger quota to 'develop the fishery,' which implied Ecuador wanted to prioritise catching its quota instead of merely selling it.[42] It argued that its current allocation was insufficient to develop profitably at its high seas jack mackerel fishery. It suggested as an alternative measure a 1.13% participation in the total allowable catch for 2018 (equivalent to 6,500 tonnes).[43]

The Review Panel rejected Ecuador's claim and alternative measures seeking more participation in the fishery. There was no discrimination in deciding an allocation scheme based primarily on historical catches and no inconsistency with the SPRFMO Convention, UNCLOS, or the Fish Stocks Agreement. However, the Review Panel dedicated key parts of its decision to encourage and delineate some principles which would guide future allocation decisions regarding Ecuador. The main message was that developing States 'should not be disadvantaged because their economic status has prevented them from developing a high seas fishery'.[44]

The Review Panel took this opportunity to adopt a constructive and proactive role in future negotiation exercises. It 'invited' SPRFMO members to 'consider whether the interests of developing States in the region might not be better taken into account in a more deliberative and specific discussion' within the decision-making process.[45] It highlighted that several members of the Commission had acknowledged that 'Ecuador's aspirations could be accommodated at future Commission meetings, provided Ecuador would submit a sufficiently compelling proposal.'[46] The Review Panel also encouraged the Commission to consider possible 'one-off' transfers outside the scope of the allocation transfer system, including the possibility of time-limited allocations and compensations by exclusion from proportional quota increases due to the rise in the total allowable catch.[47]

At the time of the hearings in 2018, SPRFMO members were holding inter-sessional discussions about possible adjustments to the allocation scheme. The Review Panel encouraged these discussions, implying these could be a way

41 Review Panel established under the Convention on the Conservation and Management of High Seas Fishery Resources in the South Pacific Ocean (Objection by the Republic of Ecuador), Findings and Recommendations, PCA Case 2018–13, 5 June 2018, para 59.

42 ibid, para 62. Ecuador did not capture the small allocation it had back then. Instead, it traded it, benefitting from quota transferring to other members with better logistical capabilities. Despite Ecuador's substantive increase in 2020, it continues to sell its allocation. Ecuador has no national industrial jack mackerel fishery.

43 ibid, paras 36 and 69. This amount was to be taken from the difference between the total allowable catch allocated on the 'applicable area' (the SPRFMO high seas area plus the exclusive economic zones of Chile and Ecuador, which consented to it) and the maximum catch defined for the entire range of the stock – which, in practice, meant to accept Ecuador's requested amount by taking it from the 58,418 tonnes that Peru was tacitly understood to catch inside its exclusive economic zone.

44 ibid, para 94.

45 ibid, para 124.

46 ibid, para 125.

47 ibid, para 127.

forward to accommodate Ecuador before the end of the five-year initial allocation agreement: 'members might also be willing to enter into an understanding that ensures that Ecuador would be among the first to benefit from it'.[48]

3.3. ***Russia (2023)***

The allocation scheme adopted for 2017–2021, and which rolled over to 2022, gave Russia 3.28% of the total allowable catch of jack mackerel to be adopted for the SPRFMO area every year. As this allocation scheme ended, the 11th Meeting of the SPRFMO Commission scheduled for February 2023 faced the challenge of allocating fishing rights again. Unsurprisingly, these negotiations proved difficult.

SPRFMO members debated three crucial aspects: accommodating Chile's demands for a larger quota as the leading and most active player in the fishery; the allocation requests from three new entrants (Belize, the Cook Islands, and Panama); and the expectations of other members not to decrease their participation percentage. These issues were closely related. For 2017–2022, Chile had 64.4% of the allocation. In practice, it caught nearly 80% by acquiring fishing rights (through quota transfers) from members whose participation in the fishery did not allow them to undertake actual commercial activities. Conversely, some members, like Russia, remained relatively active at sea and generally did not transfer their quota.[49]

The SPRFMO Commission adopted Conservation and Management Measure 01–2023 by a voting majority, which sanctioned a 10-year allocation scheme.[50] Chile's share increased to 66.36%. The three new entrants obtained a modest sum (0.10%, amounting to 1,100 tonnes). Russia experienced a slight decrease in its allocated percentage over the total allowable catch compared to the 2017–2022 period: from 3.28% to 3.02%. Russia was not the only member disappointed with the outcome: China and Peru also voted against the final decision.

On 10 April 2023, Russia objected to its share in the total allowable catch.[51] Russia challenged CMM 1–2023 on two grounds: inconsistency with the SPRFMO Convention and unjustifiable discrimination. On the first ground of inconsistency, Russia argued that the Commission had not observed the allocation criteria set in Article 21 of the SPRFMO Convention. CMM 1–2023 was 'based only on the transfers of quotas' that some Commission members had made in previous years, without this being a 'valid criteria for the allocation of quotas' or changing participation

48 ibid, para 128.

49 In the six years since the adoption of SPRFMO, CMM 01–2017, 'Conservation and Management Measure for *Trachurus murphyi*' (2017). https://pcacases.com/web/sendAttach/2374 accessed 4 December 2023, Russia had caught 1.3% of the total catches.

50 SPRFMO, CMM 01–2023, 'Conservation and Management Measure for *Trachurus murphy*' (2023). www.sprfmo.int/assets/Fisheries/Conservation-and-Management-Measures/2023-CMMs/CMM-01-2023-Trachurus-murphyi_29Mar23.pdf accessed 4 December 2023.

51 Ten days after Russia, China – having voted against the adopted CMM 1–2023 – also objected to the determination of its share in the total allowable catch of jack mackerel in 2023. However, China withdrew its objection by letter dated 2 June 2023.

percentages.[52] On the second ground of discrimination, Russia focused on the reduction of the allocated quota of affected countries which had been actively fishing since 2017. Any increased allocations for Chile and others should have come from the existing shares of those members who had transferred their quotas because they did not fish.[53] Russia also offered an alternative measure, asking the Review Panel to increase the percentage of its jack mackerel quota to 3.28% related to the total allowable catch, the same limits set for the 2017–2022 period.

The Review Panel issued its findings on 1 July 2023. The decision rejected Russia's arguments that CMM 01–2023 was inconsistent with the provisions of the SPRFMO Convention. In the Review Panel's view, the Commission had broad discretion in making allocation decisions as reflected in the words 'take into account' and 'to the extent relevant' in the *chapeau* of Article 21(1). Thus, there was no need for these allocation decisions 'to be based on all of the listed allocation criteria.'[54] Russia's reference to quota transfers as an argument to allocate fishing rights was misplaced: the SPRFMO Convention rightly considered the zonal attachment of the stock, mostly in Chilean waters, which is 'included in the words 'status of the fishery resource' in the *chapeau* of Article 21(1) or, alternatively, in Article 21(1)(a).'[55]

Most critically, the Review Panel considered the objecting ground of unjustifiable discrimination. It drew a distinction similarly to the 2018 Review Panel decision between substantive and procedural discrimination.[56] On substantive discrimination, the Review Panel concluded that Russia had not proved this claim, as the same percentage reduction was applied to members with substantial active fisheries, including Russia, and others with catch entitlements under CMM 01–2023.[57] On procedural discrimination, Russia complained that Rule 4.5 of SPRFMO had not been observed. Rule 4.5 refers to deadlines to table proposals. This suggested that any change to the jack mackerel measure needed a formal proposal, which had not happened in this case. The Review Panel rejected this argument: it is standard practice that the SPRFMO (like many RFMOs) sometimes adopts a new measure by merely changing the relevant numbers in the previous year's decision.

52 Review Panel established under the Convention on the Conservation and Management of High Seas Fishery Resources in the South Pacific Ocean (Objection by the Russian Federation), Findings and Recommendations, PCA Case 2023–33, 1 July 2023, para 81.

53 ibid, paragraph 52.

54 ibid, paragraph 118.

55 ibid, paragraph 119.

56 Review Panel established under the Convention on the Conservation and Management of High Seas Fishery Resources in the South Pacific Ocean (Objection by the Republic of Ecuador), Findings and Recommendations, PCA Case 2018–13, 5 June 2018, paras 101, 106 and 107.

57 Review Panel established under the Convention on the Conservation and Management of High Seas Fishery Resources in the South Pacific Ocean (Objection by the Russian Federation), Findings and Recommendations, PCA Case 2023–33, 1 July 2023, para 126.

3.3.1. The Finding of Discrimination: Unpersuasive Numbers

However, the Review Panel examined other facts and circumstances in the negotiations which led to CMM 1–2023. These facts were not presented directly by Russia, but the Review Panel brought them to the forefront to conclude that the allocation decision in CMM 1–2023 did amount to unjustifiable discrimination. The Review Panel's core reasoning was that the SPRFMO Commission did not devote the time needed to a complex negotiation like allocating fishing rights and had rushed into a decision that could not reach a consensus: 'there was insufficient attention paid during the negotiations to ideas, factors, criteria, and proposals of interest to Russia and similarly situated Members'.[58] The Review Panel observed that, in contrast, the Commission decided to extend the allocation agreement for ten years, unlike the previous scheme 2017–2022 which covered half that time. The Review Panel concluded that 'the relatively short duration of the negotiations, especially when compared to the relatively long duration for which the allocation percentages will in principle remain unchanged' added to a 'hurried process culminating in the adoption of CMM 01–2023 by a divided vote'. This resulted in 'unjustifiable procedural discrimination with respect to Russia's allocation interests.'[59]

Whether the fact that the negotiations should have taken time – or hurried a decision on a sensitive matter – amounts to procedural discrimination is debatable. Equally, the outcome of the alternative measures is unpersuasive. The Review Panel rejected the numbers offered by Russia, sharing the findings of the 2018 decision that, to have an equivalent effect, the alternative measure 'should seek to avoid inconsistency not only with the total allowable catch but also with the allocations to other Members'.[60] In other words, the catch limit:

> should respect the [total allowable catch] specified therein and take into account the fact that other Members and their nationals have justified expectations based on the tonnage allocations set forth in that measure for 2023 and may have already acted in reliance on those expectations.[61]

In the Review Panel's view, the alternative catch limit Russia had proposed did not satisfy that standard because it posed 'too great a risk of inconsistency not only with the total allowable catch but also with the allocations to other Members.'[62]

This principle seems correct, but the numbers proposed do not match the Review Panel's argument. Russia's allocation under CMM 1–2023 was 32,649 tonnes (3.02%). Its proposed alternative measure, rejected by the Panel, was 35,452 (3.28%). Adopting a 15% rise compared to 2022 instead of the 20% demanded by Russia, the Panel concluded that, for 2023, the catch limit 'equivalent in effect' to

58 ibid, para 135.
59 ibid, para 135.
60 ibid, para 136.
61 ibid, para 137.
62 ibid, para 137.

CMM 01–2023 amounted to 33,974 tonnes (3,14%). The difference between what Russia requested – rejected as inconsistent to the objected measure – and what the Review Panel recommended as an equivalent effect measure was 1,478 tonnes. In a total allowable catch of roughly a million tonnes, this number seems too small to make a difference between what 'poses too great a risk of inconsistency' with the total allowable catch and the allocations to other members. The Review Panel had to give a number, but it seems that it first reached a conclusion (the number) and then attempted a justification.[63] Moreover, in justifying the 33,974 tonnes, the Review Panel asserted that 'the risk that this would result in fishing in excess of the [total allowable catch] . . . is not substantial' because, among other reasons, 'Russia is not required to use all of its allotted tonnage, and has not done so in a number of years'. How this risk would increase with a 1,478 tonnes difference is more than contentious.

3.3.2. The Review Panel's Subtle Questioning of the Majority Decision

That said, the Review Panel was correct in two fundamental aspects. Its findings and recommendations illustrate the potential of the objection mechanism to solve disputes between a member and the organisation beyond legal technicalities. In this case, the decision questioned the wisdom and political judgment of the SPRFMO's majority members.

The first aspect the Review Panel correctly highlighted was the lack of preparation and adequate time given to such a sensitive matter as negotiations to allocate fishing rights. The Review Panel rightly noted that it was 'not aware of any preparatory, intersessional consultations on allocation in advance of the 11th (2023) Annual Commission Meeting' and that five days 'is a relatively short period of time in comparison with allocation negotiations in many other RFMOs.'[64] Here, it is hard to disagree with the final paragraph of the Review Panel's opinion, which elegantly rebuked the SPRFMO Commission by suggesting that 'further strengthening of the deliberative and negotiating processes would contribute to the effectiveness of the CMMs adopted in meeting the objectives of the Convention.'[65]

The second aspect that the Panel got right was a substantive issue in the allocation scheme itself: the lack of judgment of the leading members in the 2023 decision. One critical aspect was the opposition of three key players in the jack mackerel fishery and the organisation more generally: Russia, China, and Peru. When three out of six of the key States in the jack mackerel fishery were unhappy with the proposal, it is perhaps surprising this was subject to voting. Of the historical players, only Chile, Korea, and the European Union seemed satisfied with the outcome. The Review Panel wisely observed that '[t]he remaining ten Members that were entitled to vote

63 The 15% increase was based primarily on the original Scientific Committee recommendation to raise the total allowable catch in the SPRFMO area.

64 Review Panel established under the Convention on the Conservation and Management of High Seas Fishery Resources in the South Pacific Ocean (Objection by the Russian Federation), Findings and Recommendations, PCA Case 2023–33, 1 July 2023, para 134.

65 ibid, para 144.

on the adoption of CMM 01–2023 during the 11th (2023) Annual Commission Meeting either had no catch entitlements' or transferred them to other Members 'instead of actually engaging in fisheries leading to significant catches themselves,' yet '[a]ll of them voted in favour of the adoption of CMM 01–2023.'[66]

In short, members who had not fished while the 5-year allocation scheme was in place and had sold their quota were treated similarly to those members maintaining fishing activities in the SPRFMO area. As the Review Panel hinted, the push for a ten-year allocation agreement under such conditions was undoubtedly ill-advised.

3.4. Assessment

This section offers two perspectives to assess the SPRFMO experience with objections. First, it evaluates whether the Review Panel's recommendations solved the short- and long-term issues associated with SPRFMO allocation disputes. Second, it examines how the Review Panel's decisions can help the SPRFMO in accommodating or reconsidering disputed allocation schemes.

3.4.1. The Panel's Role in Solving the Issue at Hand

The SPRFMO experience demonstrates the value of objection procedures. These mechanisms can be an effective tool to achieve pragmatic solutions to disagreements between a member of the organisation and the majority. The positive outcomes can be seen through the short and mid-term impacts of the SPRFMO Review Panel's decisions adopted in 2013 and 2018, even if the effects of the 2023 decision cannot yet be assessed.

The first and most pressing question is whether the panel's findings helped the Commission solve the issue that pushed Russia in 2013 and Ecuador to object in the first place. The answer to this short-term concern is undoubtedly affirmative. Russia benefitted from a Review Panel's decision which recognised it as a legitimate player with a fishing history to be acknowledged through corresponding allocation. The Review Panel's findings were questionable on the Russian catches provenance, yet the majority accepted the outcome. The decision had little practical impact in 2013, as Russian vessels did not operate that year. Still, SPRFMO allocated 13,445 tonnes of jack mackerel to Russia at its second Commission meeting in 2014.[67] Russia expressed disappointment since it regarded the allocation as insufficient but it did not object.[68]

66 ibid, para 131.

67 SPRFMO, CMM 2.01, 'Conservation and Management Measure for *Trachurus murphyi*' (2014). <www.sprfmo.int/assets/Meetings/Archived-Meetings/Meetings-2013-plus/Commission-Meetings/2nd-Commission-Meeting-2014-Manta-Ecuador/Annex-G-CMM-2.-01-Trachurus-Murphyi.pdf> accessed 4 December 2023.

68 SPRFMO, 'Statement of the Russian Federation Delegation, Report of the Second Meeting of the SPRFMO Commission' (Manta, Ecuador 27–31 January 2014), Annex J. www.sprfmo.int/assets/

The short-term effects of the Review Panel's findings concerning Ecuador's objection were more apparent. The Commission's decision was upheld, and Ecuador accepted the result even though the Review Panel had rejected all its claims. Despite the Ecuadorian insistence, the five-year original allocation agreed upon in 2017 did not change.

Yet the recommendations given in 2018 offered another positive, mid-term effect. They were relevant beyond the procedure outcomes and influenced subsequent negotiations on the existing jack mackerel allocation. The Review Panel thoroughly understood the conflict at stake and the possible consequences for the organisation's long-term stability. While it rejected Ecuador's claims, it strongly recommended that the Commission accommodate Ecuador's legitimate aspirations even as the 5-year allocation agreement still had four years to expire. At the same time, the panel refrained from lecturing SPRFMO members on specific criteria to impact allocation decisions. It did not overstretch its role, respecting the right of SPRFMO members to decide for themselves through negotiations. In short, Ecuador did not obtain what it asked for, but the recommendations were nuanced and encouraging. SPRFMO members understood that they had to accommodate Ecuador, and the panel's findings influenced this progression. At the 2020 Commission meeting, Ecuador obtained a satisfactory allocation after two years of negotiations.[69]

Similarly, the Review Panel's recommendations in 2013 sent a straightforward message to SPRFMO members: picking up a single year to build up an allocation scheme, even if temporary, is probably not a good idea. Such recommendations in 2013 and 2018 were sensible in the mid-term, showing a 'flexibility to make suggestions for future conduct' and allowed for 'constructive outcomes beyond the confines of strict application of law to fact.'[70] SPRFMO members proved receptive to the outcomes of both cases.

One challenge to these positive aspects likely explains why objection procedures are rare in the RFMOs' practice. The objecting member (70%) and the SPRFMO Commission (30%) must bear the Review Panel's expenses.[71] According to SPRFMO documents, the organisation spent NZ$ 71,008 in 2018 (approximately 44,144 USD) to contribute to the costs related to Ecuador's objection.[72]

Meetings/Archived-Meetings/Meetings-2013-plus/Commission-Meetings/2nd-Commission-Meeting-2014-Manta-Ecuador/Annex-J-Statement-by-the-Russian-Federation.pdf.

69 SPRFMO, '8th Annual Meeting of the Commission Meeting Report' (Port Vila, Vanuatu, 14–8 February 2020) 7–12; SPRFMO, CMM 01–2020, 'Conservation and Management Measure for *Trachurus murphyi*' (2020). www.sprfmo.int/assets/Fisheries/Conservation-and-Management-Measures/2020-CMMs/CMM-01-2020-Trachurus-murphyi-31Mar20.pdf accessed 4 December 2023, Table 2.

70 Judith Levine and Camilla Pondel, 'There Are Not Plenty of Fish in the Sea: PCA Case No 2018–13 on Ecuador's Objection to a Decision of the Commission of the South Pacific Regional Fisheries Management Organisation' (2018) 24 *Australian International Law Journal* 221, 228.

71 SPRFMO Convention, Annex II, para 7.

72 SPRFMO, '6th Finance and Administration Committee Meeting Report' (The Hague, The Netherlands, 23–7 January 2019) 2 www.sprfmo.int/assets/Meetings/04-FAC/FAC-6/FAC6-Meeting-Report-rev2-edited-ADOPTED-FORMATED-v2.pdf.

Such costs may not seem excessive to bring a case before a formal dispute settlement setting, especially under the auspices of a respected institution like the Permanent Court of Arbitration. However, it is still a considerable burden for an organisation whose adopted budget is one of the smallest of all RFMOs, which for the financial year 2017–2018 was NZ$ 1,164,000 (approximately 723,618 USD).[73] Any RFMO member would likely consider this cost-related issue before moving ahead with an objection.

3.4.2. What Happens After the Russian Objection (2023) and the Review Panel's Findings?

After the 2023 Review Panel's findings, the SPRFMO probably has two options. Considering these findings only apply for the 2023 season, the first possibility is to hold to the current allocation scheme against a minority of members – Russia, China, and Peru – and force the adoption of each year's jack mackerel allocation by voting. Such a step would solve the issue for the majority: Russia and the other members would need to consider resorting to the objection procedure every year. This scenario entails two sets of costs for the organisation: financial and political. Bearing 30% of the Review Panel's expenses from its annual small budget would undoubtedly impact the SPRFMO's management and projection. More significantly, such a situation would carry long-term implications and likely deteriorate the much-needed collective trust necessary for meaningful fisheries management.

Moreover, it would be naïve to pretend the two issues are unrelated. Under the SPRMFO Convention, the annual budget is the only matter that members must always agree on by consensus.[74] Long-term dissatisfaction with the allocation scheme could quickly create resentment, and holding back the budget would be one way to pressure the majority. No one would benefit from this.

The second option, which would benefit the SPRFMO in the long term, is to move ahead based on the Review Panel's findings. As noted, the 2023 decision got a crucial point right: fishing nations operating in the fishery should not be treated in the same manner as those members which have benefitted for half a decade from merely trading quotas. Equally, the three pivotal members which are part of the majority should consider that any future conservation and management measures initiatives will require primarily fishing nations to move forward.

4. Conclusions

Objection procedures are distinct from traditional dispute settlement mechanisms. They represent an opportunity to balance the RFMOs' collective goals and the sovereign rights of their members. Modern RFMO treaties, including the WCPFC

73 ibid, 3.
74 SPRFMO Convention, art 8(n).

and NAFO, contemplate objection procedures which present similarities and differences. Still, the SPRFMO mechanism offers comparative advantages and is the only RFMO whose system has been tested in practice.

The SPRFMO experience has demonstrated the value of the objection procedure. The objection procedure is an effective tool to achieve practical solutions to overcome sharp disagreements between most RFMO participants and one member. These positive outcomes can be seen through the short-term and mid-term impacts of the SPRFMO panels' decisions adopted in 2013 and 2018. The Review Panel's findings helped the SPRFMO Commission solve the issues that had led Russia and Ecuador to oppose the original decisions. In the case of Ecuador, the decision served as a helpful instrument to guide subsequent negotiations which accommodated Ecuador's aspiration for the jack mackerel fishery in 2020. At the time of writing, the impacts of the Review Panel's findings in 2023 remain to be seen. However, the SPRFMO Commission should rethink or at least adjust the allocation scheme it adopted in 2023.

Those RFMOs that consider other objection mechanisms, such as in the WCPFC and NAFO, may reflect on the SPRFMO experience and its advantages for future disputes. It will be challenging for those RFMOs whose founding treaties do not include these mechanisms to adopt them. As experience has proven, the future application of objection procedures is likely to be limited to a handful of RFMOs and disputes.

Part IV

Combating Illegal, Unreported and Unregulated (IUU) Fishing

8 IUU Fishing Vessel Listing Cooperation and Current RFMO Practices

Eva R. van der Marel and Mercedes Rosello

1. Introduction

Regional fisheries management organisations or arrangements (RFMOs) play an increasingly important role in international fisheries governance.[1] Their number has multiplied over the years. They have adopted an increasing number and wider range of conservation and management measures (CMMs). RFMOs are also increasingly interconnected, cooperating both bilaterally and through international fora, such as the Food and Agricultural Organization of the United Nations (FAO) and the Kobe Process of Cooperation between tuna RFMOs.[2] Memoranda of Understanding (MOUs) determine and to an extent formalise these cooperative relations at the bilateral level. MOUs define the areas of cooperation across the relevant RFMOs; contribute to the visibility of their efforts; and generate goodwill in respect of data exchange and mutual observation of institutional processes.

1 Regional fisheries management organisations or arrangements (RFMOs) differ from consultative or scientific fisheries bodies in that they are intergovernmental organisations with the competence to establish conservation and management measures. See the definition in Food and Agriculture Organization of the United Nations (FAO) International Plan of Action to Prevent, Deter and Eliminate Illegal Unreported and Unregulated Fishing, 2001, para 2(6)(c) although non-binding, and FOA Agreement on Port State Measures to Prevent, Deter and Eliminate Illegal, Unreported and Unregulated Fishing, 22 November 2019, entered into force 5 June 2016, art 1(i). This chapter does not distinguish between organisations and arrangements, although an arrangement is defined in Agreement for the Implementation of the Provisions of the United Nations Convention on the Law of the Sea of 10 December 1982 relating to the Conservation and Management of Straddling Fish Stocks and Highly Migratory Fish Stocks (Fish Stocks Agreement), 4 August 1995, 2167 UNTS 3, entered into force 11 December 2001, art 1(1)(d), as

> a cooperative mechanism established in accordance with [UNCLOS] and this Agreement by two or more States for the purpose, inter alia, of establishing conservation and management measures in a subregion or region for one or more straddling fish stocks or highly migratory fish stocks.

2 See, for example, James Harrison, 'Key Regional Fisheries Governance Challenges' in Erik Molenaar and Richard Caddell (eds), *Strengthening International Fisheries Law in an Era of Changing Oceans* (Hart 2019) 97–9.

DOI: 10.4324/9781003492030-12

One area of cooperation for many RFMOs is that of combatting illegal, unreported, and unregulated (IUU) fishing.[3] A growing number of RFMOs can adopt so-called 'IUU vessel lists', which identify vessels that have engaged in fishing-related practices against the rules of that RFMO.[4] Such lists allow member States of the specific RFMO (and other States) to adopt targeted measures vis-à-vis those identified vessels or to pressure their flag State. For instance, according to the FAO Agreement on Port State Measures to Prevent, Deter and Eliminate Illegal, Unreported and Unregulated Fishing (Port States Measures Agreement), inclusion on an RFMO's IUU vessel list 'in accordance with the rules and procedures of [the RFMO] and in conformity with international law' provides sufficient proof that a vessel has engaged in IUU fishing.[5] The parties to the Port States Measures Agreement must then deny such vessels entry to port, or allow entry for inspection and taking further actions.[6]

An RFMO's IUU vessel lists may impact on the area of competence of another RFMO, either through automatic cross-listing between RFMOs or through partial recognition of each other's lists.[7] For example, the North East Atlantic Fisheries Commission's (NEAFC) Scheme of Control and Enforcement provides that vessels listed by other RFMOs will be placed 'without delay' on the NEAFC's

3 See, FAO International Plan of Action to Prevent, Deter and Eliminate Illegal Unreported and Unregulated Fishing, 2001, para 3. For a commentary on the concept IUU fishing and the implications of its definition, see for example, Andrew Serdy, '*Pacta Tertiis* and Regional Fisheries Management Mechanisms: The IUU Fishing Concept as an Illegitimate Short-Cut to a Legitimate Goal' (2017) 48 *Ocean Development and International Law* 345; Arron Honniball, 'Unilateral Trade Measures and the Importance of Defining IUU Fishing: Lessons from the 2019 USA "Concerns" with China as a Fishing Flag State' (2020) 7 *Journal of Territorial and Maritime Studies* 7; Mercedes Rosello, *IUU Fishing as a Flag State Accountability Paradigm: Between Effectiveness and Legitimacy* (Brill Nijhoff 2021) 9–28; Eva R. van der Marel, 'Problems and Progress in Combating IUU Fishing' in Erik Molenaar and Richard Caddell (eds), *Strengthening International Fisheries Law in an Era of Changing Oceans* (Hart 2019) 297.

4 RFMOs that currently operate IUU vessel negative lists are the Commission for the Conservation of Antarctic Marine Living Resources (CCAMLR), the Commission for the Conservation of Southern Bluefin Tuna (CCSBT), the Inter-American Tropical Tuna Commission (IATTC), the International Commission for the Conservation of Atlantic Tunas (ICCAT), the Indian Ocean Tuna Commission (IOTC), the General Fisheries Commission for the Mediterranean (GFCM), the Northwest Atlantic Fisheries Organization (NAFO), the North Pacific Fisheries Commission (NPFC), the South East Atlantic Fisheries Organisation (SEAFO), Southern Indian Ocean Fisheries Agreement (SIOFA), the South Pacific Regional Fisheries Management Organisation (SPRFMO), the Western and Central Pacific Fisheries Commission (WCPFC), and the North East Atlantic Fisheries Commission (NEAFC).

5 FOA Agreement on Port State Measures to Prevent, Deter and Eliminate Illegal, Unreported and Unregulated Fishing, 22 November 2019, entered into force 5 June 2016.

6 ibid, art 9(4)–(5).

7 See, for example, Zoe Scanlon, 'Safeguarding the Legitimacy of Illegal, Unreported and Unregulated Fishing Vessel Listings' (2019) 68 *International and Comparative Law Quarterly* 369; Eva R. van der Marel, 'Problems and Progress in Combating IUU Fishing' in Erik Molenaar and Richard Caddell (eds), *Strengthening International Fisheries Law in an Era of Changing Oceans* (Hart 2019) 302.

provisional list of IUU fishing vessels.[8] Similarly, the IUU vessel list of the Commission for the Conservation of Southern Bluefin Tuna (CCSBT) comprises not only vessels identified as having engaged in IUU fishing by CCSBT parties, but also vessels listed by other RFMOs.[9] Although RFMOs are increasingly interconnected in their fight against IUU fishing, '[c]oordination between RFMOs on mutual recognition of IUU vessel lists . . . remains unsystematic' as '[p]rotocols for sharing IUU vessel lists currently in place are not standardized and practices vary'.[10] Better inter-RFMO cooperation and coordination is therefore important, both for combating IUU fishing and generally for better RFMO effectiveness.

This chapter examines the nature and scope of inter-RFMO cooperation over IUU fishing. It first explores whether RFMOs are under a general duty to cooperate over IUU fishing and, if so, examines the legal basis for this duty. It then maps out how RFMOs have, in practice, formalised their cooperation over IUU fishing, including through MOUs, and by sharing and cross-listing on each other's IUU vessel lists. Finally, it provides some conclusory remarks.

2. A General Duty to Cooperate over IUU Fishing: Minimum Requirements?

A duty for RFMOs to cooperate over alleged IUU fishing is not explicitly spelt out in the United Nations Convention on the Law of the Sea (UNCLOS),[11] the Agreement for the Implementation of the Provisions of UNCLOS relating to the Conservation and Management of Straddling Fish Stocks and Highly Migratory Fish Stocks (Fish Stocks Agreement),[12] the FOA Agreement to Promote Compliance with International Conservation and Management Measures by Fishing Vessels on the High Seas (FOA Compliance Agreement),[13] and the FOA Agreement on Port State Measures to Prevent, Deter and Eliminate Illegal, Unreported and Unregulated Fishing (Port States Measures Agreement). These are the principal

8 NEAFC, 'Scheme of Control and Enforcement'. www.neafc.org/scheme/contents accessed 21 December 2023, art 44.

9 At present, the CCSBT's IUU list is not comprehensive, but contains only vessels cross-listed from the IATTC, ICCAT, IOTC, WCPFC, CCAMLR, and SEAFO, and SIOFA. The SPRFMO is mentioned for cross-listing. However, the latest (2021) SPRFMO IUU list does not contain any vessels. CCSBT, 'IUU Vessel List' (14 December 2023). www.ccsbt.org/sites/default/files/userfiles/file/docs_english/CCSBT%20IUU%20List.pdf accessed 21 December 2023.

10 Barbara Hutniczak, 'Coordination Between RFMOs on Mutual Recognition of IUU Vessel Lists' (2019) 107 *Marine Policy* 3.

11 United Nations Convention on the Law of the Sea (UNCLOS), 10 December 1982, 1833 UNTS 3, entered into force 16 November 1994.

12 Fish Stocks Agreement.

13 Agreement to Promote Compliance with International Conservation and Management Measures by Fishing Vessels on the High Seas, 24 November 1993, UNTS 2221, entered into force 24 April 2003.

instruments which together set out the international legal framework for preventing, deterring, and eliminating IUU fishing.

However, these instruments do spell out the responsibilities of States in different capacities – as flag State, coastal State, and port State – in relation to fishing-related activities amounting to IUU fishing, including through cooperation. The coastal State must regulate and enforce fishing activities in its exclusive economic zone (EEZ).[14] The flag State must regulate and enforce the activities of vessels flying its flag.[15] The flag and port State must promote the effectiveness of RFMO measures.[16] More generally, all States must cooperate with one another in the sustainable exploitation of transboundary fish stocks,[17] and in relation to enforcement, including the enforcement of CMMs of RFMOs.[18] All States are also under a general duty to, in all maritime zones, protect and preserve the marine environment and its living resources, which can be undermined by IUU fishing activities.[19] In its *Request for an Advisory Opinion Submitted by the Sub-Regional Fisheries Commission (SRFC Advisory Opinion)*, the International Tribunal for the Law of the Sea (ITLOS) stressed that this general duty cannot be discharged in isolation. ITLOS quoted from the *MOX Plant* case that 'the duty to cooperate is a fundamental principle in the prevention of pollution of the marine environment under [UNCLOS] and general international

14 UNCLOS, arts 61, 62, 73. Coastal State enforcement under UNCLOS, art 73, is phrased as a right rather than a duty. However, the International Tribunal for the Law of the Sea (ITLOS) opined in the *Request for an Advisory Opinion submitted by the Sub-Regional Fisheries Commission,* Advisory Opinion, ITLOS Rep 2015, para 104, that 'To meet its responsibilities, in accordance with [art 62(4) of UNCLOS], the coastal State *is required to adopt* the necessary laws and regulations, *including* enforcement procedures, which must be consistent with the [UNCLOS]' (emphasis added) and, para 106 concluding that

> in light of the special rights and responsibilities given to the coastal State in the exclusive economic zone under the [UNCLOS], the primary responsibility for taking the necessary measures to prevent, deter and eliminate IUU fishing rests with the coastal State.

15 UNCLOS, arts 58(3), 94, 119.

16 Fish Stocks Agreement, arts 18 and 23(1); Agreement to Promote Compliance with International Conservation and Management Measures by Fishing Vessels on the High Seas, 24 November 1993, UNTS 2221, entered into force 24 April 2003, art III(1)(a).

17 See, inter alia, UNCLOS, arts 63–67, 118; Fish Stocks Agreement, art 8.

18 Fish Stocks Agreement, arts 20 and 21.

19 The duty to protect and preserve the marine environment is codified and elaborated on in Part XII of UNCLOS at art 192. Although most of Part XII of UNCLOS deals specifically with pollution, several cases have confirmed that the conservation of the living resources of the sea is an integral element of the duty to protect and preserve the marine environment. See ITLOS, *Southern Bluefin Tuna (New Zealand v. Japan; Australia v. Japan)*, Provisional Measures, Order of 27 August 1999, ITLOS Rep 1999, para 70; *Request for an Advisory Opinion Submitted by the Sub-Regional Fisheries Commission,* Advisory Opinion, ITLOS Rep 2015, paras 120, 216; *Chagos Marine Protected Area Arbitration (Mauritius v. United Kingdom)*, Award, PCA Case 2011–03, 18 March 2015, paras 320, 538; *South China Sea Arbitration (The Republic of the Philippines v. The People's Republic of China)*, Award, PCA Case 2013–19, 12 July 2016, paras 945, 956.

law'.[20] It added that this obligation extends to cases of alleged IUU fishing activities.[21]

What the duty to cooperate requires of States varies depending on context. Sometimes, the law requires only notification, without specifying how States should act on this information. For example, the coastal State must notify the flag State of enforcement measures over illegal fishing in its EEZ, which opens the door to subsequent flag State action.[22] Sometimes, there is a clearer duty to act on certain information. For example, the flag State must investigate any report by another State of its alleged failure to exercise flag State jurisdiction.[23] This informed ITLOS' finding in the *SRFC Advisory Opinion* about the fundamental nature of cooperation. It led ITLOS to conclude that the flag State should also inform the reporting State of any action taken.[24] Elsewhere, the law explicitly requires mutual engagement, for example, to cooperate and exchange information to promote the effective implementation of the Port States Measures Agreement, including the measures adopted by RFMOs in relation to the Port States Measures Agreement's objectives.[25]

That cooperation entails something different depending on the circumstances also follows from the *SRFC Advisory Opinion.* ITLOS held that:

> The obligation to 'seek to agree…' under [Article 63(1) of UNCLOS] and the obligation to cooperate under [Article 64(1) of UNCLOS] are 'due diligence' obligations which require the States concerned to consult with one another in good faith, pursuant to [Article 300 of UNCLOS]. The consultations should be meaningful in the sense that substantial effort should be made by all States concerned.[26]

The Tribunal's conclusion relates specifically to cooperation over the sustainable management of transboundary fish stocks. Nevertheless, the same observation can be made about cooperation over alleged IUU fishing. To the extent that a general duty on States to cooperate over alleged IUU fishing exists, this is an obligation of conduct rather than result. The standard of responsibility is one of due diligence. In turn, this standard of due diligence is likely high. In the context of

20 *Request for an Advisory Opinion Submitted by the Sub-Regional Fisheries Commission,* Advisory Opinion, ITLOS Rep 2015, para 140; *The Mox Plant Case (Ireland v. United Kingdom)*, Provisional Measures, Order of 3 December 2001, ITLOS Rep 2001, para 82.

21 *Request for an Advisory Opinion Submitted by the Sub-Regional Fisheries Commission,* Advisory Opinion, ITLOS Rep 2015, para 140.

22 UNCLOS, art 73(4).

23 UNCLOS, art 94(6).

24 *Request for an Advisory Opinion Submitted by the Sub-Regional Fisheries Commission,* Advisory Opinion, ITLOS Rep 2015, para 139.

25 FOA Agreement on Port State Measures to Prevent, Deter and Eliminate Illegal, Unreported and Unregulated Fishing, 22 November 2019, entered into force 5 June 2016, arts 6 and 20(5).

26 *Request for an Advisory Opinion Submitted by the Sub-Regional Fisheries Commission,* Advisory Opinion, ITLOS Rep 2015, para 210.

environmental law and the law of the sea, due diligence has been described as 'an obligation which entails not only the adoption of appropriate rules and measures, but also a certain level of vigilance in their enforcement' and entails deploying 'adequate means, to exercise best possible efforts, to do the utmost'.[27]

This chapter raises the question of whether the various obligations to report, investigate, and engage over IUU fishing apply to States only or also to the RFMOs themselves. RFMOs are International Organisations (IOs) with legal personalities. Most constituent RFMO agreements explicitly recognise that the body they create shall have legal personality and enjoy, in its relations with other IOs and in the territories of the parties, such legal capacity as may be necessary to perform its functions and achieve its ends.[28] As described by the International Court of Justice in the *Advisory Opinion on the Interpretation of the Agreement of 25 March 1951 between the WHO and Egypt*, IOs 'are subjects of international law, and, as such, are bound by any obligations incumbent upon them under general rules of international law, under their constitutions or under international agreements to which they are parties'.[29] Scholarly views diverge over the theory of obligation which applies to Ios.[30] Kristina Daugirdas, among others, has convincingly argued that international law applies to IOs in the same manner that it applies to States.[31] As a

27 ITLOS, *Responsibilities and Obligations of States Sponsoring Persons and Entities with Respect to Activities in the Area*, Advisory Opinion, ITLOS Rep 2011, para 110; *Request for an Advisory Opinion Submitted by the Sub-Regional Fisheries Commission,* Advisory Opinion, ITLOS Rep 2015, paras 129 and 131, confirming *Pulp Mills on the River Uruguay (Argentina v. Uruguay)*, Judgment, ICJ Rep 2010, para 197.

28 For example, the constituent agreements of the Convention for the Conservation of Southern Bluefin Tuna (CCSBT Convention), 20 May 1994, 1819 UNTS, entered into force 10 May 1993, art 6(9); Convention on the Conservation and Management of Highly Migratory Fish Stocks in the Western and Central Pacific Ocean (WCPFC Convention), 5 September 2000, 2275 UNTS 43, entered in force 19 June 2004, art 9(6); Convention on the conservation of Antarctic marine living resources, 7 April 1982, 1329 UNTS 47, entered into force 7 April 1982, art 8; Convention on the Conservation and Management of High Seas Fishery Resources in the South Pacific Ocean (SPRFMO Convention), 14 November 2009, entered into force 24 August 2012, art 6(3); Convention on Cooperation in the Northwest Atlantic Fisheries (NAFO Convention), 24 October 1978, 1135 UNTS 369, entered into force 1 January 1979, art 5(3); Convention on Future Multilateral Cooperation in the North-East Atlantic Fisheries (NEAFC Convention), London, 18 November 1980, 1285 UNTS 129, entered into force 17 March 1982, art 3(2); Convention on the conservation and management of fishery resources in the South East Atlantic Ocean (SEAFO Convention), 20 April 2001, 2221 UNTS 189, entered into force 13 April 2003. Note that not all RFMOs have explicit provisions to this effect, such as the International Convention for the Conservation of Atlantic Tunas (ICCAT Convention), 15 May 1966, 673 UNTS 63, entered into force 21 March 1969, or the Agreement for the Establishment of the Indian Ocean Tuna Commission (IOTC Agreement), 25 November 1993, 1927 UNTS, entered into force 27 March 1996.

29 *Interpretation of the Agreement of 25 March 1951 between the WHO and Egypt*, Advisory Opinion, ICJ Rep 1980, para 37.

30 For an overview and discussion see Kristina Daugirdas, 'How and Why International Law Binds International Organizations' (2016) 57 *Harvard International Law Journal* 325, 331ff.

31 ibid, 328. However, note scholarly discussions around whether treaties can bind IOs without their consent, see ibid 335, referring to an earlier edition of Henry Schermers and Niels Blokker, *International Institutional Law* (Brill 2011), para 1574, which highlights that IOs are only exceptionally

result, the only obligations binding IOs are those which have been consented to, by virtue of a treaty or because they are part of customary international law or general principles of law.

The obligations to report, investigate, and engage over IUU fishing are found in treaties which are not open to participation by RFMOs. Therefore, these obligations do not bind RFMOs directly. The Fish Stocks Agreement and Port States Measures Agreement do articulate the duty to cooperate and to combat IUU fishing *around* RFMOs, and these treaties bind the States which have ratified them.[32] As a result, these States should not circumvent their own obligations when acting through an IO, including an RFMO of which they are a member.[33] This points to a duty on RFMOs to take all necessary measures to prevent IUU fishing and to ensure compliance with applicable law, including through reporting and investigating allegations of IUU fishing, and, if necessary, by blacklisting vessels, depending on their member States' own obligations.[34]

In addition to any obligations over IUU fishing resulting from the commitments of their members, and absent direct treaty obligations, customary international law binds IOs – and therefore RFMOs. The actual scope of this remains uncertain.[35] If IOs are primarily bound by the rules to which they contribute, the extent to which IOs are bound by custom relates to whether and when the practice of IOs contributes to the formation of custom.[36] To contribute to custom, IOs must act on the

---

allowed as treaty parties and that '[i]n considering the question of whether an international organization is subject to the rules of treaty law, one cannot start from the hypothesis that this is not the case unless the organization has expressly bound itself'. Conversely, Vienna Convention on the Law of Treaties between States and International Organizations or between International Organizations, 21 March 1986, UN Doc A/CONF.129/15, art 34, stipulates that '[a] treaty does not create either obligations or rights for a third State or a third organization without the consent of that State or that organization'.

32 See in particular the Fish Stocks Agreement, arts 8(3), 18(1), and 23(1); and the Port State Measures Agreement, arts 6, 9(4), 12(3).

33 See International Law Commission, 'Draft Articles on Responsibility of States for Internationally Wrongful Acts' (2001) II *Yearbook of the International Law Commission*, art 61 and the discussions on IOs as 'vehicles' for State action in Kristina Daugirdas, 'How and Why International Law Binds International Organizations' (2016) 57 *Harvard International Law Journal* 325, 342ff.

34 This however raises the issue that not all RFMO members are necessarily bound by the same treaty obligations. Neither are all non-RFMO member states whose vessels may be unduly targeted due to the exceptionally (and unhelpfully) broad description of what constitutes IUU fishing, see Andrew Serdy, 'Pacta Tertiis and Regional Fisheries Management Mechanisms: The IUU Fishing Concept as an Illegitimate Short-Cut to a Legitimate Goal' (2017) 48 *Ocean Development and International Law* 345.

35 Michael Wood, 'International Organizations and Customary International Law' (2015) 48 *Vanderbilt Journal of International Law* 609, 619, referring to similar conclusions by Jose Alvarez, *International Organizations as Law-Makers* (OUP 2006) 138 and Dapo Akande, 'International Organizations' in Malcolm Evans (ed), *International Law* (OUP 2014) 282.

36 This the reverse of the argument by Michael Wood, 'International Organizations and Customary International Law' (2015) 48 *Vanderbilt Journal of International Law* 609, 618 that '[i]t is generally assumed, and I think that this is right, that they may contribute primarily to those rules of international law by which they themselves are (or would be) bound'.

basis of *opinio juris*, the belief that something is required by law. In other words, IOs must believe that they are bound by it. The International Law Commission in its 2018 Draft conclusions on the identification of custom stated that, in certain cases, the practice of IOs does contribute to the formation, or expression, of rules of customary law.[37] As to when this may be the case, the commentary notes that such practice arises most clearly where member States have transferred exclusive competences to the IO in question.[38] It may also arise where member States have 'conferred competences upon the [IO] that are functionally equivalent to powers exercised by States', such as treaty-making or deploying forces.[39]

It follows that where RFMOs exercise powers which are functionally equivalent to the powers of States, such practice may help form custom.[40] Such custom, thereby, would bind RFMOs.[41] Arguably, the power to adopt binding CMMs to cooperate with other RFMOs over alleged IUU fishing is one such power. The exercise of this power could thereby, contribute to the recognised customary law, duty to cooperate in the protection and preservation of the marine environment and its living resources.[42] As seen previously, this duty has been held to extend to cooperation over alleged IUU fishing.[43] In turn, this bolsters our argument that the general duty to cooperate over alleged IUU fishing also applies to RFMOs.[44]

If the duty to cooperate over alleged IUU fishing applies both to RFMOs and their members, this has implications for responsibility in case of wrongful conduct. This chapter does not examine this further, although we would encourage further reflection on this elsewhere. Instead, the chapter asks what a customary law duty to cooperate over alleged IUU fishing would require of RFMOs if such duty can be established. While the standard of conduct is one of due diligence and therefore circumstantial, as discussed previously, what minimum requirements can be identified to inform this duty?

37 International Law Commission, 'Draft Conclusions on Identification of Customary International Law, with Commentaries' (2018) A/73/10 122, 131, Conclusion 4, para 2.

38 ibid, 131, para 6. In such cases, the practice of the IO may be equated with State practice, as in the case of the European Union.

39 ibid, 131, para 6.

40 The International Law Commission, however, asks for caution in assessing the weight of such practice as part of general practice, ibid, 131, para 7.

41 This is notwithstanding the unresolved question of whether they are also bound by customary law obligations to which they do not themselves contribute.

42 On the customary law status of the duty to protect and preserve the marine environment, see Detlef Czybulka 'Article 192' in Alexander Proelss (ed), *United Nations Convention on the Law of the Sea: A Commentary* (Beck, Nomos and Hart 2017) 1277, 1285. On the customary law nature of the duty to cooperate in this context, see the reference to 'general international law' in the *The Mox Plant Case (Ireland v. United Kingdom)*, Provisional Measures, Order of 3 December 2001, ITLOS Rep 2001.

43 *Request for an Advisory Opinion Submitted by the Sub-Regional Fisheries Commission*, Advisory Opinion, ITLOS Rep 2015, para 140.

44 This is notwithstanding the practical difficulty in demonstrating whether the requirements of practice and, in particular, *opinio juris* are fulfilled when considering the practice of RFMOs, something which this chapter does not attempt to do.

The first minimum requirement is to exchange IUU vessel lists and other information relevant to alleged IUU fishing. This duty appears to exist for parties to the Port States Measures Agreement. The Port States Measures Agreement requires parties to exchange data, including specifically information about relevant RFMO measures, to promote the effective implementation of the Agreement.[45] IUU fishing vessel lists by RFMOs are an integral part of the functioning of the Port States Measures Agreement by enabling port State parties to discharge their obligations. Thus, the Port States Measures Agreement implies at minimum the duty on parties to exchange information about alleged IUU fishing, including by exchanging RFMO IUU vessel lists with other RFMOs, and more widely. However, the Port States Measures Agreement cannot be ratified by RFMOs and therefore does not bind them directly. An investigation into the customary law status of its provisions falls outside the scope of its chapter.

Conversely, many provisions in UNCLOS are understood to reflect customary law. However, UNCLOS does not include a clear requirement to exchange information relevant to alleged IUU fishing cases. Where there are 'clear grounds to believe that proper jurisdiction and control with respect to a ship have not been exercised' (e.g., where some form of IUU fishing is suspected, and the flag State has not acted in response), States do not have a *duty* to report the facts to the flag State. Instead, Article 94(6) of UNCLOS provides that they *may* do so. Drawing a parallel to RFMOs, where an RFMO has clear grounds to believe that a vessel has engaged in IUU fishing and places that vessel on an IUU vessel list, it is uncertain whether the RFMO must legally notify the flag State of this. While in practice, RFMOs do, the existence of this duty is debatable, let alone whether there exists a duty to notify anyone else. Nevertheless, the publication of an IUU fishing vessel list by an RFMO, whose membership includes State parties to the Port States Measures Agreement, may pre-empt the need to engage in individual notifications on behalf of those States. Public lists more efficiently publicise the risks posed by IUU fishing vessels to port States, which might otherwise unknowingly receive IUU fishing products from such vessels.

A second minimum requirement is to assist other RFMOs in identifying (i.e., listing) vessels as having engaged in IUU fishing, to promote compliance and allow for enforcement. This duty is encouraged by the Fish Stocks Agreement, albeit in relation to State parties. The Fish Stocks Agreement requires parties to 'assist each other in identifying vessels reported to have engaged in activities undermining the effectiveness of [RFMOs]'.[46] A duty to assist goes further than exchanging information about agreed-upon RFMO IUU vessel lists. It requires cooperation during the identification or listing process. Article 10 of the Fish Stocks Agreement supports the argument that this duty should be discharged not only within the RFMO itself, but also more broadly in relation to inter-RFMO cooperation over alleged

45 FOA Agreement on Port State Measures to Prevent, Deter and Eliminate Illegal, Unreported and Unregulated Fishing, 22 November 2019, entered into force 5 June 2016, art 6.

46 Fish Stocks Agreement, art 20(4).

IUU fishing. Article 10 lists the core functions of RFMOs and requires the establishment of 'appropriate cooperative mechanisms for effective monitoring, control, surveillance and enforcement'.[47] However, the Fish Stocks Agreement does not specify the degree to which assistance is to be given, nor the 'appropriate' type of cooperative mechanism and degree of inter-RFMO cooperation in the context of IUU fishing. Similar to the Port States Measures Agreement, the Fish Stocks Agreement does not bind RFMOs directly. It is not clear whether a duty to assist can be found under customary law.

In sum, the minimum due diligence which RFMOs should demonstrate when exercising a duty to cooperate over alleged IUU fishing is to, first, exchange information over alleged IUU fishing between RFMOs and, second, provide mutual assistance in identifying IUU fishing to promote compliance and allow for enforcement. The FOA International Plan of Action to Prevent, Deter and Eliminate Illegal Unreported and Unregulated Fishing (IPOA-IUU) bolsters this argument. The IPOA-IUU is a voluntary, non-binding instrument, which nevertheless reflects the shared understandings of the international community at large. The IPOA-IUU notably encourages States, acting through relevant RFMOs, to take action to strengthen and develop innovative ways to prevent, deter, and eliminate IUU fishing. Here, consideration should be given to the 'establishment of and cooperation in the exchange of information on vessels engaged in or supporting IUU fishing'.[48] Moreover,

> objectives of institutional and policy strengthening in relevant [RFMOs] in relation to IUU fishing should include enabling [RFMOs] to . . . regularize coordination with institutional mechanisms of other [RFMOs] as far as possible in relation to IUU fishing, in particular information, enforcement and trade aspects.[49]

However, it is unclear what form the exchange of information over alleged IUU fishing between RFMOs, or mutual assistance in identifying IUU fishing, should take. Therefore, the chapter turns next to the way in which the constituent agreements of RFMOs have shaped this duty for individual RFMOs and in which RFMOs have fleshed out this duty in practice.

47 See also Takei's suggestion that some of the RFMO functions listed under Fish Stocks Agreement, art 10, which are addressed to States (what States should agree on in fulfilling their obligation to cooperate through RFMOs) could be considered as reflecting the duties of RFMOs, themselves, under customary international law, Yoshinobu Takei, 'Fisheries' in André Nollkaemper and Ilias Plakokefalos (eds), *Practice of Shared Responsibility in International Law* (CUP 2017) 362.

48 FAO International Plan of Action to Prevent, Deter and Eliminate Illegal Unreported and Unregulated Fishing, 2001, para 80(4). See also, para 81(4) on making available records of vessels engaged in IUU fishing.

49 ibid, para 82(3).

3. RFMO Practice in Cooperating over IUU Fishing: A Short Survey

Many constituent agreements of RFMOs specifically call for cooperation with other international actors. This includes the FAO;[50] other international fisheries commissions which can contribute to the work of the RFMO and further its objectives;[51] and other relevant intergovernmental and non-governmental organisations.[52] Such cooperation may be needed or desirable, in particular, where bodies have overlapping geographical or substantive mandates.[53] References to cooperation vary in constituent agreements. Some acknowledging the need for cooperation.[54] Others establish a general duty to cooperate.[55] Some include more detailed language prescribing particular cooperative arrangements.[56]

On the form that cooperation with other RFMOs (and other organisations) should take, explicit competence is usually granted to the RFMO to enter into agreements with other organisations. This is phrased as a right rather than an obligation: RFMOs 'may enter into agreements', often also 'as appropriate'.[57] No further detail is provided on the nature of such agreements, whether they should be binding or non-binding (e.g., through MOUs).[58] This demonstrates that inter-RFMO

50 This is particularly relevant for RFMOs set up under art XIV of the FAO Constitution, such as the IOTC.

51 For example, ICCAT Convention, art 11(2).

52 For example, WCPFC Convention, art 22, naming in particular the CCAMLR, the CCSBT, the IOTC, the ICCAT, and the IATTC. See also Convention on the Conservation of Antarctic Marine Living Resources (CCAMLR Convention), 20 May 1980, 1329 UNTS 47, entered into force 7 April 1982, art 22, specifically referring to both IGOs and NGOs and where due to its specific nature cooperation is moreover foreseen with Antarctic Treaty parties.

53 Raphael Billé et al. 'Regional Oceans Governance: Making Regional Seas Programmes, Regional Fishery Bodies and Large Marine Ecosystem Mechanisms Work Better Together' in *Regional Seas Reports and Studies No 197* (UNEP 2016) noting also the need to cooperate and coordinate with specific global bodies such as the International Maritime Organization and the International Seabed Authority to safeguard the latter's primacy, p. 48.

54 ICCAT Convention, art XI(1), stating that Contracting Parties 'agree that there should be co-operation between the Commission and other international fisheries commissions and scientific organizations which might contribute to the work of the Commission').

55 CCSBT Convention, art 12, stating that the CCSBT 'shall collaborate with other international organizations which have related objectives'.

56 WCPFC Convention, art 22, stating that the WCPFC 'shall make suitable arrangements for consultation, cooperation, and collaboration with other relevant international organizations'. See further, SPRFMO Convention, art 31(3), stating that the SPRFMO 'shall seek to make suitable arrangements for consultation, cooperation and collaboration with such other organisations. *In particular* it shall seek to cooperate with other relevant organisations with the aim of reducing and eventually eliminating IUU fishing' (emphasis added).

57 For example, CCAMLR Convention, art 23; IOTC Agreement, art 15(1); ICCAT Convention, art 11(2); SEAFO Convention, art 18(3); NAFO Convention, art 17(b).

58 Even if this power to enter into agreements were not granted explicitly, IOs both have the powers their constituent agreements confer directly and 'those powers which, though not expressly provided . . . are conferred upon [them] by necessary implication as being essential to the performance of [their] duties', *Reparation for Injuries Suffered in the Service of the United Nations*, Advisory

cooperation is generally called for in most RFMO constituent agreements but generally does not constitute an obligation. Further, little is included on the scope of the obligation or the modalities for cooperation.

There is nevertheless a growing practice of cooperative efforts by RFMOs over IUU fishing. In implementing the cooperative provisions in their constituent agreements, several RFMOs have concluded MOUs with other RFMOs on matters relevant to their competences and the interests of their contracting parties. These MOUs differ significantly in content: most contain generic cooperation and information-sharing commitments and typically refer to exploring and fostering institutional arrangements for cooperation.[59] Just as the cooperative provisions in RFMO constituent agreements differ in object and scope, the MOUs similarly differ.

For example, the CCSBT and Western and Central Pacific Fisheries Commission (WCPFC) have concluded an MOU to implement the CCSBT's mandate to 'collaborate with other intergovernmental organizations that have related objectives'.[60] The WCPFC's mandate is to 'avoid the duplication of measures' for species regulated by both RFMOs.[61] The CCSBT – WCPFC MOU refers to the exchange of a yearly report on stock assessment and catch data; recognition of each other's conservation and management measures; and cooperation in 'investigations and studies of mutual interest'.

By contrast, the MOU concluded between the WCPFC and the South Pacific Regional Fisheries Management Organisation (SPRFMO) is broader in scope and more detailed.[62] It includes cooperation in enforcement and details exchange of data on vessels engaged in IUU fishing. The MOU relates to a provision in the WCPFC's constituent agreement which allows it to 'make suitable arrangements for consultation, cooperation and collaboration with other relevant intergovernmental organizations'.[63] The MOU also reflects the SPRFMO's mandate to 'cooperate, as appropriate, with other relevant organisations on matters of mutual interest and to seek to make suitable arrangements for consultation, cooperation and collaboration

Opinion, ICJ Rep 1949, 182, confirming the principle of law applied by the Permanent Court of International Justice in *International Labour Organization*, Advisory Opinion, PCIJ Rep, Series B, 13.

59 The MOUs this chapter analyses contain different commitments on the substance and granularity of the information to be shared and specific information-sharing procedures. For example, the MOUs concluded between, on one hand, CCSBT and, on the other, the ICCAT, IOTC, and CCAMLR, and the MOUs entered into between, on one hand, the CCAMLR and, on the other, the SEAFO, SIOFA, and SPRFMO refer to individual vessel data, whereas other MOUs are less specific.

60 CCSBT Convention, art 12.

61 WCPFC Convention, art 22(3).

62 'MOU between the SPRFMO and the WCPFC' (6 August 2020). www.sprfmo.int/assets/Cooperation-with-others/MoUs/WCPFC-SPRFMO-MOU-signed-by-Chairs.pdf accessed 21 December 2023.

63 WCPFC Convention, art 22(2).

with such other organisations.'[64] The SPRFMO's mandate also provides that the Commission 'shall seek to cooperate with other relevant organisations with the aim of reducing and eventually eliminating IUU fishing'.[65]

Beyond the cooperation areas established in MOUs, RFMOs have also developed specific cooperative practices in elaborating and publishing IUU fishing vessel lists and related cross-listing practices. List publication and cross-listing practices are not always linked to the existence of an MOU.

Table 8.1 sets out RFMOs which have engaged in cross-listing practices, namely by including vessels already listed by other RFMOs in their own IUU fishing lists. Such cross-listing is carried out on a periodical basis, subject to objections by contracting parties.[66] In addition, many RFMOs have set out links on their websites to other RFMO IUU vessel lists for informational purposes only. By so doing, RFMOs facilitate enquiry by third parties with an interest in the data from the lists, without cross-listing the content from those lists onto the RFMO's own IUU list.

Table 8.2 sets out six MOUs which specifically define each RFMO's commitments regarding cooperation on matters involving IUU vessel lists. Three of these MOUs are with the Commission for the Conservation of Antarctic Marine Living Resources (CCAMLR). Three MOUs are with the SPRFMO. These six MOUs set out varying thresholds for information sharing, for vessels suspected of or confirmed to have engaged in IUU fishing.

Next, the chapter summarises the main provisions of these MOUs in respect of cooperation over IUU fishing data cross-listing.

3.1. CCAMLR – CCSBT MOU (2023)

The MOU between the CCAMLR and the CCSBT, concluded in 2023, provides for the exchange of data on IUU fishing vessels.[67] Although the cross-listing of IUU fishing vessels is not explicitly addressed in the MOU, the CCSBT has developed rules to this effect. It operates an IUU vessel list which is updated annually.[68] Vessels are first placed on a Draft List, primarily based on information from CCSBT's members and cooperating non-members. Then, the CCSBT's Compliance Committee adopts a Provisional List. Alongside recommendations on deletions from the list, this forms the basis for the CCSBT's IUU vessel list following a unanimous

64 SPRFMO Convention, art 31.

65 SPRFMO Convention, art 31(3).

66 Barbara Hutniczak, 'Coordination between RFMOs on Mutual Recognition of IUU Vessel Lists' (2019) 107 *Marine Policy* 3.

67 'MOU between the CCSBT and the CCAMLR' (1 May 2023). www.ccamlr.org/en/system/files/CCSBT%202023.pdf accessed 3 January 2024, para 2(ii)(b).

68 CCSBT, 'Resolution on Establishing a List of Vessels Presumed to have Carried Out Illegal, Unreported and Unregulated Fishing Activities for Southern Bluefin Tuna (SBT)' (17 October 2019). faolex.fao.org/docs/pdf/mul166050.pdf accessed 21 December 2023.

Table 8.1 Cross-listing RFMOs

Cross-listing RFMOs	*CCAMLR*	*CCSBT*	*IATTC*	*ICCAT*	*IOTC*	*SEAFO*	*SIOFA*	*WCPFC*	*NEAFC*	*NAFO*	*GFCM*
CCSBT[1]	X[2]	-	X	X	X	X	X	X			
IOTC[3]	X			X	-	X	X	X			
SEAFO[4]	X[5]					-	X		X	X	
NEAFC [A][6]				X	X			-			
NEAFC [B]	X	X	X	X	X	X	X	X			X
GFCM[7]	X		X	X		X			X	X	

[1] CCSBT, 'Resolution on Establishing a List of Vessels Presumed to have Carried Out Illegal, Unreported and Unregulated Fishing Activities for Southern Bluefin Tuna' (17 October 2019). www.ccsbt.org/sites/default/files/userfiles/file/docs_english/operational_resolutions/Resolution_IUU%20Vessel_List.pdf accessed 21 December 2023, paras 26–32 establishes the procedure for cross-listing. It indicates that the Commission may work with the IATTC, ICCAT, IOTC, CCAMLR, WCPFC, SEAFO, SIOFA, and SPRFMO to obtain their IUU lists in a timely manner and may cross-list vessels from these RFMOs unless there are objections from its contracting parties.

[2] In the MOU between the CCSBT and the CCAMLR, the two RFMOs agree to maintain consultation and cooperation and exchange data in respect of IUU fishing vessels. However, the MOU does not explicitly mention IUU vessel cross-listing. 'MOU between the CCSBT and the CCAMLR' (1 May 2023). www.ccamlr.org/en/system/files/CCSBT%202023.pdf accessed 03 January 2024.

[3] IOTC, 'Resolution18/03 on Establishing a List of Vessels Presumed to have Carried Out Illegal, Unreported and Unregulated Fishing in the IOTC Area of Competence' (1 January 2018). faolex.fao.org/docs/pdf/mul180722.pdf accessed 21 December 2023, paras 31–38, which refer to the cross-listing of vessels from the IUU lists of the CCAMLR, CCSSBT, ICCAT, SEAFO, SIOFA, SPRFMO, and WCPFC. Current practice gaps respond to blank IUU lists from other organisations. See IOTC, 'Vessels'. iotc.org/vessels accessed 21 December 2023.

[4] SEAFO, 'System of Observation, Inspection, Compliance and Enforcement' (2019). faolex.fao.org/docs/pdf/mul163878.pdf accessed 21 December 2023, art 27(18)–(20).

[5] The SEAFO and CCAMLR agree in their MOU to cooperate in matters of mutual interest, and to exchange data in respect of IUU fishing vessels and IUU Vessel Lists. However, the MOU is not explicit about cross-listing. 'MOU between the SEAFO and the CCAMLR' (2 June 2017). www.ccamlr.org/en/system/files/SEAFO.pdf accessed 21 December 2023.

[6] NEAFC, 'Scheme of Control and Enforcement'. www.neafc.org/scheme/contents accessed 21 December 2023, art 44, which indicates that vessels in the IUU lists of shall be included in its 'A' List.

[7] GFCM, 'REC.MCS-GFCM/33/2009/8 on the Establishment of a List of Vessels Presumed to have Carried out IUU Fishing in the GFCM Area Repealing Recommendation GFCM/30/2006/4' (2009). www.fao.org/3/ax890e/ax890e.pdf accessed 21 December 2023, para 16, which is an open-ended provision to cross-list from other RFMO lists.

Table 8.2 Inter-RFMO MOUs referring to the exchange of IUU vessel or list data

	CCAMLR	CCSBT
	CCAMLR	SEAFO
	CCAMLR	SIOFA
SPRFMO	CCAMLR	
SPRFMO	WCPFC	
SPRFMO	IATTC	
	NEAFC	GFCM

vote in the Extended Commission.[69] Triggers to be included on the Draft List are non-exhaustive. They can include reports from vessel inspections; catch and trade information from the FAO; and 'suitably documented' information obtained from port States or gathered from the fishing grounds. The flag State is notified and requested to notify the vessel owner in advance of the annual Compliance Committee meeting. The Compliance Committee must remove a vessel from the Draft List if the flag State demonstrates that either no IUU fishing occurred or that 'effective action has been taken in response . . . including, inter alia, prosecution and/or imposition of sanctions of adequate severity'.[70] If the vessel ends up on the final CCSBT's IUU list, its deletion can be requested by submitting 'suitable documented information' to the Compliance Committee or the Executive Secretary.[71] Inter-sessional removal is possible, although only with agreement of all contracting parties.

69 The CCSBT Commission is open to membership by States. However, to also allow the European Union and Taiwan to become CCSBT members and be bound by its measures, the CCSBT provides for membership to what it calls the Extended Commission, see CCSBT, 'Resolution to Establish an Extended Commission and an Extended Scientific Committee and Rules of Procedure of the Extended Commission for the Conservation of Southern Bluefin Tuna adopted at the Seventh Annual Meeting (18–21 April 2001), revised at the Tenth Annual Meeting (7–10 October 2003) and replaced at the Twentieth Annual Meeting (14–17 October 2013)' (17 October 2013). www.ccsbt.org/sites/default/files/userfiles/file/docs_english/basic_documents/the%20Extended%20Commission.pdf accessed 21 December 2023.

70 CCSBT, 'Resolution on Establishing a List of Vessels Presumed to have Carried Out Illegal, Unreported and Unregulated Fishing Activities for Southern Bluefin Tuna (SBT)' (17 October 2019). faolex.fao.org/docs/pdf/mul166050.pdf accessed 21 December 2023, para 14(b).

71 ibid, para 20, upon demonstrating that it a) 'has adopted measures so that this vessel complies with all CCSBT conservation and management measures'; b) 'is and will continue to assume effectively its responsibilities with respect to this vessel in particular as regards the monitoring and control of the SBT fishing activities executed by this vessel'; and c) it has taken effective action in response, the vessel has changed ownership, or '[t]he case regarding the vessel that conducted SBT IUU fishing activities has been settled to the satisfaction of the Member(s)/CNM(s) that originally submitted the vessel for listing and the flag State or entity involved'.

Cross-listing can also take place inter-sessionally. To obtain information about their IUU lists, the Secretariat of the CCSBT maintains close links to the Secretariats of the CCAMLR but also of the Inter-American Tropical Tuna Commission (IATTC), International Commission for the Conservation of Atlantic Tunas (ICCAT), the Indian Ocean Tuna Commission (IOTC), the WCPFC, the South East Atlantic Fisheries Organisation (SEAFO), Southern Indian Ocean Fisheries Agreement (SIOFA), and the SPRFMO. This is a recent development. An earlier CCSBT Resolution only provided that 'the Extended Commission may consider cross-listing IUU vessel lists with all other tuna [RFMOs] and relevant organisations on a case-by-case basis'.[72] Vessels listed by these RFMOs are then added to the CCSBT's IUU list unless a CCSBT's member gives a reasoned written objection within 30 days. If so, the case is brought to the following annual session of the Compliance Committee for examination. The Compliance Committee then issues a recommendation to the Extended Commission on the inclusion of the relevant vessel(s) on the IUU list.

The CCAMLR does not have a procedure for cross-listing IUU vessels from other RFMOs' IUU vessel lists. Instead, it operates its own separate IUU fishing vessel list for parties (CP-IUU Vessel List)[73] and non-parties (NCP-IUU Vessel List).[74] For both lists, information comes from a non-exhaustive list of sources. It can therefore be inferred that other RFMO IUU vessel lists can be a relevant source. Final lists are publicly available online. The lists are also explicitly communicated to the FAO and appropriate RFMOs to enhance cooperation. The CCAMLR's website contains links to the vessel lists of the SEAFO, SIOFA, and SPRFMO. These are RFMOs adjacent to the CCAMLR, and with which the CCAMLR has MOUs in place. No link is included to the CCSBT's IUU vessel, despite the MOU in place which refers to cooperation over IUU fishing and despite the CCSBT's website cross-listing vessels from the CCAMLR's list (as well as from other RFMOs).

3.2. CCAMLR – SEAFO MOU (2017)

The MOU between the CCAMLR and the SEAFO, concluded in 2017, also stipulates that the two RFMOs will exchange data on IUU fishing vessels and IUU vessel lists.[75] The CCAMLR's website links to the SEAFO's IUU list. The SEAFO's IUU vessel list is adopted annually. The process bears strong similarities to that of the CCSBT (i.e. non-exhaustive list of sources for evidence, standard for removal

72 Barbara Hutniczak, 'Coordination between RFMOs on Mutual Recognition of IUU Vessel Lists' (2019) 107 *Marine Policy* 3, referring to CCSBT, 'Resolution on Establishing a List of Vessels Presumed to have Carried out IUU fishing for SBT' (12 October 2017). faolex.fao.org/docs/pdf/mul166050.pdf accessed 21 December 2023, para 20.

73 CCAMLR, 'Conservation Measure 10–06: Scheme to Promote Compliance by Contracting Party Vessels with CCAMLR Conservation Measures' (2016). cm.ccamlr.org/en/measure-10-06-2016 accessed 21 December 2023.

74 ibid.

75 'MOU between the SEAFO and the CCAMLR' (2 June 2017). www.ccamlr.org/en/system/files/SEAFO.pdf accessed 21 December 2023, para 2(ii)(b).

from the draft list, etc.).[76] Once a Draft List is drawn up, this triggers a reasoned notification to the flag State. The flat State has 60 days to submit verifiable evidence to challenge the draft listing.[77] The Compliance Committee then establishes a Provisional List for adoption, which must be approved by the SEAFO's Commission. The final SEAFO's IUU vessel list and any relevant information are then transmitted to the Secretariats of the CCAMLR, the Northwest Atlantic Fisheries Organization (NAFO), and the NEAFC. According to the SEAFO's website, it is also transmitted to the Secretariats of the SIOFA and SPRFMO.

The SEAFO provides for the cross-listing of vessels from these RFMOs, provided that no SEAFO member objects within 30 days. Unlike other RFMOs, grounds for objections are well defined. A member can object if satisfactory information establishes that the vessel did not engage in IUU fishing or that effective action has been taken in response. The vessel is then placed on the SEAFO's Provisional List. Usually, this does not entail any enforcement measures.[78]

3.3. CCAMLR – SIOFA MOU (2018)

The MOU between the CCAMLR and SIOFA, concluded in 2018, provides that the two RFMOs will exchange data on vessels 'confirmed to be involved' in IUU fishing; IUU fishing vessel lists established by each RFMO; 'or other relevant information'.[79] The SIOFA establishes its own IUU fishing vessel list, following a process resembling that of the SEAFO and the CCSBT (i.e., sources of information for alleged IUU fishing, evidence required for removal from the Draft List, etc.).[80] The SIOFA's IUU vessel list should be published publicly and shared with any relevant organisation which expressed an interest and the FAO. It should also be transmitted to the Secretariats of the CCAMLR, the CCSBT, the ICCAT, the IOTC, the General Fisheries Commission for the Mediterranean (GFCM), IATTC, NAFO, NEAFC, the North Pacific Fisheries Commission (NPFC), the SEAFO, the SPRFMO, and the WCPFC 'for the purposes of enhancing co-operation between SIOFA and these organizations aimed at preventing, deterring and eliminating IUU

76 SEAFO, 'System of Observation, Inspection, Compliance and Enforcement' (2019). faolex.fao.org/docs/pdf/mul163878.pdf accessed 21 December 2023, art 27.

77 ibid, the grounds are to show that the vessels neither operated in contravention of the SEAFO's CMMs nor could engage in fishing or fishing-related activities for fishery resources covered by the SEAFO Convention.

78 ibid, as is the case also for other RFMOs, the SEAFO contains the safeguard that

> the Contracting Parties shall not take any unilateral trade measures or other sanctions against vessels on the draft or provisional IUU Vessel Lists, pursuant to paragraphs 5 or 9, or that have been removed from the IUU Vessel List, pursuant to paragraph 13, on the grounds that such vessels are involved in IUU fishing.

79 'MOU between the CCAMLR and the SIOFA' (28 August 2018). www.ccamlr.org/en/system/files/SIOFA%20Arrangement%20Signed%202018-8-28.pdf accessed 21 December 2023, para 2(ii)(b).

80 SIOFA, 'CMM 2018/06: Conservation and Management Measure on the Listing of IUU Vessels (IUU Vessel List)' (8 October 2018) siofa.org/sites/default/files/CMM%202018_06%20IUU%20Vessel%20List%20%282018.10.08%29.pdf accessed 21 December 2023.

fishing'.[81] Cross-listing is explicitly provided upon receipt of a final IUU fishing vessel list and any information regarding the lists from these RFMOs, including during the inter-sessional period. If a SIOFA member objects in writing within 30 days, the vessel is placed on the Draft IUU vessel list. Unlike the SEAFO, the SIOFA does not circumscribe the grounds for such objection.

3.4. SPRFMO – WCPFC MOU (2020)

The MOU between the SPRFMO and the WCPFC, concluded in 2020 provides for the exchange of data on vessels 'identified as having engaged' in IUU fishing activity, and on the IUU vessel lists established by each RFMO.[82] The SPRFMO establishes its own IUU fishing vessel list, which is currently empty. The SPRFMO also provides that the enforcement measures to be taken vis-à-vis listed vessels 'shall apply mutatis mutandis to fishing vessels included in the final IUU list established by another RFMO and operating in the SPRFMO Convention Area'.[83] Moreover, the SPRFMO circulates final IUU vessel lists established by other RFMOs and any other information regarding its list, which is placed on the SPRFMO's website.

WCPFC has its own IUU fishing vessel list, but the measure establishing the list contains no provisions for cross-listing.[84] The measure's preamble nevertheless explicitly considers 'the action undertaken in other regional tuna fisheries organizations to address [IUU fishing]'.[85] It lists the same non-exhaustive list of sources for evidence for presumed IUU fishing as that of the CCSBT and SEAFO. This would allow information from other RFMOs to be considered as a trigger for draft listing. Finally, the Executive Director is tasked with taking 'any measure necessary to ensure publicity of the WCPFC IUU Vessel List, in a manner consistent with any applicable confidentiality requirements, including placing it on the WCPFC website'. The Executive Director must transmit it to other RFMOs 'for the purposes of enhancing cooperation between the WCPFC and these organisations aimed at preventing, deterring and eliminating IUU fishing'.[86]

81 SIOFA, 'IUU Vessel List' (29 June 2018) siofa.org/sites/default/files/files/SIOFA%20IUU%20Vessel%20List%20-%202018_0.pdf accessed 21 December 2022.

82 'Memorandum of Understanding between the SPRFMO and the WCPFC' (6 August 2020). www.sprfmo.int/assets/Cooperation-with-others/MoUs/WCPFC-SPRFMO-MOU-signed-by-Chairs.pdf accessed 21 December 2023, para 2(ii)(c).

83 SPRFMO, 'CMM 04–2020: Conservation and Management Measure Establishing a List of Vessels Presumed to Have Carried Out Illegal, Unreported and Unregulated Fishing Activities in the SPRFMO Convention Area' (20 May 2020). www.sprfmo.int/fisheries/conservation-and-management-measures/ accessed 21 December 2023.

84 WCPFC, 'CMM 2019–07: Conservation Management Measure for the Establishment of a List of IUU Vessels for the WCPFC' (11 December 2019). cmm.wcpfc.int/measure/cmm-2019-07 accessed 21 December 2023.

85 ibid, Preamble.

86 ibid, para 23.

3.5. SPRFMO – IATTC MOU (2022)

The MOU between the SPRFMO and the IATTC, concluded in 2022, provides for data exchange in respect of vessels suspected of IUU fishing and the IUU Vessel Lists established by each RFMO.[87] The IATTC draws up its own IUU fishing vessel list. It also provides for cross-listing to the final IUU vessel lists of the CCAMLR, CCSBT, ICCAT, IOTC, GFCM, NAFO, NEAFC, NPFC, SEAFO, SIOFA, SPRFMO, and WCPFC, including during the intersessional period, unless any contracting party formally objects in writing within 30 days.[88] The grounds for objection are not circumscribed, and in the event of an objection, the case

> shall be brought to the following session of the Committee for the Review of Implementation of Measures Adopted by the Commission for its examination. The Committee shall provide a recommendation to the Commission on the inclusion of the relevant vessel/s in the IUU Vessel List.[89]

3.6. SPRFMO – CCAMLR MOU (2022)

The MOU between the SPRFMO and the CCAMLR, concluded in 2022, provides that the two RFMOs will cooperate in matters of mutual interest.[90] Specifically, the two RFMOs indicate their willingness to exchange data in support of each other's work on vessels suspected of IUU fishing activity, and the IUU vessel lists established by each RFMO.[91]

3.7. GFCM – NEAFC MOU (2019)

The MOU between the GFCM and the NEAFC, concluded in 2019, provides for the exchange 'of IUU Vessel lists and relevant information on IUU fishing activities carried out in their respective areas of application'.[92] While the constituent instrument of NEAFC makes no reference to IUU fishing, it gives the NEAFC Commission the competence to make recommendations in respect of control measures.[93] As indicated earlier, the NEAFC's Scheme of Control

87 'MOU between the SPRFMO and the IATTC' (27 January 2022). www.sprfmo.int/assets/Cooperation-with-others/MoU-SPRFMO-IATTC-27-Jan-2022.pdf accessed 21 December 2023, para 2(ii)(b).

88 ICCAT, 'Resolution 19–02: Recommendation by ICCAT to Replace Recommendation 16–01 by ICCAT on a Multi-Annual Conservation and Management Programme for Tropical Tunas' (2019). www.iccat.int/Documents/Recs/compendiopdf-e/2019-02-e.pdf accessed 21 December 2023.

89 ibid, para 22.

90 'MOU between the SPRFMO and the CCAMLR' (17 February 2022). www.ccamlr.org/en/system/files/SPRFMO-Arrangement-2022.pdf accessed 21 December 2023.

91 ibid, para 2(ii)(b).

92 'MOU between the GFCM and the NEAFC' (17 December 2019). www.neafc.org/system/files/MoU_GFCM-NEAFC_signed_dec_2019.pdf accessed 3 January 2024, para 2(f).

93 NEAFC Convention, art 8(1)–(2).

and Enforcement requires that vessels listed by other specific RFMOs must be promptly placed on the NEAFC's provisional list of IUU fishing vessels (the IUU A-list).[94] The process of being moved from the A-list to the confirmed IUU B-list is similar as that of any other vessels that the NEAFC Secretary itself has placed on the provisional A-list. The flag State is informed, and, on a yearly basis, the list is considered by the Permanent Committee for Control and Enforcement, which also recommends the removal of vessels or their transfer to the B-list to the Commission.

The GFCM's constituent agreement is not specific on IUU listing. However, it indicates that the GFCM Commission is charged with formulating and recommending measures 'to take action to prevent, deter and eliminate illegal, unreported and unregulated fishing, including mechanisms for effective monitoring, control and surveillance'.[95] The GFCM adopted a Recommendation for the Executive Secretary to set up a draft IUU Vessel List, which is compiled from information and evidence shared by contracting parties and cooperating non-contracting parties.[96] A process of notification to relevant flag States then follows. These States can refute the allegations with additional evidence.[97] Based on this information, the Executive Secretary draws a Provisional IUU Vessel List, which is further scrutinised by the Compliance Committee alongside available evidence, before the Commission approves the updated IUU Vessel List by the Commission.[98] The Recommendation specifically provides for cross-listing from other RFMO IUU Vessel lists, unless a contract party objects within 30 days and there is satisfactory information upon which to base the objection.[99]

Having set out how these RFMOs have formalised their cooperation over IUU fishing and how they put this in practice, we make four observations. First, MOU commitments to exchange information concerning IUU vessels and IUU lists do not necessarily result in cross-listing. Cross-listing practices of RFMOs are also not necessarily linked to an MOU being in place, and not always reciprocal. Second, automatic cross-linking is not necessarily the result of common and agreed process standards to ensure the objectivity, transparency, and fairness of the initial listing.[100] Third, further reflection is needed on whether cross-listing *should*

94 NEAFC, 'Scheme of Control and Enforcement'. www.neafc.org/scheme/contents accessed 21 December 2023, art 44.

95 GFCM Convention, art 8(b)(vi).

96 GFCM, 'REC.MCS-GFCM/33/2009/8 on the Establishment of a List of Vessels Presumed to have Carried Out IUU Fishing in the GFCM Area Repealing Recommendation GFCM/30/2006/4' (2009). www.fao.org/3/ax890e/ax890e.pdf accessed 21 December 2023, paras 3–4.

97 ibid, paras 3–4.

98 ibid, paras 10–11.

99 ibid, para 16.

100 Differences include the period of notification and response time for the flag State; information which must be shown to discharge the allegation; questionable burden of proof; consensus decision-making complicating the listing of vessels flagged to existing members. Meanwhile, similarities include the sources of information for a finding of alleged IUU fishing and the evidentiary standard for being removed from the draft/provisional list.

be automatic or whether there should be substantive or procedural review. For example, the grounds for objecting to cross-listing detailed by the SEAFO differ from the CCSBT. The latter lacks specificity on objection justifications. Fourth, automatic cross-listing makes sense only if the RFMO is willing to identify vessels for reasons other than undermining *their own* CMMs. For instance, the WCPFC provides that a vessel shall *not* be listed if it has 'fished exclusively for species not covered by the WCPFC Convention'.[101]

4. Conclusion

This chapter has argued that RFMOs are under a general obligation to cooperate over alleged IUU fishing. The source of this obligation can be found in customary international law. Moreover, constituent agreements of RFMOs reflect this duty for their respective RFMOs. Although uncertainty remains over the scope of this duty, it should at minimum entail, first, sharing information over alleged IUU fishing activities and, second, assisting in identifying cases of IUU fishing to promote compliance and allow for enforcement. However, the scope of the information to be shared and the method of sharing remain unclear. It is doubtful whether any cross-listing is required – or, in fact, desirable – without the assurance of robust and objective listing processes. The need for an inter-RFMO duty to cooperate over IUU fishing is evident where multiple RFMOs are competent to manage the same stock or have overlapping management areas. However, RFMOs should engage in broader cooperation strategies beyond those involving their immediate neighbours, particularly as migration and distribution patterns are likely to change with a warming climate.[102] This means that RFMOs will need to (re)consider when and how they share fisheries-related data with a wider range of RFMOs, including RFMOs with which they do not currently share a border species management.

MOUs are a useful tool for RFMOs to make their cooperation priorities more transparent and to define the implementation of the cooperation mandates set out in their respective constituent instruments. Despite their diversity and often generic nature, they confer shape and direction to RFMOs' cooperation strategies. Nevertheless, an explicit rationale for including or excluding cooperation areas or RFMO partners could be more clearly established. Similarly, where RFMOs cross-list to other IUU fishing vessels, there is no clear rationale underpinning whose IUU fishing vessel lists to list to. Some RFMOs have made provision

101 WCPFC, 'CMM 2019–07: Conservation Management Measure for the Establishment of a List of IUU Vessels for the WCPFC' (11 December 2019). cmm.wcpfc.int/measure/cmm-2019-07 accessed 21 December 2023.

102 Keith Brander, 'Impacts of Climate Change on Fisheries' (2010) 79 *Journal of Marine Systems* 389; Ussif Rashid Sumaila et al., 'Climate Change Impacts on the Biophysics and Economics of World Fisheries' (2011) 1 *Nature Climate Change* 449.

for cross-listing, but do not do so in practice.[103] Other provisions are unclear, as they fall short of cross-listing and instead implement parallel listing processes.[104] Greater coherence and transparency in listing and cross-listing practices should be encouraged. Similarly, cross-listing practices should be clearly tied in with an overarching MOU.

103 For example, the CCAMLR, WCPFC, ICCAT, NAFO, NPFC, SIOFA, SPRFMO, and WCPFC, see Barbara Hutniczak, 'Coordination between RFMOs on Mutual Recognition of IUU Vessel Lists' (2019) 107 *Marine Policy* 3, Table A2.

104 For example, the IATTC has its own list and also compiles another list where it places the IUU vessels from other organisations which fall short of cross-listing, see IATC, 'IUU Vessels Listed by Other RFMOs'. www.iattc.org/en-US/Management/Vessel-register?shortcut=IUU accessed 21 December 2023. The GFCM mentions other RFMOs in its own IUU list, but the content suggests the insertions are not to be understood as cross-listings, see GFCM, 'GFCM IUU Vessel List'. www.fao.org/gfcm/data/iuu-vessel-list/zh/ accessed 21 December 2023.

9 Indonesian Enforcement Measures Against IUU Fishing Vessels

Dita Liliansa

1. Introduction

Indonesia, the world's largest archipelagic State with over 17,000 islands, sits at the confluence between the Indian and Pacific Oceans. The United Nations Convention on the Law of the Sea (UNCLOS) has greatly benefited Indonesia, particularly by introducing the exclusive economic zone (EEZ) and archipelagic State regimes. These regimes have significantly expanded Indonesia's jurisdiction over marine living resources. In essence, Indonesia gained control over approximately three million km^2 of internal and archipelagic waters and nearly 300,000 km^2 of territorial sea, bringing almost three point five million km^2 under its sovereignty. Indonesia claims an additional three million km^2 of EEZ and an extended continental shelf. Given its sovereign rights over this extensive EEZ, Indonesia has faced challenges in ensuring compliance with its fisheries laws and regulations inside its EEZ. As a result, Indonesia has imposed various penalties to enforce its laws and regulations, including the controversial practice of blowing up illegal fishing vessels. This chapter discusses the range of Indonesian State practices employed to enforce its laws and regulations on living resources within its EEZ.

2. Rights and Jurisdiction of Coastal States Over Living Resources in the EEZ

Coastal States have sovereign rights to 'explore, exploit, conserve and manage living natural resources' within their EEZ.[1] This concept of 'sovereign rights' includes the right to take necessary enforcement measures, such as boarding, inspection, arrest, and judicial proceedings against a vessel and its crew, as necessary to ensure compliance with the coastal States' laws and regulations.[2] Sovereign rights do not equate to full sovereignty. However, they entail 'all rights necessary for and connected with the exploration and exploitation of the natural resources,' including 'jurisdiction in connection with the prevention and punishment of violations of

1 United Nations Convention on the Law of the Sea (UNCLOS), 10 December 1982, 1833 UNTS 3, entered into force 16 November 1994, art 56(1).
2 ibid, art 73(1).

DOI: 10.4324/9781003492030-13

the law.'[3] Coastal States shall determine both the total allowable catch of living resources in their EEZs, and their own capacity to harvest these resources.[4] Where they lack the capacity to harvest the entire allowable catch, they are obliged to grant other States fisheries access.[5] In exercising their sovereign rights over these living resources, coastal States shall have due regard to the rights and duties of other States and act in a manner which does not amount to an abuse of right.[6]

During the negotiation of UNCLOS, major distant water fishing States initially favoured exclusive flag State jurisdiction for violations within EEZs.[7] However, the final text of UNCLOS ultimately granted broad enforcement jurisdiction to coastal States. This jurisdiction enables coastal States to board, inspect, arrest, and initiate judicial proceedings against fishing vessels violating their laws and regulations on the exploration, exploitation, conservation, and management of living resources inside their EEZs. UNCLOS introduced certain safeguards to balance the interests of both coastal and flag States. Where a vessel is arrested or detained, the coastal State is required to notify the flag State and the arrested vessel and its crew may be released upon providing reasonable bond or other security.[8] Moreover, when violations are established, coastal States shall notify the flag State of punitive measures imposed, and these penalties may not include imprisonment or any other forms of corporal punishment unless there is an agreement with the relevant State.[9]

Article 73 of UNCLOS plays a crucial role in delineating the extent of coastal States' enforcement jurisdiction over living resources inside the EEZ. Article 73 arguably contains a non-exhaustive list of permitted coastal States' enforcement measures.[10] The use of the word 'including' in this provision implies that 'boarding, inspection, arrest, and judicial proceedings' are merely given as examples of the types of permitted measures. Whether a coastal State's enforcement measure was necessary should be assessed based on the specific circumstances of each case and the gravity of the violation. Coastal States likely enjoy a broad margin of appreciation as excessively constraining their conduct could impede their conservation and management efforts within the EEZ.[11] With the advent of modern technology, there is ample room for innovative measures so long as this margin of appreciation is

3 Myron H Nordquist et al, *United Nations Convention on the Law of the Sea 1982, Volume II: A Commentary* (Brill 1993) 541–2.
4 UNCLOS, arts 61(1) and 62(2).
5 ibid, art 62(2).
6 ibid, arts 56(3) and 300.
7 Myron H Nordquist et al, *United Nations Convention on the Law of the Sea 1982, Volume II: A Commentary* (Brill 1993) 286–91.
8 UNCLOS, art 73(2)(4).
9 ibid, art 73(3)(4).
10 Dita Liliansa, 'The Necessity of Indonesia's Measures to Sink Vessels for IUU Fishing in its Exclusive Economic Zone' (2019) 10 *Asian Journal of International Law* 125.
11 James Harrison, 'Article 73: Enforcement of Laws and Regulations of the Coastal State' in Alexander Proelß (ed), *United Nations Convention on the Law of the Sea: A Commentary* (Beck, Nomos and Hart 2017).

preserved.[12] Coastal States' enforcement measures should only be overruled when they are arbitrary or conducted in bad faith,[13] e.g., Article 73 does not explicitly mention confiscation but it also does not forbid such enforcement measures. State practice on the sanctioning of illegal fishing activities demonstrates that many States have enacted forfeiture provisions.[14] If the coastal State's penalty does not have the effect of denying a flag State's access to prompt release procedures and is not expressly prohibited by UNCLOS, the measure should be considered legal.

3. Indonesian Practice

As a civil law country, Indonesia relies on statutes and ministerial regulations to combat illegal, unreported, and unregulated (IUU) fishing. Indonesia's National Plan of Action to Prevent and to Combat IUU Fishing adopts the same definition as the International Plan of Action to Prevent, Deter and Eliminate IUU Fishing.[15] Indonesia's Fisheries Law distinguishes between fisheries-related 'crimes' and 'violations.'[16] When an offence constitutes a 'violation', it generally entails lesser punishment. In practice, Indonesia often uses the expressions 'IUU fishing' and 'illegal fishing' loosely and interchangeably. The expression 'IUU fishing' under the International Plan of Action to Prevent, Deter and Eliminate IUU Fishing encompasses a wide range of infringements. However, many, if not most, IUU fishing cases tried before Indonesian courts fall within one narrow category of illegal fishing, that is, fishing conducted by foreign nationals or foreign vessels in waters under Indonesia's jurisdiction without Indonesia's permission. Past cases have confirmed that Indonesia's fisheries courts generally view illegal fishing as simply 'fish theft,' which narrowly refers to the unlawful taking of fish from its rightful owner.[17] Other forms of infringement are rarely considered, such as fishing for non-permitted species and using illegal fishing gear. Moreover, Indonesia perceives IUU fishing within the framework of transnational crime, not solely as a fisheries management issue.[18] Indonesia's former Fisheries Minister unsuccessfully

12 Camille Goodman, 'Striking the Right Balance? Applying the Jurisprudence of International Tribunals to Coastal State Innovations in International Fisheries Governance' (2017) 84 *Marine Policy* 293.

13 James Harrison, 'Safeguards against Excessive Enforcement Measures in the Exclusive Economic Zone – Law and Practice' in Henrik Ringbom (ed), *Jurisdiction Over Ships: Post-UNCLOS Developments in the Law of the Sea* (Brill 2015).

14 *The Tomimaru Case (Prompt Release) (Japan v. Russia)*, Judgment, ITLOS Reports 2005–2007, para 72.

15 Minister of Marine and Fisheries' Regulation no KEP.50/MEN/2012 on National Plan of Action to Prevent and to Combat IUU Fishing 2012–2016.

16 Law no 31 of 2004 on Fisheries, as amended by Law no 45 of 2009, art 103.

17 *See* Decision of High Court of Jayapura no 70/Pid.Sus-PRK/2015/PT JAP (*Indonesia v. Guo Yunping*); Decision of High Court of Pekanbaru no 46/Pid.Sus/2016/PT PBR (*Indonesia v. Huynh Duy Phu*).

18 'Menteri Susi Ingin PBB Segera Tetapkan IUU Fishing Sebagai Kejahatan Transnational Terorganisir', *KKP News* (15 June 2017). https://news.kkp.go.id/index.php/menteri-susi-ingin-pbb-segera-tetapkan-iuu-fishing-sebagai-kejahatan-transnasional-terorganisir/ accessed 6 September 2023.

campaigned in numerous regional and international forums to classify IUU fishing as a transnational organised crime.[19] Indonesia also amended its anti-money laundering legislation to include assets acquired from marine and fisheries.[20]

Indonesia operates a multiple-agency structure. At least 13 agencies have responsibility over maritime law enforcement, depending on the specific activities and maritime zones. Among these 13 agencies, only seven have patrol forces tasked with conducting law enforcement activities at sea. The Fisheries Ministry is one such agency. Both the Indonesian Navy and Indonesian Water Police have similar mandates, although the Water Police are solely authorised to investigate fisheries offences within Indonesian internal waters, archipelagic waters, and territorial seas.[21] While coordination among the relevant enforcement agencies can occur, cases are typically handled on a first-come first-serve basis. The Maritime Security Agency is envisioned to become a fully-fledged national coast guard force, but it currently primarily serves a coordinating role with somewhat limited powers. Meanwhile, the Indonesian navy fulfils dual roles, with both military and constabulary functions. They are responsible not only for national defence at sea, but also for civilian law enforcement, namely enforcing national laws and maintaining security within the maritime territory under Indonesia's national jurisdiction.[22] In fact, they have the most expansive power to conduct law enforcement across all maritime zones, including pursuits, arrests, and investigations on both fisheries and shipping offences.

In recent years, Indonesia has garnered international attention for its practice of destroying IUU fishing vessels. Between 2014 and 2018, its Fisheries Ministry reported that 488 vessels had been destroyed, with the majority flagged to Vietnam.[23] Alongside this contentious practice, Indonesia has also taken other measures, including imposing fines, imprisonment, and the confiscation of vessels and catches. In the context of coastal State enforcement jurisdiction within the EEZ, some of the penalties imposed by Indonesia on foreign fishing vessels may reside in a grey area.

This section outlines various measures taken by Indonesia to enforce its fisheries laws and regulations within its EEZ.

19 'KKP Akan Jerat Pelaku Illegal Fishing dengan Pasal Pencucian Uang', *Tempo.co* (12 December 2017). https://bisnis.tempo.co/read/1041523/kkp-akan-jerat-pelaku-illegal-fishing-dengan-pasal-pencucian-uang/full&view=ok accessed 6 September 2023.

20 Law no 8 of 2010 on Prevention and Eradication of Money Laundering, art 2.

21 Law 45/2009, art 73(2).

22 Law no 34 of 2004 on Indonesia's National Armed Forces, art 9(a) and (b).

23 'Hari Kemerdekaan, Pemerintah Tenggelamkan 125 Kapal Pelaku Illegal Fishing', *KKP* (21 August 2018). https://kkp.go.id/artikel/5714-hari-kemerdekaan-pemerintah-tenggelamkan-125-kapal-pelaku-illegal-fishing accessed 6 September 2023.

1.1 Fines

Fines constitute a common form of sanctions imposed for fisheries violations under Indonesia's Fisheries Law. In numerous illegal fishing cases after 2014, Indonesian courts have imposed fines ranging from IDR one billion (about USD 65,000) to IDR six billion (about USD 400,000).[24] These amounts represent an increase of more than tenfold compared to fines in 2006.[25] Indonesia often faces challenges in recovering such fines. In these instances, pursuant to Indonesia's Criminal Code, a subsidiary punishment through confinement or jail may be applied.[26] Indonesian law specifies that confinement or '*pidana kurungan*' can last a minimum of one day and a maximum of one year, but may be extended up to one year and four months.[27] In contrast, 'imprisonment' or '*pidana penjara*' can last a lifetime.[28] For fisheries violations within the EEZ, Indonesia's Fisheries Law explicitly prohibits imprisonment in the absence of prior agreement between Indonesia and the relevant State.[29]

Nevertheless, a significant number of domestic cases have arisen. These challenge the practical application of Article 73(3) of UNCLOS given the failure of several offenders to pay fines for violating Indonesia's fisheries laws and regulations in its EEZ.[30] Two different views have emerged on whether imprisonment may serve as a secondary punishment for illegal fishing conducted by foreign nationals in the EEZ.[31] A majority of Indonesia's Supreme Court concluded that such

24 See Supreme Court Decision no 1355 K/Pid.Sus/2014 (*Indonesia v. Dao Van Tuan*); Supreme Court Decision no 131 K/Pid.Sus/2014 (*Indonesia v. Nguyen Phan Sy*); Supreme Court Decision no 168 K/Pid.Sus/2014 (*Indonesia v. Nguyen Van Be*); Supreme Court Decision no 170 K/Pid.Sus/2014 (*Indonesia v. Le Van Vuong*); Supreme Court Decision no 174 K/Pid.Sus/2014 (*Indonesia v. Bui Han Hanh*); Supreme Court Decision no 618 K/Pid.Sus/2014 (*Indonesia v. Tran Ngoc Quang*); Decision of High Court of Pekanbaru no 46/Pid.Sus/2016/Pt Pbr (*Indonesia v. Huynh Duy Phu*); Decision of District Court of Medan no 2/Pid.Sus.Prk/2016/Pn Mdn (*Indonesia v. Khin Maung Win*); Decision of High Court of Langsa no 79/Pid.Sus/2016/Pn Lgs (*Indonesia v. Montree Sama-Ae*); Decision of High Court of Jayapura no 70./Pid.Sus-Prk/2015/Pt Jap (*Indonesia v. Guo Yunping*); Supreme Court Decision no 2563 K/Pid.Sus/2015 (*Indonesia v. Chen Xiangqi*); Decision of District Court of Tanjungpinang no 23/Pid.Sus.Prkn/2015/Pn.Tpg (*Indonesia v. Dang Ngoc Quy*).

25 High Seas Task Force, 'Closing the Net: Stopping Illegal Fishing on the High Seas' (March 2006). https://wwfeu.awsassets.panda.org/downloads/high_seas_task_force_report.pdf accessed 6 September 2023, 34.

26 Indonesia's Criminal Code, art 18(1) and (3).

27 ibid.

28 ibid, art 12.

29 Law no 31 of 2004 on Fisheries, as amended by Law no 45 of 2009, art 102.

30 Dita Liliansa, 'A Quest for Meaning: Interpretation of Article 73(3) of the Law of the Sea Convention by Indonesian Supreme Court' (2023) 8 *Asia-Pacific Journal of Ocean Law and Policy* 59.

31 See Supreme Court Decision no 471 K/Pid.Sus/2013 (*Indonesia v. Nguyen Van Hai*); Supreme Court Decision no 168 K/Pid.Sus/2014 (*Indonesia v. Nguyen Van Be*); Supreme Court Decision no 99 K/Pid.Sus/2014 (*Indonesia v. Duong Van Tien*); Supreme Court Decision no 170 K/Pid.Sus/2014 (*Indonesia v. Le Van Vuong*); Supreme Court Decision no 131 K/Pid.Sus/2014 (*Indonesia v. Nguyen Phan Sy*); Supreme Court Decision no 618 K/Pid.Sus/2014 (*Indonesia v. Tran Ngoc Quang*); Supreme Court Decision no 1355 K/Pid.Sus/2014 (*Indonesia v. Dao Van Tuan*).

imprisonment contradicts Article 73(3) of UNCLOS, while the minority argued that it does not.[32] The minority contended that if imprisonment for fine default was removed as an option, there would be no remedy for the situation.

1.2 Confiscation

Given the challenges associated with collecting court-imposed fines and the varying court rulings on imprisonment, some cases have turned to confiscation as a penalty. In principle, objects or tools used in or derived from a fisheries offence can be confiscated, including fishing gear, catches, and vessels.[33] An auction may be conducted subsequently.[34] If not auctioned, vessels may also be delegated to a fisheries cooperative.[35] Confiscation is permissible while an investigation or trial is still ongoing, depending on the safety and durability of the objects or tools, and the financial considerations involved in storing them safely.[36] If a vessel is confiscated and auctioned during a trial, the revenue generated is held by the court as evidence.[37] Once the court delivers its verdict, the revenue can either be returned to the accused or expropriated for the State, depending upon the outcome. However, this measure often results in limited deterrence, as the vessel frequently returns to its owner who may later repeat the same offence.

1.3 Destruction of Vessels

In recent years, Indonesia has imposed the penalty of sinking vessels as a deterrent for fisheries offences. It argued that existing measures were insufficient to curb IUU fishing in its waters. Article 69 of Indonesia's Fisheries Law authorises Indonesian patrol vessels to employ 'special measures', such as burning or sinking foreign fishing vessels, based on sufficient preliminary evidence.[38] Indonesia adopts a broad definition of fishing vessels, which encompasses vessels, boats, or other floating devices used for fish capture, supporting fishing operations, fish aquaculture, fish transport, fish processing, fisheries training, fisheries research, or exploration.[39] As seen, Indonesia has several maritime law enforcement agencies. However, only the Navy, the Fisheries Ministry, and the Maritime Security Agency have a mandate to carry out necessary law enforcement within Indonesia's EEZ.[40] Consequently, the term 'patrol vessels' in this context should pertain to vessels

32 See, e.g., Supreme Court Decision no 174 K/Pid.Sus/2014 (*Indonesia v. Bui Han Hanh*) 12.
33 Law no 31 of 2004 on Fisheries, as amended by Law no 45 of 2009, art 104(2).
34 Law 45/2009, arts 76A and 76C(1).
35 ibid, art 76C(5).
36 Law no 8 of 1981 on the Code of Criminal Procedures, art 45(1).
37 ibid, art 45(2).
38 Law 45/2009, art 69(4).
39 Law no 31 of 2004 on Fisheries, as amended by Law no 45 of 2009, art 1(9).
40 Law 45/2009, art 73(2); Government Regulation No 13 of 2022 on Security, Safety and Law Enforcement in Indonesian Waters and Waters Within the Jurisdiction of Indonesia, art 22.

operated by these two agencies. They may conduct individual or coordinated patrols, but only the Navy and the Fisheries Ministry have a mandate to investigate fishing offences in the EEZ.

Indonesia's Supreme Court has emphasised that it lacks jurisdiction over the implementation of Article 69, indicating that it falls entirely within the purview of the authorised maritime law enforcement agencies.[41] While these 'special measures' are primarily intended for foreign vessels, Indonesian vessels are not exempt in practice. The term, 'sufficient preliminary evidence' is defined as any preliminary evidence which raises suspicion of a fisheries offence by a foreign vessel. This can include a vessel caught fishing or transporting fish without the required permits in Indonesia's fisheries zone, which encompasses the EEZ.[42] Article 69 prohibits the burning or sinking of a foreign vessel unless the vessel is 'clearly committing a fisheries offence.'[43]

Additionally, Article 76A of Indonesia's Fisheries Law permits the destruction of objects or tools associated with fisheries offence, including vessels.[44] Indonesia's Fisheries Ministry has issued a directive outlining subjective and objective requirements based on safety considerations for implementing these measures. The Navy may not necessarily adhere to this directive, which could result in different practices between the two agencies. The directive specifies that the 'special measures' involve a 'deliberate' and 'direct' destruction at sea due to safety and practical considerations. The directive's wording suggests that the practice does not involve any judicial proceedings.

The directive prescribes both subjective and objective requirements which must be met before patrol vessels can destroy a fishing vessel at sea. Subjective requirements entail considering whether a) the vessel's skipper or crew resists or engages in manoeuvres which could endanger the patrol vessel; b) weather conditions render it impractical to bring the vessel to port; or c) the vessel is so severely damaged that it poses a threat to the crew's safety and the patrol vessel.[45] These subjective requirements apply to special measures conducted in the EEZ.[46]

Meanwhile, objective requirements encompass cumulative and/or alternative requirements. Cumulative requirements apply when a) a vessel lacks a valid permit; b) is clearly engaged in illegal fishing or the illegal transportation of fish within Indonesia's fisheries management zone; and c) is a foreign vessel with an entirely foreign crew.[47] In addition to or instead of these requirements, the foreign

41 Supreme Court's Directive no 1 of 2015 on the Evidence in the Form of Vessel in Fisheries Cases, para a.

42 Law 45/2009, Commentary, art 69(4).

43 ibid.

44 ibid, art 76A.

45 Regulation of the Director General of Surveillance for Marine and Fisheries Resources no 11/PER-DJDSDKP/2014 on the Technical Guidance in Enforcing Special Measure to Foreign Fishing Vessel, art 7.

46 ibid, art 12.

47 ibid, art 8(2).

vessel must lack high economic value and/or be impossible to take to the nearest port because a) it raises concerns about safety of navigation and/or quarantine; b) it carries communicable diseases and/or poisonous and hazardous substances; c) the number of vessels captured makes it impossible to transport them to the nearest port; and/or c) transporting the vessel entails prohibitively high costs.[48]

Previously, patrol vessels were permitted to destroy a vessel after obtaining approval from the Director-General of the Fisheries Ministry. Once they obtained approval, they had to follow specific procedures. First, they were required to warn the crew to abandon the vessel; save all crew; make efforts to remove the vessel's flag; document the action; and note the vessel's position when it was burned or sunk.[49] Subsequently, the patrol vessel was required to determine a safe shooting range, considering factors such as wind, current, and safety considerations, and use explosives and/or direct the shot towards the engine room to expedite the process.[50] The Fisheries Ministry now mandates a prior environmental impact assessment and discourages the use of explosives to minimise environmental harm.[51]

The use of Article 69's special measures has declined, as patrol vessels have increasingly turned to judicial recourse to base these measures.[52] While coastal States may determine other necessary measures not explicitly mentioned in Article 73 of UNCLOS and have a margin of appreciation in selecting their preferred enforcement measures in the EEZ, such measures should be implemented with due regard to the rights of other States. The measures must not interfere with the flag State's right to prompt release and other legitimate uses of the sea by other States, such as ensuring the safety of navigation. As a coastal State, Indonesia must promptly notify the relevant flag State through appropriate channels of the measures taken and any penalties imposed so the flag State can initiate prompt release proceedings.[53] However, the time limit for such notification is unspecified. Such time limit may remain unclear unless the relevant States concerned have agreed on specific terms through bilateral agreements, e.g., Indonesia and Australia have agreed that, where their nationals have been arrested, detained, or apprehended by the other State, notification must be provided within three working days.[54]

48 ibid, art 8(3).
49 ibid, art 10.
50 ibid, art 11.
51 Interview with the Fisheries Ministry's Special Investigator of Ranai (Ranai, Indonesia 2016).
52 Article 69 has been mentioned in some cases, but discussion is often limited. Judges often treating its application as a matter of fact without reviewing the legality on a case-by-case basis. The courts generally tend to assert a pre-judgment sinking was legal where there is evidence of correspondence between the patrol vessel authorities and the Head of the relevant District Court to approve such measures.
53 UNCLOS, art 73(4).
54 The Arrangement between the Government of Republic of Indonesia and the Government of Australia on Consular Notification and Assistance, 10 March 2010, entered into force 10 March 2010, art 30.

Under Indonesia's Fisheries Law, any request for the release of a vessel or its crew can be submitted any time before a court's decision.[55] The court determines the amount of the bond based on the value of the vessel, equipment, and catches and the maximum applicable fine.[56] Despite the guaranteed right to prompt release action under Indonesian law, most defendants have not used this option. Indonesia's obligation to release promptly vessels and crews depends on the defendant or their flag State promptly requesting such a release and posting a bond or other financial security. By failing to request a release as stipulated in UNCLOS, the flag State waives its right to request the release of the vessel and crew.

In the *Tomimaru* case, ITLOS found that it retained competence to consider applications for the release of a vessel or crew, even while a decision is pending review by the domestic court of the detaining State.[57] Consequently, so long as the domestic forum of the detaining State has not issued a final and binding decision on the merits, the flag State retains the right to request a release, and the coastal State should refrain from taking actions that could prevent a prompt release. This ensures that the coastal State's measures do not obstruct the flag State's access to a prompt release action, which preserves the balance of rights between coastal and flag States. Once the decision on the merits becomes final and binding, the vessel arguably may be subject to further measures, including confiscation, destruction, or dismantling.

1.4 Law Enforcement in Undelimited Zones

Indonesia shares maritime boundaries with ten countries.[58] Most of Indonesia's territorial sea boundaries are settled and delimitation agreements have been implemented in national legislation.[59] In contrast, most of Indonesia's EEZ boundaries remain undelimited. These undelimited EEZ boundaries include those with Malaysia, Palau, Timor-Leste, India, and Thailand. Thus, there is a potential for clashes over Indonesia's enforcement measures in its undelimited EEZ. Among the undelimited EEZ boundaries with its neighbouring States, Indonesia has only reached an agreement with Malaysia on common guidelines for the treatment of fishers in all their maritime disputed areas. Indonesia and Malaysia agreed, in an encroachment incident involving their fishing boats, to limit their maritime law enforcement activities to 'inspection and a request to leave', except where fishing boats are

55 Law no 31 of 2004 on Fisheries, as amended by Law no 45 of 2009, art 104(1).

56 ibid.

57 *The Tomimaru Case (Prompt Release) (Japan v. Russia)*, Judgment, ITLOS Reports 2005–2007, para 78.

58 Australia, India, Malaysia, Palau, Papua New Guinea, Philippines, Singapore, Thailand, Timor Leste, and Vietnam.

59 Indonesia's unsettled territorial sea boundaries with Malaysia include the southern part of the Strait of Malacca and the area near Tanjung Datu.

using illegal fishing gear.[60] In practice, Indonesian courts consider this agreement when deciding cases involving a Malaysian fishing boat. However, they may still impose fines and sink the vessel where it is found to have used unlawful fishing gear.[61]

Indonesia does not claim any of the features in the South China Sea. However, China and Indonesia disagree over the status of the waters around Indonesia's Natuna Islands.[62] China claims overlapping maritime rights and interests with Indonesia in certain parts of the South China Sea. China expressed a willingness to resolve these issues through negotiation and consultation.[63] Indonesia has declined to negotiate with China on the delimitation of maritime boundaries or any other matters of claims of maritime rights or interests.[64] Indonesia does not recognise any feature in the South China Sea which could generate overlapping maritime entitlements with Indonesia's EEZ or continental shelf.[65] Additionally, Indonesia rejects China's argument on historic fishing rights in Indonesia's EEZ and continental shelf.[66]

Given Indonesia's intensified efforts against IUU fishing and the adjacent South China Sea dispute, which could potentially spill over into Indonesian waters, it is critical for Indonesia to actively pursue conflict-management provisional arrangements with the relevant States until they reach delimitation agreements. Absent such arrangements, Indonesia and the relevant States should exercise restraint and avoid actions which could provoke conflicts, including fishing or arresting each other's fishers in the disputed areas.

4. Conclusion

This paper has discussed various measures taken by Indonesia to enforce its laws and regulations concerning its sovereign rights as a coastal State over living resources in its EEZ. While some measures are controversial, it appears that coastal

60 'Memorandum of Understanding in Respect of the Common Guidelines Concerning Treatment of Fishermen by Maritime Law Enforcement Agencies of Malaysia and the Republic of Indonesia' (27 January 2012). http://treaty.kemlu.go.id/apisearch/pdf?filename=MYS-2011-0127.pdf accessed 6 September 2023, art 3.

61 See Decision of District Court of Medan no 2/Pid.Sus.Prk/2016/Pn Mdn (*Indonesia v. Khin Maung Win*) 18; Directive of the Head of Coordinating Body of Maritime Security no 1/KETUA/BAKORKAMLA/II/2013 on the Technical Guidance on the Treatment of Fishers by Maritime Law Enforcement Agencies of Indonesia in Unresolved Maritime Boundaries of Indonesia-Malaysia.

62 Damos Agusman and Citra Fatihah, 'Celebrating the 25th Anniversary of UNCLOS Legal Perspective: The Natuna Case' (2020) 17 *Indonesian Journal of International Law* 539.

63 'Note Verbale by China no CML/46/2020' (2 June 2020). www.un.org/Depts/los/clcs_new/submissions_files/mys_12_12_2019/2020_06_02_CHN_NV_UN_eng.pdf accessed 6 September 2023.

64 'Note Verbale by Indonesia no 148/POL-703/VI/20' (12 June 2020). www.un.org/depts/los/clcs_new/submissions_files/mys_12_12_2019/2020_06_12_IDN_NV_UN_002_ENG.pdf accessed 6 September 2023.

65 ibid.

66 ibid.

States which have extensive EEZs but lack policing capacity, like Indonesia, will continue to explore innovative methods to combat IUU fishing. Ensuring compliance with coastal States' laws and regulations is critical. However, it is equally critical for coastal States to ensure that their law enforcement measures align with applicable international law.

10 Addressing Transshipment as Part of an Integrated Scheme of Monitoring Measures

*Meggan Engelke-Ros**

1. Introduction

Illegal, unregulated, and unreported (IUU) fishing poses a significant threat to global fishery resources, ocean ecosystems, food security, and coastal economies.[1] Historically, conservation and management measures to ensure the sustainability of fishery resources focused almost exclusively on the control of harvesting activities. They included measures such as permitting and licensing schemes, effort controls (e.g., limits on the numbers or types of vessels which may participate in a given fishery or the amount of gear that may be deployed), harvest controls (e.g., catch or size limits), and time and/or area closures (e.g., to protect critical habitat or spawning stocks). Compliance with these measures is generally monitored through at-sea and dockside boarding and with inspection and tools like satellite-based vessel monitoring systems (VMS). This approach works well when the fishing occurs in a coastal State's own waters, by vessels flying its flag, and where the harvesting vessel lands catches in its ports.

However, fishing operations are complicated and far-ranging. Vessels may operate in waters beyond the jurisdictional or operational reach of their flag State's authorities. Fish are often harvested in one country's waters and landed in another country's port, where the laws may differ and where authorities may lack legal mechanisms to take enforcement action with respect to infractions which occurred outside their jurisdiction. Fish may be harvested on the high seas by vessels operating out of third-country ports and may rarely, if ever, enter port in their flag State. To further complicate matters, fish may be harvested by one vessel and landed by

* The views expressed in this chapter are the author's own and do not necessarily represent the views of the National Oceanic and Atmospheric Administration or the United States.

1 See Food and Agriculture Organization of the United Nations (FAO), 'Fisheries and Aquaculture Report, Report of the 33rd Session of the Committee on Fisheries' (Rome, 9–13 July 2018), FIAP/R1249, para 58; Dr Teale N Phels Bondaroff, Wietse van der Werf and Tuesday Reitano, 'The Illegal Fishing and Organized Crime Nexus: Illegal Fishing as Transnational Organized Crime', *The Global Initiative Against Transnational Organized Crime and Black Fish* (April 2015) 15. The FAO, International Plan of Action to Prevent, Deter and Eliminate Illegal, Unreported and Unregulated Fishing, 2001, para 3 defines illegal fishing, unreported fishing, and unregulated fishing.

DOI: 10.4324/9781003492030-14

another, or fish may be brought into port and be transferred directly to another vessel without being landed. This is transshipment.

For the purposes of this chapter, transshipment refers to the 'direct transfer of any quantity of fish onboard from one vessel to another vessel regardless of the location of the event, without the fish being recorded as landed.'[2] When discussing transshipment, the focus is often on the transshipment activity that occurs in large-scale fisheries where harvesting vessels transfer catch to refrigerated carrier vessels or 'reefers'.[3] However, transshipment also occurs in small-scale fisheries where small vessels tranship to 'mother ships'. Transshipment occurs in both domestic fisheries and internationally managed fisheries. While transshipment poses similar threats in both contexts, this chapter focuses primarily on the latter. It explores in turn the role of transshipment in fishing operations; the challenges to addressing transshipment; recent developments towards increased control of transshipment in international fora; and the next steps to control transshipment.

2. The Benefits and Risks of Transshipment

Transshipment is a critical part of many fishing operations because it improves efficiency and reduces the cost of fishing operations.[4] By transhipping catch, refuelling, and resupplying at sea, harvesting vessels can avoid fuel costs and lost fishing time associated with transiting back to port.[5] They can remain on the fishing grounds while their catch is landed and enters trade. However, transshipment also undermines sustainable management and efforts to combat IUU fishing.[6] In particular, transshipment masks where, when, how, and by whom the fish were harvested. Inadequately controlled and monitored transshipment can undermine an otherwise robust scheme of integrated measures of monitoring, control, and surveillance (MCS). For example, a catch documentation scheme for ensuring the legality of fish and fish products entering trade may be undermined if transshipment can occur without appropriate documentation, monitoring, and verification. Similarly, carrier vessels take on board fish from several different harvesting vessels. Thus it can be difficult, or even impossible, for port authorities to identify and verify which fish came from which vessel, which prevents authorities from confirming the conditions of harvest.

2 FAO, 'Fisheries and Aquaculture, Report of the Technical Consultation on Voluntary Guidelines for Transshipment' (Rome, 30 May–3 June and 7 July 2022), report no 1385, Appendix E, para 4(g).

3 See https://read.oecd-ilibrary.org/economics/oecd-glossary-of-statistical-terms_9789264055087-en#page455 accessed 24 January 2024.

4 Alicia Mosteiro Cabanelas et al (eds), 'Transshipment: A Closer Look – An In-Depth Study in Support of the Development of International Guidelines', *FAO Fisheries and Aquaculture Technical Paper 661* (Rome 2020) 8, noting notably the prevalence of transshipment in tuna and squid fisheries.

5 ibid, 92–4.

6 ibid, viii.

Transshipment may also facilitate criminal activity, including forced labour and human trafficking.[7] Vessels can remain at sea for long periods, sometimes years, thereby avoiding contact with port authorities who might detect such crimes.[8]

3. Challenges to Controlling Transshipment

At-sea transshipment can be expensive and difficult to monitor effectively. This problem is exacerbated by the fact that much transshipment activity occurs on the high seas.[9] Given the vastness of the areas, patrol activities on the high seas are limited. The patrol vessel will often be flagged to a different country than the vessels engaged in the transshipment activity. In many cases, the two vessels engaged in transshipment will also be flagged to different countries.

On the high seas, the flag State retains sovereignty over its vessels.[10] Therefore, boarding and inspection by another State's authorities can only occur with the flag State's consent. This consent can be provided on an ad hoc basis, or by prior agreement. Many regional fisheries management organisations or arrangements (RFMOs) have adopted high-seas boarding and inspection schemes. Any follow-up enforcement action would be taken by the flag State and perhaps the State of nationality of the captain. In some cases, the flag State of the carrier vessel is not a contracting party or cooperating non-contracting party (CNCP) to the relevant RFMO. Therefore, they are not legally bound to comply with measures adopted by the RFMO, including those applicable to transshipment and high-seas boarding and inspection. Further, they may not be subject to evaluation under the RFMO's compliance evaluation procedure. However, even flag States that are not a CNCP may be under a general obligation to ensure that their vessels do not undermine the effectiveness of conservation and management measures adopted by a relevant RFMO,[11] including through the regulation of transshipment.[12] In addition, regardless of whether or not they are flagged to a contracting party or CNCP, carrier vessels which engage in transshipment activities contravening a RFMO's

7 ibid, 21.

8 FAO, 'Global Study on Transshipment: Regulations, Practices, Monitoring and Control' (Rome June 2018) 17–18, noting that fishing vessels may remain at sea for months, or even years, regularly transshipping catch onto transport vessels and resupplying, bunkering and re-crewing via supply vessels, and enabling illegal operators to avoid port controls. See https://openknowledge.fao.org/server/api/core/bitstreams/0f38f3a7-fd75-4da1-9560-15f77a7c66f2/content accessed 4 July 2024.

9 ibid, 8.

10 United Nations Convention on the Law of the Sea (UNCLOS), 10 December 1982, 1833 UNTS 3, entered into force 16 November 1994, art 92.

11 See, for example, Agreement for the Implementation of the Provisions of United Nations Convention on the Law of the Sea of 10 December 1982 relating to the Conservation and Management of Straddling Fish Stocks and Highly Migratory Fish Stocks (Fish Stocks Agreement), 4 August 1995, 2167 UNTS 3, entered into force 11 December 2001. art 18(1); Agreement to Promote Compliance with International Conservation and Management Measures by Fishing Vessels on the High Seas, 24 November 1993, 2221 UNTS 91, art III(1)(a) and (3).

12 Fish Stocks Agreement, art 18(3)(h).

conservation measures, or otherwise support IUU fishing, could be included in that RFMO's IUU vessel list.

Even where the carrier vessel's flag State is a Contracting Party to the relevant RFMO, there may still be gaps in implementing RFMO obligations related to transshipment. This is because carrier, transport, and bunkering are likely regulated by States' transportation or maritime authorities, rather than their fisheries ministries. These authorities are less likely to participate in RFMOs, which may make them less familiar with measures adopted at the RFMO level. Thus, cooperation and information-sharing between States and between an individual States' relevant authorities are critical.

4. International Legal Framework for Addressing Transshipment

The obligation of States to address transshipment is set out in several binding or voluntary instruments, beginning with the United Nations Convention on the Law of the Sea (UNCLOS) which established the framework for ocean governance. UNCLOS does not specifically address transshipment. However, it does call on States to cooperate in conserving living marine resources, especially high seas, straddling, and highly migratory stocks.[13] This particular obligation was elaborated further for shared fishery resources in the *1995 Agreement for the Implementation of the Provisions of the United Nations Convention on the Law of the Sea of 10 December 1982 relating to the Conservation and Management of Straddling Fish Stocks and Highly Migratory Fish Stocks* (Fish Stocks Agreement). The Fish Stocks Agreement recognises the obligation of States to address transshipment because of the threat that such activity poses to the effective implementation of RFMO conservation and management measures. Thus, it requires flag States to regulate 'transshipment on the high seas to ensure that the effectiveness of conservation and management measures are not undermined'.[14]

Similar to the obligations set out in the Fish Stocks Agreement, the 1993 FAO's *Agreement to Promote Compliance with International Conservation and Management Measures by Fishing Vessels on the High Seas* (FAO Compliance Agreement) enshrines a flag State's duty to exercise effectively its jurisdiction and control over fishing vessels entitled to fly their flag, including fishing vessels and vessels engaged in transshipment. It requires flag States to ensure that their vessels do not engage in activities undermining the effectiveness of international conservation and management measures.[15] This same general obligation is identified in FAO's voluntary 1995 *Code of Conduct for Responsible Fisheries* (FAO Code of

13 UNCLOS, arts 61, 63, 64, 117, 118, 119.

14 Fish Stocks Agreement, art 18(3)(h).

15 FAO Agreement to Promote Compliance with International Conservation and Management Measures by Fishing Vessels on the High Seas, 24 November 1993, 2221 UNTS 91, art I (a) defining 'fishing vessel' to mean 'any vessel used or intended for use for the purposes of the commercial exploitation of living marine resources, including mother ships and any other vessels directly engaged in such fishing operations', art III(1)(a) and (3).

Conduct), which provides that 'States should ensure compliance with and enforcement of conservation and management measures and establish effective mechanisms, as appropriate, to monitor and control the activities of fishing vessels and fishing support vessels'.[16]

The importance of monitoring and controlling transshipment, as an integral part of effectively addressing IUU fishing, is recognised in the 2001 FAO's *International Plan of Action to Prevent, Deter and Eliminate Illegal Unreported and Unregulated Fishing* (IPOA-IUU). The IPOA-IUU calls for States to 'undertake comprehensive and effective monitoring, control and surveillance (MCS) of fishing from its commencement, through the point of landing, to final destination'.[17] The IPOA-IUU also recognises specific obligations on flag, coastal, and port States related to controlling transshipment.[18]

The 2009 FAO *Agreement on Port State Measures to Prevent, Deter and Eliminate Illegal, Unreported and Unregulated Fishing* (Port States Measures Agreement) was the first binding multilateral instrument focused on IUU fishing.[19] It prevents illegally harvested fish and fish products from entering the stream of commerce. The Port State Measures Agreement specifically includes carrier vessels in its scope and defines 'fishing-related activities' as including transshipment.[20] The Port State Measures Agreement does not specifically regulate at-sea transshipment. However, State parties must require that foreign vessels, which carry not previously landed fish and seek entry to port, report on transshipment activities.[21]

The 2014 FAO *Voluntary Guidelines for Flag State Performance* (2014 Voluntary Guidelines for Flag State Performance) are intended to serve as a tool for assessing flag States' implementation of international obligations and best practices from other instruments to develop strengthened measures and to direct capacity-building and technical assistance efforts.[22] The 2014 Voluntary Guidelines recognise the obligation of flag States to implement measures to regulate transshipment.[23] They include mandatory reporting of transshipment information as a minimum standard of an effective MCS regime.[24] They also recognise the general obligations, set out in other instruments, for the flag State to take measures to ensure that vessels flying its flag do not undermine international conservation

16 FAO Code of Conduct for Responsible Fisheries, 1995, art 6(10), see also art 6(11).

17 FAO International Plan of Action to Prevent, Deter and Eliminate Illegal, Unreported and Unregulated Fishing, 2001, para 24.

18 ibid, paras 48, 49, 50, 51(6), 53, 58.

19 Agreement on Port State Measures to Prevent, Deter and Eliminate Illegal, Unreported and Unregulated Fishing, 22 November 2019, entered into force 5 June 2016.

20 ibid, art 1(d).

21 ibid, art 8 and Annex A.

22 FAO Voluntary Guidelines for Flag State Performance, June 2014, abstract, arts 44, 46, 47, 48, 56,57.

23 ibid, art 12 (c).

24 ibid, art 31(d).

and management measures.[25] Further, the flag State should implement a system of effective control over its vessels.[26]

The 2017 FAO *Voluntary Guidelines on Catch Documentation Schemes* identifies transshipment information. This includes information on the donor and receiving vessel, area, and date, as core data elements to be captured in a catch documentation scheme.[27]

5. The FAO Voluntary Guidelines for Transshipment[28]

At its thirty-second session in 2016, the Committee on Fisheries (COFI) of the Food and Agriculture Organization of the United Nations (FAO) called on the FAO to initiate work on transshipment. It notably asked FAO to undertake a review of current regulations and at-sea transshipment practices, authorisation and notification procedures, and reporting requirements; consider which, if any, at-sea transshipment activities should be authorised; and develop guidance on specific control mechanisms where transshipment is authorised and regulated to provide independent monitoring and control over transshipment.[29]

At COFI's thirty-third session in 2018, the FAO's Global Study on transshipment was presented during a side event.[30] COFI expressed concern about the contribution of inadequately regulated transshipment activities to IUU fishing; welcomed the global study on transshipment conducted by FAO; and called for an in-depth study to support development of voluntary guidelines on the control of transshipment.[31] The in-depth study, which was undertaken by FAO with participation from the International Monitoring, Control, and Surveillance, was presented to COFI at its thirty-fourth session in 2021.[32] COFI called on the FAO to begin developing draft voluntary guidelines for the regulation, monitoring, and control of transshipment, and, then, to convene an expert consultation to review the draft. This expert consultation would be followed by a member-led negotiation known as a technical

25 ibid, art 7.
26 ibid, art 31.
27 FAO Voluntary Guidelines for Catch Documentation Schemes, July 2017, Annex, para 1(c).
28 FAO Voluntary Guidelines for Transshipment, 2023.
29 FAO, 'Fisheries and Aquaculture, Report of the 32nd Session of the Committee on Fisheries' (Rome, 11–15 July 2016), report no 1167, paras 164–5.
30 FAO, 'Global Study on Transshipment: Regulations, Practices, Monitoring and Control' (Rome June 2018), see also https://www.fao.org/iuu-fishing/news-events/detail/en/c/1145065/ accessed 4 July 2024.
31 FAO, 'Fisheries and Aquaculture, Report of the 33rd Session of the Committee on Fisheries' (Rome, Italy 9–13 July 2018), report no 1249, para 55.
32 FAO, 'Fisheries and Aquaculture, Report of the 34th Session of the Committee on Fisheries' (Rome, 1–5 February 2021), report no 1336, paras. 14(h)-(i); Alicia Mosteiro Cabanelas et al. (eds), 'Transshipment: A Closer Look – An In-Depth Study in Support of the Development of International Guidelines', *FAO Fisheries and Aquaculture Technical Paper 661* (Rome 2020), xiv.

consultation. The expert consultation was held in the fall of 2021.[33] The technical consultation followed in the late spring and summer of 2022.[34] COFI endorsed the FAO Voluntary Guidelines for Transshipment in September 2022. That endorsement was welcomed by the FAO Council and the Guidelines became final in 2023.

The Guidelines are broad in scope to reflect the range of transshipment activities taking place in domestic and internationally managed fisheries and how the monitoring and control of transshipment intersect with the overall suite of applicable monitoring measures, including at-sea and port inspections and catch documentation schemes. The Guidelines do not exclude transshipment in small-scale fisheries. Instead, they recognise that alternative measures that are comparable in effectiveness may be appropriate for transshipment between vessels flagged to a State and occurring in its waters.

Critically, the Guidelines define 'transshipment' and 'landing' and clarify that landings (including containerisation and transfers to planes) should be documented as such and are subject to measures by the port State. This was a key recommendation of the FAO's in-depth study.[35] This clarification should support more effective implementation of the Port State Measures Agreement and the port inspection measures adopted by many RFMOs. These terms are already defined in the FAO *Voluntary Guidelines on Catch Documentation Schemes*[36] and various RFMOs' catch documentation schemes.[37] However, confusion had persisted. Treating such landings as in-port transshipment created a loophole that has allowed some catches to avoid ever being subject to inspection.

In addition to clarifying the distinction between 'landing' and 'transshipment', the Voluntary Guidelines for Transshipment:

- include the broad definition of a vessel from the Port State Measures Agreement;[38]
- provide that a flag State should not authorise a vessel to act as both donor and receiving vessel on the same trip;[39]
- provide that only vessels flagged by an RFMO's CNCP should be authorised to engage in transshipment under the regulatory competence of that RFMO;[40]

33 FAO, 'Fisheries and Aquaculture, Report of the Expert Consultation on Voluntary Guidelines for Transshipment' (Virtual Meeting, 11–15 October 2021), report no 1363.

34 FAO, 'Fisheries and Aquaculture, Report of the Technical Consultation on Voluntary Guidelines for Transshipment' (Rome, 30 May–3 June and 7 July 2022), report no 1385, Appendix E.

35 Alicia Mosteiro Cabanelas et al. (eds), 'Transshipment: A Closer Look – An In-Depth Study in Support of the Development of International Guidelines', *FAO Fisheries and Aquaculture Technical Paper 661* (Rome 2020).

36 FAO Voluntary Guidelines for Catch Documentation Schemes, July 2017, para 2(7) and (10).

37 See, for example, Commission for the Conservation of Antarctic Marine Living Resource, Conservation Measure 10–05 (2021), para 1(vii) and (xi).

38 FAO Voluntary Guidelines for Transshipment, 2023, para 4(d).

39 ibid, para 11.

40 ibid, para 15.

- distinguish between authorisation, which may be for a specific time period (e.g., a fishing season), and notification, which is for a single transshipment event;[41]
- provide what should be included in pre- and post-event reporting and provide pro formas to support harmonised reporting and data sharing;[42]
- detail how transhipped fish should be documented and stowed to support inspections;[43]
- provide that there should be follow-up actions in case of infringements, linking to RFMO compliance evaluation and IUU vessel listing processes;[44]
- provide that a State should not authorise its vessels to engage in transshipment if it lacks the capacity to monitor effectively;[45]
- provide that donor and receiving vessels should be required to report near real-time VMS data to competent authorities and relevant RFMOs;[46]
- provide that there should be adequate independent verification via electronic monitoring, sensors, human observers, or a combination of these, including 100% observer coverage on the receiving vessel, except where an equivalent comprehensive set of integrated monitoring measures is in place;[47] and
- clarify that observer data related to transshipment should be available for both compliance and scientific purposes.[48]

Many of these provisions are not novel. For example, the flag State's obligation to refrain from authorising a vessel to engage in transshipment unless it can effectively monitor and control the vessel is essentially a restatement of general flag State responsibility, as set forth in the FAO Compliance Agreement, FOA Code of Conduct, and FOA Voluntary Guidelines for Flag State Performance described previously. Others have already been adopted in RFMO measures. However, some of the provisions are novel. Further, if adopted collectively, they would represent significant progress towards ensuring greater control and transparency around transshipment as well as increased clarity around the use of terms.

6. Efforts by RFMOs to Address Transshipment

The international instruments discussed previously establish general obligations and provide guidance to States on the control of transshipment and their competencies as flag, coastal, and port States. Supplementing these instruments, RFMOs have adopted detailed measures to control and monitor transshipment and to integrate these measures into MCS schemes. A review of the measures from nine

41 ibid, paras 17–22, 26–38.
42 ibid, Annexes I and II.
43 ibid, paras 27, 36, and 44.
44 ibid, paras 42–3.
45 ibid, para 22.
46 ibid, paras 13, 29, 45–47.
47 ibid, para 48.
48 ibid, para 49.

RFMOs found that the majority have adopted most of the fifteen key provisions for the control and monitoring of transshipment set out in the FAO Voluntary Guidelines on Transshipment and progress has been made in that regard since negotiation of the Guidelines concluded:[49]

- eight require that carrier vessels be included in an authorised vessel list to carry out at-sea transshipment;
- eight require both harvesting and carrier vessels to report positional data using VMS;[50]
- nine require post-event reporting and additional pre-event notification[51];
- eight require that transshipment information be reported to the State of landing or reviewed in any port inspection;[52]
- five require coastal State's authorisations for transshipment taking place in waters subject to a coastal State's jurisdiction;[53]
- six require observers onboard the carrier vessel;[54]
- five require any notification for the transfers of fuel, personnel, supplies, and other materials, and another has committed to considering that in 2024;[55] and
- five stipulate that the measures apply to all transshipment of fish harvested under the RFMO's regulatory competence, regardless of where they occur;

However, some key provisions have only been adopted by a small number of the reviewed RFMOs:

- four make the transshipment information reported to the RFMO Secretariat available to Members;

49 The Commission for the Conservation of Antarctic Marine Living Resources, CM 10–09 (2022); International Commission for the Conservation of Atlantic Tunas, Rec 21–15; Commission for the Conservation of Southern Bluefin Tuna (Resolution of Establishing a Program for Transhipment by Large-Scale Fishing Vessels (2023); Inter-American Tropical Tuna Commission, Res. C-22–03; Indian Ocean Tuna Commission (Res. 23/05); Northwest Atlantic Fisheries Organization, Conservation and Enforcement Measures (2024); North Pacific Fisheries Commission, CMM 2023–03; South Pacific Regional Fishery Management Organisation, CMM 12–2023; and Western and Central Pacific Fisheries Commission, CMM 2009–06.

50 Note that for four of these, the requirement is included in another measure and may be a requirement as the relevant Convention does not distinguish between harvesting and carrier vessels. For one of the organizations, the VMS requirement only applies to Contracting Parties and Cooperating non-Contracting Parties.

51 Note that for four the pre-notification is to the flag State and not the RFMO Secretariat.

52 Note that for three of these, the requirement is included in another measure.

53 Note that some of the RFMOs whose measures were reviewed have high seas Convention areas.

54 For one of these, the observer may be on either the harvesting or carrier vessel.

55 For one of the organisations, the notification requirement only applies to Contracting Parties and Cooperating non-Contracting Parties.

- four require that transshipment information be included in any catch documentation or statistical document programme;[56] three require that all carrier vessels be flagged to a CNCP;
- three limit the categories of harvesting vessels which may conduct at-sea transshipment (e.g., large-scale pelagic longline vessels fishing for tuna and tuna-like species);
- one prohibits a vessel from acting as the donor and receiving vessel on the same trip; and
- four require that the carrier vessel keep catches from different donor vessels separate and maintain a stowage plan onboard the vessel.

Four of the five tuna RFMOs whose measures were reviewed have adopted relatively comprehensive measures, which include similar requirements. This ensures some harmonisation which could facilitate implementation. However, the measures adopted by the other reviewed RFMOs were more varied and, as noted prevously, some key provisions set out in the FAO Voluntary Guidelines for Transshipment have not been widely implemented.

Gaps in RFMOs' monitoring and control of transshipment have been widely recognised, including in recent performance reviews of various RFMOs.[57] Strengthened measures are needed to ensure that transshipment does not facilitate IUU fishing and the entry of illegally harvested fish into commerce. Some progress has been made. However, progress in some organisations has been slow. This is due in part because participants are reluctant to agree to measures which could result in new obligations imposed on vessels flagged to non-contracting parties (e.g., VMS requirements). States fear that the consequence may limit transshipment opportunities for their industry, thereby negatively impacting their industry operations.

7. Closing the Gap and Next Steps

The FAO Voluntary Guidelines on Transshipment provide a consolidated set of best practices for the control of transshipment. Such best practices can be used by States and RFMOs in their efforts to identify gaps in their existing measures and to adopt new or strengthened measures for the monitoring and control of transshipment in various contexts.[58] Having text which was previously agreed in a multilateral setting, even in a voluntary instrument, can often help advance negotiations on binding measures. Stronger transshipment measures in internationally managed fisheries will, in

56 For one of these, the requirement is included in another measure.

57 See, for example, Report of the South Pacific Regional Fisheries Management Organisation Performance Review Panel (1 December 2018), paras 237–8; Commission for the Conservation of Antarctic Marine Living Resources, Second Performance Review of CCAMLR – Final Report of the Panel (31 August 2017), CAMLR-XXXVI/01, paras 54–5 and Recommendation 12.

58 FAO, 'Fisheries and Aquaculture, Report of the Technical Consultation on Voluntary Guidelines for Transshipment' (Rome, 30 May–3 June and 7 July 2022), report no 1385, Appendix E, para 2.

turn, improve the effectiveness of other MCS measures (e.g., port state measures, catch documentation schemes, and high seas boarding and inspection) as part of a scheme of integrated measures.

Additionally, increased harmonisation across transshipment measures will facilitate improved compliance. It will also facilitate capacity building efforts as curricula can be built around a common set of requirements. This is particularly important, not only for flag State authorities, but also for authorities in busy port States needing familiarity with the measures adopted by different RFMOs.

Part V

Substantive and Procedural Aspects in Fisheries Disputes

11 Limitations on Compulsory Settlement of Disputes with Regard to Fisheries in the EEZ Arising from Article 297(3)(a) of UNCLOS

Ben Juratowitch KC

1. Introduction

Article 297(3)(a) of the United Nations Convention on the Law of the Sea (UNCLOS) provides that:

> Disputes concerning the interpretation or application of the provisions of this Convention with regard to fisheries shall be settled in accordance with section 2, except that the coastal State shall not be obliged to accept the submission to such settlement of any dispute relating to its sovereign rights with respect to the living resources in the exclusive economic zone or their exercise, including its discretionary powers for determining the allowable catch, its harvesting capacity, the allocation of surpluses to other States and the terms and conditions established in its conservation and management laws and regulations.[1]

This provision confirms that the compulsory dispute settlement mechanisms of UNCLOS apply to disputes concerning fisheries. However, it then creates a limitation of contested scope with respect to the exclusive economic zone (EEZ). This chapter examines the scope of this limitation by proceeding in three parts. First, it considers the terms of Article 297(3)(a) of UNCLOS in their context. Second, it examines five relevant cases. Third, it identifies two general questions about the scope of Article 297(3)(a).

2. The Terms of Article 297(3)(a) in Context

Part XV of UNCLOS concerns the settlement of disputes. Section 2 of Part XV deals with compulsory dispute settlement procedures that produce binding decisions under international law. Section 3 of Part XV sets out limitations and exceptions to the application of the procedures in Section 2. Articles 297 and 298 are

1 United Nations Convention on the Law of the Sea (UNCLOS), 10 December 1982, 1833 UNTS 3, entered into force 16 November 1994.

DOI: 10.4324/9781003492030-16

located in Section 3. Article 297 establishes limitations which exist by force of the Convention. Article 298 concerns exceptions arising by declaration of a party to UNCLOS.

Broadly speaking, Article 297(3)(a) may be understood as having five aspects. The first is a positive statement of jurisdiction: 'Disputes concerning the interpretation or application of the provisions of this Convention with regard to fisheries shall be settled in accordance with section 2'. In this sense, it resembles sub-paragraph 1(a) of Article 297. Section 3 of Part XV of UNCLOS is titled 'Limitations and exceptions to applicability of section 2'. Article 297 is titled 'Limitations on applicability of section 2'. Within these, paragraph 1 of Article 297 is, ironically, devoted to positive statements of cases in which disputes concerning the exercise by a coastal State of its sovereign rights or jurisdiction shall be subject to the compulsory procedures entailing binding decisions provided for in section 2. Similarly, the first part of sub-paragraph 3(a) of Article 297 is an affirmative statement concerning jurisdiction over disputes regarding fisheries.

The second aspect of Article 297(3)(a), then, makes explicit that there is a limitation on this compulsory jurisdiction. It says, 'except that'. This is unlike paragraph 1 of Article 297, but like sub-paragraph 2(a) of the same Article.

The third aspect of Article 297(3)(a) does not exclude jurisdiction, but, where applicable, it removes its compulsory character by saying that 'the coastal State shall not be obliged to accept the submission to such settlement'. An applicant State may submit a dispute to an applicable procedure entailing a binding decision even if that dispute comes within the exception provided for in Article 297(3)(a), but the respondent State then has a choice as to whether to accept such submission and if it does not, then there will be no jurisdiction.

The fourth aspect is the content of the limitation: 'any dispute relating to its sovereign rights with respect to the living resources in the exclusive economic zone or their exercise'.

The fifth is a list of matters coming within the limitation that is illustrative rather than exhaustive:

> including its discretionary powers for determining the allowable catch, its harvesting capacity, the allocation of surpluses to other States and the terms and conditions established in its conservation and management laws and regulations.

Article 297 was negotiated from the early stages of the Third Law of the Sea Conference and went through many different drafts. Its odd formulation reflects the push and pull of divergent positions enduring over long periods. As with many provisions of the Convention, and admittedly over-simplifying, States with large numbers of long-range vessels flying their flag wanted, first, maximum freedom for such vessels, including to fish, and second, maximum review of the conduct of States off whose coasts their vessels might operate, including by fishing, which might seek to constrain that freedom. Conversely, and again over-simplifying, such coastal States wanted first, maximum power to control vessels off their coasts, even if flying a flag other than their own, and second, minimum review of their own conduct in respect of such vessels, including in relation to fishing.

3. Five Cases considering Article 297(3)(a) of UNCLOS

The first case of relevance to Article 297(3)(a) of UNCLOS is the *Chagos Marine Protected Area Arbitration* brought by Mauritius against the United Kingdom and decided in 2015.[2] The United Kingdom had declared a Marine Protected Area (MPA) around the Chagos Archipelago projected seaward to a distance of 200 nautical miles. The fourth submission of Mauritius in the case was that the MPA declared by the United Kingdom was 'incompatible with the substantive and procedural obligations of the United Kingdom under the Convention, including, *inter alia* Articles 2, 55, 56, 63, 64, 194 and 300, as well as Article 7 of [the Fish Stocks Agreement]'.[3] The United Kingdom argued that the tribunal did not have jurisdiction over this claim because the MPA was a measure relating to sovereign rights with respect to living resources in the EEZ, such that the limitation to jurisdiction in Article 297(3)(a) applied.[4]

The tribunal characterized the MPA objectively. It found that the United Kingdom had sought to justify the MPA, both before and during the arbitration, on environmental grounds broader than just the management of fisheries.[5] The tribunal, thus, refused to regard the MPA as merely a fisheries measure, and so refused to decline jurisdiction over the fourth submission as a whole.[6]

The tribunal analysed the extent to which the claims made by Mauritius were excluded by Article 297(3)(a). It noted that Mauritius sought to rely, through the reference in Article 2(3) of UNCLOS to 'other rules of international law' and the due regard obligation in Article 56(2) of UNCLOS referring to 'the rights and duties of other States', on the Lancaster House Undertakings that the United Kingdom had made to Mauritius in 1965 in connection with the separation of the Chagos Archipelago from Mauritius to form the British Indian Ocean Territory.[7] One of these undertakings related specifically to fishing rights. Thus, the tribunal had no difficulty in finding that, so far as it applied to the EEZ, issues arising in respect of this particular undertaking were excluded from the tribunal's jurisdiction pursuant

2 *Chagos Marine Protected Area Arbitration (Mauritius v. United Kingdom)*, Award, PCA Case 2011–03, 18 March 2015.

3 ibid, para 158. Citing to Agreement for the Implementation of the Provisions of the United Nations Convention on the Law of the Sea of 10 December 1982 relating to the Conservation and Management of Straddling Fish Stocks and Highly Migratory Fish Stocks (Fish Stocks Agreement), 4 August 1995, 2167 UNTS 3, entered into force 11 December 2001.

4 ibid, paras 245–6.

5 ibid, paras 286–91.

6 ibid, para 304.

7 ibid, para 294.

to Article 297(3)(a).[8] Equally, the tribunal had little difficulty finding that the claims concerning other aspects of the undertakings did come within its jurisdiction.[9]

The tribunal noted that Article 63 of UNCLOS on straddling fish stocks and Article 64 on UNCLOS on highly migratory species, as well as Article 7 of the Fish Stocks Agreement, all concerned fisheries.[10] On that basis, it found that claims that these articles had been breached were, insofar as they concerned the EEZ, excluded from the tribunal's jurisdiction by Article 297(3)(a).[11]

Mauritius had argued that there was a distinction between, on the one hand, the sovereign rights of the coastal State with respect to the living resources in the EEZ, which are excluded from a tribunal's jurisdiction pursuant to Article 297(3)(a), and, on the other hand, the rights of other States in respect of the same living resources in the same area, which, Mauritius said, would not be excluded from jurisdiction.[12] The tribunal rejected this argument. It made the obvious point that the two are intertwined, as disputes will involve a conflict between the coastal State's view of its own rights and the other State's view of its own rights.[13] Thus, the jurisdictional limitation in Article 297(3)(a) applied to the rights in respect of living resources in the MPA asserted by Mauritius just as much as it did to the rights in respect of living resources asserted by the United Kingdom by way of the MPA. Indeed, it was the conflict between these asserted rights which constituted the relevant part of the dispute.

The joint dissenting and concurring opinion of Judges Kateka and Wolfrum shared the conclusion of the majority on Article 297(3)(a), but also developed two further ideas. The first was that because Article 297(3)(a) starts with a confirmation that there shall be jurisdiction over disputes 'with regard to fisheries', the exception which follows cannot limit jurisdiction over all fisheries disputes. The two judges rightly observed that the 'second part of the clause must be narrower in scope than the scope of the first part', but wrongly said that if:

> the first part of this clause – the confirmation of jurisdiction – is to retain some meaning, not all disputes on fisheries can be interpreted as 'any dispute relating to its sovereign rights with respect to living resources.[14]

One difficulty with this statement is that it overlooks that the limitation applies only in the EEZ, whereas the positive statement of jurisdiction applies to fisheries in general, thus including high-seas fisheries.

8 ibid, para 297.
9 ibid, para 298.
10 ibid, para 300.
11 ibid.
12 ibid, para 250.
13 ibid, para 297.
14 *Chagos Marine Protected Area Arbitration (Mauritius v. United Kingdom)*, Award, PCA Case 2011–03, 18 March 2015, Dissenting and Concurring Opinion of Judge Kateka and Judge Wolfrum, para 58.

The second idea developed by the two judges was that 'it is doubtful whether a total ban on fishing is covered by the exception clause under Article 297(3)(a) of the Convention'.[15] This was said to be on the basis of UNCLOS' focus on utilising, managing, and conserving living resources.[16] In considering this issue, one should recall the terms of Article 56 of UNCLOS, defining the sovereign rights of a State in its EEZ. They include 'sovereign rights for the purpose of exploring and exploiting, conserving and managing the natural resources'. Much would depend on the contours of the measure which would be challenged. However, in general terms, the two judges' doubt may not be well founded. The limitation allows a coastal State to avoid jurisdiction over 'any dispute relating to its sovereign rights with respect to the living resources in the exclusive economic zone or their exercise'. The words 'relating to' cover quite a lot. More importantly, 'with respect to' appears broad enough to capture a ban on the exploitation of a particular living resource, just as much as it would capture a regulation specifying limitations on such exploitation. Therefore, it is hard to see how this provision would not include a dispute about a State exercising its sovereign rights, including with respect to conservation, by way of banning fishing in its EEZ, whether in respect of some or all areas within the EEZ or some or all types of fish. The remainder of the limitation is merely an inclusive list, and even that includes 'the terms and conditions established in its conservation and management laws and regulations'.

The second relevant case is the *Barbados* v. *Trinidad and Tobago* arbitration, which was decided in 2006.[17] At the hearing, Barbados claimed a right of access to flying fish stocks in the EEZ of Trinidad and Tobago.[18] This late claim was found by the tribunal to be *ultra petita*. However, the tribunal also found that it lacked jurisdiction over the claim because it concerned the rights and duties of the two States in relation to a fishery in the EEZ, as delimited by the tribunal, of one of the States.[19] On that basis, it was within the limitation in Article 297(3)(a) of UNCLOS, in circumstances where Trinidad and Tobago had made clear that it did not consent to submission of that dispute to the tribunal. The tribunal, nonetheless, recorded undertakings made by the parties in respect of Barbados' access to the fishery, including on the negotiation of an agreement.[20]

The third decision of relevance is the 2015 advisory opinion of the International Tribunal for the Law of the Sea (ITLOS) in response to the *Request for an Advisory Opinion submitted by the Sub-Regional Fisheries Commission*, and more specifically the separate opinion of Judge Paik.[21] He criticised ITLOS for not sufficiently addressing 'the relationship between the duties to cooperate and the sovereign

15 ibid, para 60.
16 ibid.
17 *Barbados v. Trinidad and Tobago*, Award, PCA Case 2004–02, 11 April 2006.
18 ibid, para 273.
19 ibid, paras 276, 283.
20 ibid, paras 287–93.
21 *Request for an Advisory Opinion submitted by the Sub-Regional Fisheries Commission*, Advisory Opinion, ITLOS Rep 2015, Separate Opinion of Judge Paik.

rights of the coastal State to conserve and manage living resources in its EEZ'.[22] He focused on the obligation to negotiate in Article 63(1) of UNCLOS, concerning fish stocks straddling the EEZs of more than one State, and noted that it is an obligation of conduct, not of result.[23] Judge Paik's thesis was twofold. First, if States do not reach an agreement, then pursuant to Articles 61 and 62 of UNCLOS each State has the obligation (and right) to conserve and manage the stocks 'occurring within' its own EEZ.[24] Second, responsibility for a breach of the obligation to negotiate, for example by refusing to consult or negotiate or by wilfully delaying responding to proposals, could be invoked through the compulsory procedures in Part XV, Section 2, of UNCLOS, and would not be excluded by Article 297(3)(a), which Judge Paik did not mention explicitly but clearly had in mind.[25] He contrasted this to disputes arising from the exercise of sovereign rights of the coastal State with respect to the living resources in its EEZ, which of course fall within the limitation to compulsory jurisdiction.[26]

Judge Paik's separate opinion does not consider the words 'relating to' and their breadth in the limitation contained in Article 297(3)(a). For his opinion to be correct, a dispute about whether an obligation to negotiate concerning fish stocks straddling the EEZs of multiple States has been breached would need not to qualify as a dispute 'relating to' a coastal State's sovereign rights with respect to fisheries in the EEZ. If this proposition ever needs to be decided, it will certainly be debated. In the meantime, it appears to be in tension with the approach adopted by the arbitral tribunal in the *Chagos Marine Protected Area Arbitration*, which regarded a claim under Article 63 as fully excluded from jurisdiction because of the limitation in Article 297(3)(a).[27]

The fourth relevant case is the *Dispute Concerning State Rights in the Black Sea, Sea of Azov, and Kerch Strait* between Ukraine and Russia, and specifically the award rendered in 2020 on Russia's preliminary objections.[28] This case involved claims to rights in maritime areas off the coast of Crimea. Sovereignty over Crimea was and, of course, remains disputed between Ukraine and Russia. The arbitral tribunal found that it lacked jurisdiction over any claim which would require it to decide, expressly or implicitly, whether Ukraine or Russia has sovereignty over Crimea.[29]

Relevantly, Russia contended that, based on Article 297(3)(a) of UNCLOS, the tribunal did not have jurisdiction over Ukraine's claim to fishing rights in these

22 ibid, para 31.
23 ibid, para 35.
24 ibid, para 37.
25 ibid.
26 ibid.
27 *Chagos Marine Protected Area Arbitration (Mauritius v. United Kingdom)*, Award, PCA Case 2011–03, 18 March 2015, para 300.
28 *Dispute Concerning Coastal State Rights in the Black Sea, Sea of Azov and Kerch Strait (Ukraine v. Russian Federation)*, Award on Preliminary Objections, PCA 2017–06, 21 February 2020.
29 ibid, para 197.

areas. The tribunal dismissed this objection as 'the interference by the Russian Federation with fisheries activities alleged by Ukraine occurred within an area that cannot be determined to constitute the exclusive economic zone of the Russian Federation or Ukraine'.[30] As a result, the conditions for applying the limitation in Article 297(3)(a) could not be met.[31] If the tribunal could not decide whether the relevant area was the EEZ of one State or the other, it could not find that the dispute related to the sovereign rights of Russia in its own EEZ.

The fifth and final case is *The South China Sea Arbitration*, commenced by the Philippines against China, in which the final award was rendered in 2016. As China did not formally participate in the proceedings, the arbitral tribunal identified potential objections to its own jurisdiction, one of which was the limitation in Article 297(3)(a). Having ruled on the maximum extent of China's maritime projections, the fisheries relevant to the potential objection under Article 297(3)(a) were all found to be contained within the Philippines' EEZ. Thus, the tribunal was able to say of Article 297(3)(a):

> These provisions serve to limit compulsory dispute settlement where a claim is brought against a State's exercise of its sovereign rights in respect of living resources in its *own* exclusive economic zone. These provisions do not apply where a State is alleged to have violated the Convention in respect of the exclusive economic zone of another State (emphasis in original).[32]

In *The Black Sea, Sea of Azov, and Kerch Strait* arbitration, a dispute about sovereignty over the territory which would generate the relevant EEZ meant that the limitation in Article 297(3)(a) could not be applied, because the tribunal did not have jurisdiction to determine the State to which the relevant maritime area appertained. By contrast, in *The South China Sea Arbitration*, where the tribunal found it had jurisdiction to determine the maximum seaward extent of China's maritime zones and did so, the limitation in Article 297(3)(a) was inapplicable because the fisheries to which the Philippines' claim related were within its own EEZ, not China's.

4. Two General Questions

The first general question is whether the limitation in Article 297(3)(a) of UNCLOS effectively swallows the rule, the rule being the affirmative statement of jurisdiction with which Article 297(3)(a) begins. The Proelss' *Commentary* to UNCLOS says that there is a risk that it does.[33] However, a lot remains that is important to the conservation and sustainable use of fish stocks. Most obviously, the limitation does

30 ibid, para 402.
31 ibid, para 402.
32 *South China Sea Arbitration (The Republic of the Philippines v. The People's Republic of China)*, Award, PCA Case 2013–19, 12 July 2016, para 695.
33 Andrew Serdy, 'Article 297' in Alexander Proelss (ed), *United Nations Convention on the Law of the Sea: A Commentary* (Beck, Nomos and Hart 2017) 1909.

not apply to fisheries in the high seas. More importantly, as far more fish are taken from EEZs than the high seas, the obligations of the flag State of a vessel which apply while it is fishing in another State's EEZ are not within the limitation. As a result, coastal States can access compulsory dispute resolution procedures against flag States of vessels when such States do not fulfil their obligations under UNCLOS in connection with fishing vessels sailing their flag and fishing in the EEZ of the putative applicant coastal State.

In Article 297(3)(a), coastal States succeeded in limiting the extent to which the compulsory dispute resolution procedures of UNCLOS could be invoked in respect of their sovereign rights to living resources in their EEZs. However, they did not truncate the ability of a coastal State, in whose EEZ a vessel sailing under another State's flag is fishing, particularly if such fishing is illegal, unreported, or unregulated, to pursue compulsory dispute resolution proceedings against the flag State if it is not fulfilling its obligations in respect of fishing vessels sailing its flag.

The second general question concerning Article 297(3)(a) arises from a later article in UNCLOS, namely Article 298(1)(b). The latter article provides that a State may declare that it does not accept the compulsory dispute resolution procedures in Section 2 with respect to:

> disputes concerning law enforcement activities in regard to the exercise of sovereign rights or jurisdiction excluded from the jurisdiction of a court or tribunal under Article 297, paragraph 2 or 3.

Logically, one might say that, if Article 298(1)(b) allows States to declare that they do not accept the compulsory procedures in Section 2 for law enforcement activities in regard to the exercise of sovereign rights excluded from jurisdiction under Article 297(3)(a), then such law enforcement activities cannot already have come within the limitation in Article 297(3)(a). If they had, they would be excluded for all parties to UNCLOS by force of the generally applicable limitation in Article 297(3)(a). If such a general limitation existed, it is difficult to see why one aspect of this limitation would also be something that States could choose to declare to exclude under Article 298(1)(b).

This logical approach would be consistent with Article 297(3)(a) concerning only prescriptive jurisdiction – the ability of a State to determine by law or other form of regulation what is and is not permitted within its EEZ. The limitation would mean that such determinations are not subject to compulsory dispute resolution procedures. By contrast, according to this approach, Article 298(1)(b) would concern enforcement jurisdiction – it specifically relates to 'law enforcement activities'. If this were the distinction, disputes concerning law enforcement activities of coastal States relating to their sovereign rights with respect to the living resources in their EEZ would not be excluded from jurisdiction by force of Article 297(3)(a). Instead, they would only be excluded if a relevant declaration had been made under Article 298(1)(b). However, disputes on the content of laws or other form of regulation being enforced would be excluded by Article 297(3)(a) by force of the terms of UNCLOS and without any declaration. This interpretation could be supported by the fact that the inclusive list in Article 297(3)(a) of matters excluded are all plainly examples of prescriptive jurisdiction. The list refers to the power of 'determining' the allowable catch and harvesting capacity; the 'allocation' of surpluses; and 'terms and conditions' in the coastal State's relevant 'laws and regulations'. None of the examples concerns enforcement jurisdiction.

If this interpretation were correct, it would allow flag States to pursue compulsory dispute resolution procedures against coastal States to challenge specific acts of law enforcement inconsistent with Article 73 of UNCLOS, which concerns the enforcement of a coastal State's laws and regulations in its EEZ. Article 73 refers to such enforcement measures 'as may be necessary' to ensure compliance with relevant laws and regulations. This language may lend itself to a similar approach taken by the tribunal in the *Duzgit Integrity Arbitration*.[34] This arbitration concerned law enforcement in archipelagic waters and was decided in 2016 between Malta and Sao Tomé and Principe. The tribunal held that, where a State derives its law enforcement powers from UNCLOS, which is certainly the case for a coastal State's law enforcement powers in the EEZ, these powers are subject to the principle of reasonableness, which in turn 'encompasses the principles of necessity and proportionality'.[35]

Arguments could also be made against such an interpretation. First, Article 297(3)(a) refers not only to sovereign rights but, also, in the alternative – 'or' – to 'their exercise'. This could reasonably include law enforcement activities as well as the content of legislation or other forms of regulation. Indeed, this is the approach which appears to have been taken in the terms of Article 73. Second, Article 297(3)(a) provides that the coastal State shall not be obliged to accept the submission of certain disputes to compulsory procedures. However, it does not similarly excuse other States, notably flag States, which a declaration under Article 298(1)(b) would do, alleviating the potential redundancy identified previously. Third, ITLOS has not favoured to date a meaningful distinction between prescriptive jurisdiction and enforcement jurisdiction, including in the *M/V Norstar* case between Panama and Italy decided in 2019.[36] Fourth, one may question whether the compromise reached in Article 297(3)(a) was objectively intended to leave law enforcement activities of coastal States in their EEZs within the scope of compulsory dispute resolution.

Irrespective of the interpretation, which is or may be found to be correct, this question might well qualify as an 'emerging' challenge in international fisheries law.

34 *The Duzgit Integrity Arbitration (Malta v. São Tomé and Príncipe)*, Award, PCA Case 2014–07, 5 September 2016.
35 ibid, para 209.
36 *The M/V "Norstar" Case (Panama v. Italy)*, Judgment, ITLOS Rep 2018–2019.

12 Compulsory Conciliation Proceedings Regarding Disputes on Conservation and Management of Fish Stocks

Alina Miron

1. Introduction

Conciliation is one of the most promising but least resorted to diplomatic means of dispute settlement. As observed by Jean-Pierre Cot, '[t]he contrast is striking between the number of important, elaborate and highly political agreements calling for conciliation . . . [and] the paucity of any effective resort'.[1] Conciliation over fisheries disputes perfectly illustrates this observation.

Article 1 of the Salzburg resolution of the Institut de Droit international defines conciliation as

> a method for the settlement of international disputes of any nature according to which a Commission set up by the Parties . . . proceeds to the impartial examination of the dispute and attempts to define the terms of a settlement susceptible of being accepted by them, or of affording the Parties, with a view to its settlement, such aid as they may have requested.[2]

Three articles in the United Nations Convention on the Law of the Sea (UNCLOS) relate to conciliation. Article 284 provides for voluntary conciliation based on an ad hoc agreement between the parties. Articles 297 and 298 provide compulsory conciliation which can be triggered unilaterally by one of the parties.[3] Compulsory conciliation is also defined as 'conciliation in which participation in the process

1 Jean-Pierre Cot, 'Expectations Attached to Conciliation Reconsidered' in Christian Tomuschat, Riccardo Pisillo Mazzeschi and Daniel Thürer (eds), *Conciliation in International Law* (Brill Nijhoff 2017) 9.

2 Institut de Droit international, 'International Conciliation' (Salzburg 1961) art 1.

3 One could add conciliation as part of the decision-making process within the International Seabed Authority per arts 161 and 162 of United Nations Convention on the Law of the Sea (UNCLOS), 10 December 1982, 1833 UNTS 3, entered into force 16 November 1994. This was revised substantially by the Agreement relating to the implementation of Part XI of the UNCLOS, 29 July 1994, entered into force 13 December 1998. These revisions have resulted in conciliation no longer being a pre-condition for using dispute-settlement procedures in arts 186–91 of UNCLOS.

DOI: 10.4324/9781003492030-17

is mandatory but the results are nevertheless non-binding'.[4] Rüdiger Wolfrum underlines that the term 'compulsory' is misleading: this 'conciliation is compulsory only as a process', not of result.[5] In UNCLOS, the scope *ratione materiae* of compulsory conciliation is extremely limited. It only applies in limited fields: the exercise of sovereign rights with regards to marine scientific research, per Article 297(2)(b);[6] sovereign rights in relation to fisheries, per Article 297(3)(b); and disputes over the delimitation of maritime boundaries when they are excluded from adjudication by an optional declaration, per Article 298(1)(a) and (b). These provisions are supplemented by Annex V to UNCLOS which provides for the conciliation procedure.

Conciliation has played a marginal role in the dispute settlement system under UNCLOS. This is not merely because of its inherent nature as an amicable procedure, but also due to its articulation with adjudication. Compulsory conciliation, as this chapter details further, has been carved as 'a fallback mechanism for certain disputes that have been excluded from compulsory dispute settlement mechanisms'.[7]

2. Conciliation is not Adjudication: General Considerations on the Nature of Conciliation

Conciliation under UNCLOS reflects the philosophy underlying this method of dispute settlement in general. Despite its adversarial aspects, conciliation is not adjudication. Instead, it is an amicable method of dispute settlement. As the International Court of Justice (ICJ) held in relation to conciliation within the framework of the International Convention on the Elimination of All Forms of Racial Discrimination,

> 'negotiation' and the 'procedures expressly provided for in [the] Convention' [i.e., conciliation] are two means to achieve the same objective, *namely to settle a dispute by agreement* (emphasis added).[8]

4 *Timor Sea Conciliation (Timor-Leste v. Australia)*, Report and Recommendations of the Compulsory Conciliation Commission between Timor-Leste and Australia on the Timor Sea, PCA Case 2016–10, 9 May 2018, para 52.

5 Rüdiger Wolfrum, 'Conciliation Under the UN Convention on the Law of the Sea' in Christian Tomuschat, Riccardo Pisillo Mazzeschi and Daniel Thürer (eds), *Conciliation in International Law* (Brill Nijhoff 2017) 186.

6 This concerns more specifically the rights enumerated in UNCLOS, arts 246, 253.

7 Shunmugam Jayakumar, 'Compulsory Dispute Settlement and Conciliation Under UNCLOS' in Hao Duy Phan, Tara Davenport and Robert Beckman (eds), *The Timor-Leste/Australia Conciliation: A Victory for UNCLOS and Peaceful Settlement of Disputes* (World Scientific Publishing 2019) 14.

8 *Application of the International Convention for the Suppression of the Financing of Terrorism and of the International Convention on the Elimination of All Forms of Racial Discrimination (Ukraine v. Russian Federation)*, Judgment on Preliminary Objections, ICJ Rep 2019, para 110.

Similarly, the objective 'to settle a dispute by agreement' permeates the different phases of conciliation in UNCLOS. Several provisions of Annex V to UNCLOS recall this fundamental nature. Article 5 notes that the conciliation commission may 'draw attention to measures [which] might facilitate an amicable settlement'. Article 6 provides that it will 'examine their claims and objections and make proposals to the parties with a view to reaching an amicable settlement'. Article 7 specifies that the report of the commission consists of 'conclusions on all questions of fact or law relevant to the matter in dispute and such recommendations as the commission may deem appropriate for an amicable settlement'. Article 7(2) also confirms the non-binding character of the outcome: '[t]he report of the commission, including its conclusions or recommendations, shall not be binding upon the parties'. Therefore, the parties may reject the recommendations and this rejection would not amount to an unlawful act.

These numerous references to the 'amicable settlement' emphasise that the objective of conciliation remains 'for the States concerned to reach an agreed settlement of their dispute'.[9] This outcome depends on the parties' will.[10] In compulsory conciliation, the difficulty is to create the appropriate conditions which can facilitate this outcome, particularly where a party challenges the competence of the conciliation commission.

On the procedural devices which can enable a successful outcome, much can be learnt from Timor-Leste/Australia Commission – the only example of compulsory conciliation held under UNCLOS so far.[11] This case concerned maritime delimitation, not fisheries. It is not suggested that its procedures should be transposed to all conciliations. However, its underpinning philosophy could serve as a guide. The key words to describe it are 'flexible pragmatism':

> Article 5 of Annex V to the Convention, however, empowers the Commission to recommend 'any measures which might facilitate an amicable settlement of the dispute.' On its own terms, this provision is extremely broad and, for the Commission, emblematic of the flexible pragmatism that lies at the heart of conciliation: the Commission's mandate is to take the steps necessary to assist the Parties in resolving their dispute.[12]

The Commission enjoyed significant discretion in conducting the proceedings and used it extensively. It thus innovated on several accounts. As a confidence-building

9 ibid, para 109.

10 ibid, para 110.

11 *Timor Sea Conciliation (Timor-Leste v. Australia)*, Report and Recommendations of the Compulsory Conciliation Commission between Timor-Leste and Australia on the Timor Sea, PCA Case 2016–10, 9 May 2018.

12 ibid, para 62. The Commission added in a footnote:

> This flexibility leaves a commission with significant discretion as to the conduct of the procedure, and the most appropriate approach may well depend upon the identity of the parties, the nature of their dispute, and the likely receptiveness of the parties to proposals for a genuine settlement.

measure, it chose to bifurcate the proceedings on competence, considering that Australia's objections should be dealt with first. Bifurcation was also justified by the fact that, unlike the report on the merits, the Commission's decision on competence was binding. Therefore, considerations of due process were of particular importance and required a different procedural approach from the merits.[13] By contrast, at the merits stage, the Commission endeavoured to reduce the adversarial charge.[14] To do so, it used informal means of communication.[15] It also preserved confidentiality to the extent necessary,[16] including through a non-prejudice clause which prevented the use of the parties' positions in any future contentious proceedings.[17] The Commission also extended the 12-month deadline, under Article 7 of Annex V, for it to produce its report. The Commission endeavoured to bring the parties closer together with such procedural devices.[18] It cultivated an agreement and encouraged unilateral commitments, which in the end proved important for success.

The Commission played close attention to the limits of its role and refrained from acting as a judge or arbitrator.[19] It assumed that the parties did not expect an award, but instead the resumption and facilitation of their negotiations on a better basis. To fulfil its role, the Commission went beyond the law and engaged with other relevant factors, including economic and financial.[20] The Commission insisted that there was a distinction between applying the law and examining the

13 ibid, para 66.

14 ibid, para 57, where the Commission stated '[i]In practice, most of the Commission's meetings with the Parties were held separately, and the Commission considers that its most important discussions with each Party would not have occurred in a joint setting'.

15 ibid, para 58, where the Commission stated

> [t]he Parties further agreed that the Commission could authorize its Chairman or a delegation of the Commission to confer or meet with either Party and report to the full Commission. In the Commission's view, this flexibility was essential to the process in two respects: first, in enabling the Commission's engagement with the Parties to continue between meetings through regular, informal discussions by telephone and e-mail exchanges and, second, by facilitating discrete discussions with the political leadership of each Party that could not have occurred in a larger or more formal setting.

16 ibid, paras 61–2.

17 ibid, para 59; see also Henri Rolin, 'Une Conciliation Belgo-Danoise' (1953) 57 *Revue Générale de Droit International Public* 359.

18 *Timor Sea Conciliation (Timor-Leste v. Australia)*, Report and Recommendations of the Compulsory Conciliation Commission between Timor-Leste and Australia on the Timor Sea, PCA Case 2016–10, 9 May 2018, para 68, where the Commission stated 'the 12-month period set out in Annex V should be understood not as the timeframe in which a successful conciliation can likely be concluded, but rather as a safeguard to ensure that an unproductive conciliation is not unduly prolonged'.

19 ibid, para 52; see also Marcelle Breton-Jokl, 'La Commission de Conciliation Italo-Suisse' (1957) 3 *Annuaire Français de Droit International* 210, 217; Jean-Pierre Cot, 'Conciliation' in Anne Peters (ed), *Max Planck Encyclopedia of Public International Law* (OUP online 2024).

20 Marcelle Breton-Jokl, 'La Commission de Conciliation Italo-Suisse' (1957) 3 *Annuaire Français de Droit International* 210, 215.

situation in light of the legal principles without applying them, but also insisted that the result should not be contrary to UNCLOS:

> The Commission has frequently noted that it is not an arbitral tribunal with the power to make a binding ruling. It follows, for the Commission, that a conciliation commission need not as a matter of course engage with the parties on their legal positions, but may engage with these matters to the extent that so doing will likely facilitate the achievement of an amicable settlement. It also follows, for the Commission, that a conciliation commission should not encourage parties to reach an agreement that it considers to be inconsistent with the Convention or other provisions of international law.[21]

In short, the goal of conciliation, in other words, facilitating the achievement of an amicable settlement, became the ultimate guide for the Commission's exercise of its broad discretion.

I. Conciliation as an Adjuvant to Adjudication

In the domain of fisheries, conciliation appears as an adjuvant to adjudication and its use speaks to States' reluctance to submit fisheries-related matters to binding judgment by a third party. Conciliation was conceived either as a substitute to adjudication (when the latter was excluded by limitations or optional declarations) or as a procedural precondition for adjudication. However, and paradoxically, there has been no practice of inter-State conciliation, whereas States have resorted to adjudication over fisheries-related matters before the International Tribunal for the Law of the Sea (ITLOS) and ad hoc tribunals. Further, in practice, conciliation competes not only with binding dispute settlement under UNCLOS, but also with mechanisms for adjudication established in other treaties.

2.1. Conciliation as a Substitute to Adjudication

Under Article 297(3)(b) of UNCLOS, conciliation is clearly a substitute for adjudication which is made unavailable under Article 297(3)(a). During the Third United Nations Conference on the Law of the Sea, the conciliation formula received 'widespread and substantial support'.[22] Such support was not for conciliation per se, but rather as a compromise allowing for the exclusion of adjudication. As Andrew Serdy noted,

21 *Timor Sea Conciliation (Timor-Leste v. Australia)*, Report and Recommendations of the Compulsory Conciliation Commission between Timor-Leste and Australia on the Timor Sea, PCA Case 2016–10, 9 May 2018, para 70.

22 Bernard Oxman, 'The Third United Nations Conference on the Law of the Sea: The Seventh Session (1978)' (1979) 73 *American Journal of International* Law 1.

> The debate at the Fourth session in 1976 highlighted the stark divide between those States wary of the extensive rights for a coastal State in the [exclusive economic zone (EEZ)] . . . who wanted them subjected to compulsory dispute settlement as a safeguard against their abuse, and the States that were the EEZ's leading proponents, for whom the prospect that *such disputes could be unilaterally referred to a settlement procedure beyond their control represented an undermining of the exclusive jurisdiction and decision-making that was the rationale for the creation of the EEZ.* . . . Owing to the continuing tension between coastal States rights fearing a plethora of legal challenges to their actions within their EEZs and other States insisting on the availability of compulsory adjudication to prevent abuse of the EEZ rights, Negotiating Group 5 was established at the Seventh Session in 1978, and developed *a compromise in the form of compulsory conciliation of the identified categories of disputes, but without an obligation to accept the ensuing report as binding* (emphasis added).[23]

However, the division between compulsory conciliation and mandatory adjudication is not clear. All that is excluded from adjudication is not necessarily included in conciliation.[24] Further, what appears included in the purview of conciliation may also fall under mandatory adjudication, pursuant to other provisions of UNCLOS. For instance, under Article 297(3)(b)(i), States may submit to conciliation the manifest failure by a coastal State 'to comply with its obligations to ensure through proper conservation and management measures that the maintenance of the living resources in the exclusive economic zone is not seriously endangered'. It is uncertain how this provision for compulsory conciliation may be combined with Article 297(1)(c) which provides for compulsory adjudication

> when it is alleged that a coastal State has acted in contravention of specified international *rules and standards for the protection and preservation of the marine environment* which are applicable to the coastal State (emphasis added).[25]

23 Andrew Serdy, 'Article 297' in Alexander Proelss (ed), *United Nations Convention on the Law of the Sea: A Commentary* (Beck, Nomos and Hart 2017) 1911–2. See also Natalie Klein, *Dispute Settlement in the UN Convention on the Law of the Sea* (CUP 2005) 177. The relevant documents of the *travaux préparatoires* are the following: Third United Nations Conference on the Law of the Sea, 'Australia, Belgium, Bolivia, Colombia, El Salvador, Luxembourg, Netherlands, Singapore and United States of America: Working Paper on the Settlement of Law of the Sea Disputes' (27 August 1974) A/CONF.62/L.7; Third United Nations Conference on the Law of the Sea, 'Informal Composite Negotiating Text: Revision 1' (28 April 1979) A/CONF.62/WP.10/REV.1; Third United Nations Conference on the Law of the Sea, 'Informal Composite Negotiating Text: Revision 2' (11 April 1980) A/CONF.62/WP.10/REV.2.

24 See section 3 of the present chapter, 'Conciliation as a Shield Against Abuse of Rights'.

25 On the obvious contradiction between these provisions, see Valentin J. Schatz, 'The Settlement of EEZ Fisheries Access Disputes Under UNCLOS: Limitations to Jurisdiction and Compulsory Conciliation' (2023) 13 *Goettingen Journal of International Law* 82, 94–5.

Indeed, it is now widely accepted that 'the conservation of the living resources of the sea is an element in the protection and preservation of the marine environment'.[26]

The same formula of compulsory conciliation as a substitute for unavailable adjudication was retained in other treaties. For example, under the Convention on Biological Diversity, States may consent to arbitration under Annex II to that treaty or to adjudication before the ICJ to resolve their disputes.[27] In the absence of such consent, compulsory conciliation is available instead.[28] Some of these treaties may encompass disputes concerning fisheries. In the *Whaling* case, Australia did invoke the Convention on Biological Diversity in its Application but dropped it subsequently.

2.2. A Procedural Condition for Resorting to Adjudication

Outside UNCLOS, conciliation is envisaged by other fisheries-related treaties as a procedural condition for resorting to adjudication. However, these compromissory clauses do not oblige the parties to exhaust conciliation before resorting to adjudication.[29] Conciliation is simply listed among the dispute settlement means available to the parties, but it is not a precondition. Thus, the typical dispute-resolution clause stipulates that

> If any dispute arises between two or more Contracting Parties concerning the interpretation or implementation of this Convention, those Contracting Parties shall consult among themselves with a view to resolving the dispute, or to having the dispute resolved by negotiation, inquiry, mediation, conciliation, arbitration, judicial settlement or other peaceful means of their own choice.
>
> Where a dispute is not resolved by recourse to other means referred to in this article within a reasonable time, such dispute shall, at the request of any

26 *Southern Bluefin Tuna (New Zealand v. Japan; Australia v. Japan)*, Provisional Measures, Order of 27 August 1999, ITLOS Rep 1999, para 70.

27 Convention on Biological Diversity, 5 June 1992, 1760 UNTS 79, entered into force 29 December 1993.

28 ibid, art 27(3)–(4), A similar dispute settlement regime is available under the United Nations Framework Convention on Climate Change, 9 May 1992, 1771 UNTS 107, entered into force 21 March 1994, art 14, and in the Paris Agreement, 12 December 2015, 3156 UNTS 79, entered into force 4 November 2016, art 24.

29 See mutatis mutandis, Article 22 of the International Convention on the Elimination of All Forms of Racial Discrimination, 7 March 1966, Treaty Series, 660 UNTS 195, entered into force 4 January 1969. While, following *Application of the International Convention on the Elimination of All Forms of Racial Discrimination (Georgia v. Russian Federation)*, Preliminary Objections, ICJ Rep 2011, there was uncertainty as to whether conciliation was a precondition to ICJ jurisdiction, the ICJ eventually decided that it would be unreasonable and against the purpose of a compromissory clause to multiply the preconditions for solving the dispute, by adding several methods of amicable settlements, *Application of the International Convention for the Suppression of the Financing of Terrorism and of the International Convention on the Elimination of All Forms of Racial Discrimination (Ukraine v. Russian Federation)*, Preliminary Objections, ICJ Rep 2019, paras 110–1.

> party to the dispute, be submitted for binding decision in accordance with procedures for the settlement of disputes provided in Part XV of the 1982 Convention or, where the dispute concerns one or more straddling stocks, by provisions set out in Part VIII of the 1995 Agreement. The relevant part of the 1982 Convention and the 1995 Agreement shall apply whether or not the parties to the dispute are also Parties to these instruments.[30]

Conventions establishing a regional fisheries management organisation or arrangement (RFMO) with competence on the high seas typically refer to conciliation either in relation to adjudication or another mechanism of dispute settlement, such as expert bodies. These conventions generally have their own mechanisms of dispute settlement. These may include compulsory conciliation or an ad-hoc expert body. The articulation with the conciliation mechanism under UNCLOS is not always obvious.

While RFMO mechanisms are not significantly used,[31] their binding nature is debated. Each constitutive treaty defines the disputes which may be submitted to panels; their composition; and the legal effect of their recommendations or decisions. Valentin J. Schatz considers that

> generally, *ad hoc* expert panels share many elements of other forms of alternative dispute resolution, most importantly conciliation and arbitration. . . . Against this background, they may be categorised as 'hybrid' or 'mixed' procedures whose features may be placed on a spectrum between what could be called 'quasi-arbitration' . . . and 'quasi-conciliation.'[32]

30 Convention on the conservation and management of fishery resources in the South East Atlantic Ocean, 20 April 2001, 2221 UNTS 189, entered into force 13 April 2003, art 24, which is applicable beyond national jurisdiction and cites to both UNCLOS and the Agreement for the Implementation of the Provisions of the United Nations Convention on the Law of the Sea of 10 December 1982 relating to the Conservation and Management of Straddling Fish Stocks and Highly Migratory Fish Stocks (Fish Stocks Agreement), 4 August 1995, 2167 UNTS 3, entered into force 11 December 2001. Similarly, see Framework Agreement for the Conservation of the Living Marine Resources of the High Seas of the South-Eastern Pacific, 14 August 2000, art 14; Agreement to Promote Compliance with International Conservation and Management Measures by Fishing Vessels on the High Seas, 24 November 1993, UNTS 2221, entered into force 24 April 2003, art IX; Food and Agriculture Organization of the United Nations Agreement on Port State Measures to Prevent, Deter and Eliminate Illegal, Unreported and Unregulated Fishing, 22 November 2019, entered into force 5 June 2016, art 22.

31 Two panel proceedings have taken place in the South Pacific Regional Fisheries Management Organization. See Robin Churchill, 'Fisheries Disputes' in Ruiz Fabri (ed), *Max Planck Encyclopedia of International Procedural Law* (OUP online 2024); Natalie Klein, 'Law of the Sea Dispute Settlement Outside of the United Nations Convention on the Law of the Sea (UNCLOS)' in Ruiz Fabri (ed), *Max Planck Encyclopedia of International Procedural Law* (OUP online 2024).

32 Valentin J. Schatz, 'Ad Hoc Expert Panels; Regional Fisheries Management Organisations (RFMOs) in Ruiz Fabri (ed), *Max Planck Encyclopedia of International Procedural Law* (OUP Online, 2024).

RFMO conventions may restrict further the scope of adjudication through additional conditions. For instance, Article 18 bis of the Convention on Future Multilateral Cooperation in North East Atlantic Fisheries provides for the exhaustion of its own panel procedure prior to triggering the UNCLOS procedure:

> Where a dispute is not resolved by recourse to the means set out in paragraphs 2 and 3, one of the parties to the dispute may refer the dispute to compulsory procedures entailing binding decisions. Such procedures shall be governed *mutatis mutandis* by the provisions relating to the settlement of disputes set out in Part XV of the United Nations Convention on the Law of the Sea of 10 December 1982 (1982 UN Convention) or, where the dispute concerns one or more straddling stocks, by the provisions set out in Part VIII of the Agreement for the Implementation of the Provisions of the United Nations Convention on the Law of the Sea of 10 December 1982 relating to the Conservation and Management of Straddling Fish Stocks and Highly Migratory Fish Stocks of 4 August 1995 (1995 Agreement). The relevant parts of the 1982 UN Convention and the 1995 Agreement shall apply whether or not the parties to the dispute are also Parties to these instruments.[33]

Similarly, the Agreement for the Establishment of the Indian Ocean Tuna Commission anticipates that State parties may consent to the jurisdiction of the ICJ if the dispute cannot otherwise be resolved through compulsory conciliation:

> Any dispute regarding the interpretation or application of this Agreement, if not settled by the Commission, shall be referred for settlement to a conciliation procedure to be adopted by the Commission. The results of such conciliation procedure, while not binding in character, shall become the basis for renewed consideration by the parties concerned of the matter out of which the disagreement arose. If as the result of this procedure the dispute is not settled, it may be referred to the International Court of Justice in accordance with the Statute of the International Court of Justice, unless the parties to the dispute agree to another method of settlement.[34]

By contrast, other treaties encourage adjudication, by transforming compulsory conciliation under UNCLOS in a system of voluntary conciliation. For example, Article 34 of the Convention on the Determination of the Minimal Conditions for Access and Exploitation of Marine Resources within the Maritime Areas under

33 North East Atlantic Fisheries, 'Proposed amendment to the NEAFC Convention' (July 2003). <www.neafc.org/system/files/Annex%20K%20_2_dispute_settlement_july_2003.pdf> accessed 23 December 2023, the amendment has not entered into force.

34 Agreement for the Establishment of the Indian Ocean Tuna Commission (IOTC Agreement), 25 November 1993, 1927 UNTS, entered into force 27 March 1996, art XXIII.

Jurisdiction of the Member States of the Sub-Regional Fisheries Commission provides that

1. Any dispute on the interpretation or implementation of the provisions of the present Convention shall be brought before the Conference of Ministers of the SRFC.
2. Disputes shall be settled amicably through conciliation, mediation or arbitration.
3. Any dispute which shall arise amongst Member States on the interpretation or implementation of the provisions of the present Convention, which may not be resolved through the afore-mentioned procedures, shall, on the request of one of the parties, be brought before the International Tribunal for the Law of the Sea.[35]

The articulation between these regional conventions and UNCLOS likely rests upon the interpretation of Articles 281 and 282 of UNCLOS. These conventions are *lex specialis* and their provisions may apply in lieu of Part XV of UNCLOS, provided that they result in a binding decision by the third body.

2.3. Concurrence with Other Modes of Dispute Settlement

Despite this plethora of dispute-settlement provisions which refers to conciliation in respect of fisheries dispute, no conciliation has taken place so far. Since UNCLOS, States have proved much less reluctant to include compulsory adjudication among the means for dispute settlement, particularly in regional conventions. The bigger the integration, the larger the trust in adjudication. Adjudication, in turn, has become an indispensable part of the governance of fisheries.

For instance, the Brexit agreement favours rather sophisticated, yet compulsory, mechanisms for dispute settlement which result in binding decisions.[36] Further, some fisheries disputes have been submitted to the World Trade Organization's dispute settlement panels. This included the herring dispute between the Faroe Islands and the European Union which led to parallel Annex VII proceedings until the

35 Convention on the Determination of the Minimal Conditions for Access and Exploitation of Marine Resources within the Maritime Areas under Jurisdiction of the Member States of the Sub-Regional Fisheries Commission, 1 June 2012, entered into force 16 September 2012. The parties to this Convention are Cabo Verde, Gambia, Guinea, Guinea-Bissau, Mauritania, Senegal and Sierra Leone. This Convention served as a basis of jurisdiction in *Request for an Advisory Opinion submitted by the Sub-Regional Fisheries Commission*, Advisory Opinion, ITLOS Rep 2015.

36 Trade and Cooperation Agreement between the European Union and the European Atomic Energy Community, of the one part, and the United Kingdom of Great Britain and Northern Ireland, of the other part, 30 December 2020, entered into force 1 May 2021, art 501. On art 501, see Valentin J. Schatz and Alexander Proelss, 'Workshop on Impacts of the EU-UK Trade and Cooperation Agreement on Fisheries and Aquaculture in the EU – Part I: Legal aspects' (December 2021). <www.europarl.europa.eu/RegData/etudes/STUD/2021/690906/IPOL_STU(2021)690906_EN.pdf > accessed 23 December 2023.

parties reached an agreement.[37] The windows of opportunities for adjudication are too open for States not to take advantage of them.

3. Conciliation as a Shield Against Abuse of Rights

Unlike maritime delimitation disputes, disputes with respect to fisheries submitted to conciliation under Article 297(3)(b) only partially overlap with disputes excluded from judicial settlement by virtue of Article 297(3)(a).[38] The jurisdiction *ratione materiae* of the Conciliation Commission under UNCLOS is defined extremely narrowly.[39] Article 297(3)(b) only considers conciliation in three situations:

1. a coastal State has *manifestly failed to comply with its obligations* to ensure through *proper conservation and management measures* that the maintenance of the living resources in the exclusive economic zone is not seriously endangered;
2. a coastal State has *arbitrarily refused to determine*, at the request of another State, the *allowable catch* and its capacity to harvest living resources with respect to stocks which that other State is interested in fishing; or
3. a coastal State *has arbitrarily refused to allocate* to any State, under articles 62, 69 and 70 and under the terms and conditions established by the coastal State consistent with this Convention, the whole or part of *the surplus* it has declared to exist (emphasis added).

Thus, in all three situations, the other party can challenge the action of the coastal State if this action amounts to an abuse of rights or discretion (or arbitrary action). The 'mere' violation of international obligations cannot be a cause of action before the Conciliation Commission. Characterising conduct by the coastal State as manifestly wrongful or arbitrary can be done only on a case-by-case basis.

As a panel from the World Trade Organization held, a decision can be arbitrary by design or in its implementation:

> the application of a measure may be characterized as amounting to an abuse or misuse of an exception of Article XX *not only when the detailed operating provisions of the measure prescribe the arbitrary or unjustifiable activity, but also where a measure, otherwise fair and just on its face, is actually applied in an arbitrary or unjustifiable manner* (emphasis added).[40]

37 See, inter alia, Jacques Hartmann and Michael Waibel, 'The 'Mackerel War' Goes to the WTO', *EJIL:Talk!* (13 November 2013). www.ejiltalk.org/the-mackerel-war-goes-to-the-wto/ accessed 23 December 2023.

38 Andrew Serdy, 'Article 297' in in Alexander Proelss (ed), *United Nations Convention on the Law of the Sea: A Commentary* (Beck, Nomos and Hart 2017) 1911–2.

39 For a more in-depth discussion, see Valentin J. Schatz, 'The Settlement of EEZ Fisheries Access Disputes Under UNCLOS: Limitations to Jurisdiction and Compulsory Conciliation' (2023) 13 *Goettingen Journal of International Law* 82, 108–17.

40 World Trade Organization, Appellate Body Report on *United States – Import Prohibition of Certain Shrimp and Shrimp Products*, WT/DS58/AB/R, adopted on 12 October 1998, para 160.

Similarly, an RFMO expert panel considered that discretion amounted to arbitrariness when it was used in a discriminatory manner, by imposing an unjustifiable difference of treatment on States in similar positions:

> for there to be unjustifiable discrimination in the procedures relating to allocation, there would for example need to be treatment . . . clearly inconsistent with the treatment of other similarly placed Members, or some unreasonable requirements made of [one State] but not applied to other Members.[41]

However, the same panel noted that 'bad faith is not necessarily a requirement for discrimination'.[42] This is not surprising, since bad faith is extremely difficult to prove.

A decision is also arbitrary if it is not based on any rational motives or if there is significant inadequacy between the motives asserted and the measures adopted:

> discrimination will be arbitrary or unjustifiable when the reasons given for the discrimination 'bear no rational connection to the objective' or 'would go against that objective'. Thus, '[o]ne of the most important factors' in the assessment of arbitrary or unjustifiable discrimination is the question of whether the discrimination can be reconciled with, or is rationally related to, the policy objective with respect to which the measure has been provisionally justified under one of the subparagraphs of article XX.[43]

The arbitrary character could also result from the coastal State's refusal to consider the positions of other States and envisage an alternative course of action, less harmful to the other States, by insisting on its unilateral position where international law prescribes some obligations of cooperation.[44]

There is no point in speculating on the standard of review which a conciliation commission, should it be convened, would retain in such cases. However, given the procedures' ultimate objective to provide a basis for an amicable settlement, a high level of review could be counterproductive.

41 Review Panel established under the Convention on the Conservation and Management of High Seas Fishery Resources in the South Pacific Ocean, Findings and Recommendations, PCA Case 2013–14, 5 July 2013, para 106.

42 ibid.

43 World Trade Organization, Panel Report on recourse to Article 21.5 on *United States – Measures Concerning the Importation, Marketing and Sale of Tuna and Tuna Products*, WT/DS381/RW, 14 April 2015, para 7.316, citing to Appellate Body Report on *Brazil – Measures Affecting Imports of Retreaded Tyres,* WT/DS332/AB/R, 3 December 2007, paras 226–7.

44 World Trade Organization, Appellate Body Report on *United States – Import Prohibition of Certain Shrimp and Shrimp Products*, WT/DS58/AB/R, adopted on 12 October 1998, paras 171–6.

Many authors have concluded that the virtues of the conciliation procedure rest less on any outcome than on the very fact that it can be unilaterally resorted to. In the words of Ian Sinclair,

> What is important – what is indeed crucial – is that there should always be in the background, as a necessary check upon the making of unjustified claims, or upon the denial of justified claims, automatically available procedures for the settlement of disputes.[45]

This may indeed be the case. However, the other reason why conciliation in fisheries-related disputes has never been resorted to is that States have increased access to judicial means and specialised bodies, established under sectorial or regional conventions. These means seem to be preferred to a method of dispute settlement which remains, in the end, amicable.

45 Ian Sinclair, *The Vienna Convention on the Law of Treaties* (Manchester: Manchester University Press 1984) 235. In the same vein, see Jean-Pierre Cot, 'Expectations Attached to Conciliation Reconsidered' in Christian Tomuschat, Riccardo Pisillo Mazzeschi and Daniel Thürer (eds), *Conciliation in International Law* (Brill Nijhoff 2017) 10–1.

13 Jurisdictional Issues in the Settlement of Disputes Concerning Straddling Fish Stocks Under UNCLOS

Yoshifumi Tanaka

1. Introduction

The international dispute settlement system set out under Part XV of the United Nations Convention on the Law of the Sea (UNCLOS) strikes a careful balance between voluntary and compulsory procedures.[1] The automatic limitations[2] and optional exceptions[3] to the compulsory dispute settlement procedures constitute a crucial balancing act. Under Article 297(3)(a) of UNCLOS, the compulsory procedures for dispute settlement will not apply to

> any dispute relating to its sovereign rights with respect to the living resources in the exclusive economic zone or their exercise, including its discretionary powers for determining the allowable catch, its harvesting capacity, the allocation of surpluses to other States and the terms and conditions established in its conservation and management laws and regulations.[4]

The practical effect of this provision is that most, if not all, fisheries-related disputes in the exclusive economic zone (EEZ) are precluded from UNCLOS' compulsory procedures. This exemption reinforces the safeguard of the coastal State's discretionary powers in the EEZ from judicial review.[5] By contrast, disputes relating exclusively to living resources in the high seas fall within the scope of the compulsory procedures.[6] The question that arises is whether international disputes

1 United Nations Convention on the Law of the Sea (UNCLOS), 10 December 1982, 1833 UNTS 3, entered into force 16 November 1994.
2 UNCLOS, art 297(2)(a) and (3)(a).
3 UNCLOS, art 298.
4 When a coastal State has manifestly failed to comply with its obligations to ensure proper conservation and management of living resources in the EEZ or arbitrarily refused to determine the allowable catch or surplus, disputes are subject to compulsory conciliation in accordance with art 297(3) of UNCLOS. Under art 297(3)(c), however, '[i]n no case shall the conciliation commission substitute its discretion for that of the coastal State.'
5 Natalie Klein, *Dispute Settlement in the UN Convention on the Law of the Sea* (CUP 2005) 177–8.
6 Alan Boyle, 'Problems of Compulsory Jurisdiction and the Settlement of Disputes Relating to Straddling Fish Stocks', (1999) 14 *The International Journal of Marine and Coastal Law* 1, 11.

DOI: 10.4324/9781003492030-18

concerning fish stocks which straddle the EEZ and the high seas are subject to the UNCLOS' compulsory procedures.[7]

The question is crucial because, as Boyle observes, '[m]ost of the more intractable fisheries disputes occur because the stocks in question straddle two or more EEZs, or straddle the EEZ and the high seas'.[8] This question is also linked to Article 63(2) of UNCLOS, which obliges the coastal State and the States fishing for straddling fish stocks in the adjacent area to seek to agree upon the measures necessary to conserve these stocks in the adjacent area. Relatedly, at the final session of the Third United Nations Conference on the Law of the Sea, a coalition of States proposed that, where conservation measures regarding straddling fish stocks in the area adjacent to the EEZ could not be reached, an appropriate tribunal would have to determine measures to be applied in the adjacent area.[9] However, the sponsors withdrew this proposal given the opposition of distant-water fishing States.[10] In the end, no explicit provision was included in UNCLOS on this matter. Thus, UNCLOS did not resolve the ambiguity as to the applicability of the compulsory dispute settlement procedures to straddling fish stocks disputes.[11]

Nor did the 1995 Fish Stocks Agreement settle the question.[12] The Fish Stocks Agreement aims to ensure the long-term conservation and sustainable use of straddling and highly migratory fish stocks beyond areas under national jurisdiction, namely the high seas.[13] The procedures for dispute settlement set out under Part XV of UNCLOS are incorporated by reference in the Fish Stocks Agreement.[14] Article 32 of the Agreement directs that Article 297(3) of UNCLOS applies to

7 The term 'straddling fish stocks' is not used in UNCLOS. Art 63(2) of UNCOS refers to 'the same stock or stocks of associated species occur both within the exclusive economic zone and in an area beyond and adjacent to the zone'. For straddling stocks, see 'Straddling Stocks', *UN Atlas of the Oceans*. <www.oceansatlas.org/subtopic/en/c/1434/> accessed 2 July 2024. Highly migratory fish stocks are listed in Annex I to the Convention.

8 Alan Boyle, 'Problems of Compulsory Jurisdiction and the Settlement of Disputes Relating to Straddling Fish Stocks' (1999) 14 *The International Journal of Marine and Coastal Law* 12.

9 Third United Nations Conference on the Law of the Sea, Amendments to art 63 by Australia, Canada, Cape Verde, Iceland, Philippines, São Tomé and Príncipe, Senegal, and Sierra Leone, A/CONF.62/L.114, 13 April 1982.

10 See, for instance, A/CONF.62/SR. 169, 96, para 43; A/CONF.62/SR.170, 100, para 7 (France). See also Edward Miles and William Burke, 'Pressures on the United Nations Convention on the Law of the Sea of 1982 Arising from New Fisheries Conflicts: The Problem of Straddling Stocks'(1989) 20 *Ocean Development and International Law* 343, 344; Andre Tahindro, 'Conservation and Management of Transboundary Fish Stocks: Comments in Light of the Adoption of the 1995 Agreement for the Conservation and Management of Straddling Fish Stocks and Highly Migratory Fish Stocks' (1997) 28 *Ocean Development and International Law* 1, 49.

11 Natalie Klein, *Dispute Settlement in the UN Convention on the Law of the Sea* (CUP 2005) 199 and 223.

12 United Nations Agreement for the Implementation of the United Nations Convention on the Law of the Sea of 10 December 1982 relating to the Conservation and Management of Straddling Fish Stocks and Highly Migratory Fish Stocks [the Fish Stocks Agreement]. Text in: 2167 UNTS 3. Adopted 4 August 1995. Entered into force 11 December 2001.

13 Articles 2 and 3(1) of the Fish Stocks Agreement.

14 See art 30(1) of the Fish Stocks Agreement.

the Agreement. Accordingly, the same question on the exemptions from the compulsory dispute settlement procedures arises under the Fish Stocks Agreement.[15] Under Article 7(4) of the Fish Stocks Agreement, if an agreement on compatible conservation and management measures cannot be reached within a reasonable time period, 'any of the States concerned may invoke the procedures for the settlement of disputes provided for in Part VIII'.[16] This provision begs the question of what procedures apply: the compulsory procedures or conciliation under Part XV of UNCLOS.[17]

Given the absence of a clear provision in UNCLOS, interpretations can be sharply divided on the question of whether the compulsory dispute settlement procedures under UNCLOS apply to disputes on straddling fish stocks. Boyle stated that '[w]hat can be observed is that neither the text of the Convention nor the negotiating records of UNCLOS III provide definitive support for either view',[18] and that 'it would be unwise to draw any firm conclusion on this point at present'.[19] Boyle may be right, but this is not the end of the consideration. An essential issue, which needs further consideration, is how to resolve the jurisdictional issue where no definitive conclusion can be drawn from the text of UNCLOS or supplementary means of interpretation, including the *travaux préparatoires*.

Noting this issue, this chapter considers the question of whether courts and tribunals acting under Part XV of UNCLOS can exercise jurisdiction over disputes concerning straddling fish stocks. It, first, highlights three key elements as the framework for analysis. It then, explores possible interpretations by applying the three elements, before offering a conclusion.

2. A Triple Approach as the Framework for Analysis

As Sir Robert Jennings stated, '[n]o reasonable litigant expects the decision of a court to be predictable, but the range of considerations used for a decision and the procedures for their application should certainly be predictable.'[20] This would hold true of the jurisdiction of a court or tribunal acting under Part XV of UNCLOS. Thus, one must identify relevant elements or criteria for judging the jurisdiction of

15 Natalie Klein, *Dispute Settlement in the UN Convention on the Law of the Sea* (CUP 2005) 201 and 223. See also Alan Boyle, 'Problems of Compulsory Jurisdiction and the Settlement of Disputes Relating to Straddling Fish Stocks' (1999) 14 *The International Journal of Marine and Coastal Law* 21.

16 See also art 16(2) of the Fish Stocks Agreement.

17 Alan Boyle, 'Problems of Compulsory Jurisdiction and the Settlement of Disputes Relating to Straddling Fish Stocks' (1999) 14 *The International Journal of Marine and Coastal Law* 21. In this regard, Boyle argued that 'it is difficult to read into it [art 7] any intention to clarify the applicability of compulsory dispute settlement in regard to straddling stocks', ibid, 22.

18 ibid, 13.

19 ibid.

20 Sir Robert Jennings, 'Equity and Equitable Principles' (1986) 42 *Annuaire suisse de droit interntional* 38.

adjudicative bodies. Even though the criteria may be context-specific, three elements must be highlighted.

The first element is the consent of States. The jurisdiction of an international court or tribunal relies on the consent of States. Thus, the consensual basis for jurisdiction is of critical importance. In this regard, the International Court of Justice (ICJ) stressed in *Djibouti v. France* stressed that '[t]he consent allowing for the Court to assume jurisdiction must be certain'.[21] The second element concerns the effective settlement of international disputes. The primary task of an international court or tribunal is to settle disputes as effectively as possible. Hence, the effectiveness of the dispute settlement also constitutes a key element. The third element relates to safeguarding community interests. As reflected in the concepts of obligations *erga omnes (partes)*[22] and *jus cogens*,[23] protection of common interests of the international community, or community interests, is increasingly important in international law.[24] In particular, obligations are key in the protection of the marine environment.[25] While further development of the jurisprudence is needed to draw more general conclusions, the jurisprudence appears to suggest that, even in the absence of an express clause giving standing in a treaty, an international court or tribunal could accept the *locus standi* of a not directly injured State regarding a breach of obligations *erga omnes*, if it could establish its jurisdiction.[26] Therefore, the protection of community interests should also be crucial when considering the jurisdiction of adjudicative bodies under Part XV of UNCLOS.

In summary, the consensual basis, the effective settlement of international disputes, and the protection of community interests provide key criteria for deciding the jurisdiction of adjudicative bodies acting under Part XV of UNCLOS. In the author's view, an appropriate interpretation of the jurisdiction of a court or tribunal rests on balancing these three elements, even though the outcome may differ depending on the members of the court or tribunal.

21 *Certain Questions of Mutual Assistance in Criminal Matters (Djibouti v. France)*, [2008] ICJ Rep. 177, 204, para 62. In this case, the ICJ's jurisdiction relied on *forum prorogatum*.

22 See definition of obligations *erga omnes* by Institut de droit international, 'Resolution: Obligation *Erga Omnes* in International Law', *Krakow Session* (2005). www.idi-iil.org/app/uploads/2017/06/2005_kra_01_en.pdf accessed 2 July 2024.

23 Vienna Convention on the Law of Treaties (Vienna, 23 April 1969, in force 27 January 1980) 1155 UNTS 331, art 53.

24 Bruno Simma, 'Universality of International Law from the Perspective of a Practitioner', (2009) 20 *European Journal of International Law* 265, at 268; Antônio Augusto Cançado Trindade, 'International Law for Humankind: Towards a New *Jus Gentium*' (2005) 316 *Recueil des Cours* 9, 35; Santiago Villalpando, 'The Legal Dimension of the International Community: How Community Interests are Protected in International Law' (2010) 21 *European Journal of International Law* 387.

25 Yoshifumi Tanaka, 'Reflections on *Locus Standi* in Response to a Breach of Obligations *Erga Omnes Partes*: A Comparative Analysis of the *Whaling in the Antarctic* and *South China Sea* Cases' (2018) 17 *The Law and Practice of International Courts and Tribunals* 527–554.

26 Yoshifumi Tanaka, 'The Legal Consequences of Obligations *Erga Omnes* in International Law' (2021) 68 *Netherlands International Law Review* 1, 30.

3. Possible Interpretations on the Jurisdiction to Address Disputes Concerning Straddling Fish Stocks Under Part XV of UNCLOS

This section explores possible interpretations of the jurisdiction of UNCLOS Part XV courts and tribunals concerning straddling fish stocks from the triple viewpoints: consensual basis, effective settlement of international disputes, and protection of community interests.

3.1 The Consensual Basis for Jurisdiction

The first element is the consensual basis for jurisdiction of UNCLOS Part XV courts and tribunals. According to one view, adjudicative bodies cannot exercise their jurisdiction without a firm consensual basis. According to this interpretation, the absence of clear provisions in UNCLOS implies that the drafters had no intension to confer the jurisdiction to address straddling fish stocks disputes to adjudicative bodies acting under UNCLOS Part XV. Thus, Boyle stated that '[i]t is at least as plausible to assume that coastal states did not want there to be compulsory jurisdiction in respect of their obligations regarding straddling stocks'.[27] According to Boyle, '[t]he conclusion may be undesirable but the interpretation is neither absurd nor unreasonable'.[28] Following this interpretation, disputes concerning straddling fish stocks would be assimilated to disputes concerning the living resources in the EEZ.

Kwiatkowska argued that the limitation under Article 297(3) of UNCLOS 'presumably applies as much to straddling and highly migratory stocks as to other fisheries, despite the fact that the coastal state's sovereign rights over the former stocks are inseparable from the high seas fishing for those stocks.'[29] This view was also supported by Orrego Vicuña.[30] This interpretation was claimed by the United Kingdom in the *Chagos Marine Protected Area* arbitration. The United Kingdom maintained that 'Article 297(3)(a) bars jurisdiction over measures relating to straddling and highly migratory stocks in the exclusive economic zone'.[31] In this case, the Annex VII arbitral tribunal held that 'Articles 63 and 64 (as well as the 1995 Fish Stocks Agreement) are, on their face, measures in respect of fisheries and in

27 Alan Boyle, 'Problems of Compulsory Jurisdiction and the Settlement of Disputes Relating to Straddling Fish Stocks' (1999) 14 *The International Journal of Marine and Coastal Law* 12–3.

28 ibid, 13.

29 Barbara Kwiatkowska, 'The Australia and New Zealand v. Japan Southern Bluefin Tuna (Jurisdiction and Admissibility) Award of the First Law of the Sea Convention Annex VII Arbitral Tribunal' (2001) 16 *IJMCL* 239, 276.

30 Francisco Orrego Vicuña, *The Exclusive Economic Zone: Regime and Legal Nature under International Law* (CUP 1989) 131.

31 Award in the Arbitration regarding the Chagos Marine Protected Area between Mauritius and the United Kingdom of Great Britain and Northern Ireland, 18 March 2015 (2018) 31 RIAA 359, 473, para 257.

their application in the exclusive economic zone are subject to the exclusion in Article 297(3)(a)'.[32]

However, there remains some scope to consider whether the absence of the firm consent of States automatically denies the jurisdiction of UNCLOS courts or tribunals. The advisory jurisdiction of the International Tribunal for the Law of the Sea (ITLOS) as a full court is a case in point. UNCLOS contains no explicit provision on the advisory jurisdiction of ITLOS as a full court, unlike for the ITLOS Seabed Disputes Chamber.[33] Furthermore, as a commentary stated, 'an advisory function for the Tribunal was not even proposed during the Third Conference on the Law of the Sea'.[34] Nonetheless, ITLOS unanimously declared in 2015 that it had jurisdiction to give the advisory opinion requested by the Sub-Regional Fisheries Commission.[35] The practice of ITLOS suggests that the absence of a clear provision conferring jurisdiction does not automatically mean that adjudicative bodies under UNCLOS Part XV do not have jurisdiction.

3.2 The Effective Settlement of International Disputes

As explained earlier, the effective settlement of international disputes is the primary task of international courts and tribunals. If disputes over straddling fish stocks are precluded from the compulsory dispute settlement procedures under UNCLOS, two options remain. First, the dispute could be submitted to a court or tribunal under UNCLOS Part XV by special agreement between the parties in dispute. Second, the dispute regarding issues over the high seas only could be submitted to a court or tribunal.[36] The weakness of the first option is clear: States rarely submit a fisheries dispute by agreement to an international court or tribunal. The second

32 ibid, at 487, para 300. For a criticism of the dictum of the arbitral tribunal, see Bjørn Kunoy, 'The Scope of Compulsory Jurisdiction and Exceptions Thereto under the United Nations Convention on the Law of the Sea' (2020) 58 *Canadian Yearbook of International Law* 78, 112–117.

33 Art 191 of UNCLOS.

34 Sotirios-Ioannis Lekkas and Christopher Staker, 'Art 21 Annex VI' in Alexander Proelss (ed), *United Nations Convention on the Law of the Sea: A Commentary* (Beck, Nomos and Hart 2017) 2381, para 16. This view was confirmed by other commentators. Miguel García García-Revillo, *The Contentious and Advisory Jurisdiction of the International Tribunal for the Law of the Sea* (Nijhoff 2015) 311; Massimo Lando, 'The Advisory Jurisdiction of the International Tribunal for the Law of the Sea: Comments on the Request for an Advisory Opinion Submitted by the Sub-Regional Fisheries Commission' (2016) 29 *Leiden Journal of International Law* 441, 450–451.

35 *Request for an Advisory Opinion Submitted by the Sub-Regional Fisheries Commission (SRFC) (Request for Advisory Opinion Submitted to the Tribunal)*, [2015] ITLOS Rep. 4, 62, para 219(1). See also *Request for an Advisory Opinion Submitted by the Commission of Small Island States on Climate Change and International Law*, [2024] ITLOS Rep (not yet reported), paras 84–87. https://www.itlos.org/fileadmin/itlos/documents/cases/31/Advisory_Opinion/C31_Adv_Op_21.05.2024_orig.pdf accessed 2 July 2024.

36 Alan Boyle, 'Problems of Compulsory Jurisdiction and the Settlement of Disputes Relating to Straddling Fish Stocks' (1999) 14 *The International Journal of Marine and Coastal Law* 13.

option is also inadequate: it only addresses one aspect of straddling fish stocks disputes.

For straddling fish stocks, it makes little sense to separate the question of high-seas fisheries from the management of fish stocks in the adjacent EEZ.[37] Given the biological unity of straddling fish stocks, a straddling fish stock dispute should be settled as a whole, without distinguishing the high seas issues from the EEZ issues. Additionally, as Boyle stated,

> there is manifest inequity in subjecting to compulsory jurisdiction states whose vessels fish on the high seas while at the same time denying these states the right to bring proceedings or counter-claims against a coastal state whose own actions may be affecting the very same straddling stock.[38]

Hence, there may be some scope to argue that the whole straddling fish stock dispute should be susceptible to the compulsory dispute settlement procedures under UNCLOS.[39] According to this view, the exceptions set out in Article 297(3) of UNCLOS are strictly limited to disputes on fisheries-related disputes in the EEZ only.[40] Relatedly, Judge Paik took the following view:

> [A]ny dispute arising from the alleged failure to comply with the obligation under article 63, paragraph 1, of the Convention, unlike those disputes arising from the exercise of sovereign rights of the coastal State with respect to the living resources in its EEZ, can be submitted to the compulsory procedure under Part XV, section 2, of the Convention.[41]

While the dictum relates to Article 63(1) of UNCLOS, the same would hold true of Article 63(2) by analogy.

3.3 The Safeguard of Community Interests

The aforementioned analysis reveals two contrasting interpretations. According to the interpretation stressing the importance of the consent of States, adjudicative bodies acting under Part XV of UNCLOS have no jurisdiction unless there is a

37 Alan Boyle, 'Dispute Settlement and the Law of the Sea Convention: Problems of Fragmentation and Jurisdiction' (1997) 46 *ICLQ* 37, 43.

38 Alan Boyle, 'Problems of Compulsory Jurisdiction and the Settlement of Disputes Relating to Straddling Fish Stocks' (1999) 14 *The International Journal of Marine and Coastal Law* 13.

39 ibid, 25; Natalie Klein, *Dispute Settlement in the UN Convention on the Law of the Sea* (CUP 2005) 204.

40 Shabtai Rosenne, 'Settlement of Fisheries Disputes in the Exclusive Economic Zone' (1979) 73 *AJIL* 89, 98.

41 Separate Opinion of Judge Jin-Hyun Paik in *Request for an Advisory Opinion Submitted by the Sub-Regional Fisheries Commission (SRFC)*, Advisory Opinion, 2 April 2015, [2015] ITLOS Rep. 4, 117, para 37.

clear provision conferring such jurisdiction to them. According to the interpretation focusing on the need to settle straddling fish stocks disputes as a whole, disputes over straddling fish stocks should be susceptible to the compulsory dispute settlement procedures under UNCLOS. The two interpretations reflect a fundamental disagreement over whether emphasis should be placed on the consent of States or the effective settlement of international disputes. The two interpretations stand in opposition and are not easily reconcilable. Here, the third element, namely the protection of community interests, comes into play.

Of note here is the *erga omnes* nature of the obligation to protect and preserve the marine environment under Article 192 of UNCLOS. The ITLOS Seabed Disputes Chamber noted that '[e]ach State Party may also be entitled to claim compensation in light of the *erga omnes* character of the obligations relating to preservation of the environment of the high seas and in the Area'.[42] The expression '[e]ach State Party' implies that the obligation on the preservation of the environment of the high seas and in the Area is an obligation *erga omnes partes*. This obligation would apply to the ocean as a whole as the obligation under Article 192 is to 'protect and preserve the marine environment'.[43] The obligation to protect and preserve the marine environment under Article 192 is now generally accepted as reflecting a rule of customary international law.[44] As a result, the environmental obligation under Article 192 can be regarded as an obligation *erga omnes*.[45] As ITLOS stated, 'the conservation of the living resources of the sea is an element in the protection and preservation

42 *Responsibilities and Obligations of States Sponsoring Persons and Entities with Respect to Activities in the Area* (Advisory Opinion), Seabed Disputes Chamber of the International Tribunal for the Law of the Sea, Case No 17, 1 February 2011, [2011] ITLOS Rep. 59, para 180.

43 Chandrasekhara Rao and Philippe Gautier, *The International Tribunal for the Law of the Sea: Law, Practice and Procedure* (Edward Elgar, 2018) 138 and 327; Rachael L. Johnstone, *Offshore Oil and Gas Development in the Arctic Under International Law: Risk and Responsibility* (Nijhoff 2015) 223.

44 The OSPAR Convention, in its Preamble, recalled 'the relevant provisions of customary international law reflected in Part XII of the United Nations Law of the Sea Convention.' Convention for the Protection of the Marine Environment of the North-East Atlantic (opened for signature 22 September 1992, entered into force 25 March 1998) 2354 UNTS 67, Preamble (OSPAR Convention). See also UNGA, *Protection and Preservation of the Marine Environment: Report of the Secretary-General* UN Doc A/44/461, 18 September 1989, 10, para 29. This view is supported by commentators, including: Alan Boyle and Catherine Redgwell, *Birnie, Boyle and Redgwell's International Law and the Environment* (4th ed., OUP 2021) 511; Philippe Sands et al., *Principles of International Environmental Law* (CUP 2018) 462; Detlef Czybulka, 'Art 192' in Alexander Proelss (ed), *The United Nations Convention on the Law of the Sea: A Commentary* (Beck, Nomos and Hart 2017) 1277, 1284–85; James Harrison, *Saving the Oceans Through Law: The International Leal Framework for the Protection of the Marine Environment* (OUP 2017) 24–25.

45 James Harrison, *Saving the Oceans Through Law: The International Leal Framework for the Protection of the Marine Environment* (OUP 2017) 24–25; Yoshifumi Tanaka, 'The Legal Consequences of Obligations *Erga Omnes* in International Law' (2021) 68 *Netherlands International Law Review* 5; Yoshifumi Tanaka, 'Changing Paradigms in the Law of the Sea and the Marine Arctic' (2020) 35(3) *IJMCL* 439, 441–443.

of the marine environment'.[46] Since marine ecosystems are part of the marine environment, the protection of marine ecosystems arguably also constitutes part of the protection of the marine environment. In fact, the Annex VII arbitral tribunal in the *South China Sea* award made clear that

> the general obligation to 'protect and preserve the marine environment' in Article 192 includes a due diligence obligation to prevent the harvesting of species that are recognised internationally as being at risk of extinction and requiring international protection.[47]

Unsustainable fishing of straddling fish stocks may affect marine ecosystems. Therefore, conservation of straddling fish stocks constitutes 'an element in the protection and preservation of the marine environment'. In this sense, the obligation to conserve straddling fish stocks can be regarded as an obligation *erga omnes*. Accordingly, coastal State interests in straddling fish stocks must be balanced with community interests. The compulsory dispute settlement procedures can provide a mechanism for checking coastal States' measures impacting those fish stocks.[48] From this viewpoint, an UNCLOS court or tribunal would be justified in establishing its jurisdiction to address disputes over straddling fish stocks.[49]

This interpretation is further supported by the increasing importance of protecting marine biological diversity. Environmentally harmful fishing is a relevant concept here. The Memorial of the Philippines in the *South China Sea* arbitration referred to environmentally harmful fishing.[50] Environmentally harmful fishing is an environment and ecology-based concept which focuses on the adverse impacts of fishing on the marine environment, including marine species and biological diversity. This broad concept seeks to protect in a comprehensive manner marine species (particularly threatened or endangered species), marine ecosystems, and their surrounding environment from the adverse impacts of fishing. The concept of environmentally harmful fishing provides a nexus between environmental protection and the regulation of fishing. This concept can be regarded as a legal device to internalise environmental norms on the conservation of marine biological diversity in UNCLOS.[51]

46 *Southern Bluefin Tuna Cases (New Zealand v. Japan; Australia v. Japan),* Provisional Measures, ITLOS Case Nos 3 and 4, Order of 27 August 1999, [1999] ITLOS Rep 280, 295, para 70. See also *Request for an Advisory Opinion Submitted by the Sub-Regional Fisheries Commission (SRFC)*, Advisory Opinion, 2 April 2015, [2015] ITLOS Rep. 4, 37, para 120.

47 PCA Case No 2013–19. The *South China Sea* Arbitral Award (The Philippines v. The People's Republic of China) (Merits), 12 July 2016, (2020) 33 *Reports of International Arbitral Awards (RIAA)* 153, 526, para 956.

48 Natalie Klein, *Dispute Settlement in the UN Convention on the Law of the Sea* (CUP 2005) 204.

49 ibid.

50 Memorial of Philippines, 174–185, paras 6.48–6.66. Yet the Philippines did not clearly define the concept of environmentally harmful fishing.

51 Yoshifumi Tanaka, 'Reflections on the Implications of Environmental Norms for Fishing: The Link between the Regulation of Fishing and the Protection of Marine Biological Diversity' (2020) 22 *International Community Law Review* 389, 393.

In the *South China* arbitration, the Annex VII arbitral tribunal examined environmentally harmful fishing, which was allegedly conducted by China, and considered 'the harvesting of sea turtles, species threatened with extinction, to constitute a harm to the marine environment as such'. Further, it had no doubt that 'the harvesting of corals and giant clams from the waters surrounding Scarborough Shoal and features in the Spratly Islands, on the scale that appears in the record before it, has a harmful impact on the fragile marine environment'.[52] According to the tribunal, 'a failure to take measures to prevent these practices would constitute a breach of Articles 192 and 194(5) of the Convention, and [the tribunal] turns now to consider China's responsibility for such breaches'.[53] After examining China's conduct, the tribunal concluded that China had breached Articles 192 and 194(5).[54] This award appear to demonstrate that environmentally harmful fishing is illegal in light of the breach of the obligation to protect and preserve the marine environment.[55]

As fish stocks are part of marine ecosystems, fishing can affect marine ecosystems. Hence, the regulation of fishing and the protection of marine ecosystems are intertwined. In fact, the distinction between fisheries disputes and disputes over the protection of the marine environment, including marine ecosystems, is not always clear-cut. A dispute over the conservation and management of straddling fish stocks could, in some instances, be characterised as a dispute over the protection of the marine environment, including marine biological diversity. Properly characterised, such a dispute could fall within the scope of the compulsory procedures for dispute settlement under UNCLOS. Hence the characterisation of the dispute may have significant jurisdictional implications.[56] One must stress here that it is for the international court or tribunal itself 'to determine on an objective basis the dispute dividing the parties, by examining the position of both parties'.[57]

4. Conclusion

This chapter has examined the question of whether adjudicative bodies acting under Part XV of UNCLOS have jurisdiction over disputes concerning straddling fish stocks. It explored this question from three viewpoints: the consensual basis for jurisdiction, the effective settlement of international disputes, and safeguarding

52 'The *South China Sea* Arbitral Award (Merits), 12 July 2016' (2020) 33 *Reports of International Arbitral Awards (RIAA)* 527, para 960.

53 ibid.

54 ibid 542, para 992.

55 Yoshifumi Tanaka, 'Reflections on the Implications of Environmental Norms for Fishing: The Link between the Regulation of Fishing and the Protection of Marine Biological Diversity' (2020) 22 *International Community Law Review* 398.

56 PCA Case No 2013–19: *The South China Sea Arbitration (The Republic of Philippines v. The People's Republic of China)*, Award on Jurisdiction and Admissibility of 29 October 2015, (2020) 33 RIAA 62, para 150. Further, see James Harrison, 'Defining Disputes and Characterizing Claims: Subject-Matter Jurisdiction in Law of the Sea Convention Litigation' (2017) 48 *ODIL* 269.

57 *Fisheries Jurisdiction (Spain v. Canada)*, Jurisdiction of the Court, Judgment, [1998] ICJ Rep. 432, 448, para 30.

community interests. Different conclusions on jurisdiction emerge depending on the relative weight given to each element. Emphasising the consent of States restricts the scope of the compulsory dispute settlement procedures. By contrast, stressing the effective settlement of disputes restricts the scope of the limitations in Article 297(3) of UNCLOS. These two interpretations reflect a fundamental opposition between two approaches to international dispute settlement: an approach safeguarding the consensual basis and State sovereignty and an approach focusing on the effective settlement of international disputes.[58] The opposition between the two approaches is difficult to reconcile.

However, introducing a third element, namely the need to protect community interests, could solve this classic dilemma in international adjudication. The law of the sea has strong environmental dimensions. Therefore, the protection of community interests in protecting the marine environment should be a crucial element. Disputes concerning the conservation and management of straddling fish stocks may at times be properly formulated as environmental disputes. If so, there may be scope to argue that these disputes over conserving and managing straddling fish stocks would fall within the scope of the compulsory dispute settlement procedures under UNCLOS. Thus, the characterisation of disputes is key to establishing the jurisdiction of adjudicative bodies acting under Part XV of UNCLOS.

58 Further, Yoshifumi Tanaka, *The South China Sea Arbitration: Toward an International Legal Order in the Oceans* (Hart 2019) 41–42 and 45.

14 The Scope of Obligations in Article 63(1) of UNCLOS on the Management of Shared Fish Stocks

Constantinos Yiallourides

1. Introducing Article 63(1)

Exclusive economic zones (EEZs) cover only 35% of the total ocean area, yet they contain about 90% of the world's commercial fish stocks.[1] Around 60% of these stocks have been 'maximally sustainably fished' and are, therefore, at risk of collapse.[2] The overfishing of a particular fish stock does not only damage the population of that stock. It may have serious ramifications on marine food webs, which could adversely affect entire marine ecosystems and even the global climate.[3]

The United Nations Convention on the Law of the Sea (UNCLOS) entrusts the management and conservation of resources in the EEZ to the coastal State.[4] The coastal State has the sole prerogative to determine the allowable catch of living resources in its EEZ and its capacity to harvest these resources.[5] This reflects coastal States' exclusive sovereign rights to explore, exploit, conserve, and manage the living resources in their EEZs.[6] However, these sovereign rights are conditioned by the coastal States' obligations to conserve and sustainably manage these resources, including transboundary resources. Transboundary fisheries resources are fish

1 Richard Barnes, 'The Convention on the Law of the Sea: An Effective Framework for Domestic Fisheries Conservation?' in Richard Barnes, David Freestone, and David Ong (eds), *The Law of the Sea: Progress and Prospects* (OUP 2006) 234; Mercedes Rosello, 'Illegal, Unreported and Unregulated Fishing Control in the Exclusive Economic Zone: A Brief Appraisal of Regulatory Deficits and Accountability Strategies' (2016) 22 *Croatian International Relations Review* 39.

2 Robin Churchill, Vaughan Lowe, and Amy Sander, *The Law of the Sea* (Manchester University Press 2022) 514, citing Food and Agriculture Organization of the United Nations (FAO), 'The State of World Fisheries and Aquaculture: Sustainability in Action' (2020) 7 and 47–8 <www.fao.org/3/ca9229en/ca9229en.pdf> accessed 23 December 2023.

3 On how overfishing affects global climate, see United Nations on Climate Change, 'Plenty of Fish?' (10 June 2022) unfccc.int/blog/plenty-of-fish accessed 23 December 2023.

4 United Nations Convention on the Law of the Sea (UNCLOS), 10 December 1982, 1833 UNTS 3, entered into force 16 November 1994.

5 UNCLOS, arts 61(1), 62(2).

6 UNCLOS, art 56(1); Robert Beckman and Tara Davenport, 'The EEZ Regime: Reflections After 30 Years', *Proceedings from the 2012 LOSI-KIOST Conference on Securing the Ocean for the Next Generation* (2012). www.law.berkeley.edu/files/Beckman-Davenport-final.pdf accessed 23 December 2023.

DOI: 10.4324/9781003492030-19

stocks which are not exclusively contained within national maritime boundaries. In such instances, two or more States must cooperate to ensure the effective and efficient conservation and development of transboundary stocks.[7] Non-cooperative management of transboundary stocks risks the unsustainable exploitation of vulnerable fishing resources.[8]

Article 63(1) of UNCLOS deals specifically with the management of transboundary fish stocks, namely stocks which migrate, are distributed, or otherwise found at various stages of their lifecycle between the EEZs of two or more States. This chapter refers to these stocks as 'shared' stocks, as is usually done in the legal literature.[9] However, the stocks are sometimes called 'joint' or 'transboundary' stocks. Transboundary stocks may also comprise species which are straddling stocks, highly migratory, anadromous, or catadromous.[10] If so, the stocks will be regulated as *leges speciales* by, respectively, Articles 63(2), 64, 66, and 67 of UNCLOS rather than Article 63(1).[11]

Article 63(1) provides that, where the same stock or stocks of associated species occur within the EEZs of two or more coastal States, the relevant States must *'seek to agree'* on a coordinated regime for conserving and developing these shared

7 Gordon Munro, Annick Van Houtte and Rolf Willman, 'The Conservation and Management of Shared Fish Stocks: Legal and Economic Aspects' (2004) 465 *FAO Fisheries Technical Paper* 59 www.fao.org/3/y5438e/y5438e.pdf accessed 23 December 2023: 'Stable cooperative management of shared fish stocks is required, if these resources are to be exploited on a sustainable basis. It is dangerous, if not foolhardy, to assume that non-cooperative management of shared fishery resources will suffice'.

8 Richard Barnes and Elizabeth Kirk, Written evidence, 'House of Lord's International Relations and Defence Committee, Enquiry: UNCLOS: Fit for Purpose in the 21st century?' (11 November 2021). committees.parliament.uk/writtenevidence/40821/html/ accessed 23 December 2023; *Request for an Advisory Opinion Submitted by the Sub-Regional Fisheries Commission (SRFC)*, Advisory Opinion, ITLOS Rep 2015, Separate Opinion of Judge Paik.

9 Moritaka defines a shared stock as one 'that occurs on both sides of a boundary at the same time in random movements or in "dynamic pool" mixing', Moritaka Hayashi, 'The Management of Transboundary Fish Stocks under the LOS Convention' (1993) 8 *International Journal of Marine and Coastal Law* 245, 247. On the typologies of shared fish stocks, see Robin Churchill, 'The Management of Shared Fish Stocks: The Neglected "Other" Paragraph of Article 63 of the UN Convention on the Law of the Sea' in Anastasia Strati, Maria Gavouneli, and Nikos Skourtos (eds), *Unresolved Issues and New Challenges to the Law of the Sea* (Brill 2006) 3, 5–6; Bjørn Kunoy, 'Assertion of Entitlement to Shared Fish Stocks' in Myron Nordquist, John Norton Moore and Ronán Long (eds), *Challenges of the Changing Arctic: Continental Shelf, Navigation, and Fisheries* (Brill 2016) 464, 471–5; James Harrison and Elisa Morgera, 'Commentary to Articles 61–65' in Alexander Proelss (ed), *United Nations Convention on the Law of the Sea: A Commentary* (Beck, Nomos and Hart 2017) 480.

10 Robin Churchill, Vaughan Lowe and Amy Sander, *The Law of the Sea* (Manchester University Press 2022) 554.

11 Churchill notes that shared straddling stocks would be regulated both by Article 63(1) and Article 63(2) of UNCLOS, see Robin Churchill, 'The Management of Shared Fish Stocks: The Neglected "Other" Paragraph of Article 63 of the UN Convention on the Law of the Sea' in Anastasia Strati, Maria Gavouneli, and Nikos Skourtos (eds), *Unresolved Issues and New Challenges to the Law of the Sea* (Brill 2006) 3, 3.

stocks (emphasis added).[12] Coastal States are required 'to seek to agree', but they are not required to reach an agreement on cooperative management measures.[13] UNCLOS does not provide guidance on the specific conduct which must be shown to discharge this obligation (e.g., guiding criteria for determining the respective allocations).[14] Neither does UNCLOS provide specific recourse where the States are unable to agree.

Therefore, the question arises as to whether Article 63(1) means something in practice. To answer this question, this chapter considers three sub-questions. First, what are the substantive and procedural obligations under Article 63(1)? Second, what would constitute a breach of these obligations? Third, what would form appropriate redress for a breach of the obligations under Article 63(1)?

2. Obligations Under Article 63(1)

This section considers the substantive and procedural obligations under Article 63(1).

2.1 An Overarching Duty of Cooperation

Article 63(1) enshrines a positive obligation on States to cooperate with a view to taking the measures necessary for conserving the shared resources concerned.[15] Cooperation to control environmental risks is a central element of international environmental law.[16] The obligation to cooperate over living marine resources is both a substantive and procedural obligation. This substantive obligation is enshrined in numerous treaties involving watercourses[17] and transboundary air pollution.[18] International courts and tribunals have recognised this obligation as a

12 Article 63(1) of UNCLOS reads:

> [w]here the same stock or stocks of associated species occur within the exclusive economic zones of two or more coastal States, these States shall seek, either directly or through appropriate subregional or regional organizations, to agree upon the measures necessary to coordinate and ensure the conservation and development of such stocks without prejudice to the other provisions of this Part.

13 Bjørn Kunoy, 'The Ambit of *Pactum de Negotiatum* in the Management of Shared Fish Stocks: A Rumble in the Jungle' (2012) 11 *Chinese Journal of International Law* 689, 698; see also Yoshifumi Tanaka, *The International Law of the Sea* (CUP 2019) 290.

14 Peter Davies and Catherine Redgwell, 'The International Legal Regulation of Straddling Fish Stocks' (1996) 97 *British Yearbook of International Law* 199, 236.

15 *Request for an Advisory Opinion submitted by the Sub-Regional Fisheries Commission*, Advisory Opinion, ITLOS Rep 2015, paras 210–2.

16 Alan Boyle, 'The Environmental Jurisprudence of the ITLOS' (2007) 22 *International Journal of Marine and Coastal Law* 369, 379.

17 For example, Convention on the Law of the Non-Navigational Uses of International Watercourses, 21 May 1997, 2999 UNTS 77, entered into force 17 August 2014, arts 11–9.

18 For example, Convention on Long-Range Transboundary Air Pollution, 13 November 1979, 1302 UNTS 217, entered into force 16 March 1998, art 5.

customary rule of international law. This includes the International Court of Justice (ICJ) in *Pulp Mills*,[19] *Gabcikovo-Nagymaros Project*,[20] and *Construction of a Road in Costa Rica along the San Juan River*.[21] The International Tribunal for the Law of the Sea (ITLOS) has considered that 'living resources and marine life are part of the marine environment'[22] and that 'the conservation of the living resources of the sea is an element in the protection and preservation of the marine environment'.[23] In *MOX Plant* and *Land Reclamation by Singapore in and around the Straits of Johor*, ITLOS stated that neighbouring States, which share a maritime space, have a duty to cooperate under Part XII of UNCLOS, and that this duty includes an obligation to consult the other State on planned activities in the shared space.[24] Although this was not mentioned by ITLOS, this duty to cooperate appears to come from Principle 19 of the 1992 Rio Declaration on Environmental and Development:

> States shall provide prior and timely notification and relevant information to potentially affected States on activities that may have a significant adverse transboundary environmental effect and shall consult with those States at an early stage and in good faith.[25]

According to Neil Craik, 'the duty to cooperate is triggered by the same condition that triggers the duty to prevent harm; namely, the risk of significant environmental harm, and thus, must also be implemented by States in the same circumstances'.[26] Prevention focuses on a State's obligation to assess and monitor the consequences of a planned activity. Conversely, cooperation over shared resources focuses on a State's obligation to inform other States and to seek their perspectives on an

19 *Pulp Mills on the River Uruguay (Argentina v. Uruguay)*, Judgment, ICJ Rep 2010, para 77, stating that

> it is by co-operating that the States concerned can jointly manage the risks of damage to the environment that might be created by the plans initiated by one or other of them, so as to prevent the damage in question.

20 *Gabcikovo-Nagymaros Project (Hungary/Slovakia)*, Judgment, ICJ Rep 1997, paras 140–7.

21 *Certain Activities (Costa Rica v. Nicaragua)*, Judgment, ICJ Rep 2015, para 106. For a complete discussion, see Neil Craik, 'The Duty To Cooperate in the Customary Law of Environmental Impact Assessment' (2020) 69 *International & Comparative Law Quarterly* 239, 246.

22 *Request for an Advisory Opinion submitted by the Sub-Regional Fisheries Commission (SRFC)*, Advisory Opinion, ITLOS Rep 2015, para 216.

23 *Southern Bluefin Tuna (New Zealand v. Japan; Australia v. Japan)*, Provisional Measures, ITLOS Rep 1999, para 70.

24 *The Mox Plant Case (Ireland v. United Kingdom)*, Provisional Measures, Order of 3 December 2001, ITLOS Rep 2001; *Land Reclamation by Singapore in and around the Straits of Johor (Malaysia v. Singapore)*, Provisional Measures, Order of 8 October 2003, ITLOS Rep 2003.

25 Rio Declaration of the United Nations Conference on Environment and Development (14 June 1992) A/CONF.151/26, Principle 19.

26 Neil Craik, 'The Duty To Cooperate in the Customary Law of Environmental Impact Assessment' (2020) 69 *International & Comparative Law Quarterly* 239, 242.

activity which may affect the other States' sovereign rights.[27] The duty to cooperate views shared fisheries resources as a shared problem. It invites States to balance their interests against the interests of their neighbours in managing and conserving the shared resources.[28]

2.2 A Duty to Notify and Share Information

Requiring prior notification based on adequate scientific information has 'a substantial pedigree of international support and is a natural counterpart of the concept of equitable utilization of a shared resource'.[29] The *Lac Lanoux* arbitration applied this principle.[30] The tribunal held that France had complied with its obligations under treaty and customary law by informing Spain of its proposal before diverting a watercourse shared with Spain; allowing consultations; and giving reasonable weight to Spain's interests.[31]

The United Nations General Assembly Resolution 3129 (XXVIII) of 1974 established certain common principles for conserving and utilising natural resources shared between two or more States. It affirms that States should cooperate 'on the basis of prior notification and information exchange'.[32] Article 3 of the 1974 Charter of Economic Rights and Duties of States sets out the same principle more fully:

> In the exploitation of natural resources shared by two or more countries each state must co-operate on the basis of *a system of information and prior consultation* in order to achieve optimum use of such resources without causing damage to the legitimate interests of others (emphasis added).[33]

On shared fisheries in the EEZ, a coastal State must notify the other State or States sharing this resource of the planned activities and exchange timely scientific

27 ibid.

28 Bjørn Kunoy, 'Assertion of Entitlement to Shared Fish Stocks' in Myron Nordquist, John Norton Moore, and Ronán Long (eds), *Challenges of the Changing Arctic: Continental Shelf, Navigation, and Fisheries* (Brill 2016) 464, 471. Judge Cançado Trindade in the *Whaling* Case considered the duty of cooperation as embedded within 'a system of collective regulation oriented towards the conservation of living species', *Whaling in The Antarctic (Australia v. Japan: New Zealand Intervening)*, Judgment, ICJ Rep 2014, Separate Opinion of Judge Cançado Trindade, para 87. See also *Barbados v. Trinidad and Tobago*, Award, PCA Case 2004–02, 11 April 2006, paras 285–94.

29 Patricia Birnie, Alan Boyle, and Catherine Redgwell, *International Law and the Environment* (OUP 2009) 175.

30 Lac Lanoux Arbitration, Award, 24 ILR 101, 16 November 1957.

31 ibid, 101.

32 UN Environment Programme Governing Council, 'Draft Principles of Conduct in the Field of the Environment for the Guidance of States in the Conservation and Harmonious Utilization of Natural Resources Shared by Two or More States' (18 May 1978) Principle 1 repr. in Vol 4(1) Environmental Policy and Law (1978) 48–56.

33 UN General Assembly, 'Resolution 3281 (XXIX): Charter of Economic Rights and Duties of States' (Resolution adopted by the General Assembly on 12 December 1974), Art 4 https://legal.un.org/avl/ha/cerds/cerds.html.

information concerning its plans.[34] The 1995 Food and Agriculture Organization of the United Nations (FAO) Code of Conduct for Responsible Fisheries provides that States with neighbouring coastal areas should cooperate with one another to facilitate the sustainable use of coastal resources and, in this regard, share 'timely information', give 'prior notification to potentially affected States', and 'consult with those States as early as possible'.[35] The Norway – FAO Expert Consultation on the Management of Shared Fish Stocks, held in 2002, laid down specific procedural principles for managing shared fish stocks.[36] The Expert Consultation noted that, where a single transboundary stock occurs wholly within two or more States' EEZs, special notification and reporting requirements (e.g., for catch, area of operation, and entry and exit from the EEZ) must be implemented to reinforce coastal States' management measures.[37]

ITLOS emphasised in its *Request for an Advisory Opinion Submitted by the Sub-Regional Fisheries Commission (SRFC Advisory Opinion)* in 2015 that the duty to share 'available scientific information, catch and fishing efforts statistics, and other data' is crucial to the conservation of shared stocks.[38] Reliable data on species to be harvested are a prerequisite for establishing an effective management regime.[39] Thus, a State, which refuses to share scientific data on the management of the shared species, would breach Article 63(1). Yet, each State must determine the precise content of the scientific data required in each case; how the data should be collected; and by whom.

2.3 A Duty to Negotiate

The duty to negotiate in good faith is another specific form of the obligation to cooperate. It requires the parties to conduct themselves to ensure the negotiations are meaningful.[40] States must enter into negotiations in good faith with a view to

34 Robin Churchill, 'The Management of Shared Fish Stocks: The Neglected "Other" Paragraph of Article 63 of the UN Convention on the Law of the Sea' in Anastasia Strati, Maria Gavouneli, and Nikos Skourtos (eds), *Unresolved Issues and New Challenges to the Law of the Sea* (Brill 2006) 537. See also, *Request for an Advisory Opinion Submitted by the Sub-Regional Fisheries Commission (SRFC)*, Advisory Opinion, ITLOS Rep 2015, Separate Opinion of Judge Paik, para 34.

35 FAO, 'Code of Conduct for Responsible Fisheries' (1995) C 95/20/Rev 1, art 10(3).

36 FAO, 'Report of the Norway-FAO Expert Consultation on the Management of Shared Fish Stocks' (Bergen, Norway, 7–10 October 2002).

37 ibid.

38 *Request for an Advisory Opinion submitted by the Sub-Regional Fisheries Commission (SRFC)*, Advisory Opinion, ITLOS Rep 2015, paras 59, 66.

39 ibid.

40 Lac Lanoux Arbitration, Award, 24 ILR 101, 16 November 1957; *North Sea Continental Shelf Cases (Germany v. Denmark; Germany v. Netherlands)*, Judgment, ICJ Rep 1969, para 85; *Fisheries Jurisdiction (United Kingdom v. Iceland)*, Judgment, ICJ Rep 1974; *Gabčíkovo-Nagymaros Project (Hungary/Slovakia)*, Judgment, ICJ Rep 1997, para 141. See also United Nations General Assembly, 'Principles and guidelines for international negotiations' (8 December 1998) A/RES/53/101.

arriving at an agreement.[41] Under Article 63(1), this obligation to negotiate arises when the same stock or stocks of associated species occur on both sides of the EEZ boundary line.[42] The coastal States must determine when such stocks have a shared transboundary nature. Thus, the duty to cooperate under Article 63(1) only becomes applicable when the relevant States determine that it is.

One could think that identifying a shared stock will rarely be difficult in practice. Indeed, that a stock is shared will often be self-evident.[43] However, States often disagree on the shared nature of a stock. One example is the dispute between the European Community and Norway over mackerel in the 1970s.[44] Neither side recognised that the fish stock in question was shared until the late 1980s. Both sides only recognised in the early 1990s that the stock was not only shared but was also a straddling one.[45]

Over time, a stock may also change its migratory pattern (e.g., due to climate variations), causing it to cease to be a single-State stock and, instead, to become a shared stock.[46] This has happened with the Atlanto-Scandian herring in the North-East Atlantic.[47] Reference here can be made to the dispute between the European Union (EU) and the Faroe Islands over the management of the Atlanto-Scandian herring.[48] This dispute was referred to arbitration under Annex VII of UNCLOS in 2013 but was settled before the proceedings started.[49] The migration pattern of mackerel in the North-East Atlantic has also changed. While

41 *North Sea Continental Shelf Cases (Germany v. Denmark; Germany v. Netherlands)*, Judgment, ICJ Rep 1969, paras 53–54.

42 Robin Churchill, 'The Management of Shared Fish Stocks: The Neglected "Other" Paragraph of Article 63 of the UN Convention on the Law of the Sea' in Anastasia Strati, Maria Gavouneli, and Nikos Skourtos (eds), *Unresolved Issues and New Challenges to the Law of the Sea* (Brill 2006) 3, 7.

43 ibid.

44 ibid.

45 ibid. See also Robin R Churchill, 'Managing Straddling Fish Stocks in the North-East Atlantic: A Multiplicity of Instruments and Regime Linkages – but How Effective a Management?' in Olav Schram Stokke (ed), *Governing High Seas Fisheries: The Interplay of Global and Regional Regimes* (OUP 2001) 235, 262–3.

46 Jóhann Sigurjónsson, 'Changes in Distribution and Migration of Fish Stocks in the Northeast Atlantic Ocean Due to Climate Variations' in Myron Nordquist, John Norton Moore, and Ronán Long (eds), *Challenges of the Changing Arctic: Continental Shelf, Navigation, and Fisheries* (Brill 2016) 405.

47 Robin R Churchill, 'Managing Straddling Fish Stocks in the North-East Atlantic: A Multiplicity of Instruments and Regime Linkages – But How Effective a Management?' in Olav Schram Stokke (ed), *Governing High Seas Fisheries: The Interplay of Global and Regional Regimes* (OUP 2001) 241–3.

48 For a discussion, see Bjørn Kunoy, 'Assertion of Entitlement to Shared Fish Stocks' in Myron Nordquist, John Norton Moore, and Ronán Long (eds), *Challenges of the Changing Arctic: Continental Shelf, Navigation, and Fisheries* (Brill 2016) 464, 466.

49 *The Atlanto-Scandian Herring Arbitration (The Kingdom of Denmark in Respect of the Faroe Islands v. The European Union)*, PCA Case 2013–30, instituted on 16 August 2013 and terminated by joint agreement on 23 September 2014.

the mackerel started migrating into the Icelandic EEZ, Iceland was not invited to participate in coastal States' negotiations until some years later.[50]

2.3.1 An Obligation of Conduct

The obligation to negotiate joint management and conservation measures is one of conduct, not an obligation to agree on any arrangement. In essence, it is 'an obligation of best efforts'.[51]

As Francisco Vicuña has noted, '[t]here is no obligation to enter into such agreements as evidenced by the expression "shall seek"'.[52] ITLOS underscored this point in its *SRFC Advisory Opinion*.[53] Indeed, if Article 63(1) had been intended as an obligation of result, it could simply have read as 'these States shall agree upon the measures necessary to coordinate the conservation and development of such stocks'. Conversely, international courts and tribunals have stressed that an obligation to negotiate in good faith 'does not imply an obligation to reach an agreement'.[54] Neither does it imply that a State, 'by undertaking to negotiate, has assumed an engagement, and is in consequence obliged to conclude . . . agreements'.[55] Thus, a State is not obliged to reach any agreement, it is under an obligation only to enter into negotiations in good faith and with a view to reaching a cooperative agreement.[56]

2.3.2 Good Faith

Article 63(1), as noted already, requires coastal States to notify and consult each other and enter into meaningful negotiations in good faith. This means that States

50 I thank Judge Tomas Heidar for suggesting this point. For a discussion, see Jessica Spijkers and Wiebren Boomstra, 'Environmental Change and Social Conflict: The Northeast Atlantic Mackerel Dispute' (2017) 17 *Regional Environmental Change* 1835.

51 Bjørn Kunoy, 'The Ambit of *Pactum de Negotiatum* in the Management of Shared Fish Stocks: A Rumble in the Jungle' (2012) 11 *Chinese Journal of International Law* 689, 692. See also *Request for an Advisory Opinion submitted by the Sub-Regional Fisheries Commission (SRFC)*, Advisory Opinion, ITLOS Rep 2015, Separate Opinion of Judge Paik, para 35.

52 Francisco Orrego Vicuña, *The Exclusive Economic Zone: Regime and Legal Nature under International Law* (CUP 1989) 61.

53 *Request for an Advisory Opinion submitted by the Sub-Regional Fisheries Commission (SRFC)*, Advisory Opinion, ITLOS Rep 2015, para 210.

54 *Railway Traffic between Lithuania and Poland*, Advisory Opinion (1931) PCIJ Rep, Series A/B, 42, para 31; see also Lac Lanoux Arbitration, Award, 24 ILR 101, 16 November 1957, 128.

55 *International Status of South West Africa*, Advisory Opinion, ICJ Rep 1950, 139, stating: '[t]he parties must be free to accept or reject the terms of a contemplated agreement. No party can impose its terms on the other party'. See also *Land and Maritime Boundary between Cameroon and Nigeria (Cameroon v. Nigeria: Equatorial Guinea Intervening)*, Judgment, ICJ Rep 2022, para 244.

56 Ellen Hey, *The Regime for the Exploitation of Transboundary Marine Fisheries Resources* (Martinus Nijhoff 1989) 81. See also Bjørn Kunoy, 'The Ambit of *Pactum de Negotiatum* in the Management of Shared Fish Stocks: A Rumble in the Jungle' (2012) 11 *Chinese Journal of International Law* 689, 692.

should not exercise their discretionary powers in a manner which constitutes an abuse of right.[57] It also means that States are vested with a mandate to make 'substantial effort' to enter into an arrangement to manage and conserve the shared stocks.[58] Such arrangements include joint determination of the total allowable catches for the shared stocks and allocation between the parties; the coordination or joint adoption of other conservation measures; and the establishment of mechanisms for effective monitoring, control, and surveillance.[59]

Failure to reach an agreement will not in itself breach Article 63(1). However, there may be a breach where the failure can be ascribed to a State's refusal to negotiate in good faith. Examples of bad faith conduct include unjustifiably breaking off of negotiations; disregarding the agreed procedure; systematically refusing to consider adverse proposals; and using economic coercion causing fisheries negotiations to collapse.[60] For example, Denmark claimed in 2013 that the EU's use of imminent threats to enforce coercive economic measures against the Faroe Islands so as to impose an allocation key of Atlanto-Scandian herring, violated the EU's obligations under Article 63(1).[61] As Bjørn Kunoy noted, such coercive measures 'were in violation of the general principle of law consistent with which coastal States endeavoring to reach an agreement on a joint management arrangement applicable to a shared fish stock should enjoy full freedom of consent'.[62]

Negotiations on shared fisheries management must be allowed to run their course. As the ICJ held:

> There would be no point to the co-operation mechanism . . . if the party initiating the planned activity were to authorize or implement it without

57 UNCLOS, art 300. See also Andreas R Ziegler and Jorun Baumgartner, 'Good Faith as a General Principle of (International) Law' in Andrew Mitchell, Muthucumaraswamy Sornarajah, and Tania Voon (eds), *Good Faith and International Economic Law* (OUP 2015) 9.

58 *Request for an Advisory Opinion submitted by the Sub-Regional Fisheries Commission (SRFC)*, Advisory Opinion, ITLOS Rep 2015; see also *Barbados v. Trinidad and Tobago*, Award, PCA Case 2004–02, 11 April 2006, para 283.

59 Daniel Owen, 'Legal and Institutional Aspects of Management Arrangements for Shared Stocks of Marine Fish' in Malgosia Fitzmaurice and Milena Szuniewicz (eds), *Exploitation of Natural Resources in the 21st Century* (Kluwer 2003) 247.

60 Lac Lanoux Arbitration, Award, 24 ILR 101, 16 November 1957, 124; Bjørn Kunoy, 'The Ambit of *Pactum de Negotiatum* in the Management of Shared Fish Stocks: A Rumble in the Jungle' (2012) 11 *Chinese Journal of International Law* 689, 724; United Nations General Assembly, 'Declaration on Principles of International Law Concerning Friendly Relations and Cooperation Among States in Accordance with the Charter of the United Nations' (24 October 1970) Resolution 2625(XXV), provides that '[n]o State may use or encourage the use of economic, political or any other type of measures to coerce any State in order to . . . to secure from it advantages of any kind'. For a discussion, Mohamed Helal, 'On Coercion In International Law' (2019) *New York University Journal of International Law and Politics* 2, 47.

61 Bjørn Kunoy, 'Assertion of Entitlement to Shared Fish Stocks' in Myron Nordquist, John Norton Moore, and Ronán Long (eds), *Challenges of the Changing Arctic: Continental Shelf, Navigation, and Fisheries* (Brill 2016) 464, 466.

62 ibid 502.

> waiting for that mechanism to be brought to a conclusion. Indeed, if that were the case, the negotiations between the parties would no longer have any purpose.[63]

However, as the Annex VII Arbitral Tribunal stated in *Mauritius* v. *United Kingdom*, 'States themselves are in the best position to determine where substantive negotiations can productively be continued'.[64] Any State can, at any time, conclude that continuing negotiations would be unproductive.[65] ITLOS later underscored this point in *Mauritius/Maldives*.[66] It found that 'the Maldives, for most of the time, refused to negotiate with Mauritius' and that 'there was nothing more that Mauritius could have accomplished in insisting on having delimitation negotiations with the Maldives'.[67] On the one hand, finding a solution in a dispute on the effective management of a shared stock depends on the States' willingness to keep negotiating. On the other hand, 'the principle of good faith does not require states subject to this duty to continue consultation and negotiation until they reach an agreement'.[68]

The duty to conduct meaningful negotiations requires that States consider the views of others and be willing to modify their own stance. As the tribunal in *Lac Lanoux* put it,

> According to the rules of good faith, the upstream State is under the obligation to take into consideration the various interests involved, to seek to give them every satisfaction compatible with the pursuit of its own interests, and to show that in this regard it is genuinely concerned to reconcile the interests of the other riparian State with its own.[69]

A State must engage with the views of other States; demonstrate respect for the other States' interests; and show readiness to modify its approach to take account of these States' views.[70] ITLOS noted in *Responsibilities and obligations of States sponsoring persons and entities with respect to activities in the Area (Request for Advisory Opinion submitted to the Seabed Disputes Chamber)* that, in fulfilling their duty, States 'must take into account, objectively, the relevant options in a

63 *Pulp Mills on the River Uruguay (Argentina v. Uruguay)*, Judgment, ICJ Rep 2010.

64 *Chagos Marine Protected Area Arbitration (Mauritius v. United Kingdom)*, Award, PCA Case 2011–03, 18 March 2015, para 379.

65 ibid.

66 *Dispute Concerning Delimitation of the Maritime Boundary Between Mauritius and Maldives in the Indian Ocean (Mauritius/Maldives)*, Preliminary Objections, ITLOS Rep 2021.

67 ibid, paras 289, 293.

68 Charles Bourne, 'Procedure in the Development of International Drainage Basins: The Duty to Consult and to Negotiate' (1972) 10 *Canadian Yearbook of International Law* 212, 221.

69 Lac Lanoux Arbitration, Award, 24 ILR 101, 16 November 1957, 139.

70 *North Sea Continental Shelf Cases (Germany v. Denmark; Germany v. Netherlands)*, Judgment, ICJ Rep 1969, para 85.

manner that is reasonable, relevant and conducive'.[71] The expectation that the views of other States will be objectively considered is inherently context-specific and is difficult to determine. On the one hand, a party cannot altogether ignore other affected parties or dictate how the shared resource must be used to other parties. On the other hand, a State's duty to engage meaningfully with other affected States and to consider their views does not constitute a duty to defer unconditionally to the views of others, even when these views appear reasonable.[72]

3. Alleging a Breach of Article 63(1) and Options for Redress

This section considers first what may constitute a breach of the substantive and procedural obligations under Article 63(1) and, second, the options for redress where such obligations have been breached.

3.1 Alleging a Breach

The relevance of Article 63(1) boils down to the following: should the provision be interpreted as permitting unilateral and uncoordinated exploitation of shared fisheries in the EEZ? Alternatively, should it be interpreted within the context of a system of mandatory collective action? Is Article 63(1) a self-judging provision so that the relevant States determine alone the conduct necessary to fulfil their obligations? Conversely, are constraints placed upon these States which may be objectively determined by an international court or tribunal?

3.1.1 A System of Mandatory Collective Action

UNCLOS establishes a 'system of collective regulation' for conserving and managing transboundary natural resources.[73] Article 63(1) must be interpreted in light of this object and purpose. The end of Article 63(1) clarifies that its substantive and procedural obligations are 'without prejudice to the other provisions of this Part'. This 'without prejudice' clause means that the States concerned remain bound by their conservation duties under UNCLOS. This is so whether the States are managing their shared fish stock cooperatively or otherwise. Article 63(1) plays a crucial role in this regard. It provides any affected State with a legal basis for initiating negotiations with relevant neighbouring States. It also enshrines a legal duty

71 *Responsibilities and Obligations of States Sponsoring Persons and Entities with Respect to Activities in the Area (Request for Advisory Opinion Submitted to the Seabed Disputes Chamber)*, Advisory Opinion, ITLOS Rep 2011, para 230.

72 The duty of cooperation presupposes that '[t]he State in question, while not bound to accept the recommendation, is bound to give it due consideration in good faith', *Voting Procedure on Questions Relating to Reports and Petitions Concerning the Territory of South West Africa*, Advisory Opinion, ICJ Rep 1955, Separate Opinion of Judge Lauterpacht, 119.

73 *Whaling in The Antarctic (Australia v. Japan: New Zealand Intervening)*, Judgment, ICJ Rep 2014, Separate Opinion of Judge Cançado Trindade, para 87.

upon these neighbouring States to conduct negotiations in good faith, as discussed previously.

Compliance with the obligations of Article 63(1) is critical to keep pace with drivers of change, notably global warming and associated challenges, such as environmental degradation, for identifying shared stocks and allocating total allowable catches. Cooperating with neighbouring States and agreeing on shared fisheries management can help respond to these challenges.[74] Acidification and ocean warming cause fish to change their patterns of feeding and reproduction. As mentioned previously, a stock may change its migratory pattern, thereby ceasing to be a single-State stock and becoming shared.[75] For example, in the North-East Atlantic, the distribution of at least 16 species has changed in recent years, with eight of these species having shifted their distribution across EEZ boundaries.[76] Such changes put pressure on existing management arrangements.[77] States are increasingly in search of alternative fishing grounds to support local fishing communities. Governments also often accuse their counterparts of doing too little to prevent overfishing. This trend is likely to continue. Accordingly, disputes arising from the interpretation and application of Article 63(1) will likely increase in the future.

Such disputes may be scrutinised by ITLOS or another court or tribunal under Part XV, Section 2, of UNCLOS. As Judge Paik noted in the *SRFC Advisory Opinion*:

> any dispute arising from the alleged failure to comply with the obligation under Article 63, paragraph 1, of the Convention, unlike those disputes arising from the exercise of sovereign rights of the coastal State with respect to the living resources in its EEZ, can be submitted to the compulsory procedure under Part XV, section 2, of the Convention . . .
>
> Thus the right course of action for a . . . [coastal] State in cases where another . . . [coastal] State sharing the transboundary stocks refuses to cooperate without justifiable reasons is to invoke the liability of that State for the

74 Keyuan Zou, 'Climate Change and Fisheries Regulation: What We Should Consider for the Future?' (2021) 13 *Sustainability* 1, 4–5.

75 Jóhann Sigurjónsson, 'Changes in Distribution and Migration of Fish Stocks in the Northeast Atlantic Ocean Due to Climate Variations' in Myron Nordquist, John Norton Moore, and Ronán Long (eds), *Challenges of the Changing Arctic: Continental Shelf, Navigation, and Fisheries* (Brill 2016) 405.

76 International Council for the Exploration of the Sea (ICES), 'EU Request on Distributional Shifts in Fish Stocks' (20 March 2017) ICES Special Request Advice sr.2017.05, cited by James Harrison, 'Written Evidence, House of Lords International Relations and Defence Committee UNCLOS: Fit for Purpose in the 21st Century?' (8 November 2021) <committees.parliament.uk/writtenevidence/40763/pdf/> accessed 23 December 2023.

77 James Harrison, 'Written Evidence, House of Lords International Relations and Defence Committee UNCLOS: Fit for purpose in the 21st Century?' (8 November 2021) <committees.parliament.uk/writtenevidence/40763/pdf/> accessed 23 December 2023.

> breach of obligations under Article 63, paragraph 1, of the Convention, not to try to restrict the exercise of its sovereign rights in the EEZ.[78]

Judge Paik emphasised that Article 63(1) of UNCLOS mandates efforts to seek agreement, rather than mandating an agreement. These efforts should be meaningful and conducted in good faith. He suggested that the obligation to cooperate may encompass duties to notify, exchange information, consult, and negotiate. Furthermore, States are under a pertinent obligation to exercise due regard and the duties under Article 63(1) connect to duties to safeguard the marine environment. These obligations are subject to compulsory jurisdiction, according to Natalie Klein.[79] This position is consistent with the authoritative *Virginia Commentary* to UNCLOS.[80] The *Commentary* distinguishes between, on the one hand, fisheries disputes relating to a coastal State's exercise of completely discretionary powers and, on the other hand, disputes which involve 'clear cases of abuse of discretion, where a State manifestly or arbitrarily has failed to comply with some basic obligations [under the Convention]'.[81] The latter category of disputes may well be scrutinised under Part XV, Section 2, of UNCLOS.[82] Thus, Article 63(1) plays a crucial role in providing a self-standing basis to found compulsory jurisdiction.[83]

3.1.2 Article 63(1) Before a Court or Tribunal

Alleging a breach of Article 63(1) before a court or tribunal under Part XV, Section 2, of UNCLOS 'could be a useful tactic, but probably one of last resort'.[84] Indeed, very few fisheries disputes have so far been referred to judicial settlement. States are reluctant to refer fisheries disputes to binding third-party settlement.[85] Other than the arbitration between the Faroe Islands and the EU, which was discontinued before the proceedings started, no State has alleged a breach of Article 63(1) before an international court or tribunal. This may be linked to the fact that

78 *Request for an Advisory Opinion Submitted by the Sub-Regional Fisheries Commission (SRFC)*, Advisory Opinion, ITLOS Rep 2015, Separate Opinion of Judge Paik, paras 37–8; for a commentary, Michael A Becker, 'Request for An Advisory Opinion Submitted by the Sub-Regional Fisheries Commission (SRFC) Case No 21' (2015) 109 *American Journal of International Law* 851.

79 Natalie Klein, 'The Many Facets of EEZ Fisheries Disputes and Their Resolution Under UNCLOS' (2023) 13 *Goettingen Journal of International Law* 14, 22–3.

80 This commentary draws on the formal and informal documentation of the Third United Nations Conference on the Law of the Sea, Myron Nordquist, Satya Nandan, and Shabtai Rosenne (eds), *United Nations Convention on the Law of the Sea 1982: Volume II: A Commentary* (Martinus Nijhoff 1989).

81 ibid, 105.

82 ibid.

83 Note however, that the tribunal in *Chagos Marine Protected Area Arbitration (Mauritius v. United Kingdom)*, Award, PCA Case 2011–03, 18 March 2015, para 300, considered that these disputes would be outside compulsory jurisdiction.

84 Robin Churchill, 'The Jurisprudence of the International Tribunal for the Law of the Sea Relating to Fisheries: Is There Much in the Net?' (2007) 22 *International Journal of Marine & Coastal Law* 383, 421.

85 ibid.

establishing a breach of Article 63(1) is generally difficult and context-specific. It will ordinarily involve answering four questions:

1. Have the parties identified a shared stock?
2. Have the parties shared relevant scientific information?
3. Have the parties consulted each other on cooperative arrangements and related measures to manage the shared stocks as necessary in the specific circumstances?
4. Have the parties negotiated in good faith?

These are all questions of fact for a court or tribunal to determine. If the evidence presented before the court or tribunal leads it to answer 'yes' to these four questions, there will be no breach of Article 63(1).

First, the court or tribunal must determine if there is, indeed, a shared stock. This is an objective determination based on science. Second, the court or tribunal must determine if the parties notified each other and shared relevant scientific information on the shared stock. This is also an objective determination. The precise content of the information or mode of communication is irrelevant to this determination. Third, the court or tribunal will assess whether the parties consulted each other on cooperative arrangements regarding the shared stock, either directly or through appropriate subregional or regional organisations. Again, this requirement is met by showing that the parties sought to exchange views or correspondence on the management of the shared fish stock. Fourth and finally, the court or tribunal will assess whether, in seeking to conclude cooperative arrangements, the parties negotiated in good faith. Here, the parties are presumed to act in good faith. The burden of proof is placed upon the party claiming the violation to show this due diligence duty was breached.[86]

To prove bad faith, 'something more must appear than the failure of particular negotiations'.[87] As the ICJ has held, proving bad faith can be made through circumstantial evidence but it should be supported 'not by disputable inferences but *by clear and convincing evidence* which compels such a conclusion' (emphasis added).[88] It is difficult to determine objectively what 'clear and convincing' evidence will establish bad faith conduct. How can we distinguish between common negotiating practices which States employ to pressure their counterparts and unlawful bad-faith conduct which violates Article 63(1)?

Another practical issue is determining the exact time when a violation occurs. For obligations of result, a violation occurs when a result is not achieved. For obligations of conduct, however, a violation occurs when the situation prohibited

86 *Application of the Interim Accord of 13 September 1995 (the former Yugoslav Republic of Macedonia v. Greece)*, Judgment, ICJ Rep 2011, para 72.

87 ibid, paras 132–4. The Permanent Court of International Justice (PCIJ) has explained that bad faith cannot be easily presumed, see *Free Zones of Upper Savoy and District of Gex (France v. Switzerland)* (1932) PCIJ Rep, Series A/B, 46, 167.

88 *Application of the Interim Accord of 13 September 1995 (the former Yugoslav Republic of Macedonia v. Greece)*, Judgment, ICJ Rep 2011, paras 132–4.

by the norm materialises (e.g., arbitrary refusal to negotiate), not when the result which may come from failing to adhere to that norm occurs (e.g., failure to reach agreement).[89]

3.2 Redress

The final issue is to consider the appropriate redress for a breach of the obligation of conduct under Article 63(1). That the obligation of conduct does not amount to a commitment to enter into an agreement does not mean that a State which has breached this obligation will not be held responsible.[90] However, as the ICJ has noted, if the obligation is one of conduct and not one of result, 'a State does not incur responsibility simply because the desired result is not achieved'.[91] Does a declaration of wrongdoing constitute the only 'appropriate satisfaction' in these cases? Alternatively, could a breach of Article 63(1) attract compensation? What can be the remedy for an injured State seeking redress?

3.2.1 Declaration of Satisfaction and Order of Compliance

A State injured by a violation of Article 63(1) cannot arguably claim *restitutio in integrum*. The State which has breached Article 63(1) cannot either be imposed a duty of reparation in the meaning of the *Factory at Chorzow*, namely a duty to 'wipe-out all the consequences of the illegal act and re-establish the situation which would, in all probability, have existed if that act had not been committed.'[92] As Kunoy writes, citing *Factory at Chorzow*, 'there could be no "obligation to restore . . . and, if this is not possible, to pay its value at the time of the indemnification, which value is designed to take the place of restitution which has become impossible" '.[93]

Insofar as a violation of Article 63(1) cannot be made good by restitution or compensation, satisfaction would typically involve a declaration of the wrongfulness of the act by the competent court or tribunal.[94] The ICJ stated in *Corfu Channel* that an acknowledgement by the Court that the responsible State committed a breach was an appropriate form of satisfaction. The ICJ found that a minesweeping operation by the British Navy was unlawful and said: '[T]o ensure respect for international law, of which it is the organ, the Court must declare that the action of

89 Medes Malaihollo, 'Due Diligence in International Environmental Law and International Human Rights Law' (2021) 68 *Netherlands International Law Review* 121, 129.

90 Bjørn Kunoy, 'The Ambit of *Pactum de Negotiatum* in the Management of Shared Fish Stocks: A Rumble in the Jungle' (2012) 11 *Chinese Journal of International Law* 689, 720.

91 *Application of the Convention on the Prevention and Punishment of the Crime of Genocide (Bosnia and Herzegovina v. Serbia and Montenegro)*, Judgment, ICJ Rep 2007, para 430.

92 *Factory at Chorzow (Germany v. Poland)* (1928) PCIJ Rep, Series A, 17, para 125.

93 Bjørn Kunoy, 'The Ambit of *Pactum de Negotiatum* in the Management of Shared Fish stocks: A Rumble in the Jungle' (2012) 11 *Chinese Journal of International Law* 689, 721.

94 International Law Commission, 'Draft Articles on Responsibility of States for Internationally Wrongful Acts, with commentaries' (2001) II *Yearbook of the International Law Commission*, 106.

the British Navy constituted a violation of Albanian sovereignty.'[95] This has been followed in many subsequent cases.[96]

Another useful tactic could be a motion seeking an order of compliance with the obligations under Article 63(1), for example, that the responsible State immediately resume good faith negotiations. However, this is less likely to succeed. For example, in *Application of the Interim Accord of 13 September 1995*, the ICJ noted that the obligation under Article 11(1) of the Interim Accord was an obligation of conduct.[97] However, the Court then refused to uphold the second plea of the applicant who sought two measures of relief: (1) a declaration that the respondent had acted illegally, and (2) an order that the respondent henceforth refrain from any action violating the specific obligation.[98] The ICJ recalled its finding in *Navigational and Related Rights* that bad faith could not be assumed.[99] It concluded that the finding that 'the Respondent has violated its obligation to the Applicant under Article 11, paragraph 1, of the Interim Accord, constitutes appropriate satisfaction'.[100]

3.2.2 Provisional Measures Under Article 290(1) of UNCLOS

Is a mere declaration of wrongfulness meaningful when States' inability to cooperate causes irreversible damage to shared fishing resources and, thus, damages the ability of the environment to provide goods and services? Here, an injured State could seek a declaration of satisfaction for a breach of Article 63(1) and, in parallel and pending a decision on the merits, seek the prescription of provisional measures pursuant to Article 290(1) of UNCLOS.[101] Article 290(1) enables ITLOS, or any other court or tribunal exercising jurisdiction under the dispute settlement framework of UNCLOS, to prescribe, pending consideration of the merits, provisional measures it considers appropriate 'to prevent serious harm to the marine environment'.[102] These provisional measures are prescribed irrespective of any

95 *Corfu Channel (United Kingdom of Great Britain and Northern Ireland v. Albania)*, Judgment, ICJ Rep 1949, 35.

96 International Law Commission, 'Draft Articles on Responsibility of States for Internationally Wrongful Acts, with commentaries' (2001) II *Yearbook of the International Law Commission*, 107.

97 *Application of the Interim Accord of 13 September 1995 (the former Yugoslav Republic of Macedonia v. Greece)*, Judgment, ICJ Rep 2011, para 168.

98 ibid.

99 *Dispute regarding Navigational and Related Rights (Costa Rica v. Nicaragua)*, Judgment, ICJ Rep 2009, para 150.

100 *Application of the Interim Accord of 13 September 1995 (the former Yugoslav Republic of Macedonia v. Greece)*, Judgment, ICJ Rep 2011, para 169.

101 I appreciate this comment from Professor James Harrison, University of Edinburgh Law School.

102 Provisional measures can be granted if the court or tribunal considers that (1) it has *prima facie* jurisdiction; (2) there is urgency in the situation; and (3) there is a risk of irreparable damage to the parties' rights or to the marine environment, see Rüdiger Wolfrum, 'Provisional Measures of the International Tribunal for the Law of the Sea' (1997) 37 *Indian Journal of International Law* 420, 423; Peter Tomka and Gleider Hernández, 'Provisional Measures in the International Tribunal for the Law of the Sea' in Peter Tomka and Gleider Hernández (eds), *Coexistence, Cooperation and Solidarity* (Brill 2002) 1763; Constantinos Yiallourides, 'Protecting and Preserving the Marine

alleged breach of the right or rights of the requesting party. Prescribing provisional measures aimed at environmental protection does not necessarily require that serious environmental harm has already occurred. Provisional measures are also aimed at countering the risk of such harm occurring before the merits are considered.[103]

ITLOS' jurisprudence on provisional measures indicates that, even where the alleged harm to the marine environment is plausible but not clear or imminent, ITLOS can nonetheless request the parties to cooperate, exchange information, and jointly assess the risks.[104] In *Southern Bluefin Tuna*, there were scientific uncertainties about the health of the southern bluefin tuna stock and the measures required to conserve it.[105] Yet, ITLOS emphasised the need for greater cooperation to ensure conservation and optimum utilisation of fishing resources. It ordered the parties to resume negotiations for that purpose 'without delay'. In *MOX Plant*, Ireland had not adduced sufficient evidence to establish that the MOX Plant operation posed imminent environmental risks. However, ITLOS ordered both parties to enter immediately into consultations and to exchange further scientific information.[106] Similarly, in *Land Reclamation*, ITLOS ordered the parties to improve their cooperation and to consult, exchange information, and monitor the effects of their respective activities on the environment.[107] Thus, ITLOS made cooperation orders notwithstanding findings that significant environmental harm was neither imminent nor likely.[108]

It is notable that during the *MOX Plant* proceedings on provisional measures, the United Kingdom gave assurances that it would abstain from transporting any radioactive material until the Annex VII arbitral tribunal heard the merits.[109] In *Land Reclamation*, Singapore committed to notify, consult, and negotiate with Malaysia before proceeding with further land reclamation works.[110] Thus, in these cases, Ireland and Malaysia secured important commitments which, in essence, provided interim protection pending a decision on the merits.

Environment in Disputed Areas: Seismic Noise and Provisional Measures of Protection' (2017) 36 *Journal of Energy and Natural Resources Law* 141, 150–2.

103 Constantinos Yiallourides and Natalia Ermolina, 'States' Environmental Obligations in Disputed Maritime Areas and the Limits of International Law' in Ishaan Madaan and Christian Campbell (eds), *Comparative Law Yearbook of International Business* (Wolters Kluwer 2021) 127, 145.

104 Alan Boyle, 'The Environmental Jurisprudence of the ITLOS' (2007) 22 *International Journal of Marine and Coastal Law* 369.

105 *Southern Bluefin Tuna (New Zealand v. Japan; Australia v. Japan)*, Provisional Measures, ITLOS Rep 1999, paras 70–79 and operative para (e).

106 *The Mox Plant Case (Ireland v. United Kingdom)*, Provisional Measures, Order of 3 December 2001, ITLOS Rep 2001, paras 78–84.

107 *Land Reclamation by Singapore in and Around the Straits of Johor (Malaysia v. Singapore)*, Provisional Measures, Order of 8 October 2003, ITLOS Rep 2003, paras 96, 106.

108 Patricia Birnie, Alan Boyle, and Catherine Redgwell, *International Law and the Environment* (OUP 2009) 176.

109 *The Mox Plant Case (Ireland v. United Kingdom)*, Provisional Measures, Order of 3 December 2001, ITLOS Rep 2001, para 78.

110 *Land Reclamation by Singapore in and Around the Straits of Johor (Malaysia v. Singapore)*, Provisional Measures, Order of 8 October 2003, ITLOS Rep 2003, para 62.

For disputes concerning shared fisheries under Article 63(1), provisional measures under Article 290(1) have the practical value of bringing environmental risks to the fore at an earlier stage, prior to considering the merits. Thus, appropriate management and conservation measures can be taken before it is too late. Of course, the probability of harm cannot be based on abstract speculations or unjustified projections.[111]

4. Conclusion

This chapter has analysed the substantive and procedural scope of Article 63(1) of UNCLOS in relation to disputes on the conservation and management of shared fishery resources in the EEZ. Article 63(1) enshrines a general obligation on States sharing fishery resources, which migrate or are distributed between their respective EEZs, 'to seek to agree' on a joint conservation and management arrangement. This obligation is one of conduct, not an obligation to agree on any arrangement. Nevertheless, it is not a mere aspiration. It encompasses specific due diligence obligations. These obligations include first, to exchange information and consult with affected States, and second, to negotiate meaningfully and in good faith with a view to arriving at a cooperative agreement.

Compliance with the due diligence obligations of Article 63(1) is critical to keep pace with drivers of change, notably global warming, and associated challenges for identifying shared stocks and allocating total allowable catches. Failure to comply with Article 63(1) may be scrutinised by a court or tribunal under Part XV, Section 2, of UNCLOS. However, proving a breach of a due diligence obligation under Article 63(1) will generally be difficult. The chapter has suggested that the optimum course of action for an injured State seeking redress is to pursue a declaration of satisfaction for a breach of Article 63(1) and, in parallel, pending a decision on the merits, request provisional measures pursuant to Article 290(1) of UNCLOS.

111 *The Mox Plant Case (Ireland v. United Kingdom)*, Provisional Measures, Order of 3 December 2001, ITLOS Rep 2001, Separate Opinion of Judge Wolfrum, 3.

15 Straddling and Highly Migratory Fish Stocks

Compatibility Requirement and Scope of Rights of High Seas Fishing Nations

Sean D. Murphy

1. Introduction

Under the law of the sea, coastal States enjoy sovereign rights within their exclusive economic zones (EEZs) to manage and exploit fishery resources. Meanwhile, all States maintain their traditional freedom to fish on the high seas, subject to some treaty obligations. These high seas obligations include those arising from regional fisheries management organisations or arrangements (RFMOs) and other treaties, such as (once it enters into force) the Agreement on the Conservation and Sustainable Use of Marine Biological Diversity of Areas beyond National Jurisdiction (BBNJ Agreement).[1] Given that straddling stocks and highly migratory species of fish move with ease between the exclusive economic zones of coastal States and the high seas, the 1982 United Nations Convention on the Law of the Sea (UNCLOS) contains provisions that seek to promote cooperation among States for their conservation and management.[2]

The UNCLOS provisions were elaborated in the 1995 Agreement for the Implementation of the Provisions of the United Nations Convention on the Law of the Sea of 10 December 1982 relating to the Conservation and Management of Straddling Fish Stocks and Highly Migratory Fish Stocks (Fish Stocks Agreement).[3] Article 7(2), in particular, provides that

> Conservation and management measures established for the high seas and those adopted for areas under national jurisdiction *shall be compatible* in

1 Agreement under the United Nations Convention on the Law of the Sea on the Conservation and Sustainable Use of Marine Biological Diversity of Areas Beyond National Jurisdiction, 19 June 2023, A/CONF.232/2023/4, opened for signature on 20 September 2023, not yet in force.

2 United Nations Convention on the Law of the Sea (UNCLOS), 10 December 1982, 1833 UNTS 3, entered into force 16 November 1994. The Convention has 169 States parties (as of July 2024).

3 Agreement for the Implementation of the Provisions of the United Nations Convention on the Law of the Sea of 10 December 1982 relating to the Conservation and Management of Straddling Fish Stocks and Highly Migratory Fish Stocks (Fish Stocks Agreement), 4 August 1995, 2167 UNTS 3, entered into force 11 December 2001. The Fish Stocks Agreement has 93 parties (as of July 2024).

DOI: 10.4324/9781003492030-20

> order to ensure conservation and management of the straddling fish stocks and highly migratory fish stocks in their entirety (emphasis added).[4]

A similar 'compatibility' concept can be found in the BBNJ Agreement, albeit in the context of the compatibility of high seas marine protected areas (MPAs) with measures adopted by RFMOs or other bodies.[5] Unfortunately, Article 7(2) of the Fish Stocks Agreement contains several ambiguities as to its interpretation. These ambiguities have not been resolved and may be inhibiting sound conservation and management measures (CMMs). Indeed, studies indicate that the current legal framework has not succeeded in addressing declines of EEZ and high seas fish stocks.[6]

This chapter considers the legal framework within which this 'compatibility requirement' rests and identifies certain ambiguities that may be impeding international cooperation. To promote greater cooperation, this chapter considers whether an advisory opinion should be sought by an RFMO from the International Tribunal for the Law of the Sea (ITLOS) on the nature and scope of the compatibility requirement. While doubts have been raised about addressing abstract legal questions through advisory proceedings,[7] an advisory opinion could allow for a more granular legal understanding as to how States should be cooperating in the management and conservation of straddling fish stocks and highly migratory species.[8]

2. Legal Framework of the Compatibility Requirement

This section considers the legal framework within which the 'compatibility requirement' rests and identifies several ambiguities of that requirement which may be impeding international cooperation.

4 ibid, art 7(2).

5 Agreement under the United Nations Convention on the Law of the Sea on the Conservation and Sustainable Use of Marine Biological Diversity of Areas Beyond National Jurisdiction, 19 June 2023, A/CONF.232/2023/4, opened for signature on 20 September 2023, not yet in force, art 22(1)(b).

6 See, for example, Food and Agriculture Organization of the United Nations (FAO), 'The State of World Fisheries and Aquaculture: Sustainability in Action' (2020) 7 <www.fao.org/3/ca9229en/ca9229en.pdf> accessed 2 July 2024, finding that the successes achieved in some States and regions have not been sufficient to reverse the global trend of overfished stocks. See also Ray Hilborn and Ulrike Hilborn, *Overfishing: What Everyone Needs to Know* (OUP 2012), identifying both failures and successes in fisheries management; Sarika Cullis-Suzuki and Daniel Pauly, 'Failing the High Seas: A Global Evaluation of Regional Fisheries Management Organizations' (2010) 34 *Marine Policy* 1036, noting that two-thirds of stocks fished on the high seas and under regional management are either depleted or overexploited.

7 See, for example, Michael Wood, 'Understanding the Advisory Jurisdiction of the International Tribunal for the Law of the Sea' in *The Contribution of the International Tribunal for the Law of the Sea to the Rule of Law: 1996–2016* (Brill 2018) 213.

8 Note that the Fish Stocks Agreement, differently from UNCLOS, uses the expression 'highly migratory fish stocks'.

2.1. 1958 Geneva Conventions on the Law of the Sea

The 1958 Geneva Conventions on the Law of the Sea provide an embryonic framework for recognising the role of the coastal State in helping to conserve and manage fish stocks on the high seas that are adjacent to its maritime space.[9] Further, the 1958 Conventions emphasise the need for all States to cooperate in that regard. While the 1958 Conventions have a limited number of States parties, they heavily influenced the adoption of UNCLOS in 1982 and the Fish Stocks Agreement in 1995.

The 1958 Convention on the Territorial Sea and Contiguous Zone does not identify the breadth of the territorial sea.[10] However, it indicates that the contiguous zone, adjacent to the territorial sea, only extends up to 12 nautical miles from the baseline.[11] The territorial sea is under the sovereignty of the coastal State,[12] thereby implicitly giving the coastal State full rights over the management and exploitation of fish stocks within the zone, without express duties in this regard. In parallel, the 1958 Convention on the High Seas confirms the freedom of fishing on the high seas for both coastal and non-coastal States,[13] defining the high seas as areas outside a State's territorial sea or internal waters.[14]

For the first time in international law, the 1958 Convention on Fishing and Conservation of the Living Resources of the High Seas addressed the importance of coastal States' conservation and management of fish stocks on the high seas in the area adjacent to that State's territorial sea (referred to here as the 'adjacent area').[15] Article 1 indicates that the freedom of high seas fishing is subject to three constraints: the interests and rights of coastal States as provided in the Convention; obligations set forth in the Convention; and other treaty obligations.[16] Moreover, Article 1 generally provides that all 'States have the duty to adopt, or to co-operate with other States in adopting, such measures for their respective nationals as may be necessary for the conservation of the living resources of the high seas'.[17]

9 The United Nations Conference on the Law of the Sea (Geneva, 24 February–27 April 1958) adopted four Conventions and an optional protocol on 29 April 1958, Final Act of the United Nations Conference on the Law of the Sea (29 April 1958) A/CONF.13/L.58.

10 The Convention on the Territorial Sea and the Contiguous Zone, 29 April 1958, 516 UNTS 205, entered into force 10 September 1964. The Convention has 52 Parties.

11 ibid, art 24(2).

12 ibid, art 1.

13 The Convention on the High Seas, 29 April 1958, 450 UNTS 11, entered into force 30 September 1962, art 2(2). The Convention has 63 Parties.

14 ibid, art 1.

15 The Convention on Fishing and Conservation of the Living Resources of the High Seas, 29 April 1958, 559 UNTS 285, entered into force 20 March 1966. The Convention has 39 Parties. For a discussion of the factors that influenced the regulation of high seas fishing in the period up to the adoption of this convention, see Yoshinobu Takei, *Filling Regulatory Gaps in High Seas Fisheries: Discrete High Seas Fish Stocks, Deep-Sea Fisheries and Vulnerable Marine Ecosystems* (Brill 2013) 16–27.

16 The Convention on Fishing and Conservation of the Living Resources of the High Seas, 29 April 1958, 559 UNTS 285, entered into force 20 March 1966, art 1(1).

17 ibid, art 1(2).

Articles 6 and 7 then identify the 'interests and rights of coastal States'. The coastal State 'has a special interest in the maintenance of the productivity of the living resources in any area of the high seas adjacent to its territorial sea'.[18] As such, if negotiations over a period of six months have not resulted in an agreement with the other relevant States, the coastal State may 'adopt unilateral measures of conservation appropriate to any stock of fish or other marine resources in' the adjacent area.[19] These measures 'shall be valid' vis-à-vis the other States if (a) urgent application of conservation measures are needed in light of the existing knowledge of the fishery; (b) the measures adopted are based on appropriate scientific evidence; and (c) such measures do not discriminate in form or in fact against foreign fishermen.[20] If any other State objects to these measures, it may pursue dispute resolution procedures under the Convention.[21]

Further, the coastal State can equally take part in any system of research and regulation to conserve the resources in the adjacent area, even if its nationals do not fish there.[22] Indeed, any State whose nationals fish in the adjacent area 'shall, at the request of that coastal State, enter into negotiations with a view to prescribing by agreement the measures necessary for the conservation of' such resources,[23] and shall not enforce conservation measures in the adjacent area 'which are opposed to those' adopted by the coastal State.[24] If the relevant States do not reach agreement over conservation measures within twelve months, either State can initiate dispute resolution procedures under the Convention.[25]

Thus, the 1958 Geneva Conventions on the Law of the Sea confirmed the right of all States to fish on the high seas. Concomitantly, they also recognised the sovereignty of the coastal State in its territorial sea and its interests in the productivity of living resources in the adjacent high seas. Balancing the interests of the coastal State with the rights of other States should be achieved through particular means: cooperation and agreement and, when necessary, also through unilateral measures by the coastal State; deference by other States to the coastal State's measures; and dispute resolution procedures.

2.2. 1982 UNCLOS

The movement toward establishing an EEZ, and the continuing strain on managing and conserving fish stocks throughout the seas, led to the inclusion in UNCLOS of numerous provisions on conservation and management replicating and expanding

18 ibid, art 6(1).
19 ibid, art 7(1).
20 ibid, art 7(2).
21 ibid, arts 7(4), 9.
22 ibid, art 6(2).
23 ibid, art 6(3)–(4).
24 ibid.
25 ibid, arts 6(5), 9.

those of the 1958 Geneva Conventions.[26] The maximum breadth of the territorial sea was set at 12 nautical miles, over which States have sovereignty.[27] Within this zone (and within archipelagic waters), the coastal (or archipelagic) State implicitly enjoys exclusive rights with respect to conserving and managing fish stocks, and only limited duties in that regard.[28] Outside this zone, UNCLOS established the concept of the EEZ, which can extend up to 200 nautical miles from the baselines.[29] Within the EEZ, the coastal State has sovereign rights and jurisdiction with respect to fish stocks, but also duties, notably to conserve the living resources and ensure their optimal utilisation.[30] Importantly, when exercising their rights and duties over the EEZ, coastal States must have 'due regard to the rights and duties of other States' and 'act in a manner compatible with the provisions of this Convention'.[31]

Outside the EEZs, a State and its flag vessels enjoy the freedom to fish, but subject to that State's treaty obligations and 'the rights and duties as well as the interests of coastal States'.[32] In this regard, UNCLOS recognises the existence of fish stocks that 'straddle' one or more EEZs and the high seas, as well as 'highly migratory species' (listed in an annex to UNCLOS) that move even more freely across the oceans.[33] For stocks straddling an EEZ and the high seas, Article 63(2) of UNCLOS provides that

> the coastal State and the States fishing for such stocks in the adjacent area shall seek, either directly or through appropriate subregional or regional organizations, to agree upon the measures necessary for the conservation of these stocks in the adjacent area.[34]

This obligation 'to seek to agree' is an obligation to cooperate in good faith, but without necessarily reaching agreement. For highly migratory species, Article 64(1) provides that the coastal State and other States 'shall co-operate directly or through appropriate international organizations with a view to ensuring conservation and promoting the objective of optimum utilization of such species throughout the region, both within and beyond the exclusive economic zone'.[35] If there is no

26 See, Yoshinobu Takei, *Filling Regulatory Gaps in High Seas Fisheries: Discrete High Seas Fish Stocks, Deep-sea Fisheries and Vulnerable Marine Ecosystems* (Brill 2013) 27–9, 33–104, focusing on high seas fishing.

27 UNCLOS, arts 2(1), 3.

28 ibid, art 24 on the duties of coastal State in the territorial sea; arts 52–3 addressing rights of passage through archipelagic waters.

29 ibid, arts 55, 57.

30 ibid, art 56 on the rights, jurisdiction, and duties of coastal State; art 61 on the conservation of living resources; art 62 on utilisation.

31 ibid, art 56(2).

32 ibid, art 116.

33 ibid, art 63 on straddling stocks; art 64 on highly migratory species; Annex 1 on highly migratory species.

34 ibid, art 63(2).

35 ibid, art 64(1).

such international organisation, 'the coastal State and other States whose nationals harvest these species in the region shall co-operate to establish such an organization and participate in its work'.[36] The obligation in Article 64(1) appears less exhortatory and more specific in nature, leading some to argue that States, whose nationals fish on the high seas, must ensure that such activities do not undermine coastal States' CMMs on highly migratory species.[37]

Separately, all States shall regulate their nationals (and cooperate with each other to this end) to conserve the living resources of the high seas.[38] Moreover, where the nationals of two or more States exploit the same area of the high seas, those States 'shall enter into negotiations with a view to taking the measures necessary for the conservation of the living resources concerned'.[39] Otherwise, they shall cooperate, as appropriate, through subregional or regional fisheries organisations.[40] Such cooperation shall pursue the maximum sustainable yield of high seas fish stocks, while paying attention to the effects of such exploitation on dependent species.[41]

Some of the concepts arising from the 1958 Geneva Conventions can be observed in UNCLOS, but they evolved to take account of the creation of the EEZ. Under UNCLOS, the coastal State has much more detailed sovereign rights to conserve and manage living resources adjacent to its territorial sea (in its EEZ). The coastal State also has cognisable interests in exploiting straddling stocks and highly migratory species on the high seas adjacent to its EEZ. In this respect, when balancing the coastal State's interests with the freedom to fish on the high seas enjoyed by other States, UNCLOS emphasises cooperation and agreement. Less attention is paid to the possibility of the coastal State adopting unilateral measures for the high seas and the deference to such measures by other States.

With overfishing becoming increasingly problematic, States decided by the early 1990s that it was important to go further and address the balance between CMMs adopted by coastal States for areas under national jurisdiction and those adopted by all States concerned for the adjacent high seas.

36 ibid. There are also provisions on cooperation with respect to anadromous stocks and catadromous species, ibid, arts 66–7.

37 See William Burke, *The New International Law of Fisheries: UNCLOS 1982 and Beyond* (Clarendon 1994) 214, stating that

> Article 116 appears to introduce a drastic change in high seas fishing rights by providing for a priority in coastal state rights and interests affecting high seas fishing states. How far this interpretation of Articles 64 and 116 can be carried is not clear.

See also Camille Goodman, 'The Cooperative Use of Coastal State Jurisdiction with Respect to Highly Migratory Stocks; Insights from the Western and Central Pacific Region' in Lawrence Martin et al (eds), *Natural Resources and the Law of the Sea* (Juris 2017) 218, stating that '[t]his provision seems to indicate that the preferential rights of coastal States with respect to highly migratory species extend (beyond the exclusive economic zone) to affect the high seas'.

38 UNCLOS, art 117.

39 ibid, art 118.

40 ibid.

41 ibid, art 119.

2.3. 1995 Fish Stocks Agreement

As noted in the introduction, the 'compatibility requirement' is embedded in Article 7 of the 1995 Fish Stocks Agreement. In all, Article 7 contains eight paragraphs addressing the need for 'compatibility' between CMMs adopted by coastal States for areas under national jurisdiction and CMMs established by all States concerned for the adjacent high seas.[42]

Subparagraphs (a) and (b) of Article 7(1) replicate almost verbatim the language on cooperation found in Articles 63(2) (straddling stocks) and 64(1) (highly migratory stocks) of UNCLOS. However, Article 7(1) opens with a chapeau stating that such cooperation is without prejudice to the sovereign rights of coastal States in their EEZs and the right of all States to fish on the high seas. Alex Oude Elferink interprets this chapeau as signalling the need, when in doubt, to balance neutrally the rights of the coastal State and all other States when considering the compatibility of CMMs.[43]

The key provision on compatibility is found in Article 7(2), which consists of a chapeau followed by a series of subparagraphs (a) through (f) indicating factors to consider when assessing compatibility. The chapeau reads:

> Conservation and management measures established for the high seas and those adopted for areas under national jurisdiction *shall be compatible* in order to ensure conservation and management of the straddling fish stocks and highly migratory fish stocks in their entirety. To this end, coastal States and States fishing on the high seas have a duty to cooperate for the purpose of achieving *compatible* measures in respect of such stocks. In determining compatible conservation and management measures, States shall: (emphasis added).[44]

Generally speaking, this chapeau requires that a coastal State, when adopting a CMM with respect to straddling or highly migratory stocks, do so in a manner 'compatible' with the measures adopted by other States for the high seas, and vice versa. The chapeau does not itself dictate that one side must conform its measure to that of the other. Rather, it underscores the possibility of competing measures and calls for a cooperative approach the 'purpose' of which is to conserve and manage the stocks 'in their entirety', given that neither side can achieve this goal on its own. The chapeau, including when read together with the associated subparagraphs, presents several ambiguities that should be clarified to strengthen their effects.

42 Such compatibility is also addressed and reinforced in the non-binding FAO Code of Conduct for Responsible Fisheries (31 October 1995) FAO Conf Res 4/95, sections 6.12, 7.3.1, 7.3.2.

43 Alex Oude Elferink, 'The Determination of Compatible Conservation and Management Measures for Straddling and Highly Migratory Fish Stocks' (2001) 5 *Max Planck Yearbook of United Nations Law* 551, 555–6.

44 Fish Stocks Agreement, art 7(2).

2.3.1. Ambiguity #1

A threshold ambiguity, which should be resolved before applying Article 7(2), is whether the compatibility requirement is an obligation arising solely under the Fish Stocks Agreement or whether it also provides content to obligations under UNCLOS. If the former, the requirement's significance is somewhat diminished, as the Fish Stocks Agreement had only 93 States Parties as of July 2024 – a respectable number, but far less than the 169 States Parties to UNCLOS.

However, if the compatibility requirement provides a means for determining the content of the general obligations arising under UNCLOS, the requirement has much greater salience.[45] In this regard, one should note that the Fish Stocks Agreement was designed to implement UNCLOS, not to change it.[46] Further, the status of the compatibility requirement under customary international law is also relevant for States that are not bound under either UNCLOS or the Fish Stocks Agreement. To the extent that some rules of UNCLOS on cooperation (whether in relation to the EEZ or high seas fishing) reflect customary international law,[47] Article 7 could simply clarify customary obligations binding upon all States. Further, the practice of non-States parties in adhering to compatibility requirements as they exist elsewhere (such as for RFMOs) may suggest acceptance of the rule reflected in Article 7 and, thus, support its customary nature.[48]

2.3.2. Ambiguity #2

A second ambiguity concerns the geographic range of Article 7(2). The Fish Stocks Agreement, as a whole, focuses on the conservation and management of straddling fish stocks and highly migratory fish stocks 'beyond areas under national jurisdiction'.[49] Yet Article 7 provides that it also applies to conservation and management of such stocks 'within areas under national jurisdiction' (and this is the case as well for Article 5 on general principles and Article 6 on the precautionary

45 See Richard Barnes, 'The Convention on the Law of the Sea: An Effective Framework for Domestic Fisheries Conservation?' in Richard Barnes, David Freestone, and David Ong (eds), *The Law of the Sea: Progress and Prospects* (OUP 2006) 233, 249, finding that 'the provisions of the [Fish Stocks Agreement] may become a means of determining the content of the general obligations set forth in [UNCLOS]'.

46 See Fish Stocks Agreement, art 4, stating that '[n]othing in this Agreement shall prejudice the rights, jurisdiction and duties of States under the Convention. This Agreement shall be interpreted and applied in the context of and in a manner consistent with the Convention.' See also Richard Barnes, 'The Convention on the Law of the Sea: An Effective Framework for Domestic Fisheries Conservation?' in Richard Barnes, David Freestone, and David Ong (eds), *The Law of the Sea: Progress and Prospects* (OUP 2006) 233, 248, noting that, while some of its provisions are innovatory, 'it is also difficult to see how the provisions of the [Fish Stocks Agreement] deviate in principle from the object and purpose of [UNCLOS]'.

47 See Ashley Roach, 'Today's Customary International Law of the Sea' (2014) 45 *Ocean Development and International Law* 239, 246–9.

48 *See* infra notes 81–84.

49 Fish Stocks Agreement, art 3(1).

approach[50]). The Fish Stocks Agreement does not define these 'areas under national jurisdiction'. According to one interpretation, the expression could be construed as covering the EEZs only.[51] However, Article 7(2) could be construed more broadly as encompassing territorial, archipelagic, and even internal waters.[52] Resolving such ambiguity could be particularly important for the conservation and management of straddling and highly migratory stocks that traverse large maritime spaces enclosed as archipelagic waters.

2.3.3. Ambiguity #3

A third ambiguity with respect to Article 7(2) is whether it binds States only when they directly adopt measures or, also, when they act collectively and indirectly adopt measures, either through an international organisation (for example, the European Union is a party to the Fish Stocks Agreement) or within RFMOs. On the one hand, the text of Article 7(2) only addresses the cooperation of 'States' and not other actors.[53] On the other hand, if State action by which measures are indirectly adopted were outside the scope of Article 7(2), this would be inconsistent with the Fish Stocks Agreement's object and purpose and would lead to an unreasonable result.

2.3.4. Ambiguity #4

A fourth ambiguity concerns the proper balance to be struck between the measures adopted by coastal States and the measures adopted by other States. As noted previously, the chapeau of Article 7(2) precedes six factors that States should 'take into account' when 'determining compatible conservation and management measures'.

Subparagraph (a) provides that States shall take into account measures adopted by a coastal State for conserving and managing straddling and highly migratory fish stocks in their EEZs (under Article 61 of UNCLOS), and shall ensure that their own measures with respect to fishing such stocks on the high seas do not undermine the measures of the coastal State.[54] When read in comparison with subparagraphs (b) and (c), this factor clearly focuses on measures unilaterally adopted by other States with respect to high seas fishing; these measures must take account of and must not undermine measures adopted by a relevant coastal State.

50 ibid, arts 5–6. For a discussion, see William Burke, 'Compatibility and Precaution in the 1995 Straddling Stock Agreement' in Harry Scheiber (ed), *Law of the Sea: The Common Heritage and Emerging Challenges* (Brill 2000) 105, 119–25.

51 See, for example, Martin Tsamenyi and Quentin Hanich, 'Fisheries Jurisdiction Under the Law of the Sea Convention: Rights and Obligations in Maritime Zones Under a Sovereignty of Coastal States' in David Freestone (ed), *The 1982 Law of the Sea Convention at 30: Successes, Challenges and New Agendas* (Brill 2013) 109, 116–8.

52 ibid, 115.

53 Fish Stocks Agreement, art 47.

54 ibid, art 7(2)(a). Additionally, art 7(7) requires coastal States to inform regularly States fishing on the high seas in the region of the coastal States' measures.

Subparagraph (b) provides that, in determining compatible measures, States shall take into account previously agreed measures reached by relevant coastal States and States fishing on the high seas that have been established to conserve and manage straddling and highly migratory fish stocks on the high seas.[55] Here, both the coastal States and other States must take account of any measures they previously agreed upon when determining if new measures they adopt are compatible.

Subparagraph (c) provides that, in determining compatible measures, States shall take into account previously agreed measures adopted by an RFMO to conserve and manage straddling and highly migratory fish stocks.[56] Here, no focus is paid on whether the RFMO's measures are directed solely at EEZs or at the high seas, given that RFMOs can have authority in both zones. In short, both the coastal States and other States must take account of any measures previously agreed upon within an RFMO when these States are determining whether measures they adopt are compatible.

When these three subparagraphs are read against each other, subparagraph (a) goes further than the others by providing that the non-coastal States shall 'ensure' that their measures taken with respect to high seas fishing 'do not undermine the effectiveness' of the coastal State's measures. Such language is not found in subparagraph (b) or (c). This difference introduces the fourth ambiguity. Arguably, the additional language in subparagraph (a) expressly tips the balance in favour of deference to the coastal State's measures.[57] If so, favouring the coastal State might be justified for two reasons. First, the coastal State must ensure that fish stocks in its EEZ are harvested at a sustainable level. In setting the sustainable level, the coastal State has incentives relating to efficiency and risk that are not shared by States fishing on the high seas. Second, the coastal State cannot uphold its obligation without assistance from other States fishing in the area adjacent to its EEZ.[58]

Yet, this is perhaps overreading subparagraph (a). The difference in wording in subparagraph (a) may simply reflect the lack of competence of a non-coastal State to regulate for others with respect to high seas fishing (and perhaps an RFMO's lack of competence to regulate for non-parties). In other words, a coastal State should not be obliged to 'avoid undermining' regulations unilaterally adopted by

55 ibid, art 7(2)(b). Additionally, art 7(7) provides that coastal States shall regularly inform States fishing on the high seas in the subregion or region of the measures the coastal States have adopted. Meanwhile, art 7(8) requires any State fishing on the high seas to inform regularly 'other interested States' (hence, any coastal States or other States fishing in the region or subregion) of the measures the State has adopted to regulate the fishing activities of its vessels in the area.

56 ibid, art 7(2)(c).

57 Tore Henriksen and Alf Håkon Hoel, 'Determining Allocation: From Paper to Practice in the Distribution of Fishing Rights Between Countries' (2011) 42 *Ocean Development and International Law* 66, 73, finding that the provision gives the coastal State 'decisive influence'. See also Peter Davies and Catherine Redgwell, 'The International Legal Regulation of Straddling Fish Stocks' (1996) 67 *British Yearbook of International Law* 199, 263, finding that the coastal State's interests are prioritised.

58 See William Burke, 'Compatibility and Precaution in the 1995 Straddling Stock Agreement' in Harry Scheiber (ed), *Law of the Sea: The Common Heritage and Emerging Challenges* (Brill 2000) 105, 111–5.

other States regarding high seas fishing, as such States are not competent in this regard except with respect to regulating their own nationals.[59] Resolving this ambiguity could draw upon practice, instruments, and jurisprudence since the adoption of the Fish Stocks Agreement.[60]

2.3.5. Ambiguity #5

Subparagraph (d) provides that States, when determining compatible CMMs, shall take into account 'the biological unity and other biological characteristics of the stocks' and 'the relationship between the distribution of stocks, the fisheries and the geographical particularities of the region concerned'.[61] This subparagraph introduces a fifth ambiguity, namely what precisely is required by these references. The expression 'biological unity' appears to refer primarily to viewing each straddling or highly migratory fish stock as a single biological unit. Therefore, measures should manage that stock as a whole, regardless of its location. The reference to 'the relationship' with other stocks and fisheries appears to invite an ecosystem approach to management and conservation. According to this approach, States should consider not just the life cycle of a particular stock (mating, spawning, and foraging) across zones, but also the inter-relationship of different stocks and their habits.[62] An ecosystem approach is sensible as such species are susceptible to regulation in numerous EEZs and different high seas areas adjacent to these EEZs, rather than just one coastal State's EEZ. Therefore, the 'compatibility' of any one coastal State's regulation must be considered vis-à-vis a much wider geographic

59 See Alex Oude Elferink, 'The Determination of Compatible Conservation and Management Measures for Straddling and Highly Migratory Fish Stocks' (2001) 5 *Max Planck Yearbook of United Nations Law* 551, 563–5; Francisco Orrego Vicuña, *The Changing International Law of High Seas Fisheries* (CUP 1999) 193–4.

60 See, for example, *Request for an Advisory Opinion Submitted by the Sub-Regional Fisheries Commission,* Advisory Opinion, ITLOS Rep 2015, paras 124–9, analysing the content of a flag State's 'responsibility to ensure' compliance with the laws and regulations enacted by a coastal State with respect to the EEZ; *Responsibilities and Obligations of States Sponsoring Persons and Entities with Respect to Activities in the Area,* Advisory Opinion, ITLOS Rep 2011, paras 107–16, analysing the content of a sponsoring State's 'responsibility to ensure' compliance with rules concerning activities in the seabed area; *Chagos Marine Protected Area Arbitration (Mauritius v. United Kingdom),* Award, PCA Case 2011–03, 18 March 2015, para 535, analysing the balancing of the United Kingdom's rights and interests with those of Mauritius; International Law Commission, 'Draft Articles on Prevention of Transboundary Harm from Hazardous Activities' (2001) II *Yearbook of the International Law Commission,* art 10, identifying factors for an equitable balancing of interests.

61 Fish Stocks Agreement, art 7(2)(d). For analysis, see Alex Oude Elferink, 'The Determination of Compatible Conservation and Management Measures for Straddling and Highly Migratory Fish Stocks' (2001) 5 *Max Planck Yearbook of United Nations Law* 551, 566–7; see also Yoshinobu Takei, *Filling Regulatory Gaps in High Seas Fisheries: Discrete High Seas Fish Stocks, Deep-sea Fisheries and Vulnerable Marine Ecosystems* (Brill 2013) 85–91.

62 The ecosystem approach is reflected in the general principles identified by the Fish Stocks Agreement, art 5(d)–(e). See generally Daniela Diz Pereira Pinto, *Fisheries Management in Areas beyond National Jurisdiction: The Impact of Ecosystem Based Law-Making* (Brill 2013) 95–6; William Burke, 'Compatibility and Precaution in the 1995 Straddling Stock Agreement' in Harry Scheiber (ed), *Law of the Sea: The Common Heritage and Emerging Challenges* (Brill 2000) 105, 125–6.

area than just the EEZ of this coastal State or even the sub-region or region. Further, species-specific regulation is increasingly seen as inferior to an ecosystem approach to regulation.[63] However, several RFMOs focus on a specific type of species (for example, species of tuna) and are limited to a particular region or sub-region. As such, it is unclear whether States must adjust their measures, unilateral or collective, to pursue an ecosystem approach.

2.3.1. Ambiguity #6

There are two final factors in Article 7(2). Subparagraph (e) provides that States shall take into account the dependence on the relevant stocks by the coastal State and by the States fishing on the high seas.[64]

Subparagraph (f) provides that States 'shall ensure' that such measures do not result in harmful impact on the living marine resources as a whole.[65] Thus, this subparagraph includes stronger language ('shall ensure') than most of the prior subparagraphs ('take into account'), suggesting that States must always exercise due diligence to ensure that the measures adopted do not harm the marine environment.[66] The stronger language is warranted as measures that have a harmful impact on the living marine resources (for example, those allowing fishing gear destructive to habitats), by definition, do not advance a management and conservation scheme.

All told, the six factors set forth in Article 7(2) are valuable, but they provide little guidance on how they should be balanced collectively in the context of a particular fishery. This presents a sixth ambiguity.[67] Arguably, such balancing might be addressed simply through negotiation or, if need be, through litigation. To date,

63 See, for example, Daniela Diz Pereira Pinto, *Fisheries Management in Areas beyond National Jurisdiction: The Impact of Ecosystem Based Law-Making* (Brill 2013) ix.

64 Fish Stocks Agreement, art 7(2)(e). See also Fish Stocks Agreement, art 11(d)–(e), noting the needs of coastal fishing communities and coastal economies that are dependent on fish stocks, and art 24 on the special requirements of developing States. For analysis, see Alex Oude Elferink, 'The Determination of Compatible Conservation and Management Measures for Straddling and Highly Migratory Fish Stocks' (2001) 5 *Max Planck Yearbook of United Nations Law* 551, 567–70.

65 Fish Stocks Agreement, art 7(2)(f). See also, Fish Stocks Agreement art 5(f), listing steps for avoiding harmful impacts; FAO Code of Conduct for Responsible Fisheries (31 October 1995) FAO Conf Res 4/95, sections 6.5–6.8, 7.2.2–7.2.3, 7.6.9, 8.5. For analysis, see Alex Oude Elferink, 'The Determination of Compatible Conservation and Management Measures for Straddling and Highly Migratory Fish Stocks' (2001) 5 *Max Planck Yearbook of United Nations Law* 551, 570–2.

66 See Alex Oude Elferink, 'The Determination of Compatible Conservation and Management Measures for Straddling and Highly Migratory Fish Stocks' (2001) 5 *Max Planck Yearbook of United Nations Law* 551, 560.

67 See, for example, Camille Goodman, 'The Cooperative Use of Coastal State Jurisdiction with Respect to Highly Migratory Stocks; Insights from the Western and Central Pacific Region' in Lawrence Martin et al. (eds), *Natural Resources and the Law of the Sea* (Juris 2017) 234, finding that the framework established by the UNCLOS for the management of tuna

> is highly ambiguous, and notwithstanding the clarifications and improvements later introduced by the [Fish Stocks Agreement], there remains a significant tension between the duty to cooperate in the conservation of highly migratory species, and the sovereign rights of the coastal State over the resources of the EEZ.

however, negotiation has not resulted in stabilizing the stress on (if not collapse of) fisheries. Litigation may be possible in some instances, provided there is a political will to pursue it. Indeed, Article 7(3) of the Fish Stocks Agreement provides that 'States shall make every effort to agree on compatible conservation and management measures within a reasonable period of time'.[68] If a lack of compatible measures leads to a dispute between States, Article 7(4) allows one of the States to invoke the dispute resolution procedures of the Fish Stocks Agreement.[69] Further, pending agreement on compatible measures, paragraphs 5 and 6 call for the relevant States to adopt provisional arrangements of a practical nature, which, again, can be submitted to dispute resolution if no agreement is reached.[70] Article 32 of the Fish Stocks Agreement, however, maintains the limitation in Article 297(3) of UNCLOS: the coastal State is not obliged to accept binding dispute settlement procedures for any dispute relating to its sovereign rights in the EEZ or the exercise of these rights.[71]

Instead of relying solely on negotiation or litigation, this ambiguity could be addressed, at least in part, by identifying a *process* for States to follow when weighing the factors (and hence fulfilling their obligations) under Article 7(2). Thus, for any given EEZ and adjacent high seas, one could imagine a series of specific steps to be taken along the following lines. First, ascertain whether there are measures adopted by a coastal State, a RFMO, and States engaged in high-seas fishing in the region.[72] Second, determine whether any of these measures appear incompatible with one another. Third, if the existing measures are incompatible, the relevant States must revise any measure deemed harmful to living marine resources so as to become compatible. Here, there may be a presumption in favour of upholding measures by the coastal State. Alternatively, or additionally, one might envisage overarching approaches or legal principles (beyond the precautionary approach set forth in Article 6) to guide the application of the factors in Article 7(2). For example, perhaps such factors should be balanced using a principle of equity (*infra legum*) to arrive at an equitable solution.[73] Fourth, any new measures to be introduced must be tested against all previously agreed or coastal State's measures.

68 Fish Stocks Agreement, art 7(3).

69 ibid, art 7(4). These procedures are found in Part VIII of the agreement. See Alex Oude Elferink, 'The Determination of Compatible Conservation and Management Measures for Straddling and Highly Migratory Fish Stocks' (2001) 5 *Max Planck Yearbook of United Nations Law* 551, 598–602.

70 Fish Stocks Agreement, art 7(5)–(6); see Alex Oude Elferink, 'The Determination of Compatible Conservation and Management Measures for Straddling and Highly Migratory Fish Stocks' (2001) 5 *Max Planck Yearbook of United Nations Law* 551, 591–7.

71 See infra note 74 on the ambiguities of the dispute resolution procedures in the Fish Stocks Agreement.

72 Alex Oude Elferink, 'The Determination of Compatible Conservation and Management Measures for Straddling and Highly Migratory Fish Stocks' (2001) 5 *Max Planck Yearbook of United Nations Law* 551, 578.

73 ibid, 573–7.

Fifth, if States cannot agree on an issue of compatibility, they should pursue dispute resolution pursuant to Article 7(4).[74]

2.4. RFMOs

RFMOs play an important role in coordinating measures taken by States to address straddling and migratory fish stocks. While each RFMO operates differently based on its constituent instrument, an RFMO generally can be defined as an inter-governmental organisation that is competent under international law to adopt legally binding CMMs over fisheries covering, at least in part, the high seas.[75] Each RFMO typically has a scientific committee that gathers data annually to recommend, for each regulated stock, the sustainable catch level for the following year. In doing so, the scientific committee may seek advice from marine science organisations, such as the International Council for the Exploration of the Sea. Then, States parties to the RFMO must agree on the catch level and its distribution, after which each State regulates its nationals to stay within its allocated catch.[76] Further, there may be various rules on the permissible means and methods for fishing the relevant stocks in the region.

74 The dispute resolution procedures, themselves, present certain ambiguities. While art 7(4) and Part VIII of the Fish Stocks Agreement contemplate stand-alone non-compulsory and then, compulsory dispute resolution, the procedures set out in Part XV of UNCLOS also apply *mutatis mutandis,* per Fish Stocks Agreement, art 30. Moreover, Fish Stocks Agreement, art 32, explicitly states that art 297(3) of UNCLOS applies to the Fish Stocks Agreement. UNCLOS, art 297(3)(a), in turn, provides that 'the coastal State shall not be obliged to accept the submission to such settlement of any dispute relating to its sovereign rights with respect to the living resources in the exclusive economic zone or their exercise'. Thus, certain disputes against a coastal State concerning sovereign rights can be excluded by the coastal State from compulsory dispute settlement. See *Chagos Marine Protected Area Arbitration (Mauritius v. United Kingdom)*, Award, PCA Case 2011–03, 18 March 2015, paras 300–1, finding that the Fish Stocks Agreement on its face concerns measures subject to that exclusion. However, other specific disputes against a coastal State arguably do not fall within the scope of this exclusion, such as any dispute arising from an alleged failure to comply with UNCLOS, art 63(1), which provides that two coastal States shall seek to agree upon the measures necessary to coordinate and ensure the conservation and development of stocks occurring in both of their EEZs. See Request for an Advisory Opinion submitted by the Sub-Regional Fisheries Commission, Advisory Opinion, ITLOS Rep 2015, Separate Opinion of Judge Paik, para 37.

75 See generally Erik Molenaar, 'Regional Fisheries Management Organizations' in Marta Chantal Riberio, Fernando Loureiro Bastos, and Tores Henriksen (eds), *Global Challenges and the Law of the Sea* (Springer 2020) 81; Mary Ann Palma, Martin Tsamenyi, and William Edeson (eds), *Promoting Sustainable Fisheries: The International Legal and Policy Framework to Combat Illegal, Unreported and Unregulated Fishing* (Brill 2010) 201–38; Tore Henriksen, Geir Hønneland, and Are Sydnes, *Law and Politics in Ocean Governance: The UN Fish Stocks Agreement and Regional Fisheries Management Regimes* (Brill 2006).

76 See Daniela Diz Pereira Pinto, *Fisheries Management in Areas Beyond National Jurisdiction: The Impact of Ecosystem Based Law-Making* (Brill 2013) 119–33.

As of July 2024, there are approximately eighteen RFMOs, covering various geographic areas and species of fish (principally commercially valuable species).[77] Some RFMOs, such as the North Pacific Fisheries Commission, have competence over all or most fisheries within their area.[78] Other RFMOs, such as the Inter-American Tropical Tuna Commission, have competence over specific species or groups of species, notably tuna.[79] However, even some of the more specialised RFMOs have begun using an ecosystem approach, whereby they consider all the marine species within the convention area.[80]

RFMOs have been established before and after the entry into force of UNCLOS and the Fish Stocks Agreement. Typically, RFMOs established after the Fish Stocks Agreement contain provisions that address the compatibility of their measures, drawing upon the language of Article 7(2).[81] Many RFMOs that predate the Fish Stocks Agreement have reviewed and updated their constituent instruments in light of that Agreement. In any event, provisions addressing management and conservation usually address the need for consistency between measures by RFMOs and coastal States,[82] or at least note the importance of considering straddling and highly migratory stocks in their entirety and the interdependence of stocks.[83] In principle, an RFMO might defer to CMMs adopted by a coastal State, which are then taken into account in developing fishing quotas on the adjacent high seas. Alternatively, the

77 For a listing, see European Commission, 'Regional fisheries management organisations (RFMOs)' <oceans-and-fisheries.ec.europa.eu/fisheries/international-agreements/regional-fisheries-management-organisations-rfmos_en> accessed 2 July 2024. 'Approximate' because some organisations may or may not be regarded as RFMOs, such as the North Atlantic Marine Mammal Commission (NAMMCO) (dealing with mammals not fish) or the International Whaling Commission (dealing with mammals and on a global not regional scale).

78 There are eight general RFMOs: Commission for the Conservation of Antarctic Marine Living Resources (CCAMLR); General Fisheries Commission for the Mediterranean (GFCM); North East Atlantic Fisheries Commission (NEAFC); North Pacific Fisheries Commission (NPFC); Northwest Atlantic Fisheries Organization (NAFO); South East Atlantic Fisheries Organisation (SEAFO); South Indian Ocean Fisheries Agreement (SIOFA); and South Pacific Regional Fisheries Management Organisation (SPRFMO).

79 There are five tuna RFMOs: Commission for the Conservation of Southern Bluefin Tuna (CCSBT); Indian Ocean Tuna Commission (IOTC); International Commission for the Conservation of Atlantic Tunas (ICCAT); Inter-American Tropical Tuna Commission (IATTC); and Western and Central Pacific Fisheries Commission (WCPFC). Three other specialised RFMOs are: North Atlantic Salmon Conservation Organization (NASCO); North Pacific Anadromous Fish Commission (NPAFC); and Convention on the Conservation and Management of Pollock Resources in the Central Bering Sea (CBS Convention).

80 See Daniela Diz Pereira Pinto, *Fisheries Management in Areas Beyond National Jurisdiction: The Impact of Ecosystem Based Law-Making* (Brill 2013) 133–56.

81 See, for example, Convention on the Conservation and Management of High Seas Fishery Resources in the South Pacific Ocean (SPRFMO Convention), 14 November 2009, 2899 UNTS 211, entered into force 24 August 2012, art 4 on the compatibility of CMMs.

82 See, for example, Convention on Cooperation in the Northwest Atlantic Fisheries (NAFO Convention), 24 October 1978, 1135 UNTS 369, entered into force 1 January 1979.

83 See, for example, International Convention for the Conservation of Atlantic Tunas (ICCAT Convention), 15 May 1966, 673 UNTS 63, entered into force 21 March 1969.

RFMO may adopt CMMs intended to operate both on the high seas and within the EEZs throughout the area of the RFMO's mandate.[84] In practice, a balancing of interests between coastal States and other States appears inevitable, such that negotiation on compatibility among the competing States is necessary.

Were the BBNJ Agreement to enter into force, it would not resolve this balancing of interests. The provisions on the management of marine genetic resources in that agreement, including the fair and equitable sharing of benefits, do not apply to fishing managed by RFMOs.[85] Moreover, if the measures for high seas MPAs, which lie at the heart of the BBNJ Agreement, overlap with those of RFMOs, the BBNJ Agreement essentially requires its States parties to collaborate with RFMOs. This is notably achieved through Article 22(1)(b) of the BBNJ Agreement, which expresses a similar 'compatibility' concept as in the Fish Stocks Agreement.[86]

2.5. *Is the Compatibility Requirement Working? A Case Study of Tuna in the Western and Central Pacific Ocean*

As is well known, regional fisheries management has led to decidedly mixed results. The proportion of fish stocks within biologically sustainable levels has decreased steadily, falling from 90 per cent in 1974 to 65.8 per cent in 2017.[87] These decreases vary widely across different species and subspecies of fish.[88] For example, the fish stock status of three out of seven major species of tuna (a highly migratory fish) has improved from unsustainable to sustainable.[89] Yet, while intensive fisheries management has led to some successes, serious problems persist in preventing illegal, unreported, and unregulated fishing of straddling and highly migratory stocks.[90]

The most detailed study of the operation of the compatibility requirement for a particular region to date is a 2018 doctoral thesis by Eric Kekoa Kingma

84 Peter Örebech, Ketill Sigurjonsson, and Ted McDorman, 'The 1995 United Nations Straddling and Highly Migratory Fish Stocks Agreement: Management, Enforcement and Dispute Settlement' (1998) 13 *The International Journal of Marine and Coastal Law* 119, 128.

85 Agreement under the United Nations Convention on the Law of the Sea on the Conservation and Sustainable Use of Marine Biological Diversity of Areas Beyond National Jurisdiction, 19 June 2023, A/CONF.232/2023/4, opened for signature on 20 September 2023, not yet in force, art 10(2)(a), stating that '[t]he provisions of this Part shall not apply to . . . [f]ishing regulated under relevant international law and fishing-related activities'.

86 ibid, art 22(1)(b), stating that

> [t]he Conference of the Parties . . . [m]ay take decisions on measures compatible with those adopted by relevant legal instruments and frameworks and relevant global, regional, subregional and sectoral bodies, in cooperation and coordination with those instruments, frameworks and bodies.

87 FAO, 'The State of World Fisheries and Aquaculture: Sustainability in Action' (2020) 7 www.fao.org/3/ca9229en/ca9229en.pdf accessed 23 December 2023.

88 ibid, 48.

89 ibid, 49.

90 See, for example, Kristina Gjerde, 'High Seas Fisheries Management under the Convention on the Law of the Sea' in Richard Barnes, David Freestone, and David Ong (eds), *The Law of the Sea: Progress and Prospects* (OUP 2006) 281, 289–90.

concerning tuna in the Western and Central Pacific Ocean.[91] The relevant RFMO is the Western and Central Pacific Fisheries Commission (WCPFC). The WCPFC was established by the Honolulu Convention, the first treaty designed in part to implement the Fish Stocks Agreement's compatibility requirement.[92] The Honolulu Convention is imbued with some of the ambiguities present in the Fish Stocks Agreement identified previously, such as the meaning of the term 'areas under national jurisdiction'.[93] Kingma's thesis uses a scoring system to evaluate implementation pursuant to Article 8 of the Honolulu Convention, which provides that '[c]onservation and management measures established for the high seas and those adopted for areas under national jurisdiction shall be compatible in order to ensure conservation and management of highly migratory fish stocks in their entirety'.[94] Article 8 then goes on to provide several provisions seeking to promote such compatibility, which echo the factors in Article 7(2) of the Fish Stocks Agreement.

For measures on catch or restrictions adopted by the WCPFC from its inception in 2004 through 2017, Kingma asks questions that generally follow the provisions in Article 8.[95] First, does the measure reference Article 8 of the Honolulu Convention? Second, does the measure recognise prior measures established for the EEZs or the high seas? Third, what is the extent of the measure's area of application, and does it take into account the biological unity of the stocks concerned and associated fisheries? Fourth, to what extent are considerations of respective dependence on the stocks concerned taken into account? Fifth, to what extent does the measure consider areas of high seas entirely surrounded by the EEZs of Commission members ('high seas pockets')? Sixth, what is the status of the relevant stocks given the collective obligation to ensure long-term conservation through effective management?

Based on the scoring,[96] Kingma concludes that the WCPFC has applied the compatibility principle inconsistently.[97] Its measures relating to tropical tunas

91 Eric Kekoa Kingma, 'The Principle of Compatibility: Its Application within the World's Largest Tuna Fishery' (2018) Doctor of Philosophy thesis, Australian National Centre for Ocean Resources and Security, University of Wollongong ro.uow.edu.au/theses1/285/ accessed 2 July 2024. For a briefer study for the same region, see Camille Goodman, 'The Cooperative Use of Coastal State Jurisdiction with Respect to Highly Migratory Stocks; Insights from the Western and Central Pacific Region' in Lawrence Martin et al. (eds), *Natural Resources and the Law of the Sea* (Juris 2017) 234. An analysis of the effectiveness of three other RFMOs from a constructivist perspective can be found Leandra Gonçalves, *Regional Fisheries Management Organizations: The Interplay between Governance and Science* (Springer 2021).

92 Convention on the Conservation and Management of Highly Migratory Fish Stocks in the Western and Central Pacific Ocean (WCPFC Convention), 5 September 2000, 2275 UNTS 43, entered in force 19 June 2004.

93 See, for example, ibid, arts 7–8.

94 ibid, art 8(1).

95 Eric Kekoa Kingma, 'The Principle of Compatibility: Its Application within the World's Largest Tuna Fishery' (2018) Doctor of Philosophy thesis, Australian National Centre for Ocean Resources and Security, University of Wollongong, 185–8. ro.uow.edu.au/theses1/285/ accessed 23 December 2023.

96 ibid, 299–303.

97 ibid, 296–7.

(skipjack, yellowfin, and bigeye) received a relatively high rating. However, the WCPFC's measures for other species, such as South Pacific albacore or Pacific bluefin, received much lower ratings. Kingma criticises, in particular, the WCPFC for following an ad hoc process when developing its measures.[98] Indeed, the RFMO has no formal process in place for methodically evaluating new proposals against Article 8 of the Honolulu Convention.

By contrast, Kingma applauds a particular type of management approach: the 'harvest strategy approach' that was adopted by the WCPFC in 2014.[99] This 'high-level' management approach 'involves assessing the consequences of a range of management options and presenting the results as trade-offs with respect to fisheries performance across a range of management objectives'.[100] According to Kingma, this mechanism can 'facilitate a more consistent application of the [compatibility requirement] by recognising compatibility as a political management objective which sits on an equal footing with social, economic and biological management objectives'.[101] Further, 'the process would involve defining operational indicators that focus on the balance of catch or fishing effort between EEZ and the high seas, including acceptable ratios of catch or effort between jurisdictions'.[102] In short, Kingma favours broadening the lens when analysing compatibility so as to bring about a more deliberative process to achieve compatibility.

3. Proposal for an ITLOS Advisory Opinion

International law entails not just codifying rules, but also illuminating them over time through the practice of States and the jurisprudence of international courts and tribunals. On straddling and highly migratory fish stocks, ample practice by States and RFMOs has emerged through CMMs. However, there is room for further clarification through jurisprudence. Litigation through an inter-State dispute is one possibility but, given the limitations in that regard,[103] a more comprehensive path is available in the form of an advisory opinion requested from ITLOS.

3.1. Ability of ITLOS to Issue an Advisory Opinion

In 2015 ITLOS issued its first advisory opinion based on a request from the Sub-Regional Fisheries Commission (SRFC), a fisheries commission comprising seven West African States.[104] The backdrop to this request was allegations by

98 ibid, 297–8.
99 ibid, 304–5.
100 ibid.
101 ibid, 327.
102 ibid.
103 See supra note 74 on the ambiguities of the dispute resolution procedures in the Fish Stocks Agreement.
104 Those States are Cape Verde; The Gambia; Guinea; Guinea-Bissau; Mauritania; Senegal; and Sierra Leone.

West African States that third-State flag vessels engaged in illegal, unreported, and unregulated fishing off the coast of West Africa imperilling fish stocks. The SRFC asked ITLOS four questions relating to the rights and obligations of flag and coastal States regarding fishing EEZs of the SRFC members.[105] Thus, the request did not relate to rights and obligations in respect of the high seas or the compatibility of measures taken in both zones.

ITLOS invited all States parties to UNCLOS to make written and oral submissions, as well as the United Nations, all RFMOs, and certain other international organisations.[106] Twenty-two State parties to UNCLOS filed written statements with ITLOS on these questions, as did the SRFC and six other international organisations.[107] Some later filed additional written statements.[108] An oral hearing was held in 2014, at which ten States parties appeared, in addition to the SRFC and two other international organisations.[109] Written responses and comments were also filed after the hearing.[110]

Importantly, ITLOS found that it could issue an advisory opinion.[111] Whether ITLOS is so empowered under UNCLOS was contested, with many States Parties arguing that it had no such advisory function, as no provision in UNCLOS clearly allows it to do so.[112] Nonetheless, ITLOS found that it had such jurisdiction provided three prerequisites were met: first, the existence of an international

105 The four questions asked were: 1. What are the obligations of the flag State in cases where illegal, unreported and unregulated (IUU) fishing activities are conducted within the Exclusive Economic Zones of third-party States? 2. To what extent shall the flag State be held liable for IUU fishing activities conducted by vessels sailing under its flag? 3. Where a fishing license is issued to a vessel within the framework of an international agreement with the flag State or with an international agency, shall the State or international agency be held liable for the violation of the fisheries legislation of the coastal State by the vessel in question? 4. What are the rights and obligations of the coastal State in ensuring the sustainable management of shared stocks and stocks of common interest, especially the small pelagic species and tuna? For ITLOS' indication that its answers only concerned the EEZs, see *Request for an Advisory Opinion submitted by the Sub-Regional Fisheries Commission,* Advisory Opinion, ITLOS Rep 2015, paras 89 (noting that question 1 only relates to EEZs) 147 (noting that question two concerns flag State's due diligence regarding its vessels in foreign EEZs) 154 (noting that question three relates to fisheries access agreements for EEZs) 179, 200, 204 (noting that question four concerns rights and obligation of coastal States in EEZs).

106 See *Request for an Advisory Opinion submitted by the Sub-Regional Fisheries Commission,* Order of 24 May 2013, ITLOS Rep 202; *Request for an Advisory Opinion Submitted by the Sub-Regional Fisheries Commission,* Order of 14 April 2014, ITLOS Rep 2014.

107 *Request for an Advisory Opinion submitted by the Sub-Regional Fisheries Commission,* Advisory Opinion, ITLOS Rep 2015, para 17. Interestingly, the United States was permitted to file a written statement even though it is not a party to UNCLOS, because it is a party to the Fish Stocks Agreement. ibid, *Request for an Advisory Opinion submitted by the Sub-Regional Fisheries Commission,* Advisory Opinion, ITLOS Rep 2015, para 24.

108 ibid, para 21.

109 ibid, para 29.

110 ibid, paras 31–5.

111 ibid, paras 37–69.

112 For a critique of ITLOS' assumption of this role, see Tom Ruys and Anemoon Soete, '"Creeping" Advisory Jurisdiction of International Courts and Tribunals? The Case of the International Tribunal for the Law of the Sea' (2016) 29 *Leiden Journal of International Law* 155; Massimo Lando, 'The Advisory Jurisdiction of the International Tribunal for the Law of the Sea: Comments on the

agreement related to the aims of UNCLOS that specifically provides for the submission of an advisory opinion request to ITLOS; a request made to ITLOS by a body authorised by or in accordance with that agreement; and a request that seeks the opinion of ITLOS on 'a legal question'.[113] Even where those requirements are met, ITLOS can decline to answer the question(s) if there are compelling reasons to do so.[114]

With respect to substance, the *SRFC Advisory Opinion* provided a robust analysis of the obligations of States on conservation and management of the living resources within the EEZs, which is relevant for conduct not just off the coast of West Africa but worldwide.[115] Much of the opinion's discussion of the general obligations of flag States under Articles 94, 192, and 193 of UNCLOS may be applicable as well to fishing activities outside of and adjacent to EEZs,[116] just as the analysis of Article 61(1) on stocks straddling EEZs may be applicable to Article 61(2) on stocks straddling EEZs and the high seas.[117] Yet, ITLOS stopped short of expressly addressing compatibility issues between measures by coastal States and measures by other States or RFMOs with respect to the high seas. In responding to the fourth question, ITLOS noted that UNCLOS called for 'cooperation between the States concerned on issues pertaining to the conservation and management of shared fisheries resources, as well as the promotion of the optimum utilization of those resources'.[118] Further, it noted that 'fisheries conservation and management measures, to be effective, should concern the whole stock unit over its entire area of distribution or migration routes'.[119] However, ITLOS went no further, stating that it 'has limited its examination and conclusions to the shared stocks in the exclusive economic zones of the SRFC Member States, constrained as it is by the limited scope of its jurisdiction in the present case'.[120]

3.2. Proposed Request for an Advisory Opinion on the Compatibility Requirement

In recent years, there has been considerable interest by States in pursuing advisory opinions from both ITLOS and the International Court of Justice.[121] In light of that

Request for an Advisory Opinion Submitted by the Sub-Regional Fisheries Commission' (2016) 29 *Leiden Journal of International Law* 441.

113 *Request for an Advisory Opinion submitted by the Sub-Regional Fisheries Commission,* Advisory Opinion, ITLOS Rep 2015, para 60.

114 ibid, para 71.

115 ibid, paras 85–219.

116 ibid, paras 116–20, 136–40.

117 ibid, paras 188–218.

118 ibid, para 213.

119 ibid, para 214.

120 ibid.

121 In 2022, the Commission of Small Island States on Climate Change and International Law requested an advisory opinion from ITLOS concerning the effects of climate change on the marine environment. Written statements were submitted by 33 States Parties and nine intergovernmental organizations. In September 2023, 33 States Parties and four intergovernmental organisations

interest, consideration should be given to a competent RFMO seeking advice from ITLOS on the compatibility of measures adopted for conserving and managing straddling and highly migratory fish stocks. Politically, it may be difficult to secure agreement within an RFMO to request such advice. However, given the problems faced with the regulation of such stocks and the value of greater legal certainty, such a request could be deemed desirable.

To this end, a discrete set of questions for an advisory opinion could centre on the compatibility requirement in Article 7(2) the Fish Stocks Agreement and the ambiguities that remain in its implementation. Considering the aforementioned analysis, such questions might include the following. First, does the compatibility requirement in Article 7(2) of the Fish Stocks Agreement clarify obligations under UNCLOS and, further, reflect customary international law?[122] Does the expression 'areas under national jurisdiction' in Article 7(2) refer solely to the EEZ or does it also encompass internal waters, the territorial sea, and archipelagic waters? Third, does Article 7(2) apply only when States unilaterally adopt measures or also when States act collectively to adopt measures, such as within RFMOs? Fourth, what is the legal significance of the second clause in Article 7(2)(a) ('and ensure that measures established in respect of such stocks for the high seas do not undermine the effectiveness of such measures') and its absence in Article 7(2)(b) and (c)? Fifth, to what extent does Article 7(2)(d) call upon States to approach each straddling and highly migratory fish stock as a single biological unit and to adopt an ecosystem approach to sustainably manage and conserve this stock? Sixth, is there an appropriate process, or overarching legal principle or approach, that should be followed when balancing the factors in Article 7(2)?

A draft text of such a request for an advisory opinion appears at the end of this chapter.

4. Conclusion

The codification that began with the 1958 Geneva Conventions on the Law of the Sea and continued with UNCLOS in 1982 and the Fish Stocks Agreement in 1995 established an important legal framework to conserve and manage straddling and highly migratory fish stocks. Yet, the compatibility requirement in Article 7(2) of

participated in the hearing, and ITLOS issued its opinion in May 2024. In 2022 and 2023, respectively, the United Nations General Assembly requested advice from the International Court of Justice on 'Israeli practices affecting the human rights of the Palestinian people in the Occupied Palestinian Territory, including East Jerusalem', and on the obligations of States in respect of climate change.

122 One could object that ITLOS is only empowered to interpret the Fish Stocks Agreement and not whether rules within this Agreement reflect customary international law. In response, one could argue that ITLOS is empowered to advise States parties on the application of the Fish Stocks Agreement's rules in complex relationships involving both parties and non-parties and, in doing so, can apply UNCLOS 'and other rules of international law not incompatible with' it. UNCLOS, art 293(1).

the Fish Stocks Agreement, which seeks to harmonise measures adopted by coastal States for their EEZs with the measures adopted for high-seas fishing, does not appear to have led to uniform results. There may be advantages – almost 30 years after the adoption of the Fish Stocks Agreement – in securing an advisory opinion from ITLOS to address outstanding ambiguities in Article 7(2). Such an advisory opinion would not be legally binding and, formally, would be given only to the RFMO seeking the opinion.[123] However, guidance by ITLOS on this matter could provide an additional layer of guidance for States and others, including RFMOs, in their continued quest to sustainably manage the living resources of the oceans.

5. Annex: Proposed Resolution Requesting an Advisory Opinion from ITLOS

The States Parties of the [name of RFMO],

Considering the United Nations Convention on the Law of the Sea (UNCLOS) signed at Montego Bay on 10 December 1982;

Considering also the Agreement for the Implementation of the Provisions of the United Nations Convention on the Law of the Sea of 10 December 1982 Relating to the Conservation and Management of Straddling Fish Stocks and Highly Migratory Fish Stocks (Fish Stocks Agreement) adopted at New York on 8 September 1995;

Reaffirming their commitment to supporting the principles and standards stipulated in the United Nations Food and Agriculture Organization (FAO) Code of Conduct for Responsible Fisheries adopted on 31 October 1995;

Recalling their resolve to implement the 2001 FAO International Plan of Action to Prevent, Deter and Eliminate Illegal, Unreported and Unregulated Fishing;

Considering the Convention of [date] on the establishment of the [name of RFMO], especially with respect to its Articles on [compatibility requirement];

Desiring to align the [RFMO] Convention and the practice thereunder with the requirements of the Fish Stocks Agreement, in particular with respect to the compatibility requirement set forth in its Article 7;

Considering the provisions of Article [XX] of the [relevant RFMO Resolution], which stipulate that [e.g., the Meeting of States Parties shall authorise the Permanent Secretary of the RFMO to seize the International Tribunal for the Law of the Sea on a specific legal matter for its advisory opinion];

Considering also Article 21 of the Statute of the International Tribunal for the Law of the Sea and Article 138 of the Rules of the Tribunal;

Decides, in accordance with Article [XX] of the [relevant RFMO Resolution], to authorise the Permanent Secretary of the [RFMO] to seize the International

123 *Request for an Advisory Opinion submitted by the Sub-Regional Fisheries Commission*, Advisory Opinion, ITLOS Rep 2015, para 76.

Tribunal for the Law of the Sea, pursuant to Article 21 of the Statute of the Tribunal and Article 138 of the Rules of the Tribunal, in order to obtain its advisory opinion on the following matters:

1. Does the compatibility requirement set forth in Article 7(2) of the Fish Stocks Agreement clarify obligations existing in UNCLOS? Does Article 7(2) also reflect customary international law?
2. Does the expression 'areas under national jurisdiction' in Article 7(2) of the Fish Stocks Agreement refer solely to the exclusive economic zone? Alternatively, does it also encompass internal waters, the territorial sea, and archipelagic waters?
3. Does Article 7(2) of the Fish Stocks Agreement only apply when States directly adopt measures or also when they act indirectly to adopt measures, such as through a regional fisheries management organisation or arrangement, or another international organisation?
4. What is the legal significance of the second clause in Article 7(2)(a) of the Fish Stocks Agreement ('and ensure that measures established in respect of such stocks for the high seas do not undermine the effectiveness of such measures') and its absence in Article 7(2)(b) and (c)?
5. To what extent does Article 7(2)(d) of the Fish Stocks Agreement call upon States to adopt compatible measures that consider each straddling or highly migratory fish stock as a single biological unit, as well as to adopt an ecosystem approach for the sustainable management and conservation of straddling and highly migratory fish stocks?
6. Is there a process, or overarching legal principle or approach, to balance the considerations set forth in Article 7(2) of the Fish Stocks Agreement?

Part VI

Trade-Related Measures and Fisheries

16 WTO Trade Disputes Concerning Marine Living Resources

Valerie Hughes

1. Introduction

Public international law does indeed play a role in WTO dispute settlement. However, how large or influential that role is or should be remains a matter of debate. This question continues to play out in the rulings of WTO adjudicative bodies. At a minimum, most WTO experts would agree that WTO law forms part of international law and is not a self-contained regime.[1] It is also clear that customary rules of interpretation of public international law, as codified in Articles 31 and 32 of the Vienna Convention on the Law of Treaties (VCLT),[2] are applicable to WTO dispute settlement.[3] Moreover, a small number of international legal principles – such as good faith, proportionality, and the non-retroactivity of treaties – have found their way into WTO rulings. Beyond this rather limited incursion, however, there remains considerable hesitancy about looking to public international law in resolving WTO disputes.

The positions of the two opposing camps in this debate break down as follows: one side argues that recourse cannot be had to public international law in settling WTO disputes other than when applying the VCLT interpretation rules, while the other side asserts that public international law is excluded only if WTO agreements contract out of it (*lex specialis*).

This chapter explores the basis for the two approaches and the extent to which they are manifested in the arguments and rulings in WTO disputes. After providing

1 See, for example, Joost Pauwelyn, 'The Role of Public International Law in the WTO: How Far Can We Go?' (2001) 95 *American Journal of International Law* 535; Giorgio Sacerdoti, 'WTO Law and the 'Fragmentation' of International Laws: Specificity, Integration, Conflicts' in Merit Janow, Victoria Donaldson, and Alan Yanovich (eds), *The WTO: Governance, Dispute Settlement & Developing Countries* (Juris Publishing 2008) 595.

2 Vienna Convention on the Law of Treaties, 23 April 1969, 1155 UNTS 331, entered into force 27 January 1980 (VCLT).

3 Understanding on Rules and Procedures Governing the Settlement of Disputes, 15 April 1994, 1869 UNTS 401, entered into force 1 January 1995 (generally referred to as the Dispute Settlement Understanding or DSU), Art 3.2 provides that the WTO dispute settlement system serves to 'clarify the existing provisions of the [WTO agreements] in accordance with customary rules of interpretation of public international law'.

DOI: 10.4324/9781003492030-22

a brief overview of the history and underlying principles of WTO Dispute Settlement, the chapter details the role of public international law in specific WTO disputes. This includes an analysis of the leading case on the United States' import prohibition of shrimp harvested using nets without turtle exclusion devices (often referred to as the Shrimp/Turtle case).[4] It also considers how public international law might have figured in the 2013 case brought by the Faroe Islands against the European Union's (EU) import prohibition on herring and mackerel caught under the control of the Faroe Islands, had the dispute not settled before a ruling was issued.[5] The chapter concludes with reflections on how the debate on the appropriate role of public international law in WTO dispute settlement may be resolved in the context of addressing the dispute settlement crisis currently facing the WTO.

2. History and Underlying Principles of WTO Dispute Settlement

To understand the role of public international law in WTO dispute settlement, it is useful to recall briefly the history of the WTO dispute settlement mechanism and its underlying principles.

The WTO dispute settlement mechanism came into effect in 1995, together with the establishment of the WTO. It replaced the dispute resolution system used under the General Agreement on Tariffs and Trade (GATT), the WTO's predecessor. The GATT system for dispute settlement operated more as a diplomatic than legal exercise: its objective was to arrive at a mutually agreed solution rather than a penalty for the wrongdoer. Throughout much of the history of GATT dispute settlement, trade negotiators conducted proceedings. Lawyers – including international law jurists – had no formal role. Although the system evolved considerably from its origins in 1947 and became more legalistic in the latter years of the GATT, it produced uneven results in terms of the legal quality of decisions, due in part to decision-makers' preference for pragmatism over legalism.[6]

In 1994, Ministers representing 'the 124 Governments and the European Communities participating in the Uruguay Round of Multilateral Trade Negotiations' saluted the 'historic achievement' of concluding the Uruguay Round of trade

4 Appellate Body Report on *United States – Import Prohibition of Certain Shrimp and Shrimp Products*, WT/DS58, adopted on 26 November 2001.

5 *European Union – Measures on Atlanto-Scandian Herring*, WT/DS469, a mutually agreed solution was notified on 24 August 2014.

6 Robert Hudec, *Enforcing International Trade Law: The Evolution of the Modern GATT Legal System* (Butterworths 1993) 353; Frieder Roessler, 'The Role of Law in International Trade Relations and the Establishment of the Legal Affairs Division of the GATT' in Gabrielle Marceau (ed), *A History of Law and Lawyers in the GATT/WTO* (Cambridge University Press 2015) 164–6;

Ernst-Ulrich Petersmann, 'The Establishment of a GATT Office of Legal Affairs and the Limits of "Public Reason" in the GATT/WTO Dispute Settlement System' in Gabrielle Marceau (ed), *A History of Law and Lawyers in the GATT/WTO* (Cambridge University Press 2015) 185.

negotiations, which led to the establishment of the WTO.[7] They 'welcomed the stronger and clearer legal framework they [] adopted for the conduct of international trade, including a more effective and reliable dispute settlement mechanism'.[8] In contrast to the GATT system that favoured diplomacy, negotiation, and mutually agreed solutions, the WTO dispute settlement system is 'rule oriented' and 'designed so as to promote as much as possible the stability and predictability of the rule system'.[9] In practice, WTO dispute settlement is very legalistic. This is due at least in part to the prominent role of lawyers in the WTO system – a marked contrast to the negotiator-led approach under the GATT. Typically, disputes address multiple claims founded on several legal provisions spanning a number of WTO agreements; pleadings run to hundreds of pages and exhibits to thousands; and disputes sometimes involve two or even three WTO members as complainants and almost always multiple WTO members as interested, non-disputing parties. Not surprisingly, rulings are commensurately long and complex with lengthy legal analyses and reasoning. They include extensive references to rulings in previous disputes, even though rulings are binding only on the parties to a specific dispute.

WTO law today comprises many dispute settlement rulings: 239 panel and 150 appellate reports.[10] These rulings cover a variety of difficult and sensitive subjects and their financial implications run in the billions of dollars.[11] To name but a few examples, WTO rulings have addressed trade restrictions on fish and agricultural products (including tuna fished using methods that cause high dolphin mortalities, shrimp harvested without using turtle exclusion devices, seal products, genetically modified products, and hormone-treated beef); discriminatory import regimes for products (such as bananas and automobiles); intellectual property rights matters (such as legislations imposing requirements for packaging of tobacco products); subsidies in various sectors (including the aircraft and steel industries); and discriminatory legislation in banking and other services.

7 'Marrakesh Declaration of 15 April 1994, Preamble'. www.wto.org/english/docs_e/legal_e/marrakesh_decl_e.htm, para 1.

8 ibid.

9 John Jackson, 'Dispute Settlement in the WTO: Policy and Jurisprudential Considerations', *Research Seminar in International Economics, University of Michigan, Discussion Paper 419* (9 February 1998) 3–4.

10 This includes rulings in original disputes and in disputes addressing whether a losing party has complied with an original ruling. The statistics reflect the situation as of 31 January 2024 as reported on the WTO website: www.wto.org/english/tratop_e/dispu_e/dispustats_e.htm.accessed 2 February 2024.

11 From 1995 through the end of January 2024, 621 requests for consultations – the first step in a WTO dispute – were filed, WTO, 'Dispute Settlement'. www.wto.org/english/tratop_e/dispu_e/dispu_e.htm accessed 24 January 2024. See also Anabel González and Euijin Jung, 'Developing Countries Can Help Restore the WTO's Dispute Settlement System', *Peterson Institute for International Economics, Policy Brief 20–1* (January 2020) 5. www.piie.com/sites/default/files/documents/pb20-1.pdf accessed 2 November 2022.

Public international law has found its way into this large body of rulings, but for the most part through only a relatively narrow window: the systematic reliance on Articles 31 and 32 of the VCLT to interpret WTO provisions. Its role otherwise has been limited. This is due at least in part to history, as international law did not figure in the GATT dispute settlement regime and so did not naturally or easily find its way into WTO dispute settlement. It is also due in part to the prescribed rules and procedures of WTO dispute settlement set forth in the Dispute Settlement Understanding (DSU).[12]

Looking first to the reliance on Articles 31 and 32 of the VCLT, Article 3.2 of the DSU provides that WTO provisions are 'clarified' (meaning interpreted) 'in accordance with customary rules of interpretation of public international law'. The WTO Appellate Body observed in its first two appeals that Articles 31 and 32 of the VCLT form part of the 'customary rules of interpretation of public international law'.[13] Every panel and Appellate Body report that followed included a legal analysis informed by the interpretation rules codified in those VCLT articles.

Article 7.1 of the DSU prescribes the terms of reference for dispute settlement panels. It states that panels must examine the matter referred to them 'in the light of the relevant provisions in [WTO] agreement(s) cited by the parties to the dispute'. It provides further that panels must 'make such findings as will assist the DSB [Dispute Settlement Body] in . . . giving the rulings provided for in that/those agreement(s)'.[14] Proponents of the view that recourse cannot be had to public international law in settling WTO disputes other than for interpretation purposes rely on Article 7.1 of the DSU to argue that panels are confined to the WTO provisions invoked by the disputing parties, both in considering the issues before them and in making their rulings. These proponents also rely on Article 3.2 of the DSU, which provides that the dispute settlement system 'serves to preserve the rights and obligations of Members *under the [WTO] agreements*' and that rulings 'cannot add to or diminish the rights and obligations *provided in the [WTO] agreements*' (emphasis added). For these proponents, the rights and obligations in play in WTO disputes are confined to those in the WTO agreements; they do not extend to rights and obligations more broadly, including those provided under public international law.[15]

12 Understanding on Rules and Procedures Governing the Settlement of Disputes, 15 April 1994, 1869 UNTS 401, entered into force 1 January 1995.

13 Appellate Body Report on *United States – Standards for Reformulated and Conventional Gasoline*, WT/DS2/AB/R, adopted 29 April 1996, 17; Appellate Body Report on *Japan – Taxes on Alcoholic Beverages*, WT/DS8/AB/R, WT/DS10/AB/R, WT/DS11/AB/R, adopted 4 October 1996, 10.

14 The Dispute Settlement Body (DSB) is comprised of all WTO Members. It generally meets monthly to establish dispute settlement panels; adopt panel and Appellate Body dispute settlement reports; monitor the implementation of rulings; and authorise suspension of trade commitments.

15 See, for example, Donald McRae, 'Treaty Interpretation and the Development of International Trade Law by the WTO Appellate Body' in Giorgio Sacerdoti, Alan Yanovich, and Jan Bohanes (eds), *The WTO at Ten: The Contribution of the Dispute Settlement System* (CUP 2006) 360; Georges Abi-Saab, 'The Appellate Body and Treaty Interpretation' in Giorgio Sacerdoti, Alan Yanovich, and Jan Bohanes (eds), *The WTO at Ten: The Contribution of the Dispute Settlement System* (CUP 2006)

Those who argue for a WTO-limited remit in WTO dispute settlement also find support in Article 11 of the DSU, which describes the function of dispute settlement panels. It states that

> a panel should make an objective assessment of the matter before it, including an objective assessment of the facts of the case and the applicability of and conformity with *the relevant [WTO] agreements*, and make such other findings as will assist the DSB . . . in giving the *rulings provided for in the covered agreements*.
>
> (emphasis added)

They also rely on Article 19.2 of the DSU, which provides that 'in their findings and recommendations, the panel and Appellate Body cannot add to or diminish the rights and obligations *provided in the [WTO] agreements*' (emphasis added). For 'WTO purists', reference to or reliance on non-WTO rules or principles would offend these DSU provisions. They argue, therefore, that WTO disputes must be decided pursuant to the provisions of WTO agreements and that it is not permissible to rely on other treaties or other principles of public international law.

Conversely, those who argue that general international law has a wide-ranging role in WTO dispute settlement maintain that the reference in Article 3.2 of the DSU to 'customary rules of interpretation of public international law' does not imply *a contrario* that other rules of international law do not apply. For these proponents, panels and the Appellate Body may apply non-WTO law when the questions before them are not regulated in WTO agreements themselves.[16] Isabelle Van Damme, for example, observes that general international law includes general principles of law, such as good faith, due process, and state responsibility, and opines that these principles 'are not intended to regulate a particular type of behaviour'; rather, they govern how international law, including WTO law, is interpreted and applied.[17] Van Damme refers to the report of the International Law Commission (ILC) on fragmentation which states that '[i]t is in the nature of "general law to apply generally" – namely inasmuch as it has not been specifically excluded'.[18]

453; Anja Lindroos and Michael Mehling, 'Dispelling the Chimera of "Self-Contained Regimes" International Law and the WTO' (2005) 16 *European Journal of International Law* 857; Isabelle Van Damme, *Treaty Interpretation by the WTO Appellate Body* (OUP 2009), chapter II, section 9; Anna Ventouratou, 'The Law on State Responsibility and the World Trade Organization' (2021) 22 *The Journal of World Investment & Trade* 759; Appellate Body Report on *European Communities and Certain member States – Measures Affecting Trade in Large Civil Aircraft*, WT/DS316/AB/R, adopted 1 June 2011, paras 844–5.

16 See, for example, Joost Pauwelyn, *Conflicts of Norms in Public International Law: How WTO Law Relates to Other Rules of International Law* (CUP 2003) 478–86.

17 Isabelle Van Damme, 'Jurisdiction, Applicable Law, and Interpretation' in Daniel Bethlehem et al. (eds), *The Oxford Handbook of International Trade Law* (OUP 2009) 319.

18 Report of the Study Group of the International Law Commission, 'Fragmentation of International Law: Difficulties Arising from the Diversification and Expansion of International Law' (13 April 2006) A/CN.4/L.682, para 185.

For Van Damme, '[t]o argue that general international law does not apply in WTO dispute settlement is to doubt the treaty basis of the WTO'.[19]

It is useful to highlight what is *not* included in the rules and procedures of WTO dispute settlement: the DSU contains no applicable law clause. Unlike, for example, Article 293(1) of the United Nations Convention on the Law of the Sea (UNCLOS), which provides that '[a] court or tribunal having jurisdiction under this section shall apply this Convention *and other rules of international law* not incompatible with this Convention' (emphasis added),[20] there is no comparable clause in the DSU. This *lacuna* may have contributed to the view that WTO adjudicators cannot rely on rules of international law beyond the WTO agreements themselves. As Donald McRae puts it, '[p]rinciples of customary international law do not leapfrog into treaty regimes and add to substantive obligations under those regimes'.[21] He explains that such principles 'exist alongside of and are relevant to the interpretation and application of substantive treaty rules'.[22]

3. The Role of Public International Law in Specific WTO Disputes

Having considered the theoretical debate around the role of public international law in WTO dispute settlement, one can now examine specific WTO disputes to determine what role – aside from applying the customary rules of interpretation codified in Articles 31 and 32 of the VCLT – public international law has played in rulings of WTO panels and the Appellate Body. As will be discussed, panels and the Appellate Body often have looked to the practice of international courts when dealing with *procedural* matters. In addition, panels and the Appellate Body have been willing to apply some principles of public international law, but they have declined to adopt others.

2.1. Drawing Inspiration from the Practice of International Courts on Procedural Matters

WTO case law suggests that WTO adjudicators readily look to the practice of international courts and tribunals when the DSU is silent on matters of procedure. For example, in an early dispute, India challenged the imposition by the United States of a quota on imports of wool shirts and blouses.[23] India asserted that the

19 Isabelle Van Damme, 'Jurisdiction, Applicable Law, and Interpretation' in Daniel Bethlehem et al. (eds), *The Oxford Handbook of International Trade Law* (OUP 2009) 319.

20 United Nations Convention on the Law of the Sea (UNCLOS), 10 December 1982, 1833 UNTS 3, entered into force 16 November 1994.

21 Donald McRae, 'Comments on Presentation by Claus-Dieter Ehlermann on the Role and Record of the Dispute Settlement Panels and the Appellate Body of the WTO', quoted in Debra Steger, 'Remarks' (2004) 98 *Proceedings of the 98th Annual Meeting of the American Society of International Law* 142.

22 ibid.

23 Appellate Body Report on *United States – Measures Affecting Imports of Woven Wool Shirts and Blouses from India*, WT/DS33/AB/R, adopted on 23 May 1997.

panel should have imposed the burden of proof solely on the United States because the United States relied on an exception in the WTO Agreement on Textiles and Clothing to justify its actions. The DSU does not address allocation of burden of proof between disputing parties. In deciding the issue, the Appellate Body looked to international practice for guidance. It observed that

> we find it difficult, indeed, to see how any system of judicial settlement could work if it incorporated the proposition that the mere assertion of a claim might amount to proof. It is, thus, hardly surprising that various international tribunals, including the International Court of Justice, have generally and consistently accepted and applied the rule that the party who asserts a fact, whether the claimant or the respondent, is responsible for providing proof thereof.[24]

Similarly, in a challenge to the European Communities' regime for importing, selling, and distributing bananas, the Appellate Body relied on the practice of international tribunals in deciding whether Saint Lucia could be represented at the oral hearing by private legal counsel rather than government employees, as had been the practice in GATT and WTO dispute settlement.[25] The Appellate Body said that it found nothing in the DSU 'nor in customary international law or the prevailing practice of international tribunals' preventing a WTO member from determining the composition of its delegation in oral proceedings.[26] Accordingly, it determined that it is for a WTO member to decide who should represent it before the Appellate Body.

In the same ruling, the Appellate Body referred to judgments from the International Court of Justice (ICJ) and the Permanent Court of International Justice when responding to a challenge that the United States lacked legal standing to bring a claim because its banana production was minimal. The Appellate Body observed that it 'did not read any of these judgments as establishing a general rule that in all international litigation, a complaining party must have a "legal interest" in order to bring a case'.[27]

In another dispute, Canada declined to provide information to a WTO panel about terms and conditions of certain debt financing activities associated with the purchase of aircraft.[28] The Appellate Body referred to the 'general practice and usage of international tribunals' in determining that WTO panels have the authority to draw adverse inferences from a WTO member's refusal to provide information sought by a panel.[29]

24 ibid, 14.

25 Appellate Body Report on *European Communities – Regime for the Importation, Sale and Distribution of Bananas*, WT/DS27/AB/R, adopted on 25 September 1997.

26 ibid, para 10.

27 ibid, para 133.

28 Appellate Body Report on *Canada – Measures Affecting the Export of Civilian Aircraft*, WT/DS70/AB/R, adopted on 20 August 1999.

29 ibid, para 202.

In another aircraft financing dispute, an arbitration panel under Article 22.6 of the DSU was set up to address the appropriate level of retaliation by Canada for Brazil's failure to comply with a WTO ruling. The panel referred to ICJ practice on applying the presumption of good faith to statements and evidence of subjects of international law (as opposed to private parties).[30]

A final example of WTO adjudicators' reliance on the practice of international tribunals when ruling on matters of procedure is the Appellate Body's treatment of municipal law in WTO dispute settlement. In a dispute involving a United States challenge to India's patent protection for pharmaceuticals, India maintained that the panel erred in its treatment of India's municipal law.[31] According to India, the panel had erred in assessing the law as a law to be interpreted and not as a fact to be established by the party relying on it. The Appellate Body stated that

> In public international law, an international tribunal may treat municipal law in several ways. Municipal law may serve as evidence of facts and may provide evidence of state practice . . . [and] may also constitute evidence of compliance or non-compliance with international obligations.[32]

2.2. *Applying Some International Legal Principles but Declining to Apply Others*

WTO panels and the Appellate Body have on several occasions considered rules of international law independently of the customary rules of interpretation codified in Articles 31 and 32 of the VCLT. In some instances, the Appellate Body readily applied the principle in question, while in other instances, it declined to do so. The following section explains the different approaches followed in those disputes.

2.2.1. *Good Faith and Pacta Sunt Servanda*

One of the most renowned WTO disputes – known as the Shrimp/Turtle case – concerned a challenge by India, Malaysia, Pakistan, and Thailand of the United States' ban on importing shrimp from countries that had not harvested their catch using nets with sea turtle exclusion devices.[33] Under WTO law, import prohibitions are generally disallowed, but the United States relied on an exception set forth in Article XX(g) of the GATT 1994. According to Article XX(g), measures (including import prohibitions) relating to the conservation of exhaustible natural resources

30 Decision of the Arbitrators on *Brazil – Export Financing Programme for Aircraft* under Article 22.6 of the Dispute Settlement Understanding and Article 4.11 of the Agreement on Subsidies and Countervailing Measures, WT/DS46/ARB, 28 August 2000, para II.17 and footnote 15.

31 Appellate Body Report on *India – Patent Protection for Pharmaceutical and Agricultural Chemical Products*, WT/DS50/AB/R, adopted 16 January 1998.

32 ibid, para 65.

33 Appellate Body Report on *United States – Import Prohibition of Certain Shrimp and Shrimp Products*, WT/DS58, adopted on 26 November 2001.

are permitted, provided that such measures are not applied in a manner that would constitute a means of arbitrary or unjustifiable discrimination between countries or a disguised restriction on international trade.[34]

In assessing whether the application of the measure constituted a means of arbitrary or unjustifiable discrimination, the Appellate Body sought guidance from general principles of international law. It stated that the non-discrimination requirement is 'but one expression of the principle of good faith . . . at once a general principle of law and a general principle of international law'.[35] It noted further that '[o]ne application of this general principle, the application widely known as the doctrine of *abus de droit*, prohibits the abusive exercise of a state's rights'.[36] Citing ICJ findings and public international law experts, the Appellate Body stated that an abusive exercise by a WTO member of its treaty right results in a breach of the other member's treaty rights and a violation of the treaty obligation of the member so acting. It concluded that the United States had applied the measure in a manner that amounted to arbitrary and unjustifiable discrimination. Therefore, it was not entitled to rely on the exception provided in Article XX(g) to justify its import prohibition.

The Appellate Body used similar language in other instances. In an appeal concerning the United States tax treatment of foreign sales corporations, the European Communities argued that this tax treatment constituted a prohibited subsidy.[37] The United States sought to have the challenge thrown out on the basis that the document filed by the European Communities in bringing the dispute was legally defective. The Appellate Body rejected the United States' claim because too much time had passed since the document was filed and the United States had not raised the issue despite numerous opportunities to do so. It observed that Article 3.10 of the DSU commits WTO members to engage in dispute settlement procedures 'in good faith in an effort to resolve the dispute' and asserted that '[t]his is another specific

34 The chapeau and subparagraph (g) of Article XX of the GATT 1994 read as follows:

> Subject to the requirement that such measures are not applied in a manner which would constitute a means of arbitrary or unjustifiable discrimination between countries where the same conditions apply, or a disguised restriction on international trade, nothing in this Agreement shall be construed to prevent the adoption by any [WTO Member] of measures . . . (g) relating to the conservation of exhaustible natural resources if such measures are made effective in conjunction with restrictions on domestic production or consumption.
>
> General Agreement on Tariffs and Trade (GATT), 15 April 1994, Marrakesh Agreement Establishing the World Trade Organization, Annex 1A, 1867 UNTS 187, entered into force 1 January 1995.

35 Appellate Body Report on *United States – Import Prohibition of Certain Shrimp and Shrimp Products*, WT/DS58, adopted on 26 November 2001, para 158.

36 ibid.

37 Appellate Body Report on *United States – Tax Treatment for 'Foreign Sales Corporations'*, WT/DS108/AB/R, adopted 20 March 2000.

manifestation of the principle of good faith which, we have pointed out, is at once a general principle of law and a principle of general international law'.[38]

In a later appeal on dumping duties imposed by the United States on Japanese steel products, the Appellate Body examined a provision of the WTO Anti-Dumping Agreement prohibiting investigating authorities from requiring exporters to complete questionnaires in a particular medium if it would entail an unreasonable extra burden.[39] The Appellate Body saw the provision as 'another detailed expression of the principle of good faith'.[40] It repeated the view that the principle of good faith is at once a general principle of law and a principle of general international law and concluded that the 'organic principle of good faith, in this particular context, restrains investigating authorities from imposing on exporters burdens which, under the circumstances, are not reasonable'.[41]

The Appellate Body has referred explicitly to the principle of *pacta sunt servanda* in a number of rulings. One example is the dispute between Peru and the European Communities about a marketing standard prohibiting exporters from using the trade description 'sardines' for a sardine species fished in waters off Peru.[42] In the course of arguments about allocating the burden of proof, Peru expressed doubts about the efficacy of a provision in the WTO Agreement on Technical Barriers to Trade requiring members to explain the rationale for their measures when requested to do so by other members. The Appellate Body rejected Peru's position stating that '[w]e must assume that Members of the WTO will abide by their treaty obligations in good faith, as required by the principle of *pacta sunt servanda* articulated in Article 26' of the VCLT.[43]

The Appellate Body relied on Article 26 of the VCLT in an appeal by the United States of a panel finding that the United States had not acted in good faith by enacting legislation under which anti-dumping and countervailing duties assessed against exporters would be distributed to domestic producers.[44] The United States argued that there was no basis in the WTO Agreement for a panel to conclude that a member had not acted in good faith, or to enforce a principle of good faith as a substantive obligation agreed to by WTO members. The Appellate Body disagreed. Referring to Article 26 of the VCLT, the Appellate Body asserted that performance of treaties is governed by good faith and noted that it had recognised the principle of good faith in other cases. It concluded that '[c]learly, therefore, there is a basis for a dispute settlement panel to determine, in an appropriate case, whether

38 ibid, para 166.

39 Appellate Body Report on *United States – Anti-Dumping Measures on Certain Hot-Rolled Steel Products from Japan*, WT/DS184/AB/R, adopted 23 August 2001.

40 ibid, para 101.

41 ibid.

42 Appellate Body Report on *European Communities – Trade Description of Sardines*, WT/231/AB/R, adopted 23 October 2002.

43 ibid, para 278.

44 Appellate Body Report on *United States – Continued Dumping and Subsidy Offset Act of 2000*, WT/DS217, WT/DS234/AB/R, adopted 27 January 2003.

a Member has not acted in good faith'.[45] Nevertheless, the Appellate Body did not agree that the record supported the view that the United States had not acted in good faith.

2.2.2. *Non-Retroactivity of Treaties*

The Appellate Body invoked the principle of non-retroactivity of treaties set forth in Article 28 of the VCLT in several disputes, including in the Philippines' challenge on countervailing duties imposed by Brazil on imports of desiccated coconut.[46] The duties were imposed after the WTO came into force on 1 January 1995, but the application and investigation which led to the imposition of duties predated the WTO. The Appellate Body upheld the decision of the panel that the WTO agreements did not apply to duties imposed as a result of an investigation initiated pursuant to an application made before the entry into force of the WTO agreements. Consequently, the Philippines' claims based in WTO law could not be considered.

2.2.3. *State Responsibility, Attribution, and Proportionality*

The ILC Articles on State Responsibility have been invoked in WTO rulings and have been characterised as reflecting customary international law.[47] In one example, the Appellate Body assessed the WTO consistency of a safeguard measure applied by the United States on cotton yarn from Pakistan.[48] Safeguard measures are duties imposed on foreign products to protect the domestic industry from serious injury when there is a surge in imports. The Appellate Body ruled that it was not permissible to attribute the totality of the damage to one member unless the imports from that member alone had caused the damage. It stated that its view was supported 'by the rules of general international law on state responsibility, which require that countermeasures in response to breaches by states of their international obligations be commensurate with the injury suffered'.[49] The Appellate Body similarly invoked the ILC Articles on State Responsibility in deciding a safeguard dispute between the United States and Korea about steel products.[50] WTO panels have

45 ibid, paras 296–7.

46 Appellate Body Report on *Brazil – Measures Affecting Desiccated Coconut*, WT/DS22/AB/R, adopted 20 March 1997.

47 International Law Commission, 'Draft Articles on Responsibility of States for Internationally Wrongful Acts' (2001) II *Yearbook of the International Law Commission*. See, for example, Panel Report on *Canada – Measures Affecting the Importation of Milk and the Exportation of Dairy Products*, WT/DS103/R, WT/DS113/R, adopted 27 October 1999, footnote 427.

48 Appellate Body Report on *United States – Transitional Safeguard Measure on Combed Cotton Yarn from Pakistan*, WT/DS192/AB/R, adopted 5 November 2001.

49 ibid, paras 119–20.

50 Appellate Body Report on *United States – Definitive Safeguard Measures on Imports of Circular Welded Carbon Quality Line Pipe from Korea*, WT/DS202/AB/R, adopted 8 March 2002, para 259.

also relied on the ILC Articles when addressing attribution and the circumstances in which the conduct of a State agency is attributable to the State.[51]

It should be noted, however, that some rules on state responsibility have been displaced in the WTO agreements through the establishment of special rules or *lex specialis* that regulate the same subject-matter for purposes of WTO law. For example, Article 23 of the DSU requires WTO members to have recourse only to the WTO dispute settlement rules and procedures in seeking redress for violations of WTO obligations. Another example is found in Article 19 of the DSU, which provides that the appropriate form of reparation is to bring an impugned measure into conformity with the WTO agreements. Finally, Article 22 of the DSU establishes a mechanism for prospective compensation in cases of non-compliance with WTO rulings.

2.2.4. Estoppel

The previous examples suggest some readiness in WTO dispute settlement to rely on public international legal principles and practices. However, there are many examples of hesitancy and even reluctance to apply such principles. One such example relates to the principle of estoppel, which was addressed in a dispute where Australia, Brazil, and Thailand challenged the European Communities' export subsidies on sugar.[52] The European Communities argued that the complainants were estopped from bringing claims due to their silence in respect of the measures and maintained that the principle of estoppel was a general principle of international law. Both the panel and the Appellate Body stated that it was 'far from clear that the estoppel principle applies in the context of WTO dispute settlement'.[53] Moreover, the Appellate Body considered that 'the notion of estoppel . . . would appear to inhibit the ability of WTO Members to initiate a WTO dispute settlement proceeding' and it saw 'little in the DSU that explicitly limits the rights of WTO Members to bring an action'.[54] Ultimately, the Appellate Body determined that even if estoppel were applicable – a matter on which it did not pronounce – the facts did not establish that the complainants were estopped from bringing their claims.

51 Panel Report on *Canada – Measures Affecting the Importation of Milk and the Exportation of Dairy Products*, WT/DS103/R, WT/DS113/R, adopted 27 October 1999, para 7.77 and footnote 427; Panel Report on *United States – Measures Affecting the Cross-Border Supply of Gambling and Betting Services*, WT/DS285/R, adopted 20 April 2005, paras 6.127–6.128.

52 Appellate Body Report on *European Communities – Export Subsidies on Sugar*, WT/DS265, WT/DS266, WT//DS283/AB/R, adopted 19 May 2005.

53 ibid, para 310.

54 ibid, para 312.

2.2.5. The Precautionary Principle

One of the early tests of the WTO dispute settlement system arose in a sensitive case in 1998 where Canada and the United States challenged the European Communities' ban on hormone-treated beef.[55] The European Communities claimed that the ban was necessary to protect human health. Canada and the United States argued that the ban had to be based on a scientific risk assessment by virtue of the WTO Agreement on Sanitary and Phytosanitary Measures,[56] and maintain that there was insufficient scientific evidence to support the European Communities' contention that the hormone residue levels in question were harmful. The European Communities invoked the precautionary principle, arguing that it was a general principle of customary international law or at least a general principle of law.

The Appellate Body was reluctant to pronounce definitively on the status of the precautionary principle. It observed that '[w]hether [the precautionary principle] has been widely accepted by Members as a principle of *general* or *customary* international law appears less than clear' (emphasis in original).[57] After considering ICJ case law and the writings of several international law experts,[58] the Appellate Body concluded that the principle 'at least outside the field of international environmental law, still awaits authoritative formulation'.[59] Ultimately, the Appellate Body determined that it was 'unnecessary, and probably imprudent, for the Appellate Body in this appeal to take a position on this important, but abstract, question'.[60] When the issue was raised in another dispute several years later in 2006, the panel declined to express a view on whether the principle had by that time attained the status of a principle of general or customary international law.[61] The panel report was not appealed.

55 Appellate Body Report on *European Communities – Measures Concerning Meat and Meat Products (Hormones)*, WT/DS26/AB/R, WT/DS48/AB/R, adopted 13 February 1998.

56 Agreement on the Application of Sanitary and Phytosanitary Measures, 15 April 1994, Marrakesh Agreement Establishing the World Trade Organization, Annex 1A, 1867 UNTS 187, entered into force 1 January 1995.

57 Appellate Body Report on *European Communities – Measures Concerning Meat and Meat Products (Hormones)*, WT/DS26/AB/R, WT/DS48/AB/R, adopted 13 February 1998, para 123.

58 ibid, footnotes 92, 93. The Appellate Body cited to the ICJ judgment in *Case Concerning the Gabčikovo-Nagymaros Project (Hungary/Slovakia)*, Judgment, ICJ Rep 1997, 7. It cited to the following authors as supporting the view that the precautionary principle is a principle of customary international law: Philippe Sands, James Cameron, and Juli Abouchar. It also cited to the following authors who were of the view that the precautionary principle had not reached this status or that such status was doubtful: Patricia Birnie, Alan Boyle, Lothar Gündling, Armand deMestral, and Daniel Bodansky.

59 Appellate Body Report on *European Communities – Measures Concerning Meat and Meat Products (Hormones)*, WT/DS26/AB/R, WT/DS48/AB/R, adopted 13 February 1998, para 123.

60 ibid.

61 Panel Report on *European Communities – Measures Affecting the Approval and Marketing of Biotech Products*, WT/DS291/R, WT/DS292/R, WT/DS293/R, adopted 21 November 2006, para 7.89.

2.2.6. Other Rules of International Law

This final subsection collates examples that do not relate to the application of international legal principles per se, but to instances when panels and the Appellate Body looked to international legal rules outside WTO agreements to give meaning to WTO provisions.

In the Shrimp/Turtle case mentioned previously, the Appellate Body had to determine whether the United States import prohibition on shrimp, which normally would have been inconsistent with WTO rules, was justified by virtue of an exception permitting measures relating to the conservation of '*exhaustible* natural resources' (emphasis added). The complainants argued that the exception did not apply as sea turtles were renewable and therefore, unlike minerals and non-living resources, cannot be 'exhaustible'. The Appellate Body disagreed, finding that living resources 'are just as "finite" as petroleum, iron ore and other non-living resources'.[62] It looked to non-WTO texts to support its position, observing that 'modern international conventions and declarations make frequent references to natural resources as embracing both living and non-living resources'.[63] It referred specifically to Articles 56, 61, and 62 of UNCLOS as well as to the Convention on Biological Diversity,[64] Agenda 21,[65] and other international legal texts.[66]

In the compliance phase of the dispute between the United States and the European Communities on tax treatment of foreign sales corporations discussed previously, the Appellate Body looked to different international instruments related to taxation when seeking to interpret the term 'foreign-source income' as used in the WTO Agreement on Subsidies and Countervailing Measures.[67] Panels and the Appellate Body have also resorted to international instruments related to customs in three separate disputes to determine the meaning of customs terms used in different WTO provisions, including 'customs', 'customs administration', 'customs fraud', 'ordinary customs duties', and 'transshipment'.[68]

62 Appellate Body Report on *United States – Import Prohibition of Certain Shrimp and Shrimp Products*, WT/DS58/AB/R, adopted on 26 November 2001, para 128.

63 ibid, para 130.

64 Convention on Biological Diversity, 29 December 1993, 1760 UNTS 79, entered into force 29 December 1993.

65 Report of the United Nations Conference on Environment and Development (12 August 1992) A/CONF. 151/26.

66 Appellate Body Report on *United States – Import Prohibition of Certain Shrimp and Shrimp Products*, WT/DS58, adopted on 26 November 2001, paras 130, 132.

67 Appellate Body Report on *United States – Tax Treatment for 'Foreign Sales Corporations'*, WT/DS108/AB/R, adopted 20 March 2000, paras 141–3.

68 See, for example, Appellate Body Report on *Thailand – Customs and Fiscal Measures on Cigarettes from the Philippines*, WT/DS371/AB/R, adopted 15 July 2011, para 193; Panel Report on *Thailand – Customs and Fiscal Measures on Cigarettes from the Philippines*, WT/DS371/R, adopted 15 July 2011, para 7.1027; Panel Report on recourse to Article 21.5 on *Thailand – Customs and Fiscal Measures on Cigarettes from the Philippines,* WT/DS371/RW, 12 November 2018, para 7.629; Appellate Body Report on *China – Measures Affecting Imports of Automobile Parts*, WT/DS339/AB/R, WT/DS340/AB/R, WT/DS342/AB/R, adopted 12 January 2009, para 7.139 and footnote

However, the approach followed in these cases may reflect the exception rather than the rule. WTO adjudicators generally have shown considerable hesitation to take into account rules of international law when determining the meaning of WTO provisions. This reluctance exists despite – or perhaps because of – the requirement in Article 31(3)(c) of the VCLT that, in interpreting treaties, '[t]here shall be taken into account, together with the context, . . . [a]ny relevant rules of international law applicable in the relations between *the parties*' (emphasis added).[69] The issue, whether the term 'the parties' refers to all WTO members or only to parties to the dispute in question has arisen in a number of disputes.

One panel ruled that 'the parties' refers to all WTO members and, therefore, for WTO adjudicators to 'take into account' in a specific dispute a rule of international law in determining the meaning of a WTO provision, all WTO members – not just the disputing parties – must be parties to the international agreement containing the rule in question.[70] Some commentators criticised this ruling, noting that not all WTO members are States. Some WTO members are separate customs territories and therefore, do not have competence to join international agreements open only to States. Another panel took the opposite approach, finding that the Revised Kyoto Convention on customs procedures 'may in principle be regarded as a "relevant rule of international law applicable in the relations between the parties" within the meaning of Article 31(3)(c) of the Vienna Convention'. It reasoned that 'even if the number of contracting parties [116 at the time compared to 164 WTO members] would be considered not to meet any requisite threshold, it still sheds light on the ordinary meaning of certain terms used in the [WTO Customs Valuation Agreement]'.[71]

The Appellate Body has yet to pronounce on the meaning of 'the parties' in Article 31(3)(c). However, the following excerpt from a WTO dispute on aircraft subsidies signals the Appellate Body's wariness on the issue, which, in turn, reflects

309; Panel Report on *Indonesia – Measures Concerning the Importation of Chicken Meat and Chicken Products*, WT/DS484/R, adopted on 22 November 2017, footnote 776. The rulings refer to the Protocol of Amendment to the International Convention on the Simplification and Harmonization of Customs Procedures (Revised Kyoto Convention), 26 June 1999 and the International Convention on Mutual Administrative Assistance for the Prevention, Investigation and Repression of Customs Offences, 9 June 1977, 1226 UNTS 143, entered into force 21 May 1980.

69 Excerpt from Article 31(3)(c) of the VCLT.

70 Panel Report on *European Communities – Measures Affecting the Approval and Marketing of Biotech Products*, WT/DS291/R, WT/DS292/R, WT/DS293/R, adopted 21 November 2006, paras 7.67–7.71. In that dispute, the panel declined to take into account the Convention on Biological Diversity, 29 December 1993, 1760 UNTS 79, entered into force 29 December 1993 and the Cartagena Protocol on Biosafety to the Convention on Biological Diversity, 29 January 2000, 2226 UNTS 208, entered into force 11 September 2003. It noted that not all parties to the dispute were parties to those instruments.

71 Panel Report on second recourse to Article 21.5 on *Thailand – Customs and Fiscal Measures on Cigarettes from the Philippines*, WT/DS371/RW/2, circulated 12 July 2019, para 7.265 (not yet adopted).

the highly sensitive nature of the issue among WTO members. The Appellate Body noted that

> one must exercise caution in drawing from an international agreement to which not all WTO Members are party. . . . In a multilateral context such as the WTO, when recourse is had to a non-WTO rule for the purposes of interpreting provisions of the WTO agreements, a delicate balance must be struck between, on the one hand, taking due account of an individual WTO Member's international obligations and, on the other hand, ensuring a consistent and harmonious approach to the interpretation of WTO law among all WTO Members.[72]

The preceding discussion demonstrates that public international law rules and principles have indeed informed WTO dispute settlement rulings. Reliance on treaty interpretation rules codified in Articles 31 and 32 of the VCLT is common and uncontroversial. The DSU provides that the WTO dispute settlement system serves to clarify WTO provisions in accordance with customary rules of interpretation of public international law and it is readily accepted that these rules of interpretation refer to Articles 31 and 32 of the VCLT. In addition, WTO adjudicators have turned to international legal principles to fill lacunae in WTO dispute settlement procedures, including in assigning the burden of proof or in determining legal standing to bring a dispute. International legal principles such as complying with treaties in good faith, the non-retroactivity of treaties, and rules on state responsibility have also found their way into WTO rulings. Nevertheless, WTO case law also reveals reticence on the part of panels and the Appellate Body to refer to some public international law rules and principles in making their rulings. This reflects a long-standing divergence of views among WTO members about the legal correctness of going beyond WTO provisions when determining compliance with WTO law.

4. The WTO Dispute Brought by the Faroe Islands

The WTO challenge brought in 2013 by the Faroe Islands against the EU's import prohibition on herring and mackerel caught under the control of the Faroe Islands and the closure of EU ports to herring- and mackerel-fishing vessels flying the flag of the Faroe Islands raised questions about the role of UNCLOS obligations in resolving WTO disputes.[73] The EU maintained that the Faroe Islands had violated its obligations under UNCLOS by virtue of its herring quota which, according to the EU, required appropriate measures for conservation purposes. The Faroe

72 Appellate Body Report on *European Communities and Certain member States – Measures Affecting Trade in Large Civil Aircraft*, WT/DS316/AB/R, adopted 1 June 2011, para 845.

73 *European Union – Measures on Atlanto-Scandian Herring*, WT/DS469, mutually agreed solution notified 24 August 2014.

Islands rejected the allegations regarding its UNCLOS obligations and claimed that the EU measures were inconsistent with WTO obligations on import prohibitions, freedom of transit, and non-discrimination.

The dispute was settled early in the proceedings. However, had the litigation proceeded, WTO adjudicators likely would have had to address the question whether a failure by a WTO member to comply with UNCLOS obligations could serve to justify measures imposed by another member that were inconsistent with WTO rules.

It is difficult to assess how a WTO panel or the Appellate Body would have looked at this issue had the case not settled. WTO panels and the Appellate Body have been reluctant in previous disputes to pronounce on a WTO member's compliance with non-WTO obligations. For example, in a case where the United States challenged taxes imposed by Mexico on certain soft drinks,[74] Mexico sought to rely on the ruling of the Permanent Court of International Justice in *Factory at Chorzów*.[75] Mexico argued that its WTO obligations towards the United States were 'call[ed] into question' because the United States had acted inconsistently with its obligations in a similar matter under the North American Free Trade Agreement (NAFTA).[76] The Appellate Body demurred, stating that, even if the legal principle on which Mexico relied applied in WTO dispute settlement, this would entail a determination that the United States had acted inconsistently with its NAFTA obligations. The Appellate Body said that it could 'see no basis in the DSU for panels and the Appellate Body to adjudicate non-WTO disputes'.[77] Therefore, it rejected Mexico's argument because its 'interpretation would imply that the WTO dispute settlement system could be used to determine rights and obligations outside the [WTO] agreements'.[78]

As mentioned earlier, WTO panel and Appellate Body rulings are binding only on the parties to a dispute, so there is no *stare decisis* in WTO dispute settlement. However, panels and the Appellate Body generally tend to follow previous decisions unless there are compelling reasons not to do so. Thus, had the dispute brought by the Faroe Islands not been resolved by way of an agreed settlement and instead proceeded to litigation, it is unlikely that a WTO panel or the Appellate Body would have sought to interpret UNCLOS provisions or make a determination whether they had been violated by the Faroe Islands by virtue of its herring quota. However, the WTO adjudicators might well have followed their approach in previous disputes, including in the Shrimp/Turtle case, and looked to relevant international instruments in determining whether challenged measures were WTO-inconsistent. In this case, UNCLOS could have been relevant in seeking to determine whether

74 Appellate Body Report on *Mexico – Tax Measures on Soft Drinks and Other Beverages*, WT/DS308/AB/R, adopted 24 March 2006.

75 *Factory at Chorzów (Germany v. Poland)* (1927) PCIJ Rep, Series A, 9.

76 Appellate Body Report on *Mexico – Tax Measures on Soft Drinks and Other Beverages*, WT/DS308/AB/R, adopted 24 March 2006, para 55.

77 ibid, para 56.

78 ibid.

the measures taken by the EU related to the conservation of exhaustible natural resources and, as such, were justified under Article XX(g) of the GATT 1994.

5. Conclusion: The Future Role of Public International Law in WTO Dispute Settlement

Going forward, the debate about the role of public international law in WTO dispute settlement may be put to rest, not through legal issues put to the test in disputes, but instead in the context of negotiations to address the so-called 'WTO Appellate Body crisis'. This crisis was precipitated by the United States, which considers that the Appellate Body acted beyond its mandate on several fronts, including by 'introducing substantive elements of public international law' into its rulings.[79] As the WTO works by consensus, the United States succeeded in blocking members' proposals to appoint new Appellate Body members when the terms of existing members expired. This has resulted in an empty appellate bench since 2020 and a non-functioning appellate process. Although first-instance panels continue to issue rulings, the lack of an appeal process has undermined the WTO dispute settlement system more generally. The United States continues to block Appellate Body appointments and maintains that the WTO dispute settlement system requires fundamental reform. Efforts to find a negotiated solution to the crisis have been unsuccessful thus far.

In June 2022, WTO members committed in the 'Outcome Document' of the 12th Ministerial Conference to 'conduct discussions with the view to having a fully and well-functioning dispute settlement system accessible to all Members by 2024'.[80] Since then, WTO members have engaged in discussions on reforming the dispute settlement system in several respects. The role of public international law in WTO dispute settlement likely has figured prominently in those discussions, which to date have been conducted behind closed doors. A key question is whether a negotiated solution – if one is reached – will include rules prescribing the precise role of public international law in WTO dispute settlement going forward.

79 United States Trade Representative, 'Report on the Appellate Body of the World Trade Organization' (February 2020) A-11. https://ustr.gov/sites/default/files/Report_on_the_Appellate_Body_of_the_World_Trade_Organization.pdf accessed 27 October 2023.

80 WTO, 'MC12 Outcome Document' (Geneva, 17 June 2022), WT/MIN/(22)/24, WT/L/1135, para 4.

17 The WTO Agreement on Fisheries Subsidies and IUU Fishing

*Clarisse Morgan**

1. Introduction

On 17 June 2022, World Trade Organisation (WTO) Ministers adopted at the 12th WTO Ministerial Conference and opened for acceptance a new binding multilateral Agreement on Fisheries Subsidies for WTO Members (the Agreement).[1] This Agreement marks a major step forward for ocean sustainability by prohibiting various forms of harmful fisheries subsidies. The Agreement is highly relevant to the topic of new international instruments, mechanisms and actors in tackling illegal, unreported and unregulated ('IUU') fishing, as it contains certain provisions specifically on IUU fishing and subsidies to IUU fishing.

Ministers at the 11th WTO Ministerial Conference in Buenos Aires in 2017 had agreed on the negotiating mandate to adopt an agreement on disciplines on subsidies to IUU fishing:

> Members agree to continue to engage constructively in the fisheries subsidies negotiations, with a view to adopting, by the Ministerial Conference in 2019, an agreement on comprehensive and effective disciplines that prohibit certain forms of fisheries subsidies that contribute to overcapacity and overfishing, and *eliminate subsidies that contribute to IUU-fishing* recognizing that appropriate and effective special and differential treatment for developing country Members and least developed country Members should be an integral part of these negotiations (emphasis added).[2]

* All views expressed in this chapter are the author's own, and do not constitute official positions of the WTO Secretariat or any WTO member.

1 Protocol Amending the Marrakesh Agreement establishing the WTO, 'Agreement on Fisheries Subsidies', not yet in force (17 June 2022). docs.wto.org/dol2fe/Pages/SS/directdoc.aspx?filename=q:/WT/MIN22/33.pdf accessed 26 December 2023.

2 WTO, 'Fisheries Subsidies: Ministerial Decision of 13 December 2017' (18 December 2017) WT/MIN(17)/64, para 1.

DOI: 10.4324/9781003492030-23

This WTO's negotiating mandate mirrors the language of Sustainable Development Goal 14.6.[3]

The core of the Agreement is its three prohibitions on:

a. Subsidies contributing to IUU fishing[4];
b. Subsidies regarding fishing on overfished stocks[5]; and
c. Subsidies to fishing on the unregulated high seas, namely outside a Member's exclusive economic zone (EEZ) and outside the competence of any regional fisheries management organisation or arrangement (RFMO).[6]

This chapter describes the provisions in the Agreement on subsidies contributing to IIU fishing. It then, discusses all of the elements included in the Agreement to implement and operationalise it, namely a) notification and transparency requirements;[7] b) dispute settlement provisions;[8] c) the establishment of a Committee on Fisheries Subsidies to oversee implementation through, inter alia, the review of notifications;[9] d) a built-in agenda for future negotiations;[10] and e) a conditional termination clause if future negotiations are unsuccessful.[11]

2. Provisions on Subsidies Contributing to IUU Fishing

The first substantive discipline of the Agreement is the prohibition of subsidies contributing to IUU fishing in Article 3. This discipline complements existing instruments against IUU fishing as it creates a binding mechanism for preventing or removing subsidies to vessels or operators found to have engaged in IUU fishing. As explained previously in sub-section 2.5, this discipline does not seek to alter existing instruments on IUU fishing or to change rights or obligations under these instruments.

The Agreement defines IUU fishing through a cross-reference to the United Nations Food and Agriculture Organization's International Plan of Action to

3 SDG Target 14.6 reads:
By 2020, prohibit certain forms of fisheries subsidies which contribute to overcapacity and overfishing, and *eliminate subsidies that contribute to IUU fishing*, and refrain from introducing new such subsidies, recognizing that appropriate and effective special and differential treatment for developing and least developed countries should be an integral part of the WTO fisheries subsidies negotiation (emphasis added).

4 Agreement on Fisheries Subsidies, art 3.

5 Agreement on Fisheries Subsidies, art 4.

6 ibid, art 5.

7 ibid, art 8.

8 ibid, art 10.

9 ibid, art 9.

10 WTO, 'Agreement on Fisheries Subsidies: Ministerial Decision of 17 June 2022' (22 June 2022) WT/MIN(22)/33-WT/L/1144, para 4.

11 Agreement on Fisheries Subsidies, art 12.

Prevent, Deter and Eliminate IUU fishing.[12] Paragraph 3 of this International Plan describes activities which constitute IUU fishing.

Article 3.1 describes the prohibition as follows: '[n]o [WTO] Member shall grant or maintain any subsidy to a vessel or operator engaged in Illegal, Unreported or Unregulated (IUU) fishing or fishing related activities in support of IUU fishing.' This chapter will later describe the provisions indicating how Members are to operationalise this prohibition on subsidies contributing to IUU fishing.

The Agreement specifies that what triggers the prohibition in Article 3.1 is an 'affirmative determination' of IUU fishing, which is made by any of the entities identified in Article 3.2, subject to the respective applicable conditions. The stipulation that an *affirmative* determination triggers the prohibition makes clear that, for example, where a Member has made an IUU finding, the subsidising Member, whose vessel or operator is implicated, cannot nullify the subsidy prohibition in respect of that vessel or operator by making its own countervailing finding that the incident in question *does not* constitute IUU fishing.[13]

The entities whose affirmative IUU determinations trigger the subsidy prohibition are:

- Coastal Members;[14]
- Flag State Members, in respect of their own-flagged vessels and/or operators;[15]
- RFMOs, for affirmative IUU determinations in areas and for species under their competence, where the determinations are made in accordance with the rules and procedures of the RFMO and relevant international law (which includes the provision of timely notification and relevant information).[16]

The Agreement defines an 'affirmative determination' as the final finding by a Member or the final listing by an RFMO that a vessel or operator has engaged in IUU fishing.[17]

2.1. Who is Implicated by the Subsidy Prohibition Triggered by an Affirmative IUU Determination and to What Extent?

The Agreement identifies two possible subjects of affirmative determinations which would trigger the subsidy prohibition: a) a vessel, or b) an operator).[18] An operator

12 Food and Agriculture Organization of the United Nations (FAO) International Plan of Action to Prevent, Deter and Eliminate Illegal, Unreported and Unregulated Fishing, 2001.

13 WTO, 'Agreement on Fisheries Draft Text: Addendum' (10 June 2022) WT/MIN(22)/W/20/Add.1, para 20, second bullet point.

14 Agreement on Fisheries Subsidies, art 3.2(a).

15 ibid, art 3.2(b).

16 ibid, art 3.2(c).

17 ibid, art 3.3 (a).

18 ibid, art 3.1.

is defined as the owner of a vessel or any person who is in charge of or directs or controls the vessel[19] at the time of the IUU fishing infraction.[20]

The Agreement elaborates, for greater certainty, that the prohibition on granting or maintaining subsidies to operators engaged in IUU fishing or fishing-related activities in support of such fishing applies to subsidies provided to the operators' fishing and fishing-related activities at sea. This clarification has the effect of focusing the Article 3 subsidy prohibition on the subsidies provided to fishing and fishing related activities at sea of the operator implicated by an IUU determination, thus excluding any other subsidies that that operator might be receiving. As explained by the Negotiating Group Chair[21], this language reflects a compromise in the drafting of Article 3 between opposing views of certain WTO Members. Some wanted any IUU determination, even involving a single vessel, to trigger the prohibition in respect of all subsidies to the operator as a whole, and not only subsidies to the vessel(s) involved in the specific incident. Others wanted to limit the subsidy prohibition in all cases to the specific vessels involved in IUU fishing, with no further implications for the operator, regardless of the scope of the subsidy or of the IUU determination.

Once an affirmative determination of IUU fishing is made in respect of a vessel or operator, and subject to the entity which made the determination following the applicable procedural rules, including notifying the WTO of the determination, the subsidising Member must stop any subsidies to the vessel or operator.

2.2. Rules on IUU Determinations by Coastal WTO Members

WTO Members struggled to agree on rules pertaining to IUU determinations by coastal Members as a trigger of the subsidy prohibition. Coastal Members wanted to ensure that the rules would fully reflect and respect their sovereignty over fishing inside their EEZs. However, many other Members wanted coastal Members' IUU determinations to be subject to due process requirements. This is linked to concerns over the potential for arbitrariness or politicisation of coastal States' determinations. There was a particular concern that, if there were no due process requirements, a coastal Member could erroneously or for political or commercial reasons make an unfounded IUU determination. The subsidising Member would then have needed to take this determination at face and be under a requirement to remove subsidies from the implicated vessel or operator.[22]

The outcome of this debate, found in Article 3.3(b), is that a coastal Member's IUU determination will only trigger the subsidy prohibition if this determination is

19 ibid, art 2(e).
20 ibid, footnote 5 to art 3.
21 WTO document WT/MIN(22)/W/20/Add.1, at paras15–18.
22 ibid, paras 23–9.

based on relevant factual evidence. In addition, the coastal Member must provide to the flag State Member, and the subsidising Member if known, the following:

a. timely notification, through appropriate channels, that a vessel or operator has been temporarily detained pending further investigation for engagement in, or that the coastal Member has initiated an investigation for, IUU fishing including reference to any relevant factual information, applicable laws, regulations, administrative procedures, or other relevant measures;
b. an opportunity to exchange relevant information prior to a determination, so as to allow such information to be considered in the final determination. The coastal Member may specify the manner and time period in which such information exchange should be carried out; and
c. notification of the final determination, and of any sanctions applied, including, if applicable, their duration.[23]

In addition to directly notifying the subsidising Member, a coastal Member making an affirmative IUU determination must also notify this determination to the Committee on Fisheries Subsidies.[24]

2.3. Rules on IUU Determinations by Flag State Members

Article 3.2(b) provides that affirmative IUU determinations by a flag State Member trigger the subsidy prohibition in respect of activities by vessels flying its flag. This provision reflects that flag States are responsible for the actions of vessels flying their flags under the United Nations Convention on the Law of the Sea (UNCLOS).[25] There are no procedural requirements in respect of such IUU determinations in the Agreement because the vessel in question is under the control of the flag State Member.

2.4. Rules on IUU Determinations by RFMOs

Article 3.2(a) provides that an affirmative IUU determination by an RFMO triggers the subsidy prohibition. Article 3.3(a) defines this type of IUU determination as a final listing by an RFMO that a vessel or operator has engaged in IUU fishing. To trigger the prohibition, Article 3.2(a) provides that this final determination must be made in accordance with the RFMO's rules and procedures, and relevant international law. Article 3.2(a) adds that such rules and procedures include 'the provision of timely notification and relevant information' in areas and for species under the RFMO's competence. The procedural language in Article 3.2(a) recognises that

23 Agreement on Fisheries Subsidies, art 3.3(b).
24 ibid, chaussette to art 3.3.
25 United Nations Convention on the Law of the Sea (UNCLOS), 10 December 1982, 1833 UNTS 3, entered into force 16 November 1994.

RFMOs have their own detailed procedures for making IUU determinations and that the WTO would not second-guess these determinations. This language also reflects the concerns of some Members that the Agreement should specify basic elements of due process which should be present for an IUU determination by an RFMO to trigger the subsidy prohibition.

2.5. Disclaimers

The Agreement contains provisions clarifying that it has no impact on how governments make and enforce IUU determinations. For one, the Agreement reflects concerns by Members that WTO subsidy rules should not impede (especially coastal) Members' rights over IUU determinations. In this context, the Agreement includes a footnote specifying that Members are not required to initiate IUU fishing investigations or to make IUU fishing determinations.[26]

Another footnote specifies that the Agreement has no effect on the competence of a coastal Member, a flag State Member, or an RFMO under relevant international instruments, and also that it confers no new rights on these entities in making IUU fishing determinations.[27] This provision makes explicit that the fact that the Agreement refers to these entities (as entities whose affirmative IUU determinations give rise to a subsidy prohibition) does not change, and particularly does not expand, the roles of these entities in making IUU determinations beyond their existing functions under other relevant instruments.

The Agreement contains a further clarifying footnote, according to which the disciplines on subsidies to IUU fishing do not delay an entity in making an IUU fishing determination nor do they have any effect on the validity or enforceability of such a determination.[28] In other words, the entities are free to make IUU determinations according to their own procedures. The Agreement has no bearing on this fact. What the Agreement does provide is that, for a determination to trigger the subsidy prohibition, the determination must conform to the relevant provisions of the Agreement.

2.6. Duration of the Subsidy Prohibition

The duration of the subsidy prohibition is based on and linked to the duration of the corresponding affirmative determination of IUU fishing. In particular, the subsidising Member must consider the nature, gravity and repetition of IUU fishing committed by a vessel or operator when setting the duration of the prohibition's application.[29] Furthermore, the prohibition must apply for at least as long as a) the sanction resulting from the IUU determination triggering the prohibition remains in

26 Agreement on Fisheries Subsidies, footnote 6 to art 3.
27 ibid, footnote 7 to art 3.
28 ibid, footnote 8 to art 3.
29 ibid, art 3.4.

force or b) the vessel or operator is listed by an RFMO, whichever is longer. Thus, the minimum duration for the subsidy prohibition is the duration of the sanction on, or the listing by an RFMO of, a vessel or operator found to have engaged in IUU fishing.

2.7. ***Provisions on Flagging***

Although not explicitly related to the IUU provisions, the Agreement contains two linked provisions on, first, responsibility for subsidisation in Footnote 3 of Article 1 on Scope and, second, due restraint when granting subsidies to vessels not flying the flag of the subsidising Member in Article 5.2. Together, these provisions could support the IUU provisions of the Agreement, especially Article 3.2(b) as flag States are responsible under UNCLOS for the conduct of vessels flying their flag. The question of a State subsidising vessels not flying its flag was the subject of extensive debate during the negotiations. Some Members called for a prohibition on all such subsidies, inter alia out of concern over a possible link between reflagging and IUU fishing. However, other Members considered that such a subsidy prohibition could have unduly harsh effects on legitimate vessel registries.[30]

Footnote 3 of Article 1 provides that '[f]or greater certainty, for the purposes of this Agreement, a subsidy shall be attributable to the Member conferring it, regardless of the flag or registry of any vessel involved or the nationality of the recipient'. This footnote was introduced to ensure that a subsidising Member retains responsibility for all the subsidies it provides which fall within the scope of the Agreement. Thus, it cannot avoid responsibility where, for example, the subsidised vessel is not flying the subsidising Member's flag.

The other provision relating to the flag of a subsidised vessel is Article 5.2. Article 5.2 obliges a Member to take special care and to exercise due restraint when granting subsidies to vessels not flying its flag.

These two provisions reflect a compromise between the two views expressed during the negotiations on how to handle subsidies given to vessels not flying the flag of the subsidising Member.

2.8. The Role of a Port State

The Agreement recognises the role of port State Members in combatting IUU fishing. Yet, it does not treat port State Members as entities whose IUU determinations could trigger the subsidy prohibition. Under the Agreement, where a port State Member notifies a subsidising Member that it has clear grounds to believe that a vessel in one of its ports has engaged in IUU fishing, the subsidising Member

30 See., for example, WTO, 'Negotiating Group on Rules – Unofficial Room Document – Fisheries Subsidies – Panama's Proposed Text for Article 5.4 on Overfishing and Overcapacity Provision of the Draft Consolidated Chair Text Contained in the Document TN/RL/W/276' (30 June 2021) RD/TN/RL/144.

shall give due regard to the information received and take such actions as it deems appropriate in respect of its subsidies.[31]

2.9. 'Peace Clause' for Developing Country and Least-Developed Country Members

The Agreement affords special and differential treatment for developing and least-developed country Members in the form of a 'peace clause' in the provisions on IUU fishing.[32] Subsidies granted or maintained by developing country Members, including least-developed country Members, up to and within their EEZ will be subject to the rules of the Agreement from its entry into force. However, these subsidies will be exempt from dispute settlement under the Agreement for two years from its entry into force. Thus, these Members will be bound by the rules, but they will be exempt from WTO dispute settlement proceedings for the first two years. This will give these Members some time to ensure that their domestic procedures are in place and operational.

3. Provisions for Notification and Transparency and Institutional Arrangements

A key element to ensure the effective implementation of the Agreement relates to notifications and transparency. As part of their periodic notifications to the WTO, the Agreement provides that subsidising Members must provide certain fisheries-related information in addition to information relating to their subsidies.[33] This includes, notably, the type or kind of fishing activity being subsidised and, to the extent possible, information on stock status; conservation measures; subsidised fleets and vessels; and catch data. Each Member must also give the Committee on Fisheries Subsidies an annual list of vessels and operators which the Member has affirmatively determined have been engaged in IUU fishing.[34] Each Member must have laws, regulations, and/or administrative procedures in place to ensure it does not grant or maintain subsidies, including pre-existing subsidies, to IUU fishing and fishing-related activities.[35] The Agreement contains several other notification provisions relating to its implementation and operation.

Upon entry into force, each Member will be required to provide information relating to each RFMO/A to which it is a party. Such notifications can be provided by Members individually or in a group. This obligation can be met by providing an electronic link to a relevant official webpage.[36]

31 Agreement on Fisheries Subsidies, art 3.6.
32 ibid, art 3.8.
33 ibid, art 8.1.
34 ibid, art 8.2.
35 ibid, art 3.7.
36 ibid, art 8.6 and footnote 16 of the Agreement.

Within one year of entry into force of the Agreement, each Member will be required to inform the Committee of measures in existence or taken to ensure the implementation and administration of the Agreement, including steps taken to implement the prohibitions on harmful subsidies, including to IUU fishing or fishing related activities in support of IUU fishing. Each Member is also required to inform the Committee promptly of any changes to such measures thereafter, and of any new measures taken to implement the prohibitions.[37]

Within one year of entry into force of the Agreement, each Member also will be required to provide to the Committee a description of its fisheries regime with references to its relevant laws, regulations and administrative procedures, and thereafter to inform the Committee promptly of any changes. To facilitate compliance with this requirement, a Member can submit an up-to-date electronic link to an official web page that sets out this information.[38] The scope of this notification requirement is relatively broad and general, and providing a link to a web page where the relevant legal instruments can be found should obviate the need to submit the full text of those instruments to the WTO.

The Committee will meet regularly to review all of the notifications through a process whereby WTO Members exchange questions and answers in a manner that is transparent for all. The Committee also will conduct periodic reviews of its operation, with a view to identifying necessary modifications to improve its operation.[39]

4. Two 'Firewalls' on 'Territoriality'

During the negotiations, some Members raised concerns over the implications of disputed territorial claims on the subsidy prohibitions, such as subsidy prohibitions based on IUU determinations. To address these concerns, the Agreement contains two provisions which ensure that the WTO, through the Agreement, will not become involved in the substance of these claims.

The first provision is Article 11.2(a). It is a disclaimer that the Agreement and any related findings, recommendations and awards, shall have no legal implications regarding territorial claims or delimitation of maritime boundaries. This is the first 'firewall' provision aimed at preventing any entity from citing the Agreement, and any outcomes under it, in respect of territorial claims in any forum.

The second 'firewall' is in Article 11.2(b). It provides that WTO dispute settlement panels and arbitration pursuant to the Agreement shall not make findings on any claim before them which would require them to base such findings on any asserted territorial claims or delimitation of maritime boundaries. This second firewall is aimed at ensuring that WTO dispute settlement proceedings do not explicitly or implicitly side with any party in a contested territorial claim.

37 ibid, art 8.3.
38 ibid, art 8.4.
39 ibid, arts .9.1, 9.2 and 9.4.

5. Other Final Provisions

The Agreement contains several additional final provisions in the form of clarifications and disclaimers. The first disclaimer, Article 11.1, pertains to subsidies for disaster relief. It provides that nothing in the Agreement can prevent a Member from granting such subsidies so long as certain conditions are met; except where such subsidies would violate the prohibitions on subsidies to IUU fishing and on subsidies in respect of overfished stocks.

The second disclaimer, Article 11.3, is general in nature. It indicates that the Agreement does not prejudice the existing jurisdiction, rights, and obligations of Members under international law, including the law of the sea. A footnote specifies that this includes the rules and procedures of RFMOs. This disclaimer clarifies that, while the Agreement does involve fisheries-related rules in addition to rules on subsidisation, it does not change any existing provisions of international law, including on fisheries.

The third disclaimer, Article 11.4, pertains to Members which are not parties or cooperating non-parties to a given RFMO. This provision clarifies that, except as otherwise provided, the Agreement does not imply that these Members are bound by measures or decisions of that RFMO or recognise the RFMO. In practice, this means that if a Member which is not a party or cooperating non-party to an RFMO applies a subsidy prohibition on the basis of an IUU listing by this RFMO, this Member's application of the prohibition has no further implications for that Member vis-à-vis that RFMO.

The fourth disclaimer, Article 11.5, specifies the relationship between the Agreement on Fisheries Subsidies and the Agreement on Subsidies and Countervailing Measures ('SCM Agreement'). In particular, it provides that the new Agreement on Fisheries Subsidies does not modify, or nullify, any rights and obligations as provided by the SCM Agreement.[40] This disclaimer ensures that the Agreement on Fisheries Subsidies establishes additional subsidy rules and does not detract from any rules in the SCM Agreement.

6. Termination Clause

Article 12, the final provision of the Agreement, states that if comprehensive disciplines are not adopted within four years of the Agreement's entry into force, and unless otherwise decided by the WTO General Council, the Agreement will immediately terminate.

This provision enshrines in the Agreement, and acts as a backstop to, the instruction by WTO Ministers to the WTO Negotiating Group on Rules to continue negotiating in paragraph 4 of the Ministerial Decision adopting the Agreement.[41] The Ministers called on the Negotiating Group to continue working on the issues which

40 ibid, art 11.5.

41 WTO, 'Agreement on Fisheries Subsidies: Ministerial Decision of 17 June 2022' (22 June 2022) WT/MIN(22)/33-WT/L/1144, para 4.

were not resolved during the 12th WTO Ministerial Conference (the so-called 'outstanding issues'), with a view to making recommendations to the 13th WTO Ministerial Conference for additional provisions which would achieve a comprehensive agreement on fisheries subsidies. The 13th WTO Ministerial Conference is scheduled for February 2024. This termination clause was added at the request of certain Members to reflect their concern that the outstanding issues would not be abandoned upon the Ministers adopting the current Agreement.

The Ministerial Decision specifically identifies subsidies contributing to overcapacity and overfishing, and related special and differential treatment provisions for developing and least-developed country Members, as outstanding issues. While this area is unrelated to the Agreement's already-agreed disciplines on subsidies to IUU fishing, the implication of the termination clause in Article 12 is that as of four years from the date of entry into force of the Agreement, if 'comprehensive disciplines' have not been adopted, the current Agreement – including its provisions relating to IUU fishing – will terminate, unless WTO Members decide otherwise. In other words, in the event the further negotiations do not result in agreement on 'comprehensive disciplines', maintaining the Agreement in force beyond its first four years of operation will require an affirmative decision by the WTO General Council.

7. Conclusion

The Agreement's operation and effectiveness in stopping subsidies to IUU fishing and the other types of subsides that it prohibits can only be assessed once it enters into force. This will happen when two-thirds of the WTO's 164 Members have accepted it.[42] To accept the Agreement, a WTO Member has to deposit an instrument of acceptance with the WTO Secretariat's Depositary. As of the date of finalization of this chapter for publication, 52 Members had deposited their instruments of acceptance[43], about half of the number needed for entry into force.

It took more than 20 years for the negotiations to deliver the Agreement on Fisheries Subsidies. During this time, the condition of the world's fish stocks steadily declined, to today's very precarious state, with IUU fishing playing a major role. It thus is a matter of urgency that this latest weapon in the fight against IUU fishing, and other harmful forms of subsidies, begin operating. It is hoped that WTO Members will accelerate their efforts to accept the Agreement so that all of its disciplines, including those related to IUU fishing, can begin to operate.

42 Marrakesh Agreement Establishing the World Trade Organization, 15 April 1994, 1867 UNTS 154, entered into force 1 January 1995, art X(1).

43 WTO, 'Members Submitting Acceptance of Agreement on Fisheries Subsidies'. www.wto.org/english/tratop_e/rulesneg_e/fish_e/fish_acceptances_e.htm accessed 26 December 2023.

18 Regulatory Space for Measures Affecting Trade in Marine Resources

*Iain Sandford and Ariane Vincent**

1. Introduction

International trade rules, such as those of the World Trade Organization (WTO), establish disciplines on measures affecting trade, including trade in products derived from marine resources. The WTO disciplines reflect the economic goals of the Marrakesh Agreement Establishing the WTO (WTO Agreement).[1] Its preamble speaks of objectives such as 'raising standards of living' and 'making optimal use of the world's resources' in pursuit of 'sustainable development'. Yet, members of the WTO, and States parties to similar trade agreements such as bilateral free trade agreements, retain regulatory space to pursue broader policy objectives. This is demonstrated by the quarter-century of WTO adjudication to date. Indeed, WTO adjudicators have frequently applied WTO rules in a manner providing expansive regulatory space. This chapter explores the balance struck between trade disciplines and regulatory space, focusing mainly, but not exclusively, on the decisions of WTO adjudicators involving marine resources to illustrate its analysis.

* At the time of writing, Iain Sandford was a Partner and Ariane Vincent was a Managing Associate at Sidley Austin LLP, Geneva.

The authors and/or Sidley Austin LLP served as counsel on a number of the disputes referenced in this chapter. Iain Sandford also served as a panellist in one of the disputes involving marine resources discussed in this chapter, namely *US – Shrimp (Viet Nam)*. The case summaries in this chapter exclusively reflect public materials. The distilled analysis and conclusions are attributable solely to the authors and are not attributable to Sidley Austin LLP, any client, or other organisation.

1 Marrakesh Agreement Establishing the World Trade Organization, 15 April 1994, 1867 UNTS 154, entered into force 1 January 1995. The WTO Agreement encompasses several Annexes. Annexes 1, 2, and 3 are deemed integral parts of the WTO Agreement, pursuant to art II.2. Annex 1 encompasses multilateral agreements on trade in goods (Annex 1A) including several agreements referenced specifically in this chapter: the General Agreement on Tariffs and Trade 1994 (GATT 1994) which incorporates each member's schedule of tariff commitments; Agreement on the Application of Sanitary and Phytosanitary Measures (SPS Agreement); Agreement on Technical Barriers to Trade (TBT Agreement); Agreement on Subsidies and Countervailing Measures; Agreement on the Implementation of Article VI of the General Agreement on Tariffs and Trade 1994 (Anti-Dumping Agreement); Agreement on Safeguards; and Agreement on Agriculture.

DOI: 10.4324/9781003492030-24

The chapter, first, provides a typology of governmental measures relevant to trade in the products of marine resources. It classifies these measures into five distinct categories by reference to identified policy objectives. Second, it describes the WTO rules and exceptions which have been invoked in disputes over products of marine resources. Third, it addresses disciplines aimed at regulating the trade effects of measures motivated by economic, sanitary and phytosanitary (SPS), environmental, or moral objectives. Fourth, it addresses the new disciplines of the WTO Fisheries Subsidies Agreement, which restrain the policy space available for pursuing economically motivated measures with the objective of preventing environmental harm.[2]

Finally, the chapter draws some conclusions. Having reviewed five categories of measure affecting trade in the products of marine resources, it observes what appears to be a continuum of regulatory space for different objectives. The continuum ranges from the strict application of trade disciplines for measures which fundamentally pursue economic objectives, to a markedly more flexible approach for measures defended by reference to public morals. In the middle, measures taken to protect the life or health of living marine resources, and trade-related environmental measures, benefit from broad regulatory space but are subject to greater discipline than measures justified by moral concerns. The chapter comments on the merits and implications of this variable balance in the application of trade rules.

2. Regulatory Objectives Involving Trade in Marine Resources Products

This chapter identifies variability in how trade law disciplines apply to measures affecting trade in products derived from marine resources. The variability is explained in part by the objectives that such measures pursue. To lay the ground for this discussion, this section considers some of the objectives pursued by measures affecting trade in marine resources and establishes a typology.

Marine resource disputes in the WTO have arisen in respect of living marine resources, including fish, shellfish, plants, reptiles, and mammals. Complainants have claimed that measures affecting trade in marine products violate trade rules – such as import restrictions or bans, marketing standards, trade descriptions, labelling requirements, and trade remedy measures. On their part, respondents have sometimes defended their measures by reference to WTO rules and exceptions, which allow members to pursue other economic and/or non-trade objectives, including social and environmental goals.

2 Protocol Amending the Marrakesh Agreement establishing the WTO, Agreement on Fisheries Subsidies, not yet in force (17 June 2022). docs.wto.org/dol2fe/Pages/SS/directdoc.aspx?filename=q:/WT/MIN22/33.pdf accessed 3 January 2024.

A review of marine resources disputes indicates that adjudicators have applied different analytical frameworks to assess measures depending on their policy objectives. Four categories can be gleaned from cases associated with measures which have economic, environmental, SPS, and public morals objectives. These four categories of measures have been challenged based on their trade impacts. A fifth category covers the new framework of fisheries subsidies disciplines.

The first category of 'economic-trade' measures covers measures which affect trade and have an economic policy objective. These economic objectives include favouring domestic competitors by reducing the competitiveness of foreign products. WTO rules allow import tariffs to be used for this purpose, so long as tariffs do not exceed levels specified in the member's schedule of commitments. However, measures favouring domestic producers often take other forms. In the marine resources context, they could include protecting domestic market share for a domestic fisheries product or ensuring that a domestic fisheries industry has access to a share of common fish stocks. Measures in this category have affected trade through import quotas, marketing standards, anti-dumping measures, and trade descriptions. They have been the subject of numerous disputes.

The second category of 'SPS-trade' measures concerns measures with an underlying SPS objective which affect trade and fall within the WTO Agreement on the Application of Sanitary and Phytosanitary Measures (SPS Agreement). An example of SPS objective is protecting animal or plant health. Marine resource disputes have dealt with measures claimed to be aimed at preventing the spread of disease from imported fish products. Measures in this category include any trade measure (e.g., import bans, licensing, or marketing requirements) which pursues an SPS objective.

The third category of 'environment-trade' measures concerns measures which impact trade and have an environmental policy objective. Environmental policy objectives in WTO cases have included, for example, preventing collateral harm to one marine resource potentially arising from fishing practices used to catch another marine resource. Measures under this category can resemble economic trade measures. Thus, past cases have addressed import bans and labelling requirements. Challenges to environment-trade measures have not been frequent in marine resources disputes. However, they have produced influential jurisprudence on the regulatory space accorded to environmental objectives at the WTO.

The fourth category of 'morals-trade' measures concerns measures which impact trade and are aimed at protecting public morals. This objective arose in the *EC – Seal Products* case in which, as will be detailed further below, public moral concerns over animal welfare were invoked to justify an import ban on products from some countries.

Finally, with the Agreement on Fisheries Subsidies, WTO members have adopted new rules to restrain policy space to pursue economic measures with the objective of preventing environmental harm. This fifth category of 'economic environment' measures marks a new frontier within the WTO framework. It broadens the focus of WTO disciplines away from trade impacts and towards new areas involving the use of trade disciplines to regulate environmental (and potentially other) impacts caused by economic policies which promote the exploitation of natural resources. This category has emerged through the negotiation of disciplines on fisheries subsidies. These disciplines will prohibit members from providing subsidies which contribute to unsustainable fishing activities.[3]

3. Relevant WTO Rules and Exceptions

The WTO Agreement encompasses multilateral trade agreements governing, inter alia, trade in goods (including products of marine resources); services; and intellectual property.[4] This section briefly describes the substantive WTO rules which restrict trade measures falling into categories identified in the previous section. It also describes exceptions or other ways in which the treaty drafters sought to accommodate additional policy concerns. The cornerstone principles of the agreements on trade in goods, notably of the General Agreement on Tariffs and Trade (GATT) 1994, include requirements not to discriminate based on the origin of products;[5] to abide by tariff commitments in a member's schedule;[6] and not to impose import bans and other quantitative restrictions.[7]

Additional multilateral agreements on trade in goods give further rules for specific kinds of measures. These include, first, disciplines on measures regulating product characteristics, such as product composition, labelling and product-related process, and production methods, per the WTO Agreement on Technical Barriers to Trade (the TBT Agreement). Second, limitations on certain measures affecting agricultural trade, per the WTO Agreement on Agriculture. Third, rules regulating the right of members to take measures to protect human, animal, or plant life against risks in food or from pests and diseases, known as SPS risks, per the SPS Agreement. Fourth, rules governing the use of so-called 'trade remedies' to counteract dumping, per the WTO Anti-Dumping Agreement; subsidies, per the WTO Agreement on Subsidies and Countervailing Measures; and certain surges in imports, per the WTO Agreement on Safeguards. This chapter refers to these additional agreements collectively as 'Trade Remedy Agreements'.

3 Note that this category already has a foothold in the wider universe of trade rules, namely under the environment chapter of the Comprehensive and Progressive Agreement for Trans-Pacific Partnership, 8 March 2018, 3346 UNTS, entered into force 30 December 2018.

4 These substantive agreements are set forth in Annex 1 to the WTO Agreement. In addition, the WTO Agreement provides basic and institutional provisions in the Marrakesh Agreement itself; Understanding on Rules and Procedures for the Settlement of Disputes (Annex 2); Trade Policy Review Mechanism (Annex 3); and as space for 'plurilateral agreements' not subject to the basic most favoured-nation treatment principle (Annex 4).

5 See, for example, GATT 1994, art I on most-favoured nation treatment principle and art III on national treatment.

6 GATT 1994, art II.

7 GATT 1994, art XI.

Besides laying down disciplines on measures affecting trade, the Trade Remedy Agreements provide exceptions or carve-outs allowing members to deviate from the disciplines when pursuing protected objectives. In other words, the agreements balance discipline with regulatory space.

For some provisions, regulatory space is baked into the rules themselves. For example, and as will be discussed, the SPS Agreement recognises the right of members to protect against SPS risks at the level they deem appropriate. However, this right is subject to discipline: the SPS Agreement, for instance, requires consistency in the application of the chosen level of protection.[8]

Other provisions contain a rule addressing solely the trade effects of a measure. However, such rules are often balanced by exceptions allowing members to pursue non-trade policies. For example, Article XI:1 of the GATT 1994 includes a clear prohibition on quantitative restrictions on imports and exports. However, this prohibition is balanced by an exception in Article XI:2 which allows import restrictions on fisheries products necessary to support domestic measures controlling consumption or production.[9] Moreover, Article XX provides generally applicable exceptions for certain listed policy objectives.[10] Protected policy objectives include measures necessary to protect 'public morals',[11] 'animal or plant life or health',[12] or which relate to 'the conservation of exhaustible natural resources . . . when applied in conjunction with restrictions on domestic consumption or production'.[13]

In the following sections, the chapter considers how WTO adjudicators and negotiators have applied the agreed balance to the products of marine resources. The analysis is ordered using the typology of trade measures outlined in the previous section. It explores how each of these categories occupies a different point on a continuum of regulatory space available to members under WTO rules. This continuum ranges from, on the one hand, requiring relatively strict adherence to the basic rules to, on the other hand, giving marked flexibility.

4. Measures Affecting Trade

This section analyses in turn the four categories of measures affecting trade identified in the second section of this chapter, namely 'economic trade' measures; 'SPS trade' measures; 'environment trade' measures; and 'moral trade' measures.

8 SPS Agreement, art 5.5.

9 GATT 1994, art XI:2(c).

10 GATT 1994, art XXI adds an exception for measures considered necessary to protect essential security and taken during time of war or other international emergency, which relate to traffic in arms or are authorised under Chapter VII of the Charter of the United Nations, 26 June 1945, entered into force 24 October 1945.

11 GATT 1994, art XX(a).

12 GATT 1994, art XX(b).

13 GATT 1994, art XX(g).

4.1. *'Economic-Trade' Measures*

WTO members have brought several cases involving marine resource measures in the economic trade category.[14] These cases have notably been brought under the GATT 1994, the TBT Agreement, and the Trade Remedy Agreements. They include challenges to:

- Scallop trade descriptions (*EC – Scallops*) and restrictions by the European Union (EU) on Faroe Islands' fishing products and vessels (*EU – Herring*) as discriminatory measures under Articles I or III of the GATT 1994;[15]
- The *EC-Scallops* measure and sardine marketing standards (*EC – Sardines*) under the TBT Agreement;[16]
- The *EU – Herring* bans, Japanese quotas on laver (*Japan – Laver*),[17] and a Chilean ban on unloading swordfish in domestic ports (*Chile – Swordfish*) as prohibited quantitative restrictions under Article XI of GATT 1994;[18] and
- Various trade remedy measures as contrary to rules in the Trade Remedy Agreements, such as anti-dumping duties by the EU over salmon from Norway

14 As discussed further in the concluding observations, the true objective of a measure will often be debated between the parties. Thus, the authors recognise that other commentators could debate the categorisation of certain measures – although well-grounded and explained. An illustration is the *EU – Herring* dispute in which Denmark in Respect of the Faroe Islands challenged trade measures by the European Union (EU) under the WTO Agreement and simultaneously challenged the EU's failure to cooperate in management of the shared herring stock, through proceedings under Annex VII of the United National Convention on the Law of the Sea, 10 December 1982, 1833 UNTS 3, entered into force 16 November 1994. Public statements by the Faroe Islands indicate that there was no dispute on the need for conservation measures in the form of a total allowable catch. However, there was a dispute about the allocation of the total allowable catch to different coastal States, see for example, WTO, 'Dispute Settlement Body: Minutes of Meeting Held in the Centre William Rappard on 22 January 2014' (25 April 2014) WT/DSB/M/341. docs.wto.org/dol2fe/Pages/SS/directdoc.aspx?filename=q:/WT/DSB/M341.pdf accessed 3 January 2024, para 5.3. Since the point of contention between the Faroe Islands and the EU was about allocation rather than conservation, this chapter treats the measures at issue as pursuing fundamentally 'economic' interests.

15 See WTO, 'DS14: European Communities – Trade Description of Scallops'. www.wto.org/english/tratop_e/dispu_e/cases_e/ds14_e.htm accessed 3 January 2024; WTO, 'DS469: European Union – Measures on Atlanto-Scandian Herring'. www.wto.org/english/tratop_e/dispu_e/cases_e/ds469_e.htm.

16 See WTO, 'DS231: European Communities – Trade Description of Sardines'. www.wto.org/english/tratop_e/dispu_e/cases_e/ds231_e.htm accessed 3 January 2024. The Philippines and the United States also engaged in consultations over a ban by the United States on the import of certain shrimp and shrimp products from the Philippines, with the Philippines alleging violations under the GATT 1994 and TBT Agreement, see WTO, 'DS324: United States – Provisional Anti-Dumping Measures on Shrimp from Thailand'. www.wto.org/english/tratop_e/dispu_e/cases_e/ds324_e.htm accessed 3 January 2024.

17 See WTO, 'DS323: Japan – Import Quotas on Dried Laver and Seasoned Laver'. www.wto.org/english/tratop_e/dispu_e/cases_e/ds323_e.htm accessed 3 January 2024

18 See WTO, 'DS193: Chile – Measures affecting the Transit and Importing of Swordfish'. www.wto.org/english/tratop_e/dispu_e/cases_e/ds193_e.htm accessed 3 January 2024, which also involved issues under GATT 1994, art V.

> (*EC – Salmon*),[19] fish fillets from Viet Nam (*US – Fish Fillets*),[20] and shrimp from various sources (e.g., *US – Shrimp (Ecuador)* and *US – Shrimp (Viet Nam)*);[21] anti-dumping and countervailing duties by the United States over frozen warmwater shrimp (*US-Customs Bond Directive*);[22] and countervailing measures and safeguards by the EU or the United States over salmon.[23]

A notable pattern for many of these disputes is the speed with which they concluded. Parties in several of these disputes ended the proceedings before the circulation of a panel report.[24] For instance, various countervailing duties and safeguards issues were resolved at the consultations stage. *Japan – Laver*, *EC – Scallops*, and *EU – Herring* were all settled through mutually agreed solutions during the panel phase. In *Chile – Swordfish*, the parties discontinued proceedings before the panel reached a decision.[25] In *US – Fish Fillets*, the parties prevented the panel report's circulation. In the cases that progressed further, there were no additional proceedings after panels found inconsistencies in *EC – Salmon, US – Shrimp (Ecuador)*, and *US – Shrimp (Viet Nam)*, or after the Appellate Body upheld findings of inconsistency in *EC – Sardines* and *US – Customs Bond Directive*.[26]

19 See WTO, 'DS337: European Communities – Anti-Dumping Measure on Farmed Salmon from Norway'. www.wto.org/english/tratop_e/dispu_e/cases_e/ds337_e.htm accessed 3 January 2024.

20 See WTO, 'DS536: United States – Anti-Dumping Measures on Fish Fillets from Vietnam'. www.wto.org/english/tratop_e/dispu_e/cases_e/ds536_e.htm accessed 3 January 2024.

21 See WTO, 'DS335: United States – Anti-Dumping Measure on Shrimp from Ecuador'. www.wto.org/english/tratop_e/dispu_e/cases_e/ds335_e.htm accessed 3 January 2024; WTO, 'DS429: United States – Anti-Dumping Measures on Certain Shrimp from Viet Nam'. www.wto.org/english/tratop_e/dispu_e/cases_e/ds429_e.htm accessed 3 January 2024.

22 See 'DS345: United States – Customs Bond Directive for Merchandise Subject to Anti-Dumping/Countervailing Duties'. www.wto.org/english/tratop_e/dispu_e/cases_e/ds345_e.htm accessed 3 January 2024.

23 On relevant countervailing duty consultations, see WTO, 'DS97: United States – Countervailing Duty Investigation of Imports of Salmon from Chile'. www.wto.org/english/tratop_e/dispu_e/cases_e/ds97_e.htm accessed 3 January 2024. On safeguards consultations, see WTO, 'DS328: European Communities – Definitive Safeguard Measure on Salmon'. www.wto.org/english/tratop_e/dispu_e/cases_e/ds328_e.htm accessed 3 January 2024.

24 Under the steps set out in the Understanding on Rules and Procedures for the Settlement of Disputes, in WTO proceedings, members must first attempt to resolve issue in consultations, before proceeding to the panel stage. Once the panel report is publicly circulated, parties may appeal the panel's decision under the Dispute Settlement Understanding, art 17. Following the circulation of an appellate report (or panel report, in the absence of an appeal), the WTO's Dispute Settlement Body (DSB) adopts the report(s) and the responding party must comply with relevant rulings and recommendations. Parties to the dispute may subsequently bring compliance proceedings (panel, and potentially appellate) to resolve disagreements over the respondent's compliance with the DSB's rulings and recommendations. Where the responding party fails to bring its measure into compliance, the DSB may authorise countermeasures with the level of countermeasures determined by arbitration.

25 See WTO, 'DS193: Chile – Measures affecting the Transit and Importing of Swordfish'. www.wto.org/english/tratop_e/dispu_e/cases_e/ds193_e.htm accessed 3 January 2024.

26 In *US – Shrimp (Viet Nam)*, the parties notified a mutually agreed solution following the expiry of the reasonable period of time for the United States to implement recommendations and rulings, see

The willingness of responding members to settle cases suggests that they generally have limited incentive to engage in a protracted defence of economic trade measures where there are plausible claims of violation. Such conduct would be consistent with an understanding, held by the respective defending parties, that adjudicators follow an orthodox and predictable application of WTO disciplines in economic-trade cases. Such strict application may be particularly expected when the cases involve cardinal principles, such as non-discrimination (e.g., under Articles I and III of the GATT 1994) or the prohibition on quantitative restrictions under Article XI of the GATT 1994. Indeed, the examples previously listed which would have required findings under these specific provisions settled *early* in the proceedings. This suggests that the respondents perceived a relatively high risk that panels would find violations, based on the claims raised and the nature of the measures at issue.[27] Moreover, relevant exceptions (such as Article XX of the GATT 1994) focus on non-economic policies.[28] This means that members have limited options to justify any findings that their economic trade measures violated other provisions.

The agreements that apply in trade remedy cases, such as *EC – Salmon* and *US – Customs Bond Directive*, establish permissive regimes.[29] These regimes allow members to impose measures to counteract a specific economic harm (thereby fulfilling an economic objective), but within narrow and rigorous parameters. The rules are detailed; they require careful adherence to a series of requirements before the measures can be applied. For example, the adjudicators' assessment under the Anti-Dumping Agreement in *EC – Salmon* focused on evidence relating to an EU determination to impose anti-dumping measures on Norwegian-farmed salmon imports, which touched on precise profit, production, finance, and other data.[30]

WTO, 'United States – Anti-Dumping Measures on Certain Shrimp from Viet Nam'. www.wto.org/english/tratop_e/dispu_e/cases_e/ds404_e.htm accessed 3 January 2024.

27 As noted in the text, *Japan – Laver*, *EC – Scallops*, and *EU – Herring* were all settled during the panel phase. The parties in *Japan – Laver* and *EC – Scallops* had additionally notified a mutually agreed solution to the DSB. In *Chile – Swordfish*, the parties discontinued proceedings before the panel reached a decision. In *US – Fish Fillets*, the parties requested the postponement of the panel report's circulation until November 2023 (after the date of writing). These cases all involved claims under one or several of the cornerstone provisions in GATT 1994, arts I, III and XI.

28 The GATT 1994, art XX exceptions for violations cover measures serving other purposes: public morals, health, exhaustible natural resources, prison labour, national treasures, essential materials, and compliance with other laws. The TBT Agreement lists similar grounds as examples when requiring that technical regulations not be more trade restrictive than necessary to fulfil a 'legitimate objective', see TBT Agreement, art 2.2. In addressing this provision, the Appellate Body considered that 'those objectives expressly listed provide a reference point for which other objectives may be considered to be legitimate in the sense of Article 2.2', Appellate Body Report on *United States – Measures Concerning the Importation, Marketing and Sale of Tuna and Tuna Products*, WT/DS381/AB/R, adopted 13 June 2012, para 313.

29 As noted previously, these agreements include the Anti-Dumping Agreement, the SCM Agreement, and the Agreement on Safeguards.

30 See, for example, Panel Report on *European Communities – Anti-Dumping Measure on Farmed Salmon from Norway*, adopted 15 January 2008, sections VII.E, F, G, and H.

There is little room for regulatory space when applying a long list of specific tests to detailed accounting or economic data.

In short, the application of basic WTO disciplines and the absence of exceptions to justify economic-trade measures restricts members' regulatory space for this category of measure. This is reflected in cases involving marine resource products: responding members have avoided drawing out proceedings in which their defensive options would be limited. As discussed in the following sub-sections, the regulatory space available for members becomes greater for measures with non-economic objectives, namely in the categories of SPS trade, environment trade, and moral trade measures.

4.2. 'SPS-Trade' Measures

The specific requirements of the SPS Agreement govern measures with SPS objectives.[31] The SPS Agreement develops the exception in Article XX(b) of the GATT 1994 for measures 'necessary to protect human, animal or plant life or health'.[32] As a result, the imposition of SPS measures becomes an 'autonomous right' rather than an exception.[33] This elaboration has dual implications for the regulatory flexibility extended to SPS measures. First, the SPS Agreement reinforces the regulatory space carved out by Article XX(b) by offering a specific niche for SPS measures. Second, it introduces objective disciplines which impose explicit, and thus more certain, limits to this regulatory space.

The SPS Agreement offers two main pathways to compliance.[34] The first pathway allows members to conform their measures to an international standard, in accordance with Article 3.1 of the SPS Agreement. If a measure complies with an international standard, it is presumed to be consistent with relevant provisions of the SPS Agreement and the GATT 1994.[35] This pathway provides members with a straightforward but narrow flexibility to deviate from trade rules on objective grounds which are determined externally by the member imposing the measure.

Under the second pathway, members may adopt higher levels of protection based on scientific risk assessments. Under this pathway, members do not benefit from a presumption of consistency with relevant SPS provisions. Instead, they are subject to an exacting set of disciplines imposing requirements which are more extensive than, for example, the environmental exception under Article XX(g) of the GATT 1994 which is discussed in the next sub-section. Under Article 5 of the SPS Agreement, members must, as a starting point, fulfil certain technical

31 SPS Agreement, art 1.1 and Annex A(1).

32 SPS Agreement, preamble.

33 See, for example, Appellate Body Report on *European Communities – Measures Concerning Meat and Meat Products (Hormones)*, WT/DS26/AB/R, WT/DS48/AB/R, adopted 13 February 1998, para 172.

34 Members may also adopt provisional measures where relevant scientific evidence is insufficient, subject to certain requirements, see SPS Agreement, art 5.7.

35 SPS Agreement, art 3.2.

requirements related to risk assessments.[36] They must also avoid 'arbitrary or unjustifiable' distinctions in the levels of protection for different but comparable situations, where these distinctions result in discrimination or a disguised restriction on international trade.[37] Additionally, members must apply SPS measures only 'to the extent necessary' to achieve SPS objectives.[38] Further, they must ensure that no reasonably available, and significantly less trade-restrictive, alternative measures could achieve the appropriate level of SPS protection.[39] SPS measures are also subject to obligations on adaptation to regional conditions;[40] transparency;[41] and control, inspection, and approval procedures.[42]

Members pursuing SPS objectives must tailor their measures to these various rules.[43] For example, the adjudicators in *Australia – Salmon* determined that an initial measure and a subsequent compliance measure did not comply with core SPS obligations.[44] In particular, Australia had failed to meet the technical risk assessment requirements under Articles 5.1 and 2.2 at both stages. First, it did not base its original measure on a risk assessment, and second, it did not ensure that there was a 'rational relationship' between its subsequent risk assessment and its compliance measure.[45]

Australia's measures also deviated from the SPS Agreement's provisions on the consistency and trade restrictiveness of the measure. Specifically, the original measure violated Articles 5.5 and 2.3 because the levels of protection applied to salmon, as opposed to certain herring and finfish, constituted 'arbitrary or unjustifiable' distinctions amounting to a disguised restriction on trade.[46] The compliance measure did not account for less-trade restrictive alternative measures which could

36 SPS Agreement, arts 5.1–5.3.

37 SPS Agreement, arts 2.3, 5.5.

38 SPS Agreement, art 2.2.

39 SPS Agreement, art 5.6 and footnote three.

40 SPS Agreement, art 6.

41 SPS Agreement, art 7.

42 SPS Agreement, art 8.

43 Other than through adherence to international standards.

44 *Australia – Salmon* is not the only dispute which has dealt with SPS measures in the context of marine resources trade. In *Korea – Radionuclides (Japan)*, Japan challenged certain import bans and testing requirements for radionuclides as discriminatory and more trade-restrictive than necessary. These import bans and testing requirements impacted both marine products as well as general food products. Although Japan prevailed before the panel, the Appellate Body identified legal errors in the panel's analysis and could not make its own findings on certain key SPS issues due to limitations in the panel's factual analysis. See WTO, 'DS495: Korea – Import Bans, and Testing and Certification Requirements for Radionuclides'. www.wto.org/english/tratop_e/dispu_e/cases_e/ds495_e.htm accessed 3 January 2024.

45 Appellate Body Report on *Australia – Measures Affecting Importation of Salmon*, WT/DS18/AB/R, adopted 6 November 1998, paras 112–38; Panel Report on recourse to Article 21.5 on *Australia – Measures Affecting Importation of Salmon*, WT/DS18/RW, adopted 20 March 2000, paras 7.84–7.85.

46 Appellate Body Report on *Australia – Measures Affecting Importation of Salmon*, WT/DS18/AB/R, adopted 6 November 1998, paras 139–78.

have achieved the appropriate level of protection, within the meaning of Article 5.6 and footnote three.[47] Ultimately, Australia committed to modify its measures under an agreement with Canada, rather than engage in proceedings beyond the first compliance panel.[48]

The multiple issues in *Australia – Salmon* illustrate that, while the SPS Agreement offers regulatory space for SPS measures which is not available for economic-trade measures, its exacting layers of rules still limit this regulatory space. Thus, SPS measures occupy a more flexible, but not unconstrained, position on the continuum of regulatory space available to members.

4.3. 'Environment-Trade' Measures

Disputes over environment-trade measures involving marine resources have generally involved lengthy proceedings, in which adjudicators have carefully assessed the relevant environmental objective.[49] *US – Shrimp* addressed a trade-restrictive certification scheme by the United States for shrimp imports from countries with programmes, waters, or methods reducing the risk, or creating no risk, of incidental capture of sea turtles through shrimp fishing.[50] *US – Tuna II (Mexico)* addressed discriminatory conditions imposed on the application of 'dolphin-safe' labels to tuna products imported, marketed, and sold in the United States to inform consumers that the tuna was not harvested in a harmful way to dolphins.[51]

In both cases, the United States sought to defend GATT violations through the exception for measures 'relating to' the conservation of exhaustible natural

47 Panel Report on recourse to Article 21.5 on *Australia – Measures Affecting Importation of Salmon*, WT/DS18/RW, adopted 20 March 2000, para 7.153.

48 On the sequence of proceedings, see WTO, 'DS18: Australia – Measures Affecting Importation of Salmon'. www.wto.org/english/tratop_e/dispu_e/cases_e/ds18_e.htm accessed 3 January 2024.

49 Relevant cases at the date of writing are *US – Shrimp* (original and compliance proceedings) and *US – Tuna II (Mexico)* (original and compliance proceedings). GATT 1994, art XX(b) and (g) have been invoked in numerous cases not involving marine resources, but in which the respondent indicated that it was pursuing environmental objectives. Such cases include *US – Gasoline, Brazil – Retreaded Tyres, Brazil – Retreaded Tyres, China – Raw Materials,* and *China – Rare Earths.*

50 In the original proceedings, the complainants were India, Malaysia, Pakistan, and Thailand; only Malaysia engaged in subsequent compliance proceedings. See WTO, 'DS58: United States – Import Prohibition of Certain Shrimp and Shrimp Products'. www.wto.org/english/tratop_e/dispu_e/cases_e/ds58_e.htm accessed 3 January 2004; Panel Report on *United States – Import Prohibition of Certain Shrimp and Shrimp Products*, WT/DS58/R, adopted 6 November 1998, paras 1.1–1.2 and 2.4–2.16. The restrictive measures were found in the original proceedings to be contrary to GATT 1994, art XI:1. This raised the question of whether they could be justified under an affirmative defence.

51 Panel Report on *United States – Measures Concerning the Importation, Marketing and Sale of Tuna and Tuna Products,* WT/DS381/R, adopted 13 June 2012, Section II. Under the Panel's GATT analysis, the discriminatory measures were found in the original proceedings to be contrary to GATT 1994, arts I:1 and III:4. This raised the question of whether they could be justified under an affirmative defence. They measures were also found to raise issues concerning the 'less favourable treatment' standard under the TBT Agreement, art 2.2.

resources.[52] The term 'relating to' is generally understood to be more flexible than the word 'necessary'. 'Necessary' appears in several other subparagraphs of Article XX – notably Article XX(b) which permits GATT-inconsistent measures 'necessary to protect human, animal or plant life or health'. In the *US – Shrimp* case, the Appellate Body held that 'relating to' requires a 'means and ends relationship' between the measure and the conservation objective.[53] The United States could, in both cases, provisionally justify the respective measures as falling within this exception.[54] This highlights the existence of regulatory space for conservation measures which is hardwired into the treaty text.

In the *US – Shrimp* case, the Appellate Body avoided the vexed question of whether defences under Article XX(g) (or, indeed, Article XX(b)) can be invoked to defend measures aimed at securing environmental outcomes beyond the national jurisdiction of the regulating member. The measure in *US – Shrimp* addressed shrimp-harvesting practices *outside* areas in which the United States enjoyed sovereign rights. However, the Appellate Body noted that the species that the United

52 That is, the defence under GATT 1994, art XX(g). See Panel Report on *United States – Import Prohibition of Certain Shrimp and Shrimp Products*, WT/DS58/R, adopted 6 November 1998, paras 3.144 and 3.146; Panel Report on recourse to Article 21.5 by Mexico on *United States – Measures Concerning the Importation, Marketing and Sale of Tuna and Tuna Products*, WT/DS381/RW, adopted 3 December 2015, para 7.507; Panel Reports on recourse to Article 21.5 by the United States and second recourse to Article 21.5 by Mexico on *United States – Measures Concerning the Importation, Marketing and Sale of Tuna and Tuna Products*, WT/DS381/RW/USA, WT/DS381/RW2, adopted 11 January 2019, para 7.730. In *US – Shrimp*, the United States also argued that in the alternative, the measure was 'necessary to protect human, animal or plant life or health' under art XX(b), see Appellate Body Report on *United States – Import Prohibition of Certain Shrimp and Shrimp Products,* WT/DS58/AB/R, adopted 6 November 1998, para 10.

53 Appellate Body Report on *United States – Import Prohibition of Certain Shrimp and Shrimp Products,* WT/DS58/AB/R, adopted 6 November 1998, para 141. In this way, the 'relating to' standard does not require a consideration of whether the member could deploy less-trade restrictive measures to meet its objective, which has been held to be a basic requirement of the necessity test in successive cases under other provisions of GATT 1994, art XX. Indeed, in its very first case, *US – Gasoline*, the Appellate Body faulted the panel for reading into the 'relating to' standard a requirement to explore less-restrictive, reasonably available alternatives, Appellate Body Report on *United States – Standards for Reformulated and Conventional Gasoline*, WT/DS2/AB/R, adopted 20 May 1996, 16.

54 This includes broad coverage of the types of resources which can be covered. In *US – Shrimp*, for example, the Appellate Body explained that measures under art XX(g) may target living resources, see Appellate Body Report on *United States – Import Prohibition of Certain Shrimp and Shrimp Products,* WT/DS58/AB/R, adopted 6 November 1998, para 128. The Appellate Body also held that the relationship with 'domestic production or consumption' can be fulfilled where there is a 'sufficient nexus' between a migratory species and the respondent's territory (para 133). The Appellate Body also emphasised the need to give the provision a contemporary reading. It stated that it 'must be read by a treaty interpreter in the light of contemporary concerns of the community of nations about the protection and conservation of the environment' and that the 'generic term "natural resources" in art XX(g) is not "static" in its content or reference but is rather "by definition, evolutionary"' (paras 129–30). This finding was significant in rejecting the argument of the complainants that 'exhaustible natural resources' were limited to minerals and did not include living marine resources capable of reproduction and hence renewal.

States sought to conserve – sea turtles – migrated in a manner which brought them into the United States' jurisdiction. On this basis, the Appellate Body found that the United States was entitled to invoke Article XX and said:

> We do not pass upon the question of whether there is an implied jurisdictional limitation in Article XX(g), and if so, the nature or extent of that limitation. We note only that in the specific circumstances of the case before us, there is a sufficient nexus between the migratory and endangered marine populations involved and the United States for purposes of Article XX(g).[55]

Over 20 years later, the jurisprudence has not resolved questions over the territorial limits of members' rights to invoke defences in Article XX.

To invoke successfully Article XX, in addition to justifying provisionally a measure under a subparagraph, a member must also demonstrate that its measure is not applied in a manner constituting 'arbitrary or unjustifiable discrimination between countries where the same conditions prevail'.[56] This language in the chapeau to Article XX limits the regulatory space conferred by exceptions in Article XX. In *US – Shrimp*, the Appellate Body explained that this prevents 'abusive' recourse to the exceptions.[57] Thus, it balances the WTO Agreement's objectives of economic efficiency and 'protecting and preserving the environment'.[58]

In *US – Shrimp*, the original measure by the United States failed under the chapeau as it arbitrarily and unjustifiably discriminated between countries where the same conditions prevailed. The measure's coercive nature discriminated by imposing a 'rigid and unbending standard', which required all exporting members to adopt measures 'essentially the same' as the United States' programme, without inquiry whether the programme was appropriate for regulatory conditions in the

55 Appellate Body Report on *United States – Import Prohibition of Certain Shrimp and Shrimp Products*, WT/DS58/AB/R, adopted 6 November 1998, para 133. The famous 'Tuna-Dolphin' panels under the GATT 1947 dispute settlement system had touched on this issue and reached contradictory findings. In the first Tuna-Dolphin case, the panel found that contracting parties to the GATT were only entitled to protect living things within their jurisdiction, see Panel Report under GATT on *United States – Restrictions on Imports of Tuna*, DS21/R – 39S/155, adopted 3 September 1991, para 5.26. By contrast in the second Tuna-Dolphin case, the Panel found in principle that a contracting party can in some circumstances protect living things outside its territory, see Panel Report under GATT on *United States – Restrictions on Imports of Tuna*, DS29/R, adopted 16 June 1994, para 5.20. the GATT Council did not adopt either of the panel reports under the opt-in dispute settlement system of the GATT 1947, meaning they did not acquire binding force between the parties.

56 The Appellate Body in *US – Shrimp* clarified that the correct sequence of analysis is to examine whether the measure fulfils the relevant requirement under the paragraph of art XX, followed by the requirements under the chapeau, see Appellate Body Report on *United States – Import Prohibition of Certain Shrimp and Shrimp Products*, WT/DS58/AB/R, adopted 6 November 1998, para 122.

57 Appellate Body Report on *United States – Import Prohibition of Certain Shrimp and Shrimp Products*, WT/DS58/AB/R, adopted 6 November 1998, para 158. The Appellate Body characterised the chapeau as expressing the concepts of good faith and *abus de droit*, making clear that the exceptions in the subparagraphs are '*limited* and *conditional* rights': see Appellate Body Report, paras 157–8 (emphasis in original).

58 See, for example, the first preambular paragraph of the Marrakesh Agreement Establishing the World Trade Organization, 15 April 1994, 1867 UNTS 154, entered into force 1 January 1995.

exporting members.[59] Additionally, the United States did not consistently seek to engage all exporting members in serious negotiations on agreements for protecting and conserving sea turtles before enforcing the measure.[60] Moreover, the measure set forth a certification process with 'little or no flexibility' and denied rejected applicants 'basic fairness and due process'.[61] In *US – Tuna II (Mexico)*, aspects of the compliance measure likewise constituted arbitrary or unjustifiable discrimination. In particular, the measure failed to provide the same conditions of access to the dolphin-safe label in circumstances of comparable risk.[62] In both cases, the United States successfully defended its measures in compliance proceedings, after adjusting its application to even-handedly address the relevant conditions prevailing in the different countries from which the fisheries products were sourced.[63]

US – Tuna II (Mexico) also sheds light on the regulatory space available to members for measures constituting 'technical regulations' under the TBT Agreement.[64] In contrast to the GATT 1994, the TBT Agreement does not set forth exceptions which are distinct from the Agreement's primary disciplines. Nevertheless, the Appellate Body interpreted the non-discrimination provision in Article 2.1 of the TBT Agreement as providing regulatory space for environmental objectives in a manner 'not, in principle, different' to that set out in the GATT 1994.[65] Specifically, the Appellate Body developed a two-step test to determine whether treatment of one product under a technical regulation is 'less favourable' than treatment of an equivalent product of different origin. First, the adjudicator considers whether the second product receives detrimental treatment. Second, the adjudicator considers whether the detrimental

59 Appellate Body Report on *United States – Import Prohibition of Certain Shrimp and Shrimp Products*, WT/DS58/AB/R, adopted 6 November 1998, para 161–5.

60 ibid, paras 166–72, 177. Interestingly, the Appellate Body the question of whether Article XX(g) could justify conservation measures targeting resources entirely outside the jurisdiction of the regulating member. The Appellate Body commented on the issue because the regulated activity – shrimp fishing – took place outside the jurisdiction of the United States. However, the Appellate Body avoided ruling on whether there is an 'implied jurisdictional limitation' in Article XX because the protected resource – turtles – were migratory, spending part of their lifecycle in waters under the jurisdiction of the United States. See ibid, para 133.

61 ibid, paras 177–84.

62 Appellate Body Report on recourse to Article 21.5 by Mexico on *United States – Measures Concerning the Importation, Marketing and Sale of Tuna and Tuna Products*, WT/DS381/AB/RW, adopted 3 December 2015, para 7.359.

63 See ibid; Appellate Body Reports on recourse to Article 21.5 by the United States and second recourse to Article 21.5 by Mexico on *United States – Measures Concerning the Importation, Marketing and Sale of Tuna and Tuna Products*, WT/DS381/AB/RW/USA, WT/DS381/AB/RW2, adopted 11 January 2019; Appellate Body Report on recourse to Article 21.5 on *United States – Import Prohibition of Certain Shrimp and Shrimp Products*, WT/DS58/AB/RW, adopted 21 November 2001.

64 'Technical regulation' is a defined expression referring to mandatory product requirements. Technical regulations are contrasted with 'standards', which are documents laying down product characteristics in a non-mandatory manner.

65 Appellate Body Report on *United States – Measures Affecting the Production and Sale of Clove Cigarettes*, WT/DS406/AB/R, 24 April 2012, para 109.

treatment stems exclusively from a 'legitimate regulatory distinction'. The measure will violate the TBT Agreement only if it fails both limbs of the test.[66]

Some have criticised this test developed by the Appellate Body to determine whether treatment is 'less favourable' in the sense of the treaty text. Others welcomed it as meeting a legitimate need to ensure members enjoy regulatory space for technical regulations. According to distinguished commentators, the TBT Agreement's 'omission of a general exception such as Article XX had to be compensated by a dogmatically tenable contextual and teleological interpretation'.[67] In any event, the United States struggled to meet the Appellate Body's test in the *US – Tuna II* proceedings. It unsuccessfully attempted to defend against Article 2.1 claims in the original and first compliance proceedings, before succeeding in subsequent compliance proceedings.[68]

Overall, the complexity of these disputes reflects the more flexible position that environment-trade measures occupy compared to economic-trade measures – and, to a lesser extent, SPS trade measures – in the continuum of regulatory space available to WTO members. It also reflects respondents' willingness to test (even repeatedly) the defensive potential of this regulatory space against its somewhat ambiguous limits.

4.4. 'Moral-Trade' Measures

This sub-section analyses measures falling under a different provision of Article XX, namely the exception under Article XX(a) GATT 1994 for measures 'necessary to protect public morals'. Members have invoked the Article XX(a) exception for various trade measures. This included in *EC – Seal Products* a measure affecting trade in products from marine resources. The analytical framework applicable under Article XX(a) follows the two-step structure of Article XX(g) discussed previously. Specifically, the respondent must, first, provisionally justify its measure on the basis that it pursues the policy objective protected by the subparagraph: under Article XX(a), the measure must be 'necessary to protect public morals'. If this requirement is met, the respondent must then demonstrate that the measure meets the requirements of the chapeau to Article XX.

66 ibid, para 215. See also, Appellate Body Report on *United States – Measures Concerning the Importation, Marketing and Sale of Tuna and Tuna Products*, WT/DS381/AB/R, adopted 13 June 2012, paras 215–6.

67 Mitsuo Matsushita et al., *The World Trade Organization: Law, Practice and Policy* (OUP 2015) 451.

68 Appellate Body Report on *United States – Measures Concerning the Importation, Marketing and Sale of Tuna and Tuna Products*, WT/DS381/AB/R, adopted 13 June 2012; Appellate Body Report on recourse to Article 21.5 by Mexico on *United States – Measures Concerning the Importation, Marketing and Sale of Tuna and Tuna Products*, WT/DS381/AB/RW, adopted 3 December 2015; Appellate Body Reports on recourse to Article 21.5 by the United States and second recourse to Article 21.5 by Mexico on *United States – Measures Concerning the Importation, Marketing and Sale of Tuna and Tuna Products*, WT/DS381/AB/RW/USA, WT/DS381/AB/RW2, adopted 11 January 2019.

However, the analysis under Article XX(a) differs from Article XX(g) in two ways. First, Article XX(a) imposes a requirement to assess alternative ways of achieving the objective by requiring that a measure be 'necessary' to protect morals (rather than simply 'relat[e] to' conservation).[69] Second, the test requires ascertaining a member's 'moral' concerns, rather than objective considerations, such as whether there are 'exhaustible natural resources' capable of 'conservation'.[70] The first difference imposes a higher standard of justification upon respondents. However, WTO adjudicators have adopted a deferential approach to the second difference, thereby expanding the regulatory space open to measures addressing 'moral' concerns.

EC – Seal Products illustrates this deferential approach to a member's 'morals'. The EU defended a ban on seal products from commercial hunts under Article XX(a). The panel accepted the EU's claims that there were seal welfare concerns in the EU and that these concerns were of a moral nature.[71] 'Morals' was defined broadly as 'standards of right and wrong' according to a community's 'own systems and scales of values'.[72] In reviewing the panel's analysis, the Appellate Body confirmed the panel's approach and stated that panels are 'not required to identify the exact content' of the moral.[73] Thus, members have extremely broad leeway to assert moral justifications. Indeed, subsequent panels applied the same approach as in *EC – Seal Products* and showed remarkable deference to respondents' asserted ethical positions. For instance, a panel accepted that the United States' unilateral imposition of tariffs against China, which addressed concerns with economic aspects, could be moral in nature.[74]

The deferential standard for identifying morals, and particularly the lack of requirement to attribute precise content, impacts the otherwise rigorous 'necessity' requirement in Article XX(a). In *EC – Seal Products*, the Appellate Body rejected a Canadian argument that, as part of its necessity analysis, a panel should ascertain

69 WTO adjudicators have operationalised the 'necessity' test in several subparagraphs of Article XX by requiring parties to address four steps: (i) the importance of the objective; (ii) the trade restrictiveness of the measure; (iii) the contribution of the measure to attaining the objective; and (iv) whether a reasonably available alternative measure would achieve the same or greater contribution. A panel assesses

> all the relevant factors, particularly the extent of the contribution to the achievement of the measures objective, in the light of the importance of the interests or values at stake. If this analysis yields a preliminary conclusion that the measure is necessary, this result must be confirmed by comparing the measure with its possible alternatives, which may be less trade restrictive while providing an equivalent contribution to the achievement of the objective pursued.

See Appellate Body Report on *Brazil – Measures Affecting Imports of Retreaded Tyres*, WT/DS332/AB/R, adopted 17 December 2007, para 156.

70 See commentary in footnote 54 on the finding in *US – Shrimp* that living resources (i.e., sea turtles) can constitute exhaustible natural resources within the meaning of GATT 1994, art XX(g).

71 Panel Report on *European Communities – Measures Prohibiting the Importation and Marketing of Seal Products*, WT/DS400/R, WT/DS401/R, adopted 18 June 2014, para 7.410.

72 ibid, para 7.384.

73 ibid, para 5.199.

74 See Panel Report, *US – Tariff Measures*, paras 7.136–7.137.

the existence of a 'risk' to animal welfare morals and should consider whether this risk is addressed consistently across species.[75] In doing so, the Appellate Body asserted that objective methods of inquiry 'do not appear to be of much assistance or relevance' when considering morals.[76] By rejecting objective comparisons and accepting subjective assertions (e.g., that the welfare of some mammals is more important than the welfare of others), the Appellate Body left the chapeau to Article XX as the only real safeguard against abuse of the 'public morals' exception.

Ultimately, carve-outs from the measure in *EC – Seal Products*, which allowed trade in seal products from certain sources (while banning it from others), meant it failed under the Article XX chapeau. However, the approach to provisional justification under Article XX(a) in *EC – Seals* highlights that trade measures with an asserted moral objective – in other words, 'moral trade' measures under this chapter's categorisation – enjoy broader space than other policy areas.

5. Economic Policy Measures Affecting the Environment or 'Economic-Environment' Measures

The four categories of measures discussed previously share an important commonality: they are subject to WTO disciplines which primarily address *trade impacts*. Since 2001, WTO members have also sought to address *environmental impacts* in WTO legal provisions.[77] These efforts resulted, in June 2022, in an initial agreement to establish disciplines on subsidies which undermine fisheries' conservation and sustainability.[78]

Once in force, this agreement will prohibit subsidies which contribute to illegal, unreported, and unregulated fishing and certain other harmful activities.[79] Fisheries subsidies are primarily an economic policy tool which alters incentives for fishing

75 Appellate Body Report on *European Communities – Measures Prohibiting the Importation and Marketing of Seal Products*, WT/DS400/AB/R, WT/DS401/AB/R, adopted 18 June 2014, para 5.201. The Canadian argument here bore a resemblance to Canada's successful argument in *Australia – Salmon* that a failure to address the same risk in herring and finfish as was the focus of the salmon measure gave rise to 'arbitrary or unjustifiable' distinctions. However, unlike in *Australia – Salmon* where claims were made under specific and detailed provisions of the SPS Agreement, Canada's argument was built simply on the word 'protect' in GATT 1994, art XX(a). In *EC – Seal Products*, the Appellate Body contrasted the two sets of legal provisions, noting that the SPS requirements are considerably more elaborate: see Appellate Body Report on *European Communities – Measures Prohibiting the Importation and Marketing of Seal Products*, WT/DS400/AB/R, WT/DS401/AB/R, adopted 18 June 2014, para 5.197.

76 ibid, para 5.198.

77 See, for the fisheries subsidies mandate, WTO, 'Fisheries Subsidies: Ministerial Decision of 13 December 2017' (18 December 2017) WT/MIN(17)/64; Sustainable Development Goal Target 14.6 indicators.report/targets/14-6/ accessed 3 January 2024.

78 The primary target under SDG 14 is to '[c]onserve and sustainably use the oceans, seas and marine resources for sustainable development'.

79 See Protocol Amending the Marrakesh Agreement establishing the WTO, 'Agreement on Fisheries Subsidies, Not Yet in Force' (17 June 2022) docs.wto.org/dol2fe/Pages/SS/directdoc.aspx?filename=q:/WT/MIN22/33.pdf accessed 3 January 2024. By addressing these subsidies, the

effort compared to a free-market situation. In this way, they most closely resemble the economic trade measures described in sub-section 4.1. As with the economic trade measures, the new agreement affords members little regulatory space within which to adopt – or defend – subsidies subject to the prohibitions.[80] However, unlike the economic-trade measures, the fisheries subsidies agreement addresses environmental, rather than trade, impacts.

6. Concluding Observations

This chapter has drawn insights from WTO marine resources disputes about the regulatory space available to members to pursue various policy objectives. The frameworks that adjudicators have applied in these disputes vary depending on the categories of measures considered. Each category corresponds with a different underlying objective. An analysis of these categories indicates that there is a continuum of policy space which begins with the strict application of trade law disciplines for economic measures affecting trade, and which broadens out into incrementally greater flexibilities for SPS, environmental, and, finally, moral measures affecting trade.

The analysis noted the emergence of a fifth category, occupying a sui generis space outside the continuum of regulatory space for measures impacting trade: economic measures affecting the environment. This category is represented in the new WTO agreement on fisheries subsidies, which will apply trade disciplines to an economic measure (subsidies) with the aim of curbing harmful impacts to conservation and sustainability.

This chapter shows that the nature and margin of regulatory space accorded under trade agreements vary depending on the policy objective for which such regulatory space is sought. Three concluding observations emerge from this insight.

First, is there a good reason for giving members greater flexibility for some policies than others? Yes and no.

On the one hand, the WTO Agreement makes clear that there must be space for certain non-trade objectives. For instance, objectives pertaining to the environment appear in the first paragraph of the preamble to the WTO Agreement and are elaborated in general exceptions or as a component of certain obligations. Where the drafters of the WTO Agreement sought to impose disciplines on the regulatory space given by environmental exceptions, they developed additional rules. An example is the SPS Agreement which sets forth procedures and objective tests elaborating on the standard initially articulated in Article XX(b) of the GATT 1994. The recent development of new fisheries subsidies disciplines emphasises the importance of environmental objectives for WTO members.

agreement contributes a puzzle piece in the broader network of international efforts addressing fisheries issues, including through fora like the United Nations Food and Agriculture Organization.

80 The limited regulatory space provided for under the agreement includes time-limited exceptions for developing country members, see ibid, arts 3.8 and 4.4.

On the other hand, adjudicators have made choices which arguably grant excessive regulatory space in some policy areas. From this point of view, the degree of deference which adjudicators have granted for measures characterised as pursuing 'moral' objectives risks undermining the integrity of otherwise applicable rules. This is because labelling many unpopular causes as matters of 'right' or 'wrong' is relatively easy. Excessive flexibility would make it relatively easier to evade WTO disciplines, impacting the security and predictability of the system of trade rules.

Second, the existence of a continuum of regulatory space in which some policy objectives are subject to stricter discipline than others impacts how litigants deal with measures affecting trade in the context of disputes. The fact that the WTO rules confer different margins of regulatory space depending on the objectives pursued provides an incentive for parties in a dispute to characterise the measure in different ways. For example, a responding member may seek to label an animal welfare measure as addressing domestic 'moral' concerns (which could vary depending on the species of animal) rather than the 'health' of the animal (which would have to be applied more consistently). This approach could give the member access to greater regulatory space under the WTO rules. Conversely, a complainant challenging such a measure could seek to argue that the measure's objective is actually to favour particular economic interests, so as to narrow the regulatory space available to the respondent. These incentives mean that identifying the true objectives of a measure can be an important threshold issue in trade disputes.

Third, the analysis shows that the priorities of international trade law continue to evolve. Traditionally, members sought to carve out regulatory space from the provisions of trade rules to pursue, inter alia, environmental objectives. Existing exceptions and other flexibilities are primarily defensive: they operate as a shield for non-trade objectives, embedded in agreements which are fundamentally about promoting economic efficiency through trade. By contrast, the new rules under the fisheries subsidy's agreement provide a discrete offensive option – a sword – to restrict members from hindering a non-trade objective. This approach turns the traditional discussion of regulatory space on its head. Instead, it provides tools to constrain members' regulatory space to prevent negative environmental externalities.

This development represents a qualitative evolution in the way that governments view the role of trade rules in facilitating non-economic objectives. In addition to fisheries subsidies, WTO members are increasingly using the WTO as a forum to advance discussions on other environment-related issues, such as fossil fuel subsidy reform, plastic pollution, sustainable agriculture, and trade in environmental goods and services.[81] Similar momentum has also influenced the content of free trade agreements. Examples include the chapter on environment, which covers

81 See, for example, information on structured discussions within the WTO, 'Trade and Environmental Sustainability'. www.wto.org/english/tratop_e/tessd_e/tessd_e.htm accessed 2 January 2024

fisheries subsidies disciplines, in the Comprehensive and Progressive Agreement for Trans-Pacific Partnership, and the focus on climate under the EU – United Kingdom Trade and Cooperation Agreement.[82] In these ways and others, international practice on trade in marine resources will likely continue to evolve to give greater weight to environmental considerations.

82 See Comprehensive and Progressive Agreement for Trans-Pacific Partnership, 8 March 2018, 3346 UNTS, entered into force 30 December 2018; Trade and Cooperation Agreement between the European Union and the European Atomic Energy Community, of the one part, and the United Kingdom of Great Britain and Northern Ireland, of the other part, 30 December 2020, entered into force 1 May 2021, which designates the 'fight against climate change' as an 'essential element' under arts 764 and 770, as well as commitments, for example, under art 401.

19 Unilateral Harmonization and the Implementation of the Import Provisions of the U.S. Marine Mammal Protection Act

*Kathleen Claussen**

1. Introduction

The United States, the world's second-largest importer of fish, is on the cusp of upending the fish trade.[1] This move is the latest in a long and well-known set of U.S. environmental regulations regarding fish and marine mammals. For over 40 years, the United States Marine Mammal Protection Act (MMPA) has been at the heart of international trade discussions on access to the United States market for fisheries products.[2] In 1972, the MMPA established a national policy to prevent marine mammal species and population stocks from declining beyond repair. The MMPA's salience has grown in recent years as U.S. lawmakers continue to revise, refine, and reform its operation. The MMPA has prompted not just extensive regulations in the United States that have re-shaped certain fishing exercises, but it also led to several disputes at the World Trade Organization (WTO), where trading partners have brought claims against the United States alleging that the application of the MMPA was discriminatory in violation of the WTO Agreements.[3]

The MMPA's Import Rule, which takes effect at the end of 2025 after a nine-year moratorium, is the latest development in this long-running international debate.[4] This chapter examines the Rule's implementation process. At the prompting of several non-governmental organisations, the United States is re-structuring the obligations placed on all fisheries exporting to the United States, requiring them to

* The author wishes to thank the several current and former United States officials who agreed to speak about the developments surrounding the Marine Mammal Protection Act (MMPA).

1 United States Government Accountability Office, 'Down on the (Fish) Farm' (26 October 2017). www.gao.gov/blog/2017/10/26/down-on-the-fish-farm accessed 8 January 2024.

2 16 USC §§ 1361–407 (1976). See, for example, Terrin Child and Jeffrey Haley, 'The Marine Mammal Protection Act and the Fishery Conservation and Management Act: The Need for Balance' (1980) 56 *Washington Law Review* 397; Eric Erdheim, 'The Immediate Goal Test of the Marine Mammal Protection Act and the Tuna/Porpoise Controversy' (1979) 9 *Environmental Law* 283.

3 See, for example, World Trade Organization (WTO), 'DS381: United States – Measures Concerning the Importation, Marketing and Sale of Tuna and Tuna Products'. www.wto.org/english/tratop_e/dispu_e/cases_e/ds381_e.htm accessed 8 January 2024.

4 Fish and Fish Product Import Provisions of the Marine Mammal Protection Act, 81 FR 54,389, effective on 1 January 2017.

DOI: 10.4324/9781003492030-25

demonstrate a threshold level of protection of marine mammals set by the United States. In so doing, U.S. regulators have sought to manage the conditions of entry to respond to both environmental and animal advocates, as well as to business and foreign trading partners. The debate surrounding the MMPA Import Rule illustrates the regulatory struggle faced by governments as they seek to achieve different important public policy aims and to meet their respective international commitments, when these aims and commitments appear at cross-purposes.

2. The Import Rule

One of the primary purposes of the MMPA was to reduce marine mammal bycatch associated with international commercial fishing operations and to do so by requiring states exporting fish and fish products to the United States to be held to standards that would achieve that goal. The legislation directed the executive branch to accomplish this in part through a ban on imports of fish from States that did not have the same standards as those to which commercial fishing operations in the United States were held.

At the time of the MMPA's enactment, the anticipated ban was heralded as the first ecosystem-based approach to legislation for protecting marine life: an approach that integrates management of land, water, and living resources to promote conservation and sustainable use in an equitable way.[5] However, these goals were not realised as no action was taken, despite the mandatory nature of the legislative provision – until about 15 years ago. This section walks through this complicated history in brief and then describes the current state of play.

2.1. History

Section 101(a)(2) of the MMPA provides

> The Secretary of the Treasury shall ban the importation of commercial fish or products from fish which have been caught with commercial fishing technology which results in the incidental kill or incidental serious injury of ocean mammals in excess of United States standards. For purposes of applying the preceding sentence, the Secretary – (A) shall insist on reasonable proof from the government of any nation from which fish or fish products will be exported to the United States of the effects on ocean mammals of the commercial fishing technology in use for such fish or fish products exported from such nation to the United States.[6]

5 Convention on Biodiversity Secretariat, 'Ecosystem Approach' (23 August 2021). www.cbd.int/ecosystem/ accessed 8 January 2024.
6 16 USC § 1371(a)(2).

Further, Section 102(c)(3) makes it unlawful to import into the United States

> any fish, whether fresh, frozen, or otherwise prepared, if such fish was caught in a manner which the Secretary has proscribed for persons subject to the jurisdiction of the United States, whether or not any marine mammals were in fact taken incident to the catching of the fish.[7]

Although these provisions were present in the MMPA since 1972, the Secretary did not impose any ban.

In 2008, environmental groups challenged the government's inaction by way of a lawsuit that ultimately prompted the United States National Marine Fisheries Service to develop a rule implementing the legislative direction.[8] A final rule outlining the ban took effect on 1 January 2017. The rule also created a five-year, one-time exemption period for United States regulatory agencies to develop an appropriate regulatory framework and to implement it in cooperation with trading partners.[9] Due to the Covid-19 pandemic, the five-year exemption was extended to nine and, as of the time of writing, will expire on 31 December 2025.[10] Thus, beginning in January 2026, the United States expects to stop at its border any fish or fish product that does not qualify for import under the newly implemented rule.

Over the last several years, the United States has worked with its trading partners to prepare them for the implementation of the rule. The implementation of the rule has had three steps: (1) categorising fisheries as being covered or not by the rule; (2) evaluating covered fisheries; and (3) determining that covered fisheries may or not continue to export to the United States. Each of these steps has proven labour-intensive for United States regulators and for international trading partners. From 2017 until 2020, the primary work was the crafting of a list of qualifying fisheries. This classification required reviewing nearly 4,000 fisheries, as the next subsection explains.

2.2. The List of Foreign Fisheries

An essential first step in implementing the Import Rule was to develop a List of Foreign Fisheries.[11] This list classifies foreign commercial fisheries that export fish

7 16 USC § 1372(c)(3).

8 See, for example, Center for Biological Diversity, Turtle Island Restoration Network, 'Petition to Ban Imports of Swordfish from Countries Failing to Submit Proof of the Effects of Fishing Technology on Marine Mammals Pursuant to Marine Mammals Pursuant to Marine Mammal Protection Act Section 101' (4 March 2008). www.biologicaldiversity.org/campaigns/fisheries/pdfs/Swordfish-PetitionL.pdf accessed 8 January 2024.

9 50 CFR 216.24.

10 National Oceanic and Atmospheric Administration (NOAA) Fisheries, 'Modification of Deadlines Under the Fish and Fish Product Import Provisions of the Marine Mammal Protection Act' (17 November 2023) 87 FR 80,193.

11 See NOAA Fisheries, 'List of Foreign Fisheries'. www.fisheries.noaa.gov/foreign/international-affairs/list-foreign-fisheries accessed 8 January 2024.

and fish products to the United States as either 'export' or 'exempt' based on the frequency and likelihood of incidental mortality and serious injury of marine mammals.[12] Export fisheries are fisheries with more than a remote likelihood of marine mammal bycatch or insufficient information available on marine mammal interactions. In contrast, exempt fisheries have a remote likelihood of, or no known, incidental mortality or serious injury of marine mammals. Fisheries labelled as exempt need not continue the process toward an additional regulatory determination for importing fish into the United States.

In the present iteration of the more than 200-page list, 720 fisheries, or 18 percent of fisheries, are classified as 'exempt'.[13] Likewise, 25 States were eliminated from consideration because their fisheries do not fall within the regulatory scope of the rule. The remaining 3,270 fisheries from 138 States continue for further evaluation as detailed in the next subsection.

This list is the only comprehensive list of commercially relevant fisheries around the world, as no international organisation has done this work. It includes critical information about each fishery, in addition to some information on the state of play for marine mammals. Nevertheless, much of the information is the result of research carried out by United States government agencies. Not all foreign governments provided data (and many did not have any) on the status and methods of their respective fisheries. Rather, to develop this list, United States regulators reviewed and considered documentation provided directly by governments or subsidiary jurisdictions together with publicly available information and information from industry participants.[14]

2.3. Comparability Findings

The next step in the implementation process was for each of the States implicated by the fisheries list to apply for permission to export fish from their fisheries to the United States. At the time of writing, United States regulators are reviewing applications to determine whether each exporting fishery will be granted a positive 'comparability finding'. The comparability finding is the determination that the regulatory system in place for that fishery is comparable to the United States' regulatory system for that fishery.

12 ibid, noting that '[e]xempt fisheries are fisheries that have no known or a remote likelihood of marine mammal bycatch and are exempt from instituting a regulatory program.'

13 '2020 Final List of Foreign Fisheries'. s3.amazonaws.com/media.fisheries.noaa.gov/2020-10/LOFF_2020_IAICRS_508.pdf?null accessed 8 January 2024.

14 NOAA Fisheries, 'Compliance Guide – Marine Mammal Protection Act Import Provisions To Reduce Marine Mammal Bycatch'. media.fisheries.noaa.gov/dam-migration/mmpa_import_rule_compliance_guide.pdf accessed 8 January 2024, stating that it

> may determine whether a fishery is an exempt or export fishery by evaluating the fishery using information such as fishing techniques, gear used, methods used to deter marine mammals, target species, seasons and areas fished, qualitative data from logbooks or fisher reports, stranding data, the species and distribution of marine mammals in the area, or other factors.

The regulations establish criteria for evaluating a State's regulatory programme for reducing marine mammal bycatch in such fisheries and the procedures required to receive the comparability finding. These criteria and procedures are complex. Again, the baseline question is whether the State has devised a system for each fishery that regulates bycatch of marine mammals in a manner comparable to that required of like fisheries in the United States. The process for determining comparability has evolved as United States agencies have developed the conditions for each determination. Many determinations are made through a carefully constructed analogy. The standard of 'comparable in effect' has been selected to provide both flexibility and effectiveness in achieving the statutory aims.[15]

One former United States official described how the work of United States agencies in this rulemaking process was difficult because the statute speaks to an 'excess of U.S. standards'. Yet, there is no single standard in the United States. Instead, the process for making determinations of this type with respect to fisheries in the United States is conducted by regionalised take reduction teams, which include government regulators, non-governmental organisations, and academics. These teams develop an often bespoke and iterative mitigation plan that may be re-evaluated and refined.

The extensive regulatory review for the Import Rule has involved internal analytical processes in which experts consider how they would handle analogous situations in the United States. The United States Department of Commerce issued criteria that vary based on species, gear, and region, among other factors. Some requirements apply universally, and others are fishery-specific. For example, all harvesting States must either prohibit the intentional killing of marine mammals or certify that their fishery products are not the 'product of intentional killing' of marine mammals.[16] Harvesting States must provide population abundance and mortality data for marine mammals, including levels of fisheries bycatch.[17] The Import Rule also requires a list of possible regulatory components to address incidental mortality and serious injury of marine mammals.[18] Effective 1 January 2026, fish and fish products may only be imported into the United States if the harvesting State has applied for and received a comparability finding for the relevant fishery.[19]

At least three features stand out in this experimental implementation process. The first is the depth of research required on the part of United States regulators to make the necessary determinations. As with the fisheries list, regulators are building analyses from statements and documents provided by other States but also from other sources for States that did not cooperate in the research process. Throughout the exercise, regulators use information gleaned from their counterparts, together

15 50 CFR § 216.24(h).

16 50 CFR § 216.24(h)(iii)(A).

17 *Natural Resources Defense Council v. Ross*, 331 F Supp 3d 1338, 1363 (2018, United States Court of International Trade), where the court held that these components are required for a comparability finding.

18 50 CFR § 216(h)(6)(iii)(B).

19 50 CFR § 216.24(h)(2)(ii).

with anecdotal public information, resources from their embassies abroad, and industry members. According to those involved, having enough capacity within the United States government to sort through these data has been a challenge.

The second feature that stands out from this review is that 'effectiveness' in protecting marine mammals is part of the United States' analysis as to whether a fishery should receive a green light to export to the United States. Comparability findings are issued to individual fisheries, although many elements of these findings depend on the laws and regulations of the harvesting State. However, unlike some other equivalency determinations in the food safety and agricultural context, this process has two distinct steps. First, does the State have the right laws on the books? Second, are these laws effective in protecting marine mammals? Once the harvesting State presents its regulatory scheme, bureaucrats in the United States are not making their findings on that schematic information alone. Rather, they are monitoring and will continue to monitor effectiveness, in other words, whether the scheme achieves the bycatch goals the United States has set. Effectiveness is part of the eligibility finding.[20] Measuring effectiveness requires a level of understanding that neither government may have at present, which leads to a third observation.

The third feature is that many States may require considerable assistance to achieve the levels of protection and monitoring required to engage with the United States on these issues. United States agencies have provided limited assistance in this regard, as described further.

3. Fishy Trade Law Consistency

The top question on the minds of most trading partners, apart from whether they will be able to continue exporting, is whether the United States' approach to implementing this provision of the MMPA complies with WTO or other trade rules. This section analyses this question and considers what the development of the Import Rule indicates more generally about trade law and its future direction.

3.1. Past and Future WTO

Past MMPA measures have faced challenges at the WTO. Thus, United States officials are acutely aware of the risk of litigation with respect to this new measure. To protect from this risk, officials documented every standard applied by the United States to allow for a transparent comparison with foreign techniques and to be able to defend any claim brought by trading partners that the United States was violating the national treatment principle of the WTO Agreements. Some officials

20 'Comparable in effectiveness' means that the regulatory program of the other States effectively achieves comparable results to the regulatory program of the United States. This approach gives harvesting States flexibility to implement the same type of regulatory program as the United States or a program which is completely different but achieves the same results, namely reducing marine mammal bycatch in an export fishery. See Fish and Fish Product Import Provisions of the Marine Mammal Protection Act, 81 FR 54,389, effective on 1 January 2017.

interviewed for this chapter acknowledged that the rulemaking process had been delayed for several years due to the trade law risks. The fish industry is so significant to the United States economy that any implementation of the statutory directive could lead to such a legal challenge – no matter how well crafted. Ultimately, however, litigation in domestic courts led the executive branch to conclude that it could no longer refrain from moving forward. Even once the rule had been issued, trade officials within the United States insisted on a five-year review process to provide trading partners an opportunity to engage with regulators. Hundreds of consultations took place over this period.

The Import Rule has certain features that suggest an intentional effort on the part of its designers to make the Rule WTO-compliant. The text of the rule includes language that WTO panels had found acceptable for other aspects of the MMPA. For example, 'comparable in effectiveness' is the language used in the revised rule governing shrimp imports, which led to a case against the United States.[21] This language is intended to give other States considerable flexibility. For instance, if the United States would use a 'gear restriction' in a certain designated area known to be frequented by marine mammals, but the other country, having established that the marine mammals are present three months a year, proceeded to ban fishing in that designated area for these three months, the United States would consider this measure as comparable. Officials highlighted the importance of close cooperation with trading partners and transparency.

The innovative features of the Import Rule make it a somewhat unique trade instrument. While it is modelled after past MMPA rules and initiatives, it also has new elements. In some ways, the rule is similar to the equivalency determinations that are frequent in the food safety context, or those used in food labelling.[22] However, those equivalency determinations are often negotiated bilaterally or through an international instrument rather than through a unilateral regulatory determination. In other respects, the rule resembles the requirements in environment chapters of free trade agreements concluded by the United States in the way the rule requires the trading partner to adopt and maintain certain laws and, then, to enforce them effectively.[23] The requirement of effective enforcement in particular, together with the requirement to adopt and maintain laws, brings together concepts that are not often grouped into a single requirement in trade law – especially one that is then enforced unilaterally. Further, unlike prior MMPA rules that were narrow by comparison, this Import Rule has a much bigger impact. Through this rule, the United States acts on a global scale and often does so through information the United States put together through its own research.

21 50 CFR § 216.24.

22 See, for example, United States Department of Agriculture, 'Organic Certification and Accreditation'. www.ams.usda.gov/services/organic-certification accessed 8 January 2024.

23 See, for example, United States – Mexico – Canada Agreement, 30 September 2018, entered into force 1 July 2020, Environment Chapter, art 24.4.

3.2. Trade's Elasticity

As the boundaries of trade law continue to evolve, the Import Rule could be a bellwether for the future elasticity of the field. States increasingly wrestle with the intersection of environmental and trade goals. Like many trade rules, the Import Rule has a liberalisation rationale: the United States has emphasised that the purpose of the rule is to 'level the playing field' for its fishers and to avoid 'unfair competition'.[24] Since fisheries in the United States will be held to high standards set by the United States, the rest of the world needs to be brought up to that same standard. It is a progressive equalisation rationale. It allows the United States to achieve an important public policy goal within international trade law so long as all other States can be brought up to these standards or otherwise differentiated.

These conversations are shifting the dynamics among trade law principles, pushing (powerful) States and markets toward regulatory means of engaging in trade actions rather than using international trade agreements. In fact, the fisheries toolkit could become one of the most diverse in this respect by including both international and domestic tools. The more diverse the toolkit becomes, the more attention will need to be spent on the intersections among them.

In the United States, these issues are made more challenging by the distribution of foreign commercial authority within the executive branch, as well as by the constraints with the public engagement process on new regulatory measures. For example, the National Oceanic and Atmospheric Administration (NOAA) is an agency within the United States Department of Commerce. While NOAA itself is not trade-oriented, higher leadership within the Department of Commerce is, and is concerned about the United States' trade deficit in fish. The Department leaders see the United States' fish import and export regime as a problem and concentrate on those issues.[25] The priorities among regulators might change if NOAA or its fish-focused sub-agency were moved away from the Department of Commerce and placed in the Department of the Interior, for instance.

4. Unilateral Harmonisation and The Other Big Fish

The strongest rationale for the Import Rule is that it could make a significant positive difference in the protection of marine mammals. One study already attempted to analyse the rule's impact on some major fish-exporting States.[26] The problem, as viewed by many, is that the protective work is carried out by a single State rather

24 NOAA Fisheries, 'Implementation of Fish and Fish Product Import Provisions of the Marine Mammal Protection Act' (30 April 2010) 75 FR 38,070.

25 See, for example, Steve Bittenbender, 'U.S. Commerce Secretary Wilbur Ross Questions Safety of Foreign Seafood Imports', *SeafoodSource* (22 March 2018). www.seafoodsource.com/news/food-safety-health/us-commerce-secretary-wilbur-ross-questions-safety-of-foreign-seafood-imports accessed 8 January 2024.

26 See, for example, Janet Bering et al., 'Will Unilateral Action Improve the Global Conservation Status of Marine Mammals? A First Analysis of the U.S. Marine Mammal Protection Act's Import Provisions Rule' (2022) 135 *Marine Policy* 104832.

than through international agreement. Such 'unilateral harmonisation' seems like an oxymoron at first, but it captures how the United States is forcing, unilaterally, a degree of harmonisation across fisheries management systems. With more than 120 States exporting fish and fish products to the United States, the Import Rule has great potential, even at this cost.

4.1. Measuring Success on a Singular Standard

On the positive side, the United States is spearheading greater protection for marine mammals. Yet, critics have noted some gaps and difficulties in achieving this important goal.[27] Measuring success along the singular standard that the United States has set is not particularly useful. According to one study, and unsurprisingly, the rule will have a variable effect on State and fishery behaviour.[28] Some States already have robust fisheries and marine mammal management systems and the data to evaluate regularly marine mammal abundance and bycatch, just as the United States' rule requires. However, other States are not near the United States' threshold. Some have information about bycatch built into their fisheries management programme but do not track data closely. Other States have no meaningful program and no data tracking.[29] This relationship is an inverse one; States like Iceland and Norway that report considerable mortality are those with the better data tracking. Meanwhile, some evidence suggests that States that do not collect the relevant data have even higher rates of mortality.

For the States that lack the resources and/or regulatory systems to meet the United States' standards, the United States has limited funding for capacity building. The comparability finding application asks that States list their needs for technical assistance, although it is unclear how that factor is being weighed in the review process. Some states that often serve as intermediary stops may also need better supply chain tracing tools connected more to the customs regulatory space than the fisheries space.

Among the many States implicated by the rule, China is critical to the regime's success. China is the world's largest seafood producer and the largest seafood exporter to the United States. China has expansive fisheries and also serves as an intermediary State for fish re-export. But little is known about China's fisheries management regime. As noted by others, '[b]ecause China is also likely to be the largest alternate market for products facing U.S. import bans, any certification requirements placed on its supply chain might indirectly increase compliance incentives for other countries'.[30] Some States may choose not to comply and may send their seafood elsewhere.

27 ibid.

28 ibid.

29 ibid.

30 Rob Williams et al., 'U.S. Seafood Import Restriction Presents Opportunity and Risk' (2016) 354 *Science* 1372.

Even where trading partners cooperate, the United States rule is limited by the constraints of technology used worldwide, despite many recent advancements. For example, only five percent of the ocean has been surveyed well enough to detect certain rare species, according to one study.[31] Further, there are some gaps in the United States regime. Scholars have noted that some of the most critically endangered marine mammals 'face their most serious threats from artisanal fisheries, which do not export'. The Import Rule does not cover these critically endangered species, although they could benefit from access to better technology stemming from the global implementation of the rule.[32]

Finally, the standards set by the United States clearly offer just one set of options. Other States that concentrate on fisheries management as well as marine mammal protection, may have other strategies that would better achieve the goals the United States has set out. Officials interviewed for this project suggested that there was some learning on the part of United States regulators, but that tracking such learning would be difficult.

4.2. International and Domestic Tensions

The Import Rule has created waves in international diplomacy. Both in formal and informal settings, States have raised concerns with the United States' unilateralism and, instead, have advocated for cooperation through regional fisheries management organisations. These States take issue with the value system and its imposition by United States regulators. Given the size of the United States market, some States have been more motivated, as well as more frustrated, to reform their regulatory systems. Market experts noted also the potential for retaliatory rules on United States' exports.

Officials in the United States maintain that they have sought to respond to these concerns and that they are providing partners with 'due process'. If they intend to reject a comparability finding, they will give the trading partner an opportunity to respond to allow for reconsideration. Regulators also noted that challenges in cooperation are particularly salient with developing coastal States, where changes in local politics can lead to a lack of continuity. A further difficulty is the inability to work with Russia at this time. As a major exporter to the United States, Russia would be a critical player in a successful implementation of the rule. Russian fisheries would also miss out on the opportunity to collaborate and learn about possible improvements in technology.

There remains a risk of litigation in the United States, as well, where non-governmental organisations or fishing groups could take issue with United States regulators' determination with respect to a particular comparability finding. It would not be the first time that civil society groups use the domestic court system to ensure greater protection for marine mammals. Throughout this process,

31 ibid.
32 ibid.

the United States executive branch has sought to balance these constraints and public policy objectives: the international trade law rules & global diplomatic efforts toward environmental goals, as well as domestic orders and pressures from interest groups.

5. Conclusion

As the MMPA Import Rule reaches its next stage, it may set a new tone for international trade law and environmental issues. Could this model provide an opportunity for regulators to meet other climate change goals? One could envision an alliance of States calculating emissions and working with partners to reach high standards, pairing those initiatives with market access controls. On the other hand, such a method has its downsides and no doubt implementing challenges. At this delicate moment in our global future, the Import Rule will be an experiment to watch.

Part VII

The Biodiversity Beyond National Jurisdiction Process (BBNJ Process) and Implications for Fisheries Management

20 The Interface Between the BBNJ Agreement and RFMOs

Daniela Diz

1. Introduction

The origins of a legally binding instrument under the United Nations Convention on the Law of the Sea (UNCLOS) on biodiversity beyond national jurisdiction date back to 2006.[1] Between 2006 and 2015, the United Nations General Assembly (UNGA) set up an Ad Hoc Open-ended Informal Working group to study issues relating to the conservation and sustainable use of marine biodiversity beyond areas of national jurisdiction between 2006 and 2015. The UNGA Resolution 66/231 agreed to a package of elements addressed by the Ad Hoc Open-ended Informal Working Group in 2011:

> the conservation and sustainable use of marine biodiversity in areas beyond national jurisdiction, in particular, together and as a whole, marine genetic resources, including questions on the sharing of benefits, measures such as area-based management tools, including marine protected areas, and environmental impact assessments, capacity-building and the transfer of marine technology.[2]

Based on the reports of the Ad Hoc Open-ended Informal Working Group, UNGA Resolution 69/292 in 2015 decided to develop an international legally binding instrument under UNCLOS. It established a Preparatory Committee (PrepCom) to make recommendations to the UNGA on the elements of the draft text. The PrepCom met between 2015 and 2017. Based on the recommendations of the PrepCom, UNGA Resolution 72/249 in December 2017 convened an Intergovernmental Conference (IGC) 'with a view to develop the instrument as soon as possible'.[3]

1 United Nations Convention on the Law of the Sea (UNCLOS), 10 December 1982, 1833 UNTS 3, entered into force 16 November 1994.

2 United Nations General Assembly (UNGA), 'Oceans and the Law of the Sea' (24 December 2011) Resolution 66/231, Annex, para (b).

3 UNGA, 'International Legally Binding Instrument under the United Nations Convention on the Law of the Sea on the Conservation and Sustainable Use of Marine Biological Diversity of Areas Beyond National Jurisdiction' (24 December 2017) Resolution 72/249, para 1.

DOI: 10.4324/9781003492030-27

The Agreement under UNCLOS on the Conservation and Sustainable Use of Marine Biological Diversity of Areas beyond National Jurisdiction (BBNJ Agreement) was adopted in June 2023 and opened for signature in September 2023. It includes the four elements from UNGA Resolution 66/231 mentioned previously, namely: (1) marine genetic resources, including the fair and equitable sharing of benefits; (2) measures such as area-based management tools (ABMTs), including marine protected areas (MPAs); (3) environmental impact assessments; and (4) capacity-building and the transfer of marine technology. It also provides relevant cross-cutting elements, such as use of terms (Article 1), general objective (Article 2), general principles and approaches (Article 7), relationship with other instruments (Article 5), and dispute settlement clauses (Article IX).

The successive UNGA resolutions had stressed that the BBNJ Agreement's negotiating process should not undermine existing legal instruments and frameworks and relevant regional and sectoral bodies. The 'non-undermining' term appeared for the first time in UNGA Resolution 69/292 in 2015.[4] It stressed that the PrepCom process 'should not undermine existing relevant legal instruments and frameworks and relevant global, regional and sectoral bodies'.[5] Then UNGA Resolution 72/249 in 2017, which convened the IGC, emphasised that 'this process *and its result* should not undermine existing relevant legal instruments and frameworks and relevant global, regional and sectoral bodies' (emphasis added).[6] Thus, while UNGA Resolution 69/292 in 2015 restricted the non-undermining concept to the PrepCom process itself, UNGA Resolution 72/249 in 2017 extended it to the results of the negotiation, namely the BBNJ Agreement per se.

Despite the integration of the non-undermining concept in these UNGA resolutions, negotiators' views have varied on how to interpret this concept. An IGC President's document entitled 'Aid to Negotiations', circulated before the second session of the IGC, provided different options for interpreting this concept:

OPTION I: This instrument shall promote greater coherence with and shall complement existing relevant legal instruments and frameworks and relevant global, regional, and sectoral bodies. This instrument shall be interpreted and applied in a manner that does not undermine those instruments, frameworks, and bodies.

OPTION II: The implementation of this instrument shall not undermine existing relevant legal instruments and frameworks and relevant global, regional, and sectoral bodies.

OPTION III: This instrument shall be implemented in a mutually supportive manner with other international instruments relevant to it. Due regard should be paid to useful and relevant ongoing work or practices under such international

4 UNGA, 'Development of an International Legally Binding Instrument under the United Nations Convention on the Law of the Sea on the Conservation and Sustainable Use of Marine Biological Diversity of Areas Beyond National Jurisdiction' (19 June 2015, Resolution 69/292, para 1.

5 UNGA, 'International Legally Binding Instrument under the United Nations Convention on the Law of the Sea on the Conservation and Sustainable Use of Marine Biological Diversity of Areas Beyond National Jurisdiction' (24 December 2017) Resolution 72/249, para 3.

6 ibid, para 7.

> instruments and relevant international organizations, provided that they are supportive of and do not run counter to the objectives of the Convention and this instrument (emphasis in original).[7]

The draft version of the BBNJ Agreement in May 2022 contained the following language, including the following text:

> This Agreement shall be interpreted and applied in a manner that [respects the competences of and] does not undermine [the effectiveness of] relevant legal instruments and frameworks and relevant global, regional, subregional and sectoral bodies and that promotes coherence and coordination with those instruments, frameworks and bodies.[8]

During the fifth session of the IGC, the draft circulated on the last day of the negotiations described the concept of non-undermining as such: 'This Agreement shall be interpreted and applied in a manner that does not undermine relevant legal instruments and frameworks and relevant global, regional, subregional and sectoral bodies and that promotes coherence and coordination with those instruments, frameworks, and bodies.'[9] Thus, this formulation encapsulates both notions: first, safeguarding the mandates of regional fisheries management organisations or arrangements (RFMOs) and other relevant bodies and instruments and, second, the need to ensure governance coherence and mutual supportiveness among applicable instruments.

By the end of the fifth session, the notion of non-undermining 'competences' had been dropped from this specific paragraph. However, in the context of the relationship with other instruments and frameworks, the concept re-appeared in draft Article 19 on ABMTs. Draft Article 19(3) stated that 'in taking decisions under this article, the Conference of the Parties shall respect the competences of [and not undermine] relevant legal instruments and frameworks and relevant global, regional, subregional and sectoral bodies.'[10]

In clarifying that the reference to 'effectiveness' concerns measures adopted by relevant bodies, draft Article 19(5) further stated that:

> Decisions and recommendations adopted by the Conference of the Parties in accordance with this Part shall not undermine the effectiveness of measures adopted in respect of areas within national jurisdiction and shall be made

7 UNGA, 'President's Aid to Negotiations' (3 December 2018) A/CONF.232/2019/1, 7.

8 UNGA, 'Further Revised Draft Text of an Agreement under the United Nations Convention on the Law of the Sea on the Conservation and Sustainable Use of Marine Biological Diversity of Areas Beyond National Jurisdiction' (30 May 2022) <www.un.org/bbnj/sites/www.un.org.bbnj/files/igc_5_-_further_revised_draft_text_final.pdf> accessed 13 January 2024, art 4(3).

9 UNGA, 'Further Refreshed Draft Text of an Agreement under the United Nations Convention on the Law of the Sea on the Conservation and Sustainable Use of Marine Biological Diversity of Areas Beyond National Jurisdiction' (26 August 2022) A/CONF.232/2022/CRP.13 <www.un.org/bbnj/sites/www.un.org.bbnj/files/crp-13_further_refreshed_text_260822_clean.pdf> accessed 13 January 2024, art 4(2).

10 ibid, art 19 (3).

with due regard for the rights and duties of all States in accordance with the Convention).[11]

Therefore, draft Article 19 clarified the application of the concept in the context of ABMTs by providing that the Conference of the Parties (COP) to the BBNJ Agreement shall, first, respect the competences of sectoral organisations such as RFMOs and, second, that it shall not undermine the effectiveness of 'measures' adopted by these bodies – rather than the effectiveness of the bodies themselves.

The adopted text of the BBNJ Agreement contains several references to the non-undermining concept. Article 5(2) notes that '[t]his Agreement shall be interpreted in a manner that does not undermine relevant legal instruments and frameworks and relevant global, regional, subregional and sectoral bodies and that promotes coherence and coordination with those instruments, frameworks and bodies'.[12] With respect to ABMTs, the BBNJ Agreement states that the COP 'shall respect the competences of, and not undermine, relevant legal instruments and frameworks and relevant global, regional, subregional and sectoral bodies'.[13]

Given the adopted text, one can argue that, overall, promoting greater policy and legal coherence or synergies is not contrary to the non-undermining concept. A systemic interpretation of norms, including in light of the obligation of States to protect marine biodiversity under the United Nations Fish Stocks Agreement, reinforces the need to create mutually supportive mechanisms under the BBNJ Agreement.[14] In practice, questions remain open, including on potential conflicts between relevant rules deriving from the BBNJ Agreement and RFMO conventions,[15] as well as in relation to the subjects bound by them.[16] The answers to these questions

11 ibid, art 19(5).

12 Agreement under the United Nations Convention on the Law of the Sea on the Conservation and Sustainable Use of Marine Biological Diversity of Areas Beyond National Jurisdiction (BBNJ Agreement), 19 June 2023, A/CONF.232/2023/4, opened for signature on 20 September 2023, not yet in force, art 5(2).

13 ibid, art 22(2).

14 Agreement for the Implementation of the Provisions of the United Nations Convention on the Law of the Sea of 10 December 1982 relating to the Conservation and Management of Straddling Fish Stocks and Highly Migratory Fish Stocks (Fish Stocks Agreement), 4 August 1995, 2167 UNTS 3, entered into force 11 December 2001, art 5(d).

15 Related to those envisioned under the Vienna Convention on the Law of Treaties (VCLT), 23 April 1969, 1155 UNTS 331, entered into force 27 January 1980, art 30. See also Report of the Study Group of the International Law Commission, 'Fragmentation of International Law: Difficulties Arising from the Diversification and Expansion of International Law' (13 April 2006) A/CN.4/L.682. But see, the Study Group's point that '[t]he criterion of 'subject-matter' leads to a *reductio ad absurdum*. Therefore, it cannot be decisive in the determination of whether or not there is a conflict' (para 22). There is also an argument that '[a] treaty may sometimes frustrate the goals of another treaty without there being any strict incompatibility between their provisions' (para 24). This could be the archetypal example of potential incompatibility between the BBNJ Agreement and RFMO conventions in relation to ABMTs.

16 Report of the Study Group of the International Law Commission, 'Fragmentation of International Law: Difficulties Arising from the Diversification and Expansion of International Law' (13 April 2006) A/CN.4/L.682.

may differ on a case-by-case basis. Decisions taken by the COP to the BBNJ Agreement will provide further clarity in due course. The ABMT establishment process, together with the compromise text on the decision-making mechanism and future mechanisms set up by the COP, may bring enhanced cooperation and mutual supportiveness across relevant instruments, such as UNCLOS, the Convention on Biological Diversity (CBD), the BBNJ Agreement, and RFMO conventions.

2. Enhancing Mutual Supportiveness on ABMT Processes Under the BBNJ Agreement

The International Law Commission noted in its report on the fragmentation of international law that '[t]he doctrine of "treaty parallelism" addresses precisely the need to coordinate the reading of particular instruments or to see them in a "mutually supportive" light'.[17] In this vein, how could negotiators of the BBNJ Agreement have designed a regime conducive to the application of the principle of systemic integration?[18] Ideally, such systemic integration would have been achieved in respect of both RFMO conventions and other relevant instruments, such as the CBD?[19]

As seen previously, ABMTs, including MPAs, are an element of the BBNJ Agreement.[20] Other global agreements have not defined ABMTs. The BBNJ Agreement defines ABMTs as 'a tool, including a marine protected area, for a geographically defined area through which one or several sectors or activities are managed with the aim of achieving particular conservation and sustainable use objectives in accordance with this Agreement.'[21]

This definition is consistent with the general understanding that ABMTs more broadly comprise: (1) spatial cross-sectoral conservation and management measures, such as MPAs[22] and arguably other effective area-based conservation measures (OECMs),[23] and (2) spatial sectoral measures, such as those taken by

17 ibid, para 417.

18 VCLT, art 31(3)(c).

19 Convention on Biological Diversity (CBD), 5 June 1992, 1760 UNTS 79, entered into force 29 December 1993.

20 UNGA, 'International Legally Binding Instrument under the United Nations Convention on the Law of the Sea on the Conservation and Sustainable Use of Marine Biological Diversity of Areas Beyond National Jurisdiction' (24 December 2017) Resolution 72/249, para 2; BBNJ Agreement, part III.

21 BBNJ Agreement, art 1(1).

22 'Protected Area' is defined in the Convention on Biological Diversity, 5 June 1992, 1760 UNTS 79, entered into force 29 December 1993, art 2 as 'geographically defined area which is designated or regulated and managed to achieve specific conservation objectives'.

23 The definition of OECM is contained in the Decision Adopted by the Conference of the Parties to the CBD, 'Protected Areas and Other Effective Area-Based Conservation Measures' (30 November 2018) CBD/COP/DEC/14/8, para 2 as:

[a] geographically defined area other than a Protected Area, which is governed and managed in ways that achieve positive and sustained long-term outcomes for the in situ conservation of biodiversity, with associated ecosystem functions and services and where applicable, cultural, spiritual, socio-economic, and other locally relevant values.

RFMOs, which could include closures of vulnerable marine ecosystem (VME).[24] More unclear is whether the BBNJ Agreement's definition of ABMTs encompasses OECMs which may not have an explicit conservation or sustainable use objective, but which could, nonetheless, achieve biodiversity conservation outcomes, in accordance with the OECM's in the CBD.[25]

Nonetheless, the BBNJ Agreement provides that its COP can take decisions on measures compatible with measures adopted by RFMOs. This is notably done through Article 22(1)(b) (on establishment of ABMTs, including MPAs) which will be discussed further in this chapter. It will be for the COP to decide what these measures may constitute. However, this provision could be interpreted to mean that coordinated efforts with other sectors, to ensure biodiversity conservation outcomes arising from RFMO measures, could facilitate identifying or recognising OECMs.

In areas beyond national jurisdiction, the absence of a process for establishing MPA at the global level is a main regulatory gap with respect to ABMTs.[26] Only a limited number of competent organisations to date can establish MPAs in areas beyond national jurisdiction (depending on their mandates and potential collaboration arrangements in place).[27] RFMOs have specific mandates to establish spatial conservation measures, such as fisheries closures and move-on rules. However, RFMO coverage vary across the globe, both geographically and in relation to their regulatory mandates on specific fish stocks. Geographic and regulatory gaps in coverage may benefit from deliberations by the BBNJ Agreement's COP in certain instances. However, in general, when RFMOs' mandates cover the specific biodiversity features which merit protection, it is difficult to imagine that the BBNJ Agreement could establish a sectoral fishery ABMT in areas covered by existing RFMOs, where such RFMOs have that specific mandate, unless the relevant RFMO agrees to it.

Part III of the BBNJ Agreement on measures such as ABMTs constitutes an improvement from previous draft versions. Indeed, it provides clearer guidance on the procedural steps for establishing ABMTs, including MPAs, and on the interface with other competent bodies. It does not expressly mention OECMs and the ABMT's definition does not encompass reference to 'conservation outcomes'. However, nothing appears to impede a future BBNJ Agreement's COP to build on

24 See Daniela Diz et al., 'Mainstreaming Marine Biodiversity into the SDGs: The Role of Other Effective Area-Based Conservation Measures (SDG 14.5)' (2018) 93 *Marine Policy* 251.

25 Decision Adopted by the Conference of the Parties to the CBD, 'Protected Areas and Other Effective Area-Based Conservation Measures' (30 November 2018) CBD/COP/DEC/14/8, para 2.

26 To give effect to the obligation to protect marine habitats, species, and ecosystems under UNCLOS, art 194(5).

27 A typical example is the MPAs of the Convention for the Protection of the Marine Environment of the North-East Atlantic, which benefit from a collective arrangement with the North East Atlantic Fisheries Commission. However, broader cooperation through the BBNJ Agreement with other sectoral bodies, such as the International Seabed Authority or the International Maritime Organization, could also be beneficial for policy coherency.

Part III by establishing clearer guidance and procedures for OECMs, especially when it comes to cross-sectoral cooperation. The next sub-section considers procedural steps for establishing ABMTs, including MPAs, and the possible recognition of OECMs, in light of the relationship between the BBNJ Agreement and RFMOs.

2.1. *Procedural Steps for Establishing ABMTs, Including MPAs, and the Role of RFMOs*

One must examine how Part III of the BBNJ Agreement describes the process for establishing ABMTs. This is necessary to assess the potential interpretation of the non-undermining concept so as to avoid conflict with other norms and to support the application of the systemic integration principle, as enshrined in the Vienna Convention on the Law of Treaties.[28] The process in the BBNJ Agreement entails the following steps.

First, a party individually or multiple parties collectively submits ABMT proposals to the secretariat. Per Article 19 of the BBNJ Agreement, such proposals should include the geographical location of the area; its biological characteristics based on indicative criteria contained in Annex I to the BBNJ Agreement and other relevant criteria; types of activities occurring in the area; status of the marine environment and biodiversity; description of conservation and sustainable use objectives for the measure; a draft management plan, including proposed measures and proposed monitoring, research, and review activities for achieving specific objectives; information on any consultation conducted with adjacent coastal States and/or relevant global, regional, subregional, and sectoral bodies; information on ABMTs, including MPAs; and relevant scientific information as well as traditional knowledge where available. The proposal may also include the duration of the measure, if any.[29]

Second, the secretariat makes the proposal publicly available and transmits it to the BBNJ Agreement's Scientific and Technical Body (STB) for a preliminary review based on elements required under Article 19.[30] The proponent or proponents will then resubmit the revised proposal based on the STB's comments.[31]

Third, the secretariat facilitates consultation.[32] Consultations on the proposals 'shall be inclusive, transparent and open to all relevant stakeholders, including States, global, regional, subregional and sectoral bodies, as well as civil society, the scientific community, Indigenous Peoples and local communities.'[33] The STB could further elaborate modalities for the consultation which could be considered by the COP.[34]

28 VLCT, art 31(3)(c).
29 BBNJ Agreement, art 19(g).
30 ibid, art 20.
31 ibid.
32 ibid.
33 ibid, art 21(1).
34 ibid, art 21(8).

Fourth, bodies of relevant legal instruments and frameworks, and relevant global, regional, subregional, and sectoral bodies, among other stakeholders, 'shall be notified and invited to submit' information. This includes views on the merits of the proposal; scientific inputs; any existing measures adopted under their frameworks; views on the proposed management plan's elements which fall within the competence of the body; views on any relevant additional measures under their competence; and any other relevant information.[35] The consultation must be time-bound.[36] The STB will develop further the consultation's modalities and duration for consideration by the COP.[37] Elaborating these modalities offers an opportunity to co-develop conservation and management measures between, on the one hand, the BBNJ Agreement's STB and COP and, on the other hand, RFMOs, notably if their scientific bodies are also involved. RFMO's scientific body typically has in-depth knowledge about the marine ecosystems and potential fishing-related threats which could, for instance, benefit from an MPA's management plan.

Fifth, the proponent revises the proposal based on the consultation inputs and the STB's views.[38]

Sixth, the revised proposal is then submitted to the STB, which provides an assessment and recommendations to the COP.[39] The STB will also elaborate on the modalities of the STB's assessment later at its first meeting for the COP's consideration.[40]

Finally, the BBNJ Agreement requires its Parties through the COP to take 'decisions on the establishment of' ABMTs, including MPAs, and related measures based on the final proposal, per Article 22(1)(a).[41]

Article 22(1)(b) provides that the COP '[m]ay take decisions on measures compatible with those adopted by relevant legal instruments and frameworks and relevant global, regional, subregional and sectoral bodies, in cooperation and coordination with those instruments, frameworks and bodies'. Thus, the COP *may* take decisions on measures compatible with measures adopted by RFMOs.[42] This could facilitate adopting cross-sectoral measures which fall outside the mandate of RFMOs. Ultimately, this would contribute not only to achieving MPAs' conservation objectives but also to achieving conservation outcomes. Achieving such outcomes is essential in the case of OECMs.[43]

35 ibid, art 21(2)(b).
36 ibid, art 21(6).
37 ibid, art 21(8).
38 ibid, art 21(5).
39 ibid, art 21(7).
40 ibid, art 21(8).
41 ibid, art 22(1)(a).
42 ibid, art 22(1)(b).
43 Decision Adopted by the Conference of the Parties to the CBD, 'Protected Areas and Other Effective Area-Based Conservation Measures' (30 November 2018) CBD/COP/DEC/14/8, para 2; Serge Michel Garcia (et al), 'OECMs in Marine Capture Fisheries: Key Implementation Issues of Governance, Management, and Biodiversity' (2022) 9 *Frontiers in Marine Science* 920051.

In addition to the non-undermining clauses,[44] another safeguard for RFMOs with regard to any potential interference by the BBNJ Agreement's COP on their areas of competence is provided by Article 22(1)(c). Article 22(1)(c) states that the COP:

> May, where proposed measures are within the competences of other global, regional, subregional or sectoral bodies, make recommendations to Parties to this Agreement and global, regional, subregional or sectoral bodies to promote the adoption of relevant measures through such instruments, frameworks and bodies, in accordance with their respective mandates.

Thus, it seems that, where no competent body exists in a given area or a body exists but it does not have competence to regulate activities regarding a biodiversity feature that the proposed ABMT aims to conserve, the COP can adopt measures in this regard.[45] Where a competent body exists and this body has competence to adopt measures regarding such biodiversity features, the COP has discretion on whether to 'take decisions' on measures compatible with these existing measures.[46] Finally, where the proposed measures fall within the mandate of an RFMO, the BBNJ Agreement's COP has discretion whether to 'make recommendations' to parties to the BBNJ Agreement and to RFMOs to promote adopting relevant measures.[47]

2.2. Compatible Measures

The BBNJ Agreement does not define compatible measures. In the context of fisheries, 'compatibility' has been incorporated into the Fish Stocks Agreement in reference to compatible conservation and management measures established for the high seas and measures adopted for areas within national jurisdiction concerning straddling and highly migratory fish stocks.[48] Coastal States and States fishing on the high seas are obliged to cooperate, and, among others, take into account the biological unity of the stocks.[49] In the BBNJ Agreement, measures adopted by the COP which would be compatible to measures adopted by RFMOs could entail, inter alia, two types of measures.

First, the first type of measures could be additional fishing measures. This could include fisheries closures for stocks which are not regulated by an RFMO in a given area (e.g., mesopelagic stocks if not regulated by any RFMO in the particular proposed ABMT area). Another possibility would be bycatch measures. In due course, the COP will most likely clarify the interpretation and application of the

44 BBNJ Agreement, arts 5(2) and 22(2).

45 ibid, art 22(1)(a),

46 ibid, art 22(1)(b)

47 ibid, art 22(1)(c)

48 Fish Stocks Agreement, art 7. See also *Request for an Advisory Opinion Submitted by the Sub-Regional Fisheries Commission*, Advisory Opinion, ITLOS Rep 2015, 4.

49 Fish Stocks Agreement, art 7(d).

compatibility clause on a case-by-case basis. The role of the COP remains to be seen in establishing, for instance, bycatch prevention measures for marine mammals, sea turtles, or seabirds, if these measures do not fall under the competence of a given RFMO or if the competent RFMO is not taking appropriate measures to address these issues. It will ultimately depend on the political will of the parties. For example, it could be that bycatch information for such species is not required by the relevant RFMO and, therefore, that there is no information on the degree to which their fishing activities constitute a threat which should be addressed and minimized.[50] In this scenario, could the BBNJ COP recommend that an RFMO collect such data to inform any needed compatible measures? This seems reasonable. Such measures could contribute to enhanced coherence on ABMT governance and greater cooperation within and across sectors, and in principle would not overstep any competent authorities' mandates.

Second, the second type of measures could be other sectoral measures or facilitation of cooperation for cross-sectoral measures. For instance, the COP could protect seamounts, which have been identified as VMEs by an RFMO and closed to fishing, from other sectors' pressures (e.g., deep seabed mining, including through consultations with the International Seabed Authority).

In theory, the COP could adopt such measures as part of the management plans of an MPA or as stand-alone ABMT measures. From a political standpoint, it is unlikely that parties to the BBNJ Agreement would focus on sectoral ABMT measures if these do not relate to establishing an MPA. However, parties could seek to ensure that areas, which have already been protected by specific sectors and could qualify as OECMs under the CBD, would also be collectively protected from other sectoral threats. In this sense, the BBNJ Agreement's COP could facilitate cross-sectoral cooperation.

2.3. Other Effective Area-Based Conservation Measures

Decisions of the CBD's COP and spatial global targets lay down OECMs.[51] The relationship between UNCLOS and the CBD is important and can be interpreted as mutually supportive. All parties to UNCLOS are also parties to the CBD. The

50 This is the case of the Northwest Atlantic Fisheries Organization for instance. See Northwest Atlantic Fisheries Organization (NAFO), 'Conservation and Enforcement Measures 2022' (2022) <www.nafo.int/Portals/0/PDFs/COM/2022/comdoc22-01.pdf> accessed 13 January 2024.

51 The term first appeared in Aichi Biodiversity 11 on protected areas, Decision Adopted by the Conference of the Parties to the CBD at its Tenth Meeting, 'The Strategic Plan for Biodiversity 2011–2020 and the Aichi Biodiversity Targets' (29 October 2010) UNEP/CBD/COP/DEC/X/2. The definition of the term was adopted by Decision Adopted by the Conference of the Parties to the CBD, 'Protected Areas and Other Effective Area-Based Conservation Measures' (30 November 2018) CBD/COP/DEC/14/8. Most recently, the Aichi Targets have been replaced by the Kunming-Montreal Global Biodiversity Framework, and the concept of OECMs was reinstated in Target 3 on spatial conservation through MPAs and OECMs, see Decision Adopted by the Conference of the Parties to the Convention on Biological Diversity, 'Kunming-Montreal Global Biodiversity Framework' (19 December 2022) CBD/COP/DEC/15/4, annex, target 3.

parties to the CBD shall implement the CBD consistently with the rights and obligations of States under UNCLOS.[52] However, provisions in the CBD may prevail over other international agreements when the exercise of such rights and obligations 'would cause a serious damage or threat to biological diversity'.[53] This should not be perceived as incompatible with provisions in UNCLOS; especially obligations related to Part XII on the protection and preservation of the marine environment.[54] On the jurisdictional scope, the CBD does not apply to components of biodiversity, such as marine genetic resources, in areas beyond national jurisdiction. However, it applies to activities and processes under the jurisdiction and control of parties to the CBD.[55] Therefore, decisions of the CBD's COP on marine and coastal biodiversity and the CBD's many voluntary guidelines are relevant to the BBNJ Agreement's context. Their implementation could be facilitated under the BBNJ Agreement for better policy coherence.

UNGA resolutions, as well as CBD decisions, have recognised that the CBD

> has a key role in supporting the work of the General Assembly with regard to marine protected areas beyond national jurisdiction, by focusing on the provision of scientific and, as appropriate, technical information and advice relating to marine biological diversity, the application of the ecosystem approach and the precautionary approach.[56]

In this context, this sub-section explores the potential role of OECMs under the BBNJ Agreement. OECMs are ABMTs, other than MPAs, which meet the following definition from the CBD:

> a geographically defined area other than a Protected Area, which is governed and managed in ways that achieve positive and sustained long-term outcomes for the *in situ* conservation of biodiversity with associated ecosystem functions and services and where applicable, cultural, spiritual, socio-economic, and other locally relevant values.[57]

52 CBD, art 22(2).

53 CBD, art 22(1). See also Alan Boyle and Catherine Redgwell, *Birnie, Boyle and Redgwell's International Law and the Environment* (OUP 2021) at 772.

54 In reference to UNCLOS, art 293(1) on applicable law, which states that 'A court or tribunal having jurisdiction under [compulsory dispute settlement procedures] shall apply this Convention and other rules of international law not incompatible with this Convention.'

55 CBD, art 4(2).

56 Decision Adopted by the Conference of the Parties to the CBD, 'Marine and Coastal Biodiversity' (9 October 2008) UNEP/CBD/COP/DEC/IX/20, 5th preambular para. See also multiple references to the CBD in the UNGA resolutions on Oceans and the Law of the Sea, including UNGA, 'Oceans and the Law of the Sea' (31 December 2020) A/RES/75/239.

57 Decision Adopted by the Conference of the Parties to the CBD, 'Protected Areas and Other Effective Area-Based Conservation Measures' (30 November 2018) CBD/COP/DEC/14/8, para 2.

The definition was developed in the context of Aichi Biodiversity Target 11, which states:

> By 2020, at least 17 per cent of terrestrial and inland water, and 10 per cent of coastal and marine areas, especially areas of particular importance for biodiversity and ecosystem services, are conserved through effectively and equitably managed, ecologically representative and well-connected systems of protected areas and other effective area-based conservation measures, and integrated into the wider landscapes and seascapes.[58]

The concept of OECM has been carried forward under the CBD's Kunming-Montreal Global Biodiversity Framework, notably in target three which was adopted by the COP 15 in December 2022.[59]

In addition to the definition, the CBD's COP has also adopted criteria for identifying measures which could qualify as OECMs.[60] The following RFMOs were notably involved in developing guidance through the Food and Agriculture Organization of the United Nations on OECMs in the marine fishery sector: the Northwest Atlantic Fisheries Organization (NAFO), the North East Atlantic Fisheries Commission, and the General Fisheries Commission for the Mediterranean.[61] These RFMOs have also initiated their own processes for identifying their ABMTs

58 Decision Adopted by the Conference of the Parties to the CBD at its Tenth Meeting, 'The Strategic Plan for Biodiversity 2011–2020 and the Aichi Biodiversity Targets' (29 October 2010) UNEP/CBD/COP/DEC/X/2.

59 Decision Adopted by the Conference of the Parties to the Convention on Biological Diversity, 'Kunming-Montreal Global Biodiversity Framework' (19 December 2022) CBD/COP/DEC/15/4, Annex, target three, reads:

> Ensure and enable that by 2030 at least 30 per cent of terrestrial, inland water, and of coastal and marine areas, especially areas of particular importance for biodiversity and ecosystem functions and services, are effectively conserved and managed through ecologically representative, well-connected and equitably governed systems of protected areas and other effective area-based conservation measures, recognizing Indigenous and traditional territories, where applicable, and integrated into wider landscapes, seascapes and the ocean, while ensuring that any sustainable use, where appropriate in such areas, is fully consistent with conservation outcomes, recognizing and respecting the rights of Indigenous peoples and local communities, including over their traditional territories.

60 See Decision Adopted by the Conference of the Parties to the Convention on Biological Diversity, 'Protected Areas and Other Effective Area-Based Conservation Measures' (30 November 2018) CBD/COP/DEC/14/8, annex III.

61 Food and Agriculture Organization of the United Nations, 'A Handbook for Identifying, Evaluating and Reporting other Effective Area-Based Conservation Measures in Marine Fisheries' (Rome, 2022). <www.fao.org/3/cc3307en/cc3307en.pdf> accessed 13 January 2024. See also NAFO, 'Report of the NAFO Commission and Its Subsidiary Bodies (STACTIC and STACFAD): 45th Annual Meeting of NAFO' (Vigo, 2023) <www.nafo.int/Portals/0/PDFs/COM/2023/comdoc23-28.pdf> accessed 13 January 2024; International Council for the Exploration of the Sea, 'ICES, Workshop to Evaluate Long-Term Biodiversity/Ecosystem Benefits of NEAFC Closed and Restricted Areas (WKECOVME)' (15 December 2023) <ices-library.figshare.com/articles/report/

which would meet the OECM's criteria. The BBNJ Agreement does not refer to the concept of OECMs.[62] The definition of ABMT contained in Article I may be broad enough to include ABMTs qualifying as OECMs where these measures have express conservation or sustainable use objectives. However, the BBNJ Agreement's text does not include a process to facilitate the cross-sectoral coordination needed to meet the OECM criteria under the CBD. For instance, the CBD's OECM criterion B requires that governance of the area, including by multiple authorities in collaboration with each other, provides the ability to address threats collectively.[63] Such enhanced cooperation would aim at ensuring consistency between conservation and management measures *across* different sectors if a sectoral OECM was proposed under the CBD or reported to the World Conservation Monitoring Centre's OECM database.

Despite the absence of an express process, the BBNJ Agreement also aims to achieve enhanced cooperation.[64] Nothing prevents its COP from adopting further processes facilitating such enhanced cooperation. The BBNJ Agreement, therefore, offers an opportunity to strengthen cooperation with the CBD by enabling enhanced cross-sectoral cooperation. This would ensure that OECMs achieve their biodiversity conservation outcomes in a holistic and coherent manner. Enhanced cooperation between the BBNJ Agreement, the CBD, and other competent organisations also offer a cost-effective solution instead of duplicating efforts. For instance, Annex I to the BBNJ Agreement includes indicative criteria for identifying areas which inform the ABMT proposals under Article 19. Among these criteria, Annex I features ecologically or biologically significant marine areas (EBSAs) under the CBD. The description of EBSA under the CBD is a scientific and technical exercise which is not foreseen in the text of the BBNJ Agreement, and which could

Workshop_to_evaluate_long-term_biodiversity_ecosystem_benefits_of_NEAFC_closed_and_restricted_areas_WKECOVME_/24198771/4 accessed 13 January 2024.

62 Decision Adopted by the Conference of the Parties to the Convention on Biological Diversity, 'Protected Areas and Other Effective Area-Based Conservation Measures' (30 November 2018) CBD/COP/DEC/14/8, para 2.

63 See also Food and Agriculture Organization of the United Nations, 'A Handbook for Identifying, Evaluating and Reporting other Effective Area-Based Conservation Measures in Marine Fisheries' (Rome, 2022) <www.fao.org/3/cc3307en/cc3307en.pdf> accessed 13 January 2024; International Council for the Exploration of the Sea, 'ICES/IUCN-CEM FEG Workshop on Testing OECM Practices and Strategies (WKTOPS)' (2 September 2022) <ices-library.figshare.com/articles/report/ICES_IUCN-CEM_FEG_Workshop_on_Testing_OECM_Practices_and_Strategies_WKTOPS_/18621746 accessed 13 January 2024.

64 BBNJ Agreement, Article 2 on general objectives states that:

> The objective of this Agreement is to ensure the conservation and sustainable use of marine biological diversity of areas beyond national jurisdiction, for the present and in the long term, through effective implementation of the relevant provisions of the Convention and further international cooperation and coordination.

Article 5(2) on the relationship between the BBNJ Agreement and other relevant frameworks and bodies, also emphasises the promotion of coherence and coordination across instruments, frameworks, and bodies.

support the BBNJ Agreement's objectives, especially on Part III (on ABMTs), Part IV (on EIAs), and Part V (on capacity building). With respect to ABMTs, proponent of an ABMT, including an MPA, under the BBNJ Agreement could build on the scientific ecological and biological information contained in the CBD's EBSA descriptions and submit these for consideration to the BBNJ Agreement's COP. Ecological and biological information is a crucial element of ABMTs if these areas are to achieve biodiversity conservation objectives (e.g. in the case of MPAs) or outcomes (e.g. in the case of OECMs).

An example of a potential OECM in the fisheries sector is VME measures adopted by NAFO on Corner Rise Seamounts. The Corner Rise Seamounts are located in the Northwest Atlantic in areas beyond national jurisdiction and under NAFO's regulatory area. Other sectoral organisations have mandates in this area: the International Seabed Authority with respect to deep seabed mining, the International Maritime Organization with respect to shipping, and the International Commission for the Conservation of Atlantic Tunas with respect to tuna and tuna-like fisheries. Furthermore, the seamounts chain falls inside the geographical scope of the Sargasso Sea Commission. Two decisions of the CBD's COP have described this seamounts chain as EBSAs: as part of the Sargasso Sea EBSA,[65] and as part of the New England and Corner Rise Seamounts EBSA.[66] Contracting parties to NAFO have also identified these as a VME[67] and as an OECM.[68] These seamounts host complex coral and sponge communities, including numerous endemic species.

NAFO has established different fisheries measures to protect these seamounts and associated species since 2006. Most notably, in 2016, bottom trawling was unauthorized, and requirements for mid-water trawl gear modification were introduced to avoid bottom contact.[69] The mid-water trawl fishery targeted the Splendid alfonsino (*Beryx* splenden) species. Uncertainties over the alfonsino stock status have prevented the NAFO Scientific Council from conducting assessments of this stock (NAFO division 6G). Consequently, the second NAFO performance review (2018) recommended that NAFO 'establishes conservation and management

65 Decision Adopted by the Conference of the Parties to the CBD, 'Marine and Coastal Biodiversity: Ecologically or Biologically Significant Marine Areas' (5 December 2012) UNEP/CBD/COP/DEC/XI/17.

66 Decision Adopted by the Conference of the Parties to the CBD, 'Marine and Coastal Biodiversity: Ecologically or Biologically Significant Marine Areas (EBSAs)' (17 October 2014) UNEP/CBD/COP/DEC/XII/22.

67 NAFO, 'Conservation and Enforcement Measures 2023' (2023). <www.nafo.int/Portals/0/PDFs/COM/2023/comdoc23-01REV.pdf> accessed 13 January 2024.

68 NAFO, 'Report of the NAFO Commission and its Subsidiary Bodies (STACTIC and STACFAD): 45th Annual Meeting of NAFO' (Vigo, 2023) <www.nafo.int/Portals/0/PDFs/COM/2023/comdoc23-28.pdf> accessed 13 January 2024.

69 NAFO, 'Report of the NAFO Fisheries Commission and its Subsidiary Body (STACTIC)' (Varadero, 19–23 September 2016) <www.nafo.int/Portals/0/PDFs/fc/2016/fcdoc16-20.pdf> accessed 13 January 2024; NAFO, 'Conservation and Enforcement Measures 2017' (2017) <www.nafo.int/Portals/0/PDFs/fc/2017/CEM-2017-web.pdf> accessed 13 January 2024.

measures for Splendid Alfonsino in Subarea 6, at the earliest opportunity'.[70] In 2019, NAFO's Scientific Council concluded that the stock was depleted and recommended a moratorium. At the subsequent NAFO Commission's Annual Meeting, parties agreed on an indefinite moratorium until the Scientific Council can conduct a full assessment of the stock and provide advice.[71] In 2021, the VME measures were reviewed and scientific proposals to expand the Corner Rise Seamounts closure were adopted.[72]

In discussing the suitability of this area as a potential OECM, an International Council for the Exploration of the Sea's expert workshop stressed the need to understand how other sectors could threaten the biodiversity conservation outcomes of the VME measures.[73] It further emphasised the need to address the fragmented governance of areas beyond national jurisdiction. In this context, the BBNJ Agreement and its COP could play an active role in facilitating cross-sectoral cooperation to 'achieve positive and sustained long-term outcomes for the *in situ* conservation of biodiversity with associated ecosystem functions and services'.[74]

This seems consistent with the requirement that the BBNJ Agreement's COP 'shall' make arrangements for regular consultations with RFMOs and other frameworks and bodies to enhance coordination and cooperation with regards to ABMTs, including MPAs, and related measures adopted by such instruments and bodies.[75] Reading these clauses altogether, it is clear that co-design and development of conservation and management measures by, on the one hand, the BBNJ Agreement's STB and COP and, on the other hand, competent bodies and frameworks' specific scientific and decision-making bodies are key to achieving international policy and legal coherence.

3. Conclusions

The BBNJ Agreement mandates its COP to adopt a management plan based on the best available science, including from the STB and from consultations held on the proposals of ABMTs developed by parties, either individually or collectively (which includes the possibility of regional coordination). The BBNJ Agreement is not overly prescriptive, and delegates to the STB and COP will further elaborate

70 NAFO, 'NAFO Performance Review Panel Report 2018' (2018) 24. www.nafo.int/Portals/0/PDFs/Performance/NAFOPerformanceReviewPanelRpt2018.pdf accessed 13 January 2024.

71 NAFO, 'Report of the NAFO Commission and its Subsidiary Bodies (STACTIC and STACFED)' (Halifax 2021). www.nafo.int/Portals/0/PDFs/COM/2021/comdoc21-21REV.pdf accessed 13 January 2024.

72 ibid.

73 International Council for the Exploration of the Sea, 'ICES/IUCN-CEM FEG Workshop on Testing OECM Practices and Strategies (WKTOPS)' (2 September 2022). ices-library.figshare.com/articles/report/ICES_IUCN-CEM_FEG_Workshop_on_Testing_OECM_Practices_and_Strategies_WKTOPS_/18621746 accessed 13 January 2024.

74 Decision Adopted by the Conference of the Parties to the CBD, 'Protected Areas and Other Effective Area-Based Conservation Measures' (30 November 2018) CBD/COP/DEC/14/8, para 2.

75 BBNJ Agreement art 22(3).

on the consultation modalities. This provides an opportunity for RFMOs to play an active role in establishing ABMTs, including MPAs, and in identifying or recognising OECMs if they so wish.

It is also clear that the BBNJ Agreement does not impose a top-down approach on RFMOs with respect to ABMTs, including MPAs and OECMs. Instead, it seeks to strike a delicate balance of empowering its COP to adopt science- and knowledge-based MPA management plans, while either co-developing with or at least meaningfully consulting RFMOs on proposed conservation and management measures. Furthermore, the recommendations by the BBNJ Agreement's COP on measures falling within the competence of RFMOs resemble those included in UNGA resolutions on sustainable fisheries regarding the protection of VMEs. Article 26(1) of the BBNJ Agreement requires that parties, individually or collectively, report to the COP on the implementation of ABMTs, including MPAs, established under the BBNJ Agreement, as well as on related measures. The Secretariat shall then make such information publicly available.[76] Although not legally binding, the review process on the implementation by States and RFMOs of measures recommended by UNGA resolutions on sustainable fisheries concerning VMEs is comparable to a COP's review of the implementation of ABMT measures.[77]

As such, the review by the BBNJ Agreement's COP could also involve RFMO scientists. This would be similar to the UNGA process for information sharing, best practices, and co-development of solutions to any implementation challenges. Cooperation between the BBNJ Agreement's STB, RFMOs' scientific bodies, and scientific programmes established under fisheries agreements could promote enhanced synergies in designing such measures at the proposal stage as well as at the implementation and review stages. As noted by David Balton, the Agreement to Prevent Unregulated High Seas Fisheries in the Central Arctic Ocean has a Joint Program of Scientific Research and Monitoring, with capacity to conduct scientific assessments in that area.[78] This Joint Program could contribute to ABMT

76 ibid, art 26(1).

77 UNGA, 'Sustainable Fisheries, Including Through the 1995 Agreement for the Implementation of the Provisions of the United Nations Convention on the Law of the Sea of 10 December 1982 Relating to the Conservation and Management of Straddling Fish Stocks and Highly Migratory Fish Stocks, and Related Instruments' (8 December 2006) Resolution 61/105; UNGA, 'Sustainable Fisheries, Including through the 1995 Agreement for the Implementation of the Provisions of the United Nations Convention on the Law of the Sea of 10 December 1982 Relating to the Conservation and Management of Straddling Fish Stocks and Highly Migratory Fish Stocks, and Related Instruments' (6 December 2011) Resolution 66/68; UNGA, 'Sustainable Fisheries, Including through the 1995 Agreement for the Implementation of the Provisions of the United Nations Convention on the Law of the Sea of 10 December 1982 relating to the Conservation and Management of Straddling Fish Stocks and Highly Migratory Fish Stocks, and Related Instruments' (7 December 2016) Resolution 71/123; UNGA, 'Sustainable Fisheries, Including through the 1995 Agreement for the Implementation of the Provisions of the United Nations Convention on the Law of the Sea of 10 December 1982 Relating to the Conservation and Management of Straddling Fish Stocks and Highly Migratory Fish Stocks, and Related Instruments' (8 December 2020) Resolution 75/89.

78 David Balton, 'What Will the BBNJ Agreement Mean for the Arctic Fisheries Agreement?' (2022) 142 *Marine Policy* 103745.

proposals, in addition to the International Council for the Exploration of the Sea, the North Pacific Marine Science Organization, and relevant Arctic Council bodies. This scientific coordination could enable a mutually supportive interface between the BBNJ Agreement and RFMOs, as well as with the CBD with respect to EBSA and OECMs to achieve global spatial targets for conservation of the marine environment.

21 The Impact of the BBNJ Agreement on Regional Fisheries Management Organisations or Arrangements

Kentaro Nishimoto

1. Introduction

After two decades of deliberations, the Agreement under the United Nations Convention on the Law of the Sea on the Conservation and Sustainable Use of Marine Biological Diversity of Areas beyond National Jurisdiction (BBNJ Agreement or Agreement) was adopted on 19 June 2023.[1] The BBNJ Agreement seeks to 'ensure the conservation and sustainable use of marine biological diversity of areas beyond national jurisdiction, for the present and in the long term', through the effective implementation of the United Nations Convention on the Law of the Sea (UNCLOS) and further international cooperation and coordination.[2] To achieve this objective, the Agreement introduces detailed rules and procedures relating to marine genetic resources; area-based management tools (ABMTs), including marine protected areas (MPAs); environmental impact assessments (EIAs); and capacity-building and transfer of marine technology. Moreover, it establishes an institutional framework to implement the Agreement, including a Conference of the Parties (COP), an independent secretariat, and a Clearing-House Mechanism, a platform for parties to access, provide and disseminate relevant information.

The decision to develop the Agreement was made in 2015 by United Nations General Assembly (UNGA) Resolution 69/292. This decision resulted from discussions on the need to fill 'legal gaps' and strengthen the governance of areas beyond national jurisdiction (ABNJ).[3] However, the existence of a 'legal gap' did not mean that there was a legal vacuum. Various legal instruments, frameworks, and bodies (IFBs) exercise regulatory powers over certain activities or regions. In regard to fishing, the Agreement for the Implementation of the Provisions of UNCLOS

1 Agreement under the United Nations Convention on the Law of the Sea on the Conservation and Sustainable Use of Marine Biological Diversity of Areas Beyond National Jurisdiction (BBNJ Agreement), 19 June 2023, A/CONF.232/2023/4, opened for signature on 20 September 2023, not yet in force.

2 ibid, art 2.

3 Dire Tladi, 'Conservation and Sustainable Use of Marine Biodiversity in Areas Beyond National Jurisdiction: Towards an Implementing Agreement' in Rosemary Rayfuse (ed), *Research Handbook on International Marine Environmental Law* (Elgar 2015) 263.

DOI: 10.4324/9781003492030-28

relating to the Conservation and Management of Straddling Fish Stocks and Highly Migratory Fish Stocks (Fish Stocks Agreement) provided the legal regime for managing straddling fish stocks and highly migratory fish stocks.[4] Within this framework, measures adopted by regional fisheries management organisations or arrangements (RFMOs) apply to fish stocks in different areas of the world's oceans.

On the one hand, regulating activities in ABNJ through sector-specific or region-specific IFBs was seen as illustrating the shortcoming of the governance of ABNJ given that 'the problems of ocean space are closely interrelated and need to be considered as a whole'.[5] This problem was considered especially acute for the conservation and sustainable use of biodiversity, which is threatened by the cumulative impacts of various forms of human activity.[6] The development of the BBNJ Agreement represented an opportunity to overcome the fragmented nature of ABNJ's governance.

On the other hand, some States held concerns about overlapping mandates between the BBNJ Agreement and existing IFBs.[7] Specifically in relation to RFMOs, certain tensions existed between the focus of RFMOs on 'sustainable use' and the objective of the Agreement, namely 'conservation and sustainable use'.[8] These concerns were particularly prevalent among States with fishing interests in relation to ABMTs/MPAs. During the process which led to the UNGA's decision to develop the Agreement, these States argued that fisheries should be excluded from the scope of the Agreement.[9] Such positions were abandoned early in the subsequent phase of negotiations. However, concerns over the possible impact of the Agreement on the operation of existing regulatory regimes resulted in the mandate of the negotiating process being constrained. It was specified that the process

4 Agreement for the Implementation of the Provisions of the United Nations Convention on the Law of the Sea of 10 December 1982 relating to the Conservation and Management of Straddling Fish Stocks and Highly Migratory Fish Stocks (Fish Stocks Agreement), 4 August 1995, 2167 UNTS 3, entered into force 11 December 2001.

5 United Nations Convention on the Law of the Sea (UNCLOS), 10 December 1982, 1833 UNTS 3, entered into force 16 November 1994, preamble.

6 Kristina Gjerde, Nichola Clark, and Harriet Harden-Davies, 'Building a Platform for the Future: The Relationship of the Expected New Agreement for Marine Biodiversity in Areas beyond National Jurisdiction and the UN Convention on the Law of the Sea' (2019) 33 *Ocean Yearbook* 3, 8.

7 See, for example, International Institute for Sustainable Development, 'Summary of the First Session of the Preparatory Committee on Marine Biodiversity of Areas Beyond National Jurisdiction: 28 March – 8 April 2016' (11 April 2016) 25(97) *Earth Negotiations Bulletin* 2, recording that Japan stressed that the Agreement 'should not overlap with the mandates of RFMOs and other existing instruments'.

8 Konrad Jan Marciniak, 'New Implementing Agreement under UNCLOS: A Threat or an Opportunity for Fisheries Governance?' (2017) 84 *Marine Policy* 320, 323.

9 Dire Tladi, 'The Proposed Implementing Agreement: Options for Coherence and Consistency in the Establishment of Protected Areas beyond National Jurisdiction' (2015) 30 *International Journal of Marine and Coastal Law* 654, 660; Richard Barnes, 'The Proposed LOSC Implementation Agreement on Areas Beyond National Jurisdiction and Its Impact on International Fisheries Law' (2016) 31 *International Journal of Marine and Coastal Law* 583, 592–5.

'should not undermine existing relevant legal instruments and frameworks and relevant global, regional and sectoral bodies'.[10]

As a consequence, a critical question for the negotiations was how the BBNJ Agreement could fill gaps and realise a coherent system for governing ABNJ without undermining relevant IFBs.[11] Thus, the relationship between the BBNJ Agreement and relevant IFBs was treated as a central issue impacting the architecture of the Agreement and led to intensive discussion throughout the negotiation process.[12] Now that an agreement has been reached, this chapter examines how this issue was resolved and the resulting impact of the BBNJ Agreement on RFMOs. For this purpose, it first examines the provisions of the Agreement which are relevant to the relationship between the Agreement and IFBs. It then considers the specific impact of the Agreement on the operation of RFMOs. Finally, it offers some concluding observations on the balance between the need to achieve coherent governance of ABNJ and not to unduly interfere with relevant IFBs.

2. The Relationship between the BBNJ Agreement and Relevant IFBs

The BBNJ Agreement does not contain any reference to RFMOs. Instead, it deals with its relationship with RFMOs entirely within the broader issue of its relationship with relevant IFBs. The provisions which are relevant to this issue are found both in the general provisions (Part I) which apply to the entire Agreement and in specific sections on ABMTs/MPAs (Part III) and environment impact assessments (EIAs) (Part IV).

2.1. General Provisions

Article 5(2) sets out the overall relationship between the BBNJ Agreement and IFBs. It states that the Agreement shall be interpreted and applied 'in a manner that does not undermine relevant [IFBs] and that promotes coherence and coordination with those [IFBs]'. This provision consists of two elements reflecting the overall philosophy of the Agreement, which is to promote coherent governance of ABNJ without 'undermining' IFBs. The first element is that the Agreement's provisions must be construed in a way that does not undermine relevant IFBs. This first

10 United Nations General Assembly (UNGA), 'Development of an International Legally Binding Instrument Under the United Nations Convention on the Law of the Sea on the Conservation and Sustainable Use of Marine Biological Diversity of Areas Beyond National Jurisdiction' (19 June 2015) Resolution 69/292, para 3.

11 Veronica Frank, 'Options for Marine Protected Areas under a New Agreement on Marine Biodiversity of Areas Beyond National Jurisdiction' in Tomas Heidar (ed), *New Knowledge and Changing Circumstances in the Law of the Sea* (Brill 2020) 101, 111.

12 Efthymios Papastavridis, 'The Negotiations for a New Implementing Agreement Under the UN Convention on the Law of the Sea Concerning Marine Biodiversity' (2020) 69 *International and Comparative Law Quarterly* 585, 601–3.

element reflects the basic premise of the Agreement set out in UNGA Resolution 69/292 which decided to develop the Agreement. Originally, this instruction was framed in relation to the Agreement's negotiating process.[13] Yet, the instruction not to undermine IFBs in Article 5(2) is formulated as a method of interpretation and application of the Agreement itself. The first element is, thus, intended as a safeguard against the Agreement encroaching on matters within the competence of IFBs. The second element is to interpret and apply the Agreement in a manner that promotes coherence and coordination with IFBs.

One major difficulty with this provision is that the meaning of 'not undermine' is unclear. This term first appeared in UNGA Resolution 69/292 and was thoroughly discussed in academic literature during the negotiation process, leading to different interpretations.[14] The points raised in these discussions seemingly continue to be relevant when interpreting Article 5(2). However, some additional observations can be attempted based on the provision's drafting history. First, a proposal to add 'the effectiveness of' after 'does not undermine' was reflected in the draft text at one point in the negotiations.[15] The omission of this wording in the final text strengthens the argument that it is not the effectiveness of an IFB which is relevant in determining whether this IFB is undermined. Second, the proposal to add 'respect the competences of and' before 'not undermine' appears in various versions of the negotiating text until the final stages of the negotiations.[16] The omission of the reference to competence in the final text could support the interpretation that not all consideration of issues under an IFB's competence would undermine this IFB. However, in Article 22(2) on ABMTs, which may be considered a specific application of this provision, the term 'respect the competences of' was deliberately included in addition to 'not undermine'.

13 UNGA, 'Development of an International Legally Binding Instrument under the United Nations Convention on the Law of the Sea on the Conservation and Sustainable Use of Marine Biological Diversity of Areas Beyond National Jurisdiction' (19 June 2015) Resolution 69/292, para 3. The resolution to convene the BBNJ Intergovernmental Conference expanded the scope of the instruction 'not [to] undermine' the negotiation process *and its result*, see UNGA, 'International Legally Binding Instrument Under the United Nations Convention on the Law of the Sea on the Conservation and Sustainable Use of Marine Biological Diversity of Areas Beyond National Jurisdiction' (24 December 2017) Resolution 72/249, para 7.

14 Zoe Scanlon, 'The Art of 'Not Undermining': Possibilities within Existing Architecture to Improve Environmental Protections in Areas beyond National Jurisdiction' (2018) 75 *ICES Journal of Marine Science* 405, 406–9; Richard Barnes, 'Fisheries and Areas Beyond National Jurisdiction: Advancing and Enhancing Cooperation' in Tomas Heidar (ed), *New Knowledge and Changing Circumstances in the Law of the Sea* (Brill 2020) 124, 136–9.

15 UNGA, 'Further Revised Draft Text of an Agreement under the United Nations Convention on the Law of the Sea on the Conservation and Sustainable Use of Marine Biological Diversity of Areas Beyond National Jurisdiction: Note by the President' (1 June 2022) A/CONF.232/2022/5 undocs.org/A/CONF.232/2022/5 accessed 14 January 2024, art 4(3).

16 ibid; UNGA, 'Updated Draft Text of an Agreement Under the United Nations Convention on the Law of the Sea on the Conservation and Sustainable Use of Marine Biological Diversity of Areas beyond National Jurisdiction as of 25 February 2023' (25 February 2023) A/CONF.232/2023/CRP.1, art 4(2).

Article 8 on international cooperation is another general provision of the BBNJ Agreement relevant to its relationship with IFBs. Article 8(1) sets out a general obligation for parties to cooperate to achieve its objective and explicitly provides that cooperation in this regard would include two forms of cooperation involving IFBs. The first is 'strengthening and enhancing cooperation with' IFBs, which refers to the cooperation between IFBs and parties acting to achieve the Agreement's objectives. The explicit reference to this form of cooperation underscores the crucial role of IFBs in achieving the objective of the Agreement. The second is 'promoting cooperation among' IFBs. This form of cooperation would improve the fragmented governance of ABNJ by requiring parties to promote cooperation among different IFBs.

The general obligation to cooperate under Article 8(1) is detailed in other provisions of the Agreement. First, Article 8(2) provides that 'Parties shall endeavour to promote, as appropriate, the objectives of this Agreement when participating in decision-making under other relevant [IFBs]'. This provision seeks to achieve coherence in efforts toward conserving and sustainably using marine biological diversity in ABNJ by requiring parties to the Agreement, which may also be parties to or members of various IFBs, to behave in a certain way when participating in IFBs. The concern about the Agreement encroaching upon matters within the mandate of IFBs likely explains the general wording in Article 8(2). This provision only requires parties to 'endeavour to promote' the Agreement's objectives, rather than to adhere strictly to specific decisions adopted by the BBNJ Agreement's COP. The obligation is also further qualified by the term 'as appropriate'. While Article 8(2) applies to the entire treaty, a more specific version of this obligation can be found in Article 25(4) on ABMTs/MPAs and Article 29(1) on EIAs.

Second, under Article 47(6)(c) of the Agreement, the BBNJ Agreement's COP is tasked with promoting the two forms of cooperation referred to in Article 8(1). The obligation under Article 8(1) refers to cooperation 'in the achievement of the objectives of this Agreement'. Conversely, Article 47(6)(c) highlights a more specific agenda and refers to cooperation 'with a view to promoting coherence among efforts towards the conservation and sustainable use of marine biological diversity of [ABNJ]'. It also identifies 'establishing appropriate processes' as a possible means through which the COP could promote cooperation and coordination. While Article 47(6)(c) only refers to establishing appropriate processes as one means of promoting cooperation, Article 22(3) on ABMTs/MPAs provides that the COP 'shall make arrangements for regular consultations to enhance cooperation and coordination with and among relevant [IFBs]'. Similarly, Article 29(2) on EIAs provides that the COP 'shall develop mechanisms under this Part for the Scientific and Technical Body to collaborate with relevant [IFBs]', although this cooperation is only between the Agreement and IFBs.

2.2. *Area-based Management Tools, Including Marine Protected Areas*

Part III of the BBNJ Agreement introduces rules and processes regarding ABMTs/MPAs in ABNJ. The centrepiece of Part III is the procedure by which the COP can establish ABMTs/MPAs and related measures based on a 'hybrid approach' championed in the Agreement's negotiations.[17] The procedure reflects the 'global approach' as the COP is given the power to take decisions on establishing ABMTs and related measures in accordance with the procedures set out in Part III. However, the procedure also reflects the 'regional/sectoral approach' as it recognises the role of IFBs in establishing ABMTs/MPAs and adopting related measures.

Article 22(1) of the Agreement sets out the COP's power to take decisions on establishing ABMTs/MPAs and related measures. According to this provision, the COP '[s]hall take decisions on the establishment of [ABMTs/MPAs] and related measures' per subparagraph (a); '[m]ay take decisions on measures compatible with those adopted by relevant [IFBs], in cooperation and coordination with those [IFBs]' per subparagraph (b); and per subparagraph (c):

> May, where proposed measures are within the competences of other global, regional, subregional or sectoral bodies, make recommendations to Parties to [the] Agreement and to global, regional, subregional or sectoral bodies to promote the adoption of relevant measures through such [IFBs], in accordance with their respective mandates.

Article 22(2) then introduces a limitation to the COP's power by providing that '[i]n taking decisions under this Article, the [COP] shall respect the competences of, and not undermine, relevant [IFBs]'.

These provisions are not entirely clear on whether the COP could adopt measures which would fall within the mandate of RFMOs. To begin with, Article 22(1) is open to multiple interpretations. One reading would be to interpret the explicit reference to measures in subparagraphs (b) and (c) as restricting the general power of the COP under subparagraph (a) to take decisions on these two types of measures. However, the use of the term 'may' in subparagraphs (b) and (c) – in contrast to 'shall' in subparagraph (a) – could suggest that these are options available to the COP at its discretion and do not limit the power conferred to the COP under subparagraph (a).

In contrast, it is reasonably clear that Article 22(2) limits the COP's power to take decisions on ABMTs/MPAs under Article 22(1). As previously discussed, the meaning of the term 'not undermine' is notoriously vague. However, the further inclusion of the expression 'respect the competences of' suggests that the boundaries

17 On the origins of the hybrid approach as a compromise between the global and regional/sectoral approach, see Kristine Dalaker Kraabel, 'The BBNJ PrepCom and Institutional Arrangements: The Hype About the Hybrid Approach' in Myron Nordquist, John Norton Moore and Ronán Long (eds), *The Marine Environment and United Nations Sustainable Development Goal 14* (Brill 2018) 137. On the implications of the different approaches for ABMTs/MPAs, see Veronica Frank, 'Options for Marine Protected Areas Under a New Agreement on Marine Biodiversity of Areas beyond National Jurisdiction' in Tomas Heidar (ed), *New Knowledge and Changing Circumstances in the Law of the Sea* (Brill 2020) 111, 112–22.

of the COP's competence are defined by the competence of IFBs.[18] Other provisions in Part III and the Agreement's drafting history also support the interpretation that the COP may not take measures under the competence of RFMOs. For example, the rule requiring consultations with IFBs for adopting measures on an emergency basis, when an immediate response may be required, could reflect the understanding that the COP must not adopt measures where IFBs have competence.[19] In addition, the existence of a rule relating to the measures adopted by the COP, where such measures subsequently fall within the competence of IFBs due to their establishment or an amendment of their competence, could reflect the precedence of IFBs where they have competence.[20] Proposals to list the powers of the COP, based on whether the measures fall within the competence of IFBs, were not successful in the negotiating process.[21] Such proposals were finally dropped in exchange for adding the language 'respect the competences of'. This could indicate that this expression was intended to allow the COP only to make recommendations when measures are within the competence of IFBs. However, a contrary interpretation might still be attempted, based on the ambiguous wording of Article 22(1) and the unclarity of the expression 'respect the competences of, and not undermine'. Further, it may not always be appropriate if an IFB with the competence to adopt a measure could block the COP from adopting a measure, particularly when the IFB was not exercising its competence in the face of scientific information evidencing the need to take measures.[22]

On ABMTs/MPAs and related measures adopted under IFBs, Article 22(4) allows the COP to decide to develop a mechanism where such mechanism is required to achieve the objectives and implementation of Part III. This provision originates from an unsuccessful proposal to have a procedure for 'recognition' of

18 The term 'respect' is used in various provisions of UNCLOS which requires strict observance of what must be respected, rather than merely to take them into account. This usage can be seen in UNCLOs, arts 41(7), 47(6), 51(1), 51(2), 53(11), 60(6), 168(1), 233, 240(c), 242.

19 BBNJ Agreement, art 24(2).

20 BBNJ Agreement, art 22(7).

21 UNGA, 'Updated Draft Text of an Agreement Under the United Nations Convention on the Law of the Sea on the Conservation and Sustainable Use of Marine Biological Diversity of Areas Beyond National Jurisdiction as of 25 February 2023' (25 February 2023) A/CONF.232/2023/CRP.1, art 19. See also, International Institute for Sustainable Development, 'Summary of the Resumed Fifth Session of the Intergovernmental Conference on an International Legally Binding Instrument under the UN Convention on the Law of the Sea on the Conservation and Sustainable Use of Marine Biodiversity of Areas Beyond National Jurisdiction: 20 February – 4 March 2023' (7 March 2023) 25(250) *Earth Negotiations Bulletin* 8, explaining that '[i]n a breakthrough, delegations agreed on the option that allows the COP to take decisions on measures compatible with those adopted by IFBs, and to propose measures that are within the competencies of "and not undermine" other IFBs'.

22 Barnes points out that the mandates of many RFMOs are widely drawn in terms of power, but are weak in terms of duties, see Richard Barnes, 'Fisheries and Areas beyond National Jurisdiction: Advancing and Enhancing Cooperation' in Tomas Heidar (ed), *New Knowledge and Changing Circumstances in the Law of the Sea* (Brill 2020) 124, 137.

ABMTs/MPAs.[23] This procedure would have allowed the COP to grant ABMTs/MPAs adopted by IFBs the same status as those adopted by the COP, making them binding on non-members of IFBs under the Agreement.[24] In the case of RFMOs, the Fish Stocks Agreement already prevents non-members from authorising fishing operations for the straddling fish stocks or highly migratory fish stocks subject to measures adopted by RFMOs, unless they agree to apply the measures.[25] However, the future development of a mechanism could benefit RFMOs by further extending the binding effect of their measures.

Once the COP adopts decisions, parties must ensure that activities under their jurisdiction or control in ABNJ are conducted consistently with these decisions.[26] With respect to IFBs, Article 25(4) provides that parties have an obligation to 'promote, as appropriate, the adoption of measures within relevant [IFBs] of which they are members, to support the implementation of the decisions and recommendations made by the [COP] under this Part'. This provision is a specific application of the more general provision in Article 8(2). Like Article 8(2), Article 25(4) is broadly worded: it only requires parties to 'promote . . . the adoption of measures' rather than to require the parties to adopt measures, which would, in any event, be impossible to guarantee given the collective decision-making in IFBs. The obligation is further qualified by the term 'as appropriate'. Based on this wording, it is doubtful whether the obligation under Article 25(4) could compel the parties to the Agreement to propose conservation measures in RFMOs in order to implement recommendations by the COP or to vote in favour of such proposals. The Article appears intended to encourage parties' actions within relevant IFBs in a general manner.

As mentioned previously, Part III also includes provisions for enhancing coherence among IFBs. Article 22(3) provides that the COP is to make arrangements for regular consultations to enhance cooperation and coordination with and among relevant IFBs over ABMTs/MPAs, as well as coordination over measures adopted by IFBs. In addition, Article 26(2) provides that relevant IFBs shall be invited to provide information to the COP on implementing measures adopted by these IFBs to achieve the objectives of ABMTs/MPAs established under the Agreement. Finally, provisions are made to incorporate IFBs in the process of establishing ABMTs/

23 On recognition of ABMTs, see Bastiaan Ewoud Klerk, 'Recognizing Recognition: An Indispensable Element in a Global Regime for High Seas Marine Protected Areas', *The NCLOS Blog* (27 July 2022). site.uit.no/nclos/wp-content/uploads/sites/179/2022/07/Bastiaan-E-Klerk_270722_NCLOS_blog-post.pdf accessed 14 January 2024.

24 For example, UNGA, 'Further Revised Draft Text of an Agreement Under the United Nations Convention on the Law of the Sea on the Conservation and Sustainable Use of Marine Biological Diversity of Areas Beyond National Jurisdiction: Note by the President' (1 June 2022) A/CONF.232/2022/5. undocs.org/A/CONF.232/2022/5 accessed 14 January 2024, art 19, Option II, para 1.

25 Fish Stocks Agreement, art 17(1)–(2). Moritaka Hayashi, 'The 1995 Agreement on the Conservation and Management of Straddling and Highly Migratory Fish Stocks: Significance for the Law of the Sea Convention' (1995) 29 *Ocean and Coastal Management* 51, 58.

26 BBNJ Agreement, art 25(1).

MPAs and related measures from an early phase. During consultations on a proposal, bodies of relevant IFBs are notified and invited to submit, inter alia, views on the merits of the proposal and any aspects of the measures or draft management plan which fall within the competence of the body.[27] In practice, issues regarding the competence of IFBs could be addressed at this stage.

2.3. Environmental Impact Assessments

Part IV of the BBNJ Agreement provides rules and procedures to implement the obligation to conduct EIAs under UNCLOS with respect to activities in ABNJ. Article 206 of UNCLOS requires States to conduct EIAs when States have reasonable grounds to believe that planned activities under their jurisdiction or control may cause substantial pollution of or significant and harmful changes to the marine environment. Part IV of the BBNJ Agreement provides additional guidance on implementing this obligation. It notably clarifies the threshold and factors for conducting EIAs;[28] outlines the EIA process,[29] and establishes procedural requirements relating to notification, consultation, and preparation of EIA reports.[30] Part IV also includes provisions on the monitoring and review of activities authorised based on an EIA.[31]

Part IV of the Agreement would require parties, whose vessels fish on the high seas, to conduct EIAs where fishing could cause significant and harmful changes to the marine environment. Besides Article 206 of UNCLOS, the obligation to assess the impact of fishing can also be found in international fisheries law but lacks specificity on the content of the assessment to conduct.[32] Article 5(d) of the Fish Stocks Agreement lists assessing the 'impacts of fishing, other human activities and environmental factors' as a means through which the duty of States to cooperate in conserving and managing straddling fish stocks and highly migratory stocks shall be given effect. The Food and Agriculture Organization of the United Nations developed International Guidelines for the Management of Deep-Sea Fisheries in the High Seas to provide guidance to States and RFMOs on appropriate measures for managing deep-sea fisheries in the high seas.[33] This includes guidance on conducting assessments if deep-sea fishing activities are likely to produce significant adverse impacts. Further, although some RFMOs require EIAs, specific

27 ibid, art 21(2)(b).
28 ibid, art 30.
29 ibid, art 31.
30 ibid arts 32–3.
31 ibid, arts 35–7.
32 Simon Marsden, 'Environmental Assessment and International Fisheries Law' in Richard Caddell and Erik Molenaar (eds), *Strengthening International Fisheries Law in an Era of Changing Oceans* (Hart 2019) 219.
33 Food and Agriculture Organization of the United Nations, 'International Guidelines for the Management of Deep-Sea Fisheries in the High Seas' (Rome 2009), paras 47–9.

requirements for conducting EIAs are limited to new or exploratory fisheries and bottom-sea fisheries.[34]

Recognising that some IFBs, including RFMOs, require EIAs for activities they regulate, Part IV of the BBNJ Agreement contains provisions on the relationship between the Agreement and EIA processes under relevant IFBs. There are two aspects to this relationship. First, to achieve consistent implementation of EIAs for activities in ABNJ across different sectors, 'standards and/or guidelines' on EIAs will be developed under the Agreement for use in IFBs. Second, to avoid duplication of efforts under the Agreement and under relevant IFBs, the Agreement will not require EIAs if EIAs are conducted under IFBs and meet certain requirements under the Agreement.

The BBNJ Agreement's Scientific Technical Body (STB) will develop the standards and/or guidelines for adoption by the COP.[35] They will address issues such as determining thresholds and assessing cumulative impacts and impacts in areas within national jurisdiction.[36] They could also include an indicative list of activities which require or do not require an EIA, and the conduct of EIAs in areas identified as requiring protection or special attention.[37] The difference between standards and guidelines appears to be whether they are legally binding or not. A provision in the Agreement explicitly states that standards will be set out in an annex to the Agreement, which forms an integral part of the Agreement.[38] In contrast, the Agreement is silent on the status of EIA guidelines.

Despite this difference between standards and guidelines, the only specific obligation on their use in IFBs is in Article 29(1). Article 29(1) requires parties to 'promote . . . the adoption and implementation of the standards and/or guidelines developed under article 38 in relevant [IFBs] of which they are members'. This obligation parallels the obligation under Article 25(1) on ABMTs/MPAs to promote the adoption of measures within IFBs to support the implementation of the COP's decisions and recommendations. The observations on the general nature of the obligation under Article 25(1) equally apply to Article 29(1). It is difficult to read this obligation as directly requiring parties to take specific actions in IFBs. Since this general obligation equally applies to standards and guidelines, the distinction between standards and guidelines may not have significant implications for the work of IFBs, including RFMOs. Thus, the effect of Article 29(1) would be to

34 Robin Warner, 'Conservation and Management of Marine Living Resources Beyond National Jurisdiction: Filling the Gaps' in Robert Beckman et al. (eds), *High Seas Governance: Gaps and Challenges* (Brill 2018) 179, 186–7. For practice on these types of fisheries, see Simon Marsden, 'Environmental Assessment and International Fisheries Law' in Richard Caddell and Erik Molenaar (eds) *Strengthening International Fisheries Law in an Era of Changing Oceans* (Hart 2019) 219, 239–41; Richard Caddell, 'Precautionary Management and the Development of Future Fishing Opportunities: The International Regulation of New and Exploratory Fisheries' (2018) 33 *International Journal of Marine and Coastal Law* 199, 252–7.

35 BBNJ Agreement, art 38(1).

36 ibid, art 38(1).

37 ibid, art 38(2).

38 ibid, arts 38(3), 74(1).

encourage parties to implement the standards and/or guidelines to achieve convergence in how IFBs implement EIAs.

Planned activities regulated by IFBs will be exempt from the obligation to conduct a screening or a full EIA when these activities fulfil the requirements under Article 29(4). This provision requires, first, that the potential impacts of the planned activity or category of activity have been assessed in accordance with the relevant IFBs' requirements. Second, one of two elements must be satisfied: (a) the undertaken assessment must have been equivalent to the assessment required under Part IV of the Agreement, or (b) the relevant IFB's regulation or standards arising from the assessment must have been designed to prevent, mitigate, or manage potential impacts below the threshold for EIA under Part IV and were complied with. In addition, there are related requirements for parties to publish EIA reports for EIAs conducted under IFBs through the BBNJ Agreement's Clearing-House Mechanism,[39] and to publish monitoring and review reports unless the activities are subject to monitoring and review under relevant IFBs.[40] Thus, parties would have to conduct EIAs for fishing activities unless the regulations under the RFMOs fulfil these requirements. This should prompt RFMO members to revisit the requirements in RFMOs to conduct EIAs and the basis of RFMO's conservation measures. However, one weakness of Article 29(4) is that it is the party with jurisdiction or control over the planned activity which determines the applicability of the exemption.

Part IV mirrors the approach in Part III in mandating the COP to develop mechanisms for the STB to collaborate with IFBs which regulate activities in ABNJ or protect the marine environment.[41] A collaborative approach is also envisaged in the process of developing the EIA standards or guidelines, wherein the STB is instructed to collaborate with relevant IFBs as appropriate.[42] These provisions will serve to ensure that expertise and experience accumulated in IFBs will be utilised in moving toward a coherent regime of EIAs for activities in ABNJ.

3. The Impact of the BBNJ Agreement on RFMOs

The examination of the relevant provisions in the previous section indicates that the rules and procedures under the BBNJ Agreement will not replace RFMOs' role in managing high seas fisheries resources. On the contrary, effective fisheries management through RFMOs will be vital in achieving the Agreement's objectives. Nevertheless, the Agreement will require RFMOs to re-evaluate their functions within the context of global efforts to conserve and sustainably use marine biological diversity in ABNJ. The Agreement contains limited prescriptive rules requiring RFMOs or their members to adopt or abstain from specific measures. However, it nudges RFMOs and their members toward a coherent approach under the direction

39 ibid, art 29(5).
40 ibid, art 29(6).
41 ibid, art 29(2).
42 ibid, art 29(3).

of the Agreement and its COP. The Agreement has three main mechanisms serving this purpose: creating a platform for interaction with and among IFBs; issuing non-binding recommendations on appropriate measures; and influencing parties' behaviour within RFMOs.

First, the Agreement contains mechanisms for cooperation and coordination designed to facilitate interaction not only between the Agreement's institutional arrangements and IFBs, but also among IFBs. One significant mechanism for RFMOs is the arrangement of regular consultations by the COP on ABTMs/MPAs and related measures (Article 22(3)). Although there are some attempts to enhance coordination between sector-specific IFBs for certain areas of ABNJ, these efforts remain limited.[43] Establishing a new forum for consultations to enhance coordination among IFBs may help identify issues and good practices and foster arrangements between RFMOs and other IFBs. While the BBNJ Agreement's COP can only establish such mechanisms and invite IFBs, including RFMOs, to participate, RFMOs may find participation beneficial in effectively implementing their mandate.

Second, notwithstanding the lack of complete clarity on this issue, the COP does not appear to have the power to impact the work of RFMOs by directly adopting measures which fall within their mandates or by prescribing obligatory minimum standards for assessments. However, the work of RFMOs may be impacted by the COP's power to indicate to RFMOs and their members what it considers desirable by adopting recommendations to promote the adoption of measures in relation to ABMTs/MPAs (Article 22(1)(c)) and by developing standards/guidelines on environmental impact assessments (Articles 29(1) and 38). The recommendations on measures and standards and/or guidelines do not legally bind RFMOs. Therefore, an RFMO may decide not to follow the recommendations or standards and/or guidelines and, instead, adopt or maintain their own measures. However, the BBNJ Agreement's wider participation could create a perception of greater legitimacy. This could create political pressure on RFMO members to follow the recommendations or standards and/or guidelines adopted by the COP. This may be the case, especially when there is uncertainty in scientific information supporting the decision. Additionally, as will be discussed, the obligation to cooperate under the Agreement could be construed as requiring members of RFMOs which are parties to the Agreement, at least, to consider the COP's recommendations or standards and/or guidelines within RFMOs.

Third, the provisions requiring parties to behave in a specific manner when participating in RFMOs may significantly impact the operation of RFMOs by guiding the parties' actions. These are the provisions setting out the obligations to promote

43 For examples, see Ellen Hey, 'The OSPAR NEAFC Collective Arrangement and Ocean Governance: Regional Seas Organisations as the Setters of Conservation Standards in ABNJ?' (2022) 37 *International Journal of Marine and Coastal Law* 610; David Freestone and Kate Killerlain Morrison, 'The Signing of the Hamilton Declaration on Collaboration for the Conservation of the Sargasso Sea: A New Paradigm for High Seas Conservation?' (2014) 29 *International Journal of Marine and Coastal Law* 345.

the objectives of the Agreement (Article 8(2); to promote the implementation of measures within IFBs to support the COP's decisions and recommendations (Article 24(4)); and to promote the use of EIAs and implementation of EIA standards and/or guidelines (Article 29(1)). As previously discussed, these obligations are couched in general terms: it is difficult to interpret them as requiring parties to take specific actions within the RFMOs of which they are members. The general nature of these obligations reflects a balance between the need for coherent governance of ABNJ under the guidance of the BBNJ Agreement's COP and the need to allow IFBs, including RFMOs, to make decisions according to their respective mandates. These obligations provide a subtle mechanism to induce IFBs, including RFMOs, to adopt measures which are consistent with the decisions and recommendations of the COP.

However, because these obligations are legally binding, they could also be powerful mechanisms affecting the operation of RFMOs in different ways. On the one hand, although the general nature of these obligations makes assessing their compliance difficult, non-compliance would be more discernible in extreme situations, such as where members of an RFMO manifestly disregard the COP's decisions, recommendations, or standards/guidelines. Parties which wish to hold RFMO members accountable in such situations could bring this issue to the compulsory dispute settlement procedure under the Agreement,[44] or to the Implementation and Compliance Committee.[45] On the other hand, these obligations could lead to the polarisation of positions within RFMOs and complicate decision-making where some of RFMO members, as parties to the Agreement, strictly adhere to the obligations and endeavour to promote the COP's decisions and recommendations, while others opt to distance themselves from the COP's direction. However, this scenario is unlikely if the Agreement achieves widespread ratification by RFMO members.

4. Conclusion

In the early stages of negotiation of the BBNJ Agreement, some States feared that the Agreement might unjustly encroach on the mandate of RFMOs. These concerns appear to have not materialised in its final text. Under the Agreement, RFMOs will be invited and expected to interact within the new legal framework through various mechanisms. Nevertheless, if this chapter's analysis of the relevant provisions is correct, the core function of RFMOs in managing fisheries resources under their mandate will remain intact. However, this may not necessarily mean business as usual for RFMOs. Their performance could come under increased scrutiny in relation to possible recommendations regarding ABMTs/MPAs and guidelines and/or standards on EIAs adopted by the BBNJ Agreement's COP.

44 BBNJ Agreement, art 60. The Agreement adopts a compulsory dispute settlement procedure based on Part XV of UNCLOS.

45 BBNJ Agreement, art 55.

Overall, the provisions on the relationship between the BBNJ Agreement and IFBs reflect a balanced approach. This could foster a more coherent system of governance for ABNJ to achieve the objectives of the Agreement while, at the same time, not undermining relevant IFBs. In particular, it seeks to achieve coherence among IFBs by creating a general obligation on their members to cooperate and promote the adoption of measures within IFBs which support the implementation of decisions and recommendations by the COP. This innovative approach strikes a balance between the two considerations. In addition, the procedures and bodies which envisage interaction with IFBs should support finding acceptable solutions, even where there are conflicting positions on establishing ABMTs/MPAs and related measures.

Because the BBNJ Agreement is a product of compromise, its text is ambiguous on some crucial aspects. However, once the Agreement enters into force, its parties will be able to clarify any remaining issues through discussions at the COP.

Part VIII

Climate Change and Fisheries

22 International Fisheries Law and the Anthropocene

A Challenge to Foundational Narratives

Ethan Beringen

1. Introduction

The effects of human activities on the environment are becoming ever more clearly understood. Simultaneously, it is becoming clear that international law will have to take steps to adapt to changing conditions. Whether because of climate change or rapidly declining biodiversity, the planet appears to have reached a tipping point, beyond which prevailing environmental conditions will dramatically change.[1] This is the thinking behind the concept of the Anthropocene, which goes so far as to state that human beings now drive change in planetary systems more than any other factor.[2] The geological era of the last 11,700 years is called the Holocene and has been characterised as stable and predictable.[3] Yet, in the face of human-induced environmental change, the future of planetary systems looks to be the opposite.[4] The marine environment is particularly vulnerable to the effects of climate change and other human impacts on oceans.[5] Oceanic conditions are expected to change rapidly in response to the emerging new era. It is therefore important to consider existing international fisheries law in this context.

International environmental law more broadly has faced similar challenges. It has been argued that international environmental law focuses particularly on ensuring the continuation of historic environmental baselines which may no longer be relied upon.[6] This approach is built into international environmental legal regimes, including international fisheries law, particularly through foundational legal

1 See, for example, Will Steffen, Paul Crutzen, and John McNeill, 'The Anthropocene: Are Humans Now Overwhelming the Great Forces of Nature?' (2007) 36 *Ambio* 614; Yadvinder Malhi, 'The Concept of the Anthropocene' (2017) 42 *Annual Review of Environment and Resources* 77, 89.

2 Will Steffen, Paul Crutzen, and John R McNeill, 'The Anthropocene: Are Humans Now Overwhelming the Great Forces of Nature?' (2007) 36 *Ambio* 614.

3 Yadvinder Malhi, 'The Concept of the Anthropocene' (2017) 42 *Annual Review of Environment and Resources* 77.

4 ibid.

5 See, for example, Edward Allison and Hannah Bassett, 'Climate Change in the Oceans: Human Impacts and Responses' (2015) 350 *Science* 778.

6 Louise du Toit and Louis J Kotzé, 'Reimagining International Environmental Law for the Anthropocene: An Earth System Law Perspective' (2022) 11 *Earth System Governance* 1, 4.

DOI: 10.4324/9781003492030-30

principles. These principles play a key role in the narrative of the fisheries regime, and how it operates in practice. The work of Hey has highlighted how a regime's foundational principles can develop into enduring regime-based narratives, which influence how decisions are made and the goals and values of the regime.[7] Thus, regimes are not simply a collection of norms, institutions, and actors. Regimes also reflect collective understandings about the function of these regimes and represent what Hey calls 'epistemic communities'.[8] These collective narratives shape what is to be regulated, how it is to be regulated, and who has the responsibility for and gains from regulation.[9] According to Hey, regime-based narratives often form around the regime's foundational principles and result in path-dependent development of the regime.[10] In other words, political choices at the start of a regime continue to influence its direction into the future.[11]

This chapter considers three fundamental narratives within the regime of international fisheries law and examines how anticipated Anthropocene conditions challenge the continued relevance of these narratives. As the Anthropocene is an expansive concept, there is a broad range of human-induced changes to the marine environment which may fall under its umbrella. Such impacts stem from climate change, pollution, overfishing, shipping, and more.[12] Given word constraints, this chapter cannot fully elucidate the complex and overlapping impacts of all human activities encompassed by the Anthropocene concept. Instead, this chapter focuses on some specific anticipated impacts of climate change and biodiversity loss to demonstrate how human-induced changes to the oceans challenge three narratives of international fisheries law.

The first narrative is the long-held belief that there is a measurable point at which target fish species can be maximally sustainably caught, which allows exploitation to continue indefinitely.[13] This is the thinking underpinning the concept of maximum sustainable yield (MSY), which was entrenched as a foundational principle in the 1982 United Nations Convention on the Law of the Sea (UNCLOS).[14]

The second narrative of international fisheries law is that fish stocks should be managed and allocated to various fishing interests based on geographically

7 Ellen Hey, 'Regime Interaction and Common Interests in Regulating Human Activities in Areas Beyond National Jurisdiction' in Seline Trevisanut, Nikolaos Giannopoulos, and Rozemarijn Holst (eds), *Regime Interaction in Ocean Governance Problems, Theories and Methods* (Brill Nijhoff 2020) 98–9.

8 ibid, 85–6.

9 ibid, 87.

10 ibid, 115.

11 ibid, 115.

12 See, for example, Angela Arthington et al., 'Fish Conservation in Freshwater and Marine Realms: Status, Threats and Management' (2016) 26(5) *Aquatic Conservation and Freshwater Ecosystems* 807.

13 See, for example, United Nations Convention on the Law of the Sea (UNCLOS), 10 December 1982, 1833 UNTS 3, entered into force 16 November 1994 (UNCLOS), arts 61(3) and 119(1)(a).

14 ibid.

determined legal boundaries created by UNCLOS.[15] The zonal approach to resource management in the world's oceans, combined with various regional bodies, geographically limits fisheries allocation and management.[16]

The third narrative is that the implementation of international fisheries law contains an inordinate focus on single species assessment of fish stocks.[17] Attempts have been made to introduce a broader ecosystem approach to fisheries. However, many existing fisheries bodies only focus on a limited number of species and extensively rely on assessments of individual populations.[18]

This chapter examines, in turn, each of the three narratives and the legal principles that they stem from. The analysis highlights their origin, their current role within the regime of international fisheries law, and the way in which the onset of Anthropocene conditions challenges the suitability of these narratives for future oceanic conditions.

2. Maximum Sustainable Yield as a Foundational Narrative

MSY is a particularly persistent principle in international fisheries law.[19] MSY originated in in Article 61(3) and Article 119(1)(a) of UNCLOS, which respectively deal with fishing in the Exclusive Economic Zone (EEZ) and the high seas.[20] These provisions similarly provide that States shall determine a total allowable catch (TAC) based on the need to:

> maintain or restore populations of harvested species at levels which can produce the ***maximum sustainable yield***, as qualified by relevant environmental and economic factors, including the economic needs of coastal fishing communities and the special requirements of developing States, and taking into account fishing patterns, the interdependence of stocks and any generally

15 ibid, arts 2, 55, 56, and 86.

16 ibid.

17 See, for example, Mariana Tolotti et al., 'Unintended Effects of Single-Species Management' (2022) *Environment, Development and Sustainability* 1; Howard Schiffman, 'Moving from Single-Species Management to Ecosystem Management in Regional Fisheries Management Organisations' (2007) 13(2) *ILSA Journal of International and Comparative Law* 387; Daniel Howell et al., 'Combining Ecosystem and Single-Species Modeling to Provide Ecosystem-Based Fisheries Management Advice Within Current Management Systems' (2021) 7 *Frontiers in Marine Science* 1.

18 Mariana Tolotti et al., 'Unintended Effects of Single-Species Management' (2022) *Environment, Development and Sustainability* 1, 2; Stefán Ásmundsson, 'Regional Fisheries Management Organisations (RFMOs): Who are They, What is Their Geographic Coverage on the High Seas and Which Ones Should be Considered as General RFMOs, Tuna RFMOs and Specialised RFMOs?' (2016) <www.cbd.int/doc/meetings/mar/soiom-2016-01/other/soiom-2016-01-fao-19-en.pdf> accessed 27 March 2022.

19 Ellen Hey, 'The Persistence of a Concept: Maximum Sustainable Yield' (2012) 27 *The International Journal of Marine and Coastal Law* 763.

20 UNCLOS, arts 61(3) and 119(1)(a).

> recommended international minimum standards, whether subregional, regional or global (emphasis added).[21]

The content of this obligation is two-fold. States must first monitor and determine the level of a TAC at which MSY can be attained, including by considering the listed factors, and then take measures to put this TAC into practice.[22] In the EEZ, this obligation is paired with another obligation to ensure 'optimum utilisation of the living resources'.[23] Importantly, this applies both to species found in the EEZ and to 'highly migratory' species which move between EEZs and the high seas.[24] The 1995 Agreement for the Implementation of the Provisions of the United Nations Convention on the Law of the Sea of 10 December 1982 relating to the Conservation and Management of Straddling Fish Stocks and Highly Migratory Fish Stocks (Fish Stocks Agreement) reinforced these obligations. The Fish Stocks Agreement also requires States to 'maintain or restore stocks at levels capable of producing maximum sustainable yield'.[25] However, this agreement also introduced new restrictions on this concept, essentially establishing that MSY is an upper limit on fisheries effort rather than an ultimate goal.[26]

The concept of MSY has long been convincingly critiqued, even before it was enshrined in international fisheries law.[27] It has been dubbed a 'policy disguised as science', given the difficulty of gaining the requisite information to determine accurately the MSY of any given target stock.[28] Determining the MSY of one species requires a broader understanding of the whole ecosystem given the interdependent nature of such ecosystems.[29] Hey demonstrates that MSY has been a persistent and influential concept in international fisheries law despite these critiques.[30] MSY has created inherent issues by legitimising, and indeed requiring, fishing effort which

21 ibid, art 61(3).
22 ibid, art 61(1)–(5).
23 ibid, arts 62(1) and 64.
24 ibid.
25 Agreement for the Implementation of the Provisions of the United Nations Convention on the Law of the Sea of 10 December 1982 relating to the Conservation and Management of Straddling Fish Stocks and Highly Migratory Fish Stocks, 4 August 1995, 2167 UNTS 3, entered into force 11 December 2001 (Fish Stocks Agreement), art 5(b).
26 Abdullah Al Arif, 'Legal Status of Maximum Sustainable Yield Concept in International Fisheries Law and Its Adoption in the Marine Fisheries Regime of Bangladesh: A Critical Analysis' (2017) 32 *The International Journal of Marine and Coastal Law* 551.
27 See, for example, Ellen Hey, 'The Persistence of a Concept: Maximum Sustainable Yield' (2012) 27 *The International Journal of Marine and Coastal Law* 763, 766–7.
28 Carmel Finley and Naomi Oreskes, 'Maximum Sustained Yield: A Policy Disguised as Science' (2013) 70 *ICES Journal of Marine Science* 245.
29 See, for example, Peter Anthony Larkin, 'An Epitaph for the Concept of Maximum Sustained Yield' (1977) 106 *Transactions of the American Fisheries Society* 1, 3–6.
30 Ellen Hey, 'Regime Interaction and Common Interests in Regulating Human Activities in Areas Beyond National Jurisdiction' in Seline Trevisanut, Nikolaos Giannopoulos, and Rozemarijn Holst (eds), *Regime Interaction in Ocean Governance Problems, Theories and Methods* (Brill Nijhoff 2020) 115; Ellen Hey, 'The Persistence of a Concept: Maximum Sustainable Yield' (2012) 27 *The International Journal of Marine and Coastal Law* 763.

can come just up to the limit of being unsustainable. While the Fish Stocks Agreement marked a shift by qualifying MSY as a limit rather than a goal,[31] it remains that States, to fulfil their obligations, must determine a TAC while operating with necessarily limited information.[32] Hence, a significant margin for error exists when aiming for MSY given the myriad of factors that affect fish stocks, including interactions between and within ecosystems.[33]

Fishing statistics from the Food and Agriculture Organization of the United Nations (FAO) raise concerns about the accuracy of current calculations of MSY. Only 7.2% of stocks are 'underfished', 57.3% of stocks are fished at the maximum sustainable level and the remaining 35.5% are either over-exploited or depleted.[34] These figures suggest that the majority of the world's fisheries are being pushed to the brink of unsustainable exploitation and that another large proportion has tipped over that edge. This raises questions about the appropriateness of MSY as a management goal or even as a limit on fisheries efforts. The point at which MSY is reached may be too close to the point at which fisheries catastrophically deplete, with overfishing being far more common than under-fishing.[35] Hence, the entrenched narrative that it is possible to calculate and stick to a TAC with the limit of fishing up to MSY has been proven to be ineffective in practice.

When examining this narrative in the context of the Anthropocene, its flaws are even more readily apparent. Due to the advent of climate change and its observable impacts on the world's oceans, the narrative of MSY needs to be critically re-examined. Ocean warming and ocean acidification are expected to alter species distributions,[36] abundance,[37] and ecosystem structures.[38] These effects will result

31 Abdullah Al Arif, 'Legal Status of Maximum Sustainable Yield Concept in International Fisheries Law and Its Adoption in the Marine Fisheries Regime of Bangladesh: A Critical Analysis' (2017) 32 *The International Journal of Marine and Coastal Law* 551.

32 See, for example, Peter Anthony Larkin, 'An Epitaph for the Concept of Maximum Sustained Yield' (1977) 106 *Transactions of the American Fisheries Society* 1.

33 ibid.

34 Food and Agriculture Organization of the United Nations, 'The State of World Fisheries and Aquaculture' (Rome, 2022) 46 www.fao.org/3/cc0461en/cc0461en.pdf accessed 16 October 2023.

35 Pamela Mace, 'A New Role for MSY in Single-Species and Ecosystem Approaches to Fisheries Stock Assessment and Management' (2001) 2 *Fish and Fisheries* 2, 5, and 17.

36 See, for example, Intergovernmental Panel on Climate Change, 'Synthesis Report of the IPCC Sixth Assessment Report' (2023) 4. https://report.ipcc.ch/ar6syr/pdf/IPCC_AR6_SYR_SPM.pdf accessed 16 October 2023; Daniel Suman, 'Oceans and the Changing Climate' in Ana Spalding and Daniel Suman (eds), *Oceans and Society* (Routledge 2023) 99; Shuyang Ma et al., 'Climate Risks to Fishing Species and Fisheries in the China Seas' (2023) 857 *Science of the Total Environment* 1, 2; William Cheung et al., 'Projecting Global Marine Biodiversity Impacts Under Climate Change Scenarios' (2009) 10 *Fish and Fisheries* 235, 243.

37 See, for example, Dan Laffoley et al., 'Ocean Acidification: Scientific Understanding and Challenges' in David VanderZwaag, Nilüfer Oral, and Tim Stephens (eds), *Research Handbook on Ocean Acidification Law and Policy* (Edward Elgar 2021) 14; Heike Lotze et al., 'Global Ensemble Projections Reveal Trophic Amplification of Ocean Biomass Declines with Climate Change' (2019) 116 *The Proceedings of the National Academy of Sciences* 12907, 12908.

38 See, for example, Malin Pinsky and Rebecca Selden, 'Climate Variability, Climate Change, and Conservation in a Dynamic Ocean' in Phillips Levin and Melissa Poe (eds), *Conservation for the Anthropocene Ocean: Interdisciplinary Science in Support of Nature and People* (Elsevier Inc

in greater uncertainty in ocean ecosystems, which scientists already struggle to monitor.[39] This could pose insurmountable challenges in determining and setting a TAC based on attaining MSY. With scientists already doubting the utility of the MSY concept to begin with,[40] this uncertainty will exacerbate the problems with relying on this narrative within the Anthropocene. Some have suggested that, in such conditions, economic concepts like MSY and optimum utilisation must be replaced with an international fisheries system which focuses, first and foremost, on food security and is not a vehicle for economic goals,[41] particularly for wealthy States that dominate high seas fishing.[42]

The concept of MSY is particularly reliant on monitoring and setting fisheries limits based on achieving the maximum sustained economic value possible. This concept will need to be rethought in the Anthropocene context. Accurately determining an MSY, something that was already a fraught prospect in any case,[43] will only become more difficult. Driving for maximum sustainable exploitation will become increasingly risky as monitoring information becomes less reliable and predictable. In the face of these drastic changes, a precautionary approach is needed. Such approach could focus on securing adequate food supply over maximising economic opportunities.[44]

3. The Zonal Approach as a Foundational Narrative

The second foundational narrative is that of the zonal approach to resource allocation found in the law of the sea. This is one of UNCLOS' most significant contributions to international law. UNCLOS established a series of jurisdictional zones at

2017) 26; Daniel Suman, 'Oceans and the Changing Climate' in Ana Spalding and Daniel Suman (eds), *Oceans and Society* (Routledge 2023).

39 See, for example, Francisco Ramírez et al., 'Challenges for Marine Ecological Assessments: Completeness of Findable, Accessible, Interoperable, and Reusable Biodiversity Data in European Seas' (2022) 8 *Frontiers in Marine Science* 1.

40 See, for example, Abdullah Al Arif, 'Legal Status of Maximum Sustainable Yield Concept in International Fisheries Law and Its Adoption in the Marine Fisheries Regime of Bangladesh: A Critical Analysis' (2017) 32 *The International Journal of Marine and Coastal Law* 551, 557–60; Ellen Hey, 'The Persistence of a Concept: Maximum Sustainable Yield' (2012) 27 *The International Journal of Marine and Coastal Law* 763, 766–7; Carmel Finley and Naomi Oreskes, 'Maximum Sustained Yield: A Policy Disguised as Science' (2013) 70 *ICES Journal of Marine Science* 245.

41 Salvador Lluch-Cota, Pablo del Monte-Luna, and Helen Gurney-Smith, 'Transformational Adaptation in Marine Fisheries' (2023) 60 *Current Opinion in Environmental Sustainability* 1.

42 Douglas McCauley et al., 'Wealthy Countries Dominate Industrial Fishing' (2018) 4 *Science Advances* 1.

43 See, for example, Peter Anthony Larkin, 'An Epitaph for the Concept of Maximum Sustained Yield' (1977) 106 *Transactions of the American Fisheries Society* 1.

44 See, for example, Salvador Lluch-Cota, Pablo del Monte-Luna, and Helen Gurney-Smith, 'Transformational Adaptation in Marine Fisheries' (2023) 60 *Current Opinion in Environmental Sustainability* 1.

sea within which States had different rights and obligations.[45] The first 12 nautical miles (nm) from a State's coastline is the territorial sea, within which the State has complete sovereignty and right over living resources.[46] Up to 200 nm from the baseline is the EEZ, which gives the State sovereign rights to the living resources within.[47] Finally, the high seas are open to all States and there is an established freedom of fishing, subject to some requirements to conserve and manage the 'living resources of the high seas'.[48] These are the key aspects of the zonal approach for fisheries, although the regime for the continental shelf is relevant for other living resources, such as sedentary species.[49]

Importantly, the rights and obligations of States regarding living resources vary within the territorial sea, EEZ, and high seas. First, within the territorial sea, States have exclusive rights to fish, only tempered by the general obligation to 'protect and preserve' the marine environment.[50] Second, more extensive obligations come into play in the EEZ. States have 'sovereign rights for the purpose of exploring and exploiting, conserving and managing' the natural resources found within the EEZ.[51] However, States are subject in the EEZ to Article 61 of UNCLOS on the conservation of living resources, which requires States to establish a TAC based on the concepts of MSY and optimum utilisation discussed previously.[52] This includes obligations to allow other States to fish in the EEZ if the State cannot reach TAC on its own.[53] Some further obligations apply in relation to cooperation in the management of shared and migratory stocks. These obligations were expanded upon in the Fish Stocks Agreement.[54] Third, in the high seas, there is a general freedom of fishing, but this is accompanied by requirements on the conservation of resources, namely through cooperation,[55] and determining a TAC based on MSY.[56]

This zonal approach largely gave States certainty about the kinds of resources which States can claim and the extent of their maritime territory.[57] This is an understandable goal as a fundamental aim of international law more generally is to establish certainty in interstate relations. However, the borders drawn by UNCLOS clearly never held any sway over the fish themselves. This led to extensive consideration of transboundary fish stocks, most significantly through the Fish Stocks

45 UNCLOS, arts 2, 55, 56, and 86.
46 ibid, art 2.
47 ibid, art 56(1)(a).
48 ibid, arts 87(1)(e) and 119.
49 ibid, art 77(4).
50 ibid, arts 192 and 193.
51 ibid, art 56(1)(a).
52 ibid, art 61.
53 ibid, 62(2).
54 See, for example, Fish Stocks Agreement, arts 5, 7(1)(b), 7(3), 7(5), and Part III.
55 UNCLOS, art 118.
56 ibid, art 119(1).
57 See, for example, Tulio Treves, 'Historical Development of the Law of the Sea' in Donald Rothwell et al (eds), *The Oxford Handbook of the Law of the Sea* (OUP 2015).

Agreement.[58] Likewise, many regional fisheries management organisations or arrangements (RFMOs) have been established to fulfil States' obligation to cooperate in managing such stocks.[59] This zonal approach is now well entrenched in the regime-based narrative of a number of sub-fields of the law of the sea, including international fisheries law. However, the zonal approach is likely to encounter significant challenges in the face of the Anthropocene.

Ocean warming resulting from climate change will cause significant poleward shifts as fish species attempt to migrate to cooler waters.[60] This will result in commercial stock leaving warmer equatorial waters in pursuit of more livable conditions.[61] Other stocks are expected to shift in different ways, such as towards deeper and cooler waters.[62] Given that human-induced climate change will likely result in the mass movement of species, the static geographical zonal approach to fisheries allocation will likely become more contested.[63] For example, some stocks may shift from EEZs to high seas. Meanwhile, stocks that were once shared between multiple States may end up entirely within the waters of one State, or high-seas stocks may shift into national waters. Up to 78% of EEZs worldwide could lose at least one species through these shifts by 2030 if carbon emissions remain high.[64] These potential changes would likely cause inequality, as States in warmer waters lose access to fisheries which they rely on.[65] Drastic shifts in species range could also lead to conflicts between States over resources.[66] For instance, States which are used to relying on a particular transboundary stock are unlikely to welcome losing the stock entirely to a neighbour. Furthermore, the shifts of species may result in currently well-managed stocks moving to unregulated waters.[67] This could result

58 Fish Stocks Agreement.

59 ibid, art 9.

60 See, for example, William Cheung et al., 'Projecting Global Marine Biodiversity Impacts Under Climate Change Scenarios' (2009) 10 *Fish and Fisheries* 235, 243.

61 ibid.

62 Malin Pinsky and Rebecca Selden, 'Climate Variability, Climate Change, and Conservation in a Dynamic Ocean' in Phillips Levin and Melissa Poe (eds), *Conservation for the Anthropocene Ocean: Interdisciplinary Science in Support of Nature and People* (Elsevier Inc 2017) 26.

63 See, for example, Anastasia Telesetsky, 'Cross Regime UNCLOS and UNFCCC Cooperation to Address Loss and Damage from Climate-Shifted Transboundary Fisheries' (2023) 148 *Marine Policy* 1, 3; Cecilia Engler, 'Transboundary Fisheries, Climate Change, and the Ecosystem Approach: Taking Stock of the International Law and Policy Seascape' (2020) 25(4) *Ecology and Society* 43, 46.

64 Juliano Palacios-Abrantes et al., 'Timing and Magnitude of Climate-Driven Range Shifts in Transboundary Fish Stocks Challenge Their Management' (2022) 28 *Global Change Biology* 2312, 2312.

65 Anastasia Telesetsky, 'Cross Regime UNCLOS and UNFCCC Cooperation to Address Loss and Damage from Climate-Shifted Transboundary Fisheries' (2023) 148 *Marine Policy* 1; Cecilia Engler, 'Transboundary Fisheries, Climate Change, and the Ecosystem Approach: Taking Stock of the International Law and Policy Seascape' (2020) 25(4) *Ecology and Society* 43.

66 ibid.

67 Cecilia Engler, 'Transboundary Fisheries, Climate Change, and the Ecosystem Approach: Taking Stock of the International Law and Policy Seascape' (2020) 25(4) *Ecology and Society* 43, 48.

in opportunistic exploitation, which in turn could damage the health of particular species.

Sea level rise is another potential impact of climate change.[68] This phenomenon has already received particular international legal scrutiny, given the potential legal effects of baselines shifting landward.[69] As maritime zones are measured from each State's baseline, this could result in an ultimate loss of territory for affected States.[70] This problem is particularly acute for small island States, such as Pacific Island States, which have limited land space already and strongly rely on their ocean territory.[71] If a State's territory shrank landwards, fisheries over which the State previously had a claim would become transboundary or even entirely based in the high seas. The International Law Commission found that the caselaw does not directly answer whether the baseline moves with the low water line or can be fixed by States when delimitating their maritime zones.[72] However, the International Law Commission also noted that there is no mention of amending baselines within international law. Seeing as most States wish to maintain predictable baselines, a concept of ambulatory baselines would seemingly not be fit for purpose.[73] Some States support this fixed baseline view. The Pacific Islands Forum notably declared the participating States' mutual intention to fix their baselines in place regardless of sea level rise, with support from some other States.[74]

The difficulties faced by the zonal approach in dealing with sea level rise also demonstrate the way that maritime zones can be challenged by human-induced shifts in the marine environment. This has implications for resource access, including fisheries, and demonstrates that fish species may shift distribution but that the zones themselves may also become increasingly uncertain. While some States have proposed addressing the issue of sea level rise through fixing baselines,[75] such issues illustrate the challenges posed by the zonal approach.

68 Nadine Heck et al., 'Global Climate Change Risk to Fisheries: A Multi-Risk Assessment' (2023) 148 *Marine Policy* 1.

69 See, for example, Nilufer Oral, 'UNCLOS and Sea Level Rise' (2023) 149 *Marine Policy* 1.

70 ibid, 2–3.

71 See, for example, Pacific Islands Forum, 'Declaration on Preserving Maritime Zones in the Face of Climate Change-Related Sea-Level Rise' (6 August 2021). www.forumsec.org/2021/08/11/declaration-on-preserving-maritime-zones-in-the-face-of-climate-change-related-sea-level-rise/ accessed 16 October 2023.

72 Nilufer Oral, 'UNCLOS and Sea Level Rise' (2023) 149 *Marine Policy* 1, 5; International Law Commission, 'Sea-Level Rise in Relation to International Law: First Issues Paper by Bogdan Aurescu and Nilüfer Oral, Co-Chairs of the Study Group on Sea-Level Rise in Relation to International Law' (2020) A/CN.4/740.

73 ibid.

74 See, for example, Pacific Islands Forum, 'Declaration on Preserving Maritime Zones in the Face of Climate Change-Related Sea-Level Rise' (6 August 2021). www.forumsec.org/2021/08/11/declaration-on-preserving-maritime-zones-in-the-face-of-climate-change-related-sea-level-rise/ accessed 16 October 2023; Alliance of Small Island Developing States, 'Launch of The Alliance of Small Island States Leaders' Declaration' (2021). www.aosis.org/launch-of-the-alliance-of-small-island-States-leaders-declaration/ accessed 16 October 2023.

75 ibid.

Indeed, the inability of the rigid zonal approach to account for shifts in fisheries distribution illustrates another fundamental part of the regime-based narrative which must be re-examined in Anthropocene conditions. Some have already suggested alternatives to static spatial management, such as dynamic area-based management tools on the high seas.[76] More broadly, the future of the law of the sea will need to embrace such creative approaches to ensure dynamic management of marine biodiversity. These static maritime zones, particularly the EEZ, primarily act to predictably allocate access to resources. Yet, potential shifts in fisheries distribution challenge their effectiveness at achieving this purpose due to the limits of this approach. As such, allocations lose their certainty which will likely lead to increased contestation.

4. Single Species Management as a Foundational Narrative

The third and final narrative this chapter examines is that of single species management. International fisheries law often includes references to 'associated' 'dependent' and 'non-target species'.[77] Yet, it is fundamentally built around the idea of a single target species which must be monitored and managed.[78] Meanwhile, the broader ecosystem remains a secondary concern. This narrative also arises out of the concept of MSY, as it is the requirement of establishing a TAC which focuses on a singular species from a monitoring point of view. This is perhaps the narrative which has been most subject to attempts at reform, aiming to integrate the ecosystem approach into international fisheries law.[79] However, in practice, it has been difficult for an ecosystem approach to influence fisheries management decisions, particularly when it comes to which fish are monitored and targeted.[80] This is clearly shown by the RFMOs established to manage fisheries cooperation in the high seas.[81] Five RFMOs exclusively focus on managing tuna fisheries.[82] It

76 See, for example, Guillermo Ortuño Crespo et al., 'Beyond Static Spatial Management: Scientific and Legal Considerations for Dynamic Management in the High Seas' (2020) 122 *Marine Policy* 1.

77 See, for example, UNCLOS, arts 61(4), 119(1)(b); Fish Stocks Agreement, arts 5(d)–(f), 6(3)(c)–(d), 6(5), 10(d).

78 See, for example, Mariana Tolotti et al., 'Unintended Effects of Single-Species Management' (2022) *Environment, Development and Sustainability* 1; Howard Schiffman, 'Moving from Single-Species Management to Ecosystem Management in Regional Fisheries Management Organisations' (2007) 13(2) *ILSA Journal of International and Comparative Law* 387; Daniel Howell et al., 'Combining Ecosystem and Single-Species Modeling to Provide Ecosystem-Based Fisheries Management Advice Within Current Management Systems' (2021) 7 *Frontiers in Marine Science* 1.

79 See, for example, Abdullah Al Arif, 'Exploring the Legal Status and Key Features of Ecosystem-Based Fisheries Management in International Fisheries Law' (2018) 27 *Review of European, Comparative and International Environmental Law* 320.

80 Mariana Tolotti et al., 'Unintended Effects of Single-Species Management' (2022) *Environment, Development and Sustainability* 1, 2.

81 See, for example, Geographic Coverage on the High Seas and Which Ones Should be Considered as General RFMOs, Tuna RFMOs and Specialised RFMOs?' (2016). www.cbd.int/doc/meetings/mar/soiom-2016-01/other/soiom-2016-01-fao-19-en.pdf accessed 27 March 2022.

82 ibid, 4–5.

has been observed that, while these five tuna RFMOs have all incorporated the ecosystem approach into their mandate, they still rely heavily on individual stock assessments.[83]

Meanwhile, some general RFMOs focus on fishing in a specific region.[84] However, the diversity of targeted fish species is still very low. This further emphasises international fisheries' narrow focus on individual species. Indeed, of all finfish captured in 2020, just 14 species made up 38% of total landings.[85] This contrasts with the 20,000 fish species thought to exist in the ocean.[86] As a result, some have advocated for 'balanced harvesting', in which fishing effort is spread among a range of species in the ecosystem, which lessens overfishing of particular target species.[87]

Furthermore, given their focus on commercial fisheries, RFMOs have been shown to not effectively monitor up to 95% of high-seas fish species.[88] The most commonly proposed method to address this is the greater use of ecosystem-based management. Yet, this is difficult to implement fully within existing international fisheries law.[89] The 2001 Reykjavik Declaration on Responsible Fisheries in the Marine Ecosystem developed a non-binding process within the FAO on preliminary guidelines for an ecosystem approach to fisheries.[90] However, UNCLOS and the Fish Stocks Agreement only make passing references to ecosystems and associated and dependent species, which indicates at best an implied ecosystem approach.[91]

There have been numerous attempts to broaden the focus of fisheries towards the wellbeing of all species. However, the narrative remains well-entrenched that international fisheries law should primarily focus on individual species of commercial value.[92] Early fisheries law focused most clearly on commercial species

83 Mariana Tolotti et al., 'Unintended Effects of Single-Species Management' (2022) *Environment, Development and Sustainability* 1, 2.

84 ibid, 3–4.

85 Food and Agriculture Organization of the United Nations, 'The State of World Fisheries and Aquaculture' (Rome 2022) 6. www.fao.org/3/cc0461en/cc0461en.pdf accessed 16 October 2023.

86 Oceana, 'Ocean Fishes', *Marine Life Encyclopedia*. https://oceana.org/ocean-fishes/ accessed 16 October 2023.

87 See, for example, Shijie Zhou et al, 'Balanced Harvest: Concept, Policies, Evidence, and Management Implications' (2019) 29 *Reviews in Fish Biology and Fisheries* 711.

88 Guillermo Ortuño Crespo et al., 'High-Seas Fish Biodiversity is Slipping Through the Governance Net' (2019) 3 *Nature Ecology & Evolution* 1273.

89 See, for example, Abdullah Al Arif, 'Exploring the Legal Status and Key Features of Ecosystem-Based Fisheries Management in International Fisheries Law' (2018) 27 *Review of European, Comparative and International Environmental Law* 320.

90 Food and Agriculture Organization of the United Nations, 'The Reykjavik Declaration on Responsible Fisheries in the Marine Ecosystem' (October 2001). www.fao.org/fishery/docs/DOCUMENT/reykjavik/y2198t00_dec.pdf accessed 16 October 2023.

91 See, for example, UNCLOS, art 61(4); Fish Stocks Agreement, art 5(d).

92 Howard Schiffman, 'Moving from Single-Species Management to Ecosystem Management in Regional Fisheries Management Organisations' (2007) 13(2) *ILSA Journal of International and Comparative Law* 387; Mariana Tolotti et al., 'Unintended Effects of Single-Species Management' (2022) *Environment, Development and Sustainability* 1; Walters et al., 'Possible Ecosystem Impacts

and their management, with only passing references to other related species. This makes implementing an ecosystem-based approach difficult.[93] However, the impetus for an ecosystem approach continues to build and is made more salient by the impacts of climate change on the world's oceans.

Changes in the range, abundance, and health of species, already discussed, result in what can be described as ecosystem shifts.[94] Ecosystem shifts occur where the structure of the overall ecosystem changes due to, for example, the migration of a new predator species into a distant ecosystem or the knock-on effects of the depletion of a particularly vulnerable species.[95] This has been a key concern in the Arctic Ocean, as species are expected to move towards the poles.[96] Due to ocean warming, predator species may migrate and interfere with the hunting of existing predators in the Arctic Ocean.[97]

Over-exploitation of certain fish stocks will also likely change the structure of ecosystems, due to fishing pressures on target species and stock collapse.[98] Such shifts will need to be considered in any commercial fishing in the Anthropocene. The ecosystem approach shifts the analysis away from the targeted species and directly related species. Instead, this approach seeks a holistic understanding of the ecosystem in which the species exist to make informed management decisions.[99] While the ecosystem approach is not infallible and is difficult to implement,[100] international fisheries law must continue to move away from the pervasive narrative centred on individual species.

of Applying MSY Policies from Single-Species Assessment' (2005) 62 *ICES Journal of Marine Science* 558.

93 ibid.

94 Malin Pinsky and Rebecca Selden, 'Climate Variability, Climate Change, and Conservation in a Dynamic Ocean' in Phillips Levin and Melissa Poe (eds), *Conservation for the Anthropocene Ocean: Interdisciplinary Science in Support of Nature and People* (Elsevier Inc 2017) 26.

95 ibid.

96 William Cheung et al., 'Projecting Global Marine Biodiversity Impacts Under Climate Change Scenarios' (2009) 10 *Fish and Fisheries* 235, 243.

97 Malin Pinsky and Rebecca Selden, 'Climate Variability, Climate Change, and Conservation in a Dynamic Ocean' in Phillips Levin and Melissa Poe (eds), *Conservation for the Anthropocene Ocean: Interdisciplinary Science in Support of Nature and People* (Elsevier Inc 2017).

98 See, for example, Robert Steneck and Daniel Pauly, 'Fishing Through the Anthropocene' (2022) 29 *Current Biology* R942; Joël Durant, Leana Aarvold and Øystein Langangen, 'Stock Collapse and Its Effect on Species Interactions: Cod and Herring in the Norwegian Barents Seas System as an Example' (2021) 11 *Ecology and Evolution* 16993; Malin Pinsky and Rebecca Selden, 'Climate Variability, Climate Change, and Conservation in a Dynamic Ocean' in Phillips Levin and Melissa Poe (eds), *Conservation for the Anthropocene Ocean: Interdisciplinary Science in Support of Nature and People* (Elsevier Inc 2017).

99 See e.g., Abdullah Al Arif, 'Exploring the Legal Status and Key Features of Ecosystem-Based Fisheries Management in International Fisheries Law' (2018) 27 *Review of European, Comparative and International Environmental Law* 320.

100 ibid.

Ecosystems in the Anthropocene are expected to shift due to species over-exploitation, migration, and loss.[101] Catch limits and other measures should be understood in this context, where monitoring will become increasingly important. The entrenched narrative of single species assessment and management cannot respond to unexpected shifts within ecosystems and understand the reasons behind those shifts. Hence, single species approaches, which have long dominated international fisheries law, will become increasingly unworkable due to human impacts on the world's oceans.

5. Conclusion

International fisheries law faces a decisive moment, as the world stands on the threshold of a new geological epoque. Human-induced shifts in ocean conditions will significantly impact fish life. Climate change and biodiversity loss are driving changes in species distribution, abundance, ecosystem composition, and more. These changes create new prevailing conditions in the oceans which are not yet properly understood. The foundational narratives of the current regime are not built to respond to such uncertainty. These foundational narratives will struggle to be effective and relevant in projected future conditions.

This chapter has given an overview of three prominent foundational narratives of international fisheries law to highlight the challenge that the Anthropocene poses to international fisheries law. The concept of MSY continues to be challenged by the lack of information available to decision-makers in setting a TAC. This will become even more difficult as species distribution, abundance, and ecosystem health become less predictable due to ocean warming and acidification. Likewise, the zonal approach faces challenges associated with fish migration to avoid climate effects. Species are expected to move into other ocean areas than those that they have long occupied. This will likely result in unequal outcomes for geographically disadvantaged States and an increase in fisheries conflicts. Finally, international fisheries law has never quite broken away from the traditional focus on single-species assessment and management. However, to understand the changes in marine environments as accurately as possible, a more holistic view of ecosystem health will be needed in the future.

101 See, for example, William Cheung et al., 'Projecting Global Marine Biodiversity Impacts Under Climate Change Scenarios' (2009) 10 *Fish and Fisheries* 235; Intergovernmental Panel on Climate Change, 'Synthesis Report of the IPCC Sixth Assessment Report' (2023). https://report.ipcc.ch/ar6syr/pdf/IPCC_AR6_SYR_SPM.pdf accessed 16 October 2023; Daniel Suman, 'Oceans and the Changing Climate' in Ana Spalding and Daniel Suman (eds), *Oceans and Society* (Routledge 2023); Shuyang Ma et al., 'Climate Risks to Fishing Species and Fisheries in the China Seas' (2023) 857 *Science of the Total Environment* 1; Dan Laffoley et al., 'Ocean Acidification: Scientific Understanding and Challenges' in David VanderZwaag, Nilüfer Oral, and Tim Stephens (eds), *Research Handbook on Ocean Acidification Law and Policy* (Edward Elgar 2021); Heike Lotze et al., 'Global Ensemble Projections Reveal Trophic Amplification of Ocean Biomass Declines with Climate Change' (2019) 116 *The Proceedings of the National Academy of Sciences* 12907.

The three narratives explored in this chapter have remained persistent in the international fisheries law regime due to the entrenchment of foundational legal principles. Path dependency constrains the evolution of these legal regimes to conform to the decisions taken early in their development.[102] To adapt to the challenges of the Anthropocene, one must understand how these narratives continue to influence modern fisheries management. This chapter has demonstrated that some foundational narratives of international fisheries law must be rethought if this body of law is to remain fit for purpose in the Anthropocene era.

102 Ellen Hey, 'Regime Interaction and Common Interests in Regulating Human Activities in Areas Beyond National Jurisdiction' in Seline Trevisanut, Nikolaos Giannopoulos, and Rozemarijn Holst (eds), *Regime Interaction in Ocean Governance Problems, Theories and Methods* (Brill Nijhoff 2020) 115.

23 Climate Change and Management of Shared and Straddling Fish Stocks

Nothing (New) to See Here, Folks?

Andrew Serdy

1. Introduction

The task allotted to the author is to discuss the effect of climate change on conservation and management of shared and straddling fish stocks through its impact on the zonal attachment and migratory pattern of the stocks concerned. To begin by defining terms, shared and straddling stocks are the usual international fisheries law shorthand for stocks that respectively occur in the exclusive economic zones (EEZs) of two or more neighbouring States, or in one or more neighbouring EEZs and the adjacent area of high seas.[1] These are respectively addressed in paragraphs 1 and 2 of Article 63 of the United Nations Convention on the Law of the Sea,[2] both calling for the cooperative management of these stocks. Climate change in this chapter is used in a sense broader than anthropogenic global warming attributable to the increased concentration of greenhouse gases in the atmosphere since the beginning of the industrial age; it includes past cyclical changes too. Zonal attachment refers to the spatio-temporal distribution of fish stocks with respect to an international boundary, in other words, what proportion of a stock can be expected to be found on one side of a given boundary over the course of a year.[3] Despite the

1 See, for example, Annick van Houtte, "Legal Aspects in the Management of Shared Fish Stocks – A Review," *Papers Presented at the Norway-FAO Expert Consultation on the Management of Shared Fish Stocks, Bergen, Norway (FAO Fisheries Report No 695, Supp)* (7–10 October 2002) 30, 30.

2 (adopted 10 December 1982), 1833 UNTS 3 (UNCLOS).

3 The best-known recent instance of zonal attachment being pursued as an explicit allocative policy aim was by the United Kingdom in the Fisheries White Paper issued as its departure from the European Union loomed: Department for Environment Food and Rural Affairs, "Sustainable Fisheries for Future Generations," *White Paper*, Cm 9660 (2018) 12 and 26; see also ibid, 44–56 (Annex C, "Zonal Attachment Evidence," showing that there are different ways to measure this). Ultimately, however, the aim was not achieved: there is no mention of zonal attachment in the fisheries chapter of the Trade and Cooperation Agreement between the United Kingdom of Great Britain and Northern Ireland, of the one part, and the European Union and the European Atomic Energy Community, of the other part (Brussels and London, 30 December 2020), UKTS No 8 (2021), Arts 493–511 and Annexes 35–38.

DOI: 10.4324/9781003492030-31

"intuitive fairness appeal" of zonal attachment as a basis for allocating shared and straddling stocks, the incentives for cooperation do not align perfectly with it.[4]

Fisheries themselves are not significant contributors to global warming, so, while there is no reason to exempt them from general economy-wide policies to reduce greenhouse gas emissions, equally the case for singling them out for special attention in this regard is weak. Regional fisheries management organisations (RFMOs) cannot cure climate change,[5] all that can realistically be expected of them is not to make the problems worse by mismanaging their stocks.

According to Rayfuse,[6] "The challenge of climate change can . . . be viewed not just as a question of ecosystem resilience, but also of the institutional robustness and resilience of the regimes charged with the conservation and management of international fisheries." One reason for this is that, although climate change complicates considerably the cooperative task of States mandated by UNCLOS Article 63, its effect is not uniform. The more elaborate the structures for management have been to date, the greater the challenge posed; conversely, where the cooperation occurs solely through less formalised arrangements such as occasional government-to-government talks, the change in the facts on the ground is merely one more factor to take into account, and the change is one of degree rather than quality, since fish stocks have never been static, but have often redistributed themselves spatially in response to altered environmental conditions. Where allocation of catch limits is based wholly or partly on zonal attachment data collected over many years,[7] this will be all the more vulnerable to the change in availability of the fish. Unless the States on both sides of the boundary are roughly equally affected, political pressures can be expected to develop to reopen the allocation to redress the new imbalance.

4 Rögnvaldur Hannesson, "Sharing the Northeast Atlantic Mackerel" (2013) 70 *ICES Journal of Marine Science* 259, 259. It is also supported by Peter Ørebech, "The 'Lost Mackerel' of the North East Atlantic – The Flawed System of Trilateral and Bilateral Decision-making" (2013) 28 *International Journal of Marine and Coastal Law* 343.

5 Rosemary Rayfuse, "Addressing Climate Change Impacts in Regional Fisheries Management Organizations" in Richard Caddell and Erik J Molenaar (eds), *Strengthening International Fisheries Law in an Era of Changing Oceans* (Hart Publishing 2019) 247, 251 acknowledges that "the solution to climate change lies not with RFMOs but rather with the climate regime."

6 ibid 249.

7 A rare instance of this being enshrined in a treaty relates to the Atlanto-Scandian or Norwegian spring-spawning herring stock. When the stock size is small it is present only in Norwegian waters, whereas when it becomes larger it moves into neighbouring coastal States' EEZs and the adjacent high seas. In these periods the stock was managed by way of bilateral agreements concluded by Norway with other participants that "permitted [them] to target herring when the fish were in their most valuable condition," in other words by catching them in Norway's EEZ rather than their own. Their fleets were moreover "allowed to land their catches in Norway, thereby reducing the transportation that the herring would have to undergo before processing," leading, in turn, to "a superior final product." The allocation formula was based on zonal attachment. See Kathleen A Miller et al., "Governing Marine Fisheries in a Changing Climate: A Game-Theoretic Perspective" (2013) 61 *Canadian Journal of Agricultural Economics* 309, 324.

International fisheries have long been exposed to changes in catchability of targeted stocks due to long-term climatic cycles. The Pacific Decadal Oscillation and North Atlantic Oscillation "provide striking examples of modes of atmospheric circulation having substantial, long-term impacts on a variety of fish populations."[8] The former "involves long-term shifts in predominant patterns of sea-surface temperatures, wind stress and coastal upwelling across the North Pacific, with associated changes in food-web dynamics."[9] Moreover, it has been possible to reconstruct "[d]ramatic swings in abundance over a roughly 2,000-year time horizon . . . for Alaskan salmon . . . and for California sardine and anchovy stocks,"[10] long before anthropogenic climate change began. What is new, and has been wrought by global warming, is thus that over and above both random short-term fluctuations and slow cyclical fluctuations which there is no reason to expect to cease, there is now superimposed an additional motor of change whose effect may be to slow down such cycles, speed them up, or replace them altogether with something else. Often this is in a predictable direction: if the habitat of a given fish species is waters within a certain ocean temperature band, the overall effect of global warming transmitted through the rising temperature of the oceans will be to push the ranges of such stocks away from the equator into higher latitudes.[11] (This does not preclude local exceptions where the existing migratory path of a stock depends on an ocean current whose strength or direction is appreciably shifted, or a new current flowing towards the equator develops in an area where previously there was none, confounding the expected effect.)

As Miller *et al.* warn, however,

> the complexity of marine ecosystems creates distinct limits to predictability. Such complexity is characterized by interacting nonlinear processes that can lead to abrupt changes in the abundance or trophic interactions of one or more species within an ecological community. Once such a hidden threshold has been crossed, the structure of a marine community can rapidly change, with perhaps irreversible impacts on the productive potential of targeted species.[12]

The reaction of international bodies, however, as shown in Section II, has been little more than paying lip service to anticipating and countering the effects of

8 Kathleen A. Miller and Gordon R. Munro, "Climate and Cooperation: A New Perspective on the Management of Shared Fish Stocks" (2004) 19 *Marine Resource Economics* 367, 369.

9 Kathleen A Miller et al., "Governing Marine Fisheries in a Changing Climate: A Game-Theoretic Perspective" (2013) 61 *Canadian Journal of Agricultural Economics* 321.

10 Kathleen A Miller and Gordon R Munro, "Climate and Cooperation: A New Perspective on the Management of Shared Fish Stocks" (2004) 19 *Marine Resource Economics* 369 (footnote two and source there cited).

11 William W.L. Cheung et al., "Modelling Future Oceans: The Present and Emerging Future of Fish Stocks and Fisheries," in Richard Caddell and Erik J Molenaar (eds), *Strengthening International Fisheries Law in an Era of Changing Oceans* (Hart Publishing 2019), 13, 15.

12 Kathleen A Miller et al., "Governing Marine Fisheries in a Changing Climate: A Game-Theoretic Perspective" (2013) 61 *Canadian Journal of Agricultural Economics* 311.

climate change. Bilaterally too, it might have been expected that the movement of stocks across boundaries which pits States against each other whose interests were formerly aligned would lead to debates among them as to where the onus of proof lies of stocks becoming, or ceasing to be, shared or straddling, a matter not addressed by UNCLOS Article 63.[13] In practice, however, this has not occurred and States are content to abide by the usual international law rule that the party asserting a fact – in effect, any change to the *status quo* – bears the burden of proving it. Instead, as seen in section III on the most prominent legal controversies prompted by changed zonal attachment of stocks, they tend to argue about whether States in whose waters stocks newly appear are, in fact, coastal States with respect to those stocks. Section IV then surveys suggestions for tackling the issues, one dramatic but misplaced, the others more prosaic, and conclusions are ventured in Section V.

2. Climate Change in International Fisheries Bodies

As observed by Rayfuse, "there is little evidence . . . to suggest that RFMOs are explicitly absorbing climate change into their decision rules for stock assessment and harvest rules, or into their catch allocations."[14] Rather, in her survey of how RFMOs are reacting to the phenomenon, there is a tendency for their meeting reports to mention climate change in general terms as a factor affecting the oceans and fisheries they manage, "but little by way of explicit engagement with . . . relevant science or substantive suggestions to remedy or address the issue."[15]

A rise in the frequency of mention of climate change is detectable in the reports of successive resumed sessions of the UN Fish Stocks Agreement Review Conference. That of the 2010 session recommended that "where possible" impacts of climate change be considered "in establishing conservation and management measures for straddling . . . and highly migratory fish stocks."[16] This was repeated and elaborated in the report of the next (2016) session of the Conference, which devotes

13 This will in due course affect, for example, the *Agreement to Prevent Unregulated High Seas Fisheries in the Central Arctic Ocean* (adopted 3 October 2018), text available at <www.mofa.go.jp/files/000449233.pdf> accessed 28 August 2023, which seeks to prevent the emergence of an unregulated fishery in the high seas part of the Arctic Ocean once stocks arrive there, which will *ex hypothesi* entail straddling at least one EEZ/high seas boundary. So far this is the sole fisheries treaty negotiated because of global warming: Erik J. Molenaar, "Integrating Climate Change in International Fisheries Law" in Elise Johansen, Signe Veierud Busch and Ingvild Ulrikke Jakobsen (eds), *The Law of the Sea and Climate Change: Solutions and Constraints* (CUP, 2020) 263, 285.

14 Rosemary Rayfuse, "Addressing Climate Change Impacts in Regional Fisheries Management Organizations" in Richard Caddell and Erik J Molenaar (eds), *Strengthening International Fisheries Law in an Era of Changing Oceans* (Hart Publishing 2019) 263.

15 ibid, 260–262.

16 "Report of the resumed Review Conference on the Agreement for the Implementation of the Provisions of the United Nations Convention on the Law of the Sea of 10 December 1982 relating to the Conservation and Management of Straddling Fish Stocks and Highly Migratory Fish Stocks Prepared by the President of the Conference" (27 July 2010) UN Doc A/CONF.210/2010/7, https://documents-dds-ny.un.org/doc/UNDOC/GEN/N10/465/87/PDF/N1046587.pdf?OpenElement> accessed 24 August 2023 42 (para I(n) of the Outcomes section).

several paragraphs to it, though no specific guidance on measures to counteract or deal with its effects is offered.[17] The trend continues in the 2023 session report, but still contains no concrete way in which either the Conference or RFMOs should address it, beyond the advice, of dubious utility, that it be "mainstream[ed]."[18]

Exemplifying how individual RFMOs have reacted to the problem, the Commission for the Conservation of Antarctic Marine Living Resources (CCAMLR) began by passing a resolution on climate change in 2009,[19] but a 2014 proposal by a non-governmental organisation to introduce climate change impact statements in all CCAMLR papers and fisheries reports met opposition and was not put to a vote.[20] The following year, a proposal by Australia and Norway for an intersessional correspondence group to develop approaches for integrating considerations of the impacts of climate change into the Commission's work succeeded,[21] but the group appears to have been ineffectual.[22] A more recent resolution with the same title adopted in 2022 is no less hortatory than the previous one.[23]

CCAMLR has taken the initiative to pursue cooperative arrangements with neighbouring RFMOs whose stocks are likely to follow the predicted southward shift of the Antarctic Polar Front,[24] bringing them increasingly into its Convention

17 "Report of the resumed Review Conference on the Agreement for the Implementation of the Provisions of the United Nations Convention on the Law of the Sea of 10 December 1982 relating to the Conservation and Management of Straddling Fish Stocks and Highly Migratory Fish Stocks Prepared by the President of the Conference" (1 August 2016) UN Doc A/CONF.210/2016/5, https://documents-dds-ny.un.org/doc/UNDOC/GEN/N16/244/06/PDF/N1624406.pdf?OpenElement> accessed 24 August 2023 10 (paras 40–43) and 36 (para 4(a) of the Outcomes section).

18 "Report of the Resumed Review Conference on the Agreement for the Implementation of the Provisions of the United Nations Convention on the Law of the Sea of 10 December 1982 Relating to the Conservation and Management of Straddling Fish Stocks and Highly Migratory Fish Stocks Prepared by the President of the Conference" (20 June 2023) UN Doc A/CONF.210/2023/6, https://documents-dds-ny.un.org/doc/UNDOC/GEN/N23/178/62/PDF/N2317862.pdf?OpenElement> accessed 25 September 2023 10–11 and 26 (paras 49–53 and 141).

19 CCAMLR Resolution 30/XXVIII, https://cm.ccamlr.org/en/resolution-30/xxviii-2009 accessed 24 August 2023.

20 See CCAMLR, "Report of the Thirty-third Meeting of the Commission, Hobart, Australia 20–31 October 2014," >https://meetings.ccamlr.org/system/files/e-cc-xxxiii.pdf> accessed 24 August 2023 33 (paras 5.93–5.97).

21 See CCAMLR, "Report of the Thirty-fourth Meeting of the Commission[,] Hobart, Australia 19–30 October 2015," >https://meetings.ccamlr.org/system/files/e-cc-xxxiv_0.pdf> accessed 24 August 2023 33 (para 7.12) and 207–209 (Annex 8).

22 Lynda Goldsworthy, "Consensus Decision-Making in CCAMLR: Achilles' Heel or Fundamental to Its Success?" (2022) 22 *International Environmental Agreements* 411, 423–424.

23 CCAMLR Resolution 36/41, "Climate change," https://cm.ccamlr.org/en/resolution-36/41-2022 accessed 24 August 2023.

24 Referred to as the "Antarctic Convergence" in the Convention for the Conservation of Antarctic Marine Living Resources (adopted 20 May 1980), 1329 UNTS 47, which uses an approximation of it as the northern boundary of the Convention Area: Art I. It constitutes a major circum-Antarctic, biogeographic boundary where cold, northerly-flowing Antarctic waters sink beneath warmer southerly-moving subtropical waters: CCAMLR, "Information on CCAMLR and Its Links to the Antarctic Treaty," <www.ccamlr.org/en/system/files/e-linkages_0.pdf> accessed 29 August 2023 4 (para 9).

Area.[25] This shows that adjustments may be called for, not only between neighbouring States but also neighbouring RFMOs. A specific example is the late 20th-century migration of oceanic redfish from waters regulated by the North-East Atlantic Fisheries Commission (NEAFC) into those of the Northwest Atlantic Fisheries Organization (NAFO).[26] Four solutions were under consideration: (1) expansion of the NEAFC regulations into NAFO waters, NEAFC thus setting the total allowable catch (TAC) for the entire stock, with any catch taken in NAFO waters counting against NEAFC quotas; (2) NEAFC setting the TAC for the entire stock, but leaving an agreed portion of it for NAFO to allocate; (3) the two RFMOs regulating separately the redfish fisheries occurring in their respective waters, with separate TACs; (4) as a last resort in the event of dispute, pending its resolution, a temporary moratorium on fishing in NAFO waters. A variant of (2) was eventually chosen, but some NAFO members objected to the resolution enacting it and thus escaped being bound by it.[27]

While the areas on both sides of the boundaries in question here are high seas, where no restriction applies on access to fish (leaving aside the possible but tenuous application of Article 8(4) of the UN Fish Stocks Agreement,[28] contrasted with the clear authority of a coastal State to prohibit foreign fishing in its EEZ to which it has not previously consented), there are inexact but instructive parallels with straddling stocks where there is a tension between RFMOs and coastal States. UNCLOS Article 119 is applicable to straddling but not shared stocks moving from the EEZ into the high seas but not *vice versa*; in determining the TAC and establishing other conservation measures for fish stocks on the high seas it requires fishing patterns to be taken into account, which Thomson in the NEAFC/NAFO interaction takes as a "presumption in favour of the established use of the redfish."[29] He adds that the "due regard for the existing NEAFC management measures" that NAFO had agreed should characterise the ultimate solution "implies the respect

25 Rosemary Rayfuse, "Addressing Climate Change Impacts in Regional Fisheries Management Organizations" in Richard Caddell and Erik J Molenaar (eds), *Strengthening International Fisheries Law in an Era of Changing Oceans* (Hart Publishing 2019) 255, and see <www.ccamlr.org/en/organisation/cooperation-others> accessed 28 August 2023, with links to its arrangements with four RFMOs and the secretariat of the Southern Indian Ocean Fisheries Agreement (adopted 7 July 2006) 2835 UNTS 409.

26 See A. Thomson, "The Management of Redfish (Sebastes Mentella) in the North Atlantic Ocean – A Stock in Movement," in *FAO Fisheries Report No 695, Supp* (7–10 October 2002) 192.

27 ibid 196.

28 Agreement for the Implementation of the Provisions of the United Nations Convention on the Law of the Sea of 10 December 1982 relating to the Conservation and Management of Straddling Fish Stocks and Highly Migratory Fish Stocks (adopted 4 August 1995) 2167 UNTS 3. Art 8(4) provides that where a relevant RFMO exists and a non-member State involved in the fishery declines both to become a member and to apply its conservation and management measures, vessels of its flag lose the right to fish the stocks managed by the RFMO – but what if membership of the organisation depends on admission by the existing members, and it is withheld, or they are unwilling to award the applicant any quota?

29 A Thomson, "The Management of Redfish (Sebastes Mentella) in the North Atlantic Ocean – A Stock in Movement" in *FAO Fisheries Report No 695, Supp* (7–10 October 2002) 196.

of existing fishing rights and therefore the rights already established" by NEAFC members.[30] But measures are not the same as rights; the proposition that States can, by exploiting stocks on the high seas, acquire property-like rights in them, is one that may someday benefit international fisheries management if carefully introduced, but, for the time being, such rights are not widely accepted,[31] so their proponents need to advocate them rather than simply assume their existence. The compatibility provisions in Article 7 of the Fish Stocks Agreement also have a role to play, even if they fall short of the gloss put on them by Thomson's reference to "the pre-eminence of established regulated fisheries."[32]

3. Disputes Occasioned by Changing Distribution of Fish Stocks

Northeast Atlantic Mackerel

The management of this stock became the object of tension early in the new millennium between Norway and the EU on one hand, and the Faroe Islands and Iceland on the other, when it expanded out of Norwegian and EU waters into those of Denmark (in respect of the Faroes and Greenland) and Iceland, a development attributed to "[c]limate change, leading to ocean warming and a related shift in environmental conditions."[33] Ørebech is sharply and persuasively critical of the attempt by the EU and Norway to resist not only Iceland's claim to reflect their new abundance there by a substantial increase in its previously small share of the TAC, which it had no role in setting at a time when there were no mackerel in its waters, but also Iceland's status as an equal partner in decision-making on the stock as a coastal State once it was established in those waters.[34] The development of a fishery for this stock in the Faroe Islands waters similarly led to a dispute

30 ibid.

31 See, for example, *The South China Sea Arbitration between the Republic of the Philippines and the People's Republic of China, Award of 12 July 2016*, XXXIII RIAA 153, 290 (para 270): fishing beyond the territorial sea "cannot" form the basis for the emergence of a historic right, since "such activity was merely the exercise of freedoms already permitted by international law."

32 A Thomson, "The Management of Redfish (Sebastes Mentella) in the North Atlantic Ocean – A Stock in Movement" in *FAO Fisheries Report No 695, Supp* (7–10 October 2002) 196. Article 7 constrains RFMOs establishing rules for the high seas portion of straddling stocks not to undermine existing measures for the same stock maintained by the coastal State in its EEZ, and *vice versa*. See Alex G. Oude Elferink, "The Determination of Compatible Conservation and Management Measures for Straddling and Highly Migratory Fish Stocks," (2001) 5 *Max Planck Yearbook of United Nations Law* 551.

33 Kathleen A Miller et al., "Governing Marine Fisheries in a Changing Climate: A Game-Theoretic Perspective" (2013) 61 *Canadian Journal of Agricultural Economics* 320; Rosemary Rayfuse, "Addressing Climate Change Impacts in Regional Fisheries Management Organizations" in Richard Caddell and Erik J Molenaar (eds), *Strengthening International Fisheries Law in an Era of Changing Oceans* (Hart Publishing 2019) 255.

34 Peter Ørebech, "The 'Lost Mackerel' of the North East Atlantic – The Flawed System of Trilateral and Bilateral Decision-Making" (2013) 28 *International Journal of Marine and Coastal Law* 354–363.

with the EU, settled in 2014, in which the EU had maintained that the allocative shares previously fixed for the North Sea mackerel fishery wholly conducted in EU waters (assuming, though it was certainly not incontrovertible, that it was the same stock that migrated into Faroese waters), must remain immutable no matter where the fish were caught.[35] As parties to UNCLOS all were subject to the Article 63 duty of cooperation, but the economic incentive to comply with it or not has been shown to differ radically depending on whether migration into another State's waters occurs only in years when the stock is large (yes, because it is vulnerable to retaliation by other parties who can increase their own removals to return the stock to a smaller size), or randomly (no, at least not until its own rights as a coastal State are recognised).[36]

Pacific Salmon

Salmon as anadromous species are governed by Article 66 rather than Article 63 of UNCLOS, but the factual situation is nonetheless comparable, as Article 66 is designed specifically for circumstances where salmon spawned in rivers of one State reach the high seas not directly through that State's own EEZ but via the EEZ of another State, where they would ordinarily be subject to capture under that other State's sovereign rights over the living resources per Article 56(1)(a). Such stocks in other words would fall within Article 63 were it not for the more particularised provisions of Article 66, which aims to preserve each coastal State's ability to catch the fish originating in its own rivers and to that extent imposes a regime of cooperation to a specific end, contrasted to the more general prescriptions of Article 63. This is true of the five species of Pacific Salmon governed by a treaty between Canada and the United States,[37] which struck trouble when the Pacific Decadal Oscillation reduced the survival prospects of salmon spawned in rivers draining Oregon and Washington states vulnerable to interception in Canadian waters, but benefited those spawned in Alaskan rivers which were not at risk from the fleet based in British Columbia.

The parties had differing interpretations of Article III(b) of the treaty: "each Party shall conduct its fisheries . . . so as to (a) prevent overfishing and provide for optimum production; and (b) provide for each party to receive benefits equivalent to the production of salmon originating in its waters."[38] Canada argued for many years that the number of interceptions by each side of fish originating in rivers of the

35 Parallel proceedings were brought before an UNCLOS Annex VII arbitral tribunal and a World Trade Organization panel (see https://pca-cpa.org/en/cases/25/> and <www.wto.org/english/tratop_e/dispu_e/cases_e/ds469_e.htm> respectively).

36 Rögnvaldur Hannesson, "Sharing the Northeast Atlantic Mackerel" (2013) 70 *ICES Journal of Marine Science* 263–268.

37 Treaty between the Government of the United States of America and the Government of Canada Concerning Pacific Salmon (adopted 28 January 1985), 1469 UNTS 357.

38 See generally Kathleen A Miller and Gordon R Munro, "Climate and Cooperation: A New Perspective on the Management of Shared Fish Stocks" (2004) 19 *Marine Resource Economics* 380–387.

other should remain in balance, but eventually had to accept the impracticality of this and settled instead in 1999 for indirect monetary compensation through starkly unequal contributions to two endowment funds.[39]

4. Suggested Solutions to Date

A Non-Solution: Moving EEZ Boundaries

While Árnadóttir has argued that climate change may be a sufficient reason to invoke the *rebus sic stantibus* provision of the Vienna Convention on the Law of Treaties[40] to allow unilateral termination of fisheries-related treaties where a fundamental change of circumstances has occurred,[41] there are two reasons for doubting whether this will be helpful in the type of situation envisaged in this chapter. One is that all this achieves is to cast aside a treaty whose constraints one party has come to find intolerable; it does nothing to put an alternative solution in its place. The other is that she writes of "access to resources [being] radically transformed", but this distorts one of the cumulative tests for applicability of Article 62 of the Vienna Convention laid down by the International Court of Justice in the *Fisheries Jurisdiction Cases*:[42] that the effect of the fundamental change must be to bring about a radical transformation of the obligation still to be performed. Yet even where the shift of a stock across a boundary gravely disadvantages the State on one side of it, if its obligation pursuant to the treaty is to limit its catch from that stock to either a certain tonnage or a certain percentage share of a periodically (often annually) calculated TAC, that does not change at all; what will have changed is instead the ability of that State's fishing fleet to take its full allocated limit. Nor can it be an answer to terminate the boundary treaty, the question to which Árnadóttir devotes the bulk of her attention, unless it can be shown that the course of the existing boundary was dictated by fisheries considerations to the exclusion of virtually all

39 See T.L. McDorman, Salt Water Neighbors: International Ocean Law Relations Between the United States and Canada (OUP, 2009), 289–307. The post-1999 endowments were updated and renewed in a 2013 revision of the 1999 treaty: Kathleen A Miller et al., "Governing Marine Fisheries in a Changing Climate: A Game-Theoretic Perspective" (2013) 61 *Canadian Journal of Agricultural Economics* 323.

40 (adopted 23 May 1969) 1155 UNTS 331, Art 62. This provision was applied by the International Court of Justice before the entry into force of the Convention in 1980, and hence on the footing that it represented a customary international law rule, in the *Fisheries Jurisdiction Cases (United Kingdom v. Iceland; Federal Republic of Germany v. Iceland), Jurisdiction of the Court* [1973] ICJ Rep 3, 18 [36] and 49, 63 [36] respectively.

41 S Árnadóttir, "Ecological Changes Justifying Termination or Revision of EEZ and EFZ Boundaries" (2017) 84 *Marine Policy* 287, 290: "ecological changes . . . can affect the essential basis of treaties that establish boundaries by reference to fisheries or boundaries that have been arrived at on the basis of ecological circumstances."

42 *Fisheries Jurisdiction Cases (United Kingdom v. Iceland; Federal Republic of Germany v. Iceland), Jurisdiction of the Court* [1973] ICJ Rep 3, 19–20 [40] and 64 [40] respectively.

else. The *Aegean Sea Continental Shelf* case[43] and *Bay of Bengal* arbitration[44] both support the proposition that the need for stability and permanence brings all maritime boundaries, not just those delimiting the territorial sea, within the Article 62 exception for boundaries. This is reinforced by UNCLOS Article 76(9), as the "natural prolongation of a State's land mass is much less prone to changes than ambulatory coastlines or migratory fish stocks"[45] – Árnadóttir, though unconvinced, thus concedes the point for boundaries delimiting continental shelves, leaving the EEZ isolated as the only maritime zone for which she would deny the exception. But since the EEZ encompasses seabed, as well as water column jurisdiction, States negotiating their maritime boundary, or international courts or tribunals where they have been unable to agree on one, have invariably preferred coastal geography as a neutral factor as between living and mineral resources.[46] This produces boundaries that normally depart very little if at all from a median line, in other words, one whose every point is equidistant from the nearest points on each of the two States' baselines from which the breadth of their maritime zones is measured.

While it is not unknown for access to particular fishing grounds to influence the course of treaty delimitations,[47] most boundary treaties are silent on why the negotiated line runs precisely where it does. Rarely, if ever, do these institute a comprehensive regime for shared and straddling stocks, let alone dictate what should happen if the stocks redistribute themselves across the boundary. This is unsurprising, as the few such treaties predate the rise of global warming as a major regulatory concern. Most are interim agreements governing fisheries in areas of overlapping EEZ entitlements yet to be delimited, and thus generally are left to expire when the boundary is agreed, typically in a treaty that, if not altogether silent, has relatively little to say on the subject of fisheries. The 2010 Norway-Russia maritime boundary delimitation treaty[48] is unusual in having three preambular paragraphs acknowledging the fisheries background, on which Article 4 expands, but mostly still in general terms serving to underline the parties' common desire to maintain

43 *Aegean Sea Continental Shelf (Greece v. Turkey)* [1978] ICJ Rep 3, 35–36 [85].

44 *The Bay of Bengal Maritime Boundary Arbitration between the People's Republic of Bangladesh and the Republic of India, Award of 7 July 2014*, XXXII RIAA 1, 74 [215]-[218].

45 S Árnadóttir, "Ecological Changes Justifying Termination or Revision of EEZ and EFZ Boundaries" (2017) 84 *Marine Policy* 289.

46 In the *Arbitration between Barbados and the Republic of Trinidad and Tobago, relating to the delimitation of the exclusive economic zone and the continental shelf between them, Decision of 11 April 2006*, XXVII RIAA 147, 211–212 [228], the tribunal noted that, with very few exceptions, geographical circumstances have "prevailed . . . over area-specific criteria such as geomorphological aspects or resource-specific criteria such as the distribution of fish stocks."

47 A handful are identified by R.R. Churchill, "Fisheries Issues in Maritime Boundary Delimitation," (1993) 17 *Marine Policy* 44, 53–55.

48 Treaty between the Kingdom of Norway and the Russian Federation concerning Maritime Delimitation and Cooperation in the Barents Sea and the Arctic Ocean (adopted 15 September 2010), 2791 UNTS 3.

the *status quo* under an earlier treaty.[49] It too makes no link between catch allocation (paragraph 2) and the course taken by the boundary:

1. The fishing opportunities of either Party shall not be adversely affected by the conclusion of the present Treaty.
2. To this end, the Parties shall pursue close cooperation in the sphere of fisheries, with a view to maintain their existing respective shares of [TAC] volumes and to ensure relative stability of their fishing activities for each of the stocks concerned.
3. . . .
4. Except as provided for in this Article and in Annex I, nothing in this Treaty shall affect the application of agreements on fisheries cooperation between the Parties.[50]

But this makes no mention of movement of fish and their habitats triggered by climate change or any other cause. At most, therefore, paragraph 2 goes only as far as implying that maintenance of their existing catch shares and relative stability of fishing activities would not cease to be a goal in that event, but does not transform these things into obligations.

More likely is that baselines will recede in a way that "eradicate[s] the lawful entitlement of a State to an area subject to a boundary treaty,"[51] which might, at first sight, seem a stronger reason for terminating the treaty, but the boundary will shift in a random direction rather than necessarily following the fish polewards and thus risks exacerbating instead of alleviating the imbalance of benefits.

What then Instead?

One can readily agree with the predictions from sources pitched at a high level of generality such as those quoted by Rayfuse, noting that the greater level of uncertainty will impel management measures to become more conservative and that management practices will have to "be flexible enough to account for changes

49 Agreement between the Government of the Union of Soviet Socialist Republics and the Government of the Kingdom of Norway concerning Mutual Relations in the Field of Fisheries (adopted 15 October 1976), 1157 UNTS 139.

50 Annex I consists of four articles. The first keeps the existing bilateral fisheries treaties between the parties, notably that in the previous footnote, in force for at least fifteen years after entry into force of the 2010 treaty, and potentially indefinitely thereafter. Article 2 provides for a two-year transitional period from entry into force during which each party's technical regulations for its own fishing vessels in the previously disputed area within 200 nautical miles from the Norwegian or Russian mainland continue to apply. Articles 3 and 4 deal with the extant processes for negotiating TACs, mutual quotas of catches and other regulatory measures as well as other matters under the purview of the Joint Fisheries Commission established under the treaties preserved by Article 1, again underlining the lack of change.

51 S Árnadóttir, "Ecological Changes Justifying Termination or Revision of EEZ and EFZ Boundaries" (2017) 84 *Marine Policy* 290.

in stock distribution and abundance."[52] This, it may be added, is over and above any reduction in a stock's maximum sustainable yield (MSY) due to a reduction in its size.[53] The legal tools for doing so do not need to be invented: "On paper, at least, recent studies suggest that RFMO management frameworks are already generally adequate to manage resources effectively in a climate-changed world."[54] This would require "[s]tock assessments, catch limits and quota allocations . . . to be reviewed periodically and adjusted to take account of climate-induced changes in stock abundance and distribution."[55] This suggests that the longer the duration of a negotiated allocation, the greater the need for inbuilt flexibility mechanisms.

What is missing are the detailed processes for making these adjustments as routine and close to automatic as possible. Miller *et al.* recommend "building resilience and the capacity to adapt to changes that cannot be predicted in detail. This might entail replacing allocations based on fixed national shares" with formulae "explicitly allowing shares to adjust to shifting migratory patterns, or transferable quotas that maintain a rough balance of fishery benefits while allowing fishing effort to efficiently follow the fish."[56] Miller and Munro aver that while the "timing, location, and magnitude of significant changes in fish stock dynamics will likely remain unpredictable," nonetheless they can be anticipated (as distinct from predicted, likened in this sense to earthquakes, for which it would be foolhardy not to plan in regions prone to them).[57] They go on: "the possibility of significant, imperfectly predictable regime shifts highlights the need for management systems that can minimize the cost and disruption of potentially large and long-term adjustments in effort and allowable harvests."[58]

They point to the new abundance-based approach for Pacific salmon which makes it easy to reduce or raise catch in response to fluctuations in the condition of the stocks, in the form of a "clearly articulated set of rules for adjusting quotas and allocations as a function of mutually agreed upon indicators of changes in the shared stock."[59] They could have added that there would be a need to develop a

52 Rosemary Rayfuse, "Addressing Climate Change Impacts in Regional Fisheries Management Organizations" in Richard Caddell and Erik J Molenaar (eds), *Strengthening International Fisheries Law in an Era of Changing Oceans* (Hart Publishing 2019) 257 (footnotes 60 and 61 with further references).

53 UNCLOS Arts 61 (in the EEZ) and 119 (on the high seas) prescribe as the goal of fisheries management to keep stocks at, or restore them to, the size at which they generate the MSY, adjusted for economic and environmental factors.

54 Rosemary Rayfuse, "Addressing Climate Change Impacts in Regional Fisheries Management Organizations" in Richard Caddell and Erik J Molenaar (eds), *Strengthening International Fisheries Law in an Era of Changing Oceans* (Hart Publishing 2019) 265.

55 ibid 268.

56 Kathleen A Miller et al., "Governing Marine Fisheries in a Changing Climate: A Game-Theoretic Perspective" (2013) 61 *Canadian Journal of Agricultural Economics* 327.

57 Kathleen A Miller and Gordon R Munro, "Climate and Cooperation: A New Perspective on the Management of Shared Fish Stocks" (2004) 19 *Marine Resource Economics* 372–373.

58 ibid 387–388.

59 ibid 388.

trusted and binding method of calculating the quantum of such changes that is not open to manipulation by any individual member, such as the scientific staff of the Inter-American Tropical Tuna Commission who serve that RFMO's membership as a whole, making national scientific delegations unnecessary, or the International Council for the Exploration of the Sea which contractually performs the same task for NEAFC.

The point is that although the large and disruptive changes were the result of factors other than global warming, it is not obvious how if at all, the situations would have been different if that had indeed been the cause. Despite the wording of RFMO resolutions, it is probably not sensible to devote effort to planning specifically for changes caused by global warming, partly because it will mostly not be possible to tell reliably which changes are caused by it and which not, but the frequency of them is likely to rise and potentially also the likelihood of them predictably favouring certain members at the expense of others.

Molenaar's suggestion that quota transfers could be a mitigation method in RFMOs,[60] though useful in theory, may encounter difficulties in practice. The record of RFMOs accepting this technique in other contexts is patchy, and they are unlikely to relinquish control to the extent of allowing willing buyers to transact directly with willing sellers of quota. Since any transfer would need to be from the loser to the gainer from the ecological change, the most durable solution may be where the loser accepts a permanent loss of share of the fishery but is able to exact economic compensation for this. Transfers in the opposite direction would superficially be more equitable, but will not help if the fish are no longer there to be caught.

5. Concluding Observations

Policy should aim for equality or at least symmetry of risk so that climate-induced change is just as likely to favour one party as the other. Where this is not possible and it is only the geographical distribution rather than the size of the stock that is affected, so that the loss suffered by one State is matched by a corresponding gain to the other, it would be preferable for the fleet of the losing State to be granted access to fish its pre-agreed share of the TAC in the waters of the gaining State. This could apply equally in situations where the biomass too is diminished – along with, as a quantity related to it, the MSY – and there is only a loss on one side but no matching gain on the other. If it is predictable that this will be the case, the other State may be reluctant to bear any share of the loss and insist that it should lie where it falls, but where there remains uncertainty, perhaps a formulaic solution could be found that covers all eventualities, even if imperfectly, allowing both States' fleets to continue fishing to a comparably reduced extent. Failing that,

60 Erik J Molenaar, 'Integrating Climate Change in International Fisheries Law' in Elise Johansen, Signe Veierud Busch and Ingvild Ulrikke Jakobsen (eds), *The Law of the Sea and Climate Change: Solutions and Constraints* (CUP 2020) 286.

monetary compensation according to a pre-agreed formula may be the least damaging solution, as was eventually found in the case of the Pacific salmon settlement. Such "side payments", as they are known in game theory parlance, tend to find favour with fisheries economists, as they make agreement far easier to reach and cooperative solutions hence more likely.[61] Reopening of settled boundaries should be avoided except in those rare instances where this is expressly contemplated in the treaties by which they are established.

Because of the relatively underdeveloped state of international fisheries law, the scope for disruptive effects on zonal attachment caused by climate change is correspondingly modest. In these circumstances, States through RFMOs and other international bodies have done little more than tip their collective hat to the problem, yet it is not obvious what more they could reasonably be expected to do that they should not already have been doing anyway. Molenaar's advocacy of restricting TACs below MSY, for example, is less radical than it may seem, as this is already mandated for straddling stocks by Annex II to the UN Fish Stocks Agreement,[62] which transforms the corresponding level of biomass from a target into a lower limit.

Rather, climate change adds another powerful reason to accelerate the slow progress towards the elaboration of robust allocative rules that can withstand short-term fluctuations and secular trends in zonal attachment, and this may yet be what ultimately generates the political will to take the necessary steps, which has not so far been in evidence. While it cannot be excluded that in due course it could bring about some radical new redirection of the thrust of international fisheries law, that is far from inevitable and the outlines of it are not yet discernible. Meanwhile, since changes that are foreseen do not justify invoking the *rebus sic stantibus* rule,[63] future negotiators for States, whether in relation to fish, boundaries or both, should not assume that the distribution of the fish will never change, but instead provide expressly for what is to happen if it does, as a safeguard against risk from that quarter.

61 See, for example, Kathleen A Miller and Gordon R Munro, "Climate and Cooperation: A New Perspective on the Management of Shared Fish Stocks" (2004) 19 *Marine Resource Economics* 378.

62 ibid.

63 ILC, "Second Report on the Law of Treaties, by Mr G.G. Fitzmaurice, Special Rapporteur" (15 March 1957) UN Doc A/CN.4/107, 32–33.

Index

For Product Safety Concerns and Information please contact our
EU representative GPSR@taylorandfrancis.com Taylor & Francis
Verlag GmbH, Kaufingerstraße 24, 80331 München, Germany